THE CAMBRIDGE HISTORY OF THE
COLD WAR

Volume II of *The Cambridge History of the Cold War* examines the developments that made the conflict between the United States and the Soviet Union a long-lasting international system during the 1960s and 1970s. A team of leading scholars explains how the Cold War seemed to stabilize after the Cuban Missile Crisis in 1962 and how this sense of increased stability evolved into the détente era of the early 1970s. The authors outline how conflicts in the Third World, as well as the interests and ideologies of the superpowers, eroded the détente process. They delve into the social and economic roots of the conflict, illuminate processes of integration and disintegration, analyze the arms race, and explore the roles of intelligence, culture, and national identities. Discussing the newest findings on US and Soviet foreign policy as well as examining key crises inside and outside Europe, this authoritative volume will define Cold War studies for years to come.

MELVYN P. LEFFLER is Edward Stettinius Professor of American History at the Department of History, University of Virginia. His previous publications include *To Lead the World: American Strategy After the Bush Doctrine* (2008, as co-editor), *For the Soul of Mankind: The United States, the Soviet Union, and the Cold War* (2007, winner of the AHA George Louis Beer Prize), and *A Preponderance of Power: National Security, the Truman Administration and the Cold War* (1992, winner of the Bancroft Prize, the Robert Ferrell Prize, and the Herbert Hoover Book Award).

ODD ARNE WESTAD is Professor of International History at the London School of Economics and Political Science. His previous publications include *The Global Cold War: Third World Interventions and the Making of Our Times* (2005, winner of the Bancroft Prize, the APSA New Political Science Prize, and the Akira Iriye Award), *Decisive Encounters: The Chinese Civil War, 1946–1950* (2003), and *Brothers in Arms: The Rise and Fall of the Sino-Soviet Alliance, 1945–1963* (1999, as editor).

THE CAMBRIDGE HISTORY OF THE COLD WAR

GENERAL EDITORS

MELVYN P. LEFFLER, *University of Virginia*

ODD ARNE WESTAD, *London School of Economics and Political Science*

The Cambridge History of the Cold War is a comprehensive, international history of the conflict that dominated world politics in the twentieth century. The three-volume series, written by leading international experts in the field, elucidates how the Cold War evolved from the geopolitical, ideological, economic, and sociopolitical environment of the two world wars and the interwar era, and explains the global dynamics of the Cold War international system. It emphasizes how the Cold War bequeathed conditions, challenges, and conflicts that shape international affairs today. With discussions of demography and consumption, women and youth, science and technology, ethnicity and race, the volumes encompass the social, intellectual, and economic history of the twentieth century, shedding new light on the evolution of the Cold War. Through its various geographical and national angles, the series signifies a transformation of the field from a national – primarily American – to a broader international approach.

THE CAMBRIDGE
HISTORY OF THE
COLD WAR

*

VOLUME II
Crises and Détente

*

Edited by
MELVYN P. LEFFLER
and
ODD ARNE WESTAD

CAMBRIDGE
UNIVERSITY PRESS

CAMBRIDGE
UNIVERSITY PRESS

University Printing House, Cambridge CB2 8BS, United Kingdom

Cambridge University Press is part of the University of Cambridge.

It furthers the University s mission by disseminating knowledge in the pursuit of
education, learning and research at the highest international levels of excellence.

www.cambridge.org
Information on this title: www.cambridge.org/9780521837200

First published 2010
First Paperback edition 2011
Reprinted 2017

Printed in the United Kingdom by Clays, St Ives plc.

A catalogue record for this publication is available from the British Library

Library of Congress Cataloguing in Publication data
The Cambridge history of the Cold War / edited by Melvyn P. Leffler and Odd Arne Westad.
p. cm.
Includes bibliographical references.
ISBN 978-0-521-83720-0
1. Cold War. 2. World politics – 1945–1989. 3. International relations – History –
20th century. I. Leffler, Melvyn P., 1945– II. Westad, Odd Arne. III. Title.
D842.C295 2009
909.82′5–dc22
2009005508

ISBN 978-0-521-83720-0 Hardback
ISBN 978-110760230-4 Paperback

Contents

Contents

Contents

Illustrations

Maps

Graphs

xi

Contributors to volume II

CHRISTOPHER ANDREW is Professor of Modern and Contemporary History at Cambridge University. He has published *Secret Service: The Making of the British Intelligence Community*; *KGB: The Inside Story of Its Foreign Operations from Lenin to Gorbachev* (with Oleg Gordievsky), and *The Mitrokhin Archive* (with Vasili Mitrokhin).

FRÉDÉRIC BOZO is Professor of Contemporary History at the Sorbonne (University of Paris III). He has published *Two Strategies for Europe: De Gaulle, the United States, and the Atlantic Alliance*, and *Mitterrand, la fin de la guerre froide et l'unification allemande: De Yalta à Maastricht*.

WILLIAM BURR, a senior analyst at the National Security Archive, George Washington University, directs the archive's project on Nuclear History Documentation. He edited *The Kissinger Transcripts* (1998) and has published on US nuclear history in scholarly journals.

RICHARD N. COOPER is Maurits C. Boas Professor of International Economics at Harvard University. He has served in the US government, including as chairman of the National Intelligence Council (1995–97). His most recent books include *Boom, Crisis, and Adjustment* and *Environment and Resource Policies for the World Economy*.

FRANK COSTIGLIOLA is Professor of History at the University of Connecticut. A former Guggenheim Fellow, he is the author of *Awkward Dominion: American Political, Economic, and Cultural Relations with Europe, 1919–33* and *The Cold Alliance: France and the United States Since World War II,*

NICHOLAS J. CULL is Professor of Public Diplomacy at the Annenberg School for Communication, University of Southern California, and the current president of the International Association for Media and History. He is author of *The United States and the Cold War: American Propaganda and Public Diplomacy, 1945–1989*.

ENNIO DI NOLFO is Professor Emeritus of History of International Relations at the University of Florence. He has published *Dagli Imperi militari agli imperi tecnologici: La politica internazionale dal XX secolo a oggi* and *Storia delle relazioni internazionali 1919–1999*.

JOHN LEWIS GADDIS is Robert A. Lovett Professor of History at Yale University. He is the author of *Strategies of Containment: A Critical Appraisal of Postwar American National Security*, *The Long Peace: Inquiries into the History of the Cold War* and *We Now Know: Rethinking Cold War History*.

FRANCIS J. GAVIN is the Tom Slick Professor for International Affairs at the LBJ School of Public Affairs and the Director of Studies at the Robert S. Strauss Center for International Security and Law at the University of Texas. He is the author of *Gold, Dollars, and Power: The Politics of International Monetary Relations, 1958–1971*.

PIERO GLEIJESES is a professor of American foreign policy at Johns Hopkins University (SAIS). He is the author of *Conflicting Missions: Havana, Washington, and Africa, 1959–1976* and *Shattered Hope: The Guatemalan Revolution and the United States, 1944–1954*.

JUSSI HANHIMÄKI is Professor of International History and Politics at the Graduate Institute of International and Development Studies in Geneva, Switzerland. He is the author of *The Flawed Architect: Henry Kissinger* and *American Foreign Policy* and *The United Nations: A Very Short Introduction*.

JAMES G. HERSHBERG is Associate Professor of History and International Affairs at George Washington University and Director Emeritus of the Cold War International History Project. He is author of *James B. Conant: Harvard to Hiroshima and the Making of the Nuclear Age*.

ROBERT JERVIS is Adlai E. Stevenson Professor of International Politics at Columbia University. He is the author of *American Foreign Policy in a New Era* and *The Politics and Psychology of Intelligence and Intelligence Failures*.

ANTHONY KEMP-WELCH is Senior Lecturer at the School of History, University of East Anglia. He is author of *Poland under Communism: A Cold War History* and *Stalin and the Literary Intelligentsia, 1928–39*.

MICHAEL E. LATHAM is Associate Professor of History at Fordham University. He is the author of *Modernization as Ideology: American Social Science and "Nation Building" in the Kennedy Era*, and a co-editor of *Staging Growth: Modernization, Development, and the Global Cold War*.

MELVYN P. LEFFLER is Edward Stettinius Professor of American History at the University of Virginia. He is the author of *A Preponderance of Power: National Security, the Truman Administration, and the Cold War* and *For the Soul of Mankind: The United States, the Soviet Union, and the Cold War*.

DOUGLAS LITTLE is Professor of History at Clark University in Worcester, Massachusetts. He is the author of *Malevolent Neutrality: The United States, Great Britain, and the Origins of the Spanish Civil War* and *American Orientalism: The United States and the Middle East since 1945*.

FREDRIK LOGEVALL is Professor of History at Cornell University. His publications include *Choosing War: The Lost Chance for Peace and the Escalation of War in Vietnam*, *The Origins of the Vietnam War*, and *Terrorism and 9/11: A Reader*.

WILFRIED LOTH is Professor of Modern and Contemporary History at the University of Duisburg-Essen. He is author of *The Division of the World 1941–1955* and *Overcoming the Cold War. A History of Détente, 1951–1991*.

N. PIERS LUDLOW is Reader in International History at the London School of Economics and Political Science. He is the author of *The European Community and the Crises of the 1960s: Negotiating the Gaullist Challenge* and the editor of *European Integration and the Cold War: Ostpolitik/Westpolitik, 1965–73*.

SERGEY RADCHENKO is Lecturer in History at the University of Nottingham, Ningbo. He is the author of *The Atomic Bomb and the Origins of the Cold War* (with Campbell Craig) and *Two Suns in the Heavens: The Sino-Soviet Struggle for Supremacy*.

DAVID ALAN ROSENBERG is Professorial Lecturer in History at Temple University. He has published widely on issues of strategic and nuclear planning.

SVETLANA SAVRANSKAYA is a research fellow at the National Security Archive in Washington, DC, where she directs cooperative projects with Russian archives and institutes and edits the Russian and East Bloc Archival Documents Database.

ROBERT D. SCHULZINGER is Professor of History and Director of the International Affairs Program at the University of Colorado, Boulder. He has published *Henry Kissinger: Doctor of Diplomacy, Present Tense: The United States since 1945* and *A Time for Peace: The Legacy of the Vietnam War*.

JEREMI SURI is Professor of History at the University of Wisconsin. He is the author of *Power and Protest: Global Revolution and the Rise of Détente* and *Henry Kissinger and the American Century*.

WILLIAM TAUBMAN is Bertrand Snell Professor of Political Science at Amherst College. He is the author of *Khrushchev: The Man and His Era* and *Stalin's American Policy: From Entente to Détente to Cold War*.

MARC TRACHTENBERG, a historian by training, is a professor of political science at UCLA. He is the author of *History and Strategy* and *A Constructed Peace: The Making of the European Settlement, 1945–1963*.

ODD ARNE WESTAD is Professor of International History at the London School of Economics and Political Science. Among his publications are *Decisive Encounters: The Chinese Civil War, 1946–1950* and *The Global Cold War: Third World Interventions and the Making of Our Times*.

Preface to volumes I, II, and III

Since the beginning of the twenty-first century, the Cold War has gradually become history. In people's memories, the epoch when a global rivalry between the United States and the Soviet Union dominated international affairs has taken on a role very much like that of the two twentieth-century world wars, as a thing of the past, but also as progenitor of everything that followed. As with the two world wars, we now also have the ability to see developments from the perspectives of the different participants in the struggle. Declassification, however incomplete, of a suggestive body of archival evidence from the former Communist world as well as from the West makes this possible. The time, therefore, is ripe to provide a comprehensive, systematic, analytic overview of the conflict that shaped the international system and that affected most of humankind during the second half of the twentieth century.

In this three-volume *Cambridge History*, the contributors seek to illuminate the causes, dynamics, and consequences of the Cold War. We want to elucidate how it evolved from the geopolitical, ideological, economic, and sociopolitical environment of the two World Wars and the interwar era. We also seek to convey a greater appreciation of how the Cold War bequeathed conditions, challenges, and conflicts that shape developments in the international system today.

In order to accomplish the above goals, we take the *Cambridge History of the Cold War* (CHCW) far beyond the narrow boundaries of diplomatic affairs. We seek to clarify what mattered to the greatest number of people during the Cold War. Indeed, the end of the conflict cannot be grasped without understanding how markets, ideas, and cultural interactions affected political discourse, diplomatic events, and strategic thinking. Consequently, we shall deal at considerable length with the social, intellectual, and economic history of the twentieth century. We shall discuss demography and consumption, women and youth, science and technology, culture and race. The evolution of the Cold War cannot be comprehended without attention to such matters.

The *CHCW* is an international history, covering the period from a wide variety of geographical and national angles. While some chapters necessarily center on an individual state or a bilateral relationship, there are many more chapters that deal with a wider region or with global trends. Intellectually, therefore, the *CHCW* aspires to contribute to a transformation of the field from national – primarily American – views to a broader international approach.

The authors of the individual chapters have been selected because of their academic standing in the field of Cold War studies, regardless of their institutional affiliation, academic discipline, or national origin. Although the majority of contributors are historians, there are chapters written by political scientists, economists, and sociologists. While most contributors come from the main research universities in North America and Britain – where Cold War studies first blossomed as a field – the editors have also sought to engage scholars working in different universities and research centers around the globe. We have included a mixture of younger and more established scholars in the field, thereby seeking to illuminate how scholarship has evolved as well as where it is heading.

The *CHCW* aims at being comprehensive, comparative, and pluralist in its approach. The contributors have deliberately been drawn from various 'schools' of thought and have been asked to put forward their own – often distinctive – lines of argument, while indicating the existence of alternative interpretations and approaches. Being a substantial work of reference, the *CHCW* provides detailed, synthetic accounts of key periods and major thematic topics, while striving for broad and original interpretations. The volumes constitute a scholarly project, written by academics for fellow academics as well as for policymakers, foreign affairs personnel, military officers, and analysts of international relations. But we also hope the *CHCW* will serve as an introduction and reference point for advanced undergraduate students and for an educated lay public in many countries.

The present *Cambridge History* was first conceived in 2001 and has therefore been almost ten years in the making. It has been a large, multinational project, with seventy-three contributors from eighteen different countries. We have met for three conferences and had a large number of hours on the phone and in conference-calls. Most chapters have been through three, if not four, different versions, and have been read and commented upon – in depth – not only by the editors, but also by other participants in the project. In the end, it was the spirit of collaboration among people of very different backgrounds and very different views that made it possible to bring this *Cambridge History* to completion in the form that it now has.

While the editors' first debt of gratitude therefore is to the contributors, a large number of others also deserve thanks. Jeffrey Byrne, our editorial assistant, did a remarkable job organizing meetings, keeping track of submissions, and finding maps and illustrative matter, all while completing his own doctoral thesis. He has been a model associate. Michael Watson, our editor at Cambridge University Press, helped keep the project on track throughout. Michael Devine, the director of the Harry S. Truman Presidential Library, worked hard to set up the conferences and provide essential funding for the project. At the London School of Economics and Political Science (LSE), the wonderful administrative staff of the International History Department, the Cold War Studies Centre, and LSE IDEAS provided help far beyond the call of duty; Arne Westad is especially grateful to Carol Toms and Tiha Franulovic for all the assistance rendered him during a difficult period when he juggled the *CHCW* editorship with being head of department and research center director.

Both editors are grateful to those who helped fund and organize the three *CHCW* conferences, at the Harry S. Truman Presidential Library in Independence, Missouri; at the Lyndon B. Johnson Presidential Library in Austin, Texas; and at the Woodrow Wilson International Center for Scholars in Washington, DC. Besides the Truman Library director, Michael Devine, we wish to thank the director of the Johnson Library, Betty Sue Flowers, the director of the History and Public Policy Program at the Wilson Center, Christian Ostermann, and the director of the National Security Archive, Thomas S. Blanton. We are also grateful to Philip Bobbitt, H. W. Brands, Diana Carlin, Francis J. Gavin, Mark Lawrence, William Leogrande, Robert Littwak, William Roger Louis, Dennis Merrill, Louis Potts, Elspeth Rostow, Mary Sarotte, Strobe Talbott, Alan Tully, Steven Weinberg, and Samuel Wells.

Being editors of such a large scholarly undertaking has been exhausting and exhilarating in turns (and roughly by equal measure). The editors want to thank each other for good comradeship throughout, and our families, students, and colleagues for their patience, assistance, and good cheer. It has been a long process, and we hope that the end product will serve its audiences well.

Melvyn P. Leffler
and
Odd Arne Westad

Note on the text

All three volumes use the simplified form of the Library of Congress system of transliteration for Cyrillic alphabets (without diacritics, except for Serbian and Macedonian), Arabic, and Japanese (modified Hepburn), Pinyin (without diacritics) for Chinese, and McCune-Reischauer (with diacritics) for Korean. Translations within the text are those of the individual contributors to this volume unless otherwise specified in the footnotes.

Grand strategies in the Cold War

JOHN LEWIS GADDIS

Wars have been around for a very long time. Grand strategies for fighting wars – if by "grand strategy" one understands the calculated use of available means in the pursuit of desired ends – have probably been around almost as long; but our record of them dates back to only the fifth century BCE when Herodotus and Thucydides set out to chronicle systematically how the great wars of their age had been fought. We do have, however, in the greatest of all poems, mythologized memories of a war fought centuries earlier, none of whose participants appear to have known how to write. But they did know about the need to connect ends with means: "Put heads together," Homer has wise Nestor admonishing the Achaeans at a desperate moment in the long siege of Troy, "if strategy's any use."[1]

The ancient Greeks made no sharp distinction between war and peace. Wars could last for years, even decades; they could pause, however, to allow the sowing and harvesting of crops, or for the conduct of games. The modern state system, which dates from the seventeenth century, was meant to stake out boundaries that did not exist in the era of Homer, Herodotus, and Thucydides: nations were either to be at war or they were not. But the boundaries blurred again during the Cold War, a struggle that went on longer than the Trojan, Persian, and Peloponnesian wars put together. The stakes, to be sure, were higher. The geographical scope of the competition was much wider. In its fundamental aspects, however, the Cold War more closely resembled the ancient Greek wars than it did those of the eighteenth, nineteenth, and early twentieth centuries.

It is hardly surprising, then, that grand strategies dominated Cold War statecraft. They could no longer be deployed when military operations began, and retired when hostilities ended. Nor could such strategies remain static,

---

1 Homer, *The Iliad*, trans. by Robert Fagles (New York: Penguin Books, 1990), 371. For the illiteracy of Homer's characters, see Bernard Knox's introduction to this edition, 7–8.

for the Cold War's particular combination of limited violence with long duration required responding not only to the actions of adversaries but also to the constraints of resources, the demands of constituencies, and the persistent recalcitrance of reality when theory is applied to it. The grand strategies of the United States, the Soviet Union, and their allies therefore evolved in relation to one another, much as competitive species do within common ecosystems.

Here too an ancient Greek provides a guide. Thucydides' great history of the Peloponnesian War gives equal weight to the strategies of all its belligerents, to the ways in which each shaped the other, and to the manner in which none escaped the unexpected. Even more strikingly, Thucydides does this with *us* in mind: he writes for "those inquirers who desire an exact knowledge of the past as an aid to the understanding of the future, which in the course of human things must resemble if it does not reflect it."[2]

Stalin's grand strategy

Before there can be a grand strategy there must be a need for one: a conflict that goes beyond the normal disputes of international relations, for which diplomacy is the remedy. Because *we* know that the Cold War followed World War II, it is easy to assume that the leaders of the victorious coalition knew this too and were preparing for the struggle that lay before them. This was not the case. Indeed, it is doubtful that any of those leaders, prior to 1945, anticipated a "cold war" as we have come to understand that term – with the sole exception of Iosif Stalin.

We do not often think of Stalin as a grand strategist, but perhaps we should. He rose to the top in the Kremlin hierarchy by systematically eliminating rivals who underestimated him. He transformed the Soviet Union from an agrarian state into an industrial great power. He then led that state from a devastating military defeat to an overwhelming triumph in less than four years. When World War II ended, Stalin had been in power for almost two decades: he alone among postwar leaders had had the time, the experience, and the uncontested authority to shape a long-term plan for the future.

Stalin's strategy had several objectives, the first of which was to continue the acceleration of history his predecessor Vladimir Ilich Lenin had begun. Karl Marx had identified class conflict as the mechanism that would cause

---

2 Robert B. Strassler (ed.), *The Landmark Thucydides: A Comprehensive Guide to the Peloponnesian War*, revised edition of the Richard Crawley translation (New York: Simon & Schuster, 1996), 16.

capitalism to give way to socialism and then to Communism, at which point states would wither away. But Marx had been as vague about when this would happen as he had been precise about where it would occur: in the great industrial societies of Europe. Lenin sought to hasten the process by starting a revolution from the top down in Russia, with the expectation that it would spark revolutions from the bottom up in Germany, Britain, and other countries in which workers were supposedly waiting to overthrow their capitalist masters. They had not done so, however, by the time Lenin died in 1924.

That disappointment led Stalin toward another method of advancing the Communist cause: he would industrialize Russia, and then use it as a base from which to spread revolution elsewhere. He undertook this process during the 1930s with little regard for the human or material costs. He also knew, though, that his accomplishments would mean little unless the USSR was safe from external attack. One could hardly expect capitalists to welcome the emergence of a strong socialist state whose goal it was to end their own existence.

This led to the second of Stalin's objectives: a fusion of traditional Russian imperialism with Marxist–Leninist ideology. Lenin regarded imperialism as the highest form of capitalism, but since capitalism was doomed he thought imperialism was also. He never saw the reconstruction of empire as a way to speed the destruction of capitalism. Stalin's strategy, however, required extending the Soviet Union's boundaries as far as possible, for with Nazi Germany and Imperial Japan on the rise, the international environment was hardly benign. The most plausible justification was to claim all the lands the Russian tsars had once possessed, together with spheres of influence beyond them that would allow only "friendly" neighbors.

From this perspective, Stalin's apparent inconsistencies between 1935 and 1945 – his call for the League of Nations to resist the aggressors, his support for the Republicans in the Spanish Civil War, his 1939 "non-aggression" pact with Adolf Hitler, his alliance with the United States and Great Britain after Germany attacked in 1941, his determination to retain his wartime gains after the war – reflected a single underlying priority, which was to ensure the safety of the Soviet state, the base from which the international proletarian revolution would in time spread. Imperialism now had a revolutionary purpose.

The third and final objective in Stalin's grand strategy was to await the self-destruction of capitalism. Stalin firmly believed, as had Lenin, that "internal contradictions" arising from an inability to resolve economic crises would produce rivalries among capitalist states which would eventually lead them to attack one another. The two world wars had arisen, after all, from just such causes: why should there not be a third that would bring about capitalism's demise once and for all?

Until that happened, the Soviet Union would rebuild its strength, absorbing the new possessions victory had brought it while letting the United States, Great Britain, and the other capitalist countries stumble into the next war. It was a curiously passive program for a revolutionary, but it reflected Stalin's conviction that the forces of history were on his side: the "science" of Marxism–Leninism guaranteed it. At no point did he share the capitalists' interest in a stable postwar order. Such a system could only come, he believed, with a victory for Communism everywhere. It was in this sense, then, that Stalin anticipated a "cold war," and developed a grand strategy for conducting it.

Roosevelt's response

No equally comprehensive strategy for confronting the Soviet Union emerged anywhere in the capitalist world before 1945. One reason was the absence of a single manager for the global economy, Britain having relinquished that role after World War I, and the United States not having yet assumed it. The rise of authoritarianism in Italy, Germany, and Japan further fragmented capitalism. By the mid-1930s, the remaining European democracies were too preoccupied with the Great Depression to devise common approaches in foreign affairs – beyond the vague hope that appeasing the fascists might somehow satisfy them. Stalin's diagnosis in this sense was correct: divisions among capitalists prevented their devising a plan comparable to his own.

Despite their power, the Americans during these years were particularly purposeless. Woodrow Wilson had called, in response to the Bolshevik Revolution, for a new international order based upon principles of collective security, political self-determination, and economic integration. Before he even left the White House, however, the United States had reverted to its traditional posture of avoiding entanglements beyond its hemisphere. It thereby dodged the responsibility for defending ideas it valued – democracy and capitalism – at a time when no other state had the strength to do so. Franklin D. Roosevelt had hoped to revive Wilson's cause after becoming president in 1933, but he made domestic economic recovery the greater priority, while the appeasement policies of the British and the French left him little basis upon which to seek an end to American isolationism.

All of this changed with Hitler's seizure of Czechoslovakia in 1939, the outbreak of war in Europe later that year, and the fall of Denmark, Norway, the Netherlands, Belgium, and France to the Germans in the spring of 1940.

By this time, Roosevelt had a grand strategy: it was to do everything possible to save Britain, defeat Germany, and contain Japan. That meant *cooperating* with the Soviet Union, however, because Hitler's invasion in June 1941 had made that country an informal ally of the British and the Americans. Germany's declaration of war on the United States following the Japanese attack on Pearl Harbor closed the circle, creating the Grand Alliance.

It was almost as if Roosevelt had foreseen these events, for from the moment he extended diplomatic recognition to the USSR in 1933, he had sought to bring it within a shared international system. He consistently assumed the best of Stalin's intentions, even when the Kremlin dictator – with his brutal purges and his cynical pact with Hitler – made this difficult. After they became wartime allies, Roosevelt deferred generously to Stalin's postwar territorial demands. But he also expected Stalin to respect an American design for a postwar world that would combine great power collaboration with a new set of international institutions – most significantly the United Nations – based on Wilsonian principles.

Was Roosevelt naïve? It is difficult to say for sure because his death, in April 1945, prevents our knowing what he would have done once it became clear that Stalin was no Wilsonian. We do know, though, that Roosevelt left his successor, Harry S. Truman, in a strong position to confront the Soviet Union if that should become necessary. Roosevelt had kept wartime casualties to a minimum, relying on the Red Army to do most of the fighting against the Germans. He had agreed to few, if any, territorial changes that Stalin could not have brought about on his own. He had doubled the size of the American economy during a war that had devastated the economies of most other belligerents – including that of the USSR – and he had authorized the building of an atomic bomb. Roosevelt's did not seem, to Stalin, to have been a naïve grand strategy.

None of this changes, however, a fundamental asymmetry. Roosevelt allowed for the possibility that a "cold war" might not happen. Stalin regarded it as inevitable.

Kennan and containment

But no grand strategy fails to produce feedback. What if Stalin's own brutality – the harsh nature of his dictatorship and the unilateral manner in which he had imposed Soviet influence in Eastern and Central Europe – should frighten other Europeans into settling their differences? What if the United States should commit itself to reviving capitalism and democracy among them?

For someone who used fear with such success in gaining and consolidating power, Stalin was strangely oblivious to the possibility that fear might rally his adversaries.

The chief wartime priority of the United States and Britain had been to secure the Eurasian balance of power against future threats like those of 1914 and 1939–41. Stalin shared that objective to the extent that it meant defeating and totally disarming Germany and Japan. By the spring of 1946, however, the Soviet Union itself seemed, to the Americans and their West European allies, to be threatening postwar stability.

Few officials in Washington, London, or Paris expected a Soviet military attack, but there were fears that war-weary Europeans – recalling the prewar failures of capitalism and democracy – might vote their own Communist parties into power, in effect *inviting* the Soviet Union to dominate them. The crisis was one of confidence, in the absence of which any positive program might prevail. The Truman administration had made it clear that it was not going to be another Harding administration: that however frustrating the European situation might be, it would not produce yet another American withdrawal from overseas responsibilities. But that was only a promise. It was not a strategy for countering European despair.

It fell to George F. Kennan, an American Foreign Service expert on Russian history and Soviet ideology, to show how such a strategy might work. Kennan agreed with Marx, Lenin, and Stalin that industrialized states held the key to power in the modern world, but he did not accept their view that capitalism carried within itself the seeds of its own destruction. Stalin's own system, he pointed out, contained more serious "internal contradictions." These included its lack of legitimacy – the fact that it had never risked free multiparty elections – together with the tendency of all multinational empires to over-expand, provoke resistance, and break apart. Here Kennan cited Gibbon on Rome.[3] He could as easily have invoked Thucydides on Athens.

Democracy embodied legitimacy, Kennan pointed out, and that made it stronger than most of its practitioners realized. If they could muster the self-confidence in their institutions that Stalin claimed to have in his – and if they could keep remaining centers of industrial power from falling under his control – then future Soviet leaders could hardly continue to see history as on their side. The United States and its allies would have found a path between renewed appeasement and a new world war.

---

3 George F. Kennan, *Memoirs: 1925–1950* (Boston, MA: Little, Brown, 1967), 129–30.

That was the *theory* behind what Kennan called "containment," but it took leadership to put it into practice. This came in June 1947 when the Truman administration offered Europeans the resources necessary to rebuild their economies and revive their societies. The Marshall Plan's beneficiaries in turn agreed to subordinate their historic rivalries to the common *European* task of reconstruction, integration, and democratization. That meant including an old enemy – the western parts of Germany then under British, American, and French occupation – within the new Europe. The United States in 1948 embraced a similar set of priorities for occupied Japan.

Stalin had not expected any of this because Leninist theory said it could not happen: capitalists were supposed to fight, not help, one another. Caught off guard, he authorized a Communist coup in Czechoslovakia, denounced Yugoslav Communists for insubordination, and blockaded the city of West Berlin. These measures backfired: they ensured public support for the Marshall Plan within the United States, they hastened the creation of a democratic capitalist West German state, and they led the other European democracies to request inclusion within a formal military alliance organized by the United States. Meanwhile Josef Broz Tito's regime in Belgrade survived – with discreet American help – thereby showing that international Communism could fragment, just as Stalin had expected international capitalism to do.

With the success of the Marshall Plan, the establishment of the North Atlantic Treaty Organization (NATO), the rehabilitation of West Germany and Japan, and the Yugoslav defection, Stalin's strategy of exploiting capitalist rivalries lay in ruins. His "scientific" theory had run up against an emotional reality, which was that the Soviet Union frightened the capitalists – even some other Communists – more than the capitalists did each other. All that the Americans and their allies needed to do henceforth, Kennan claimed, was to wait for a Soviet leader to detect this fact, abandon his nation's revolutionary-imperial aspirations, and transform the USSR into a satisfied member of the international system. History, it appeared, was not on Stalin's side after all.

The global Cold War

Kennan too, though, failed to anticipate feedback, notably the risk that selective containment – protecting only the industrial regions of Western Europe and Japan – might not sustain self-confidence within the democracies over however long it might take for Soviet behavior to change. Self-confidence is an *emotion*, which Kennan hoped to produce through *rational* argument. So had Pericles when he advised the Athenians to rely exclusively on their naval strength and the wealth it brought them, while watching impassively from atop their walls as the Spartans ravaged their countryside.[4] Strategy depends as much on morale as on logic, and Pericles found the Athenians unready for the path he meant to follow. Kennan's experience was similar.

Containment, Kennan acknowledged, was like walking a tightrope. It was an economical way to cross an abyss, but it was important not to look down. That meant maintaining composure when Stalin succeeded – unexpectedly early – in building his own atomic bomb. It meant not worrying about Communist victories in non-industrial regions like China, where Mao Zedong had defeated Chiang Kai-shek's Nationalists and was poised to take power. Neither of these developments significantly shifted the global geopolitical balance, Kennan argued at the end of 1949: deterrence would still work, Mao might not follow Moscow's orders, and even if he did China would absorb whoever tried to run it. The United States should simply stick to reviving capitalism and planting democracy in Western Europe and Japan – lest it too succumb, as the Soviet Union had, to imperial temptations.

But the Americans were no more prepared than the Athenians had been to suffer setbacks with equanimity. The Truman administration, under congressional pressure, had to agree to build a thermonuclear bomb, a weapon so powerful that war planners had no idea how it might be used. The president also commissioned a reassessment of containment, NSC-68, which concluded that no parts of the world were now peripheral, that no means of protecting them could now be ruled out, and that the existing defense budget was woefully inadequate. Then, in June 1950, the North Koreans invaded South Korea, a country whose defense no one in Washington had regarded as a vital interest. Now everyone, including even Kennan, believed it to be.

Historians have generally argued that Stalin blundered in authorizing this attack. He had not expected the United States to intervene; when it did military spending tripled, while Truman used the crisis to justify rearming the West Germans and stationing American troops permanently in Europe. From the Soviet leader's perspective, however, Korea also brought benefits. The United States suffered major military reversals there without using the atomic bomb. Chinese involvement ended any hope in Washington that Mao might become another Tito. And the war convinced Truman and his advisers that the authors of NSC-68 were right: any part of the world threatened or even apparently threatened by international Communism – industrial or not – would have to be protected.

---

4 Strassler (ed.), *The Landmark Thucydides*, 98, 125.

So the Americans, like the ancient Greeks, lost the self-confidence to leave anything undefended. They gained in its place the insecurity that accompanies expansion: "fear [was] our principal motive," Thucydides has the Athenians tell the Spartans. '[I]t appeared no longer safe to give up our empire; especially as all who left us would fall to you."[5] From a strategy meant to retain the initiative by distinguishing vital from peripheral interests, the United States shifted to one that yielded the initiative to its enemies. Wherever *they* chose to challenge, it would have to respond.

Stalemate: ideology

Therein lay the makings of a grand strategic stalemate, like the one that perpetuated the Peloponnesian War. Its roots lay in frustrated hopes: those of Soviet leaders that capitalism would collapse; those of American leaders that it would be enough simply to ensure that capitalism survived. The Cold War shifted now to strategies for breaking this stalemate, none of which proved decisive. Their effect instead was to stabilize and therefore prolong the Cold War – to transform it into a new international system that closely resembled a very old one.

The first of these efforts focused on reforming Marxism–Leninism. Stalin saw little need to make his dictatorship popular because he assumed that capitalist economic crashes and the wars they produced would do that for him. But as his successors watched the growing prosperity and political legitimacy of postwar capitalism, they lost any illusions that its self-destruction was imminent. Instead, they began wondering how their own system was going to sustain itself and spread its influence if it could not demonstrably improve the lives of the people who lived under it.

The problem became clear as early as June 1953 when workers in East Germany – the very class, according to Marx, that should have most welcomed Communist Party rule – instead rebelled against it. The Red Army quickly crushed the uprising and the hardline East German leader Walter Ulbricht survived, but the experience convinced Nikita Khrushchev, soon to emerge as the Soviet Union's new leader, that "socialism" had to be given "a human face." That meant disavowing Stalin and promising something better – even if still within the framework of a command economy and one-party rule.

---

5 *Ibid.*, 43. Compare with Melvyn P. Leffler, *A Preponderance of Power: National Security, the Truman Administration, and the Cold War* (Stanford, CA: Stanford University Press, 1992), 445.

Conceding the necessity of reform, though, made it hard to control the pace. Khrushchev's attacks on Stalin's legacy – most dramatically his February 1956 "secret" speech – had the unintended effect of encouraging attacks on Soviet authority, for how could the two be separated? By the end of that year, Khrushchev had narrowly avoided a revolution in Poland, only to face one in Hungary that he suppressed by harsher means than Stalin had ever employed in that region. Meanwhile, an open border with West Berlin was allowing millions of East Germans to emigrate. When Khrushchev and Ulbricht built a wall to prevent this in 1961, they gave up any pretense that the people they governed preferred "socialism" over democratic capitalism. The Soviet sphere of influence in Eastern and Central Europe would remain, but only against the wishes of those included within it.

Khrushchev's reforms provoked an equally unanticipated response from the Chinese, a people he could not shoot down or wall in. It had been one thing for Tito to challenge Stalin and stay in power: Yugoslavia was a small country, and the Soviet dictator's influence within the international Communist movement remained dominant. It was quite another thing for the volatile and inexperienced Khrushchev to condemn Stalin without consulting Mao, the leader of the most significant revolution since Lenin's who now ruled the world's most populous country – and who had patterned his leadership on the example Stalin had set. With the Sino-Soviet split, the fragmentation of international Communism became irreversible just as the revival of market capitalism and democratic politics was also becoming so.

Leonid Brezhnev and Aleksei Kosygin, Khrushchev's successors, did no better. Having encouraged reforms in Czechoslovakia, they concluded in 1968 that these had gone too far and ended them with yet another military intervention. It was the Soviet Union's right, they claimed, to intervene whenever "socialism" seemed to be in danger. But the Brezhnev Doctrine frightened whatever Marxist sympathizers were left in Europe, while Mao saw it as aimed at China and began preparing for war with the USSR. By the end of the decade, the Communist world had two centers whose hostility toward one another was at least as great as that of each toward the capitalists they had sworn to overthrow.

However well-intentioned it may have been, then, Khrushchev's strategy of reforming Marxism–Leninism instead diminished its legitimacy and shattered its unity. It showed that any withering away of state authority – or any wavering of resolve among leaders – could cause that ideology itself to implode. This was disconcerting indeed for ruling Communist parties because it suggested that change carried within itself the seeds of *their* own destruction.

Stalemate: nuclear weapons

Why, then, did the Cold War continue? Why did the Americans and their allies fail to confront a dysfunctional adversary and claim victory? The best answer is that this crisis within an ideology coincided with a quantum leap in the lethality of weaponry. By the early 1960s, tolerating a Cold War stalemate – even if one side lacked the legitimacy the other side thrived on – seemed safer than trying to end it.

The United States tested its first thermonuclear weapon in November 1952, but the Soviet Union quickly followed with one of its own in August 1953. Hydrogen bombs were at least a thousand times more powerful than the atomic bombs that had devastated Hiroshima and Nagasaki: it quickly became clear that their mass use might render the northern hemisphere uninhabitable. For only the second time in modern military history – the first was the non-use of poison gas in World War II – competing war plans came up against a common ecological constraint.

This danger discouraged the exploitation of vulnerabilities. The United States did nothing to assist the rebellious East Germans, Poles, or Hungarians – despite the fact that it had earlier aided the rebellious Yugoslavs. It assumed that the Soviet Union would fight to retain its sphere of influence in Europe, if necessary with nuclear weapons, and that the results would be catastrophic. It insisted that it would do the same to defend its NATO allies, and especially the exposed Anglo-American-French outpost in West Berlin. As a consequence, the political asymmetry that dominated postwar Europe – the legitimacy of democratic capitalism and the illegitimacy of Marxism–Leninism – did nothing to change its political boundaries, which remained frozen through the end of the 1980s.

There lingered, however, the lurking sense that there must be some way to extract advantages from nuclear weapons without actually using them. President Dwight D. Eisenhower thought that threats to use these devices might lower the costs of containment while deterring Soviet and Chinese challenges outside of Europe, but the results were unimpressive. Meanwhile, Khrushchev seized upon a rare Soviet technological "first" – the launching of an earth satellite in October 1957 – to claim that the USSR had surged ahead of the United States in strategic rocketry and to attempt to extract concessions from this feat. That strategy failed even more thoroughly than Eisenhower's, though, because the Soviet Union had not in fact surged ahead, a fact the Americans soon confirmed from secret reconnaissance flights and later satellite photography.

The nuclear-arms race, then, reinforced the Cold War status quo, a fact made dramatically evident in 1962 when Khrushchev undertook one more effort to change it. In a risky attempt to redress the strategic balance – and to defend Fidel Castro's revolution – he sent medium- and intermediate-range missiles equipped with nuclear warheads to Cuba. He thereby brought the world as close as it came during the Cold War to a nuclear war, but in the end the crisis changed little. Khrushchev withdrew his missiles, the Americans promised not to invade Cuba, and the Soviet–American rivalry went on as before – except in one respect. The confrontation had been sufficiently alarming that Soviet and American leaders agreed tacitly not to use nuclear weapons again to try to break the Cold War stalemate. That was one promise they kept.

Stalemate: tails wagging dogs

The United States and the Soviet Union were not alone in seeking to shape Cold War strategy, however, and here, too, there were ancient echoes. One of the striking things about the Peloponnesian War is the extent to which smaller powers maneuvered the superpowers of their day. For in so delicately balanced a situation, small shifts in allegiance could make big differences.[6] The same was true in the Cold War.

Small powers had several sources of strength during that conflict. One came from the simultaneous dismantling – in some cases collapse – of the great European colonial empires in Asia, the Middle East, and Africa. All at once dozens of new states were appearing that had not yet taken sides in the Soviet–American conflict. Few, if any, could expect by doing so to tilt the global balance in any measurable way. But fears in Washington and Moscow had gone beyond the measurable: the critical balance was now a *psychological* one in which appearances meant as much as hard facts. That empowered regimes that only recently had lacked power.

If there was a grand strategist of tilt it was Tito, whose defection from Moscow and subsequent success in winning American aid first demonstrated the possibility of playing off one superpower against the other. He, in turn, became close to Jawaharlal Nehru in India and Gamal Abdel Nasser in Egypt, who also saw the leverage such a strategy could provide and encouraged other new states to embrace it. By 1955, the three of them had organized the "Non-Aligned" Movement: a Third World, as it came to be called, where

6 Strassler (ed.), *The Landmark Thucydides*, especially 24, 365.

power resided in the possibility that the countries that constituted it might cease to remain non-aligned.

The United States and – later – the Soviet Union tried persistently to shape such choices through diplomacy, economic and technological assistance, even covert and overt intervention. Their successes, however, were problematic because none of these measures could prevent future defections, whether as the result of revolutions, coups, dissatisfaction, neglect, or simply the other side's offer of a higher price. The Third World, then, was both victim and manipulator of the "first" and "second."

Alliances – formal and informal – provided another way to transform weaknesses into strengths. States generally join alliances because they lack power: they have either sought protection or been forced to accept it. But if the leading nation of an alliance has lost the ability to discriminate – if it has put its credibility on the line everywhere by declaring everything vital – then it has passed the initiative to its weaker partners, who can often use that advantage to get what they want.

Hence Ulbricht in East Germany undermined Khrushchev's attempts to reform Marxism–Leninism by repeatedly warning that, if pressed too hard, his regime might collapse. Similarly, Syngman Rhee in South Korea and Chiang Kai-shek on the Nationalist-held island of Taiwan coerced a reluctant Eisenhower into giving them security guarantees, on the grounds that without these the North Koreans and the Chinese Communists would attack, with devastating results for American credibility. Rhee and Chiang were hardly democratic allies – they were not even predictable allies. But by flaunting their weakness they made themselves, like Ulbricht, necessary allies.

The risks of *not* defending allies became clear in 1963 when the administration of John F. Kennedy decided to abandon Ngo Dinh Diem of South Vietnam. It thereby left, for Lyndon B. Johnson, a leadership vacuum he was never able to fill. Fearing that the North Vietnamese, with the help of their Soviet and Chinese allies, would take over the country, Johnson embarked upon a full-scale military intervention that would cost the lives of 58,000 Americans, an unknown but far larger number of Vietnamese, and would bring the United States close to domestic paralysis.

It later became clear that neither the Soviet Union nor China had authorized Ho Chi Minh's war against South Vietnam. In yet another demonstration of strength through weakness, he had acted on his own, confident that neither Moscow nor Beijing would disavow him. He was right: these large Marxist–Leninist states let a small one tell them what to do because they feared their own loss of ideological credibility if they failed to support it. Ho's strategy produced impressive results. The long and costly war in Vietnam dissipated American resources and shook American resolve – even though, in retrospect, the global balance of power was never really at stake there to begin with.

One additional effect of the Vietnam War was to help mobilize a new generation of educated young people who were less prepared than their elders to accept the Cold War stalemate. Their energies manifested themselves, to be sure, in anti-war protests, but also in challenges to "establishments" everywhere: to governments, corporations, and universities throughout the United States and Western Europe, to Marxist–Leninist regimes that had suppressed dissent in Eastern Europe, even to the state and party bureaucracy in China, where Mao himself launched his destructive "Cultural Revolution" – a rare instance of an establishment igniting an insurrection against itself.

By the end of the 1960s, the grand strategic flexibility available to the Cold War great powers had narrowed significantly. Leaders in the United States, the Soviet Union, Europe, and even China found themselves frustrated in winning support for their ideologies, frightened by the prospect of nuclear war, worried about the solidity of their alliances – and even about the cohesion of their own societies. The Cold War was now not only a stalemate: it seemed to be diminishing the influence of the states that supposedly dominated it.

Détente: a failure of stabilization

Détente was a cooperative superpower effort to reverse this trend, but also a competitive superpower attempt to regain the advantage in the Cold War. It was, thus, the first grand strategy to reflect common interests in Washington, Moscow, and the capitals of their respective allies – beyond the obvious desirability of avoiding a nuclear holocaust. But détente was never meant to end the Cold War: instead its designers sought to set rules for what they all understood would continue to be a contest. What none had anticipated was that setting rules would sharpen the conflict.

By 1969, all sides had an interest in cooling off the Cold War. The Americans were failing in Vietnam. The Soviet Union had suppressed the "Prague spring," but only by alienating ideological allies elsewhere. Sensing the unlikelihood of reunification, West and East Germans had begun easing tensions across the walls that divided them. And in China, Mao Zedong had convinced himself that the Soviet Union was now a greater threat to his country's safety than the United States would ever be: his diplomatic revolution was about to overshadow – though not yet end – his cultural revolution.

These converging circumstances made it possible for the new president of the United States, Richard M. Nixon, and his assistant for national security affairs, Henry Kissinger, to make the most radical shift in American grand strategy since NSC-68. They had several objectives: to get the United States out of Vietnam without appearing to have been forced out; to engage the Soviet Union in negotiations on arms control, economic contacts, and the management of Third World conflicts; to open relations with China as a way of applying pressure in Moscow, and to restore presidential authority at home. By the end of 1972, it all seemed to have worked: Nixon had traveled to Beijing and Moscow, signed the first Strategic Arms Limitation Treaty with the USSR, come close to a Vietnam ceasefire, and won reelection triumphantly. It looked as though the Americans had become grand strategic wizards.

But the wizardry rested on shaky foundations. The Nixon–Kissinger strategy required a carefully controlled "linkage" of inducements with constraints – of sticks with carrots – leaving little room for leaks to the press, complaints from critics, or congressional oversight. It implied an equal distribution of calculable benefits to the United States and the Soviet Union, but their rivalry had long been propelled by incalculable fears. It expected saintliness on the part of the superpowers – that they would resist Third World temptations – but it did nothing to prevent Third World regimes from continuing to offer them. And it conflated stability with justice: the relief that would come from lessening the danger of nuclear war, Nixon and Kissinger believed, would overcome whatever resentments would arise from locking the Cold War stalemate into place.

None of these assumptions held up. Domestic critics assailed the Nixon administration for giving away too much on strategic arms, and for not having done enough for human rights. The president's insistence on centralizing power led to abuses of power, with the Watergate crisis forcing his resignation in August 1974. Meanwhile, Nasser's successor in Egypt, Anwar Sadat, had tempted the United States by expelling Soviet advisers from his country: when Washington failed to seize this opportunity, he attacked Israel, forcing an American-imposed settlement from which Kissinger excluded the USSR – a bitter humiliation for Moscow. That left Kremlin leaders with little sympathy for Nixon's successor, Gerald Ford, when he and Kissinger tried to save South Vietnam from a North Vietnamese invasion in the spring of 1975, or when they sought to prevent Cuban and Soviet intervention on behalf of Marxist rebels in the former Portuguese colony of Angola later that year.

American unilateralism in the Middle East was not the only reason, though, that the Soviet Union went on the offensive in the Third World. Brezhnev worked hard for détente and wanted it to succeed; but within the Soviet Communist Party and especially the emerging regional institutes – Moscow's equivalent of think tanks – a new generation of experts was insisting that this was the time to seize the initiative. The United States had shown itself unexpectedly irresolute in Vietnam. The USSR now had the naval and air strength to project power into distant parts of the world. The Cuban revolution had shown that Marxism–Leninism could thrive in "developing" countries, and the Cubans themselves had become adept at playing Ho Chi Minh's game: embracing causes – Angola was an example – which Moscow could not easily disavow. Perhaps history was again moving toward revolution, this time in Southeast Asia, Southern Africa, and Latin America.

So while the plans of Nixon and Kissinger, by the mid-1970s, had fallen into disarray, so too had those of the Soviet Union. The international Communist movement had long ceased to be monolithic; now leadership in Moscow was becoming pluralistic. Détente, which began as a joint superpower effort to stabilize the Cold War, instead destabilized the priorities of both superpowers. It was not even clear anymore what each side's grand strategy was, much less how one might measure its effectiveness. The resulting confusion left a vacuum in which the long-obscured ecology of the Cold War – the environment within which all of its antagonists operated – began to manifest itself.

Soviet strategic overstretch

One reason we still read Thucydides on the Peloponnesian War is that he allows us to see the underlying structural features of that conflict. One of these was dissimilar capabilities: the fact that Athens was a naval power while Sparta relied on a land army meant that neither could easily defeat the other. Structures in this ancient war, however, were never completely stable. If one side could master the skills of the other, or if one side blundered into situations that favored the other, then the stalemate could end. This happened when the Athenian assembly approved a land war in Sicily for which its army was ill-prepared, after which the Spartans found ways to harass and then defeat it by sea. Athens never recovered from this reversal of roles – this failure to respect structures that had sustained its power, even as it exposed itself to those that had favored its enemy.

Something like this happened to the Soviet Union after détente collapsed. At first the United States seemed weakened: Jimmy Carter's administration found it difficult to devise any consistent grand strategy with respect to the USSR, while that country's leadership appeared, from the outside at least, to be increasingly self-confident. In retrospect, though, Carter and his critics were debating how to *adapt* American strategy to the realities of a post-détente era. Brezhnev and his colleagues fundamentally *misjudged* those realities, with far more devastating consequences.

Soviet leaders now concluded – as if to echo the Americans a decade earlier – that the global balance of power required demonstrations of resolve wherever Moscow's reputation might be at stake. Following the fall of South Vietnam and the unexpected success of the Angolan revolution, Brezhnev found it necessary to aid new insurrections that claimed to be Marxist in Yemen, Ethiopia, and Afghanistan. History seemed to be vindicating Marx in places Marx had hardly heard of. If the most powerful Marxist state failed to help history along, however, it might lose credibility with more militant Marxists like the Cubans while creating opportunities for renegade Marxists like the Chinese. It hardly mattered that the Yemenis, Ethiopians, and Afghans had only the vaguest idea of Marxism, Leninism, Stalinism, Maoism, and even Castroism. Like the Americans in Vietnam – and like the Athenians in Sicily – the aging Brezhnev regime lost the ability to distinguish what was vital from what was not.

Soviet interventions in these countries weakened what little support was left for détente within the United States, even though Carter had hoped to revive that strategy. They left Moscow's agents at the mercy of forces they did not understand: the analytical categories of Marxism–Leninism were of little use in societies dominated by warlords, tribalism, and deeply held but violently manifested religious convictions. And when the Afghan revolution began to fail, in 1979, Brezhnev ordered military intervention on a massive scale, at great cost to the Afghan people, to the Soviet Union itself, and to its own anti-imperialist reputation. He thereby empowered an improbable coalition that included the Afghan mujahedin as well as Pakistanis, Iranians, Saudis, Chinese, and Americans – who employed the tactics of Ho Chi Minh against Ho's former superpower ally.

Meanwhile, in another misjudgment of Cold War structures, Soviet leaders had abandoned their long-time policy of isolating Marxist–Leninist countries from the global economy. With the inefficiencies of that ideology having become obvious and with popular discontent growing, they had little choice by the early 1970s but to relax either authoritarianism or autarchy. They chose the latter, gambling that by importing technology and even food from the United States and Western Europe, they could buy the time necessary for yet another attempt at reform at home and in Eastern Europe – this time one that would *not* get out of control and have to be suppressed.

As it happened, though, Moscow lost control in another way. Capitalist credits left the East Europeans – apart from the enterprising Hungarians – with few incentives to undertake reforms: they simply borrowed the money to finance their imports. Meanwhile, the Soviet Union, a major oil producer, was hooked on the artificially high price of that commodity brought about by the 1973 Middle East War, and that too induced complacency. As the decade ended, the Soviet and East European economies were much more closely tied to the global economy than they had been at its beginning. That solved some problems but created others: notably a contraction of credit when the Eastern Europeans found it difficult to repay their loans, and – even more devastatingly for the USSR – a sharp decline in oil prices during the early 1980s.

All of this took place as Soviet military expenditures were soaring, owing to the collapse of détente, the Afghan war, and support for Third World revolutions elsewhere. By some calculations, the USSR was spending as much as 25 percent of gross domestic product on defense – the equivalent figure for the United States, on a far larger economic base, was about 5 percent. Meanwhile, living standards were worse than they had been when Kremlin leaders first decided to reverse autarchy and risk integration into what was still a capitalist world.

The most surprising way in which Brezhnev and his advisers misjudged structures, however, had to do with human rights. The Soviet Union had long sought recognition of post-World War II boundaries in Eastern Europe, and in the spirit of détente persuaded the United States and its NATO allies to sign a formal agreement to that effect at Helsinki in the summer of 1975. In return, and with remarkable short-sightedness, Brezhnev committed his country to the principle that sovereignty could no longer shield brutality – that the manner in which a state treated its own citizens was a legitimate matter for international concern.

He did this in the belief that Soviet and East European authorities could easily contain whatever disruptions the concession might cause: it was more important to get the boundaries recognized. But no one had any intention of challenging boundaries in the first place. Challenging authoritarian rule, however, was now a legitimate enterprise, because Brezhnev's signature on the Helsinki Final Act formally endorsed the argument that the Soviet Union's adversaries had been making throughout the Cold War: that the people, not the party and its leaders, had the right to organize, vote, and thereby determine their own future.

Dissidents who had long hoped for reform could now claim it as their right, and within months their demands were sweeping the Soviet bloc. Several circumstances prevented Moscow from crushing these movements as it had in the past. One was the economic dependence on the capitalists that had come with the abandonment of autarchy: any replay of Budapest 1956 or Prague 1968 would cause an immediate cut-off in credits, technology, and food imports, worsening an already deteriorating situation. Another was dispropor-tionate military spending, which left little room – especially after the invasion of Afghanistan – for taking on still greater military burdens. But a third was what Soviet leaders had themselves pledged at Helsinki: a public commitment to respect precisely the processes that were eroding their own authority.

Each of these miscalculations – these failures to respect structures that had sustained Soviet power – became, for Moscow, what the Sicilian expedition had been for Athens: an ill-considered departure from a long-held strategy, with results that overstretched resources, exposed vulnerabilities, and thus handed enemies the means to break a long stalemate.

Reagan, Gorbachev, and the end of the Cold War

By 1981, the Soviet Union had many enemies: in China, where the twice-purged Deng Xiaoping had succeeded Mao Zedong and shown that a single-party Marxist state could indeed reform its economy – but only by moving toward capitalism; in Czechoslovakia, where the playwright Vaclav Havel and the movement he founded, Charter 77, were pressing Soviet leaders to honor their Helsinki human rights commitments; in the Vatican, where a papal conclave surprised the world – and especially the Kremlin – by electing a Polish pope determined to challenge Moscow's influence in Eastern Europe; in Britain, where Margaret Thatcher had become prime minister by attacking planned economies; in Poland, where a persistent Gdansk shipyard worker, Lech Wałęsa, had forced the government in Warsaw to recognize Solidarity, the first independent trade union within the Soviet bloc; and in the United States, where Ronald Reagan had become president after decisively defeating Carter's bid for reelection – with an explicit promise to kill détente.

The simultaneous appearance of so many adversaries suggests several things. One is a major failure of strategy in Moscow, since an obvious standard for success in strategy is to decrease, not increase, the number of opponents one faces. Another is that the shaking up of the Cold War stalemate – the destabilizations of the 1970s and the misjudgment of structures into which these lured the USSR – destroyed the sense of inevitability that had come to surround bipolarity: they opened minds to the possibility that a superpower rivalry was not the only conceivable way to organize the world. Still another is that détente, which had been meant to institutionalize such a system, instead wound up de-institutionalizing it.

For it now had become apparent that détente could never end the Cold War: it could at best only make the struggle safer and more predictable. That was progress, but it still meant that half the world would live under governments it had not chosen. Détente's gravediggers – Havel, John Paul II, Thatcher, Wałęsa, Reagan – were determined to change that situation. Deng was content with it but sought something else equally radical: to make the world's most populous country a prosperous country. There was no common strategy in all of this – the anti-Soviet movement was too diverse and disconnected – but there was a convergence of strategies with a common objective. That was to move beyond the Cold War.

No one was sure, though, how this might happen. Many people still feared a nuclear war, not least the dying Brezhnev and his equally feeble successors Iurii Andropov and Konstantin Chernenko. Others hoped for a negotiated settlement, but the Reagan administration at first seemed uninterested, and even if it had been interested, the old men in the Kremlin would hardly have been capable of negotiating. A few prophets predicted the collapse of the Soviet Union but found it difficult to specify how or when that might occur. A few officials in Washington and London foresaw the possibility that a Soviet leader might emerge, as Kennan decades before had foreseen, who would sense the "internal contradictions" of his own system and seek to change it. But it was not at all evident, even to Kennan, how the Soviet system of the early 1980s, which had never been more set in its ways, could ever produce such a visionary.[7]

In the end, as often happens in history, all expectations were confounded. The nuclear danger was greater than at any point since the Cuban missile crisis, but Reagan turned out to be a nuclear abolitionist – the only one ever to occupy the White House – and upon recognizing the risks quickly moved to diminish them. The ossified Soviet system did produce a negotiating partner in Mikhail Gorbachev, who succeeded Chernenko in 1985, but it also produced much more: Gorbachev turned out to be the Soviet leader Kennan had hoped for. To everyone's surprise including probably his own, Gorbachev abandoned the Soviet Union's revolutionary-imperial aspirations and set out to make his state a normal member of an international system in which the Cold War itself would cease to be "normal."

7 John Lewis Gaddis, *The United States and the End of the Cold War: Implications, Reconsiderations, Provocations* (New York: Oxford University Press, 1992), 126–27.

But Gorbachev too misjudged a structure, which was that of the Soviet Union itself. It turned out that to give up its ideology, to relinquish its sphere of influence, and to acknowledge the right of non-Russian nationalities to secede – without at the same time transforming that state into a multiparty democracy and a market economy – was to hollow it out from within: Gorbachev left it no reason to exist. He could never bring himself to acknowledge that reality, but his successor, Boris Yeltsin, saw it clearly. For just as the visionaries of the 1980s understood that détente, having perpetuated the Cold War, had to be eliminated, so this visionary of the early 1990s concluded that the same was now true of the Soviet Union itself.

A Clausewitzian conclusion

The Cold War ended differently from the Peloponnesian War, indeed from all the other great wars of which we know: with the peaceful collapse – no surrender was necessary – of one of its participants. Grand strategies on all sides contributed to this outcome because none valued violence as an end in itself. Each respected the teaching of the greatest of all students of strategy, Carl von Clausewitz, who insisted that war must always and in all of its aspects reflect policy. During the Cold War, strategy went beyond this principle to substitute for war in most of its aspects. And so modern civilization – except for Marx and his ideological descendants – did not follow the trajectory of Greek civilization, which survived the Peloponnesian War only as art, ideas, and ruins.

No single strategy, strategist, or state was responsible for this achievement. Rather, they each adapted to and evolved within their common ecosystem or, where they could not, they accepted extinction gracefully. As a consequence, the Cold War resembled the past, but did not in all respects reflect it. Thucydides would not have been surprised.

2

Identity and the Cold War

ROBERT JERVIS

The question for this chapter is how Soviet and American national identities shaped and were shaped by the Cold War. Defining identity is not easy, however.[1] Is it the same as self-image or self-perception? How does it relate to ideology and political culture?[2] Can we treat national identity as singular in the face of internal differences? What evidence can establish the content or even the existence of identities, and how do we go about determining their causes and effects?

Although in the end perhaps we have to settle for the Potter Stewart definition of knowing it when we see it, more formally national identity can be seen as the set of values, attributes, and practices that members believe characterize the country and set it off from others. Identity is the (shared) answer to central if vague questions: Who are we? What are we like? Who are we similar to and different from? Identity is at work when people say "We must act in a way that is true to what we are," as Jimmy Carter did in his 1978 state of the union address when he declared that "the very heart of our identity as a nation is our firm commitment to human rights."[3] Identities thus carry

---

1 For a good review, which also includes a discussion of methods for determining the substance of identities, see Rawi Abdelal, Yoshiko Herrera, Alastair Iain Johnston, and Rose McDermott, "Identity as a Variable," *Perspectives on Politics*, 6 (2006), 695–712. For identity and political conflict, see, for example, Alexander Wendt, *Social Theory of International Politics* (New York: Cambridge University Press, 1999), and Consuelo Cruz, *Political Culture and Institutional Development in Costa Rica and Nicaragua: World-Making in the Tropics* (New York: Cambridge University Press, 2005).

2 The literature on ideology and the Cold War is extensive: for good recent statements, see Mark Kramer, "Ideology and the Cold War," *Review of International Studies*, 25 (1999), 539–76; Nigel Gould-Davies, "Rethinking the Role of Ideology in International Politics During the Cold War," *Journal of Cold War Studies*, 1 (1999), 90–109. Important older treatments include Samuel Huntington and Zbigniew Brzezinski, *Political Power: USA/USSR* (Westport, CT: Greenwood Press, 1982), ch. 9; Carew Hunt, "The Importance of Doctrine," in Alexander Dallin (ed.), *Soviet Conduct in World Affairs* (New York: Columbia University Press, 1960), 37–46.

3 See www.let.rug.nl~usa/P/jc39/speeches/su78jec.htm, 8.

heavy affective weight, and this helps explain why scholarly arguments about the Cold War are often very bitter because the stakes include what the Soviet Union and the United States are like or should be like.

Soviet and American identities

As the preceding paragraph indicates, identities are like stereotypes in being over-generalizations. With this in mind, I think it is fair to say that characteristics of the American identity during the Cold War included democracy; individualism and voluntarism as contrasted to strong direction – let alone compulsion – from the government; opposition to concentrated power, especially when wielded by the government; the belief in a supreme being that supplies meaning to life; and a faith that this model or "way of life" can, should, and eventually will be adopted by others as well. To say that the United States saw its model as potentially universal is not to say that it was viewed by Americans as yet widely shared. Quite the contrary: the idea of American exceptionalism is not merely an academic construct but has deep roots in American society. The United States was founded to be different from the rest of the world (meaning Europe), and it would or at least could remain uncorrupted. As Thomas Paine explained, "We have it in our power to begin the world over again."[4] Much of this can be traced back to the fact that the thirteen colonies were dominated by a middle-class fragment which, as Louis Hartz argued, meant that unlike Europe the United States never had a bourgeois revolution or a strong socialist movement, and this in turn helps explain why the United States feared and failed to understand revolutions and radicalism abroad.[5]

The Soviet identity also held out its system as one that would eventually spread throughout the world, but its content was very different in being built around the proletariat, the centrality of class conflict, and the transformation of individuals and societies. As Stephen Kotkin puts it: "From its inception, the Soviet Union had claimed to be an experiment in socialism, a superior alternative to capitalism, for the entire world. If socialism was not superior to capitalism, its existence could not be justified."[6]

---

4 Thomas Paine, *Basic Writings of Thomas Paine* (New York: Willey, 1942), 65.
5 Louis Hartz, *The Liberal Tradition in America* (New York: Harcourt, Brace & World, 1955).
6 Stephen Kotkin, *Armageddon Averted: The Soviet Collapse, 1970–2000* (New York: Oxford University Press, 2001), 19. Melvyn Leffler sees the Cold War as a struggle in these terms: *For the Soul of Mankind* (New York: Hill and Wang, 2007).

An additional aspect of Soviet identity, one about which Soviet leaders were ambivalent, came from interaction with the United States. This is the Soviet Union as a superpower, equal in status and rights to its rival. The ambivalence stemmed from the fact that at least some Soviets associated being a great power with behaving like a "normal" state – i.e., seeking narrow advantage and exploiting others rather than behaving in accord with socialist principles. But as Soviet power grew and a global reach became possible, the sense of the Soviet Union as being an equal of the United States became much more important. It increasingly rankled Soviet leaders that the United States consistently upheld a double standard and denied them the right to do things that the United States did routinely – for example, intervene in the Third World, establish bases all over, and play a central role in the Middle East. The Soviets then bent their efforts less to restricting American activities than to establishing the right for them to behave in the same way. Leonid Brezhnev and his colleagues placed great store in the Basic Principles Agreement of 1972 because it seemed to ratify their equality (Richard Nixon and Henry Kissinger did not take the agreement seriously and signed it just to humor the Soviets); détente broke down in part because of disagreements over whether the Soviets could emulate American behavior in the Third World. Status as well as specific privileges were involved. As Kissinger put it in a memo to prepare Nixon for a possible meeting with Aleksei Kosygin: "It has always been one of the paradoxes of Bolshevik behavior that their leaders have yearned to be treated as equals by the people they consider doomed."[7]

Symmetries and asymmetries in Soviet and American identities

Soviet and American identities had four major similarities or parallelisms, but they heightened rather than dampened the conflict. First, each implied a form of universalism in that there was nothing unique about the country that meant its values could not spread. Some countries do have identities that are bounded in this way. Thus, while the British believe they have a distinctive and highly valued way of life that has much to offer others, they do not expect the world ever to be entirely British. But for somewhat different reasons,

7 "Memorandum from the President's Assistant for National Security Affairs (Kissinger) to President Nixon," (undated), US Department of State, *Foreign Relations of the United States, 1969–1976*, vol. XII, *Soviet Union, January 1969–October 1970* (Washington, DC: Government Printing Office, 2006), 603 (hereafter, *FRUS*, with year and volume number).

neither the United States nor the Soviet Union felt this way: both were founded not on nationality or myths of blood and common heritage, but on ideas. The United States is famously a country of immigrants, one in which it was possible to be "un-American" by believing incorrect ideas. For the Soviets, universalism was built into the ideology from the start. There was nothing particularly Russian about Marxism, and indeed the triumph of this doctrine in a backward country was regarded as a fluke. Indeed, for the Soviets, and to a lesser extent the Americans, the validity of the founding principles would be upheld only if they triumphed elsewhere.

Second and relatedly, both the United States and the Soviet Union saw themselves as the standard-bearers of progress and modernity. It was taken for granted that historical advancement is real and that while there might be setbacks, other peoples would eventually follow the same path that they did. Furthermore, within the world and within each country, there were progressive and regressive forces, and the former deserved encouragement if not active support.

Third, in a break from traditional European thinking about international politics, both the Soviet and the American ideologies implied that states' foreign policies were deeply influenced by their domestic systems. In the framework of Kenneth Waltz, they were "second-image" thinkers.[8] A balance of power might temporarily yield peace and security, but because of the primary role of the nature of the domestic regime, the world could be made safe for democracy (for the United States) or for Communism (for the Soviet Union) only if it became dominant if not universal throughout the world.

Finally, perhaps because the United States and the Soviet Union emerged as the result of revolutions, each was prone to expect and seek transformations of politics. For the USSR, the nature of the class struggle meant that gradual change was unlikely. Politics was not about small advantages and adjustments of interests, but about the basic question of *Kto-Kogo* – who-whom, who is going to dominate and who is going to be dominated. Transformationism was not as prominent an element in the American worldview, but President George W. Bush did not have to conjure it up from nowhere. As Steven Sestanovich has argued, during the Cold War the United States often reacted to setbacks not by limiting its goals or adjusting its tactics, but by seeking major changes, and this approach had deep roots in American history.[9]

---

8 Kenneth Waltz, *Man, the State, and War* (New York: Columbia University Press, 1959).
9 Stephen Sestanovich, "American Maximalism," *The National Interest*, no. 79 (2005), 13–23.

These similarities created a malign environment. Most fundamentally, they meant that while temporary agreements were possible, especially to minimize the danger of war, deep and long-run cooperation was not. A second-image view of international politics implies that the international conflict can end only when the other's fundamental beliefs and domestic arrangements change.[10]

One shared belief restrained conflict, however, and indeed may have saved the world from war. Each side believed that time was on its side, and that if war could be avoided, the long term would bring not only survival but victory. The most dangerous combination of beliefs is short-run optimism coupled with long-run pessimism, which gives great impetus to preventive wars; fortunately, most of the Cold War was characterized by long-run optimism even as predictions about the short-run oscillated.

As important as these similarities are four asymmetries between Soviet and American identities. First, Soviet identity came from the top down, and it remains unclear exactly how much of it was adopted by the population at large. This made Soviet leaders wary of permitting contact between their citizens and outsiders, and indeed their worries were well founded. Second, the American identity was much less self-conscious than the Soviet self-image. The lack of American awareness gave a certain flexibility to policy and a resilience to its sense of self. Third, Soviet identity pivoted not on what Soviet society was, but what it could be, and, relatedly, on what it should lead the world to be. American identity, although also looking to the future, was based on a view of what American society actually was (of course an idealized one). Because the Soviet identity represented beliefs about what would develop, it could lead to grave disappointments. Fourth, Soviet identity grew out of an explicit ideology, one that both predated the Soviet state and was formed in explicit opposition to capitalism, the main force it would confront during the Cold War. American identity developed more slowly, and, although it could readily be pressed into service against the Soviet Union, originated in differentiation from Europe, and especially Britain, which was seen as tyrannical.

Perhaps the most important implication of the asymmetries was that domestic reverses and the failure of the world to move in desired directions would be corrosive to the Soviet regime and identity. This also helps explain

10 This is why I think the Cold War can be described as a "deep security dilemma" in which each side was an inherent threat to the other's security: Robert Jervis, "Was the Cold War a Security Dilemma?" *Journal of Cold War Studies*, 3 (2001), 36–60.

what I think is the fact that the American identity was left relatively unscathed by the Cold War. This conflict left its mark on US domestic society, politics, and economy, but sense of self was altered relatively little. Hartz hoped that its encounter with the world in the Cold War would lead the United States to better understand itself and the range of social processes operating in the world. This turned out not to be the case, however.

The theoretical context

At first glance, the disputes over the importance of identity as a cause of Soviet or American foreign policy would seem to be a classic example of what international relations (IR) scholars call the level of analysis question and historians talk of as "Primat der Innerpolitik" versus "Primat der Aussenpolitik." Much traditional IR and diplomatic history argues that the main determinant of states' foreign policies is their external environments. This means not only the general context of international anarchy (i.e., the lack of sovereign power above national governments), but also the particular landscape of adversaries and allies through which the state must navigate. The fundamental contrast is to arguments asserting that internal characteristics and domestic politics are crucial, that different states will behave differently despite similarities in their external situation, and that foreign policies are guided by domestic factors and often aimed at producing domestic change in others.[11]

How identities operate

While identity is internal, in two crucial ways it operates differently from the factors discussed in the previous paragraph. By its very nature, an identity cannot be completely internal because it forms in response to others. To hold an identity is to set a boundary, to separate Self from Others, to exclude as well as include. Furthermore, the very act of separating people into groups, even without any rational basis, leads to an in-group bias. Conversely, conflict usually leads the actor to see the adversary in a way that maximizes contrast with it. Thus, differences between the United States and the Soviet Union, great as they were, were often exaggerated in the United States, especially at

---

11 For more discussions of the empirical implications of theories at different levels of analysis, see Robert Jervis, *Perception and Misperception in International Politics* (Princeton, NJ: Princeton University Press, 1976), ch. 1.

the start of the Cold War when differentiation was most necessary. Although the totalitarian model of the USSR had significant validity and was readily accessible because of the previous experience with Nazi Germany, its widespread acceptance owed at least something to the contrast it provided to American individualism, freedom, and lack of state control.

The links between seeing others as different and having a hostile relationship with them are reciprocal. To paraphrase Charles Tilly, "identity makes conflict, and conflict makes identity." Although more attention has been paid to the influence of identity on conflict, the reverse is at least as strong. Thus, while feelings of racial superiority may underlie much imperialism, the perception of racial differences and their central importance often follows rather than precedes conflict and domination. For the United States in much of the nineteenth and twentieth centuries, when leaders or countries became targets of enmity or acquisition, they developed darker skins. Similarly, conflict can magnify, or even create, a collective sense of self. Catholics and Protestants in Northern Ireland deepened their communal ties and identity when they were attacked for being Catholic or Protestant; Bosnians had little sense of this as a meaningful category and held a relaxed view of Islam until they were driven from their homes for being Bosnian and Muslim. Identity can then come from how others define you.

In the modern era when states must claim and believe to be fighting for more than simple material advantage, the need to differentiate will entail both real and perceived changes. Thus, with the violent breakup of Yugoslavia, Serbs and Croats tried to develop distinct languages from what had been a shared Serbo-Croatian. They claimed to be purging "their" language of words introduced by the other and to be returning to the ancient and pure version but in fact often achieved the differentiation by developing new words. In the Cold War, each side shunned anything that smacked of the other. In the mid-1950s, in addition to adding the phrase "under God" to the Pledge of Allegiance, Congress replaced "E pluribus unum" as the official national motto with "in God we trust," which was also put on paper money. Arguments against increased federal spending for education received added power from the association of central control of education with Soviet indoctrination, and measures of community that smacked of compulsion rather than voluntarism had to be avoided. Along with actual changes came perceptual changes and exaggerations. The degree to which American society was in fact individualistic was exaggerated and episodes and areas that were communal or communitarian were downplayed. The role of government, including state governments, in American economic development was slighted and the quality of American democracy was exaggerated.

The conception of democracy was also at least marginally influenced by the Cold War, just as American ideas on this topic had been shaped by previous encounters with enemies. For scholars in the 1930s influenced by the Great Depression, democracy had a significant economic dimension, and substantive outcomes were included. As the Cold War developed, scholars came to define democracy solely in terms of procedures such as competitive elections and a free press. There are good intellectual reasons for this formulation and it might have been adopted in any event, but it was no accident that it provided a sharper contrast between the United States and the Soviet Union than did the older one.[12]

Tensions, détentes, and identities: the limits of sustainable claims

If identities can be shaped by conflict, perhaps one of the root causes of conflict is the need of one or both sides to establish and maintain an identity, which is difficult to do in a relaxed international system. This need could be conscious or unconscious and could arise either from popular pressures or elite manipulation. We should then expect the Cold War to be at its most bitter when identity is under most pressure and, conversely, cooperative policies to be pursued when identities are secure. The argument is not without some plausibility, and we could see the early Cold War years as ones in which each side, having been challenged by world war and domestic upheavals, felt a loss of self and turned to a foreign enemy for confirmation and consolidation. But it is difficult to see later periods of détente as arising from secure identities,[13] and counterfactuals illustrate how the supposed connections between posited identity considerations and foreign-policy behavior can all too easily be fitted to any history that unfolded. Had the United States and the Soviet Union reached out to each other in the early period, one could attribute this behavior to the social and psychological security that came from winning the world war, and if the Cold War had coincided with extensive immigration into the United States, this line of thinking would lead us to conclude that American elites conjured up a foreign threat in order to Americanize the newcomers.

12 Ido Oren, *Our Enemies and Us: America's Rivalries and the Making of Political Science* (Ithaca, NY: Cornell University Press, 2003).
13 Indeed, it can be argued that it was domestic unrest that forced the leaders into détente: Jeremi Suri: *Power and Protest: Global Revolution and the Rise of Détente* (Cambridge, MA: Harvard University Press, 2003).

If the argument that conflicts are created in order to differentiate between populations and produce unity within them is too Machiavellian, the less extreme claim that conflict induces homogeneity is worth more consideration. This claim implies that conformity will rise and fall with international tensions. There is something to this, especially on the Soviet side. At the start of the Cold War, Iosif Stalin launched a campaign to denigrate the West and ensure that Soviet citizens had no contact with it. But we should not be too quick to accept the common claims for a parallel process in the United States. Although the stereotype of the late 1940s and 1950s is indeed one of conformity, it is far from clear that this is accurate. Abstract Expressionism, often held up as an example of the way in which the United States differentiated itself from the Soviet Union and sought to win over the Europeans by showing them that it had a significant culture, was transgressive and met with fierce resistance, not least from conservatives who strenuously objected to government-sponsored exhibits of it abroad.[14] While McCarthyism policed the liberal flank of acceptable views, its success was less attributable to widespread domestic sentiment than to calculations and maneuvers by the mainstream Republican leaders.[15] The foundations for the later success of the civil rights movement were also laid down in the early Cold War years, and Cold War concerns were largely responsible for the limited support for racial equality that was provided by the Dwight D. Eisenhower administration. International tension did not consistently solidify a narrow identity or slow social change in the United States.

The early Cold War years also saw heightened homophobia, justified in part by the claim that homosexuals were security risks, which was a self-fulfilling prophesy because as long as being gay was stigmatized, homosexuals were vulnerable to blackmail. But the subsequent changing course of American attitudes toward homosexuality does not track with increases and decreases in international tensions. Here as elsewhere, the influences on American culture were numerous and the Cold War was not the most potent one.

Even more strikingly, the economic policies not only of Harry S. Truman but even of Eisenhower did not maximize the differentiation from socialism. Although the onset of the Cold War may have diminished liberal impulses, the role of the government in the economy in the 1940s and 1950s looks very

14 Taylor Littleton and Maltby Sykes, *Advancing American Art: Painting, Politics, and Cultural Confrontation at Mid-Century* (Tuscaloosa, AL: University of Alabama Press, 1989).
15 Michael Rogin, *The Intellectuals and McCarthy: The Radical Specter* (Cambridge, MA: MIT Press, 1967).

large from today's perspective, with vigorous anti-trust measures, a degree of economic planning, the consolidation of the welfare state, and high taxes on upper-income brackets. Many of the measures undertaken to meet the perceived Soviet threat increased federal direction of the society, most obviously the increased role of Washington in education, and an interstate highways project that literally reshaped the American landscape. Two general conclusions follow. First, international competition can lead to measures that do not easily fit with identity or can undermine it. Second, the fact that the United States, unlike the Soviet Union, has a relatively strong society and a relatively weak state means that many of the forces acting on it came internally, and, while not unaffected by the course of the Cold War, had much autonomy from it.

Identity and the standard view of the Cold War

Arguments for the importance of identity come through most clearly by contrast with what is the standard account, at least in IR, which is that the United States and the Soviet Union were "enemies by position," to use the felicitous phrase by Raymond Aron.[16] They emerged from World War II as the only superpowers; no other state could menace them and each by its capabilities menaced the other. The normal frictions of international politics, the desire by each country to ensure its own security, and – perhaps – expansionism by one or both sides then made the latent Cold War manifest.

This story is not all wrong, but it is incomplete. First, although both the United States and the Soviet Union were potential superpowers by dint of their size, they were able to play this role only when they mobilized significant domestic resources and placed themselves at the head of their respective blocs, something that only followed their clashes. Second and relatedly, bipolarity may tell us that each superpower will view the other warily, but structure and even specific instances of friction do not automatically produce the degree of hostility and fear that characterized the Cold War. Would hostility have grown as it did if the two superpowers had had compatible identities? Third, while it is true that each side thought that the other was menacing its interests, only to some extent can we explain how each conceived of its interests by reference to uniform and unchanging factors of

16 Raymond Aron, *Peace and War: A Theory of International Relations*, trans. by Richard Howard and Annette Baker Fox (Garden City, NY: Doubleday, 1966), 138, see also p. 544. I am indebted to Marc Trachtenberg for noting that this phrase does not fully reflect Aron's views of the conflict, which is less deterministic than this.

1. Stalin claimed that the creation of NATO led to an enemy encirclement of the Soviet Union. Some Western cartoonists saw it differently; here is Leslie Illingworth's illustration from 1949.

international politics. Identity and interest can shape each other or even merge. Each side's interest in many questions was defined in part by its identity, and the interactions of the contending interests in turn affected each side's sense of self. While the competition for Western Europe can perhaps be understood in terms of the need for countries to contend for the potential centers of power, the conflict over the Third World is not explicable in this framework, and it is to this topic that we will now turn.

Conflict in the Third World

At first glance, it might seem that Soviet–American competition in the Third World can be readily explained by traditional IR theories.[17] These tell us, after

17 For the best survey, see Odd Arne Westad, *The Global Cold War* (New York: Cambridge University Press, 2006). See also Robert McMahon, *The Cold War on the Periphery: The United States, India, and Pakistan* (New York: Columbia University Press, 1994); Jerry Hough, *The Struggle for the Third World: Soviet Debates and American Options* (Washington, DC: Brookings Institution, 1986).

all, that major states struggle for power and advantage, that each will try to match what the other does, and that clients will be sought. Just as the European powers divided Africa and much of Asia during the period of imperialism, so the United States and the Soviet Union sought to spread their influence around the globe. But in fact the competitive logic of international politics does *not* lead to this conclusion. The most prominent IR theory, Waltz's neorealism, argues that because the superpowers were so much stronger than everyone else and able to balance against the adversary by mobilizing their internal resources, they did not need to pay much attention to the Third World.[18]

The power of identities and the related fact that each side understood the Cold War as a clash of social systems explains much here. With Europe and China having chosen one way of life or the other, the Third World represented the uncommitted states and peoples. What was at stake was nothing less than each side's view of the rightness of its cause, the universalism of its values, and the answer to the question of whose side history was on. Kissinger's reaction to Salvador Allende's election in Chile was particularly telling: "I don't see why we have to let a country go Marxist just because its people are irresponsible."[19] The idea that an educated and sophisticated country would choose a different path was deeply upsetting for reasons that go beyond standard interstate power competition.

The Soviets felt that supporting revolutionary forces was not only good international politics because it weakened the adversary, but also a revolutionary duty. The whole purpose of the Bolshevik Revolution was to lead others to the same path. One of the great surprises in Soviet archives was that the elites spoke the same way in private as they did in public. Politburo stationery bore the heading "Proletariats of the world unite!" and while this did not mean that Soviet security was to be risked to help foreign comrades, this mission was a central part of Soviet identity. Class conflict was the driver of politics, and without its revolutionary mission the Soviet Union would have no convincing self-justification.

The sense of being on the right side of historical forces and the duty to help them along come out nicely in the Kennedy–Khrushchev discussions – a mild word for the exchange – at Vienna. To the president's plea that events in the

18 Kenneth Waltz, *Theory of International Politics* (Reading, MA: Addison-Wesley, 1979); for a critique, see Jervis, *System Effects: Complexity in Political and Social Life* (Princeton, NJ: Princeton University Press, 1997), 118–22.
19 Quoted in Walter Isaacson, *Kissinger* (New York: Simon & Schuster, 1992), p. 290.

Third World had to be managed so that they were not unduly upsetting to either side,

> Mr. Khrushchev said that the West and the U.S. as its leader must recognize one fact: Communism exists and has won its right to develop ... The Soviet Union is for change. It believes that it is now in the political arena and it is challenging the capitalist system just as that system had challenged feudalism in the past. Mr. Khrushchev ... wondered whether the United States wanted to build a dam preventing the development of human mind and conscience. To do such a thing is not in man's power. The Spanish Inquisition burned people who disagreed with it but ideas did not burn and eventually came out as victors. Thus if we start struggling against ideas, conflicts and clashes between the two countries will be inevitable. Once an idea is born it cannot be chained or burned. History should be the judge in the argument between ideas ... Did the President want to say that Communism should exist only in those countries that are already Communist and that if Communist ideas should develop the U.S. would be in conflict with the USSR? Such an understanding of the situation is incorrect, and if there really is such an understanding, conflicts will be inevitable. Ideas do not belong to any one nation and they cannot be retracted.[20]

Although Nikita Khrushchev may have enjoyed tweaking his younger and less experienced counterpart, there is no reason to doubt his sincerity, just as there is no reason to doubt that he shared the sentiment that Mikoyan expressed to him that meeting Castro made him feel young again.[21]

Since the Third World started out as non-Communist, if not always friendly to the United States, the main American objective was to keep it that way. Although it always hoped for the spread of democracy and American values, the primacy of blocking the Soviet Union meant that it was relatively open-eyed in its support of tyrannies when this proved necessary, as it often did. As President John F. Kennedy explained in the aftermath of the assassination of Rafael Truillo in the Dominican Republic: "There are three possibilities in descending order of preference: a decent democratic regime, a continuation of the Truillo regime, or a Castro regime. We ought to aim at the first, but we really can't renounce the second until we are sure that we can avoid the

20 Memorandum of conversation, June 3, 1961, FRUS, 1961–1963, vol. V, Soviet Union, 174–76; for an interesting discussion of this conversation, see Vladislav Zubok and Constantine Pleshakov, Inside the Kremlin's Cold War (Cambridge, MA: Harvard University Press, 1996), 243–48.
21 Aleksandr Fursenko and Timothy Naftali, "One Hell of a Gamble": Khrushchev, Castro, and Kennedy, 1958–1964 (New York: Norton, 1997), 39.

2. Communism and capitalism compete for attention on walls in Calcutta.

third."[22] The Soviets were also willing to be pragmatic and often supported friendly Third World countries that repressed the local Communist parties, such as in Egypt. But on these occasions they had to tell themselves that these regimes, as bourgeois nationalists, were historically progressive and would eventually lead to socialism. This helps explain their continuing faith in the Third World despite the almost unbroken record of disappointment.

Of course, neither side reacted to the Third World as it actually was, but to what they perceived, and each saw events and possibilities through the lenses of their own experiences, hopes, and fears. For both sides, modernization was crucial, but in quite different ways. The United States believed that revolutions and Communism grew out of poverty and despair. If countries could be launched on the path of economic development, and if the difficult years of destabilizing transition could be weathered, then they would begin to resemble the West. Walt Rostow's *The Stages of Economic Growth* was the clearest statement, but it was only one of a whole shelf of related volumes. The Soviet Union also placed great faith in modernization, which it was undergoing itself. The model of how it was leading its Asian populations to modernity was

---

22 Quoted in Arthur Schlesinger, Jr., *A Thousand Days: John F. Kennedy in the White House* (Boston, MA: Houghton Mifflin, 1965), 769.

particularly important to it. This produced optimism, the sense that many Third World regimes were or soon would be ripe for revolution, and led to the perception that many Third World leaders had the skill and will to lead their countries to socialism at home and alignment with the USSR. If the United States suffered from exaggerated fears, the Soviet Union held exaggerated hopes. Both saw the Third World through the lenses of their understanding of their own history.

Khrushchev, the thaw, and the Third World

Both Soviet identity and its response to the Third World changed more than the American, and this was not a coincidence. Khrushchev's de-Stalinization was built on a less rigid view of the role of class and class conflict, just as the earlier perception of great threat from the capitalists made it seem dangerous to permit domestic relaxation. As Ted Hopf explains, acknowledging difference at home made the acceptance of differences abroad less threatening. When the distinction between workers and members of the bourgeoisie was taken to be either–or, with no mixtures or complex combinations possible, compromise was difficult at home and abroad; by making class only one of many possible identities for another state, the Soviet Union multiplied its possible relationships in the world.[23] The wider scope for what it meant to be a good Soviet citizen or to be on the path to socialism made it much easier for Khrushchev to see the bourgeois nationalist regimes as potential allies, as countries that were moving in the right direction rather than being irretrievably non-Communist. Indeed, local Communist parties could be sacrificed because the local regime was acceptable and a more progressive outcome would come in due course. Of course, there was more than a dose of hypocrisy and traditional international political calculation in this, but we may wonder whether it would have been possible without a change in the sense of what the USSR was.

The relations among the thaw, modifications of Soviet identity, and external relations bring us back to interactions. Identities are shaped by existing and desired relations abroad as well as shaping them. The realization that the Third World was the best ground on which to compete with the West and that this would be possible only if the USSR courted regimes that were constituted differently was conducive to constructing a less rigid Soviet

23 Ted Hopf, *Social Construction of International Politics: Identities and Foreign Policies, Moscow 1955 and 1999* (Ithaca, NY: Cornell University Press, 2002), 41, 92.

identity. What the Soviet *New Times* said in its retrospective survey of 1955 also characterized the changes in domestic attitudes: "The desire to find what unites countries, not disunites them, became a universally accepted slogan."[24] Similarly, the pressing need for relaxing tensions with the West in order to decrease the danger of war and gain access to Western economic resources and technology not only provided a strong impetus to peaceful coexistence, but also made it more likely that Soviet leaders would adjust their self-image to be consistent with the new policy. People want to think of themselves as principled and consistent, and so their beliefs about many things, including themselves, will be modified to justify their behavior.

Détente, identity, and the end of the Cold War

The relations between identity and foreign policy are brought out well by the 1969–1975 détente and the end of the Cold War, and to compare them brings us back to the asymmetry between the Soviet and American identities. What is most important for my analysis is the decline of détente, but this cannot be examined without some discussion of its origins and course. As usual, we know more about the American side, for which Vietnam was central. Nixon inherited a bloody and unpopular war and, like Lyndon B. Johnson before him, could neither win it nor afford a defeat. For Johnson and Nixon, what was at stake was the credibility of American commitments around the world, and the importance of credibility was greatly enhanced by a nuclear strategy that stressed the role of resolve and signals in producing deterrence in an era when nuclear war meant total destruction. This also meant that it was not so much defeat that was unacceptable as it was defeat of a type that would produce these unfortunate effects. Thus, if the Communists won not by pushing out American troops, but only after a decent interval following their removal, the harm to the United States would be less and the domino effects could be greatly attenuated. Furthermore, if the Soviet Union could be pressured into helping end the war, it might not take the American actions as indications of weakness.[25]

Such a "soft landing" was also needed for reasons more closely related to identity, as an open defeat in Vietnam could undermine the self-confidence of the American public, and perhaps of US leaders. From the start of the Cold

24 Quoted in Hopf, *Social Construction of International Politics*, p. 94.
25 For further discussions of US policy, see the chapters by Frank Costigliola, Robert D. Schulzinger, and Marc Trachtenberg.

War, the US elite worried that the public lacked the steady nerves that the struggle required and was prone to vacillate between defeatism and excess fear on the one hand and unwise bellicosity on the other. Defeats were particularly dangerous because they could lead to an over-reaction in either direction, and if the United States was to keep on track, the war had to be ended in a way that minimized its adverse consequences.

The Nixon administration also sought to limit Soviet advances in the Third World through the policy of linkage – i.e., making arms-control agreements, treaties formalizing the European settlement, and access to American economic resources contingent on Soviet restraint in the Third World. This assumed that the United States could afford to withhold these benefits if the Soviet Union did not cooperate. And that, of course, was the problem. Although in earlier periods the United States had resisted negotiating from a perceived position of weakness, Nixon and Kissinger had no choice. American opinion had turned against the war in Vietnam and it simply had to be ended. Furthermore, the war had undercut the domestic support for vigorous defense programs and measures to counter Soviet penetration of the Third World.

Soviet motives for détente both overlapped and differed, and also in part related to identity. For them, Vietnam was both a danger and an opportunity. The danger was that the war could spread, Chinese influence could grow, and chances for economic relations with the West would decline. (In fact, Soviet–American relations entered such a deep freeze that President Johnson and Soviet ambassador Dobrynin were reduced to discussing whether the Broadway musical *Hello Dolly* would be permitted to travel to the USSR.) The benefits of the war were equally obvious: the United States was wasting its efforts, dividing its alliances, and alienating much of the Third World. Furthermore, for the Soviets, Vietnam had intrinsic value as a revolutionary movement, and they had the duty to support it as this was the *raison d'être* for the Soviet existence. Even had it not been for competition with the People's Republic of China (PRC), it would have been very difficult for the Soviets to cooperate with the United States in a way that kept South Vietnam non-Communist.

For them, as for the Americans, the Third World was also important, but in a quite different way. As Brezhnev explained in 1976: détente did "not abolish or alter the laws of class struggle."[26] The Soviets hoped that by stabilizing the

26 Quoted in John Soares, Jr., "Strategy, Ideology, and Human Rights: Jimmy Carter Confronts the Left in Central America, 1979–1981," *Journal of Cold War Studies*, 8 (2006), 59.

central issues of arms and Europe, détente would allow them to proceed with competition in the Third World from a position of equality. Being treated as an equal was both a necessary part of a robust policy in the Third World and a valued end in itself. The Revolution had truly arrived: Moscow was recognized as a power equal to Washington; the capitalists finally realized that Communism was permanent; this would now set the stage for its eventual triumph. For the Soviets, détente offered a great opportunity to confirm what they were.[27]

The decline of détente

At bottom, détente failed because the two sides had incompatible expectations.[28] The United States saw the easing of tensions as a way to maintain the status quo in the face of American weakness; the Soviets saw it as a way to attain equal status and gains in the Third World. Although a variety of calculations, miscalculations, and accidents were at work, even under the best circumstances détente could not have brought the Cold War to an end because the United States and the Soviet Union, being founded on such different principles, were inherently a threat to each other as long as they were what they were. For the Soviets, there were then real limits beyond which détente could progress if it meant restraining itself in the Third World; the policies that were dictated by the Soviet conception of its interests and duties meant that it would be hard to maintain good relations for long in the face of US resistance.

It remains unclear whether Nixon and Kissinger pursued détente in truly cooperative terms and thought that it might be semi-permanent. This is the view expounded by Kissinger in the first two volumes of his memoirs and vigorously attacked by Raymond Garthoff, who argues that the administration never ceased pursuing unilateral advantage.[29] In the aftermath of the fall of the Soviet Union, however, Kissinger dropped his earlier stance and endorsed Garthoff's, using the third volume of his memoirs to argue that he saw détente as a way of gaining breathing space until the public would support a harder line, and claiming that the United States made no concessions in the hope of establishing long-run cooperation. For our purposes, what is crucial is

27 For Soviet policy, see William Taubman and Svetlana Savranskaya's chapter in this volume and Vladislav M. Zubok's chapter in volume III.
28 For assessments of détente, see Jussi Hanhimäki's, chapter in this volume and Olav Njølstad's chapter in volume III.
29 Raymond Garthoff, *Détente and Confrontation: American-Soviet Relations from Nixon to Reagan* (Washington, DC: Brookings Institution, 1994).

that Kissinger's second view implies that the USSR remained a revolutionary power, driven by its ideology and identity. Whether or not the latter view was correct, to the extent that American policymakers believed it, détente in fact could not have been permanent.

From the start, détente was opposed by neoconservatives who argued not only that the United States was getting the worse part of the bargain, but that the very notion of détente was flawed because it abandoned America's deepest ideals of supporting the forces of freedom throughout the world. Although some of the critics were opportunistic in seeking their own domestic political advantage, their stance was effective because it represented a strong reaffirmation of American identity and the parallel claim that the Soviets were driven by theirs. A détente that accepted a Communist Soviet Union was a betrayal of American values and would at most buy a temporary respite since it could not tame the expansionist Soviet policy that stemmed from its identity. Furthermore, such a policy would sacrifice domestic support because even if Kissinger, Nixon, and Gerald Ford were realists, the bulk of the American population remained truer to traditional American values.

Jimmy Carter's presidency embodied and magnified the contradictions in Kissinger's views. On the one hand, Carter and some of his advisers thought the United States had exaggerated the Soviet threat and believed that there was a great deal of common interest that could be realized through diplomacy – the United States and Soviet Union were, after all, normal states. On the other hand, he and others in his administration believed that the Soviet Union would press the United States wherever possible throughout the world, yet was vulnerable because its domestic system, which drove its foreign policy, was increasingly recognized as a failure. While this view was skeptical about détente, it recognized that a crucial lever could be American insistence that the Soviet Union grant human rights to its citizens. It appears that Carter's stance here was simultaneously instrumental and principled.

But even had Carter ignored human rights, détente probably would have failed. The Soviets saw a number of opportunities to support movements and states in Africa that they believed to be progressive, if not revolutionary. The United States was being forced to grudgingly acknowledge Soviet equality, and even if the Soviet moves harmed relations with the United States, this was a price worth paying. Some of the gains came in traditional power-political terms, but at least as important was the Soviet feeling that they could not be true Soviets if they abandoned the progressive cause. This played a role in the dispatch of troops to Afghanistan that gave the *coup de grâce* to détente. The potential loss was not only of a client on their borders, but that a potentially socialist state would revert to the forces of reaction.

Identity and the end of the Cold War

The Cold War ended when Soviet identity shifted, and Reagan refused to reciprocate Soviet concessions until he believed that this was occurring.[30] This provides a fundamental contrast with the earlier détente. The change in Soviet policy and identity, furthermore, grew out of comparisons and interactions with the West.

Mikhail Gorbachev and his colleagues realized that the Soviet system was failing. But this failure was relative not absolute. The economy was not collapsing, indeed it was growing a bit. There was no starvation or privation, and despite the concern of Soviet military leaders, the large and secure nuclear arsenal was adequate to deter an American attack. The inadequacies of the Soviet performance appeared only when compared to the capitalist world. This had always been true, but in the past Soviet leaders could tell themselves that they were catching up. The contrast between East and West Germany was particularly striking since many of the other excuses of the weak socialist performance were implausible here. Furthermore, increased travel and contacts with the West meant that more members of the Soviet elite understood the situation, which undermined the leaders' confidence in their system and the beliefs that had produced it. Competition in the Third World by military activities, foreign aid, or serving as a model of development was obviously being crippled. Since the Third World represented the future, impending failure there cast doubt on Soviet prospects. Even more centrally, the knowledge that socialism had failed to out-compete capitalism struck at the core of Soviet beliefs about themselves and the world.

To reform the Soviet economy, Gorbachev needed better relations with the West in order to reduce military spending and gain access to Western investment and technology. Thus, he began a series of initiatives and concessions, mostly dealing with arms control. These were accompanied by a basic shift in outlook toward world politics, summarized in the phrase "new thinking." Whether these ideas were largely rationalizations for policies forced on him by pressing circumstances or whether they were autonomous and more freely adopted is heatedly debated but is of less importance here than the fact that the

---

30 For a similar argument, see John Mueller, "What Was the Cold War About? Evidence from Its Ending," *Political Science Quarterly*, 119 (2004–05), 609–32.

new thinking implicitly if not explicitly contradicted key elements of Soviet identity. Not only was lowering international tensions given priority over supporting progressive movements, but the sources of tension were located in the traditional dynamics of international conflict, especially misperceptions and spirals of unnecessary hostility and fears. In arguing that Soviet isolation and Western belligerence were largely brought on by ill-advised Soviet actions, Gorbachev adopted what IR scholars call a security dilemma analysis. Although not new to Western observers, this line of thought was not only innovative in the Soviet context but constituted a denial of the crucial idea that politics pivots around class conflict. Thus, at the XXVIIth Party Congress in 1986, for the first time there was no mention of the "world revolutionary process," and by December 1988 Gorbachev abandoned talk of defending the "Socialist Commonwealth," of supporting progressive revolutions, and of the dangers from "American imperialism."[31]

Once Gorbachev and his colleagues concluded that they needed a solid rapprochement with the West, it was hard for them to maintain that the difference between the Soviet and American social systems had to be central to their relationship. So it is no accident that Yegor Ligachev, who opposed Gorbachev's policies, claimed that "We proceed from the class nature of international relations. [Any other approach] only confuses the Soviet people and our friends abroad."[32] Once class conflict was dropped, little remained of the unique Soviet identity and mission in the world. Even if the Soviets thought that their system was more humane and progressive than capitalism, there was no reason to believe that Soviet security required keeping the West on the defensive, and little need to resist concessions on arms control or maintain Soviet clients in the Third World. As Marx and Engels had said, the revolutionizing power of capitalism was so great that under its influence "All that is solid melts into air."[33]

Gorbachev famously said that he was going to do something terrible to the United States – he was going to deprive it of an enemy. In fact, what is striking is how little the United States actually changed after the Cold War. While

---

31 Jon Jacobson, *When the Soviet Union Entered World Politics* (Berkeley, CA: University of California Press, 1994), 30; minutes of the Politburo, December 27–28, 1988, *Cold War International History Project Bulletin*, 12/13 (Fall–Winter 2001), 24–29.
32 Quoted in Robert English, *Russia and the Idea of the West* (New York: Columbia University Press, 2000), 225.
33 Karl Marx and Friedrich Engels, *The Communist Manifesto* (New York: Monthly Review Press, 1968), 7. Of course, Marx and Engels were referring to the displacement of pre-capitalist systems by the rise of the bourgeoisie, but the point seems to have more general validity.

Soviet identity was formed in opposition to a capitalist world, American identity did not need Communism, and the United States came out of the Cold War with little more knowledge of itself or others then it had at the start. Whether the American identity would have withstood prolonged reversals abroad or falling behind the USSR in economic and technological competition is an interesting question. Certainly, American self-confidence was shaken at a number of points, especially in the late 1950s and early 1960s. But having deeper roots in its own society and history, the American identity had a resilience that the Soviet one did not. Although American society changed markedly during the Cold War, it is far from clear that it would have been much different had those years been peaceful or characterized by conflict with a different adversary. Furthermore, to the extent that American identity did change during the Cold War, there was a broadening of sense of self, a greater tolerance for diversity, and, at least until the late 1970s, the acceptance of a greater role for government in many spheres of life, just the opposite of what we would expect if the Cold War had led to an exaggeration of those features that separated the United States from the USSR.

It is not hindsight that leads to the conclusion that the asymmetries outlined earlier were crucial. Maintaining Soviet identity depended on the future unfolding according to plan: a cooperative worker's society was to be put in place, the Soviet Union was to modernize, class conflict would dominate until the workers prevailed, and the superiority of Communism would be demonstrated by overtaking the West and by the triumph of revolutions abroad. Until these hopes were dashed only limited détentes were possible, and these would be undermined by the refusal of either side to give up the competition. Conversely, when the hopes faded and politics was not seen as dominated by class conflict, there was no reason for the Soviet Union to either menace or fear the US, and once American leaders concluded that the Soviet domestic system was changing, issues that had bedeviled the relationship for so long were easily resolved. The Cold War ended only when one side's identity did; it could not have ended peacefully otherwise.

3

Economic aspects of the Cold War, 1962–1975

RICHARD N. COOPER

US objectives during the Cold War were to prevent Soviet attacks on the United States and its allies and to prevent the spread of Communism as a political and economic system to other countries, whether by force or by threat, subversion, persuasion, or bribery. The principal instrument to prevent attack was an extensive build-up of defensive and retaliatory military forces, combined with political and military alliances that extended US protection to other countries in exchange for their engagement and support. The principal instruments for preventing the spread of Communism by nonmilitary means involved building an international economic system conducive to economic prosperity; engaging in persuasion, providing incentives, and occasionally imposing economic sanctions; and, not least, promoting a robust US economy that could serve as a stimulant to others and as a beacon for the benefits of a free, enterprise-based, market-oriented economy.

This chapter will examine the second set of instruments, usually neglected by historians of the Cold War in favor of a focus on the actual or threatened military actions and the diplomacy associated with them. Following some introductory remarks, the chapter will discuss developments in the world economy and will highlight the comparative economic performance between Communist countries and what was called the "free world." I will then analyze the actions taken by the United States, including public expenditures on national security and international affairs that were motivated, at least in part, by their international implications. Subsequent sections will consider US economic policies toward the Communist countries, toward US allies (mainly Western Europe and Japan), and toward the international economic system as a whole. The chapter will conclude with a discussion of actions toward other non-Communist countries, often loosely albeit unhelpfully called the Third World, where the competition was most visible. The main focus will be on the United States, which typically took the initiative, but other countries played important, somewhat critical, supporting roles.

Economic policy, broadly interpreted, was an essential complement to the policy of deterrence. In the end, the Soviet Union was not defeated in military combat, but rather it collapsed because of internal economic weaknesses that were increasingly evident to the Soviet people and, more gradually, to their leaders. These emergent internal weaknesses marked a sharp contrast to the robust performance of economies in the orbit of the United States and its allies – first in Western Europe and in Japan, followed soon by southern Europe and the four Asian tigers (South Korea, Taiwan, Hong Kong, and Singapore), with Thailand, Malaysia, Indonesia, and others starting down the same successful path. It was increasingly evident that Communism did not work well economically – it did not deliver significantly higher standards of living to ordinary people – as became evident especially with the growing contrast between Eastern and Western Europe, between North and South Korea, and between the People's Republic of China (China hereafter) and Taiwan and Hong Kong. After some initial successes, the Communist countries became mired in inflexible systems of resource allocation and low levels of innovation in a world increasingly dominated by rapid technological advances. Not that all countries in the non-Communist world did well. But many did, yet after an initial spurt of capital-intensive industrialization, economic performance deteriorated significantly in all Communist countries. Gradually those countries in the non-Communist world that experimented with central planning and control drew away from it – including eventually even China and Vietnam, which remained under political control by Communist parties.

It is necessary to recall the high promise which Communism and central planning of the economy held out to many. Kim Philby, the Russian spy who was high in the British diplomatic corps, could still write from his Moscow exile as late as 1968 that he had no doubt that the verdict of history would be victory for Communism.[1] The battle of ideas was not decisive; but the cumulative experience was increasingly difficult to ignore. In the end, this cumulative comparative experience was at least as important in preventing the spread of Communism as was deterrence. And, of course, economic prosperity in the West made it easier to carry the financial burdens of defense, deterrence, and containment.

All this would become evident with the passage of time. In the 1960s, however, Communism was still seen as an aggressive, vigorous ideology, with continuing support from the Soviet Union but drawing also on indigenous

---

[1] Kim Philby, *My Silent War* (New York: Grove Press, 1968), 90.

revolutionary groups and idealistic new leaders around the world. Nearly every year brought forth some perceived new Communist threat. Fidel Castro's Cuba became increasingly Communist from 1960. The Soviet Union sent funds and advisers to the leftist prime minister Patrice Lumumba of Congo immediately following the abrupt abandonment of its colony by Belgium, threatening the break-up of that newly independent country, and leading President John F. Kennedy to take countervailing measures. The Soviet Union under Nikita S. Khrushchev tried once again to isolate Berlin in 1961, and a wall was built to prevent increasing migration of East Germans into more appealing West Berlin, thence into Western Europe. The Soviet Union tried, with Cuban encouragement, to place missiles in Cuba in 1962, leading to the Cuban missile crisis. In 1962, China, still (erroneously) considered by many Americans to be a surrogate of the USSR, fought Indian troops in areas claimed by India. In 1964, indigenous Communist groups were disciplined enough to emerge successfully from anarchy in the Dominican Republic, prompting President Lyndon B. Johnson to send in US marines to reestablish order and an interim government. In 1965, Communists in Indonesia staged a coup, possibly with the support of President Sukarno, threatening to take the world's fourth most populous country into the Communist "orbit"; it was brutally suppressed by Indonesia's army. In 1967, Syria, with Soviet encouragement and support, promoted terrorist raids in Israel, leading ultimately to the Six Days War in June. In 1968, Soviet troops marched into Czechoslovakia, suppressing the "Prague Spring" and ushering in the Brezhnev Doctrine. In 1971, a left-wing president, Salvador Allende, was contentiously elected in Chile. Even as late as 1975, Communists made a serious run at taking over Portugal after the collapse of the dictatorship there; immediately thereafter they tried to do the same in Angola, newly liberated from Portugal.

And, of course, the conflict in Vietnam ran right through the entire period. So while the Communists had few successes between 1960 (Cuba) and 1975 (Vietnam), they were vigorously pursuing opportunities around the world, always with encouragement and often with material support from the Soviet Union. President Richard M. Nixon could say to his senior officials in 1971 "the impressive thing about the Communist leaders is their total absolute conviction that they're going to win, and their determination to do everything to win."[2]

---

2 H. R. Haldeman, *The Haldeman Diaries: Inside the Nixon White House* (New York: Putnam, 1994), entry for September 13, 1971.

These continuing episodes provide a backdrop for the efforts by leaders in the United States, Western Europe, Canada, and Japan to attempt to assure economic prosperity, both through national policy and through international cooperation. The main components of the strategy were already laid down in the late 1940s, with Marshall Plan aid to Europe, trade liberalization through the General Agreement on Tariffs and Trade (GATT), and President Harry S. Truman's "Point Four," calling for aid to developing countries. Private US investment abroad typically followed, although it was not a reliable instrument of policy. The International Monetary Fund (IMF) and the World Bank, created in 1946, were also important features of the international economic architecture. The United States, with the sometimes reluctant cooperation of others, tried also to penalize countries within or too close to the Soviet orbit.

World economic performance

The 1960s was a decade of high global economic growth, perhaps the highest decadal growth in history. US growth was interrupted by recessions – declines in total production – in 1960–61, 1970–71, and 1975. The rest of the world continued to grow during the first two US downturns, but global output declined following the nearly fourfold increase in world oil prices in 1974, resuming in 1976. Inflation increased in the major economies in the late 1960s but remained modest compared with the acceleration of inflation associated with the two sharp oil price increases of 1974 and 1979–80.

Continental Western Europe and Japan, in particular, experienced extraordinary growth in the 1960s and early 1970s. This performance was no doubt influenced, in the case of Europe, by the formation of the European Economic Community (EEC) in 1958 and the trade liberalization that ensued within Europe, as well as by the global trade liberalization brought about by successive GATT rounds of negotiation. In particular, imports of merchandise into the United States, the world's largest national economy, grew by 170 percent during the 1960s, from $15 billion in 1960 to $40 billion in 1970. Both the fact and the prospect of selling into the large US market stimulated growth-enhancing investment in Europe, Japan, and elsewhere.

The USSR and its Warsaw Pact allies were also growing rapidly during this period. There are serious measurement problems for any growing economy whose structure of production is changing rapidly, and those problems become acute for an economy, such as the Soviet Union, where resource allocation occurs on the basis of quantitative targets rather than through market-determined prices. Moreover, official Soviet growth figures are known to have an upward bias, due partly to some double counting, partly to the exclusion of the (slower growing) service sector. For all these reasons, considerable disagreement surrounds estimates of Soviet growth rates during this period. Thus, official Soviet figures, which undoubtedly influenced the perceptions and the self-confidence of Soviet leaders, show growth of 10.1 percent a year during the 1950s, declining to a still high 7.0 percent during the 1960s and to 5.3 percent during the 1970s. America's Central Intelligence Agency (CIA), in contrast, basing its analysis on work by Abram Bergson and other American scholars, estimated Soviet growth rates at 6.0, 5.1, and 3.7 percent, respectively, during these three periods.[3] On either measure, the USSR in the early 1960s was on a roll, reflected in the frequent exuberant boasts of the Soviet premier, Khrushchev. Growth gradually declined on both measures, and the USSR had increasing difficulty in maintaining its economic growth, and particularly its growth of oil production, the major source of hard currency export earnings as well as a critical input into the Soviet economy and military machine. Inability to innovate, or even to absorb foreign innovations, loss of discipline among Soviet workers, and failure to maintain installed equipment and to scrap obsolete equipment have all been given as explanations for the gradual but steady decline in economic growth.

Foreign trade did not fit comfortably into national central planning. In 1949, the Soviet Union formed the Council for Mutual Economic Cooperation (Comecon) with its Eastern European satellites, and over time developed a concept of the "socialist division of labor." But it was never received enthusiastically by many of Comecon's members, there was no effective mechanism for multilateral trade or for balancing trade over time, and trade was not thoroughly integrated into the five-year planning process. As a consequence, trade within Comecon was limited (compared, for example, to that within Western Europe), although the Soviet Union was the major source of oil for East European countries and Cuba. Trade with non-Communist countries, sometimes occurring within the framework of barter agreements (for example, with India), sometimes carried on in "hard" currency (mainly US dollars), was even more limited – partly because of the unfavorable treatment of Soviet exports, to be discussed further below, partly because of the cumbersome and awkward institutional arrangements for trade within the Soviet Union.

Trade with non-Communist countries gradually increased during the 1960s and especially after Germany's *Ostpolitik* and the promulgation of détente in

---

3 Paul R. Gregory and Robert C. Stuart, *Russian and Soviet Economic Performance and Structure*, 6th ed. (Reading, MA: Addison-Wesley, 1998), 225.

Table 1. *Annual percentage-wise growth in gross domestic product*

	USSR	Eastern Europe	USA	Western Europe	Japan
1950–60	5.2	5.1	3.5	4.9	8.8
1960–70	4.8	4.3	4.2	4.8	10.5
1970–80	2.4	3.8	3.2	3.0	4.5
1980–90	1.5	−0.2	3.2	2.2	4.0

Source: calculated from Maddison, *The World Economy*, 275, 298, 329.

the 1970s. Exports by industrialized countries to the Comecon countries, partly on the basis of credits, grew from $2.8 billion in 1960 to $8.7 billion in 1970 to $34 billion in 1975 to $58 billion in 1980, before a cutback in the early 1980s following the Soviet invasion of Afghanistan.[4] The share of market-oriented countries in total Comecon imports grew from 27 percent in 1960 to 34 percent in 1970 to 46 percent in 1975. World trade grew modestly more rapidly than total Comecon trade, but trade within Comecon grew more slowly. The main earner of hard currency for the Soviet Union was exports of oil, whose price rose gradually in the early 1970s and sharply in 1974, thus improving its export earnings and its terms of trade. Prices of oil exports to other Comecon countries were raised only gradually, thus implying a subsidy to those countries, but oil exports over allotment were priced at world prices and payable in dollars, a practice that did not please the Soviet Union's fraternal allies.

Table 1 provides estimates of annual average growth rates in gross domestic product (GDP), by decade, for the USSR, Eastern Europe, the United States, Western Europe, and Japan. Several points are noteworthy. First, the USSR grew faster than the United States to 1970, raising Soviet GDP on one estimate from 35 percent of the US level in 1950 to 44 percent in 1975, before declining to 34 percent in 1990.[5] Second, economic growth declined over time in all countries, but especially sharply in the Soviet Union and Eastern Europe, less markedly in the United States. Third, these

4 *International Trade 1975–76*, Geneva: General Agreement on Tariffs and Trade (GATT), Table F.
5 Calculated from Angus Maddison, *The World Economy: A Millennial Perspective* (Paris: Organization for Economic Development, 2001), 274–75.

measures are for total output, not consumption or standards of living. In the Soviet Union, 15 to 17 percent of GDP was devoted to equipping and supporting the military, and an even larger and growing portion was devoted to investment, which by all accounts was used very inefficiently. Thus, the high growth in output was not always reflected in equally high growth in consumption. After the Hungarian revolt of 1956, in which workers conspicuously participated, Khrushchev worried that the standard of life of ordinary Soviet citizens was not improving sufficiently. He therefore tried to cut down on military spending and redirected resources into consumer goods, particularly food production. Without formally reversing this emphasis on agriculture, Leonid Brezhnev increased military spending in the mid-1960s. However, Soviet standards of living increased respectably during the 1960s.

Fourth, a division of GDP by population yields output per capita, which showed Soviet "productivity" growing from 30 percent of the US level in 1950 to 38 percent in 1975, and declining to 30 percent by 1990. These figures are based on purchasing power parity calculations for the Soviet Union, which have always been problematic and contentious because of the absence of meaningful prices for Soviet-produced goods and services; it is now believed that they overstate the quality of Soviet goods and services, hence of Soviet GDP and output per capita.

Finally, post-1991 work by Russian economists has judgmentally lowered growth rates during the Soviet period even below those estimated by the CIA, from which the growth rates reported in Table 1 have been adapted.[6] But Soviet leaders in the 1960s and early 1970s may not have been aware of this weaker performance, since production in sectors in which they were especially interested, such as steel, cement, and oil, were continuing to grow rapidly, and indeed by 1975 had overtaken that of the United States.

In any case, during the period covered by this chapter the Soviet economy was performing reasonably well, although market-oriented economies in Europe and Japan were growing even more rapidly, and in the case of Europe from a significantly higher base. Soviet leaders had reason to be confident in their economy – serious weaknesses showed up later – but also to be concerned about the long-term prospects of Communism as a method for organizing production compared with market capitalism.

---

6 Gregory and Stuart, *Russian Economic Performance*, 227.

Economic and other policies within the United States

President Kennedy was convinced that US policy toward the USSR, and toward the world, must be based on a robust US economy. On the basis of its lackluster performance in the late 1950s, he campaigned in 1960 that he would "get the economy moving again." To that end, he proposed significant trade liberalization. To stimulate growth and domestic demand, he proposed an investment tax credit, and eventually a significant reduction in income taxes, which was finally legislated in 1964. As expected, economic growth improved, and indeed became too robust after the sharp buildup in military expenditures associated with Vietnam, such that President Johnson (belatedly) proposed a tax increase in 1967, enacted in 1968. As the economy grew, so did government revenues.

A government's spending priorities can be found in its budget. Defense expenditures in the United States declined from a Korean War high of $49 billion (13 percent of GDP) in 1953 to $38 billion in 1955, and then rose gradually to $45 billion (8.8 percent of GDP) in 1960 and to $49 billion in 1965 (7.1 percent of a significantly larger GDP). The Vietnam War built them up to $77 billion in 1968 (8.8 percent of GDP), whereupon they rose to $86 billion (representing a sharp decline in real terms, because of inflation), 5.0 percent of GDP in 1976, and fell below 5 percent in the years 1977–79.

During this period, the United States also expanded its expenditures on "international affairs," mainly foreign assistance, but also including the Peace Corps and the US Information Agency (USIA). In addition, Federal government expenditures on higher education increased under the National Defense Education Act, as did the space program, both launched in 1958. Kennedy promised in 1961, following the manned earth orbit by Russian Yuri Gagarin, to land a man on the moon "before the decade is out" – an achievement accomplished in July 1969. Kennedy wanted to reestablish the United States as being on the frontiers of technology in the eyes of Americans and of those around the world – not least in the Soviet Union. The expenditures of the National Aeronautics and Space Administration (NASA) rose from nothing in 1958 to a peak of $5.1 billion in 1965 before receding to below $3 billion in 1974–75.[7] These government expenditures did not impose severe strains on the US economy except during the years of the rapid military buildup in Vietnam in the late 1960s.

---

7 US Bureau of the Census, *Statistical Abstract of the United States 1991* (Washington, DC: US Government Printing Office 1991), 597.

Trade and financial policy toward Communist
countries

The use of economic sanctions was an ongoing feature of US foreign economic policy. In the context of the Cold War, specific sanctions were used against North Korea, China, Cuba, and North Vietnam. But they were also used against the thoroughly anti-Communist Trujillo regime of the Dominican Republic, against neutral India, and against Portugal, a member of the North Atlantic Treaty Organization (NATO). The United States often resorted to sanctions when a foreign government's behavior displeased it. Other countries also used economic sanctions, although not so frequently as the United States, where members of Congress individually and collectively complained about foreign behavior and wanted to employ economic sanctions against the offending foreign government.

Specific sanctions were threatened, introduced, or tightened against Cuba, the German Democratic Republic, the United Arab Republic (Egypt), North Vietnam, Chile, and Kampuchea (Cambodia); they were relaxed against Laos. But it needs to be emphasized that the United States threatened or imposed economic sanctions twenty-six times during the period 1960–75, not counting US participation in United Nations' (UN) sanctions against South Africa (1962), Portugal (1963), and Rhodesia (1965).[8]

Before addressing specific episodes, we need to describe US trade policy toward Communist countries in the absence of specific sanctions. This consisted of three components: treatment of imports from Communist countries; controls on exports to Communist countries; and granting of official credits to foreign countries, for example, by the Commodity Credit Corporation (CCC) for the purchase of US agricultural products or by the Export–Import Bank for the purchase of US equipment.

The basic tariff legislation of the United States was (and in 2008 remained) the infamous Smoot–Hawley Tariff Act of 1930. These high tariffs had been greatly reduced through a series of reciprocal trade negotiations, bilateral in the 1930s, multilateral (under the auspices of GATT) thereafter. Tariff reductions to any country were typically extended to other countries under so-called most-favored-nation (MFN) treatment, both by US policy and as required by GATT for all signatories to GATT. The United States did not, however, extend MFN treatment to Communist countries (except Yugoslavia

---

8 Gary C. Hufbauer, Jeffrey Schott, and Kimberly Elliot, *Economic Sanctions Reconsidered*, rev. ed. (Washington, DC: Institute for International Economics, 1990).

and, after 1960, Poland). Thus, while the Soviet Union, for example, could export to the United States, its goods had to pay the typically high 1930 tariffs, except for those goods on the duty-free list, mostly raw materials. A combination of central planning in the USSR, with tight control over foreign trade, and high import duties into the United States assured little trade between the United States and the USSR and other Communist countries.

The United States also limited sales to the Soviet Union and its allies of military goods and of "strategic" goods that might have direct or indirect military application. This process started in 1948 and was formalized in the Export Control Act of 1949, which, with amendments, governed US exports thereafter. The United States also enlisted the cooperation of West European countries, and of Japan, in limiting such sales to the USSR and East European communist countries, and to Communist China and North Korea – covering both strategic goods originating locally and reshipment of such goods from the United States. An initially secret Coordinating Committee (COCOM) was established to agree on lists of goods considered "strategic" and to discuss enforcement of the export controls.

Like other countries, the United States had mechanisms for extending official credits or credit guarantees to foreign purchasers of US exports, through CCC, Exim Bank, the Defense Department (for credit on sales of military equipment), and the Agency for International Development (AID) or its predecessors (for foreign economic assistance to poor countries). In general, Communist countries were denied access to these credits, although occasional exceptions were made for CCC credits.

In addition to the "penalties" imposed on Communist countries affiliated with the Soviet Union (Yugoslavia was exempt after Josip Broz Tito's break with Stalin in 1948), specific sanctions – effectively, a total embargo – had been applied to trade with North Korea after its invasion of South Korea in 1950, and to China after its entry into that war. Chinese and North Korean assets in the United States were also frozen, and all financial transactions between American residents and those countries required a license. These embargoes continued through the 1960s; that against China was relaxed following President Nixon's visit to China in 1972; that against North Korea continued into the twenty-first century.

Trade with Cuba was partially embargoed, with increasing severity, starting in 1960, following nationalization of American-owned property, with inadequate promised compensation; the embargo persists (as of 2009), nearly five decades later. In 1961, the German Democratic Republic (GDR), with the approval of the Soviet Union, put an economic squeeze on West Berlin, which was viewed increasingly as a disruptive island of growing prosperity surrounded by the GDR and an unwanted source of attraction to East Germans, many of whom worked in the western sector. The United States and its allies protested vigorously and sent additional troops; economic sanctions against the GDR were seriously, and openly, considered. In the end, the GDR backed off and instead built the infamous Berlin Wall between the east and west sectors of the city, closing West Berlin to East Germans, and the sanctions were not applied.

In 1963–65, the United States first threatened and then cut foreign aid and agricultural credits to the United Arab Republic (Egypt), following its intervention in Yemen, its alienation of Saudi Arabia, and its support for rebels in Congo. In May 1964, after Hanoi augmented its support for the Viet Cong in South Vietnam, the United States imposed an embargo on all economic transactions between the United States and North Vietnam and froze North Vietnamese assets in the United States – an embargo that was terminated only in 1994. In 1975, President Gerald Ford imposed a total trade embargo on and froze the US assets of Kampuchea (Cambodia), after the Khmer Rouge (Cambodian Communists) seized power, sought to be self-sufficient, and forced many Cambodians into the countryside (and ultimately to their deaths).

The United States attempted to reward actions it considered positive as well as penalize countries that moved in the wrong direction. Thus, in 1960, the United States extended MFN treatment to goods from Communist Poland, as it had earlier done for Yugoslavia, as that country showed greater autonomy with respect to the USSR. Aid, turned off and on since 1956 as the Communist Pathet Lao moved in and out of coalition governments and attempted to establish diplomatic relations with the USSR and China, was finally resumed to Laos in 1962, following the Geneva accords; it was suspended again in 1975 after a takeover by the Pathet Lao. Although rigidly authoritarian, Romania increasingly distanced itself from the USSR, and gained MFN treatment from the United States in 1975.

This is not the occasion to evaluate the effectiveness of the sanctions, or the rewards. Suffice it to say that one detailed analysis found a mixed picture. Many of the sanctions were judged to have had negligible effect on their stated objectives, such as the long-lasting embargo on Cuba, which arguably contributed to keeping Castro in power for more than four decades. But others, such as the cut-off of critical agricultural credits to Gamal Abdel Nasser's Egypt, may have encouraged that country to pull back from its foreign interventions.[9]

9 Ibid.

By the mid-1960s, the time seemed ripe to improve relations with the USSR – what later was called détente. Kennedy and Johnson started the process, banning atmospheric testing of nuclear weapons in 1963 and concluding the important non-proliferation agreement in 1968 to inhibit the spread of nuclear weapons. Johnson had hoped also to start negotiations on limiting nuclear arms, anti-ballistic missiles, and multiple independently targetable re-entry vehicles (MIRVs), but an upcoming summit in Leningrad was cancelled following the Soviet invasion of Czechoslovakia. The process eventually led to the Anti-Ballistic Missile Treaty and an interim Strategic Arms Limitation Treaty (SALT I) finally agreed at a Brezhnev–Nixon summit in May 1972.

Détente also involved increased East–West trade. As part of his bridge-building effort, Johnson tried to alter the discriminatory US trade policy in 1966, but failed to persuade the Congress.[10] Germany's foreign minister (later chancellor) Willy Brandt inaugurated *Ostpolitik*, with tacit US approval. In July 1972, after Nixon's trip to China, the United States agreed to sell $750 million of grain to the Soviet Union over the following three years (which was implicit acknowledgment that the Soviet economy could not by itself provide meat to its people on the scale desired). In October 1972, the two countries initialed a trade agreement that would extend MFN treatment to Soviet goods sold in the United States (which would have reduced US tariffs by on average about 64 percent, from 24 percent to 8.6 percent), while the USSR agreed to a significant partial payment (of $722 million) on its 1945 Lend Lease debts to the United States.

Some Americans were concerned about the inability of minorities, especially Jews, to emigrate from the USSR. The Soviets responded quietly by allowing more emigration, rising from 400 in 1968 to 35,000 in 1973. Senator Henry M. Jackson (D–Washington) and Congressman Charles Vanik (D–Ohio) added an amendment to the trade bill that was then passing through Congress to the effect that MFN could not be extended to non-market (i.e., Communist) countries that restricted emigration. Soviet officials suggested privately that emigration might reach 45,000, but bristled at any open US intervention in what they considered their internal affairs. In the end, Nixon resigned over Watergate, the newly installed president, Gerald Ford, signed the Trade Act of 1974, including the Jackson–Vanik amendment (and a parallel

---

10 Lyndon Baines Johnson, *The Vantage Point: Perspectives on the Presidency 1963–1969* (New York: Holt, Rinehart, and Winston, 1971), 472–73.

piece of legislation that restricted – but did not prohibit – Export–Import Bank loans to the Soviet Union). The USSR backed out of the 1972 trade agreement, and Soviet goods never received MFN treatment.

The Jackson–Vanik amendment is an example of the ability of a determined Congress to thwart an American president's foreign policy. More generally, presidents must constantly seek at least the acquiescence of Congress for the actions they wish to pursue, and must work diligently for legislative support when additional funds are required.

The Yom Kippur War between Israel and Egypt of October 1973 led to an Arab oil embargo on the United States and a nearly four-fold increase in oil prices in 1974. This relieved the hard currency shortage of the oil-exporting Soviet Union and diminished its eagerness to receive MFN treatment from the United States.

Trade and financial policies toward allies

The economic dimension of Cold War policy was not confined to penalizing Communist countries or rewarding those who resisted the embrace of the Soviet Union. There was a more affirmative agenda. As often, its roots go back to the late 1940s. But the young President Kennedy became an articulate spokesman of the need for vigorous US leadership of an economically vital Western world. He sounded the theme in his inaugural address in January 1961. His first year in office was plagued by the Bay of Pigs fiasco in Cuba and by the crises over Berlin and the Congo.

A major element of the world economic system was the General Agreement on Tariffs and Trade, adopted by twenty-three countries in 1947, which promulgated rules to guide states in their trading relationships and provided a forum for reducing tariffs and other restrictions on imports from their high levels of the late 1940s. By 1961, this liberalizing process seemed to have run out of steam. Moreover, six European countries had in 1958 created the EEC, which when completed (in 1970) would become a trading entity larger than the United States, with a single negotiating authority. The United States desired the reluctant United Kingdom to join the EEC. With all this in mind, in January 1962, Kennedy proposed a bold new round of trade negotiations. In contrast to earlier multilateral negotiations, he wanted to cut tariffs (with selected exceptions) across the board by to 50–100 percent on products for which the United States and the EEC together accounted for more than 80 percent of world exports. This was a respectable list if the UK joined the EEC, but not otherwise. It provided for elimination of duties on tropical products. And, domestically, it called for the first time for adjustment assistance for firms and workers who were hurt by the trade liberalization.

Kennedy cited five important changes in the world as reasons for proposing legislation, one of which was the "communist aid and trade offensive." The Soviet bloc had trebled its trade with forty-one non-Communist developing countries, and Soviet trade missions had been active around the world. Kennedy's trade proposal was to be his top legislative priority in 1962. It created the basis for the subsequent Kennedy Round of trade negotiations. The president identified the basis for the subsequent Kennedy Round of trade negotiations. The president identified seven benefits expected to flow from the legislation and subsequent trade liberalization. The first three concerned benefits to the US economy, including enhancing its capacity to bear burdens of defense, as well as that of its allies. The remaining four reasons – promoting the strength and unity of the West, proving the superiority of free choice, aiding developing nations, and maintaining US leadership of the free world – were suffused with references to competition with the "Sino-Soviet world" and the importance of a liberal trading regime for winning that competition.

The results of the Kennedy Round, concluded in 1967, were less than hoped for, but nonetheless impressive. Britain did not join the EEC until 1973, delayed by a veto by President Charles de Gaulle of France. As a result, the provision for elimination of tariffs on manufacturing goods went unused. But tariffs were reduced by an average of about 35 percent on $40 billion of world trade in the base year, 1964. Above all, it was a successful cooperative venture, overcoming parochial domestic interests, and bringing the "free world" closer together economically.

President Johnson faced the domestic challenge of ensuring civil rights to American blacks and the domestic objective of introducing publicly financed medical care for the aged and the poor – furtherance of Franklin D. Roosevelt's New Deal, as he saw it. Apart from relations with the Soviet Union and the escalating conflict in Vietnam, Johnson faced the challenge – as did other Europeans – of dealing with de Gaulle's aspirations and ambitions for establishing France's independence of the United States and its primacy in Europe. De Gaulle aggressively questioned the international role of the dollar in early 1965 and withdrew French forces from NATO's integrated command (but did not withdraw from NATO) in March 1966. De Gaulle had earlier vetoed Britain's application for EEC membership and had stymied the EEC by prohibiting his ministers from attending the decisionmaking Council of Ministers. De Gaulle desired France to have a relationship with the Soviet

Union independent of, and different from, that of the United States and other European countries. The Soviets responded politely but warily. Their main concern was with Germany, and they flirted with various ideas for weaning Germany away from the Western alliance. Johnson worked hard (and successfully) to keep Germany firmly with the West, even while making overtures to the Soviet Union on non-proliferation (which would effectively deny Germany nuclear weapons) and on strategic arms control.

Johnson unsuccessfully sought new tariff-negotiating authority in May 1968. President Richard Nixon, breaking with the protectionist tradition in the Republican Party and reflecting his view of America's proper role in the world, renewed the request in November 1969. New authority was finally granted by Congress in December 1974 (after Nixon had resigned), which provided the basis for US participation in the next major trade-liberalizing round of multilateral negotiations, the Tokyo Round, begun in 1973 and concluded in 1979.

The other main strand of post-1960 foreign economic policy with respect to Europe was mainly defensive. In 1944, forty-four nations had agreed at Bretton Woods, New Hampshire, to postwar rules governing financial transactions among countries, and to the creation of two new implementing institutions, the IMF and the International Bank for Reconstruction and Development (later known as the World Bank). The rules *inter alia* required restriction-free access to currency for current account transactions (for example, trade and travel), nearly fixed exchange rates among currencies, and currency convertibility into gold for monetary authorities (but not for ordinary citizens), a commitment adopted only by the United States. As the Bretton Woods system came under increasing strain after the late 1950s, one strand of US policy was to avoid a collapse of this system. Various currencies, including the US dollar, came under pressure from time to time, and adjustments had to be made to deal with imbalances in international payments. The main thrust of US policy during the 1960s was to pursue actions that forestalled a serious financial crisis while still preserving high-priority US objectives, which included maintaining the Atlantic alliance, keeping British and US troops in Germany, extending an open trading system, and pursuing the non-proliferation treaty and other initiatives. The cooperation of other countries was required, and the United States did not want to jeopardize that cooperation. Thus, a series of temporizing measures were taken to head off periodic US payments crises. As President Johnson once said to a startled William McChesney Martin, chairman of the Federal Reserve Board, "I will not deflate the American economy, screw up foreign policy by gutting aid or pulling troops out, or go protectionist just so we can continue to pay out gold to the French at \$35 an ounce."[11]

One mechanism for supporting countries in financial trouble, especially if the trouble was due to currency speculation on a change in the official exchange rate, was to provide short-term credit to the country's monetary authorities enabling them to ride out the speculation until it reversed. Thus, a mechanism was put in place to provide such credits, partly by the US Treasury's Exchange Stabilization Fund, partly through "swap" lines extended by the Federal Reserve System to other central banks. Through these mechanisms the United States provided short-term credits to Canada (1962, 1968), Italy (1963–64, 1975), Britain (many times), and France (1968, 1969). If the short-term credits could not be repaid quickly from reversals of speculative capital flows, they could be repaid by drawing on the IMF, another cooperative arrangement, for longer-term credit.

Britain's budget and balance of payments were so heavily burdened that Prime Minister Harold Wilson considered not only pulling British troops east of Suez into Britain, which was ultimately done, but also cutting significantly the British Army on the Rhine. If he had done so, he would have increased pressure in the United States to reduce its own forces in Germany and elsewhere in NATO, actions that were already being advocated in the US Senate, especially by Senator Mike Mansfield (D–Montana), during a period of intense fighting in South Vietnam. In addition to short-term financial support to Britain, the United States, itself facing financial pressure, launched in 1967 a tripartite burden-sharing discussion with Britain and Germany. The three governments worked out financial arrangements that increased German purchases in Britain and, secondarily, in the United States. These accords deflected pressure in both countries to reduce troop levels in Germany.

The leading Western countries, joined by all members of the IMF, also agreed on a major reform of the international monetary system. They created a new, international money (for monetary authorities), the Special Drawing Right (SDR). The financial journalists dubbed it "paper gold" because it was to replace gradually the international monetary role of gold and ease the demand for dollars by central banks. The SDR was seen at the time as a major step forward toward international monetary cooperation, although it subsequently failed to live up to expectations.

---

11 As paraphrased by Francis M. Bator, "Lyndon Johnson and Foreign Policy: The Case of Western Europe and the Soviet Union," in Aaron Lobel (ed.), *Presidential Judgment: Foreign Policy Making in the White House* (Hollis, NH: Hollis Publishing, 2001), 175.

Britain's balance-of-payments problems were eased following a 14 percent devaluation of the pound in November 1967. US balance-of-payments problems came to a head in August 1971, when President Nixon ceased convertibility of the US dollar into gold (for foreign monetary authorities). At the same time, he imposed a wage/price freeze in the United States to stop the momentum of inflationary pressures that had built up in the preceding four years, and levied a 10 percent surcharge on all dutiable imports into the United States – the last mainly to force other countries to negotiate seriously on a realignment of exchange rates. These tense negotiations were concluded in December 1971 with the Smithsonian agreement. It realigned exchange rates of the leading currencies against the dollar and provided for an increase in the official dollar price of gold. However, pressures continued in foreign exchange markets, and in March 1973 major currencies were allowed to float against the US dollar (Canada and Britain had earlier switched to floating exchange rates). Continental Europeans struggled to maintain a higher degree of exchange rate stability among their currencies, leading to the European monetary system in 1979 and eventually to a common European currency in 1999.

Thus, in the early 1970s, two key features of the Bretton Woods system were abandoned: gold convertibility of the dollar and fixed exchange rates among major currencies (many other countries around the world maintained fixed exchange rates with respect to the dollar, the French franc, the British pound, or some other currency). This traumatic period of financial turmoil prompted serious discussions of reform of the international monetary system, which in some respects has not matured even in the early twenty-first century, but those issues lie outside a discussion of the Cold War, except insofar as they affected Western cohesion and prosperity. Despite occasional monetary turmoil, the Western economies generally performed well, as noted above.

Economic policies toward developing countries

The United States pursued an active policy toward the Third World, or "developing countries," as they were designated in UN jargon – as did Canada and West European countries, joined by Japan as it became richer. Soviet interventions in developing countries, especially in the Middle East and Africa, mainly in the form of grants of military equipment and training and resident technical advisers, more rarely as financial assistance, were a source of frustration and irritation to successive American administrations during the 1960s and 1970s. The US government tried to counter these measures, both by preemption and by direct response.

The program that captured most imagination in the United States and indeed in many developing nations was the Peace Corps. President Kennedy created it in 1961 to mobilize the energy, enthusiasm, and idealism of young adults, as he thought the Communist countries (especially Cuba) were able to do. This program sent volunteers (only expenses were covered by the government) to developing countries to work in towns and villages on anything that could be helpful, mainly teaching and public health. Starting from nothing, the program grew to over 10,000 volunteers by 1964, in forty-six countries.[12] It reached a peak expenditure of $110 million in 1968, before declining as Nixon showed less interest in it. The volunteers went abroad neither as diplomats nor intelligence agents, but to do good in ways envisioned largely by each individual. The experience exposed young Americans to different and much less privileged parts of the world; the program also exposed people in developing countries to idealistic Americans, unencumbered by the exigent requirements of US government policy. By all accounts, the Peace Corps was highly successful. In recipient countries, the demand for volunteers often greatly exceeded the supply. Many of the Americans who volunteered felt their careers were decisively shaped by their Peace Corps experience.

Kennedy also altered the guidelines of the United States Information Agency (USIA). Previously, it had disseminated information about the United States around the world and had focused on doctrinaire material about the merits of capitalism. Now, it provided more realistic and pluralistic accounts of life in the country. Its budget, moreover, was nearly doubled over the decade, 1960–70.

Kennedy also built on earlier legislation and created a "Food for Peace" program. American agricultural products were exported to developing countries not only in humanitarian emergencies (for example, due to drought), but more generally to alleviate malnutrition and to contribute to development projects through the budget of the recipient country. This program grew sharply from $350 million in 1960 to over $1.6 billion in 1965 before stabilizing between $1–2 billion annually. It had the advantage of appealing greatly to US farmers, who under US agricultural support programs were producing surpluses of several products that periodically became fiscally burdensome.

12 Arthur M. Schlesinger, Jr., *A Thousand Days: John F. Kennedy in the White House* (Boston, MA: Houghton Mifflin, 1965), 607.

It had the disadvantage, as was later discovered, of diverting the attention of recipient governments away from improving their indigenous agricultural production and productivity, and sometimes depressing the incomes of their farmers. But it was typically appreciated by recipient governments, and it created a source of US leverage insofar as the threat of cutting food aid could occasionally be used to alter undesired behavior, as noted above in the case of Egypt and perhaps most dramatically in the case of India.

The United States had had foreign assistance programs since the late 1940s, most notably the Marshall Plan to help Europe recover from World War II (Eastern European countries were invited to join, but at Soviet insistence declined to participate – one of the earliest signs of the sharp division of Europe that was to persist for four decades). After the Marshall Plan, US bilateral aid (as opposed to loans for development projects from the World Bank) was largely in the form of technical assistance until the Development Loan Fund was created by the Eisenhower administration in 1958. Kennedy felt that the US aid program lacked overall strategic vision and that it was guided too much by short-term, Cold War considerations. Earlier programs were combined in 1961 into the Agency for International Development, with the charge of focusing on economic development and taking a longer-term view of each recipient country's prospects and how they could best be assisted. Kennedy tried but failed to get congressional support for multiyear appropriations, and his Department of Defense objected to incorporating military assistance in AID's mandate. Moreover, economic assistance levels actually declined for several years due to congressional skepticism combined with outright opposition. Nonetheless, US economic assistance was somewhat reoriented toward development objectives. The largest recipients of US economic assistance during the period 1966–72 were, in order of amount received, India, South Vietnam, Pakistan, South Korea, Israel, Brazil, Turkey, and Colombia, ranging from $3.7 billion for India to $600 million for Colombia.

A component of economic assistance that received special attention was the Alliance for Progress. Latin America, it was felt, had been neglected by US policymakers, and such attention as they did focus on the region went mainly to protecting American business interests. After the unhappy developments in Cuba, Kennedy felt the need for a more affirmative, preemptive program for Latin America, and the Alliance for Progress was his response. This component of the aid budget grew sharply during the 1960s – possibly with some effect. Soviet adventurism there was notably lower than in some other parts of the world, although it was not altogether absent. Cuba, however, sometimes encouraged and assisted revolutionary groups and local Communist parties.

Finally, just as the Soviet Union supported many governments by providing arms and other military equipment, so did the United States. Indeed, the United States in total exported nearly twice the value of military equipment – some as sales to allies, some provided as foreign assistance to developing countries. The assistance sometimes included money for training. Military grants generally exceeded $1.5 billion a year in the early 1960s, then rose steadily to a peak of $4.5 billion in 1972. The steep increase reflected the US attempt to shift military responsibility to the government of South Vietnam for defending the South against Communist North Vietnam and its Viet Cong allies. Thereafter, it receded to under $3 billion (less in dollars of 1960, due to the inflation that occurred between 1967 and 1975). The main recipients of military assistance in the early 1970s, apart from Vietnam, were Turkey and Greece in NATO, Israel, South Korea, Cambodia, Laos, Republic of China (Taiwan), Thailand, and Jordan, in that order, but many other countries received smaller amounts on a regular basis.[13]

One further channel of economic assistance needs to be mentioned: discriminatory trading arrangements. The newly established EEC, with its common external tariff, provided preferential access to the European market (through lower tariffs, or higher quotas on selected agricultural products) for former European colonies in the so-called ACP (for Africa, Caribbean, Pacific) regions, but excluding larger former colonies such as India, Pakistan, Indonesia, and Vietnam. Thus, goods from selected small countries got preferential access to the European market. In the mid-1960s, the developing countries, through the newly created UN Conference on Trade and Development (UNCTAD), called upon all rich countries to extend tariff preferences to all poor countries. The Generalized System of Preferences (GSP), as it was called, was first embraced by Australia, Europe, and Canada, and only later by a more reluctant Japan and United States. President Johnson accepted GSP for the United States only in 1967. Since it required legislation, it was not legally adopted until the Trade Act of 1974, and could not be implemented until 1976. Neither the European nor the US scheme, which differed in important details, was nearly as generous as liberal trade advocates had in mind; but these schemes arguably encouraged some private investment in developing countries to take advantage of the tariff preferences.

The Soviet Union also purchased products from its client states, most notably sugar from Cuba, which could not be sold to the United States because of its embargo, or to Europe because of its agricultural protection. But Soviet trade

---

13 *Statistical Abstract 1978*, Table 1508.

was undertaken by a monopoly trading ministry, so sales were subject to government-to-government negotiation and had to fit into the requirements of the five-year economic plan or else was regarded as outright aid.

The real "battleground" of the Cold War after the early 1960s was thus competition for influence in developing countries through trade, financial and technical aid, and military assistance in the form of equipment and training. Both the USSR and the United States also had programs for bringing students to their respective universities. The Soviet ambassador to the United States, Anatolii Dobrynin, lamented, in his memoirs, published many years later, that "détente was to a certain extent buried in the fields of Soviet–American rivalry in the Third World."[14]

Recession and recovery

From the perspective of Soviet leaders, the Soviet Union in the mid-1970s was doing very well in its economic competition with the United States. Its aggregate production had risen slowly but steadily relative to US production, and output of products of special interest, such as steel, had come to exceed US production. The major hard-currency exports of the Soviet Union, crude oil and gold, had enjoyed substantial increases in price on the world market. At the same time, the "capitalist" world economy was in turmoil, experiencing in 1975 its worst recession since the 1930s. The Bretton Woods system of financial cooperation was in disarray, and the onset of "stagflation" created serious dilemmas of policy in most market-oriented economies. In short, Communists still confidently expected the ultimate victory of Communism against the ailing capitalist system.

This self-satisfaction neglected the fundamental recuperative capacities of market capitalism. Incentives for adaptation, innovation, and private initiative remained strong. To take only one example, the integrated circuit, introduced in the early 1970s, was to revolutionize computation, communication, and much else, including military applications.[15] While the Communist system could dictate heavy investment in traditional products, it did so inefficiently and inflexibly, without extensive innovation. It could not adapt well to changes in technology and to changes in the composition of demand. By the mid-1980s, Soviet president Mikhail Gorbachev would declare, "We cannot go on like this," and inaugurated his ultimately unsuccessful economic reform of the Soviet system of Communism.

14 Anatoly Dobrynin, *In Confidence: Moscow's Ambassador to America's Six Cold War Presidents, 1962–1986* (New York: Times Books, 1995), 473.
15 See David Reynolds's chapter in volume III.

4

The Cuban missile crisis

JAMES G. HERSHBERG

In October 1962, the Cold War endured its most perilous passage – and humanity survived its closest brush with the ultimate man-made catastrophe: a thermonuclear war between the United States and Soviet Union that could have incinerated scores of cities and killed half a billion people, rendered much of the northern hemisphere uninhabitable, lacerated industrial civilization, and stamped a lethal exclamation point on a century already twice bloodied by outbursts of global carnage that would now pale in comparison.

On its surface, the Cuban missile crisis involved a single discrete set of circumstances: It stemmed from Soviet leader Nikita S. Khrushchev's secret dispatch of nuclear missiles to Fidel Castro's revolutionary Cuba and US president John F. Kennedy's determination to reverse that deployment – and climaxed during the famous "13 Days" "eyeball-to-eyeball" "on the brink" (the crisis birthed so many clichés that one can string them together to evoke it) extending from Washington's detection of the missiles in mid-October to Khrushchev's coerced consent to remove them on October 28.

Yet, any serious analysis requires assessing how multiple narratives converged to bring the Cold War to its tensest apex. Most broadly, the crisis starkly dramatized the chasm between ends and means that Hiroshima portended for international affairs. Cuba itself represented a vital interest for neither the United States nor the Soviet Union; both proclaimed their ideological contest should be decided through gradual historical processes, not war; and both Khrushchev and Kennedy sought their political goals short of a hazardous military collision.

Nevertheless, in the supercharged atmosphere of the missile crisis, with forces on high alert, any direct clash, whether intentional or accidental, was fraught with the danger of uncontrollable escalation. As Khrushchev wrote Kennedy, "if indeed war should break out, then it would not be in our power to stop it, for such is the logic of war. I have participated in two wars and know that war ends when it has rolled through cities and villages, everywhere sowing death and destruction."[1]

Had full-scale war erupted, it would have dwarfed all others since humans bashed each other with stone clubs over raw meat and choice cave locations: though the nuclear balance overwhelmingly favored Washington – possessing, in 1962, about 27,300 nuclear warheads, including more than 7,000 strategic thermonuclear weapons, to Moscow's roughly 3,300 nuclear warheads, about 500 of them strategic[2] – the two countries had more than enough firepower to justify Kennedy's acknowledgment that "even the fruits of victory would be ashes in our mouth" and Khrushchev's warning that a lack of wisdom could lead to "a clash, like blind moles, and then reciprocal extermination will begin."[3]

Kennedy and Khrushchev managed to avoid yanking their fellow lemmings over the precipice – though how close they came remains disputed – and as the fear and patriotic fervor faded, the ludicrous dissonance between the crisis's nearly apocalyptic outcome and ephemeral causes began to inspire ridicule, symptomatic of a slackening of reverence for Cold War orthodoxies. Stanley Kubrick's *Dr. Strangelove or: How I Learned to Stop Worrying and Love the Bomb* (1964) fused subversive humor and technical verisimilitude to depict accidental nuclear war and hilariously mock Cold War paranoia. "So long, Mom, I'm off to drop the bomb," sang Tom Lehrer a year later in a bit of "pre-nostalgia" (since ditties commemorating World War III had to be composed beforehand). Promising mom he'd "look for her when the war is over – an hour and a half from now," the soldier marching off to Armageddon jauntily juxtaposes the impending conflict's devastation and gripping entertainment value:

> While we're attacking frontally
> Watch Brinkally and Huntally[4]
> Describing contrapuntally
> The cities we have lost.
> No need for you to miss a minute
> Of the agonizing holocaust ...

1 Nikita S. Khrushchev (NSK) to John F. Kennedy (JFK), October 26, 1962, US Department of State, *Foreign Relations of the United States, 1961–1963*, vol. XII, *Cuban missile crisis and Aftermath* (Washington, DC: Government Printing Office, 1996), 236 (hereafter, *FRUS*, with year and volume number).

2 Natural Resources Defense Council website, www.nrdc.org/nuclear/nudb/datab10. asp.

3 JFK address, October 22, 1962; NSK to JFK, October 26, 1962, *FRUS, 1961–1963*, vol. XI, 240.

4 NBC-TV nightly news co-anchors David Brinkley and Chet Huntley.

In Cold War history, the crisis culminated a decade-and-a-half of superpower jousting and groping toward tacit "rules of the game." To block Communist expansion, John Foster Dulles had espoused "brinkmanship" – the doctrine to display unflinchingly, when challenged, the nerve to risk nuclear war – and Khrushchev embraced this recipe for his own ratcheting up of tensions to discover whether the West would cave. In no place was his strategy more apparent than Berlin, where, in late 1958, he launched a drive to expel US and allied military forces from the western sector of the divided capital and, eventually, ease its absorption into East Germany. Though Dwight D. Eisenhower and Kennedy (JFK) vowed they would stay put, Khrushchev repeatedly turned up the heat. At a June 1961 summit in Vienna, he brusquely told JFK that he had until the end of the year to relent or else Moscow would sever West Berlin's access routes to West Germany, and rebuffed his cautions against "miscalculation" (yet he would let the ultimatum lapse). Khrushchev once likened the isolated city to the "testicles of the West" – it hollered whenever he squeezed – but to colleagues in January 1962, he used a more genteel metaphor to describe his tactic of keeping East–West relations on a knife-edge to extract maximum concessions: filling a wineglass just past the brim, so the liquid formed a "meniscus" yet never quite overflowed.[5]

So harrowing were the years leading up to the Cuban crisis that they were compared to the atmosphere pervading J. R. R. Tolkien's *Lord of the Rings*, laden with evil and imminent doom.[6] Sooner or later, the superpowers would have to break their habit of meeting at the brink – because a crisis exploded into all-out war, or grew so terrifying as to sober them up.

Countdown to crisis: Khrushchev's decision

Why did Khrushchev send nuclear missiles to Cuba? The question has gnawed at officials and analysts since they were first discovered. "Well, it's a goddamn mystery to me," JFK confessed, as to why the "awfully cautious" Soviets would take this most provocative step since the Berlin blockade.[7] "It's all gray to me, this whole Russian thing," he mused," … ahh … someday."[8]

---

5 Aleksandr Fursenko and Timothy Naftali, *Khrushchev's Cold War: The Inside Story of an American Adversary* (New York: Norton, 2006), 414.
6 Louis J. Halle, *The Cold War as History* (New York: Harper & Row, 1967), 138n.
7 Meeting transcript, 6:30 p.m., October 16, 1962, in Ernest R. May and Philip D. Zelikow (eds.), *The Kennedy Tapes: Inside the White House during the Cuban Missile Crisis* (Cambridge, MA: Harvard University Press, 1997), 107.
8 Sheldon M. Stern, *Averting 'The Final Failure': John F. Kennedy and the Secret Cuban Missile Crisis Meetings* (Stanford, CA: Stanford University Press, 2003), 432.

At the time, secrecy shrouded Kremlin decisionmaking, but since the Cold War's fading, inside information has illuminated Operation ANADYR, Khrushchev's initiative (and it's now clear it was *his* rather than the military's or Castro's). On May 21, 1962, he formally proposed secretly deploying medium- and intermediate-range nuclear missiles (MRBMs and IRBMs) to Cuba; the Presidium provisionally approved his concept three days later and, once a delegation to Havana secured Castro's wary approval, ratified it on June 10. The "joint defense" plan envisioned shipping 24 R-12 (SS-4) MRBMs with a 1,100-mile range and 16 R-14 (SS-5) IRBMs with a range roughly double that – plus half that amount of missiles in reserve – equipped with 200 kt-1 MT warheads. Khrushchev also sent tactical nuclear weapons. After JFK publicly warned in early September against introducing "offensive weapons" to Cuba, the Soviet leader upped the ante by augmenting (and sending nuclear-armed submarines to escort) this battlefield atomic arsenal, which ranged from eighty short-range FKR-1 nuclear cruise missiles to nine warheads for Frog/Luna battlefield missiles to six warheads for short-range (about 600 miles) IL-28 bombers. The total buildup, apparent to US reconnaissance by late summer, also included tanks, surface-to-air missiles (SA-2s), MiG-21 jet fighters, and roughly 50,000 soldiers and technicians.

Khrushchev's venture defies mono-causal explanation; like Harry S. Truman's dropping of the atom bomb on Japan (which combined short-term military and postwar political aims), it had overlapping objectives. Seeking a panacea to alleviate manifold ailments, Khrushchev prescribed "a cure-all, a cure-all that cured nothing."[9]

Most US officials presumed Khrushchev's decision stemmed from a desire to redress Soviet nuclear inferiority, which Washington (after fretting over a purported "missile gap") had trumpeted the previous fall to deflate his truculence on Berlin. By establishing Cuba as an unsinkable strategic missile base, Americans guessed, Khrushchev sought to double Soviet capacity to hit targets in the continental United States more cheaply and easily than with intercontinental ballistic missiles (ICBMs) stationed at home. The nuclear balance did, indeed, vex Khrushchev – especially in view of his lagging ICBM program – and enhance the deployment's attractions. Yet, attributing it to this motive alone shortchanges other considerations.

For instance, Americans generally derided as a patent propaganda ploy Khrushchev's claim that he acted to defend Havana from aggression. But information emerging from US and then Russian sources has gradually led

9 William Taubman, *Khrushchev: The Man and His Era* (New York: Norton., 2003), 532.

historians to take his assertions more seriously. Besides its open campaign to isolate Havana diplomatically, politically, and economically following the failed April 1961 Bay of Pigs invasion, the Kennedy administration sponsored secret actions – covert harassment ("Operation Mongoose"), assassination plots, military muscle-flexing – that might have fanned fears of attack both in Havana and in Moscow, even as Washington grossly underestimated Khrushchev's personal commitment to Castro's revolution. Safeguarding Cuba – strategic missiles to "restrain the United States from precipitous military action,"[10] tactical weapons to fight if deterrence failed – was a key Khrushchev aim.

Other Cold War hot spots may also have swayed the Kremlin boss. He hatched the idea of sending missiles to Cuba while visiting Bulgaria in May 1962, as he paced a Black Sea beach and brooded over nuclear-tipped Jupiter MRBMs pointing at his homeland from over the horizon in Turkey. Forcing the Americans to swallow comparable rockets on their doorstep would merely dispense "a little of their own medicine."[11] (Khrushchev's bid to swap the missiles in Cuba for the Turkish Jupiters, however, was improvised rather than premeditated.)

Aleksandr Fursenko and Timothy Naftali speculate that Laos, of all places, may have been the "ultimate trigger for the decision to put missiles in Cuba." On the eve of his Cuban venture, Khrushchev raged at JFK's rushing troops to northern Thailand (to counter a Communist offensive) and grumbled that he was pursuing a Dulles-like "position-of-strength policy."[12]

Looming over everything, however, was Berlin, where Khrushchev had been stymied. Kennedy suspected that leverage there was the Cuban deployment's real aim, and during the missile crisis set up a special high-level group to deal with a possible counter-blockade around West Berlin. Though it didn't happen, a successful Cuban gambit might have emboldened the Soviet leader to resume squeezing.

Though it remains uncertain whether Khrushchev devised any specific plan, timetable, or "grand strategy" to exploit a fait accompli in Cuba (as Fursenko and Naftali contend), he counted on it to enhance his overall position on the Cold War chessboard for subsequent moves in Berlin or elsewhere. More important than the missiles' military impact, the Kremlin

10 Nikita S. Khrushchev, *Khrushchev Remembers*, trans. and ed. Strobe Talbott (Boston, MA: Little, Brown, 1970), 494.
11 *Ibid.*, 492–94.
12 Fursenko and Naftali, *Khrushchev's Cold War*, 433, 513.

leader hoped they would alter the political and psychological "correlation of forces" in his favor. "This will be an offensive policy," he vowed to associates.[13]

Khrushchev's ploy also promised to boost his leadership of international Communism. Acting decisively to protect revolutionary Cuba would counter Chinese claims that the Soviet "revisionists" had gone soft. Khrushchev also wanted to avoid losing ground to Beijing in Havana itself. While dependent on Soviet economic aid since the rupture with Washington, Cuban leaders such as Che Guevara ideologically skewed closer to Beijing's avid support for armed uprisings throughout Latin America. With Soviet–Cuban ties strained in early 1962 as Castro purged pro-Moscow Communists, Khrushchev believed that sending missiles might reinforce the alliance and fence out China.

Khrushchev also had economic incentives. Like Mikhail Gorbachev, he genuinely wished to reduce Soviet military spending drastically in order to improve his people's lot. Yet, unlike his reformist successor, Khrushchev also indulged in threatening behavior that undercut East–West progress. The first half of 1962 impaled him on the horns of this contradiction: secret plans to expand commitments abroad coincided with discontent at home at the poorly performing economy. As Khrushchev puzzled over how to save Cuba, the prohibitive cost of fending off its giant neighbor magnified the allure of a nuclear deterrent – much as his enemy had laid a tripwire in West Germany rather than match Soviet conventional forces. Khrushchev thereby emulated not only Dulles's "brinkmanship," but also Eisenhower's "New Look" of seeking "more bang for the buck" through increased reliance on nuclear weapons.

Finally, personality mattered, not just abstract historical forces. Khrushchev steamrollered the Presidium, but odds are remote that his associates, if in power, would have chanced nuclear war for Cuba's sake. Though hardly irrational, the deployment did not simply flow from a detached reckoning of Soviet interests. Khrushchev's idiosyncratic sensibilities and temperament – and misjudgment of his youthful adversary – produced a step the Central Intelligence Agency (CIA) judged "incompatible with Soviet practice to date and with Soviet policy as we presently estimate it."[14]

---

13 Presidium notes, May 21, 1962, University of Virginia Miller Center of Public Affairs website, http://millercenter.org/scripps/archive/kremlin. On Khrushchev's foreign policy aims, see also Taubman and Savranskaya's chapter in this volume.

14 Special National Intelligence Estimate (SNIE) 85-3-62, "The Military Buildup in Cuba," September 19, 1962, Mary S. McAuliffe (ed.), *CIA Documents on the Cuban Missile Crisis* (Washington, DC: History Staff, CIA, October 1992), 93.

The crisis arrives: Kennedy's response

The news Kennedy received on the morning of Tuesday, October 16, 1962, came as a shock. Throughout the late summer and early autumn, his administration had watched with mounting unease the Soviet military buildup in Cuba and, as the mid-term congressional elections in November neared, sustained barbed Republican criticism for allowing it to proceed. Secretly, JFK stepped up military contingency planning and covert operations against Havana. Yet publicly he resisted calls for immediate military action and hewed to the line that the Soviet aid appeared purely "defensive," even while warning Khrushchev that if his military aid crossed the line into "offensive" weaponry, such as ground-to-ground missiles, "the gravest issues would arise."[15]

Khrushchev, while intimating in private correspondence that he planned to reopen Berlin later in the fall, sent reassurances through his Washington embassy – both new ambassador Anatolii F. Dobrynin and military intelligence officer Georgii Bolshakov, who maintained a back channel to the White House via the president's brother, Attorney General Robert F. Kennedy (RFK) – that he would not embarrass Kennedy before the vote and certainly not send offensive or nuclear weapons to Cuba. Though CIA director John McCone, dissenting from his own analysts, argued from his French honeymoon that the SA-2s were probably meant to hide the installation of surface-to-surface missiles, JFK preferred to believe Khrushchev. As late as Sunday, October 14, national security adviser McGeorge Bundy reiterated on national television that there was neither "present evidence" nor a "present likelihood" of an offensive threat.

Even as he spoke, a U-2 spy plane snapped damning photographs of MRBM sites under construction southwest of Havana. On Monday evening, word seeped through top administration ranks, and the next morning, Bundy broke the bad news to JFK in his bedroom as he breakfasted and read the papers. At 11:50 a.m., the first meeting convened of what would become known as the Excomm (Executive Committee of the National Security Council). The ad hoc group varied – Dean Acheson, Robert Lovett, Adlai Stevenson, and others came and went – but regulars included Bundy; Secretary of State Dean Rusk, his deputy, George Ball, Deputy Under Secretary U. Alexis Johnson, and Soviet expert Llewellyn E. Thompson, Jr.; Defense Secretary Robert S. McNamara and his deputy, Roswell Gilpatric, and chair of the Joint

15 JFK press release, *New York Times*, September 5, 1962; also JFK press conference, *New York Times*, September 14, 1962.

Chiefs of Staff, General Maxwell D. Taylor; Vice President Lyndon B. Johnson; CIA director McCone; Secretary of the Treasury C. Douglas Dillon; speechwriter Theodore C. Sorensen; and most importantly, the president's brother. As later caricatured, Excomm "hawks" favored military action, while "doves" preferred political and diplomatic pressure. In fact, debate frequently shifted, as participants oscillated between camps or advanced arguments that combined approaches.

From the outset, all agreed the United States could not passively accept the missiles. Debate revolved around the *means* of removing them – if possible without sparking World War III. The option of doing nothing received scant consideration, though JFK mused that a month earlier, "I should have said that we don't care ... What difference does it make? They've got enough to blow us up now anyway."[16] Kennedy leaned strongly toward a no-warning attack, and his brother belligerently exhorted the CIA to intensify Mongoose operations and brainstormed a provocation to justify an invasion "through Guantánamo Bay or ... you know, sink the *Maine* again or something."[17]

By Tuesday evening, McNamara had limned the parameters of the secret debate. Fearing escalation after a first strike and less concerned than the uniformed military over the missiles' strategic impact (primarily a "domestic political problem"), he shunned either preemptive military action or a purely political-diplomatic path and instead proposed, as a moderate alternative, a blockade on offensive weapons shipments to Cuba.[18]

Over the next few days, Kennedy felt rising pressure to act: U-2 flights spotted more MRBMs plus IRBM bases; the clock ticked toward the missiles going operational; and worries of a leak grew. Amidst the intense deliberations came one of the Cold War's most duplicitous encounters: On October 18, Kennedy and Andrei Gromyko conversed politely for more than two hours in the Oval Office. Neither put his cards on the table. JFK hid the fact that he had caught the Kremlin red-handed and, resisting temptation to display the incriminating U-2 photos in his desk drawer, reaffirmed warnings against introducing offensive weaponry to Cuba. The unsuspecting foreign minister repeated Moscow's false assurances and, despite noticing Rusk's "crab red" face, blithely cabled home that the situation seemed "completely

16 Excomm meeting transcript, 6:30 p.m., October 16, 1962, in May and Zelikow (eds.), *Kennedy Tapes*, 92.
17 *Ibid.*, 100–01.
18 *Ibid.*, 86–87, 89, 112–13.

satisfactory."[19] (Khrushchev, disdaining Castro's argument that a no-invasion vow couldn't be trusted, later noted that Gromyko had told JFK "that we have no atomic missiles in Cuba. And he was lying. And how! And that was the right thing to do; he had orders from the Party. So, the imperialists cannot trust us either."[20])

By Thursday, the Excomm had swerved behind the blockade. Most important, JFK had edged away from his initial impulse toward an airstrike (although hearing General Curtis LeMay, the cigar-chomping air force chief, growl that a blockade would be "almost as bad as the appeasement at Munich" bluntly reminded him of the domestic political hazards of appearing weak).[21]

Maintaining the charade of normality, the president left for a scheduled campaign swing. To convince hardliners they were getting a fair hearing, he secretly instructed Bundy to keep the airstrike option alive. But after cutting short his trip on Saturday (on the pretext of a cold) to return to Washington, and hearing closing arguments from the bitterly split Excomm, he reaffirmed his preference for a limited blockade.

Attention turned to divulging the news before it leaked. By Monday afternoon, when the White House announced that the president would address the nation at 7 p.m. on a "matter of highest national urgency," a crisis atmosphere gripped Washington. After sending special envoys to brief key allies (Harold Macmillan, Charles de Gaulle, Konrad Adenauer) and telephoning predecessors (Hoover, Truman, Eisenhower), Kennedy informed congressional leaders and heard some of them rip the blockade as a futile half-measure. Irked, he then walked to the Oval Office to tell the world of its predicament.

Why did Kennedy ultimately choose the blockade? First – McNamara disclosed decades later – JFK felt deterred by the prospect of a single Soviet nuclear warhead detonating on an American city,[22] and his military advisers could not guarantee a surprise airstrike would wipe out all the missiles. Second, Kennedy derived thin comfort from the hawks' forecasts that the Soviets would swallow a first strike on Cuba without retaliating elsewhere. He expected a

19 Andrei Gromyko cables, October 19, 20, 1962, *Cold War International History Project Bulletin* (hereafter, *CWIHP Bulletin*), 5 (Spring 1995), 66–67 and 8–9 (Winter 1996/97), 278–82.
20 Memorandom of conversation between NSK and A. Novotný, Moscow, October 30, 1962, briefing book, National Security Archive conference, "The Cuban Missile Crisis: A Political Perspective after 40 Years," Havana, October 11–13, 2002.
21 JCS meeting transcript, 9:45 a.m., October 19, 1962, in May and Zelikow (eds.), *Kennedy Tapes*, p. 178.
22 Robert McNamara, "The Military Role of Nuclear Weapons: Perceptions and Misperceptions," *Foreign Affairs*, 62, 1 (Fall 1983), 59–80.

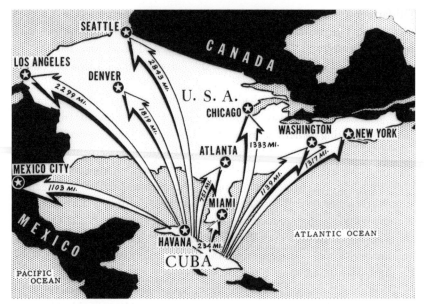

3. During the Cuban missile crisis, US newspapers carried maps showing that Soviet nuclear missiles in Cuba could reach any point in the continental United States except the Pacific northwest.

strike on Cuba to provoke Khrushchev to seize West Berlin, "which leaves me only one alternative, which is to fire nuclear weapons – which is a hell of an alternative ..."[23] Third, Kennedy worried that military action to erase a threat Europeans had learned to endure, risking Berlin or general war, would undermine the support of the North Atlantic Treaty Organization (NATO). Fourth, a limited blockade could be intensified.

Finally, Kennedy recoiled at a surprise attack liable to kill thousands of Cubans and Soviets. "I now know how Tojo felt when he was planning Pearl Harbor," his brother jotted wryly.[24] Though hawks bitterly rejected the analogy, RFK passionately argued that a sudden strike would be "very, very difficult indeed for the President ... with all the memory of Pearl Harbor and with all the implications this would have for us in whatever world there would be afterward. For 175 years we had not been that kind of country. A sneak attack was not in our traditions."[25]

23 JCS meeting transcript, 9:45 a.m., October 19, 1962, in May and Zelikow (eds.), *Kennedy Tapes*, 176.

24 Arthur M. Schlesinger, Jr., *A Thousand Days: John F. Kennedy in the White House* (Boston, MA: Houghton Mifflin, 1965), 803.

25 Excomm meeting transcript, 11 a.m., October 19, 1962, *FRUS, 1961–1963*, vol. 11, 119.

Crucible of the Cold War: how close did they come?

"Good evening, my fellow citizens," a somber Kennedy began. On Monday evening, October 22, 1962, the president opened the public phase of the crisis by revealing that "unmistakable evidence" had confirmed the presence in Cuba of Soviet missile bases whose purpose could only be "to provide a nuclear strike capability against the Western Hemisphere." Calling on Khrushchev "to halt and eliminate this clandestine, reckless and provocative threat to world peace and to stable relations between our two nations" and "move the world back from the abyss of destruction," JFK declared that this "secret, swift, and extraordinary buildup" constituted a "deliberately provocative and unjustified change in the status quo which cannot be accepted by this country, if our courage and our commitments are ever to be trusted again by either friend or foe."

To persuade the Kremlin to reverse course, he announced a "strict quarantine on all offensive military equipment" bound for Cuba, effective from Wednesday morning. Invoking Munich – the 1930s' "clear lesson" that "aggressive conduct, if allowed to go unchecked and unchallenged, ultimately leads to war" – Kennedy vowed neither to "prematurely or unnecessarily risk the costs of worldwide nuclear war" nor to "shrink from that risk at any time it must be faced." Abandoning flexible response for massive retaliation, he warned Washington would "regard any nuclear missile launched from Cuba against any nation in the Western Hemisphere as an attack by the Soviet Union on the United States, requiring a full retaliatory response upon the Soviet Union."[26]

In Moscow, Krushchev had already called an unusual late-night Presidium meeting. When the text of JFK's speech arrived, he was relieved the president had not announced an actual assault on Cuba yet feared one was still likely and "may end in a big war." At first, Khrushchev did not shy away from nuclear conflict *in Cuba*: while withholding permission to fire strategic missiles, he was inclined to authorize use of tactical nuclear weapons if needed. Pleas from associates (particularly Anastas Mikoyan) convinced him to moderate his course and issue a diluted directive to "take immediate steps to raise combat readiness and to repulse the enemy together with the

---

26 *Public Papers of the Presidents of the United States: John F. Kennedy: containing the Public Messages, Speeches, and Statements of the President, January 1 to December 31, 1962* (Washington, DC: US Government Printing Office, 1963), 806–09.

Cuban army and with all the power of the Soviet forces, *except"* nuclear warheads.[27]

The next day, both sides dug in. US, Soviet, and Cuban military establishments went on high alert. Rusk quipped mordantly to an aide that they had won a "considerable victory" since they were still alive – Khrushchev had not retorted with a preemptive strike.[28] As the United Nations (UN) Security Council opened emergency debate, Kennedy secured unanimous endorsement of the blockade by the Organization of American States (OAS), and NATO allies also quickly closed ranks.

In a private letter, Khrushchev curtly demanded Kennedy renounce the quarantine, a "gross violation" of international law threatening "catastrophic consequences."[29] Less belligerently, the Soviet leader deflected suggestions to erect a retaliatory blockade around Berlin. Ready to settle for a "halfway successful" outcome, he ordered two IRBM-transporting ships to stop shy of the quarantine line while instructing one vessel to run for Cuba before it went into effect. He leaned toward Mikoyan's cautious advice to order nuclear-armed Foxtrot submarines to avoid the area around Cuba over his defense minister's brash confidence that the noisy vessels could evade US detection – but that instruction seems never to have reached the commanders of the submarines.[30]

Rebutting Khrushchev, Kennedy warily stressed that both leaders should "show prudence and do nothing to allow events to make the situation more difficult to control than it already is."[31] To convey his rage more vividly, he sent his brother to see Dobrynin on Tuesday evening, opening a vital back channel (replacing Bolshakov). RFK vented the president's ire at being "deceived intentionally," and the two argued hotly. Leaving, the attorney general asked what orders Soviet captains approaching the blockade held. Standing instructions "not to obey unlawful demands to stop or be searched on the open seas," Dobrynin presumed. Robert Kennedy waved good-bye and said: "I don't know how all this will end, for we intend to stop your ships."[32]

27 R. Malinovskii to P. S. Pliev, October 22, 1962 (emphasis added), in General Anatoly I. Gribkov and General William Y. Smith, *Operation ANADYR: U.S. and Soviet Generals Recount the Cuban Missile Crisis* (Chicago: edition q, 1994), 62.
28 Elie Abel, *The Missile Crisis* (New York: Bantam, 1966), 110.
29 NSK to JFK, October 23, 1962, *FRUS, 1961–1963*, vol. XI, 170–71.
30 Fursenko and Naftali, *Khrushchev's Cold War*, 476–80 ("halfway," 477).
31 JFK to NSK, October 23, 1962, *FRUS, 1961–1963*, vol. XI, 174–75.
32 A. Dobrynin cable, October 24, 1962, *CWIHP Bulletin*, 5 (Spring 1995), 71–73; Robert F. Kennedy, *Thirteen Days: A Memoir of the Cuban Missile Crisis* (New York: Norton, 1969), 63.

Wednesday was the day JFK – and much of the globe – dreaded. Once the quarantine started at 10 a.m., no one knew whether Soviet ships would respect or flout it. The president commented glumly that the situation looked "really mean," but seconded his brother's comment that if he hadn't acted firmly "you would have been impeached."[33] Waiting for news of the first intercept, hearing McNamara explain that US ships would use depth charges to force Soviet subs to surface, John Kennedy felt unbearable suspense. "This was the moment we had prepared for," recalled RFK,

> which we hoped would never come. The danger and concern that we all felt hung like a cloud over us all … These few minutes were the time of greatest worry by the President. His hand went up to his face & covered his mouth and he closed his fist. His eyes were tense, almost gray, and we just stared at each other across the table. Was the world on the brink of a holocaust and had we done something wrong?[34]

Then reports arrived that Soviet ships had stopped "dead in the water" or reversed course. Rusk whispered to Bundy, "We're eyeball-to-eyeball, and I think the other fellow just blinked."[35]

The Excomm exhaled, but the crisis continued. Kennedy remained bent on evicting the missile bases already in Cuba, work on which was accelerating. Khrushchev still exuded belligerence. Besides telling an American businessman that JFK better not hit Cuba or they would all "meet in Hell,"[36] he sent Kennedy a note blasting the blockade as "outright banditry or, if you like, the folly of degenerate imperialism," an "act of aggression which pushes mankind toward the abyss of a world nuclear-missile war."[37]

On Thursday, the international spotlight shone on the UN Security Council. Dramatically, Stevenson insisted his Soviet counterpart answer the "simple question" of whether Moscow was placing MRBMs and IRBMs in Cuba. *"Yes or no?"* the US ambassador demanded. "Don't wait for the translation, *yes or no?*"

Removing his earphone, to nervous laughter, Valerian Zorin demurred. "I am not in an American courtroom, and therefore I do not wish to answer a question that is put to me in the fashion in which a prosecutor puts questions."

33 Kennedy, *Thirteen Days*, 67.

34 Arthur M. Schlesinger, Jr., *Robert Kennedy and His Times* (Boston, MA: Houghton Mifflin, 1978), 514; Kennedy, *Thirteen Days*, 69–70.

35 Stewart Alsop and Charles Bartlett, "In Time of Crisis," *Saturday Evening Post*, December 8, 1962, 16–20.

36 William E. Knox *Oral History*, JFKL, in Robert Dallek, *An Unfinished Life: John F. Kennedy, 1917–1963* (New York: Little, Brown, 2003), 563–64.

37 NSK to JFK, October 24, 1962, *FRUS, 1961–1963*, vol. XI, 185–87.

"You are in the courtroom of world opinion right now," Stevenson shot back, "and you can answer yes or no."

"You will have your answer in due course."

Indicating he could wait "until hell freezes over," the American then achieved a public relations coup by unveiling enlarged U-2 images of the missile bases.

Combining pressure and restraint, Kennedy had McNamara keep tight reins on navy commanders implementing the blockade and scotched any boarding of Eastern bloc ships; but he added, "we must act soon because work on the missiles sites is still going on and we must back up very soon the firmness we have displayed up to now."[38]

Behind Moscow's outward defiance, Khrushchev decided to cut his losses. Masking his retreat with gibes at JFK's cowardice, the Soviet leader scaled back visions of a Cold War masterstroke. Confirming a decision that ships ferrying nuclear hardware to Cuba should not defy the blockade, he confided a "fallback position." If Washington "pledges not to touch Cuba," he would dismantle the missile sites under UN inspection. Such an outcome, leaving the tactical nuclear weapons undiscovered, would be "not bad." More candidly, he admitted his venture had "succeeded with some things and not with others." You had to play this game "without losing your head" – war was "not advantageous."[39]

Unaware of his adversary's modified stand, Kennedy seemed gloomy, even fatalistic. Convinced the quarantine would merely hasten an eventual confrontation ("which may or may not be desirable"), he suspected the only realistic ways to expel the missiles were negotiations or "to go over and just take them out."[40]

But during the evening of Friday October 26, a long private telegraph from Khrushchev – one of the Cold War's most remarkable communications – clattered in. Reaching out in personal, emotional terms, Khrushchev viscerally evoked the horrors of war and also implied a deal. If JFK ended the blockade and foreswore attacking Cuba, "this would immediately change everything."

> Let us therefore show statesmanlike wisdom. I propose: we, for our part, will declare that our ships, bound for Cuba, are not carrying any armaments. You would declare that the United States will not invade Cuba with its forces and will not support any sort of forces which might intend to carry out an invasion

38 Excomm minutes, October 25, 1962, *ibid.*, 209.
39 Presidium notes, October 25, 1962, Miller Center website.
40 Excomm meeting transcript, 10 a.m., October 26, 1962, in May and Zelikow (eds.), *Kennedy Tapes*, 464, 468.

of Cuba. Then the necessity for the presence of our military specialists in Cuba would disappear.

... Mr. President, we and you ought not now to pull on the ends of the rope in which you have tied the knot of war, because the more the two of us pull, the tighter that knot will be tied. And a moment may come when that knot will be tied so tight that even he who tied it will not have the strength to untie it, and then it will be necessary to cut that knot. And what that would mean is not for me to explain to you, because you yourself understand perfectly of what terrible forces our countries dispose.

Consequently, if there is no intention to tighten that knot and thereby to doom the world to the catastrophe of thermonuclear war, then let us not only relax the forces pulling on the ends of the rope, let us take measures to untie that knot. We are ready for this.[41]

Khrushchev's proposal also arrived more explicitly through an unorthodox channel: a journalist related that a Soviet embassy contact (KGB *rezident* Aleksandr Feklisov, under diplomatic cover) had urgently inquired whether Washington might agree not to invade Cuba if Moscow dismantled the missile bases under UN scrutiny – terms mirroring Kremlin thinking so closely that it almost certainly was an authorized feeler.

In Havana, meanwhile, Castro geared for apocalyptic battle. Judging an attack "almost imminent within the next 24 to 72 hours," he composed a letter on Friday night advising Khrushchev that if "the imperialists invade Cuba with the goal of occupying it, the danger that the aggressive policy poses for humanity is so great that following that event the Soviet Union must never allow the circumstances in which the imperialists could launch the first nuclear strike against it ... that would be the moment to eliminate such danger forever through an act of clear legitimate defense, however harsh and terrible the solution would be, for there is no other."[42]

For Kennedy, October 27 ("Black Saturday") started out bad and steadily deteriorated. First, the Federal Bureau of Investigation (FBI) reported that Soviet diplomats in New York were preparing to burn their papers. Then, Radio Moscow broadcast a tougher, more impersonal Khrushchev message demanding that in exchange for removing Soviet missiles from Cuba, Kennedy withdraw "analogous means" from Turkey.[43] Inspired by a

---

41 NSK to JFK, October 26, 1962, *FRUS, 1961–1963*, vol. XI, 235–41.
42 F. Castro to NSK, October 26, 1962, in James G. Blight, Bruce J. Allyn, and David A. Welch, *Cuba on the Brink: Castro, the Missile Crisis, and the Soviet Collapse* (New York: Pantheon, 1993), 509–10.
43 NSK to JFK, October 27, 1962, *FRUS, 1961–1963*, vol. XI, 257–60.

Thursday column by journalist Walter Lippmann, Khrushchev hoped this new demand might yet enable him to "win" the duel.[44]

Confused by the discordant messages, some on the Excomm blanched at rewarding nuclear blackmail. JFK, however, saw that stand as untenably rigid. Long wishing to replace the obsolete, vulnerable Jupiters with nuclear-armed Polaris submarines, he observed that the United States would be hard-pressed to justify war over "useless missiles in Turkey" and "to any man at the United Nations or any other rational man, it will look like a very fair trade."[45] Washington couldn't openly pressure Ankara, but the Turks themselves might request the Jupiters' departure given the "great danger in which they will live during the next week and we have to face up to the possibility of some kind of a trade over missiles."[46]

As the Excomm squirmed on Saturday afternoon – "Let's not kid ourselves," said JFK, Khrushchev made a "very good proposal"[47] – U-2 incidents jangled already frayed nerves. A weather-sampling mission strayed over Siberia, rousing Soviet interceptors to scramble. US fighters escorted the petrified pilot to safety, but Khrushchev later admonished Kennedy that at such an anxious moment "an intruding American plane could easily be taken for a nuclear bomber, which might push us to a fateful step."[48] Over Cuba, an SA-2 missile downed a U-2, killing its pilot. The news stoked fear on the Excomm – uncertain whether Moscow had authorized the act (it hadn't) – that the Soviets had deliberately "fired the first shot" in the crisis. "Well, this is much of an escalation by them, isn't it?" the president remarked.[49]

But Kennedy cautiously deferred authorizing a reprisal against the SAM site and prodded aides to refocus on Moscow's "inconsistent and conflicting proposals." Most Excomm members adamantly opposed a public swap and several advisers, including RFK, Bundy, and Thompson, urged JFK to eschew the Turkish offer and instead "accept" the deal implicit in Khrushchev's private letter – an idea that would go down in crisis lore as

---

44 Fursenko and Naftali, *Khrushchev's Cold War*, 488.
45 Excomm meeting transcript, 10 a.m., October 27, 1962, in May and Zelikow (eds.), *Kennedy Tapes*, 498.
46 Excomm minutes, 10 a.m., October 27, 1962, *FRUS, 1961–1963*, vol. XI, 252–56 (quotation 255–56).
47 Excomm meeting transcript, 10 a.m., October 27, 1962, in May and Zelikow (eds.), *Kennedy Tapes*, 512.
48 NSK to JFK, October 28, 1962, *FRUS, 1961–1963*, vol. XI, 282.
49 Excomm meeting transcript, 4 p.m., October 27, 1962, in May and Zelikow (eds.), *Kennedy Tapes*, 571.

the "Trollope Ploy," after the Victorian novelist's description of a damsel's interpreting an innocuous gesture as a marriage proposal.

Kennedy grew dismayed as conversation turned toward the likelihood of imminent combat, especially if firing at surveillance flights persisted. When General Taylor reported that the Joint Chiefs of Staff urged a "big strike" no later than Monday, followed by an invasion, RFK drolly remarked, "Well, that was a surprise."[50] McNamara hawkishly advised removing or defusing Jupiters in Turkey and Italy to dissuade Moscow from reprisals – and *then* invading Cuba … nonplussing CIA director McCone and Lyndon Johnson, who wondered, then, why not trade and avoid the casualties?

The president – freshly sensitized to history's judgment from reading Barbara Tuchman's *The Guns of August* – feared the consequences of rash military action or political intransigence more than anyone:

> We all know how quickly everybody's courage goes when the blood starts to flow, and that's what's going to happen to NATO. When we start these things and they grab Berlin, everybody's going to say: "Well, that was a pretty good proposition" … I think we're better off to get those missiles out of Turkey and out of Cuba because I think the way of getting them out of Turkey and out of Cuba is going to be very, very difficult and very bloody, in one place or another … Of course, what we would like to do is have the Turks come and offer this … We can't very well invade Cuba, with all the toil and blood it's going to be, when we could have gotten them out by making a deal on the same missiles in Turkey. If that's part of the record, then I don't see how we'll have a very good war.[51]

In his reply to Khrushchev, JFK converted the private letter's hazy terms into a firm proposition: should Moscow "agree to remove these weapons systems from Cuba under appropriate United Nations observation and supervision" and prevent their reintroduction, Washington would lift the quarantine and "give assurances against an invasion of Cuba." "[S]uch a settlement on easing world tensions," he noted, "would enable us to work toward a more general arrangement regarding 'other armaments,' as proposed in your second letter which you made public."[52]

But Kennedy anticipated only further stalling from Khrushchev, and on Saturday night he desperately searched for an escape hatch from the crisis. As ships, warplanes, and troops massed around Cuba, and pressure for an attack built – a conference ended with the wisecrack, "Suppose we make Bobby

50 *Ibid.*, 563 51 *Ibid.*, 548–49, 578, 602.
52 JFK to NSK, October 27, 1962, *FRUS, 1961–1963*, vol. XI, 268–69.

mayor of Havana?"[53] – he took a series of secret initiatives to create alternatives to using force.

First, he had his brother assure Dobrynin that if Khrushchev removed his missiles, the Jupiters would be gone from Turkey within four to five months. But in a de facto ultimatum, RFK stressed that Khrushchev must answer *tomorrow*: his brother faced intense pressure to respond violently should flights over Cuba be fired on again, and a grave danger existed that "a chain reaction will quickly start that will be very hard to stop," killing millions of American and Soviet citizens. "Time is of the essence and we shouldn't miss the chance."[54]

Second, JFK authorized Rusk to telephone an associate of UN secretary-general U Thant with the terms of an appeal Thant might issue (if prompted) calling on Washington and Moscow to remove their respective missiles in Turkey and Cuba. Finally, Kennedy's ambassador in Rio was instructed to give the Brazilian government a message it could present (in its own name) to Castro, prodding him to evict the missiles in exchange for a rapprochement with the United States.

None of these efforts struck Kennedy as promising, so it was with surprise bordering on disbelief that he learned the next morning that Khrushchev had agreed, in exchange for the no-invasion vow, "to dismantle the arms which you describe as offensive, and to crate and return them to the Soviet Union," and even to permit the UN to verify the process.[55]

Why had Khrushchev folded so quickly? After all, JFK (via RFK) had only requested a commitment to withdraw the missiles sometime on Sunday, so he had more hours to haggle. Yet, the Kremlin leader rushed to accept Kennedy's proposal in the belief that he needed to "act very quickly" since Washington might soon attack, and before the belligerent Castro dragged the USSR into mortal conflict. Appalled by the Cuban's implicit advocacy of a preemptive nuclear strike, he scorned: "Only a person who has no idea what nuclear war means, or has been so blinded, for instance, like Castro, by revolutionary passion, can talk like that."[56] The headstrong Castro might have seen an invasion of his country as the start of World War III, but Khrushchev did not, and on Saturday he had "categorically" re-ordered his commanders in

---

53 Excomm meeting transcript, 9 p.m., October 27, 1962, in May and Zelikow (eds.), *Kennedy Tapes*, 628.
54 Dobrynin cable, October 27, 1962, *CWIHP Bulletin*, 5 (Spring 1995), 79–80.
55 NSK to JFK, October 28, 1962, *FRUS, 1961–1963*, vol. XI, 279–83.
56 NSK to Novotný, October 30, 1962.

Cuba not to fire any nuclear charges without Moscow's express consent.[57] (Contrary to long-held belief, JFK's secret Turkish concession did *not* influence Khrushchev's move.[58])

Khrushchev's surrender ended the crisis's most acute phase, but it took several weeks for US and Soviet negotiators to sort out the debris. To surmount Castro's balking at inspections, the Americans monitored the missiles' departure by flying low over the ships carrying them away as sailors pulled back the covering tarpaulins, a procedure that humiliated Soviet naval commanders. After Khrushchev grudgingly accepted Washington's demand to remove the IL-28 bombers, JFK lifted the quarantine on November 20. Khrushchev assured Kennedy that all Soviet nuclear weapons were gone from Cuba – but the tactical nuclear weapons weren't shipped out until early December. (Had US intelligence uncovered this fresh deception, the crisis might have restarted amid irresistible pressure for an invasion.) Though Kennedy never formalized the no-invasion vow due to Cuba's blocking of on-site inspection, on January 7, 1963 Washington and Moscow jointly requested the issue's removal from the Security Council agenda.

How dangerous was the crisis? How close did it come to nuclear catastrophe? Those at the top concurred that it came very close indeed. "This time we were really on the verge of war," Khrushchev told a visitor.[59] Kennedy independently agreed, estimating the odds of the Soviets going to war at "somewhere between one and three and even."[60]

Though scholars still hotly debate the level of nuclear danger, evidence suggests a mixed retrospective judgment. Probably the peril of *intentional* escalation was less acute than once formerly believed. As the crisis climaxed, Khrushchev and Kennedy veered toward compromise rather than belligerence. The Soviet leader, as noted above, secretly resolved by October 25 to settle for terms Washington could accept, and JFK's frantic search for an escape hatch two days later suggests that, rather than approve an airstrike or invasion early the next week, he would have tightened the blockade, or even publicly bartered missiles. Both leaders increasingly recognized their shared, transcendent interest in avoiding the ultimate catastrophe.

Yet, the risk of *inadvertent* escalation appears to have been even greater. Contingent events might have been disastrously misinterpreted or caused an

57 Malinovskii to Pliev, October 27, 1962, in Gribkov and Smith, *Operation ANADYR*, 63.
58 Fursenko and Naftali, *Khrushchev's Cold War*, 490.
59 NSK to Novotný, October 30, 1962.
60 Theodore C. Sorensen, *Kennedy* (New York: Harper & Row, 1965), 795.

MISSILE EQUIPMENT
MARIEL PORT FACILITY
4 NOVEMBER 1962

LAUNCH STANDS

17 MISSILE ERECTORS

4. US spy planes photographed Soviet missile equipment as it arrived in Cuba and as it was sent back. Here missile launchers are waiting to be sent back to the USSR from the port of Mariel, west of Havana.

accidental clash, and revelations about Soviet nuclear weapons in and around Cuba *other than* the strategic missiles – including the tactical nuclear weapons (which local commanders under attack might have used regardless of Moscow's edicts), and nuclear-armed submarines maneuvering around the blockade – suggest even a limited or accidental collision risked ballooning to general war, since *any* nuclear use against US forces would have provoked instant nuclear retaliation. At least one frazzled Soviet submarine commander on the blockade line, stalked and harassed by American ships and planes and out of touch with Moscow, is reported to have concluded that war had begun and considered firing his nuclear torpedo.

In sum, the crisis still earns its status as the most dangerous moment in history.

Consequences and controversies

The crisis had important consequences for the subsequent course of the Cold War and nuclear-arms race, and for the fates of its principal figures. Kennedy's success in compelling Khrushchev to pull out the missiles struck most Americans as a glorious victory. He won kudos for toughness in domestic politics (the Jupiter deal remained safely buried) and gained confidence and stature for the duration of his shortened presidency, at home and abroad.

Khrushchev had a tougher time coping with the fallout. Castro was enraged at the Soviet leader both for his concessions to JFK and for his failure to consult before making them. To mollify him, Khrushchev sent Mikoyan to Havana for weeks of tense secret negotiations, a hidden November Crisis that buffeted Soviet–Cuban ties. The Kremlin's decisions to extract additional hardware (the IL-28s, the tactical nuclear weapons) only intensified Castro's fury, while Khrushchev grew increasingly exasperated at the Cuban leader's intransigence. Though the alliance survived, the crisis's humiliating outcome gravely impaired Khrushchev's standing within the Kremlin. Together with other missteps, it solidified a sense that his erratic foreign policy had to end and ultimately hastened his ouster in October 1964. By contrast, Castro remained atop the Cuban government for decades. Despite chagrin at the way the crisis had ended, he owed his regime's long-term survival partly to JFK's no-invasion vow. Khrushchev's claims to have "saved" Cuba, hollow at the time, in retrospect have some validity.

In the Cold War and nuclear arms race, the crisis heralded an era of relative stability in superpower relations. In June 1963, JFK made a singularly conciliatory speech toward the USSR, hailing its World War II role and emphasizing the two nations' common humanity and interest in avoiding nuclear ruin. Shortly thereafter, Washington and Moscow established an emergency hot line – a step directly attributable to exasperation over the cumbersome methods used during the crisis – and agreed to a limited nuclear test ban, a major arms control advance that pointed the way towards a 1968 nuclear non-proliferation pact and also exacerbated the Sino-Soviet split as Beijing (nearing its own first atomic blast) decried superpower collusion.

Perhaps even more significant was what *didn't* happen after the crisis. Convinced now that "Imperialism, as can be seen, is no paper tiger [but] can give you a nice bite in the backside,"[61] Khrushchev lost his appetite for a new Berlin showdown. Within a decade, Moscow and Washington ratified the

61 NSK to Novotný, October 30, 1962.

status quo of a split Berlin and Germany. After Cuba, neither side wanted to risk a repetition along the heavily armed divide in Europe – as the Americans showed by wary responses to upheavals in Czechoslovakia (1968), Poland (1970, 1980–81), and all of East-Central Europe (1989).

The waning of superpower tensions fostered speculation that Kennedy and Khrushchev, had they lasted in power longer, might have ended the Cold War altogether. That seems unlikely. Neither yielded fundamentally incompatible views of ideology or the legitimacy of the postwar international order. Though military friction in Europe subsided, the superpowers repeatedly clashed indirectly in the Third World – and success in Cuba may have facilitated disaster in Vietnam. In 1965, when Johnson decided to bomb the north and send hundreds of thousands of US troops to the south, his entire national security team consisted of missile crisis veterans; McNamara later acknowledged that his experience with the quarantine directly influenced his thinking on the bombing.[62] To the extent that Cuba inculcated confidence (or hubris) that calibrated force could compel a Communist adversary to capitulate, this may have been a fateful misreading: if Khrushchev had "blinked," Castro never did – and nor did Ho Chi Minh, demonstrating anew the ferocity of revolutionary nationalism and leaving Washington painfully quagmired.

In arms control, too, the consequences varied. Furious at being forced to back down – and submit to mortifying close-range inspection – Moscow resolved to catch up in the nuclear competition as rapidly as possible and never again be vulnerable to American pressure. US leaders rationalized the rapid expansion of the Soviet ICBM force as a stabilizing component of what McNamara dubbed mutual assured destruction (MAD), and Nixon and Brezhnev enshrined it in 1972 as a state of nuclear parity. Some scholars argue the crisis reinforced a process of superpower "nuclear learning" – increasing judiciousness and responsibility, cementing a stable "long peace" – but this runs up against evidence that in late 1983 nuclear tensions led to another comparably perilous trip to the brink.

More than any other single Cold War event, the Cuban missile crisis stimulated a voluminous historiography and contentious public debate, not only over what actually happened but its implications for national security policy controversies, international relations theories, bureaucratic politics models, and a host of other fields and sub-fields. Since the rise of Gorbachev's *glasnost*

---

62 McNamara interview, May 21, 1987, in James G. Blight and David A. Welch, *On the Brink: Americans and Soviets Reexamine the Cuban Missile Crisis*, 2nd ed. (New York: Hill and Wang, 1989, 1990), 193–94.

and the fall of Soviet Communism, the partial yet substantial release of Russian, Cuban, CIA, and other formerly inaccessible primary source materials has spawned a new generation of accounts and arguments and allowed scholars to reconstruct and assess the crisis more deeply and broadly than previously possible.

While it is impossible to do justice in a few words to the richness of this new evidence and scholarship, one may advance two tentative hypotheses. First, both Khrushchev and Kennedy come off looking worse in terms of their actions *before* the crisis – more irresponsible and reckless, less heedful of the risks and potential unintended and disproportionate consequences of their actions (for example, Khruschev's deployments of tactical nuclear weapons and nuclear-armed submarines; Kennedy's obsessive anti-Castro campaign) – yet, once *in* the crisis, their shared achievement in escaping it appears even more impressive. It required not only bridging the gulf between them, but mastering their own bellicose initial impulses, and those of some in their own camps. And second, even with the Cold War a receding memory, the persistence of acute fears over nuclear proliferation and confrontation into the twenty-first century suggests that the missile crisis will retain its relevance, as well as its fascination, for the foreseeable future.

5

Nuclear competition in an era of stalemate, 1963–1975

WILLIAM BURR AND DAVID ALAN ROSENBERG

During the years after the Cuban missile crisis, both superpowers treaded more warily to avoid direct confrontations, but traditional Cold War concerns kept them expanding their nuclear arsenals and preparing for the possibility of World War III. Motivated by fear and suspicion, but also by diplomatic and political purposes, both Moscow and Washington invested huge sums in thousands of nuclear weapons and intercontinental delivery systems. During the 1960s, the United States deployed over a thousand intercontinental ballistic missiles (ICBM), hundreds of submarine-launched ballistic missiles (SLBMs), and took the arms race in a new qualitative direction by developing accurate multiple independently targetable re-entry vehicles (MIRVs). The Soviets, determined never to be outmatched again in a crisis, began to field a formidable ICBM force. Before Moscow reached strategic parity with Washington, and ended US nuclear supremacy, however, a stalemate had emerged, where neither side could launch a preemptive strike to gain a military advantage without incurring horrific losses. While the leaders of the superpowers recognized that nuclear weapons were militarily unusable, except in the most extreme circumstances, they nevertheless wanted them for deterrence and for diplomatic leverage.

In Europe, the cockpit of Cold War rivalries, apprehensions about military force imbalances and fears of nuclear blackmail and first strikes gave nuclear weapons a central role in alliance policies and politics. To validate security guarantees and to deter political and military threats, both the Soviet Union and the United States stockpiled thousands of tactical nuclear weapons on European soil. In light of the terrible danger of a nuclear conflagration in Central Europe, both superpowers searched for "flexible response" options to raise the threshold for nuclear weapons use in a confrontation.

The emergence of strategic parity at the close of the 1960s provided the context for superpower détente. US and Soviet leaders wanted to moderate

Cold War rivalries and avoid confrontations, but those goals uneasily co-existed with commitments to preserving and developing strategic advantages. Despite efforts at strategic arms control, innovations such as MIRVs and cruise missiles provided new fields for the nuclear competition and renewed apprehension about the vulnerability of strategic forces. With Moscow and Washington relying on electronic systems to enhance warning of strategic attack, both governments headed toward risky launch-on-warning capabilities, which raised the chances of nuclear catastrophe. While the United States and the Soviet Union continued to avoid nuclear weapons use, the practice of nuclear deterrence and nuclear blackmail remained risk-laden enterprises.

The dilemmas of nuclear stalemate

On the morning of September 12, 1963, President John F. Kennedy directly confronted the reality of nuclear stalemate in the Cold War nuclear-arms competition between the United States and the Soviet Union. General Leon Johnson, director of the National Security Council's Net Evaluation Subcommittee (NESC), briefed the president and senior advisers on the NESC's 1963 report detailing the estimated future results of general war nuclear exchanges between the United States and the Soviet Union between 1964 and 1968 based on war game analyses conducted under various conditions of preemption and retaliation. The US war objective in all cases was to "limit damage to the U.S. and destroy the ability of the USSR and China to wage war." Yet, the report concluded that whichever side initiated an attack, "neither the U.S. nor the USSR can emerge from a full nuclear exchange without suffering very severe damage and high casualties." In the event of Soviet preemption in 1964, the NESC estimated US fatalities at 93 million, a number that rose to 134 million in 1968. If the United States preempted in 1964, NESC estimated that 63 million Americans would die; in 1968, more than 108 million would die. "There is no way," General Johnson told Kennedy, "no matter what we do, to avoid unacceptable damage in the U.S. if nuclear war breaks out."[1]

---

1 Summary record of the 517th Meeting of the National Security Council, September 12, 1963, US Department of State, *Foreign Relations of the United States, 1961–1963* (Washington, DC: US Government Printing Office, 1996), vol. VIII, 499–507; Net Evaluation Subcommittee, "Oral Report," August 27, 1963, copy at the National Security Archive, George Washington University, Washington, DC (hereafter, NSA).

Having contemplated preemptive options during the Berlin crisis, Kennedy now recognized that the strategic advantage the United States had long enjoyed – the ability to destroy much of the Soviet strategic nuclear arsenal in a preemptive strike – was gone. When asked how the United States might reestablish nuclear superiority, General Johnson thought it was impossible. The positive side, he noted, was that the Soviets were equally aware of "the unsatisfactory estimated results of an all-out nuclear war." If both countries recognized that a nuclear war would be a disaster, then "nuclear war is impossible if rational men control governments." That might be true, Secretary of State Dean Rusk observed, but he saw a danger that "one side or the other would be tempted to act in a way which would push the other side beyond its tolerance level." In addition, pressures could reach the point that one side or the other acted in a suicidal way, just "to get it over with." "We can't assume nuclear war won't happen," Rusk said. There was no certainty in "[t]his God Damn poker game."[2]

This briefing marked an unheralded milestone in the history of the arms competition between the United States and the Soviet Union, which now had such dangerous potential that challenges to each other's vital geopolitical interests, as in Europe or East Asia, could have unimaginably destructive results. A condition of nuclear stalemate between the two nuclear superpowers had long been forecast as coming. It had its origins in the pressures to expand the US nuclear arsenal, which derived from several major objectives: treaty guarantees for West European security and the need to stay ahead of the Soviets for military and diplomatic reasons after Moscow tested its first nuclear weapon. Confronted by a nuclear-capable USSR, the Joint Chiefs of Staff (JCS) identified destruction of the Soviet ability to deliver nuclear weapons against the United States and its allies as the highest priority for targeting. This essentially preemptive nuclear strategy, along with the need to ensure that a sufficient number of US forces would survive a Soviet surprise attack, became one of the key forces driving the expansion of the US strategic nuclear arsenal. A complex calculus of attack and counterattack, which blurred the distinction between war-fighting and deterrent capability, fueled the arms race of the 1950s. Although US officials now understood that nuclear

2 For Kennedy and preemption, see Lawrence Freedman, *Kennedy's Wars: Berlin, Cuba, Laos, and Vietnam* (New York: Oxford University Press, 2000), 97. See also Marc Trachtenberg, *A Constructed Peace: The Making of the European Settlement, 1945–1963* (Princeton, NJ: Princeton University Press, 1999), 183.

stalemate had emerged, the same dynamic continued to propel nuclear war planning and military budgets.[3]

Lyndon B. Johnson, who succeeded to the presidency in November, had not been present at the September 1963 briefing, and it is not clear whether he had been back-briefed. Nevertheless, early in his presidency, Johnson received a memorandum from Secretary of Defense Robert McNamara that included alarming details of the costs and consequences of nuclear exchanges with the Soviet Union that were consistent with the NESC briefing. Remarks made by Johnson during the 1964 campaign about the unique destructiveness of nuclear weapons and the horrific casualty levels of nuclear war strongly suggest that he drew the same lesson that Kennedy had: US nuclear superiority was fading and nuclear weapons could be used only for deterrence, not for preemption or war-fighting.[4]

That both superpowers were entering a period of stalemate showed the basic irrelevance of President Dwight D. Eisenhower's 1959 guidance that nuclear planning should ensure that the United States should "prevail and survive" after a war. The NESC exercise did, however, confirm the value of strategic theorist Bernard Brodie's observation that in the nuclear age the chief goal of military establishments was not to "win wars ... but to avert them." After 1963, US policymakers, and later Soviet leaders, widely shared this perception, but that could not solve key problems: what force structures and plans would suffice for deterrence? Would military planners abandon preemptive options? Moreover, would deterrence itself make the superpowers secure?[5]

US nuclear posture and force levels

US presidents wanted to avoid nuclear war but nevertheless agreed that a robust nuclear posture, that is, a large nuclear arsenal backed by elaborate war plans, was the deeply implicit threat that Washington needed in order to play a central role in shaping world affairs. Since the late 1940s, US policymakers,

---

3 David A. Rosenberg, "The Origins of Overkill: Nuclear Weapons and American Strategy, 1945–1960," in Steven Miller (ed.), *Strategy and Nuclear Deterrence* (Princeton, NJ: Princeton University Press, 1984), 113–82.

4 Draft memorandum for the President, "Recommended FY 1965–1969 Strategic Retaliatory Forces," December 6, 1963, NSA; Nina Tannenwald, *The Nuclear Taboo: The United States and the Non-Use of Nuclear Weapons since 1945* (Cambridge: Cambridge University Press, 2007), 206–07.

5 David A. Rosenberg, "Nuclear War Planning," in Michael Howard, George J. Andreopoulos, and Mark R. Shulman (eds.), *The Laws of War: Constraints on Warfare in the Western World* (New Haven, CT: Yale University Press, 1994), 173; Bernard Brodie (ed.), *The Absolute Weapon: Atomic Power and World Order* (New York: Harcourt Brace & Co., 1946), 76.

worried about shifts in the balance of power that could threaten US security and economic interests, believed that a capability to wield the worst possible threat would preserve US influence, discourage Moscow from using military power to coerce US allies, and otherwise deter an attack.

By stationing troops in Western Europe and offering security guarantees through the North Atlantic Treaty Organization (NATO), the United States established a tripwire that raised the stakes if an East–West confrontation turned violent. Even after conditions of nuclear stalemate emerged, key officials such as Secretary of Defense McNamara believed that US strategic forces were necessary not only to deter nuclear attacks against the United States, but also to discourage lesser military challenges to US interests, for example, probes against West Berlin or nuclear "blackmail" of NATO allies. This emphasis on deterrence and diplomatic advantage was inconsistent with the preemptive logic of US, as well as Soviet, nuclear war-planning, and threatened to weaken deterrence, but it was a risk that defense officials accepted.[6]

The eight years of the Eisenhower administration bequeathed the weapons technology programs and choices of the 1960s. Those weapons – subsonic manned bombers, land- and sea-based ballistic missiles with intercontinental reach – were key elements of US forces for the next three decades. Networks of military services, government scientists, and contractors made new weapons possible, but development and deployment depended on the support of top-level Pentagon officials as well as members of Congress. The Kennedy and Johnson administrations shaped the strategic landscape by eliminating cumbersome liquid-fueled Atlas ICBMs and setting force levels for new solid-fueled missiles, Polaris SLBMs and rapid-firing Minuteman ICBMs. Although the Air Force sought thousands of Minutemen, President Johnson eventually approved 1,000, a politically negotiated number representing McNamara's thinking on what the services would accept. Long-range weapons deployed later in the 1960s and the 1970s would largely be improved versions of existing delivery systems, such as B-52s, Poseidon and Trident SLBMs, and Minuteman II and III ICBMs.[7]

6 Melvyn P. Leffler, *A Preponderance of Power: National Security, the Truman Administration, and the Cold War* (Stanford, CA: Stanford University Press, 1992), 331; Rosenberg, "The Origins of Overkill"; William Kaufmann, *The McNamara Strategy* (New York: Harper & Row, 1964), 76, 130–32.
7 Desmond Ball, *Politics and Force Levels: The Strategic Missile Programs of the Kennedy Administration* (Berkeley, CA: University of California Press, 1980); Lawrence S. Kaplan, Ronald D. Landa, and Edward J. Drea, *History of the Office of the Secretary of Defense*, vol. V, *The McNamara Ascendancy 1961–1965* (Washington, DC: Historical Office,

Since the late Eisenhower years, Pentagon officials had supported the emerging mixture of forces with what became known as the "strategic triad" concept; each element of the mix of bombers, SLBMs, and hardened ICBMs would hypothetically provide a separate retaliatory capability in the event that the others were destroyed or otherwise failed. Defense officials routinely assumed that hardened Minutemen and relatively invulnerable SLBMs would have the greatest survivability compared to bombers on the ground. While the Strategic Air Command (SAC) kept nuclear-armed B-52s on airborne alert during 1960–68, this was a risky enterprise. Nuclear accidents over Spain (1966) and Greenland (1968) led the Pentagon to cancel the program, although SAC continued putting some 40 percent of its bombers on ground alert.[8]

In 1962, McNamara and his advisers began using concepts of "assured destruction" and "damage limiting" to justify levels of strategic forces that would preserve a US edge. If the Soviets launched a first strike on the United States, SLBMs, surviving ICBMs, and alert bombers would provide a retaliatory force capable of the "assured destruction" of the Soviet Union: one-third of the population, 150 cities, the command-and-control system, and 50 percent of its industrial capability. McNamara saw the existence of such a capability as a basic deterrent. While rejecting the air force's demands for more Minutemen to permit a full first strike, McNamara supported enough forces for a "damage limiting" mission that could destroy Soviet nuclear threat targets in either retaliatory or preemptive strikes.[9]

A US decision in the mid-1960s to produce MIRVs for ballistic missile forces significantly changed the dynamics of the nuclear rivalry. Produced to penetrate Soviet missile defenses, but also to hit strategic nuclear targets more accurately, MIRVs greatly increased the capability of US missile forces, without changing their numbers. The air force and the navy respectively developed and deployed MIRVs, first on Minuteman III (1970) and then on Poseidon SLBMs (1972). While important military organizations and interests supported MIRVs and the inertial guidance systems that made them possible, few worried about the arms-control implications. With the US

Office of the Secretary of Defense, 2006), 57–67, 478–79, 490; Graham Spinardi, *From Polaris to Trident: The Development of Fleet Ballistic Missile Technology* (Cambridge: Cambridge University Press, 1994).

8 Peter J. Roman, *Eisenhower and the Missile Gap* (Ithaca, NY: Cornell University Press, 1995); Stephen Schwartz (ed.), *Atomic Audit: The Cost and Consequences of U.S. Nuclear Weapons since 1940* (Washington, DC: Brookings Institution, 1998), 189; Scott Sagan, *The Limits of Safety: Organizations, Accidents, and Nuclear Weapons* (Princeton, NJ: Princeton University Press, 1993).

9 Deborah Shapley, *Promise and Power: The Life and Times of Robert McNamara* (Boston, MA: Little, Brown, 1993), 193–201; Kaplan, Landa, and Drea, *The McNamara Ascendancy*, 322.

5. Minuteman III in silo. Introduced in 1970, the Minuteman III intercontinetal ballistic missile (ICBM) had three nuclear warheads and a range of more than 6,000 miles. It remained the mainstay of the US strategic nuclear arsenal for more than forty years.

MIRV decisions, the strategic rivalry moved from quantities of bombs and missiles to such qualitative and quantitative issues as the yield, accuracy, and numbers of warheads that could be mounted on each launcher.[10]

10 Ted Greenwood, *Making the MIRV: A Study of Defense Decision Making* (Cambridge, MA: Ballinger, 1975); Donald MacKenzie, *Inventing Accuracy: A Historical Sociology of Nuclear Missile Guidance* (Cambridge, MA: MIT Press, 1990).

Despite the innovations in strategic technologies, US war-planning, largely determined by the air force, did not stray from patterns set during the 1950s. War planners divided targets into nuclear, other military, and urban-industrial categories, with time-urgent nuclear targets – missile silos, bomber bases, command and control – driving increases in the US nuclear stockpile. Nuclear planners ignored the devastating fire effects of nuclear weapons, which may have kept estimates of weapons requirements unrealistically high. The US nuclear weapons stockpile deployed at bases throughout the United States and overseas stood at 29,000 in 1963 and peaked in 1966–67 at nearly 32,000. The decline in the following years, however, was irregular owing to the introduction of MIRVs, which, during 1969 to 1975, brought the total number of US ICBM and SLBM warheads from over 2,500 to over 7,000.[11]

US war plans posited huge nuclear strikes, but more options became available during the 1960s. When Secretary of Defense McNamara received his first briefing on the Single Integrated Operational Plan (SIOP), he was appalled by its "rigidity" and "overkill" because it posited a single massive nuclear strike involving thousands of weapons with high damage expectancy. While McNamara wanted more flexibility and more choices for the president, including a counter-force attack for limiting damage ("no cities"), the JCS made only marginal changes. They broke up the SIOP into five options, all of which involved massive strikes with high damage requirements, which could be launched either in retaliation or preemptively. Even if the NESC had shown that preemption was not feasible, war planners wanted the possibility of striking quickly if intelligence detected Soviet attack preparations. Other emerging options included attacks against Soviet nuclear capability, other military forces, and urban-industrial targets, as well as options to defer strikes on Warsaw Pact countries and the People's Republic of China (PRC) and even national capitals, like Moscow. Force levels and their composition changed, but the SIOP remained essentially the same until the mid-1970s.[12]

While senior US officials treated nuclear weapons as central to Western defense, since the late 1950s they had recognized that as nuclear stalemate emerged, threats to use them, except in response to a surprise attack, could

---

11 Schwartz (ed.), *Atomic Audit*, 85; Lynn Eden, *Whole World on Fire: Organizations, Knowledge, & Nuclear Weapons Devastation* (Ithaca, NY: Cornell University Press, 2004); Natural Resources Defense Council, "Archive of Nuclear Data From NRDC's Nuclear Program," www.nrdc.org.

12 Rosenberg, "Origins of Overkill," 177; William Burr, (ed.), "New Evidence on the Origins of Overkill," National Security Archive Electronic Briefing Book No. 236, November 22, 2007, www.nsarchive.org.

lack credibility. They (and the Europeans) questioned whether the United States would risk destruction by launching a nuclear strike if conflict broke out in Europe. In 1970, President Richard M. Nixon privately acknowledged that the "nuclear umbrella was no longer there." Although Nixon could not say this publicly, for fear that it would increase Soviet leverage, he and US defense officials continued to search for ways to buttress the credibility of nuclear threats. This concern shaped US nuclear strategy and planning throughout the period.[13]

Following patterns set during World War II, US nuclear planning occurred under conditions of deep secrecy; for example, the terms "Single Integrated Operational Plan" and "SIOP" were secret for years. As justifiable as some of the secrecy was, it was inconsistent with US political traditions of open government and raised enduring questions about accountability.[14]

Soviet nuclear posture and force levels

During the NESC briefing, General Johnson expressed his firm belief that the Soviets must have made the same calculations as the Americans and must have been equally convinced of the futility of nuclear war, but this conviction was based on "mirror imaging" rather than concrete intelligence. After the Cuban missile crisis, Soviet leaders wanted to avoid crises and risks of nuclear war, but they supported nuclear force buildups to minimize risks of exposure to political coercion and to be in a more advantageous position should super-power conflict break out. Indeed, to deter and thwart feared US aggression, military planners embraced a preemptive strategy which shaped Soviet war plans until the early 1970s.[15]

---

13 Robert Jervis, *The Meaning of the Nuclear Revolution: Statecraft and the Prospect of Armageddon* (Ithaca, NY: Cornell University Press, 1989), 38–39; Robert J. McMahon, "Credibility and World Power: Exploring the Psychological Dimension in Postwar American Diplomacy," *Diplomatic History*, 15 (1991), 469–70; "Notes on NSC Meeting 14 February 1969," box H-20, folder: NSC Meeting, Biafra Strategic Policy Issues, 2/14/69 (1 of 2), National Security Council (NSC) Institutional Files, Nixon Presidential Library, National Archives, College Park, Maryland (hereafter, NA) (materials will be moving to Yorba Linda, California), and memorandum of conversation, "NSC Meeting: NATO and MBFR," November 19, 1970, box 109, folder: NSC Minutes Originals 1970 (1 of 3), NSC Institutional Files, Nixon Presidential Library, NA.

14 Schwartz (ed.), *Atomic Audit*, 433–84.

15 Christoph Bluth, *Soviet Strategic Arms Policy Before SALT* (Cambridge: Cambridge University Press, 1992), 78, 157; Vladislav M. Zubok, *A Failed Empire: The Soviet Union in the Cold War from Stalin to Gorbachev* (Chapel Hill, NC: University of North Carolina Press, 2007), 193, 203.

In a major open-source publication in 1962, senior Soviet officers headed by Marshal V. D. Sokolovskii showed how their apprehensions shaped preemptive thinking. Should conflict break out, it would be a "nuclear rocket war." Of "decisive importance" to the outcome of war would be the immediate destruction of the adversary's nuclear weapons complex, chief military installations, and military-industrial resources. Sensitive to the danger of first strikes because of the German attack in June 1941, Sokolovskii and his colleagues feared that Washington was preparing for a "sudden nuclear attack against the Soviet Union." Recognizing the devastating potential of a single nuclear strike, they underscored the need to repel a surprise attack with the "timely infliction of a shattering attack upon [the adversary]." While the massive destruction of nuclear war would be catastrophic, allegedly the Soviet Union would prevail to the extent that its counterattack destroyed the "aggressor."[16]

Secrecy, even more pervasive than on the US side, makes it impossible to know how Soviet war planners targeted their nuclear capabilities in the Plan of Operation of the Strategic Nuclear Forces. But they were determined to frustrate the enemy's "aggressive designs" and, just like SIOP planners, most likely gave priority to strikes on their adversary's nuclear forces. Nevertheless, they also recognized that the limited accuracy of their forces and the dangers of a US retaliatory strike made preemption a perilous choice. In fact, the civilian leadership never supported it.[17]

The "aggressive definition of deterrence" assumed by Soviet strategy required, first of all, continued rapid expansion of the Soviet nuclear stockpile and the production and deployment of nuclear delivery systems. This stockpile had increased rapidly during the late 1950s, but not quickly enough to overcome the US lead; between 1956 and 1961, the Soviet stockpile of warheads increased from about 400 to 2,450 (compared to 3,620 and 23,200 respectively for the United States). Moscow especially lagged in the production of intercontinental delivery systems. In 1960, the newly organized Soviet

16 V. D. Sokolovkii, *Soviet Military Strategy: Soviet Doctrine and Concepts* (Englewood Cliffs, NJ: Prentice-Hall, 1963); R. Craig Nation, *Black Earth, Red Star: A History of Soviet Security Policy, 1917–1991* (Ithaca, NY: Cornell University Press, 1992), 214–17; Matthias Uhl, "Storming on to Paris: The 1961 Buria Exercise and the Planned Solution of the Berlin Crisis," in Vojtech Mastny, Sven S. Holtsmark, and Andreas Wenger (eds.), *War Plans and Alliances in the Cold War: Threat Perceptions in the East and West* (London: Routledge, 2006), 46–52.

17 Steven Zaloga, *The Kremlin's Nuclear Sword: The Rise and Fall of Russia's Strategic Nuclear Forces* (Washington, DC: Smithsonian Institution Press, 2002), 79–80 and 137. For targeting, see Bruce Blair, *The Logic of Accidental Nuclear War* (Washington, DC: Brookings Institution, 1993), 61.

Strategic Rocket Forces (SRF) had hundreds of medium-range ballistic missiles (MRBMs) capable of striking NATO Europe but, despite three years of testing and Nikita S. Khrushchev's missile rattling, the Soviets probably had only four ICBMs capable of reaching the United States. The Kremlin's strategic bomber force remained small compared to Washington's because missiles were its chief priority.[18]

US plans to build and deploy hundreds of Minutemen ICBMs, along with lessons drawn from the Cuban missile crisis, motivated Khrushchev and the high command to develop a missile force rivaling that of the United States. Determined never again to be caught in a strategically vulnerable position, Soviet leaders decided to deploy large numbers of ICBMs, including the huge SS-9s, designed to match the US Titan, and the relatively cheap SS-11, designed to be produced in large numbers so that Moscow could reach parity quickly and end US nuclear preponderance. The Soviets aimed some SS-11s east to counter Beijing's developing nuclear capabilities. While the Soviets were building formidable numbers of missiles, unlike US ICBMS, theirs had short service lives, making it necessary to build new generations on a regular basis. Moreover, Moscow's SLBM program was underfunded and Soviet submarines were vulnerable to detection.

Alliances and nuclear weapons

As a central front in the Cold War, Europe became a focal point for super-power nuclear rivalries. Both Washington and Moscow deployed thousands of nuclear weapons in Europe and their allies played integral roles in operating systems to deliver them. Both superpowers kept tight control over the weapons themselves, but Moscow's nuclear policies toward European allies were top-down, while US policy involved the construction of a shaky NATO consensus on nuclear planning. Both superpowers came to support "flexible response" strategies to avoid use of nuclear weapons, although by the early 1970s the Soviets eventually supported "no first use," which Washington consistently rejected.

US nuclear weapons policies in NATO Europe reflected military, security, and political priorities. Unease about the size of Soviet conventional forces served as an enduring justification for fielding US nuclear weapons in Europe,

18 This and the following paragraph draw on Nation, Black Earth, Red Star, 217; Zaloga, The Kremlin's Nuclear Sword, 61–66, 75–76, 80; Pavel Podvig (ed.), Russian Strategic Nuclear Forces (Cambridge, MA: MIT Press, 2001), 121–26, 145–47, and 196–205.

even though tactical nuclear deployments was one area where the United States retained an edge over the Soviets. Although US nuclear deployments were often controversial in Western Europe, US leaders assumed that their presence was necessary to reinforce security guarantees and maintain the confidence of allies. According to McNamara, a strong US military posture was important not only for maintaining NATO cohesion, but also to check "Soviet political pressure and blackmail" and avert changes in West German policy – either a militaristic revival or the negotiation of special security arrangements with Moscow – that could disrupt the Western security system.[19]

The Pentagon fielded growing numbers of theater and tactical nuclear weapons during the 1960s to support security guarantees and reinforce deterrence. In 1960, the United States had deployed only a few hundred weapons in NATO Europe; by 1967, it had stockpiled over 7,000. They were designed for a variety of missions, including anti-submarine, air defense, battlefield use, and strikes on Soviet bases and command posts. In part, the deployments flowed from the decisions of the Kennedy and Johnson administrations to continue Eisenhower's NATO nuclear stockpile program by negotiating nuclear-sharing agreements with European allies. To prevent unauthorized use of the weapons, Kennedy's advisers tightened up control of the weapons by installing Permissive Action Locks (PALs) on weapons deployed in Europe.[20]

The danger of nuclear weapons use in a Central European confrontation shaped Washington's search for non-nuclear options that raised the threshold for nuclear weapons use. NATO's General Strike Plan (later known as the Nuclear Options Plan) included a wide array of "package" nuclear options for clashes with Warsaw Pact forces as well as for strikes against fixed targets. Nevertheless, during the 1960s and 1970s, senior Pentagon officials found it difficult to visualize plausible scenarios for using tactical weapons that did not involve risks of escalation and nuclear conflagration. Those dangers made the Kennedy and Johnson administrations want to strengthen the credibility of nuclear threats with a NATO capability for "flexible," nonnuclear, responses

---

19 Matthew Evangelista, *Innovation and the Arms Race* (Ithaca, NY: Cornell University Press, 1988); R. McNamara to President Johnson, "NATO Strategy and Force Structure," September 21, 1966, copy at NSC. Francis J. Gavin, "The Myth of Flexible Response: United States Strategy in Europe during the 1960s," *International History Review*, 23 (December 2001), 858.

20 Trachtenberg, *A Constructed Peace*, 193–200, 304–09; Ivo Daalder, *The Nature and Practice of Flexible Response: NATO Strategy and Theater Nuclear Forces since 1967* (New York: Columbia University Press, 1991), 108–11.

to less than all-out Soviet conventional attacks. While US defense officials rejected a "no-first-use" nuclear policy, they hoped that "flexible response" would make it possible to avoid early, or even any, use of nuclear weapons in a European conflict. This was a difficult objective, complicated by balance-of-payments pressures, French withdrawal from NATO forces, and opposition from European partners, who refused to expand conventional forces.[21]

A growing belief that the threat of general war had receded and US–European agreement that NATO needed conventional capabilities to deal with limited nonnuclear attacks created conditions for the formal revision of NATO strategy along "flexible response" lines. In October 1967, NATO approved MC-14/7, which emphasized the need for both conventional and nuclear options so that NATO could react "appropriately" to any level of attack. Thus, MC-14/7 straddled US support for nonnuclear approaches and British and German beliefs that deterrence required a commitment to early nuclear use. It did not, however, resolve a question that would be an enduring dilemma for military planners: just how long could alliance forces hold against Soviet attack before resorting to nuclear weapons.

The growing stockpile of US nuclear weapons in Europe raised another basic problem: how to give NATO allies a voice in nuclear use and war planning, especially so that some, such as West Germany, did not become motivated to acquire their own nuclear forces. While NATO guidelines gave "special weight" to the views of governments, and Washington made loose consultative arrangements with Bonn and London on nuclear weapons use, the United States retained final control over the weapons. NATO's Nuclear Planning Group (NPG), created in the mid-1960s, was a significant US-led effort to ensure alliance participation in the complexities of nuclear use. The NPG focused on such problems as consultation and preliminary guidelines for firing tactical nuclear weapons. That it would take the NPG nearly two decades to agree on a full statement of political guidelines on nuclear use suggests the depths of controversy over this sensitive problem.[22]

The Soviets saw their large conventional forces in Eastern Europe as a necessary counter to US strategic forces as well as valuable for local political

21 The following paragraphs draw on Kaplan, Landa, and Drea, *The McNamara Ascendancy*, 313; Trachtenberg, *A Constructed Peace*, 188–89, 289; John S. Duffield, *Power Rules: The Evolution of NATO's Conventional Forces Posture* (Stanford, CA: Stanford University Press, 1995); and Helga Haftendorn, *NATO and the Nuclear Revolution: A Crisis of Credibility, 1966–1967* (New York: Oxford University, 1996).
22 Paul Buteux, *The Politics of Nuclear Consultation in NATO 1965–1980* (Cambridge: Cambridge University Press, 1983); Daalder, *Nature and Practice of Flexible Response*, 80–84, 90–93.

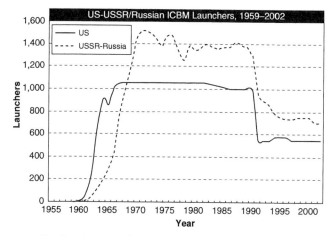

Graph 1. US–USSR/Russian ICBM Launchers, 1959–2002

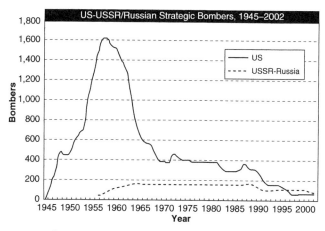

Graph 2. US–USSR/Russian Strategic Bombers, 1945–2002

control. US deployments of theater nuclear forces in NATO Europe stimulated the Soviets to field tactical nuclear weapons in Eastern Europe, but their stockpile was half the size of NATO's, and most of the weapons were high-yield and not suited for battlefield use. Using storage sites in several Warsaw Pact countries, Moscow kept tight control of its weapons. Local Warsaw Pact forces received training from the Soviets in using them for their role in the war plan, but they would not gain possession of them until war broke out. In spite of these plans and deployments, by the 1970s, Warsaw

Pact leaders understood that even though they had advantages in numbers of troops and heavy armor, NATO had a "qualitative edge" in nuclear weapons and aircraft.[23]

While little is known about Soviet nuclear plans, archival releases from the former Eastern bloc show how concern about escalation also led them to raise the nuclear threshold. A Warsaw Pact Command Post exercise held during the 1961 Berlin crisis showed the Soviet bloc striking NATO Europe with a massive nuclear attack of over 1,000 weapons in response to warning of impending US and allied airstrikes. General nuclear war was expected to quickly ensue. Similar assumptions informed Pact war plans in 1964. Beginning in the mid-1960s, however, the Soviets began to change their doctrine because they recognized the nuclear stalemate and saw the emergence of US flexible response strategies. The high command no longer assumed that war in Europe would be automatically nuclear and Soviet/ Pact planning anticipated fighting a conventional war first, with nuclear weapons introduced only if the Western powers used them first or threatened to do so. That the NATO powers would use nuclear weapons first remained a Warsaw Pact planning assumption.[24]

Intelligence, war plans, and warning

To improve their strategic position and to secure early warning of hostile moves, Moscow and Washington tried to perfect intelligence capabilities. On the US side, reconnaissance satellites transformed nuclear planning by settling the missile gap controversy in 1961 and then discovering in 1966 that the Soviets were heading towards parity. More accurate knowledge of Soviet force levels would help defense planners forecast nuclear weapons requirements and configure US strategic forces, while satellite technology made it possible to target Soviet installations with high levels of precision.[25]

---

23 Evangelista, *Innovation*, 215; Daalder, *Nature and Practice of Flexible Response*, 119; Uhl, "Storming on to Paris," 59–62; Christoph Bluth, "The Warsaw Pact and Military Security in Central Europe During the Cold War," *Journal of Slavic Military Studies*, 17 (2004), 299–311.

24 See Uhl, "Storming on to Paris," Petr Luňák, "War Plans from Stalin to Brezhnev: The Czechoslovak Pivot," and Frede P. Jensen, "The Warsaw Pact's Special Target," in Mastny, Holtsmark, and Wenger (eds.), *War Plans and Alliances in the Cold War*, 52–56, 81–84, and 105–08; Raymond Garthoff, *Deterrence and the Revolution in Soviet Military Doctrine* (Washington, DC: Brookings Institution, 1990), 52–69.

25 Eden, *Whole World on Fire*, 99–107, 225–26; Dwayne A. Day, John M. Logsdon, and Brian Latell (eds.), *Eye in the Sky: The Story of the Corona Spy Satellites* (Washington, DC:

Acquiring "real-time" warning of a strategic missile attack became a high-priority goal of the intelligence services. Unless detected in time, a surprise attack would not give SAC bombers enough warning to take off or US political authorities time to respond. By the late 1960s, Defense Support System satellites provided at best a twenty-seven minutes warning. That could give time for bombers to launch and the president to authorize a retaliatory strike, but US military experts still worried about the vulnerability of the US command-and-control system to disruption by a paralyzing attack. While US presidents, beginning with Eisenhower, had approved "predelegation" arrangements (depicted in *Dr. Strangelove* as "Plan R") authorizing top commanders to launch strikes in the event that an attack had incapacitated the president, the Pentagon kept searching for methods to improve command-and-control and communications. Such innovations as ARPANET, the forerunner of the Internet, emerged in that context.[26]

The problem of inadequate warning time provided the context for the launch-on-warning capability. By the late 1950s and early 1960s, White House advisers recognized that warning systems could make it possible to launch quick-reaction Minutemen almost automatically, although the possibility of a false alarm made that option perilous. With the Defense Support System, launch-on-warning became technically feasible; some analysts argue that the "U.S. strategic posture gravitated to [that] option" by the early 1970s. Later in the decade, the closely related launch-under-attack option became part of the SIOP in order to facilitate a quick Minuteman strike of a foe's targets. That both the US and the Soviet deterrence postures rested on such a potentially catastrophic basis was one of the most worrisome secrets of the Cold War.[27]

The Nixon administration, like its Democratic predecessors, recognized that under conditions of stalemate first strikes and preemption were not workable. Nevertheless, seeking more freedom of action, Nixon and Henry Kissinger wanted to find ways to make nuclear weapons useful for political coercion. Based on his interpretation of Eisenhower's conduct during the 1950s crises, Nixon's "madman theory" – the "principle of a threat of excessive force" to coerce Moscow or a Soviet ally – informed a number of his actions.

Smithsonian Institution Press, 1998), 26, 184, 204–06, 209; Lawrence Freedman, "The CIA and the Soviet Threat: The Politicization of Estimates," *Intelligence and National Security* (1997), 124–26.

26 Leonard Wainstein, C. D. Cremeans, J. K. Moriarty, and J. Ponturo, *The Evolution of U.S. Strategic Command and Control and Warning, 1945–1972*, Study S-467, Institute for Defense Analyses, June 1975, Top Secret (declassified 1992); Jeffrey Richelson, *America's Space Sentinels: DSP Satellites and National Security* (Lawrence, KS: University Press of Kansas, 1999); Schwartz (ed.), *Atomic Audit*, 218.

27 *Ibid.*, 216–17; Blair, *Logic of Accidental Nuclear War*, 186–87.

Thus, in October 1969, Nixon ordered a secret alert of US nuclear and conventional forces to "jar" the Soviets into cooperating with his Vietnam War diplomacy. Nixon and Kissinger continued to employ the "madman" strategy, e.g., raising alert levels of Mediterranean forces during the Jordan crisis (1970) and going to a DEFCON 3 alert during the October War (1973), but Kissinger eventually recognized that nuclear threats in diplomatic risk-taking had become too dangerous to use.[28]

Ironically, "madman" tactics, with their risks of unintended consequences, went hand in hand with US efforts to reform the SIOP to give more options to the president and minimize risks of escalation to all-out nuclear war. Feeling "horror" over the SIOP's massive destructiveness and believing that more limited nuclear options would make deterrence and nuclear threats more credible, a persistent Kissinger induced the Pentagon to undertake major studies of strategic targeting policy during 1972 and 1973. Secretary of Defense James Schlesinger also favored changing the SIOP. By 1974, in response to Nixon's instructions, defense planners began creating a range of attack options for a variety of possible confrontations with the Soviet Union (as well as China), with preemption remaining an option. Change was slow and some questioned whether escalation could be controlled once nuclear weapons had been used, even on a "limited" basis. Moreover, the war plan produced under the new guidance, SIOP-5, had few limited options. It shifted some emphasis from military targets by stressing the importance of destroying "military forces" and "critical industries" that would be needed for Soviet postwar recovery. While secretaries of defense had publicly declared that "we do not ... target civilian population *per se*," nuclear planners were, in effect, treating urban workers as high-priority targets.[29]

The Soviets also began to recognize that preemption was unfeasible, although later than US leaders. Even if Minutemen ICBMs were vulnerable to attack, secure US missile-launching submarines put the Soviets at risk, and the constant training and retraining for successive generations of ICBMs

28 "Notes on NSC Meeting February 14, 1969" and Minutes, MBFR Verification Panel meeting, July 30, 1970, box 109, NSC Institutional Files, Nixon Presidential Library. For the October 1969 alert, see William Burr and Jeffrey Kimball, "Nixon's Secret Nuclear Alert: Vietnam War Diplomacy and the Joint Chiefs of Staff Readiness Test, October 1969," *Cold War History*, 3 (January 2003), 113–56; Brzezinski to Carter, "Weekly National Security Report #8," 9 April 1977, Jimmy Carter Presidential Library, Atlanta, Georgia.

29 Terry Terriff, *The Nixon Administration and the Making of U.S. Nuclear Strategy* (Ithaca, NY: Cornell University Press, 1995); William Burr, "The Nixon Administration, the 'Horror Strategy,' and the Search for Limited Nuclear Options, 1969–1972," *Journal of Cold War Studies*, 7 (2005): 34–78.

caused "turmoil" in Soviet rocket forces. Those problems greatly complicated the possibility of a successful preemptive strike. Instead of preemption, the Soviet military headed toward reliance on a launch-on-warning concept, which new warning systems supposedly made conceivable. During the late 1960s and the 1970s, the Dnestr-M radar system provided a ten-minute warning, but it may have been unreliable, and a satellite warning system was not available until the 1980s. The warning gap continued to make launch-on-warning problematic, especially when US submarines could launch missiles with little warning to Soviet command and control.[30]

Much about Soviet strategic intelligence and targeting remains secret. The Soviet spy satellite, the Zenit, was deployed in August 1962, with a more precise system deployed a year later. Soviet military intelligence sought such precision to help create the accurate maps needed for targeting. Later in the 1960s, the Soviets deployed Sfera geodetic satellites that collected information on gravitational and magnetic fields needed to make trans-polar ICBM flights more accurate. Although the satellites were designed to enhance targeting and facilitate an attack, they eased the problem of verifying arms-control agreements. "National means of verification" ensured that each side could monitor the other's force deployments.

Nuclear taboos and arms control

Despite Dean Rusk's fears of suicidal conduct, during the period between the missile crisis and the Helsinki summit, the superpowers avoided direct confrontations where nuclear use was a possibility. During the tense October War, Leonid Brezhnev acted with more restraint than Kissinger by eschewing nuclear readiness measures. During the Vietnam War, when some US officials and scientists studied the possibility of nuclear use, no one saw any military advantage in such action. Some analysts have argued that in the United States a deep-rooted predisposition emerged, a "nuclear taboo" against the military use of nuclear weapons, except in retaliatory circumstances, based on such concerns as adverse international reaction and the disproportionate effects of the weapons. McNamara's private understandings with Presidents Kennedy and Johnson that the United States would not use

---

30 This and the next paragraph draw on Zaloga, *The Kremlin's Nuclear Sword*, 123, 127, 163–166, 177; Podvig, *Russian Strategic Nuclear Forces*, 420–32; Peter Gorin, "Zenit: The Soviet Response to CORONA," Day, Logsdon, and Latell (eds.), *Eye in the Sky*, 157–72.

nuclear weapons first reflected that inclination. That the Soviet leadership had similar concerns is suggested by the Politburo's early 1970s decision that military plans should reflect a "no-first-use" doctrine. Although the civilian leaders of the superpowers believed that nuclear weapons were valuable politically and diplomatically, they found them virtually unusable militarily, except for the most unlikely circumstance (response to a first strike). This may have been one of the biggest secrets of the Cold War.[31]

Widespread public anxiety about nuclear testing led Kennedy and Khrushchev to reach agreement on the Limited Nuclear Test-Ban Treaty (1963). Stopping atmospheric testing by the superpowers, the treaty left them free to test nuclear weapons underground, thus facilitating the development of new weapons, such as MIRVs. While the superpowers negotiated an agreement to ban nuclear weapons from space (1966) and sponsored the Nuclear Non-Proliferation Treaty (1968), arms-control achievements were scarce during the 1960s. Nuclear taboos did not discourage either side from fielding new weapons systems or from searching for nuclear options.[32]

ABMs and SALT

The fear of surprise attack created significant pressure for anti-ballistic missile (ABM) systems, which were highly controversial. Both sides spent huge sums for research and development, but even the ABM system that was developed to defend Moscow could stop only a few missiles. Realizing that "absolute protection" was impossible, top political leaders, such as Brezhnev and Aleksei Kosygin favored negotiations to limit ABMs, but the Defense Ministry and military-industrial complex wanted to work on a national missile defense sytem. McNamara opposed missile defense, not only because of technological uncertainties, but also because both sides could defeat it by building more missiles and MIRVs. Nevertheless, the Joint Chiefs of Staff strongly favored an ABM deployment, and President Johnson would not oppose it unless the Soviets agreed to discuss mutual limitations. The Soviets, however, were not yet interested in talks on freezing strategic force levels. Therefore, in a September 1967 speech, McNamara reluctantly announced that Washington

---

31 Tannenwald, *Nuclear Taboo*, 1–25, 190–240; Garthoff, *Deterrence and the Revolution in Soviet Military Doctrine*, 80–89; Kaplan, Landa, and Drea *The McNamara Ascendancy*, 322.
32 Kendrick Oliver, *Kennedy, Macmillan, and the Nuclear Test-Ban Debate, 1961–63* (New York: St. Martin's Press, 1998); Lawrence Wittner, *Resisting the Bomb: A History of the World Nuclear Disarmament Movement, 1954–1970* (Stanford, CA: Stanford University Press, 1997), 414–41. For non-proliferation, see Francis M.Gavin's chapter in this volume.

would deploy Sentinel, a "thin" ABM system, mainly aimed at an alleged Chinese missile threat in the 1970s.[33]

Progress in arms control partly depended on Moscow's attaining strategic parity with Washington. By 1968–69, Soviet ICBM forces were close to matching those of the United States in size, the Soviet leadership was more worried about a ruinous ABM competition, and interested in limiting US forward-based systems (aircraft and SLBMs) in Europe and the Mediterranean. What gave compelling stimulus to Brezhnev's support for Strategic Arms Limitation Treaty (SALT) negotiations and détente policies was his personal commitment, formed by his World War II experience, to avoiding war and to promoting peaceful relations between the superpowers. That, however, did not rule out pursuing an ICBM buildup to maintain Soviet strength.[34]

The Soviet invasion of Czechoslovakia derailed initial plans for SALT talks, and internal problems on both sides led to delays until November 1969. Nixon supported SALT in part because he wanted a reputation as a peacemaker to offset public apprehension about Vietnam. Worried about the erosion of US power signaled by parity and determined to preserve a central US position in world affairs, he and Kissinger also pursued arms control and détente as a subtle form of anti-Soviet containment. At first, they wanted to delay negotiations by trying to "link" SALT to progress on Vietnam War and Middle East settlements. That failed, but Nixon gave the go-ahead to a limited, but highly controversial, ABM deployment plan to strengthen his leverage in the SALT talks.[35]

A central issue in the negotiations was the status of MIRVs, where the United States enjoyed a temporary advantage. For State Department and Arms Control and Disarmament Agency (ACDA) officials, banning multiple warheads could prevent a spiraling arms race, but the Joint Chiefs saw strategic advantages in deploying the MIRVed Minuteman III, and neither Nixon nor Kissinger wanted to oppose them. To protect Pentagon interests, the White House instructed negotiators to make an offer that Moscow would have to refuse, because it would have left the US Air Force with a stockpile of already-tested MIRVs, while the Soviets would have to freeze

---

33 Victor Gobarev, "The Early Development of Russia's Ballistic Missile Defense System," *Journal of Slavic Military Studies*, 14 (June 2001), 29–48; Podvig (ed.), *Russian Strategic Nuclear Forces*, 412–20; Shapley, *Promise and Power*, 389–95.

34 Zaloga, *Kremlin's Nuclear Sword*, 141–43; Gobarev, "The Early Development of Russia's Ballistic Missile Defense System," 40–43; Zubok, *Failed Empire*, 201–05.

35 Raymond Garthoff, *Détente and Confrontation: American–Soviet Relations From Nixon to Reagan*, rev. ed. (Washington, DC: Brookings Institution, 1994), 28–68, 78, 146–50; also see Robert Schulzinger's chapter in this volume.

their development work. Whether an effective MIRV ban could have been negotiated or not, Kissinger suggested an opportunity had been missed when he later observed that he should have "thought through the implications of a MIRVed world more thoughtfully in 1969 and 1970."[36]

The complex SALT negotiations produced agreements, signed at the Moscow summit (May 1972), which confirmed each side's strategic advantages. An "Interim Agreement" had less consequence; it froze US and Soviet ICBMs at 1054 and 1618 respectively, but the Soviet lead in missiles was offset by the US advantage in MIRVs. Reflecting Kissinger's oversight in excluding SLBMs from his original back-channel freeze proposal, the final agreement froze US SLBM levels at 656 and 44 submarines, while allowing the Soviets to build up to 950 SLBMs and 62 submarines, as long as they retired over 200 old ICBMs. The "Interim Agreement" left untouched strategic bomber forces, preserving SAC's three to one advantage, as well as US forward-based systems (FBS) in NATO Europe. The most significant achievement, however, was the ABM Treaty, which sharply checked an arms race in this area by barring national missile defense systems altogether.[37]

With the SALT I Interim Agreement permitting modernization and replacement of old ICBMs, the Soviets moved ahead on the third generation of ICBMs that they had begun planning in 1969. In this way, the Soviets hoped to match US qualitative improvements but also compensate for FBS, British, French, and Chinese nuclear forces. After major controversy between design bureaus, defense industry leaders, and technologically conservative military officers over the degree of innovation, Brezhnev and the Politburo approved the development of three new MIRV-capable ICBMs: the SS-17, the SS-18, which would replace the SS-9, and the SS-19, slated to replace the SS-11. With these decisions, the defense industry sector, which was becoming a decisive player in setting force levels, secured more work, but the Strategic Rocket Forces became "saddled with three entirely different missile systems ... with entirely different infrastructure, training requirements and maintenance demands."[38]

By the mid-1970s, the Soviets had begun to offset the US advantage in MIRVs. The SS-17 and SS-18 were especially formidable, with hardened silos, significant accuracy, and improved fuel storage and command-and-control

36 Garthoff, *Détente and Confrontation*, 153–61; Jussi Hanhimäki, *The Flawed Architect: Henry Kissinger and American Foreign Policy* (New York: Oxford University Press, 2004), 51, 83.
37 The following paragraphs draw on Podvig (ed.), *Russian Strategic Nuclear Forces*, 8–9, 130–32; Zaloga, *Kremlin's Nuclear Sword*, 135–53; Garthoff, *Détente and Confrontation*, 180–97; Hanhimäki, *Flawed Architect*, 220–24, Zubok, *Failed Empire*, 243.
38 Zaloga, *Kremlin's Nuclear Shield*, 135–41.

systems. US intelligence was well aware of these developments, having detected testing activity in 1972 and 1973. While the deployments would eventually fuel alarmist rhetoric in the United States about a "window of vulnerability," they did not threaten parity or give the Soviets a first-strike capability. Brezhnev saw them as legitimate moves wholly compatible with détente.

The protracted SALT II negotiations reflected a more complex political context for arms control, especially in Washington. Kissinger's secretive negotiating style antagonized the Pentagon and his position further weakened when Nixon purged ACDA in early 1973 in response to pressure from SALT critic Senator Henry Jackson (D-Washington). Removing moderate arms controllers from the internal debate strengthened hardliners like Secretary of Defense James Schlesinger and limited Kissinger's maneuverability. Kissinger himself complicated SALT II by pressing for the development of nuclear-tipped cruise missiles to increase US negotiating leverage. While Brezhnev remained strongly committed to the SALT process, his top commanders were highly suspicious of the negotiations.[39]

After two years of difficult negotiations, at the November 1974 Vladivostok summit, Brezhnev and Gerald Ford, Nixon's successor, reached an understanding that sought to limit the drive for strategic advantage. Based on the principle of equal aggregates, the agreement allowed each side up to 2,400 launch vehicles, bombers, and missiles, with a 1,320 sub-limit of MIRVed missiles. Both sides could improve strategic systems qualitatively. For senior US officials, the understanding reduced concern that the Soviets could get a numerical edge that would improve their political and diplomatic position. The agreement included no compensation to the Soviets for US forward-based systems; the Soviet high command thought this concession was unjustifiable, but Brezhnev forced them to accept it.[40]

Negotiations to fill in the details of the Vladivostok agreement bogged down during 1975 and 1976. Washington sought broad freedom of action to deploy cruise missiles, but the Soviets wanted limits on US deployments. Even more controversial was whether to count the Soviet Backfire bomber as a strategic system. Despite the disagreements, by late 1975, Kissinger and Soviet

---

39 Garthoff, *Détente and Confrontation*, 369–71, 467–73, 493–505; Zubok, *Failed Empire*, 221, 245.

40 Podvig (ed.), *Russian Strategic Nuclear Forces*, 14; Garthoff, *Détente and Confrontation*, 369–71, 467–73, 494–505; Minutes, National Security Council, January 29, 1975, Gerald Ford Presidential Library website, www.fordlibrarymuseum.gov/library/document/nscmin/750129.pdf.

negotiators were heading toward an understanding, but the Ford administration, facing re-election in 1976 and political challenges to détente and controversies over Angola and CIA estimates of Soviet forces, was losing its freedom of action. Kissinger's position was now weaker, and opposition from Secretary of Defense Donald Rumsfeld's Pentagon made completing a worthwhile agreement impossible in 1976.[41]

The SALT II stalemate dovetailed with other emerging US–Soviet controversies generated by routine pressures to improve weapons systems. Soviet decisions to replace obsolete MRBMs with up-to-date MIRVed SS-20 mobile missiles, and thereby preserve a full range of nuclear systems to meet all military needs, triggered questions in the West about the impact of the SS-20 on the nuclear balance. Senior Defense Department and West German officials, already supporting modernization of NATO nuclear forces, and misconceiving the SS-20 as a force for blackmailing NATO, wanted to find ways to counter the new missile. Moreover, in late 1976, Secretary of Defense Rumsfeld pushed for accelerated development of the highly accurate MX ICBM, as well as a more accurate Minuteman MIRV, which could destabilize US–Soviet strategic relations because of their counterforce and preemptive potential. All of these developments foreshadowed some of the US–Soviet tensions that emerged later in the decade.[42]

The nuclear Cold War

The US–Soviet nuclear competition of the 1960s and early 1970s saw the end of US nuclear superiority and the emergence of the strategic parity that would characterize the remainder of the Cold War. Driven by fear, credibility concerns, and organizational interests, both sides made massive investments in weapons systems whose use would have horrible consequences. Preemption came to be understood by both sides as highly dangerous and highly difficult technically. Indeed, US defense officials, and possibly their Soviet counterparts, were not sure how tactical nuclear weapons could be used without inviting catastrophe. As the nuclear danger increased and as

---

41 Garthoff, Détente and Confrontation, 502, 517, 596–601; Anne Hessing Cahn, Killing Détente: The Right Attacks the CIA (University Park, PA: Pennsylvania State University Press, 1998); Podvig (ed.), Russian Strategic Nuclear Forces, 13–14, 390–94; Zaloga, Kremlin's Nuclear Sword, 175.

42 Garthoff, Détente and Confrontation, 872, 958–74; Christoph Bluth, Britain, Germany, and Western Nuclear Strategy (Oxford: Clarendon Press, 1995), 114–21; John Edwards, Superweapon: The Making of MX (New York: W. W. Norton, 1982), 95–121.

taboos against the use of nuclear weapons strengthened, US and Soviet leaders sought to avoid high-stakes nuclear "poker games." They moved toward military strategies that postponed nuclear weapons use (flexible response), but also engaged in strategic arms control.

Even while détente and SALT were unfolding during the early 1970s, Cold War concerns continued to shape strategic policy. Both sides prepared for the worst by developing high-tech warning systems and heading toward launch-on-warning capabilities. Also making deterrence hazardous and uncertain, both sides developed new weapons systems, cruise missiles on the one hand, and MIRVed missiles on the other, that raised apprehensions about vulnerabilities to attack. By the mid-1970s, the prospects for an end to the Cold War were hard to imagine as arms control faltered and arms builders on both sides continued to develop and deploy new strategic weapons. US and Soviet leaders knew that it was insane to use nuclear weapons, but they wanted to keep them because of their fears and pursuit of national advantage.

6

US foreign policy from Kennedy to Johnson

FRANK COSTIGLIOLA

Like their predecessor Dwight D. Eisenhower, Presidents John F. Kennedy and Lyndon B. Johnson adhered to the major tenets of post-World War II US foreign policy. They saw the Cold War as a long-term struggle played out in military, ideological, political, economic, scientific, and cultural arenas. All three leaders sought to contain the Soviet Union while advancing US influence around the globe. They agreed that radical revolution threatened US interests, and that such upheavals were instigated by the Soviets, "Red China," or Fidel Castro's Cuba. All three presidents believed that Western-style modernization – and particularly American values and institutions – offered the best model for developing nations. They also concurred on the strategy of tightening links with European allies in order to win the Cold War, head off potential problems with Germany, and compensate for the relative decline in US economic predominance. Kennedy (JFK) and Johnson (LBJ) differed from Eisenhower, however, in embracing an exuberant activism that "Ike" distrusted. In their respective presidencies, Kennedy and Johnson saw greater opportunities and threats than Eisenhower perceived in his time.[1] While Kennedy and Johnson differed in background, style, and the relative emphasis each placed on domestic or foreign initiatives, they shared similar ideological assumptions and policy goals. Both had competitive personalities.

Kennedy and Johnson regarded the Cold War as the defining paradigm for international relations in their time. They interpreted almost all events and trends in terms of this struggle. On the one hand, this view was nearly inevitable. These men faced the unrelenting reality of East–West propaganda barrages, nuclear and conventional arms rivalries, a space race, troops glaring across the tense borders dividing Germany and Korea, tension over Berlin, civil wars in Vietnam and Laos, revolution in Cuba, and competition for new African states and non-aligned nations in Asia and Latin America. Kennedy and

---

1 See Robert J. McMahon's chapter in volume I.

Johnson worried that Soviet premier Nikita S. Khrushchev, egged on by a militantly anti-American "Red China," might indeed try to "bury" the United States, if not militarily, at least economically. Indeed, the Cold War intensified in 1961–62 as the Berlin and Cuban missile crises brought the superpowers to the brink of nuclear war.

On the other hand, the Cold War, like other paradigms, entailed some distortion of perceptions. Long-term changes that probably would have occurred in the absence of the East–West struggle were interpreted by Kennedy and Johnson as Cold War phenomena. With historical hindsight, decolonization appears as the nearly inevitable redress of power by Africans and Asians temporarily overwhelmed by Europeans in the nineteenth century. From the perspective of Kennedy and Johnson, however, the breakup of colonial empires upset the established order they had known since youth. They regarded the new nations as malleable objects of Cold War competition that might be won for the West or lost to the East. Another secular trend largely independent of the Cold War was China's recovery of great power status after its century of neocolonialism and civil war. JFK and LBJ, however, interpreted this development as a Cold War disaster. In a telling Cold War discourse, a senior adviser recalled that Kennedy "always regarded the Chicom nuclear explosion as likely to be historically the most significant and worst event of the 1960s."[2]

Kennedy, Johnson, and most of their advisers overestimated both the threats and promises facing them. The excitement greeting the dawn of the 1960s was overblown. Caution ended up prevailing in the Berlin crisis and the Cuban missile crisis. New nations in Africa and turbulent ones in Latin America resisted both Communist-exported revolution and US-inspired modernization. Structural problems, such as the US balance-of-payments deficit and the disparity between the US and European wings of the North Atlantic Treaty Organization (NATO), persisted despite efforts to fix them. Although the worst dangers of the Cold War did not materialize, neither did the promise of détente for Kennedy in 1963 or for Johnson in 1966–68. Historical memory, ideology, and personality encouraged Kennedy and Johnson to overrate the potential of the new decade.

Most of them born in the 1910s, the men in the Kennedy and Johnson administrations reflected their generation's memories of the 1930s–40s, when aggressive nations marched into one country after another. Imprinted with what they regarded as the lesson of Munich, this generation concluded that

---

2 James Fetzer, "Clinging to Containment: China Policy," in Thomas G. Paterson (ed.), *Kennedy's Quest for Victory* (New York: Oxford University Press, 1989), 182.

"totalitarian" states, including the Soviet Union and the People's Republic of China, were expansionist and ideological. As a consequence, the democracies had to remain armed, vigilant, and opposed to "appeasement." Kennedy and Johnson feared "Red China" as particularly dangerous because it seemed to be in a highly ideological, "Stalinist" phase. Notions about historical development had another consequence. Kennedy and Johnson shared the prevailing belief that the decade of the 1960s portended extraordinary change. Pundits tried to decide on a unifying "national purpose." A blue ribbon panel that featured a number of Kennedy's and Johnson's appointees, including Secretary of State Dean Rusk, published *Prospect for America* (1958), which predicted a decade of challenge. Presidential adviser Arthur M. Schlesinger, Jr. recalled that at Kennedy's inauguration, "we thought ... the world was plastic and the future unlimited."[3]

Such assumptions stemmed in part from rarely questioned ideological beliefs. Kennedy and Johnson assumed that their nation had the power and the obligation to lead others toward adopting American-style institutions and values, particularly elections, gradual reform, and free markets. This doctrine, flattering to American sensibilities, incorporated elements of John Winthrop's 1630 dream of a model "city upon a hill"; mid-nineteenth-century faith in manifest destiny; and twentieth-century confidence in US superiority in production, technology, and societal institutions. Woodrow Wilson synthesized these notions into an ideology of mission to the rest of the world. Wilson believed that the United States – close to God and superior in its economic, political, and cultural institutions – not only offered a model, but also had the obligation to help other nations become like itself. Wilson and his successors believed that adopting US-style institutions would enable other nations to become more prosperous, modern, stable, and friendly. In turn, the more other nations modeled themselves on the United States, the greater would become US security and the opportunity for Americans to do business and feel comfortable overseas. Radical change, such as in the Russian Revolution of Wilson's time and the Cuban and Vietnamese revolutions during the Kennedy–Johnson era, appeared as the arch enemy to these ideas and to American opportunity.

Kennedy

This ideology informed Kennedy's inaugural address. The new president argued that American freedom packed such transforming power that the

3 Thomas G. Paterson, "Introduction: Kennedy and Global Crisis," in Paterson (ed.), *Kennedy's Quest for Victory*, 15.

6. President Kennedy's oratory moved a nation, here delivering his inauguration speech, January 20, 1961.

1776 revolution remained the touchstone for all peoples. He asserted that "the same revolutionary beliefs for which our forebears fought are still at issue around the globe."[4] In January 1962, he declared that "people everywhere ... look to us," especially to "the splendor of our ideals." Affirming manifest destiny, he said: "our Nation is commissioned by history to be either an observer of freedom's failure or the cause of its success."[5] The phrase "commissioned by history" indicated, with the difficult-to-contest logic of the passive voice, that history itself had ordained the US mission. According to this logic, the United States could either stand idly by as freedom failed, or "cause" it to succeed around the world.

Kennedy's personality also inclined him to tackle challenges. In JFK's boyhood, ambition, contact sports, risk-taking, performance, and, above all, winning were mandated by his father, Joseph P. Kennedy. After his eldest brother died on a bombing mission, JFK inherited the mandate to fulfill the family's presidential destiny. In 1946, JFK's appeal as a war hero helped him win election to Congress. In 1952, he ascended to the Senate. As his brother

4 Theodore C. Sorensen, *Kennedy* (New York: Harper and Row, 1965), 242–48.
5 Fred L. Israel (ed.), *The State of the Union Messages of the Presidents 1790–1966* (New York: Chelsea House, 1966), 3132.

Robert F. Kennedy recalled, JFK spent half his days on earth in pain. He suffered back spasms, Addison's disease, and gastrointestinal problems. Kennedy responded by trying to demonstrate manliness and courage. His philandering was extraordinary for the sheer number of women he slept with and the risks he took in choosing such partners as the Mafia moll Judith Campbell Exner. After Kennedy proved his calm toughness to Khrushchev and to the world in the Cuban missile crisis, he seems to have settled into a more relaxed, confident appraisal of risk and dangers.

Before October 1962, however, Kennedy exaggerated crisis. In his inaugural address, he dramatically declared: "In the long history of the world only a few generations have been granted the role of defending freedom in its hour of maximum danger."[6] By characterizing January 1961 as an historic "hour of maximum danger," the new president was invoking memories of his generation's formative experience. In 1941–42, the Germans and Japanese threatened to link up and isolate the rest of the world. But that was not the danger the United States faced in 1961, regardless of how enthusiastically the Soviets and Chinese might support "wars of liberation." Ten days after he took office, Kennedy warned that in the next four years, "we shall have to test anew whether a nation organized and governed such as ours can endure. The outcome is by no means certain."[7] This was astounding hyperbole. As Kennedy noted, he was speaking on Franklin D. Roosevelt's birthday. Kennedy might have considered that even after the devastation of Pearl Harbor, Roosevelt had voiced nothing but confidence in the nation's institutions.

Kennedy probably expected that a sense of emergency would spur Congress, the bureaucracy, and the allies to accept his proposals. He secured a 15 percent increase in military spending. The Kennedyites' confidence that they could achieve the extraordinary was reflected in how they labeled their programs: the "New Frontier" at home, the "Grand Design" for Europe, the "Alliance for Progress" for Latin America, and the "New Africa" policy. Equally ambitious was the "Peace Corps," which would mobilize American youth to win hearts and minds in the Third World. If revolutionary guerrillas threatened, Kennedy would counter with the "Green Berets," special forces trained in guerrilla tactics. To deter aggression while heading off a nuclear holocaust, Secretary of Defense Robert McNamara developed the concept of careful escalation of force through "flexible response." Despite their differences, these programs were alike in promising so much that they were bound

6 Sorensen, *Kennedy*, 242–48.
7 Israel (ed.), *State of the Union Messages*, 3122.

to disappoint. Neither other nations nor structural problems proved as malleable as Kennedy and his advisers hoped.

As Kennedy took office, a National Intelligence Estimate (NIE) predicted that though the Soviets and the Chinese would promote revolution, they would not risk "recklessness." Another NIE opined that "stresses and strains" would "weaken the Communist world posture and diminish the effectiveness of world Communism outside the bloc."[8] After the aborted May 1960 summit froze relations with Eisenhower, Khrushchev anticipated the new president. "What can we do to help the new administration?" the deputy Soviet foreign minister asked Kennedy's advisers.[9] Khrushchev sought help with his problem: the hemorrhaging of people and talent from East Germany through Berlin. The open city also offered Western espionage and propaganda entry into the Soviet bloc. Khrushchev "had nightmares about it," his son recalled. "The German problem gave him no peace; instead it kept slipping out of his hands."[10] The Kremlin leader also acted on his Marxist–Leninist ideology, out of sincere belief and to stave off competition from Mao Zedong. On January 6, 1961, Khrushchev lauded "wars of liberation." The US ambassador in Moscow pointed out that the speech also reaffirmed peaceful coexistence and declared that wars of liberation must not become wars between states.[11] Kennedy, however, feared that Khrushchev's tactics could slice away pieces of the Third World. He determined not to lose but rather to win the Cold War.

Although Kennedy and his advisers worried about the Third World, they also understood that wealth and political influence remained concentrated in the northern half of the globe. Indeed, advisers regarded links with Europe as key to winning the Third World and the Cold War. Rusk laid out this thinking.

> Western Europe if it were really unified, and the North American Community, if we really developed the relationships that all of us have been discussing ... would be a nexus of special relationships reaching right around the world, with our relations with Latin America, and with the countries in the Pacific, the British with the Commonwealth, and the French with the French-speaking countries. Germany [too] is establishing some interesting relationships with selected countries.

As Rusk saw it, the United States would be the hub, with direct and indirect spokes of influence radiating to most of the world. Such organization would

---

8 National Intelligence Estimates (NIE), December 1, 1960, and January 17, 1961, US Department of State, *Foreign Relations of the United States, 1961–1963* (Washington, DC: US Government Printing Office, 1998), vol. V, 2, 17–18.
9 William Taubman, *Khrushchev: The Man and His Era* (New York: Norton, 2003), 486.
10 *Ibid.*, 482. 11 *Ibid.*, 487–88.

isolate the Communists and, he predicted, "would be reflected in growing caution on the part of the Soviet Union." The Communists would be reduced, as State Department adviser Walt Whitman Rostow put it, to a "relatively minor power in the world."[12]

Western Europe figured at the center of Kennedy's concerns. Like Eisenhower, Kennedy worried that the US balance-of-payments deficit, foreign distrust of the dollar, and the resulting gold outflow could weaken the nation's vitality. "What matters," Kennedy declared to an adviser, "is the strength of the currency. It is this, and not its nuclear weapons, which makes France a factor. Britain has nuclear weapons, but the pound is weak, so every one pushes it around."[13] The European Common Market and Japan were presenting tough competition. US exports could no longer pay for the nation's imports, capital investments, tourist expenditures, foreign aid, and military expenditure overseas. Kennedy told the National Security Council, "we have been very generous to Europe," but now "it is time to look out for ourselves." Cognizant of the crippling impact on Britain of its chronic payments crises, Kennedy warned that "if we cannot keep up our export surplus, we shall not have the dollar exchange with which to meet our military commitments. We must either do a good job of selling abroad or pull back."[14] Part of JFK's solution was the Trade Expansion Act, which facilitated tariff decreases to expand markets for US exporters. (This proved another exercise in overconfidence. The reduced tariffs boosted US imports more than exports.) Kennedy also advocated Britain's admission into the Common Market (the European Economic Community) to keep it looking outward and receptive to US interests. Given French President Charles de Gaulle's opposition to allowing the "Anglo-Saxons" into the Common Market, the Kennedy administration deputized West Germany to check de Gaulle. In January 1963, however, de Gaulle shocked Washington and London by vetoing British entry to the Common Market and by signing a friendship treaty with Germany's octogenarian leader, Konrad Adenauer.

An astonished Kennedy wondered "what kind of a deal [could] de Gaulle make with the Russians which would be acceptable to the Germans?"[15] The phrasing of this question highlighted key assumptions. Almost every international development was interpreted by the administration in terms of the Cold War. An underlying fear was that a diplomatic revolution could overturn the

12 Frank Costigliola, "The Pursuit of Atlantic Community: Nuclear Arms, Dollars, and Berlin," in Paterson (ed.), *Kennedy's Quest for Victory*, 29.
13 Andrew Schlesinger and Stephen Schlesinger (eds.), *Journals, 1952–2000: Arthur M. Schlesinger, Jr.* (New York: Penguin, 2007), 186.
14 Costigliola, "Pursuit of Atlantic Community," 30.   15 *Ibid.*, 50.

NATO alliance that anchored the Federal Republic of Germany (FRG) and the rest of Western Europe to the United States. The Achilles heel of the alliance was the reality that the Soviet Union, which controlled East Germany, held the key to German reunification.

Throughout the forty-five-year history of the Cold War, Germany remained the principal prize of the conflict. Neither the Americans nor the Soviets could permit the other to control all of Germany. Both superpowers and their allies felt more comfortable with a divided Germany, though no one wanted to antagonize the Germans by admitting this attitude. Washington exercised much of its influence in Europe through the FRG and through the integrated military command of NATO, to which the Germans made the largest European contribution. Though it remained impolite to say so, the 300,000 US troops in the FRG had a mission of double containment: blocking a Soviet invasion and keeping the West Germans facing west. As former Secretary of State Dean Acheson, who had helped create the FRG, reminded McNamara: "Germany is the most important country in the world to us. It is subject to be influenced by us ... as the Soviet Union, France, and Britain are not."[16] Under Secretary of State George Ball recalled that Americans counted on West Germany's burgeoning payments surplus "as a bank ... for our grandiose Third World programs."[17]

The importance of both Germanys raised the stakes of the Berlin crisis. In 1961, Khrushchev renewed his 1958 threat to sign a peace treaty with the German Democratic Republic (GDR). The treaty would turn over to the GDR regulation of access to the democratic-capitalist enclave of West Berlin. Aside from the danger that the GDR might isolate West Berlin, the treaty could douse hopes for eventual reunification. Americans worried that such disappointment could unleash unrest. Desperate East Germans might revolt, call on their western brethren for aid, and drag Washington into a nuclear confrontation with Moscow. Bitter West Germans might strike a deal with de Gaulle or the Soviets, or seek an independent nuclear capability as an avenue toward reunification. Rostow warned that "the Soviet strategy will certainly be to try to demonstrate to West German nationalists that the West could not give them unity and that they should break out and make a private deal with Moscow. It's not too hard to imagine [Minister of Defense Franz Josef] Strauss playing that game, despite his tough talk."[18] Rostow's warning of a West

16 *Ibid.*, 35.
17 George W. Ball, *The Past Has Another Pattern* (New York: Norton, 1982), 184–85.
18 Frank Costigliola, "The Failed Design: Kennedy, de Gaulle, and the Struggle for Europe," *Diplomatic History*, 8 (1984), 232–33.

German "break out" and shift in alliances demonstrated the tendency to overestimate dangers while underestimating the tenacity of the status quo.

The projected multilateral force (MLF) illustrated the mirror tendency of Americans to overestimate their ability to craft institutions. The MLF idea grew out of concern that as the FRG developed its economic and political clout, it would overthrow the restrictions that kept it a nonnuclear power. De Gaulle's development of an independent nuclear force seemed to set a dangerous example. Joined by other nations, the Soviet Union adamantly opposed a West German nuclear force. After all, many Germans wanted to reunify their nation. Moreover, the FRG, pending a peace treaty, refused to accept as final Germany's postwar losses of territory. Americans hoped that the MLF could square the circle. Conceived in the Eisenhower years, the MLF was planned as a fleet of surface ships, manned by a mix of NATO nationalities (including Germans) and armed with nuclear missiles. The missiles could not be launched without Washington's approval. The MLF would give the Germans a finger near, though not on, the nuclear button. Kennedy appreciated the MLF as a device to "increase our influence in Europe and provide a way to guide NATO."[19] Although quickly dubbed the Multilateral Farce, the scheme was embraced by Kennedy, who swallowed his skepticism. The fact that the unwieldy proposal survived into the Johnson years testified to the persistence of US efforts, as a top aide put it, to "contain and provide a creative outlet for a West Germany which might be tempted to seek reunification with East Germany through bilateral arrangements with Moscow."[20]

Kennedy believed that the United States could not hope to win in far-off Berlin and Vietnam unless it secured what he saw as the nation's backyard, Latin America. JFK probably paid more attention to Latin America than did any other president of the Cold War era. He toured southern neighbors, met with leaders, and devoured economic and political reports. Despite his familiarity with the region, however, Kennedy overrated the threats and possibilities.

He called Latin America "the most dangerous area in the world."[21] In retrospect, this designation appears odd because the Soviets had only a minimal presence in Latin America, aside from Cuba. Again, apart from Cuba, there was little possibility of a US or Soviet provocation or miscalculation escalating into a major war, as could happen along the nuclear-armed

---

19 Costigliola, "Pursuit of Atlantic Community," 51.   20 *Ibid.*, 39.
21 Stephen G. Rabe, *The Most Dangerous Area in the World* (Chapel Hill, NC: University of North Carolina Press, 1999), 7.

border between the two Germanys. Kennedy feared that Castro's charismatic appeal could spread revolution to the dispossessed of the region. Eliminating the Cuban revolutionary grew into an obsession. McNamara remembered that "we were hysterical about Castro at the time of the Bay of Pigs and thereafter."[22] Castro survived this April 1961 US-sponsored invasion and the Central Intelligence Agency's (CIA) Operation Mongoose designed to assassinate him and sabotage the Cuban economy. Trying to eliminate Castro helped set in motion a chain of events leading to the worst confrontation of the Cold War. Concern about another US invasion induced the Cuban dictator to welcome the installation of Soviet nuclear-tipped missiles as a deterrent. That led to the US–Soviet missile crisis of October 1962.[23] Although Castro's revolution sparked a nuclear confrontation, the Cuban model ended up being difficult to export. A year after Kennedy's death, Castro concluded that Latin America presented poor prospects for revolution. The Soviets remained unwilling to commit resources to the region. Latin American Communists resented the Cubans' know-it-all attitude. In November 1964, Castro shifted his revolutionary efforts to Africa.[24]

Kennedy exaggerated the promise as well as the danger in Latin America. He probably agreed with Schlesinger, who described "the atmosphere" of the region as "set for miracles."[25] In a speech broadcast throughout the hemisphere on March 13, 1961, Kennedy announced a signature initiative, the Alliance for Progress. He called for sweeping changes to promote economic growth, redistribution of wealth, education, and democracy. His administration pledged $20 billion in public and private US capital, to which Latin Americans were to add $80 billion. The Kennedyites expected that this investment would double real growth rates and foster more equitable, democratic, and stable societies. The hope was that the Alliance could immunize Latin America against Castro-type revolutions. Although such revolutions failed to materialize, it was not because the Alliance reinvigorated economies. Despite the growth in US aid, private capital inflows and internal investment remained disappointing. US modernization theories proved ill adapted to Latin American realities. Elites and middle-class groups clung to their privileges. Economic growth stagnated, and wealth remained concentrated. Despite their

---

22 Thomas G. Paterson, "Fixation with Cuba: The Bay of Pigs, Missile Crisis, and Covert War against Castro," in Paterson (ed.), *Kennedy's Quest for Victory*, 123.
23 See James G. Hershberg's chapter in this volume.
24 See Piero Gleijeses's chapter in this volume.
25 Thomas G. Paterson, "Kennedy's Quest for Victory and Global Crisis," in Paterson (ed.), *Kennedy's Quest for Victory*, 15.

soaring rhetoric about democracy, the Kennedyites chose anti-Communist stability rather than risk radical change. US Army Special Forces trained policemen and soldiers in techniques for suppressing popular discontent. Washington accepted military coups in Peru and elsewhere and destabilized democratic, leftist governments in Argentina, Brazil, British Guiana, and Guatemala. The Kennedy administration may have launched more covert operations in Latin America than any other Cold War president. Before his death, Kennedy realized that the Alliance for Progress was sputtering. He remained uncertain how to respond.

Kennedy also perceived serious challenges in Africa and South Asia. The rush to independence by scores of African nations – seventeen in 1960 alone – excited imaginations. Kennedy saw supposedly malleable societies that could drift toward capitalist or Communist models of development. Africa appeared a battleground. "We cannot simply sit by and watch on the sidelines," JFK declared. "There are no sidelines."[26] Although Kennedy realized that these nations preferred non-alignment, he remained anxious that neutrality not slide toward hostility. Moreover, his competitive nature impelled him to jockey for advantage. Discussing with Rusk which countries were willing to accept Peace Corps volunteers, Kennedy said, "If we can successfully crack Ghana and Guinea, Mali may turn to the West. If so, these would be the first Communist-oriented countries to turn from Moscow to us."[27] Also concerned with populous, non-aligned nations such as India, Kennedy told his advisers, "We cannot permit all those who call themselves neutrals to join the Communist bloc." If "we lose them, the balance of power could swing against us."[28] The Kennedyites believed their support of India in its 1962 border skirmish with China provided the opportunity to win an ally. But aid to India alienated rival Pakistan. And India was not about to abandon its neutrality in the Cold War. African nations also proved resistant to blandishments. Neither Western nor Eastern models of development met the needs of extractive economies suffering a dearth of infrastructure and trained personnel. Moreover, most Africans remained loath to trade colonialism for some new tutelage. Kennedy also met frustration with the problems of Portuguese rule in Angola and Mozambique, chaos in the Congo, and apartheid in South Africa. Although the United States voted against Portugal in the United Nations, most African nations still

---

26 Thomas J. Noer, "New Frontiers and Old Priorities in Africa," in Paterson (ed.), *Kennedy's Quest for Victory*, 256.
27 Paterson, "Kennedy's Quest for Victory and Global Crisis," 15.
28 Melvyn P. Leffler, *For the Soul of Mankind: The United States, the Soviet Union, and the Cold War* (New York: Hill and Wang, 2007), 177.

regarded Washington as Lisbon's ally. While the CIA helped assassinate Congo premier Patrice Lumumba, whom Americans and Belgians feared as unstable and radical, peace did not return to that resource-rich nation. And South Africa resisted Kennedy's efforts to moderate apartheid.[29]

Vietnam became the most grievous instance of Kennedy's tendency to overvalue both dangers and opportunities. JFK developed a special relationship with South Vietnam. Although Senator Kennedy in the early 1950s criticized French colonialism in Vietnam, he welcomed Washington's client government in Saigon as an independent, vital partner.[30] In 1956, Kennedy declared South Vietnam "the cornerstone of the Free World in Southeast Asia, the keystone to the arch, the finger in the dike."[31] Subscribing to Eisenhower's "domino theory," JFK argued that keeping this "finger in the dike" was crucial to preventing Communists from flooding into all of Southeast Asia, which would deprive Japan of markets and raw materials. Senator Kennedy traveled in the American Roman Catholic circles that lauded President Ngo Dinh Diem as the Christian savior of his country.

As president, Kennedy deepened commitments to South Vietnam. Meanwhile, Diem's unpopular government persecuted non-Communist opponents and botched the suppression of the pro-Communist National Liberation Front (NLF) guerrillas. After Kennedy suffered embarrassment with the Bay of Pigs invasion, a rough-and-tumble summit with Khrushchev in June 1961, and the erection of the Berlin Wall that August, he believed he simply had to "win" on some Cold War battlefield. He took seriously the reports of Vice President Johnson, who journeyed to Vietnam in May 1961, and Rostow and General Maxwell Taylor, who visited in October. Johnson exaggerated the stakes in Vietnam. He praised Diem as the "Winston Churchill of Asia" and framed the issue as a "fundamental decision" between trying "to meet the challenge of Communist expansion now in Southeast Asia" or "throw[ing] in the towel."[32] Rostow and Taylor advised sending more US military advisers. By the end of his presidency, JFK had raised their number from 600 to 16,000. Some became casualties.

The Kennedyites chose escalation because they overrated the ability of foreign military forces to achieve political aims in a culturally different society such as Vietnam. They underplayed the determination of the Vietnamese,

---

29 See Michael E. Latham's chapter in this volume.
30 See Fredrik Logevall's chapter in this volume.
31 Walter LaFeber, *America, Russia, and the Cold War, 1945–2006* (New York: McGraw-Hill, 2008), 242.
32 *Ibid.*, 226.

who had a two-thousand-year history of expelling invaders. Wilsonian ideology proved naïve in its underestimation of the resolve of non-Americans to achieve their own goals in their own way. Having raised military spending from his first months in office, Kennedy had at his disposal overwhelming forces: the troops and ships of the US Pacific Command, the Green Berets, and innovative weaponry such as helicopters. After the Soviets backed down when confronted with US superiority during the Cuban missile crisis, Kennedy drew the conclusion that escalation of force could impel the Communists in Vietnam likewise to back down. He regarded the conflict as an opportunity to demonstrate that "wars of liberation" could be defeated. The deepening war proved the most tragic element in Kennedy's legacy to Johnson.

But that legacy also included steps toward détente. The accolades that Kennedy won after his perceived victory in October 1962 seem to have eased his burning need to best the Soviets at every opportunity. The brush with nuclear war tempered him. Khrushchev's many letters awakened Kennedy to the Soviets' legitimate concerns about nuclear war, possible German revenge, and improving the lives of the Russian people. In December 1962, JFK mused to Schlesinger that "Khrushchev makes much the same set of charges against the West that the West makes against him." The president added that this "mirror effect reinforces his own detachment and his refusal to regard the world contest as a holy war."[33] Kennedy and Khrushchev opened a direct "hot line" to ensure communication should another crisis strike. They also renewed efforts to reach a nuclear test ban treaty. On June 10, 1963, at American University, Kennedy called for a relaxation of tensions and "genuine peace" with the Soviet Union. Implicitly recognizing that Khrushchev had reason to dread a remilitarized Germany, Kennedy recalled that "no nation in the history of battle ever suffered more than the Soviet Union in the course of the Second World War."[34] In August 1963, US, Soviet, and British negotiators signed the treaty to ban all but underground nuclear tests. Underground tests, which required greater technical sophistication, would add another hurdle for nations bent on developing nuclear weapons. While a step toward détente, the treaty was also aimed at the nuclear aspirations, real or feared, of China and West Germany. When Kennedy was struck down, his advisers were still divided on détente. Rostow warned that a relaxation of tensions with Moscow would legitimize Communism and induce people in the West to let down their guard. Rusk,

33 Schlesinger and Schlesinger (eds.), *Journals*, 181.
34 Leffler, *For the Soul of Mankind*, 183.

however, believed that détente with the Soviets "was bound to work in favor of the West."[35]

From Kennedy to Johnson

This split on détente highlights Kennedy's mixed legacy to Johnson. Kennedy's crises gave Johnson breathing space. As leaders, Kennedy and Khrushchev were both highly competitive while entertaining exaggerated hopes and fears. This volatile mix had brought the world close to nuclear war. Faced with apocalypse, Washington and Moscow had accepted common-sense mitigation of the under-lying problems. The Berlin Wall ended the hemorrhage of East Germans while allowing West Berliners their freedom and ties with the outside world. The Cuban crisis subsided with the missiles withdrawn and the Americans promis-ing not to invade the island unless provoked. This easing of the issues that had preoccupied Americans and the Soviets in 1958–62 enabled the Johnson admin-istration to pursue détente, especially in 1966–68. Happily, there was no serious Soviet–American confrontation during LBJ's term. Unhappily, the retreat from Armageddon enabled Johnson to focus his foreign policy on a disastrous project, the Vietnam War. Kennedy had deepened the US commitment to South Vietnam. Despite his rhetoric and activism, Kennedy did not solve but rather passed on to Johnson structural problems he had inherited from Eisenhower. The balance-of-payments deficit and gold drain continued. With Germany's division dramatized by the Berlin Wall, the FRG remained frustrated. The problem of containing West German nuclear aspirations persisted. France defied US leadership, and Britain continued its quest for a post-imperial eco-nomic and political role. The Alliance for Progress did little to ease Latin American stagnation, inequality, and frustration. Non-aligned nations in Africa and Asia remained volatile and resistant to blandishments from East and West.

In terms of personality, Kennedy and Johnson presented a mix of similar-ities and contrasts. Although Johnson's family did not approach Kennedy's family in wealth or eminence, both produced intensely competitive sons bent on redressing grievances over status. While Kennedy vaulted the barriers imposed on nouveau-riche Irish-Americans, Johnson outgrew the limitations of his central Texas upbringing. During the late 1930s, when JFK was being escorted around Europe by William C. Bullitt, George F. Kennan, and other diplomats, LBJ gained entry into Roosevelt's circle of congressmen. Roosevelt admired this intelligent, hard-working acolyte and recruited him to run

---

35 *Ibid.*, 191.

for senator after only four years in Congress. Johnson's roots among hard-scrabble farmers and his close association with Roosevelt imprinted him with a fierce commitment to domestic reform that Kennedy never matched. Differences in background also conditioned their approaches to personal diplomacy. Comfortable with a wide range of people, Kennedy could turn on the charismatic charm. In his short presidency he met with many foreign chiefs, including twenty-eight African leaders invited to the White House. In contrast, Johnson kept foreign trips and visitors to a minimum. The problem with foreigners, LBJ explained, "is that they're not like the folks you were reared with."[36]

Johnson shared Kennedy's tendency to personalize foreign-policy contests. Tragically, however, Johnson never gained the confident perspective and release that Kennedy won from his perceived victory in the Cuban missile crisis. Instead, Johnson waded deeper into the morass of Vietnam. Haunting him were fears that if one showed cowardice, enemies would breach the most private refuge. "What in the hell is Vietnam worth to me?" Johnson asked in 1964. Then he answered himself: "Of course, if you start running from the Communists, they may chase you right into your own kitchen."[37] He had learned early in life that if you ran from a bully, "he is going to wind up chasing you right out of your own house."[38] Explaining to Martin Luther King, Jr., his February 1965 decision to bomb North Vietnam, Johnson alluded to unspecified demons invading not just his home but also his inner self. He said he preferred not to escalate the war. "But they kept coming. They just kept coming and I couldn't stand it any longer."[39] George Reedy, a close associate, recalled of Johnson, "whatever may be said about him, he was a tormented man. I don't know what tormented him."[40] The president was certainly cognizant of the supposed strategic rationale for fighting in Vietnam. Nevertheless, he couched the consequences of pulling out in personal terms: "They'd impeach a president that would run."[41] He feared that the American people will "forgive you for anything except being weak."[42]

Johnson coupled his personal and political determination to stave off foreign-policy threats with faith in the righteousness of America's mission to remake the world. As he put it: "Woodrow Wilson once said: 'I hope we shall

---

36 LaFeber, *America, Russia*, 265.   37 Leffler, *For the Soul of Mankind*, 213.

38 James Fetzer, "Clinging to Containment: China Policy," in Paterson (ed.), *Kennedy's Quest for Victory*, 182.

39 Leffler, *For the Soul of Mankind*, 220.

40 Randall B. Woods, *LBJ: Architect of American Ambition* (New York: Free Press, 2006), 646.

41 Leffler, *For the Soul of Mankind*, 224.   42 *Ibid.*, 211.

7. The war in Vietnam became President Johnson's worst nightmare; here the president is reacting to news about the war from Secretary of Defense Robert McNamara in December 1964.

never forget that we created this nation, not to serve ourselves, but to serve mankind.'"[43] In early 1965, Johnson invoked Wilsonian ideology to justify his plans for two simultaneous initiatives, an expanded war overseas and a Great Society reform program at home. He believed that domestic and foreign affairs remained inseparable: "The state of the Union depends, in large measure, upon the state of the world."[44] When protesters later criticized the war, Johnson countered that the United States risked "decay and even disaster" if it looked "only through a narrow glass." Johnson believed that America could fulfill the promise of economic opportunity and civil rights at home only if it was expanding those promises abroad. He warned that a United States "living in a hostile or despairing world would be neither safe nor free to build a civilization to liberate the spirit of man."[45]

The outline for détente with Moscow that Johnson inherited was only partly fleshed out during his presidency. Two weeks after taking office, Johnson both began and ended a meeting by reiterating a first principle: "A nuclear war will be the death of all of our hopes and it is our task to see that it does not happen."[46] Johnson and his advisers did not, however, believe that nuclear war

43 LaFeber, *America, Russia*, 247.
44 Israel (ed.), *Messages of the Presidents*, 3162.   45 Ibid., 3176.
46 Warren I. Cohen, "Introduction," in Warren I. Cohen and Nancy Bernkopf Tucker (eds.), *Lyndon Johnson Confronts the World* (New York: Cambridge University Press, 1994), 2.

threatened. This confidence enabled them to put other priorities ahead of improved relations with Moscow. Johnson wanted to ensure his victory in the November 1964 election as someone "tough" on Communism. He also sought to defeat the NLF and North Vietnam. Although cognizant of the Soviets' worries about a remilitarized West Germany, he preferred to co-opt rather than frustrate that vibrant nation. Johnson remained suspicious of the Soviets and even more so of the Chinese. Khrushchev and his successors, more eager for a breakthrough, reached out to the new president. The Kremlin chiefs sent detailed letters after Johnson became president and again after his election victory. Johnson responded less effusively. He did not meet with the Soviet ambassador until four months after he became president and he delayed two months before replying to the Kremlin's post-election proposals. Sidetracking the Soviets' suggestion for solidifying the division of Germany, which would infuriate the FRG, Johnson knitted what Rusk called "the little threads that bind."[47] These were noncontroversial, bilateral agreements that fostered trust, such as an accord on rescuing astronauts.

Johnson and his advisers dealt with Cold War adversaries along three tracks. They sought to isolate "Red China," minimize disputes with Moscow, and quash Hanoi's will to fight. The contradictions in this policy became apparent in February 1965, when Johnson chose to bomb North Vietnam even though Premier Aleksei Kosygin (who had helped overthrow Khrushchev in October 1964) was just then visiting Hanoi. LBJ explained that he "wanted to impress Kosygin and a number of others in the world."[48] While Johnson may have "impressed" Kosygin with US military power, he failed to win Soviet aid in pressing North Vietnam and the NLF to give up their fight. Though unwilling to pay a high price for détente with the Soviets, Johnson hoped to move in that direction. In his January 1967 state of the union message, he declared: "Our objective is not to continue the cold war but to end it." Eschewing the verbal barrage that extended back to the Truman Doctrine speech, LBJ pledged to avoid "both the acts and the rhetoric of the cold war."[49] He called for "bridge-building" to Poland, Romania, and other Soviet satellites eager to trade and establish cultural ties with the West.

The shifting nuclear balance propelled Johnson toward détente. Kennedy had deployed preponderant military power to persuade the Soviets to back

47 Ibid., 4.   48 Leffler, For the Soul of Mankind, 219.
49 Lyndon B. Johnson, "Annual Message to the Congress on the State of the Union," www.presidency.ucsb.edu/ws/index.php?pid=28338.

down in the missile crisis. Yet this superiority proved fleeting. Afterward, a Moscow official warned an American, "you'll never be able to do that to us again."[50] In the ensuing decade, the Soviets, despite a slowing economy, secured nuclear parity and built a blue-water navy. Johnson sought agreement with Moscow to head off a race in anti-ballistic missiles, which could destabilize the deterrence of "mutual assured destruction." After his June 1967 summit with Kosygin in Glassboro, New Jersey, Johnson boasted of their agreements. The accords regulated consular affairs and commercial air travel and banned weapons in outer space. Always competitive, Johnson contrasted this comity with Kennedy's calamities: "We have made some progress since Vienna, the Berlin Wall, and the Cuban missile crisis."[51] In August 1968, however, Soviet tanks crushed prospects for an anti-ballistic missile accord when they rolled into Czechoslovakia to put down the reformist "Prague Spring."[52] After a few months, Johnson resumed negotiations in hope of achieving a missile agreement before he had to relinquish the presidency. In this instance, too, Johnson overestimated his opportunity.

Johnson could move toward détente in part because the German issue was stabilizing. "I know my Germans," Johnson liked to say, having grown up with a German grandmother near German settlements in the Texas hill country. He determined to keep the Germans in Europe "by my side where I can count on them and where I can watch them." He acknowledged that his "overwhelming interest was to make sure that the Germans did not get us into World War III."[53] Since the late 1940s, Americans and their European allies had kept the West Germans contained and busy by integrating them into supranational economic and military structures, such as the European Coal and Steel Community, the Common Market, and NATO. Americans valued the MLF scheme, despite its farcical aspects, because it promised to apply the supranational formula to the hypersensitive issue of a possible German nuclear bomb. In an elaborate dance from 1963–66, the Americans and the allies tiptoed around the fact that the MLF remained, despite the camouflage, a ruse. The scheme was not substantive enough to give West Germany a real voice in the decision to use nuclear weapons. Yet it contained enough substance to scare the Russians. The French, who had their own bomb,

---

50 LaFeber, *America, Russia*, 268.
51 *Public Papers of the Presidents of the United States: Lyndon B. Johnson 1968–69* (Washington, DC: US Government Printing Office, 1970), vol. I, 27.
52 See Anthony Kemp-Welch's chapter in this volume.
53 Frank Costigliola, "Lyndon B. Johnson, Germany, and the 'End of the Cold War,'" in Cohen and Tucker (eds.), *Johnson Confronts the World*, 173–74.

vehemently opposed the plan since it threatened their superior status. Finally, Johnson's advisers and their FRG counterparts opted for a "non-hardware" solution. McNamara's Defense Department agreed to admit German and other NATO defense officials into the technical process of nuclear war-planning.

Meanwhile, the mood in the FRG was changing. The Berlin Wall underscored that reunification was unlikely to be achieved through ritual pledges made by Americans and others to placate their German allies. Foreign Minister and later Chancellor Willy Brandt began reaching out to the East Germans, Soviets, Poles, and others with a policy that became known as *Ostpolitik*. As part of these policies, the FRG accepted the 1968 Nuclear Non-Proliferation Treaty negotiated by the Americans and Soviets.

The Vietnam War and its impact on US global standing

Two days after becoming president, Johnson, who had disapproved of the overthrow of Diem, nonetheless affirmed determination "to win the war."[54] Although Johnson positioned himself in the 1964 election as a moderate against the Republican candidate, Barry Goldwater, he also encouraged planning for escalation afterward. Johnson refused to become the first president to lose a war. He dreaded abandoning the South Vietnamese to what he saw as ruthless Communism. In the summer of 1964, the US Navy assisted South Vietnamese raids on North Vietnam. During the night of August 2, North Vietnamese torpedo boats in the Tonkin Gulf fired at the *U.S.S. Maddox*. Two nights later, jittery crews reported another attack. The next morning there was no evidence of a second assault. No matter. Johnson was looking for an opportunity to hit both the North Vietnamese and Goldwater, who was accusing the administration of timidity. Johnson ordered an airstrike on North Vietnam. He sent to Congress a resolution, prepared months before, authorizing broad military actions. Passed by the Senate with only two dissenting votes, the Gulf of Tonkin Resolution became Johnson's legal basis for escalating the war. In February 1965, LBJ responded to an attack on a US airbase with "Rolling Thunder," a sustained bombing campaign against North Vietnam.

In July 1965, Johnson multiplied the number of US troops in South Vietnam. As he later told Senator Eugene McCarthy, "I know we oughtn't be there, but

---

54 Leffler, *For the Soul of Mankind*, 210.

I can't get out. I just can't be the architect of surrender."[55] To avoid surrender, Johnson kept increasing US troops in Vietnam until they reached a half-million in early 1968. Despite White House predictions that victory was near, the North Vietnamese and NLF in February 1968 launched the devastating Tet offensive. Enemy troops surged through most South Vietnamese cities, nearly breaking into the US embassy in Saigon. As US public opinion turned against the war, LBJ convened a bipartisan group of Cold War veterans. The "Wise Men" warned that the war was tearing apart society at home and failing in Vietnam. Johnson called for a limited bombing halt to jumpstart negotiations. He also launched what would become Richard Nixon's policy of replacing US troops with South Vietnamese forces. On March 31, 1968, Johnson announced he would not run for re-election.

Johnson's hope for an historic legacy of beneficial reforms at home and abroad was only one of the dreams soured by the Vietnam War. The conflict undermined US prestige and reduced the funds available for foreign aid. In Latin America, the Alliance for Progress shifted priorities from development and equality to foreign investment. Kennedy's lip service to democracy was replaced by a blatant support for supposedly stable, military-run governments. In Africa, US tacit acceptance or support of Portuguese colonialism, the all-white government in Southern Rhodesia, and a Congolese dictatorship supported by white mercenaries alienated most leaders. Johnson lacked Kennedy's personal interest in Africa and Latin America. Moreover, he grew so preoccupied with Vietnam that he neglected other issues. Protests aggravated Johnson's defensiveness. During an interview with *New York Times* columnist Cyrus R. Sulzberger, Johnson kept thumbing through a folder of papers while asserting, "I'm spending most of my time on Europe these days." The president insisted his administration had a global agenda, "despite Vietnam, despite what 'intellectuals' and the *New York Times* and those people in Georgetown say." But when he tried to talk with reporters about these other matters, "all they did was to keep whining Veetnam, Veetnam, Veetnam," protested the president, himself imitating a whining baby. Sulzberger recorded that after this performance, Johnson "suddenly … opened the folder of papers he had been browsing over – and started to read a cable sent him by [Ambassador Henry Cabot] Lodge in Saigon."[56]

The Vietnam War had other consequences. In much of the world, repugnance for the war fostered broader skepticism and eroded US power – as

---

55 Lyndon B. Johnson telephone conversation with Eugene McCarthy, February 1, 1966, Lyndon Baines Johnson Presidential Recordings Project, Miller Center, University of Virginia, Charlottesville, Virginia.
56 Costigliola, "Johnson, Germany," 176.

illustrated by the worsening gold drain. In Western Europe, increasing numbers of people grew horrified as television brought home images of heavily armed Americans and napalm-dropping jets terrorizing Vietnamese villagers. De Gaulle cited the war as further reason for European independence from both superpowers. In 1966, he pulled France out of the integrated NATO military command. This veteran of the pre-Cold War era looked toward a post-Cold War reunification of "Europe from the Atlantic to the Urals."[57] Spending on the war prompted a March 1968 panic in the international gold market. The dumping of dollars for gold forced the Johnson administration to close the gold window of the US Treasury to all holders of dollars except other governments, which could be pressured to hold onto their greenbacks. Meanwhile, Japan boomed with orders to supply both the United States and North Vietnam. One of the many ironies of the war entailed China. Although the containment of China was cited as justifying the war, China itself retreated into self-imposed isolation with its cultural revolution.

Kennedy, Johnson, and US foreign policy

Despite their contrasts in background, style, and personality, Kennedy and Johnson differed little in many aspects of foreign policy. Kennedy paid more attention to Latin America and to Africa, which, however, yielded only limited gains. Johnson never acquired Kennedy's ease in dealing with foreign leaders and problems. Nor did LBJ acquire JFK's comfort in his own skin. Although attracted to détente, both Kennedy and Johnson found difficulty in escaping the premises of Cold War policies codified in the Eisenhower and Truman eras. The confines of Wilsonian ideology narrowed what JFK and LBJ regarded as acceptable change around the world. They remained committed to the belief that the United States was an exceptional nation whose values and institutions offered the best model for others. The Vietnam War helped frustrate Johnson's striving toward détente. If Kennedy had lived, he probably would have encountered Johnson's difficulty of fighting in Vietnam to contain Communism while trying simultaneously to engage the Soviet Union.

Neither the prospects nor the problems Kennedy and Johnson perceived evolved as they had expected. The Alliance for Progress did not yield the economic growth or political stability that Americans had hoped would innoculate Latin America against more Castros. In spite of these setbacks, Castro failed to export his revolution. The NLF and North Vietnam refused to

---

57 See Frédéric Bozo's chapter in this volume.

surrender despite the terrible pounding meted out in years of war. Nevertheless, the eventual US defeat in Vietnam did not pull down a long chain of dominos, as Kennedy and Johnson had feared. Notwithstanding Germans' frustration at continued division, de Gaulle's arguments for an independent Europe, and Bonn's overtures to the East in the late 1960s, the FRG remained allied to the United States. As the labels "New Frontier" and "Great Society" suggest, the domestic and foreign policies of Kennedy and Johnson – like the decade of the 1960s – stand out in history for grand promises unfulfilled.

7

Soviet foreign policy, 1962–1975

SVETLANA SAVRANSKAYA AND WILLIAM TAUBMAN

The span of Soviet foreign policy that is the subject of this chapter covers two distinct periods, 1962 to 1964, and 1964 to 1975. The first period consists of Nikita Khrushchev's last three years in power; the second covers the first eleven of Leonid Brezhnev's. Because of the centralized nature of the Soviet system, with so much power concentrated in the Communist Party Politburo, and especially in the hands of the top party boss, Khrushchev and Brezhnev had immense influence over Soviet policy. But the two men were very different leaders with contrasting approaches to governing: by 1962 the impulsive, explosive Khrushchev hardly listened to his Kremlin colleagues. Brezhnev, on the other hand, had to struggle to consolidate his power for the first few years, and even after that, he preferred to preside over the Politburo instead of dominating it. Moreover, the Brezhnev regime came to power determined to alter, although not entirely reverse, the foreign-policy pattern Khrushchev had followed. It is not surprising, therefore, that the two sub-periods are notable for significant differences of both substance and style. Yet, there is an overall trend that characterizes the whole period – movement from the Cold War's most dangerous episode, the 1962 Cuban missile crisis, to the high point of détente in 1975.

This trend reflects various Soviet domestic and international circumstances, which helped to convince both Khrushchev and Brezhnev that the USSR needed more than a short-term respite from the kind of Cold War over which Stalin had presided. Escalating numbers of nuclear weapons on both sides, along with the dangers they posed of a catastrophic war, placed a premium on limiting tensions, while Moscow's achievement of strategic parity with the United States, obtained under Brezhnev, gave him the confidence to negotiate arms-control agreements from a "position of strength" that Khrushchev lacked. The vulnerability of Soviet allies in Eastern Europe, dramatically visible in Poland and Hungary in 1956, and again in the Prague Spring of 1968, heightened Soviet interest in European détente. In contrast to

Khrushchev, who responded to Chinese charges of being soft on capitalism by getting tough with the United States, Brezhnev moved toward a new relationship of détente with Washington.

The détente achieved by Brezhnev and company stabilized Cold War competition in Europe while braking the arms race and expanding East–West ties. But it contained the seeds of its own eventual disintegration. The growing power and prestige of the USSR, sharply contrasting with America's retreat from Vietnam, offered new opportunities to expand Soviet power and influence in the Third World. Marxist–Leninist ideology helped to ensure that Moscow would try to exploit those new opportunities, thus seeming to confirm to many in the West that Moscow was engaged in another round of global expansionism. As a result, even as détente reached its peak, it began to unravel.

Khrushchev's last years in power

When the XXIInd Congress of the Soviet Communist Party convened on October 17, 1961, Khrushchev seemed at the height of his powers. He delivered two long reports, taking a total of ten hours, on the general state of the Union, and on the new party program. That program, prepared under his close supervision, promised that within twenty years "Communism in our country will be just about built," and that after "steadily winning victory after victory" in economic competition with the United States, the USSR would "rise to such a great height that, by comparison, the main capitalist countries will fall far below and way behind." Before the Congress closed, Brezhnev hailed Khrushchev's "indefatigable energy and revolutionary passion," while Nikolai Podgornyi, who was to join Brezhnev in a successful anti-Khrushchev conspiracy a mere year and a half later, extolled Khrushchev's "indissoluble bond with the people, humanity, simplicity, his ability to learn constantly from the masses and to teach the masses ..."[1]

Although the Congress seemed Khrushchev's hour of glory, problems were growing at home and abroad. The 1961 harvest proved disappointing, although not as bad as the year before when Khrushchev warned, "If we don't take measures, we could slide back to where we were in 1953."[2] Particularly devastating was the sharp contrast between the resulting food shortages and the new party program's promise of abundance. Relations with

1 *Pravda*, October 20, 1961, 2; October 21, 1961, 2.
2 See William Taubman, *Khrushchev: The Man and His Era* (New York: Norton, 2003), 480, 516.

China, already tense, further deteriorated when Zhou Enlai walked out of the XXIInd Party Congress. As for Soviet relations with the West, Khrushchev's Berlin ultimatum, first proclaimed in November 1958 and then renewed in the summer of 1961, had borne little if any fruit.

In the winter of 1961–62, it appeared as if Khrushchev were still intent on forcing the German issue. He sounded desperate in a November 9, 1961 secret letter to President John F. Kennedy: "You have to understand, I have no ground to retreat further, there is precipice behind me." When Kennedy's December 2 reply took no notice of Khrushchev's plight, the latter accused the United States of "megalomania," and swore, "We must conclude a German peace treaty and we will conclude it even if you do not agree."[3]

These and other Khrushchev signals on Berlin form the basis for one interpretation of why Khrushchev decided in the spring of 1962 to send missiles capable of striking the United States to Cuba. When a U-2 overflying Cuba on October 14 discovered those missiles, Kennedy himself guessed the rockets were somehow linked to Berlin, a hypothesis later developed by scholars who believe, among other things, that Khrushchev sent them there in preparation for talks he hoped to hold with Kennedy in Washington in November.[4] If such speculation seems strained, that is partly because of the vast geopolitical distance between Berlin and Cuba, but also because another explanation focused on Cuba itself seems more likely.

After Fidel Castro declared himself a Communist, Khrushchev viewed Cuba as "a beacon, a hopeful lighthouse for all the unfortunate, exploited peoples of Latin America."[5] Khrushchev feared an American invasion designed to finish the job US-supported Cuban émigrés had botched at the Bay of Pigs in April 1961. Former Soviet policymakers and Russian historians have insisted that the missiles sent to Cuba were supposed to prevent that. If so, Khrushchev clearly meant to deter the Americans, not actually to fire the missiles, an approach that reflected his longstanding attachment to diplomatic bluster backed by nuclear bluff.

---

3 *Ibid.*, 538–39.
4 Ernest R. May and Philip Zelikow (eds.), *The Kennedy Tapes: Inside the White House during the Cuban Missile Crisis* (Cambridge: Belknap Press, 1997), 175–76. See also Taubman, *Khrushchev*, 537–41. For a brief summary of various Berlin-related motives that have been attributed to Khrushchev, see Dan Munton and David A. Welch, *The Cuban Missile Crisis: A Concise History* (New York: Oxford, 2007), 22. For emphasis on Berlin-related motivations, see Graham Allison and Philip Zelikow, *Essence of Decision: Explaining the Cuban Missile Crisis* (New York: Longman, 1999), 99–109.
5 Nikita S. Khrushchev, "Memuary Nikity Sergeevicha Khrushcheva" [Memoirs of Nikita Sergeevich Khrushchev], *Voprosy istorii*, 7 (1993), 93.

8. The Cuban leader Fidel Castro was a particularly welcome guest for the Soviets; here with Leonid Brezhnev (left) and Nikita Khrushchev at Khrushchev's *dacha* in April 1963.

"Khrushchev possessed a rich imagination," his former foreign-policy assistant Oleg Troianovskii later observed, "and when some idea took hold of him, he was inclined to see in its implementation an easy solution to a particular problem, a sort of 'cure-all'" for many problems.[6] Other international challenges to which Khrushchev imagined Cuban missiles could serve as a response were the apparent strategic superiority the United States had attained by 1962, and the doubts the Chinese were spreading that Khrushchev was strong enough to stand up to the Americans. But the results of Khrushchev's Cuban gamble were disastrous.[7]

Khrushchev depicted his retreat as a triumph, with *Pravda* claiming that the Soviet government's "calm and wisdom" saved the world from a "nuclear catastrophe."[8] But as his Kremlin colleague Petr Demichev later recalled,

6 Oleg Troyanovsky, "Nikita Khrushchev and the Making of Foreign Policy," paper prepared for delivery at Khrushchev Centennial Conference, Brown University, December 1994, 39
7 For more details on the crisis, see James G. Hershberg's chapter in this volume.
8 *Pravda*, December 13, 1962, 2.

Khrushchev "made a show of having been brave, but we could tell by his behavior, especially by his irritability, that he felt it had been a defeat."[9] Castro's angry sense of betrayal when Moscow withdrew the missiles helps to explain Khrushchev's dismay. So did the initial failure of Khrushchev's attempt, which began even before the crisis ended, to parlay a Cuban settlement into broad new negotiations with the United States. His letters to Kennedy on October 27, 28, and 30 proposed talks on a nuclear test-ban treaty, liquidating military bases, and even "general and complete disarmament."[10] Impressed by Kennedy's handling of the crisis, Khrushchev was ready at last for the sort of relationship of mutual restraint that Kennedy had offered at the June 1961 Vienna summit but that he, Khrushchev, had spurned. Unfortunately for Khrushchev, Kennedy was no longer in a hurry. Only during the following summer was a treaty banning nuclear weapons testing in the air, underwater, and in outer space negotiated by the United States, USSR, and the United Kingdom concluded. Khrushchev assumed he had six more years (if the president were reelected) to build a real partnership. But several months later, Kennedy was assassinated, and before his successor, Lyndon B. Johnson, could get serious about seeking a summit, Khrushchev was ousted from power on October 14, 1964.

Other setbacks contributed to that outcome. Sino-Soviet peace talks, begun in Moscow on July 5, 1963, dissolved in mutual recriminations several weeks later, with the polemics soon culminating in clashes over the Sino-Soviet border and in violent personal attacks on both Khrushchev and Mao Zedong. When the USSR's 1963 grain harvest proved disappointing (only 107.5 million tons compared with 134.7 in 1958, and with the Virgin Lands producing their smallest crop in years, although the sown area was now 10 million hectares larger than in 1955), Khrushchev had no choice but to buy grain from the very capitalists he had once promised to "bury."

The conspiracy to remove Khrushchev was set in motion as early as March of 1964, when Brezhnev and Podgornyi began approaching other Presidium members. Over the summer and early autumn, the plotters secretly secured the support of Central Committee members so as to avoid the fate of Khrushchev's "anti-party group" rivals, who outvoted him in the Party Presidium in 1957, only to be trounced when Khrushchev succeeded in transferring the issue to the larger Central Committee for final resolution. The head of the KGB joined the plot, and the Soviet military, disenchanted with

---

9 William Taubman's interview with Petr N. Demichev, Moscow, August 1993.
10 See Taubman, *Khrushchev*, 583.

what they regarded as Khrushchev's precipitous arms cuts, his emphasis on nuclear as opposed to conventional weapons, and his reckless risk-taking in Berlin and Cuba, stood aside.

On October 13, 1964, Khrushchev returned to Moscow from a vacation on the Black Sea to face a withering indictment, which his accusers later summarized publicly as "subjectivism and drift in Communist construction, hare-brained scheming, half-baked conclusions and hasty decisions and actions divorced from reality, bragging and bluster, attraction to rule by fiat, [and] unwillingness to take into account what science and practical experience have already worked out."[11] Most of the charges concerned his sins in domestic policy, but in a report prepared for delivery at the October 14 Central Committee plenum that ratified his ouster, Politburo member Dmitrii Polianskii said the following: During the Suez crisis, "We were a hair away from a big war," yet "we didn't have a mutual assistance agreement with Egypt, and hadn't even been asked to help them." As for Berlin, "only a fool would have thought it necessary to fight a war to make Berlin a 'free city.'" And the main effect of sending missiles to Cuba "was to produce a global crisis, bring the world to the edge of war, and terrify the very organizer of this dangerous undertaking."[12]

The next day the Central Committee named Brezhnev to replace Khrushchev as Soviet party leader. Khrushchev comforted himself by saying to Anastas Mikoyan, his only remaining friend in the party leadership, "I've done the main thing. Could anyone have dreamed of telling Stalin that he didn't suit us anymore and suggesting he retire? Not even a wet spot would have remained where we had been standing. Now everything is different. The fear is gone, and we can talk as equals. That's my contribution."[13]

Khrushchev was correct. In his time in power, he had succeeded in curbing the worst of Stalinism. At home, he had ended arbitrary terror, revived agriculture, allowed a cultural thaw, and fostered renewed social optimism. Abroad, he had ended Soviet isolation, eased the Cold War, and opened new contacts with the Third World. But by 1964, he had alienated all sectors of Soviet society; even the working class itself, in whose name the party had ruled since 1917, was in near revolt – witness riots in Novocherkassk in June 1962, provoked by food price rises, increased work-norms, and terrible working conditions, which were crushed by police and army troops at the cost of twenty-six dead and nearly a hundred injured. In foreign affairs as well, despite

---

11 *Pravda*, October 17, 1964.
12 "Takovy tovarishchi, fakty" [Such, Comrades, Are the Facts], *Istochnik*, No. 2 (1988), 112–13.
13 Cited in Sergei N. Khrushchev, *Khrushchev on Khrushchev*, trans. and ed. William Taubman (Boston, MA: Little, Brown, 1990), 154.

Khrushchev's efforts to ease East–West tensions, the Soviet leader had provoked the Berlin and Cuban crises, and escalated the arms race he had set out
to slow down.

Brezhnev's rise

Leonid Brezhnev came to power as a member of the "collective leadership."
His major colleagues / rivals were Prime Minister Aleksei Kosygin, Politburo
member Mikhail Suslov, chairman of the Presidium of the Supreme Soviet,
Nikolai Podgornyi, and former KGB chairman and Politburo member
Aleksandr Shelepin, whose nickname in the Kremlin was "Iron Shurik."
Early in his tenure, some well-placed observers regarded Brezhnev as a
transitional figure. But as Anatolii Cherniaev, who worked for Brezhnev
before he became Mikhail Gorbachev's chief foreign policy assistant points
out, once Brezhnev took full command of Soviet foreign policy, he became
the driving force for détente. According to Cherniaev, Brezhnev "believed in
the possibility of 'peacemaking with imperialism.' ... He differed from his
colleagues in that, as General Secretary, he was less dependent on ideological
stereotypes ... and it was permissible for him, unlike the others, to ignore
sacred cows, when necessary."[14]

The role of ideology in shaping Brezhnev-era foreign policy should not be
underestimated. The cause of "world revolution" had long helped to legitimize Soviet rule in the USSR itself. But equally important were national
interests, including a stake in "peaceful coexistence" with capitalist states,
because to lead the world to socialism, the Soviet Union itself had to survive as
a great power. This dual nature of Soviet foreign policy persisted into the
1970s. Moreover, ideology provided a framework for interpreting and advancing national interests themselves. It portrayed the West as inevitably hostile
to the Soviet camp, but also prescribed ways of coping with the class enemy –
by playing off one capitalist country against another (especially the West
Europeans against Americans), and by collecting allies in the Third World.

In domestic politics, too, ideology loomed large. To be sure, discontent was
emerging, reflecting the frustration of many that Khrushchev's de-stalinization
campaign had not been completed. Intellectuals were attracted to the idea
that the rival social systems might yet converge, and many young people,
exposed to Western influence through music and literature, had lost faith in

14 A. S. Cherniaev, *Moia zhizn i moe vremia* [My Life and My Times] (Moscow:
Mezhdunarodnye otnosheniia, 1995), 292.

Marxism–Leninism.[15] The second half of the 1960s gave rise to the human rights movement in the Soviet Union. In 1968, a dissident journal, the *Chronicle of Current Events*, appeared in Moscow with the cover page titled "Human Rights Year in the Soviet Union," and quoting Article 19 of the *Universal Declaration of Human Rights*. In May 1968, Andrei Sakharov, the famous Soviet nuclear physicist and father of the Soviet thermonuclear bomb, wrote "Progress, Coexistence and Intellectual Freedom," in which he promoted the idea of East–West convergence based on "democratization, demilitarization, and social and technological progress."

But the Soviet political system was still guided by a class of ideological "clergy," apparatchiks who staffed ideological departments and positions at every level of the Communist Party and Soviet state, and ideology was still entrenched in the minds of the Kremlin leadership, as many memoirs of the late Soviet period, even of the most enlightened functionaries, like Anatolii Cherniaev, attest. Aleksandr Iakovlev himself, who was to become Mikhail Gorbachev's prime ally in transforming the Soviet Union, did not question the "socialist choice" that Russia made (or, rather, one should say, had had made for it by the Bolsheviks) in 1917.[16] The new dissidents, who were mostly from the intelligentsia, hardly made up a mass movement. But the potential for mass unrest, on the model of the 1962 Novocherkassk riots, alarmed the Kremlin, prompting the post-Khrushchev leadership to try to energize the economy, and especially agriculture.

Brezhnev's highest foreign-policy priority was to prevent war. He had experienced enough of it in World War II (beginning on the Southern Front in July 1941, and ending in May 1945 in Prague with the rank of major general) to resolve never to allow another one. Above all else, Brezhnev was concerned about peace and stability in Europe. For him and other Soviet leaders, the blood of Soviet soldiers sanctified the postwar European borders that they were determined to preserve. It also cemented the new socialist alliance, making it impossible for the Soviet leadership until Gorbachev to "lose" any of its East European allies.

Brezhnev wanted to be seen as a peacemaker. In addition, as former Soviet ambassador to the United States Anatolii Dobrynin notes in his memoirs, by the late 1960s, "the party establishment gradually began to realize the need to satisfy the population's basic requirements more fully and to narrow the gap

---

15 Robert English, *Russia and the Idea of the West* (New York: Columbia University Press, 2000), 100–07.

16 Aleksandr Iakovlev, *Sumerki* [Twilight] (Moscow: Materik, 2003), 32, 587.

with the West in technology and the economy itself."[17] Brezhnev was especially interested in expanding trade ties with the West but also believed that the resources spent on the arms race could be reoriented toward production of consumer goods if stability and a relaxation of tensions were achieved. However, the fear of a sudden attack brought on by "inferiority" in armaments and the Soviet military-industrial complex's sense of having to "catch up" with the West made serious pursuit of détente impossible without first achieving full strategic nuclear parity.

The result was a rapid military buildup. In comparison to the Khrushchev period, Soviet defense spending rose 40 percent between 1965 and 1970, and the US–Soviet ratio of strategic nuclear missiles fell from a seventeen to one US advantage during the Cuban missile crisis to rough parity in 1972. By 1967, the USSR was deploying about 200 intercontinental ballistic missiles (ICBMs) a year in an attempt eventually to pull ahead of the United States in this category. The United States developed multiple independently targetable re-entry vehicle (MIRV) technology and, therefore, had more warheads, but the Soviets possessed more deliverable nuclear firepower atop its bigger land-based heavy missiles.

In the early 1970s, the USSR finally achieved the goal that had eluded Khrushchev. Achieving strategic parity, in the view of Soviet leaders, established the Soviet Union as a true superpower, able to expand its power and influence globally, while actively pursuing détente with the West. Moreover, building up the Soviet military for the purpose of making the country invulnerable to any adversary was hard to argue against in the leadership, and it was acceptable to and understandable by ordinary people. Brezhnev's promotion in 1956 to candidate member of the Politburo in charge of the defense industry had strengthened his already existing ties with the Soviet military-industrial complex. Having been alienated by Khrushchev, the military was quick to give its support to Brezhnev.

Before he could pursue his domestic and foreign priorities, Brezhnev had to prevail in the Kremlin competition for power, and it took him several years to do so. He did not challenge his rivals openly but gradually undermined their political base and removed them from power while refraining almost entirely from persecuting them. With the exception of Kosygin, all his opponents were more conservative than he. According to Georgii Arbatov, at the time a Central Committee consultant, a "struggle for the soul of Leonid Brezhnev

17 Anatoly Dobrynin, *In Confidence: Moscow's Ambassador to America's Six Cold War Presidents* (New York: Times Books, 1995), 217–18.

took place in the Central Committee in 1965–1967 as the conservatives tried to co-opt him."[18]

Brezhnev came to power without any experience in international relations, a fact he readily confessed to his colleagues, especially in the early years. He quickly learned to rely on policy experts among his colleagues, like Foreign Minister Andrei Gromyko. At the start of the Brezhnev period, Prime Minister Kosygin represented the Soviet Union in meetings with foreign leaders. His June 1967 summit meeting with President Johnson in Glassboro, New Jersey, seemed to establish him (at least in Western eyes) as Brezhnev's equal, if not superior. The main issue at Glassboro was Vietnam, but the meeting did not bring the Soviet cooperation that the United States was hoping for. Kosygin's hopes for increased East–West trade proved to be stillborn when the next planned summit between the two leaders and the start of arms-control negotiations were both canceled because of the Soviet invasion of Czechoslovakia in August 1968.

As Brezhnev gradually prevailed in the Kremlin, he elevated himself over Kosygin. His consolidation of power culminated in April 1973 at a Central Committee plenum that endorsed East–West détente and reconfirmed the highly publicized Peace Program that had been adopted at the XXIVth Party Congress in April 1971. The plenum also removed from office the last members of the Shelepin group – Gennadii Voronov and Petr Shelest – and promoted Brezhnev's allies, Gromyko, Defense Minister Andrei Grechko, and KGB chairman Iurii Andropov, to full Politburo membership. After this, Brezhnev's dominance in domestic and foreign policy was never challenged again.

The Soviet invasion of Czechoslovakia

If the post-Khrushchev leadership's goals included maintaining domination over Eastern Europe, as well as firm control at home, the Prague Spring of 1968 challenged both. Brezhnev felt he had to intervene to prevent the "domino effect" in the Warsaw Pact and to nip in the bud the liberalizing influence of Czechoslovak reforms on Soviet society. Soviet intervention was also a show of strength to the West – a reaffirmation of the postwar spheres of influence in Europe. However, the decision to intervene was made only after

---

18 Georgy Arbatov, *The System: An Insider's Life in Soviet Politics* (New York: Times Books, 1992), 127.

sharp disagreements within the Soviet Politburo and agonizing indecision by Brezhnev himself.[19]

As Czechoslovakia moved toward reform, Moscow initially played the role of a concerned but supportive outsider. When Brezhnev visited Prague in December 1967, his intention was to save Antonin Novotný, the conservative first secretary, who was under heavy criticism within the Czechoslovak leadership, but in the end the Soviet leader agreed to have Novotný removed from power, and Alexander Dubček was elected first secretary.

On January 18, 1968, the Soviet ambassador to Prague, Stepan Chervonenko, characterized Dubček as an "unquestionably honest and dedicated person, a very loyal friend of the Soviet Union."[20] By March 15, however, after the gradual removal of censorship in Czechoslovakia, which coincided with student protests in Poland, KGB chairman Andropov compared the events in Prague to the upheaval in Hungary in 1956, which he experienced as the Soviet ambassador: "The situation is really very serious. The methods and forms, which are being used now in Czechoslovakia, are very reminiscent of the Hungarian ones. In this seeming chaos, ... there exists a certain order. This is how it began in Hungary."[21]

The threat to stability of the socialist bloc was an especially sensitive issue for Brezhnev because he was embarking on arms-control negotiations with the United States and envisioned a European security system linking the two blocs. Throughout the winter and spring of 1968, East European Communist leaders repeatedly expressed their concerns about Dubček's ability to maintain control. They and their Soviet counterparts were particularly alarmed by his gradual recognition of non-Communist parties in Czechoslovakia, and by the "Program of Action of the Czechoslovak People's Army," which called for a reassessment of the country's military policy and its membership in the Warsaw Pact.

Practically every Soviet Politburo session in the spring and summer of 1968 registered alarm about Czechoslovakia. Brezhnev, who maintained close contact with Dubček, and Kosygin were cautious, preferring to rely on Dubček to limit the reforms. However, Andropov, Gromyko, and Shelest were inclined toward more radical measures, hoping to find replacements for

---

19 On Soviet internal debate and institutional interests, see Jiri Valenta, *Soviet Intervention in Czechoslovakia, 1968: Anatomy of a Decision*, rev. ed. (Baltimore, MD, and London: John Hopkins University Press, 1991).

20 Rudolf Pikhoia, *Sovetskii soiuz: istoria vlasti, 1945–1991* [The Soviet Union: A History of Power, 1945–1991] (Novosibirsk: Sibirskii khronograf, 2000), 273.

21 *Ibid.*, 275.

the current reformist leaders among Central Committee members who were closer to Moscow, such as Vasil Biłak.[22] On March 21, 1968, Andropov went so far as to propose to his Politburo colleagues that "we should undertake measures along the military line, at least we should prepare them." Documents justifying a military intervention were prepared by July, and in early August, during a meeting of leaders of Communist parties in Bratislava, Biłak's group asked for military assistance.

Meanwhile, not only Soviet dissidents, but the Soviet liberal intelligentsia were looking at Prague with awe and hope to see whether socialism could be reformed peacefully, some even learning Czech in order to be able to read *Rude Pravo*. Petr Shelest expressed concern about possible disturbances in Ukraine because of its proximity to Czechoslovakia.[23]

After a last conversation between Brezhnev and Dubček on August 13, which persuaded the Soviet leader that Dubček was not in control of the situation, the Politburo decided to use military force. Warsaw Pact leaders met in Moscow on August 18 and agreed to send troops to Prague. Forces of five countries invaded Czechoslovakia on August 21, encountering no armed resistance from the Czechs. Up to the very end, Brezhnev was reluctant to use force and modified his position many times, but as a consensus-oriented leader, he eventually sided with his Politburo colleagues (in particular Andropov, Shelest, and Podgornyi). According to Arbatov, Brezhnev was convinced he would have been forced to resign as general secretary if he had "lost Czechoslovakia."[24]

The formal basis for the invasion, which subsequently became known as the Brezhnev Doctrine, was the claim that in the spirit of proletarian inter-nationalism, every Communist party was responsible not only to its own people, but also to "other socialist countries and to the entire Communist movement." In fact, the intervention was a fiasco in the sense that the Soviets were unable to find any reliable allies in the Czech leadership, and at first had to keep Dubček at least nominally in power. In addition to shattering the image of the Soviet Union in the eyes of the Czechoslovak population, the invasion alienated many in the Soviet public and among the party elite itself. Intellectual circles in Moscow reacted with shock, considering the invasion a crime and seeing it as the end of their hopes for reform. Arbatov reports that the invasion "played an important role in the growth of the conservative tendencies that eventually led to the period of stagnation."[25]

---

22 Valenta, *Soviet Intervention*, 20–22   23 *Ibid.*, xvii, 15, 21.
24 Arbatov, *The System*, 141.   25 *Ibid.*, p. 13.

The invasion had wider implications for Soviet foreign policy. The lack of a strong Western response to the invasion "proved to Moscow that Western governments were not prepared to commit themselves militarily on the territory of the Warsaw Treaty powers."[26] This was a huge relief for Brezhnev. It meant that existing European borders were, in effect, final, and that it was now time to render that *de facto* situation *de jure* in an international agreement.

Détente in Europe

The first steps toward détente in Europe were taken before the Prague Spring. In March 1966, Brezhnev blasted the United States in his report to the XXIIIrd Party Congress, but also called for "achieving European security" on the basis of the territorial status quo.[27] That same year, President Charles de Gaulle of France, responding to repeated Soviet appeals for broader cooperation, visited Moscow. While de Gaulle was seeking an independent role for France in bridging the East–West confrontation, Brezhnev and Gromyko saw France as the key to a new relationship with Europe.

French–Soviet détente survived the test of Czechoslovakia. It was invigorated by President Georges Pompidou's visit to Moscow in October 1970 and Brezhnev's visit to France in the spring of 1971. France and the Soviet Union signed a declaration on relations between the two countries, which became a tentative model for European security principles. France then became the first country officially to endorse the Soviet proposal for a European security conference.

As for West Germany, it was slowly moving away from its earlier policy of no contact with the Eastern bloc, while not abandoning its ultimate goal of unification. When Willy Brandt was elected chancellor of West Germany in October 1969, he launched a program of *Ostpolitik* aimed at relaxing tensions in Europe by recognizing East Germany, along with post-World War II territorial changes in Europe. Brandt chose to deal directly with the Soviet Union first (rather than with its East European allies) as a way of allaying Moscow's concerns about West German–East German rapprochement.

---

26 Dobrynin, *In Confidence*, 184.
27 Raymond L. Garthoff, *Détente and Confrontation: American–Soviet Relations from Nixon to Reagan*, rev. ed. (Washington, DC: Brookings Institution, 1994), 123.

As a result of very fast-moving and productive negotiations, the USSR and West Germany signed a non-aggression pact (the Moscow Treaty) in 1970. Next, Brandt signed similar treaties regulating the borders of the two Germanys with Poland, Czechoslovakia, and the German Democratic Republic (GDR). The process was completed in 1971 by a Quadripartite Agreement on Berlin signed by the USSR, the United States, Britain and France. The Soviets, for their part, pressured the Stalinist East German leader Walter Ulbricht to step down and be replaced by a more open-minded Erich Honecker. After this leadership transition, the two Germanys extended recognition to each other and signed a bilateral treaty in December 1972. In this way, Brezhnev and company achieved through careful, steady negotiation what Khrushchev had failed to achieve through ultimatums, bluster, and bluff.

Sino-Soviet relations

After Khrushchev was removed, the new collective leadership reconsidered the USSR relationship with China. China seemed poised to usher in the beginning of multipolarity on the international stage – by emerging as a challenger both to the Soviet Union and the United States. The Chinese detonated their first nuclear device in the fall of 1964 and successfully tested a ballistic missile in 1966. In the same year, responding in part to this development, the USSR began deploying the first elements of an anti-ballistic missile (ABM) system around Moscow.

At the heart of the Sino-Soviet split, which began under Khrushchev but grew deeper in the late 1960s, was the struggle for ideological leadership of the Communist bloc, with the Third World being the main target of that competition. The Chinese leadership came to believe that the Soviet Union was abandoning the purity of the Marxist–Leninist teaching and the idea of world revolution for the benefits of cooperating with the imperialists. Yet, several members of the post-Khrushchev leadership sought to mend the relationship. While Brezhnev was not overly enthusiastic about reaching out to Mao, Kosygin saw improvement of relations with the Chinese as one of his personal priorities.[28]

---

28 Vladislav M. Zubok, *A Failed Empire: The Soviet Union in the Cold War from Stalin to Gorbachev* (Chapel Hill, NC: University of North Carolina Press, 2007), 462.

Kosygin anticipated that a rapprochement with China would be easier because of the growing American involvement in Indochina, which underlined the need for the two Communist states to defend their common ally. During a February 1965 trip to Hanoi, with a stop along the way in China, Kosygin failed to persuade the Vietnamese Communists to abstain from open hostilities against the South once the United States got involved, and failed to reach any agreement with the Chinese. It did not help that while Kosygin was in North Vietnam, the United States bombed Hanoi and Haiphong. The Chinese criticized the Soviets for their "revisionism" and declined to attend the XXIIIrd Party Congress in March of 1966. Later the same year, China officially launched its Great Proletarian Cultural Revolution, and relations with the Soviet Union dramatically worsened.[29]

Mao made no secret of his extensive territorial claims to Soviet Siberia. Alarmed by these demands, as well as by the radical character of the Cultural Revolution, the Soviet Union began a massive buildup of forces along the Chinese border. This buildup, which continued through the end of the 1960s, suggested to the Chinese that Soviet forces might be used in a preemptive attack. In 1969, major border clashes erupted between the Soviet and the Chinese forces on Damansky Island. Responding to the Chinese attack, Soviet troops made a short but deep intrusion into Chinese territory. Moscow's last illusions about the possibility of improving relations with China were dispelled by the Damansky hostilities.

During the same year, the administration of Richard M. Nixon began trying to open channels to Beijing through Pakistan and Romania. In July 1971, Henry Kissinger made a secret visit to China, where he explicitly discussed the Soviet threat with the Chinese and even provided them with some sensitive intelligence information on Soviet military activities. President Nixon himself visited China in February 1972.

The Soviets repeatedly urged the United States not to exploit the Sino-Soviet split, but the very possibility that Washington might do so prompted Moscow to try to improve relations with both the Americans and the Chinese. On October 20, 1969, the same day that Dobrynin informed Nixon of the Soviet agreement to open Strategic Arms Limitation Treaty (SALT) talks, the USSR and China resumed talks on their disputed border. By the early 1970s, with Sino-Soviet relations seeming beyond repair for the time being, Moscow moved to prevent a possible US–Chinese rapprochement by proposing just such a détente between itself and Washington.

29 See also Sergey Radchenko's chapter in this volume.

Superpower détente

Although the drive toward détente was mutual, the United States and the USSR entertained quite differing views of it. Neither of the two countries was willing to forgo competition in pursuit of its interests internationally. For each of them, détente meant a limited accommodation that would allow those interests to be pursued at a lower level of tension.

For Soviet leaders, détente would confirm not only military, but political, parity with the United States. That meant that, like US policymakers, Soviet officials wanted to exert their influence and support their allies globally while relying on the other side to accept such actions as a military and political reality. The Soviet concept of "peaceful coexistence," understood as a form of "class struggle," would allow Moscow to promote proletarian international-ism and support national liberation movements in the Third World. The two main pro-détente arguments in Moscow – that the Soviet Union needed the West to improve its own economic situation, and that its growing military might could produce geopolitical gains at the West's expense – were not seen as contradictory in the Kremlin.[30]

On the US side, President Nixon and his national security adviser and later secretary of state Henry Kissinger wanted to prevent US–Soviet competition from escalating into confrontation, while at the same time gaining Soviet assistance in resolving international conflicts in Vietnam and the Middle East. Nixon, Kissinger, and Brezhnev resembled each other in their aspiration to be great statesmen and peacemakers, in their generally Realpolitik worldview, and in their preference for secrecy and personal diplomacy in conducting policy. That is why the idea of regular summitry was so attractive to both sides. The presence of a very talented Soviet ambassador in Washington, Anatolii Dobrynin, who also shared those views, contributed significantly to the rapid development of US–Soviet détente.

Just one month after Nixon's inauguration, in February 1969, a secret personal "back channel" between Kissinger and Dobrynin began to function, with arms control being the first subject under consideration. With the Soviet Union on the verge of pulling ahead of the United States in ICBM launchers, and the United States actively engaged in developing the MIRV technology, both sides recognized that without agreed limits, the nuclear-arms race threatened international stability and imposed significant economic costs on both countries.

---

30 Garthoff, *Détente and Confrontation*, 40–73.

Signed on May 26, 1972, during President Nixon's visit to Moscow, SALT I did not actually reduce any armaments; rather, it froze the number of nuclear weapons at the levels existing on both sides, while failing to address the most destabilizing issue, MIRV technology. That technology allowed the side that employed it to increase the actual throw weight of its warheads many times without adding any new launchers, thus rendering the nuclear balance less predictable and therefore less stable. When the treaty was signed, MIRV technology gave an advantage to Washington because the Soviet Union was falling far behind the United States in this area. However, potentially, it was the Soviet side that could gain most from this technology because of its bigger ICBMs.

Along with SALT I, the US and Soviet leaders signed the Anti-Ballistic Missile Treaty limiting strategic defenses, which in the future came to be perceived as critical to nuclear deterrence by both sides. Yet, even though arms control soon became the centerpiece at the summits, the May 1972 meeting did not produce other key results the two sides hoped for: "for the U.S., a definitive pledge of Soviet help in settling the Vietnam war, for the USSR some kind of understanding concerning China."[31]

SALT II negotiations began soon after the signing of SALT I. However, the negotiations were more difficult than expected because of increasing tensions in overall US–Soviet relations, growing doubts about détente in US domestic politics, plus the sheer difficulty of limiting forces that had very different components and structures. After President Nixon resigned in 1974, Gerald Ford moved quickly on SALT II, picking up where Nixon and Brezhnev left it. In late November 1974, Ford and Brezhnev met in the Soviet Far East, near the city of Vladivostok, and negotiated the basic framework of the treaty.

Brezhnev made a significant concession in Vladivostok against the advice of his own defense minister, Andrei Grechko. He agreed to an overall ceiling of 2,400 strategic launchers (including ICBMs, submarine-launched ballistic missiles (SLBMs), and strategic bombers), of which 1,320 could be equipped with MIRV technology, while not counting either American nuclear systems "forward-based" in Europe or the nuclear weapons of other members of the North Atlantic Treaty Organization (NATO). However, to the dismay of Soviet leaders, President Jimmy Carter soon abandoned the Vladivostok framework.

31 Adam B. Ulam, *Dangerous Relations: The Soviet Union in World Politics, 1970–1982* (New York: Oxford University Press, 1983), 75.

9. President Ford and Leonid Brezhnev at the conclusion of the SALT II talks in Vladivostok in November 1974. Brezhnev made détente the key point in his relations with the United States.

Proletarian internationalism and competition in the Third World

Détente began to unravel in the Third World. Khrushchev had reached out to national liberation movements in an ostentatious but tentative fashion. In the early 1960s, the Soviet Union had almost no specialists on Africa: a subsection on Africa was just being created in the International Department of the Central Committee in 1961. Under Brezhnev, Soviet support for real or potential Third World allies shifted in emphasis from economic to military aid. The Kremlin sold arms, sent military advisers, and sought bases in some Third World Countries. Moscow's most important Third World allies were Cuba, India (after the signing of the Soviet–Indian Treaty of Friendship and Cooperation in August 1971), and Vietnam. In the Middle East, Syria, Iraq, Libya, and Egypt were particularly significant. While there was no Soviet master plan for the Third World, the Soviet Union, trying to emulate the United States, was becoming a global power, with a growing naval presence in

SVETLANA SAVRANSKAYA AND WILLIAM TAUBMAN

all parts of the world. However, there was a strong perception of a Soviet master plan within the Carter administration, championed by national security adviser Zbigniew Brzezinski, who had significant influence on the new president's thinking, especially through his weekly national security reports.[32]

Even as Soviet aid to Third World countries grew, some in the Soviet leadership, especially Kosygin, tried to limit it. He hoped to make relations with Third World countries more "mutually beneficial," by basing them on the "distribution of labor." Kosygin was especially interested in expanding Soviet influence in South Asia. During the September 1965 hostilities between India and Pakistan, Kosygin successfully mediated the conflict and persuaded the two countries to sign the Tashkent Declaration in January 1966. In the late 1960s, especially after the Soviet–Indian Treaty was signed, Moscow's Indian connection helped to balance the US–Chinese rapprochement. The alliance between the USSR and India was cemented during the Indo-Pakistani war of December 1971, which India fought successfully with Soviet armaments. The Chinese were deterred from intervening on Pakistan's side by the Soviet–Indian alliance.

Meanwhile, in the Middle East, the post-Khrushchev leadership initially tried to deemphasize the former leader's support for Arab states as the main source of Soviet influence in the region. Kosygin's successful mediation of the conflict between India and Pakistan kindled Soviet aspirations to replace the United States as the main Middle East peace mediator. However, Egypt, the most important Soviet ally in the area, resisted this idea.

In the spring of 1967, the Soviets found themselves being manipulated by Syria and Egypt. Soviet arms sales to these two countries encouraged their belligerence toward Israel, while Soviet pressure on them to be more conciliatory had no effect. Shortly before the outbreak of the June 1967 war, the Soviets allowed Egypt to mobilize troops to deter a possible Israeli attack against Syria, about which Podgornyi informed the Egyptian government in May 1967. Strong rhetorical support for the Arabs then undermined Soviet ability to serve as a mediator.

Once hostilities broke out, and the devastating defeat of Egypt, Syria, and Jordan became apparent, Moscow felt it had no choice but to threaten intervention if Israel did not stop its advance. At the same time, however, the Kremlin turned to the United States for joint mediation. The shift from seeking to be the sole peacemaker in the Middle East to understanding the

---

32 Melvyn P. Leffler, *For the Soul of Mankind: The United States, the Soviet Union, and the Cold War* (New York: Hill and Wang, 2007), 269–84 See also Nancy Mitchell's chapter in volume III.

need for US–Soviet cooperation was a turning point in Soviet Middle East policy. In July 1967, the Soviet Union and the United States successfully collaborated on UN resolution 242, which envisioned an Israeli withdrawal from the occupied lands in exchange for Arab recognition of Israel's right to exist. In 1970, Brezhnev even proposed a gradual restoration of relations with Israel, but Suslov and Gromyko opposed it. They insisted that Soviet policy toward the Middle East stay the same until a full peace settlement in the region was reached. According to Dobrynin, Brezhnev gave in and continued the pro-Arab policy.[33]

Notwithstanding the lessons learned during the 1967 war, and the newly found joint mission with the United States in the region, the Soviet Politburo, acting in response to the urgent requests of its Arab allies, decided to resupply their armies. Thousands of Soviet military personnel were sent to Syria and Egypt, and the Soviet Union acquired naval rights in Arab countries. Although Egypt and Syria were resupplied with up to $5 billion worth of military equipment, Egypt wanted even more, and so during the war of attrition in 1969–70, Soviet fighter pilots were dispatched there. A treaty with Egypt was signed in May 1971, and a similar treaty with Iraq in April 1972. Driven by fear that the United States would marginalize Soviet efforts to be a leading mediator in the region, Moscow was seeking to consolidate its own sphere of influence in the Middle East,

Soviet interests suffered a major setback when, just six weeks after the Moscow Brezhnev–Nixon summit, Egyptian president Anwar Sadat expelled over 20,000 Soviet military advisers, technicians, and military aircraft from Egypt. Sadat had pursued secret contacts with Kissinger for a long time before that decision was made, apparently exploring a more promising alliance. His turnaround made it even more important for the Soviet Union to reach an understanding with the United States on their joint role in the Middle East, an effort that jibed with Brezhnev's personal dream of joining with Nixon to exert pressure on Soviet and American allies in a crisis situation. During his second American summit with Nixon in San Clemente, California, in June 1973, Brezhnev had a famous middle-of-the-night three-hour session with the president. Among other things, Brezhnev proposed that it was time for the two leaders to reach an agreement on the Middle East among themselves and then to "bring to bear [their] influence" on their respective allies to reach the settlement that would bring a lasting peace to the region. Brezhnev was

33 Dobrynin, *In Confidence*, 162.

153

passionate and unrelenting, urging Nixon to step in personally before it became too late.[34]

Nonetheless, US–Soviet collaboration failed its first test in the region just a couple of months after the summit. After the Egyptian and Syrian attack against Israel on October 6, 1973, Moscow and Washington accused each other of using delaying tactics in order to assist their allies in gaining more territory. When the ceasefire collapsed, and the Arabs seemed to have gained momentum, the United States put its forces on a very high level of alert, precipitating a crisis that threatened a direct US–Soviet clash. The ceasefire was eventually reestablished and hostilities ended, but this episode undermined Washington's reliability as a partner in Moscow's eyes, thus compromising the overall health of US–Soviet détente.

Conference on security and cooperation in Europe: the Final Act

Arguably the most important diplomatic process of the period between 1964 and 1975, at least symbolically, was the ambitious attempt to bring the United States, the Soviet Union, and the Europeans together within one new integrative security framework. This process, which unfolded in Europe in the early 1970s, resulted in what came to be known as the Helsinki Accords of 1975.

The idea of a European security conference, which would legitimize the postwar borders in Europe and reconfirm the Soviet Union's status as a great European power, was one of the top priorities of the post-Khrushchev leadership, and one which especially suited Brezhnev is his role as a peacemaker.

A secondary Soviet goal was to expand trade relations and achieve some degree of integration into the European economy. Initial Soviet proposals did not include humanitarian issues, which later were commonly referred to as Basket III of the Helsinki Accords. Basket III, which included human rights provisions and other nonmilitary aspects of security such as domestic security of citizens, freedom of information, freedom of movement, and availability of cultural and educational contacts between citizens of different countries, provoked sharp differences of opinion among Soviet leaders. Brezhnev and Gromyko cautiously favored including Basket III in the negotiations, Suslov

---

34 Memorandum of conversation, President Richard Nixon's Meeting with General Secretary Leonid Brezhnev, June 23, 1973, San Clemente, California. document no. 00766, Kissinger Memcons Collection, National Security Archive, Washington, DC.

was against, and Andropov took a cautious position. He understood the need to confirm borders and expand economic contacts, but sensed the potential dangers of the human rights provisions. According to Melvyn Leffler, the Soviet leaders were faced with the "tradeoff: recognition of human rights in return for recognition of the territorial status quo."[35]

The attention that the Conference on Security and Cooperation in Europe (CSCE) negotiations received at the highest level is evident in the fact that April 1973 and April 1975 Central Committee plenums – the only ones from 1973 to 1980 that dealt specifically with foreign-policy matters – discussed the CSCE negotiations, and that several Politburo sessions addressed CSCE-related issues, with at least one meeting, on January 7, 1974, largely devoted to it.

The Final Act of the CSCE was signed in Helsinki on August 1, 1975, and printed in full in *Pravda*. Brezhnev's goals seemed to be achieved: postwar European borders were confirmed in an international agreement; the Soviet Union was recognized as a member of the European great power concert; and relations with the United States were firmly set within the framework of arms-control agreements. Upon signing the Final Act, Brezhnev probably felt he was at the peak of his political career. Yet, even as Soviet leaders were celebrating the Helsinki Accords, the fruits of the perceived victory were beginning to turn sour.

Soviet human rights activists quickly began using the Helsinki Final Act as a way to make their case abroad. The first Helsinki Watch Group was established in Moscow on May 12, 1976, by the prominent dissident, physicist Iurii Orlov. The Soviet government cited other provisions of the act to accuse foreign governments of interference in Soviet domestic affairs. The dissidents retorted that the Helsinki Accords legitimized human rights movements in the USSR and other socialist countries.[36]

Western support for the new wave of human rights movements combined with other irritants, which by the mid-1970s had accumulated in US–Soviet bilateral relations and in the Third World, to start pulling détente apart just as it seemed to reach its apogee.[37] Instead of becoming the year that consolidated détente, 1975 became the watershed between détente and what seemed like a second round of the Cold War.

35 Leffler, *For the Soul of Mankind*, 249
36 Paul Goldberg, *The Final Act: The Dramatic, Revealing Story of the Moscow Helsinki Watch Group* (New York: William Morrow & Co., 1988).
37 See Marc Trachtenberg's chapter in this volume and Olav Njølstad's chapter in volume III.

The end of détente

The period of 1962–75 was when the Central European theater of the Cold War stabilized. The European status quo was affirmed, first, in a series of treaties with two German states, and, finally, by the Helsinki Accords. At the same time, arms-control agreements were signed, which, while not reducing armaments, put significant brakes on the arms race. The fear of nuclear war subsided. East–West ties of all sorts – economic, political, social, and cultural – expanded.

The Soviet leadership seemed to have learned the lessons of the almost disastrous Cuban missile crisis. Brezhnev's ascendance meant moderation in foreign policy, and the achievement of détente. But détente did not remove competition in the Third World. If anything, Moscow's growing international prestige, as well as its growing arms sales to developing countries, made the Soviet Union a more attractive ally for Third World leaders at a time when the United States was suffering a major defeat in Vietnam. As more opportunities presented themselves in the Third World, the Soviet Union gradually got sucked into conflicts. When African and Asian leaders employed Marxist revolutionary rhetoric and called themselves countries of a "socialist orientation," the Soviet Union, as the leader of the socialist camp, felt it had to respond.[38]

The fall of the last colonial empire – the Portuguese – at the very peak of détente triggered just such a Soviet response in Angola. The USSR and the United States came to support two opposing sides in the civil war there, and China also meddled in the strife to thwart Soviet influence in Africa. When the Cubans pushed the Soviets to widen their military involvement in the civil war, and the first battles were won by the faction favored by the Kremlin, Brezhnev took that to confirm that class struggle could proceed in the Third World while superpower relations improved.[39] In reality, however, the Soviet role in Angola strengthened the perception in the United States that the Soviet Union was using détente to lull the West into a false sense of security while driving for global dominance.

A truly cooperative relationship between East and West required a deeper consensus on basic values and principles that would not be within reach for

38 See Vladislav Zubok's chapter in volume III.
39 For the most recent detailed account of US and Soviet involvement in Angola, see Odd Arne Westad, *The Global Cold War: Third World Interventions and the Making of Our Times* (New York: Cambridge University Press, 2006), 222–36; see also Piero Gleijeses's chapter in this volume.

another ten years. Such a consensus, as détente had shown, could not come about while the two main ideologies – capitalist democracy and Communism – continued to clash. Only after 1985 would Mikhail Gorbachev transform the Soviet approach to international relations, reining in the ideological clergy and the military-industrial complex, and resisting temptations to expand Soviet power in the Third World. Until then, the conflict would not only continue but worsen. As Robert Gilpin pointed out in his analysis of US–Soviet relations, "in the absence of shared values and interests, the mechanism of peaceful change [had] little chance of success."[40]

40 Robert Gilpin, *War and Change in World Politics* (Cambridge: Cambridge University Press, 1981), 209.

8

France, "Gaullism," and the Cold War

FRÉDÉRIC BOZO

The importance of France's role in the Cold War is often overlooked when compared with that of both the two superpowers and the other major West European countries. Germany self-evidently occupied a central position in the East–West conflict from its inception and was a decisive actor at its end, and Britain's role during the Cold War was much enhanced thanks to the "special" relationship with the United States. By contrast, the French contribution often comes across as less important. This may be partly explained by a comparatively modest French input in the historiography, especially in the English-speaking literature. Yet the perception of France as a lesser player in the Cold War is misleading.

To be sure, the country was in a somewhat peripheral position at the very beginning of the East–West conflict. Wartime leader Charles de Gaulle and – following his withdrawal from politics in January 1946 – his immediate successors were indeed reluctant to accept the emerging logic of the Cold War and its consequences. By the late 1940s, however, the intensification of the Cold War had led to the country's active alignment within the West, thus making France a key protagonist in the East–West conflict. Yet France's position in the Cold War soon provoked a number of frustrations that the country's painful decolonization process and chronic internal instability only aggravated, and these tensions together played no small part in the demise of the Fourth Republic and General de Gaulle's return to power in 1958. Seeking to reestablish France's "rank," de Gaulle was determined to challenge the international status quo which corseted the country on the world scene. By the mid-1960s, France's concept and practice of East–West relations had become premised on the objective of overcoming "Yalta," thus leading France to assume an influential role in the long-term transformation of the East–West conflict. After his departure in 1969, de Gaulle's successors as presidents of the Fifth Republic by and large continued to shape France's international policies according to this grand design. Although events subsequently confirmed the durability of the bipolar order and the persistence of the European status quo contrary to Gaullist expectations, de Gaulle's legacy remained the yardstick of French diplomacy during the second half of the Cold War and until its end.

If France's posture in the Cold War were to be summarized in one word, "Gaullism" should be considered an appropriate one. The term indeed captures the overwhelming influence of Charles de Gaulle and his legacy on France and its international role throughout the period, as well as the specificity of the French input in the conflict. France's role reflected not only its intrinsic geopolitical importance in the Cold War but, perhaps more significantly, a distinctive approach to East–West relations that resulted from a complex and, at times, paradoxical combination of accommodation and dissatisfaction with the status quo. Because dissatisfaction by and large prevailed, "Gaullism" became a synonym for the Cold War revisionism which – although culminating under de Gaulle's presidency in the 1960s – characterized France's policy during most of the period. And because it rested on a forceful and coherent concept of transcending the bloc system, "Gaullism" may be seen historically as having represented one of the most significant alternative conceptions of the evolution of the Cold War beyond the established order of the East–West conflict.

France's hesitant entry into the Cold War

France's entry into the East–West conflict in the immediate aftermath of World War II was characterized by more hesitation and second thoughts than was the case for the other major Western powers. For de Gaulle and, after his withdrawal, for his successors as heads of the "tripartite" governments (a coalition of Christian Democrats, socialists, and Communists that remained in power until spring 1947), there were, by and large, three main reasons to observe the emergence of the Cold War with concern. First, international status: for a country still under the trauma of its defeat of 1940 and whose "rank" as a great power had been only halfheartedly recognized by the Big Three in 1945, there was an obvious interest in the preservation of the wartime "club" to which it had been admitted belatedly; the French, therefore, had strong misgivings as cracks began to develop in the victorious alliance between the Western powers and the Soviet Union soon after the end of the war.[1] In addition, the emerging East–West divide carried the risk of

---

1 Although France was not invited to Yalta in February 1945 (nor to Potsdam in July 1945), it was formally granted the status of permanent member of the UN Security Council and that of occupying power in Germany during the Crimea conference. "Yalta" subsequently became the motto of Gaullist denunciations of the Cold War system.

cutting France's ties with its traditional Central and East European allies, which had contributed to its standing after World War I, as exemplified by France's links with the "Petite Entente" in the 1920s and 1930s.

The second reason was linked to national security. Because the potential resurgence of Germany as a long-term threat remained a major French concern after the war, in spite of the total defeat of the Nazi Reich, preserving a strong connection with Moscow was key in terms of military reassurance, hence the alliance treaty that de Gaulle had signed with Iosif Stalin in Moscow in December 1944. The connection with Moscow was also important in order to gain Soviet support for what was then France's German policy, one of opposing the restoration of a central state across the Rhine and of amputating the territory of Germany while incorporating its western segments in a West European "grouping" of sorts, (such a grouping, in de Gaulle's eyes, would also help France check the growing influence and power of Russia in Eastern Europe).

Finally, there was the issue of internal stability. With a significant participation in government, the French Communist Party (PCF) was then a decisive element in France's diplomatic posture. Because it made alignment with the United States and confrontation with the USSR potentially troublesome in domestic terms, the Communist factor was a strong incentive for the maintenance of France's proclaimed role as a "bridge" between the West and the East as set forth by de Gaulle, a policy staunchly defended by his early successors, especially the foreign minister, Georges Bidault, until 1947.

Perceptions of the Soviet Union and of East–West relations evolved rapidly, however. French decisionmakers were in fact quite lucid with regard to the Soviet challenge as early as 1945. While primarily the result of his impatience with the parliamentary system of the nascent Fourth Republic, de Gaulle's withdrawal in January 1946 also reflected his frustration with France's impotence against the backdrop of a quickly deteriorating East–West context. Yet these changing perceptions did not immediately lead to the adoption of new policies, if only because the domestic situation, still marked by the politics of "tripartism," made it difficult to change the course of French diplomacy. The turning point was reached in spring 1947. France, owing to converging factors, was now forced to acknowledge Cold War realities and the necessity for alignment in the East–West conflict. By then de Gaulle, now in the opposition, had adopted a hardline stance in these matters; in April, he launched the *Rassemblement du peuple français* (RPF), a right-wing party built on a staunchly anti-Soviet posture. And in May, the Communist ministers were dismissed from government by the socialist premier, Paul Ramadier. Although primarily a matter of domestic politics (in fact, most observers expected the

Communists to quickly come back in government), the move no doubt reflected the internalization of the East–West divide. By then, the Cold War had clearly settled into French politics.

Yet the shift in France's East–West posture was primarily the result of the international context. It was the consequence, first and foremost, of increasingly aggressive Soviet behavior, which ran counter to France's interests, especially in Eastern and Central Europe where the strengthening of Moscow's grip cut France off from traditional allies. Moscow's policies with respect to Germany were also a growing concern. The Four Powers' foreign ministers conference in Moscow in March–April 1947 had shown that Stalin was not ready to support French territorial claims, in particular over the Saarland. Soviet aims vis-à-vis Germany were, in fact, increasingly seen as threatening to the West and to France. Not only was Moscow determined to incorporate the eastern part of the country in its sphere, but Stalin's objective of securing Soviet influence over Germany as a whole by playing the "German card" was now seen as a major challenge by the French. In short, the perception of a Soviet threat was now looming larger in Paris than the fear of a restoration of an increasingly hypothetical German danger, a decisive and durable shift that the events of the following years – from the Prague coup to the Berlin blockade and the Korean War – would but confirm.

France's gravitation to the West in 1947, therefore, was a result of the centrality of the German question in French perceptions: because the scheme of a Germany lastingly kept down jointly by France and the Soviet Union was now precluded and because the United States and the United Kingdom were increasingly pressuring them to that effect, the French, starting in 1948, recognized that solving the German problem implied just the reverse – rebuilding West Germany on Western terms and establishing a separate West German democratic state closely integrated into Euro-Atlantic institutions. This was a watershed in French diplomacy. In the wake of the creation of the Federal Republic of Germany (FRG) in 1949, it opened the way to the Schuman declaration of May 9, 1950, which laid a solid groundwork for Franco-German reconciliation and European integration. These twin objectives would, from then on, constitute France's most consistent project, exerting a major influence on French policies throughout the Cold War (in turn, Franco-German reconciliation and European integration would profoundly change French perceptions of the German question over time, a development which also influenced France's policies significantly, as would be seen at the end of the Cold War).

FRÉDÉRIC BOZO

Evidently, none of the foregoing would have occurred without another, equally decisive, factor: the US engagement in Europe, which, starting in 1947, became massive. For France, as for other West European nations, the announcement of the Marshall Plan carried the promise of economic recovery and political stability; it was no surprise that Paris and London took the lead in organizing the West European response to the offer in the summer of 1947. Yet the prospect of a political alliance between America and Europe, which was discussed throughout 1948 and became a reality with the signing of the Washington Treaty in April 1949, was even more decisive. The Atlantic alliance indeed offered the country both a guarantee against the danger of Soviet belligerence *and* an insurance against the possibility of German resurgence. The alliance's transformation into an integrated organization starting in 1950 and the stabilization of the US military presence in Europe confirmed this. The agonizing German rearmament question, from 1950 onwards, certainly revealed how delicate the balance between those two concerns was in those years as seen from Paris. However, the unfolding of the crisis over the European Defense Community (EDC) in the fall of 1954 and the FRG's accession to the North Atlantic Treaty Organization (NATO) and the Western European Union (WEU) in 1955 definitively established the "double containment" (of the USSR, thanks to the Western alliance, and of West Germany within that same alliance) that would ensure France's security and status in the decades to come. By the mid-1950s, the country had settled into the structure of the Cold War for good.

The Fourth Republic's Cold War

Accommodation, however, did not mean satisfaction. Beginning in the early 1950s, the policies of the Fourth Republic were characterized by a growing sense of frustration. This reflected, first of all, a widening gap between the country's ambitions and its limited economic, political, and military means. As a result, France faced growing dilemmas when confronted with major international choices or crises. Yet Paris's frustration was also, to a significant extent, fostered by the rules of the Cold War, which France never wholeheartedly accepted. Nonetheless, the fundamentals of the country's posture in the East–West conflict and, most of all, its Atlantic and European orientations were at no point called into question after 1947. Although some of the factors that explained France's reluctance to enter the conflict in the early years were now less salient, they still continued to operate. On the domestic scene, the influence of neutralist tendencies remained important in political and intellectual circles, especially in the early 1950s, and, in strategic terms, the fear of a confrontation with Moscow, in particular over the German rearmament question, continued to loom large.

The foregoing helps explain French thinking about East–West relations during the 1950s, which in some ways foreshadowed de Gaulle's policies in the next decade. Most important was the notion – at least in the early years of the decade – that the Cold War was a transitory state of affairs and that alternative schemes were conceivable; the belief that a more independent Europe could alleviate the East–West divide in the long run, for example, played a significant role in the thinking of Jean Monnet. Also important was the thought that France had to temper what were now and then seen as exceedingly confrontational US policies (again, the German rearmament debate revolved largely around this issue as viewed from Paris). And last, but not least, was the belief that it was important to preserve contacts with the Soviet Union for the sake of European security. Pierre Mendès France was thinking this way when he broached the theme of disarmament and détente at the United Nations in November 1954 and when his successor, Edgar Faure, pushed for the convening of the meeting of the Big Four in Geneva in July 1955. Although the international policies of the Fourth Republic can hardly be viewed as "revisionist" in the sense of de Gaulle's in the 1960s, they did reflect the country's growing sense of unease with the constraints and dilemmas imposed by the East–West situation.

Yet it was within the US-dominated Western alliance that the strictures of the Cold War were felt most bitterly by the French during the Fourth Republic. To be sure, the country had a fundamental choice in the late 1940s and the early 1950s: along with the UK, France had been the most important European supporter of the Atlantic political alliance and its military organization. Yet if "Atlanticism" prevailed under the Fourth Republic, the consequences of that choice were felt with increasing dismay. The country quickly found itself in the position of a junior partner of the "Anglo-Saxons" within the Western bloc, especially with regard to nuclear weapons, of which it was deprived. As a result, France's NATO policy, starting in the early 1950s, amounted to an uphill battle for recognition as the alliance's third big power, along with the United States and the United Kingdom. Meanwhile, the establishment of the Atlantic system inevitably led to the blurring of the European project which, by then, had become a central element of France's foreign policy and the principal justification of its claim to international leadership.

The 1956 Suez crisis, however, even more decisively affected France's disgruntlement with US domination of the Atlantic alliance. Its humiliating outcome, which Washington had forced upon London and Paris, dramatically illustrated France's and Europe's diminished margin of maneuver vis-à-vis the United States. This feeling of humiliation was aggravated by the fact that the crisis had taken place, as seen from Paris, against the backdrop of de facto Soviet–American collusion, illuminating a new phase of the Cold War, characterized by the emergence of bipolarity at the global level. But whereas the Suez crisis had led Britain to seek a reaffirmation of its "special relationship" with the United States, France, in the last years of the Fourth Republic, chose a different course and relaunched its search for strategic autonomy. Suez was the real starting point of a process that would culminate under de Gaulle in 1966.

By the end of the 1950s, the principal source of French frustration was the agonizing decolonization process that the country was experiencing in the aftermath of World War II and that was now circumscribing its ability to act freely in international affairs. France's colonial wars were without doubt only partially the consequence of the East–West conflict. The perception nevertheless prevailed that the former were exacerbated by the latter; this was in fact the case in Indochina, which had become a theater of the Cold War after the outbreak of the Korean War in 1950, but not in Algeria, where the motivations of the "rebels" had little to do with international Communism. Moreover, the French felt that, although the country was fighting these wars in the interest of the "West," their task was made more difficult, if not jeopardized, by their allies, especially the United States. In Indochina, Paris had quickly come to resent Washington's growing influence in the conflict, which was seen as being at odds with French objectives. This led to French–American friction culminating in the Dien Bien Phu crisis in the spring of 1954. In Algeria, the perception arose – especially after Suez – that not only did the United States call into question the legitimacy of France's fight, but that Washington acted against France's interests by encouraging Algerian nationalists. This pattern eventually led to the final crisis of the Fourth Republic in the spring of 1958. Washington and London imposed their good offices in the French–Tunisian crisis that had developed alongside the war in Algeria, thus paving the way for the return of General de Gaulle. By then, France's international impotence had become glaring, and it reflected the country's dissatisfaction with its place in a world increasingly dominated by the realities of the Cold War.

The return of de Gaulle

In spite of his increasing aloofness from active politics, de Gaulle had proved an implacable critic of the regime throughout the decade. Because he had consistently presented himself as offering an alternative to a weak Fourth Republic and an answer to the nation's growing frustrations, his return to power in June 1958 was a turning point. While the Fourth Republic had proved unable to transcend these frustrations, de Gaulle was determined to do so. From then on, France's policies were shaped by his desire to restore the country's international status and by his revisionist objectives with regard to the Cold War system.

De Gaulle's foremost ambition was to reestablish France's "rank." This implied, first of all, the restoration of internal stability and international credibility – hence the tailor-made, presidential constitution of the Fifth Republic, which gave him and his successors a robust instrument to assert French influence in international politics. His next priority was to solve the Algerian problem, which severely reduced France's margin of maneuver. Although this was by no means a foregone conclusion in 1958, de Gaulle quickly understood that no solution short of Algeria's independence would allow the country to regain a diplomatic "free hand." This result was achieved in July 1962, putting an end to a painful decolonization and enabling France to adopt a higher profile on the world scene. Finally, while de Gaulle fully recognized France's status as a medium power, he also understood that the country's ability to regain international influence would be a function of the fundamentals of power, whether economic or military. In this respect, France's economic growth and dynamism in the 1960s were exceptionally strong, enabling de Gaulle to move ahead and develop France's nuclear deterrent, which became a reality when the "force de frappe" went operational in 1964. It was on this solid ground that de Gaulle would soon base his policy of challenging the Cold War status quo.

De Gaulle's ambition to restore France's rank was indeed inseparable from his determination to transform the international system as a whole. By the time of his return to power, his dissatisfaction with the established order was no secret: although he had essentially been a cold warrior during his opposition years, he had developed a long-term vision of the end of the Cold War, a vision that stemmed from a combination of historical analysis and political anticipation. First, Communism in the East was not eternal. Sooner or later, the Soviet Union would cease to be and Russia would reappear as a "normal" power – though not necessarily a benign one. In fact, de Gaulle believed that, under the mask of ideology, Stalin and his successors in many ways behaved internationally as the followers of the tsars. As for East European countries, de Gaulle thought they would eventually free themselves from Soviet tutelage and regain their national personalities. Second, America's role as a European power would also prove transitory. Once the Soviet threat receded, the United States would inevitably withdraw and return to its traditional aloofness from the Old World, thus allowing Western Europe to regain its autonomy. Hence, for de Gaulle, the prevailing East–West order was doomed, at least in the long run. Down the road, the loosening of the superpowers' grip would lead to the obsolescence of the bloc system, allowing for the reemergence of European nations "from the Atlantic to the Urals." Needless to say, France, in this vision, would play a prominent role, in particular as the leader of an assertive, political Western European "grouping" that de Gaulle had envisioned since World War II. After he came to power in 1958, de Gaulle labored diligently to move beyond "Yalta" and to realize this vision of a transformed international system.[2]

In spite of early attempts at engaging the Soviet Union (Khrushchev made a colorful but rather unproductive visit to France in 1960), de Gaulle's international policies in the first years focused primarily on the Western bloc, a priority which reflected his growing dissatisfaction with the existing Atlantic order and his conviction of the need for a profound overhaul of the alliance in accordance with his long-term vision. His views were outlined in the memorandum of September 1958 that he sent to President Dwight D. Eisenhower and Prime Minister Harold Macmillan, in which he famously advocated a tripartite "directorate" of the United States, Britain, and France in the alliance. When Eisenhower rejected the idea and when the incoming Kennedy administration reiterated US disapproval, de Gaulle tried to use the lever of Franco-German cooperation and European unification: hence the Fouchet Plan of 1961–62, a blueprint to build the European Economic Community (EEC) into an intergovernmental "union of states" endowed with a large degree of strategic autonomy vis-à-vis the United States. The idea, however, was defeated in the spring of 1962 as a result of overt hostility on the part of Europeanists and Atlanticists and tacit opposition in Washington. These initiatives nonetheless illustrated de Gaulle's long-term aspirations to strengthen France's position as an interlocutor in relations with

---

2 See Stanley Hoffmann, *Decline or Renewal? France since the 1930's* (New York: Viking, 1974), 304 (Hoffmann's analysis of the Gaullist vision remains the most thorough and cogent to this day).

the Soviet Union and the Eastern bloc and as the leader of a cohesive Western Europe in the pursuit of East–West détente. In fact, the Fouchet Plan was clearly premised on ideas similar to those of the US diplomat George Kennan who believed that a more assertive, less US-dominated Western Europe would be in a better position to engage the Soviet Union and thereby overcome the East–West divide. Still, until at least 1962, de Gaulle's international revisionism had more to do with intra-West relations than with East–West transformation. Although both dimensions were linked from the outset, the priority was the redistribution of power within the Atlantic alliance rather than actively challenging "Yalta."

In any event, the East–West confrontation – which reached a peak during the second Berlin crisis in 1958–61 and the Cuban missile crisis in 1962 – precluded an assertive policy of reaching out to the East. De Gaulle's attitude toward Moscow in the first few years of his term was unyielding: hence his refusal to negotiate over Berlin as long as the Soviets maintained a threatening posture and, most of all, his unconditional support of President John F. Kennedy's

10. Charles de Gaulle and Konrad Adenauer shaking hands during their meeting in Bad Kreuznach, West Germany, in December 1958. De Gaulle made Franco-German friendship and cooperation a key foreign-policy aim.

stance during the missile crisis. De Gaulle's behavior was, first and foremost, an expression of his conviction that Western cohesion was indispensable in order to prevent Moscow from carrying out its threats, and that yielding to blackmail would only encourage further aggression. As a result, the French rebuffed negotiations with the East well into 1963. Of course, there were ulterior motives as well: de Gaulle's show of solidarity with Konrad Adenauer over Berlin was meant to emphasize the importance of the Franco-German rapprochement (the two statesmen had developed a close relationship as early as September 1958 when they met at de Gaulle's home in eastern France). Likewise, his attitude during the Cuban crisis demonstrated France's commitment to the Western alliance in spite of an already diminishing French participation in NATO and increasing disagreements over nuclear strategy. De Gaulle, in other words, was strengthening his Western credentials with a view to his future East–West moves. Be that as it may, de Gaulle, in those years, was still perceived on the world scene as a consummate cold warrior.

The emergence of de Gaulle's "politique à l'Est"

France's rapid shift in the next few years was all the more spectacular in view of the foregoing. Although his Western objectives remained unchanged, by 1964 the search for a new model in East–West relations had become the keystone of the Gaullist international strategy. His goal now was to overcome the Cold War status quo. This change may be explained by three factors. First, the state of East–West relations after the Cuban missile showdown: if the crisis had confirmed the risk of nuclear confrontation, it also heralded, in de Gaulle's view, a new phase of Soviet–American rapprochement that could strengthen the superpowers' shared control over Europe. In this respect, in the immediate aftermath of the crisis, French diplomacy was highly wary of the strategic dialogue between Moscow and Washington and, in particular, of the Limited Nuclear Test-Ban Treaty of August 1963, which was seen as portending a Soviet–American condominium. De Gaulle's shift toward an active East–West policy, in other words, was a response to the challenge of a bipolar international system. If Europe was to be spared a "new Yalta," France had to take the lead in the quest for détente *in* Europe and, indeed, for a *European* détente.

Developments in the east of Europe constituted a second important factor influencing de Gaulle. The fall of Khrushchev in 1964 marked the end of a period of "adventurism" and appeared to set the stage for more predictable

11. De Gaulle wanted to defuse East–West tensions and nurture ties with Eastern Europe; here he is seen visiting the Polish city of Gdańsk in 1967.

and reasonable Soviet behavior in the international arena. This was all the more likely, in de Gaulle's view, because the Sino-Soviet rift was growing and would, in all probability, encourage Soviet moderation toward the West. Moreover, Moscow's satellites in Eastern Europe were beginning to show more autonomy, as illustrated by the more independent course of Nicolae Ceauşescu's Romania. In brief, by the mid-1960s, de Gaulle realized that there was a serious chance to inject fluidity into the Eastern European status quo, and he was intent on seizing the opportunity.

Last but not least, the shifting dynamics in the Western alliance also played a role in de Gaulle's evolving policies. In May 1963, the German Bundestag voted for an Atlanticist preamble to the treaty that de Gaulle and Adenauer had signed at the Elysée palace in January 1963. This, combined with Washington's pressure on European allies to set up a US-led multilateral nuclear force (MLF), was a clear illustration that Washington, while engaging in strategic rapprochement with Moscow, was also determined to block de Gaulle's design for a more "European" Europe and to insist on US primacy in the Western alliance, especially after Adenauer left office in West Germany. De Gaulle wanted to counter this trend and thought he could do so, thanks to the development of his relations with the East. For de Gaulle, an active policy of détente, in other words, was also an antidote to US hegemony: hence his determination, from 1963 onwards, to step up France's *politique à l'Est*.

In de Gaulle's view, change in East–West relations required, first of all, the intensification of concrete exchanges, especially in the economic, scientific, technological, and cultural domains. Starting in early 1964, French diplomacy began to increase contacts with Moscow with a view to enhancing bilateral cooperation. This pattern was highlighted by de Gaulle's spectacular visit to the USSR in June 1966. Because of the warm welcome staged by the Soviets, the trip arguably marked the apogee of the Gaullist *politique à l'Est*. While seeking not to antagonize Moscow in Eastern Europe, the French president also tried to increase contacts with satellite countries, especially those with historic ties to France like Poland and Romania, where de Gaulle also made high-profile visits in September 1967 and May 1968. Although in the mid-1960s Gaullist France was not alone in advocating the intensification of concrete East–West ties – Bonn had begun to cultivate economic contacts in Eastern Europe as early as 1963 and US president Lyndon B. Johnson had famously declared the need for building bridges with the East in 1964 – France remained in the lead. Washington, in fact, kept a back seat until Johnson's landmark New York speech in September 1966, and Bonn remained hostage to the Hallstein Doctrine until the new government of the Grand Coalition came into office in December of that year. For a while, French diplomacy was thus in a position to set the East–West agenda in Europe, and it clearly played a role in the evolution of its Western allies' more active East–West policies. Bonn's nascent *Ostpolitik* and Washington's careful search for détente with Moscow were a response to de Gaulle's activism.

Yet beyond the intensification of France's *politique à l'Est*, de Gaulle's East–West challenge was of a broader, fundamentally political nature. Starting in 1964, he began to spell out a road map – no longer an abstract vision – of how to *effectively* overcome the Cold War. He did so most famously in his press conference of February 4, 1965, held exactly twenty years after the Yalta conference, which of course was no accident.[3] De Gaulle's reasoning was as follows: two decades of East–West confrontation in Europe had led to a dead end exemplified by the division of Germany and it could not be overcome short of all-out war. Therefore, the stalemate could be ended only by calling into question the very logic of blocs. This required the USSR's transformation into a cooperative power and the gradual emancipation of its East European

---

3 Text of the press conference, in Charles de Gaulle, *Discours et messages*, vol. IV (Paris: Plon, 1970), 325–42.

satellites, as well as the emergence of Western Europe as an autonomous political entity with redefined ties to the United States. This dialectical process would progressively establish new patterns of continental cooperation that could eventually lead to a pan-European settlement with, at its core, a reunified Germany – an outcome which de Gaulle had described as early as 1959 as "the natural destiny of the German people."[4] While this would be a long-term process – it would take "a generation," he prophesied – and would require preconditions such as Germany's definitive recognition of its borders and renunciation of nuclear weapons, de Gaulle nonetheless placed the settlement of the German question at the top of the international agenda at a time when the confirmation of the European status quo seemed to freeze it durably. De Gaulle's concept of détente, in sum, was not just about the relaxation of tensions between the two halves of the divided continent: it was about the progressive healing of East–West relations and constituted a radical departure from the Cold War system, an ambition which his motto "détente, entente, and cooperation" was meant to underscore.

"Détente, entente, and cooperation"

For the first time in two decades, a prominent European leader thus offered a credible alternative to the order of "Yalta." The challenge was acutely felt on both sides. At a time when Soviet diplomacy had exchanged its past activism for a conservative policy aiming at the consecration of its domination of Eastern Europe and of the division of Germany, de Gaulle's essentially revisionist approach was unsettling. Although Moscow was evidently satisfied by de Gaulle's assault on US hegemony and his policy toward NATO, the Soviet leadership did not welcome his desire for a more autonomous Eastern Europe. Moreover, while Soviet officials shared his views on Germany's borders and its nonnuclear status, they were clearly disappointed by de Gaulle's refusal to ratify Germany's partition and to recognize the German Democratic Republic (GDR). And while they hoped to use relations with Gaullist France to promote their vision of European security, they deplored his reluctance to endorse their project of a pan-European conference, now a key objective for Moscow. Despite common interests, the limits of Franco-Soviet convergence were quite clear. Yet France's Western partners were perhaps even more disturbed by Gaullist revisionism. Washington was

---

4 Press conference of March 25, 1959, in Charles de Gaulle, *Discours et messages*, vol. III (Paris: Plon, 1970), 84–85.

dismayed by what amounted to a refutation of the very premises of the strategy of containment and by what it perceived as a blueprint for a European settlement excluding the United States. In Bonn, many leaders were distrustful of a policy which essentially reversed the traditional doctrine with regard to the German question by making reunification the long-term outcome of détente, and not the other way round. And some were – wrongly – suspicious of a "deal," if not an old-style *alliance de revers* between Paris and Moscow in order to maintain the division of Germany.

De Gaulle's ambitious East–West policy was all the more upsetting for France's allies because it was coupled with his equally disturbing NATO policy. On the one hand, developments in the East and the emerging détente were used as a justification for France's disengagement from NATO. The military bloc that had been created at the height of the Cold War, the French argued, had become a liability for improved East–West relations. Hence there was a need to transform NATO into a less bellicose, less US-dominated body that would be more attuned to the new East–West context. France's withdrawal from the integrated organization, announced in March 1966, therefore, was not only the result of the general's quest for "independence," which he had pursued since 1958, but also designed to promote his vision of a new European order.

Accordingly, de Gaulle was more and more tempted to use France's estrangement from NATO as an asset in reaching out to the East. France's withdrawal from military integration, French decisionmakers believed, would stimulate in the long run similar centrifugal tendencies in the East and, therefore, contribute to the dismantling of blocs on both side of the Iron Curtain. In the short run, however, French officials recognized that their country's growing distance from NATO and the United States intrigued Moscow, making France an even more valuable interlocutor in the eyes of the Soviets. It was thus no accident that de Gaulle's visit to the USSR took place barely three months after he had announced his decision regarding NATO, creating an unsettling conjunction as seen from Washington and other Western capitals where his policies were now perceived as verging on neutralism – wrongly, since France's withdrawal never implied a rupture of military solidarity with the rest of the alliance.

By then, de Gaulle's East–West design had also become inseparable from what may be described as his "global" revisionism, which – although nominally directed at both superpowers – was increasingly identified with his assault on US "hegemony" worldwide. His recognition of the People's Republic of China in January 1964, much to Washington's dismay, was a clear sign of his determination to challenge US policies. De Gaulle wanted to use his growing reputation as a maverick to reach out to the Third World. He wanted to position his country as an advocate of North–South cooperation as well as a champion of self-determination. He made this clear in a speech he gave in Phnom Penh in September 1966, in which he resoundingly condemned the US war in Vietnam and vibrantly called for the emancipation of subject peoples.[5] De Gaulle's challenge to the United States – especially his assault on the Vietnam War, which he saw as likely to lead to an escalation of tension in the East–West conflict – vested him with additional capital in his dealings with the East and enhanced his global reputation as an imaginative and independent statesman. By 1968, de Gaulle's foreign policy had turned into an all-out crusade against US preponderance and against the established global order.

The watershed of Gaullist diplomacy

The year 1968, however, was to be a watershed for Gaullist France as well as a turning point in East–West relations. The students' revolt and the social unrest which paralyzed the country in May signaled a serious internal crisis. Although the situation was rapidly brought under control, the regime was deeply weakened, as de Gaulle's resignation would illustrate in less than a year's time. Moreover, the events provoked a financial crisis and weakened the French franc, thereby eroding the power base of Gaullist diplomacy. In brief, the limits of "grandeur" were now clearly visible. Perhaps even more importantly, international developments did not conform to de Gaulle's vision. As Władysław Gomułka had warned in no uncertain terms a year earlier during de Gaulle's visit to Poland, the time was not ripe for Soviet satellites to free themselves from Moscow's control.[6] The Soviet-led invasion of Czechoslovakia at the end of the summer came as a dramatic confirmation. Although the crushing of the Prague Spring was only a temporary blow to the amelioration of East–West relations, and détente was back on track in a matter of months, the détente that began to emerge was very different from the one envisioned by de Gaulle. As evidenced by the multiplication of calls on both sides, it was a détente in which the superpowers and their respective alliances played a major role, that is, the very kind of détente "between blocs"

---

5 Text of the speech in Charles de Gaulle, *Discours et messages*, vol. IV (Paris: Plon, 1970), 325ff.
6 See Jean Lacouture, *De Gaulle*, vol. III, *Le souverain* (Paris: Seuil, 1986), 541.

that de Gaulle had persistently rejected because it sustained the East–West status quo. This was what the Harmel Report of December 1967 called for. Named after Belgian foreign minister, Pierre Harmel, who had taken the initiative, the report was adopted by the NATO allies in spite of French reservations. Focused on the "future tasks" of the alliance, the report made the case for an increased role for the Atlantic alliance in East–West relations, in effect making the argument – much to the dismay of Gaullists – that the conduct of détente should become a NATO policy.

The adoption of the Harmel Report illustrated the limits of de Gaulle's revisionist design on the Western alliance. Far from triggering the "disinte-gration" of the Western bloc, France's withdrawal from the allied integrated bodies actually led to a reaffirmation of US leadership and a consolidation of the Atlantic alliance. This was made clear by the adoption, in 1967, of the new strategy of flexible response that Paris had obstructed for years, thus ending a divisive intra-alliance debate. By the time of his resignation in April 1969, de Gaulle's all-out revisionism, in short, had failed to shatter the status quo, both in East–West relations and within both blocs.

The balance sheet of de Gaulle's policies must be nuanced in terms of both their impact on the Cold War system and their effects on France's international standing. In spite of the failure – at least for the time being – of his revisionist design, de Gaulle had succeeded in shaping a vision of East–West relations that represented a valid alternative to the bipolar model. To be sure, the prevailing model was compatible with a measure of East–West change, as illustrated by the intensification of détente in Europe in the after-math of the Czechoslovakia crisis. In fact, the crisis arguably made détente easier to accept both in the East and in the West, as Soviet worries that the satellites would leave the Warsaw Pact and declare their neutrality were allayed and US fears of a dilution of the Atlantic alliance were also put to rest. Yet the American version of détente seemed more likely to preserve the division of the continent and of Germany for the foreseeable future than to create a dynamic which would bring about structural change. The Gaullist model thus remained an enduring alternative in the debate about the future of the European system in the decades to come.

As for France's international standing, it was, from then on, premised on the self-proclaimed validity of the Gaullist vision in the long term. France's interna-tional reputation stemmed from its support of an international system freed of the logic of blocs. This vision underscored France's unique approach to East–West as well as to North–South relations and illuminated its commitment to national self-determination as well as to European autonomy. In this way, the

Gaullist ambition to overcome the Cold War status quo justified the country's independent profile and its assertive foreign policy. This was perhaps de Gaulle's most significant achievement: by restoring France's sense of a distinctive international role and status, he reconciled the French to their international environment. There was a paradox here: by making the overcoming of Cold War realities the *raison d'être* of France's international policies, de Gaulle somehow turned his country into a satisfied power – and this at a time when events seemed to be freezing those very realities.

The Gaullist legacy

This paradox remained at the core of France's international policies in the last two decades of the Cold War period, most notably during the 1970s. French foreign policy gave increasing signs of satisfaction with the established order during the presidencies of Georges Pompidou (1969–74) and Valéry Giscard d'Estaing (1974–81). Indeed, in some important ways, the status quo could be seen as increasingly favorable to France's security and "rank." On the West–West level, relations with the United States were now exempt from the drama of the Gaullist period. The Cold War stalemate guaranteed the maintenance of the US commitment to the defense of Europe. At the same time, the country's claim to independence and non-alignment justified France's distinctive position within the Atlantic alliance. (The French position in the Euromissile debate at the end of the decade was an illustration: Paris could support the deployment of US missiles in Europe in response to Soviet SS-20s without having to accept these missiles on French territory.)

On the East–West level, Franco-Soviet ties, against the backdrop of the evolution of détente, were now a permanent factor in France's international posture. Pompidou and Giscard were willing to institutionalize the bilateral relationship beyond what de Gaulle had been prepared to accept and to maintain, to the extent possible, close contact with Soviet leaders. This orientation was much to the liking of Soviet officials: relations with post-Gaullist France were clearly an important asset for Moscow throughout the 1970s. While Pompidou was careful to avoid creating the impression of a Franco-Soviet "special relationship," Giscard proved ready to go quite far in that direction in spite of the deterioration of East–West relations at the end of the decade. His controversial meeting with Leonid Brezhnev in Warsaw in the spring of 1980 in the aftermath of the Soviet invasion of Afghanistan was an illustration of his strong desire to maintain an ongoing relationship with the Kremlin.

Last but not least, although the FRG had become a pivotal power as a result of its growing economic weight and political role in East–West relations, the confirmation of the European status quo now seemed to offer a long-lasting solution to the German question. The French, therefore, seemed willing to accept the stable balance of power. Accordingly, Pompidou maintained a somewhat ambivalent attitude toward Willy Brandt's *Ostpolitik* (which he welcomed as a German variant of détente, although it aimed to achieve long-term German national unity), and Giscard went even further, tacitly accepting the reality of Germany's division. In short, France, in the 1970s, could denounce the consolidation of the established order while enjoying its advantages.

Still, continuity with the Gaullist revisionist design prevailed over the temptation of accommodation. The objective of overcoming the system of "Yalta" remained a key element in France's rhetoric and policies in the 1970s and 1980s. True, de Gaulle's far-reaching vision of a Europe from the Atlantic to the Urals was now replaced by a more modest approach. Yet the French concept of East–West relations remained fundamentally revisionist: hence the increasingly supportive French attitude vis-à-vis the project of a Conference on Security and Cooperation in Europe (CSCE), which the Pompidou administration officially championed in the fall of 1969. Of course, the French realized that the Soviets' foremost objective in the CSCE was to consecrate the European political and legal status quo and the division of Europe. French diplomacy – like that of other Western allies – was therefore adamant that borders should not be recognized as permanent as a result of the Helsinki negotiation (a key Soviet aim) and that their peaceful change should be allowed. Moreover, Paris remained watchful that the pan-European process not hinder prospects for an autonomous West European entity, which remained France's long-term priority for severing the grip of "Yalta." French officials were also active in promoting the newly established European political cooperation, or EPC, as an instrument for coordinating West European diplomacy into the CSCE framework. Yet in the context of the 1970s, the CSCE was seen in Paris as the best instrument to undercut the blocs, especially in the East, where it was hoped the CSCE would contribute to the loosening of the Soviet grip. The French therefore insisted that the Helsinki process should bring together individual nations rather than organized blocs, and that issues of culture as well as freedom of opinion be included in Basket III of the conference. Moreover, French diplomats helped devise the three-step process of the CSCE, a schema that aimed at keeping pressure on Soviet diplomacy throughout the negotiation by making the conclusion of the deliberations conditional on substantive progress in human rights and economic and cultural exchange as well as security. In 1975, Giscard was the first Western leader to accept the Soviet proposal to hold the final meeting at the heads of states level, thus opening the way to the Helsinki summit which, as seen from Paris, marked the apogee of détente in Europe.

France's continued rejection of the bipolar logic in East–West relations during the 1970s was classically illustrated by Paris's refusal to participate in the negotiations on mutual and balanced force reductions (MBFR) and by its defiance of the Strategic Arms Limitation Treaty (SALT), which the French regarded as a Soviet–American attempt to establish a condominium over the divided continent. French diplomacy, meanwhile, also pursued its long-term revisionist course within the Western alliance. Although Pompidou had tried to revive the idea of European strategic autonomy, it had remained a distant goal since the 1960s. Yet at the end of the 1970s, Giscard, together with Chancellor Helmut Schmidt of West Germany, resumed efforts toward this goal, as illustrated by their willingness to step up Franco-German political-military cooperation in the framework of the Elysée Treaty. With the erosion of détente after the Soviet invasion of Afghanistan, a more assertive Western Europe was again seen as a possible mediator between an aggressive Soviet Union and an overly reactive United States. In the long term, the French and the Germans might thereby help to ease the bipolar confrontation. French public opinion continued to support this aspect of Gaullism. While de Gaulle's policies a decade earlier had been at times hotly debated, by the end of the 1970s a much-famed "national consensus" by and large prevailed among the political class and in the wider public on the importance of an independent foreign and security policy, an autonomous Europe, and an end to blocs dividing the continent.

As seen from Paris, the events of the late 1980s were in line with the foregoing. A few years after his election in 1981, François Mitterrand found himself presiding over Europe's exit from the East–West conflict. A socialist and a longtime opponent of de Gaulle, Mitterrand had come to espouse de Gaulle's vision, declaring in 1981: "all that contributes to the exit from Yalta is good."[7] Although Mitterrand had adopted a strongly pro-Western stance in the "new" Cold War after 1979 – his January 1983 speech in the Bundestag in support of the deployment of US missiles was a defining moment – the French president proved eager to engage Mikhail Gorbachev after he came to power

---

7 François Mitterrand's New Year's Eve statement on French TV, December 31, 1981, *Politique étrangère de la France. Textes et documents* (Nov.–Dec. 1981), 85.

in March 1985 and to take the lead in a "new" détente. At the same time, he and Chancellor Kohl nurtured Franco-German cooperation and European integration (the main objective, starting in 1988, was economic and monetary union). By 1989, against the background of rapid changes in the USSR and in Eastern Europe, France's international policy sought to overcome Yalta progressively and establish a new European order in line with France's long-term Gaullist vision. Democratization in the East and integration in the West, Mitterrand believed, would gradually allow Europeans to overcome the East–West divide and end the dominance of the superpowers.

This progressive scenario for the end of the Cold War was clearly outpaced by the fall of the Berlin Wall and the dramatic developments that followed. Yet the French by no means attempted to slow down, let alone impede, these events, as often argued. In spite of brief misunderstandings in the fall and winter of 1989–90, Mitterrand and Kohl quickly determined to use *German* unification as an opportunity to make a decisive step in *European* unification. The 1992 Maastricht Treaty and the creation of the European Union were therefore the real endpoint of France's policies at the conclusion of the Cold War and was the logical outcome of four decades of Franco-German reconciliation and European construction. These had been the two central objectives of French policy throughout the period; they constituted the groundwork for the kind of "European" Europe that had been at the center of the Gaullist vision since "Yalta."

9

European integration and the Cold War

N. PIERS LUDLOW

European integration and the Cold War were separate but intertwined. Chronologically, the two share the same formative decades – although the basic idea of uniting the separate states of Europe into a single political and economic entity long predates the East–West conflict. Both European unity and the course of the Cold War became, moreover, central preoccupations of Western leaders on both sides of the Atlantic throughout the 1947–89 period. Yet more often than not, European integration and the Cold War have been studied in near total isolation from one another, the subject of separate journals, academic conferences and books, and the primary interest of two distinct groups of specialist scholars who have rarely exchanged ideas. This chapter will hence begin with a brief explanation of why this separation has occurred, before going on to argue that the interaction between the evolution of the Cold War and the gradual development of today's European Union (EU) was so intimate as to make it vital for historians to break down the barriers between the two fields.

One of the reasons why the two historiographies have diverged is that the most consistently successful forms of European integration have been primarily concerned with economic matters rather than military or political cooperation. Of the two economic and military plans launched within months of each other in 1950, the Schuman Plan – intended to pool the coal and steel industries of France, Germany, Italy, and the Benelux countries – succeeded in bringing the European Coal and Steel Community (ECSC) into being in 1952. The Pleven Plan, designed to create a European Defence Community (EDC), encountered far rougher waters, was fiercely criticised from the outset and, ultimately, voted down by the French parliament in August 1954. Furthermore, since 1958 the dominant manifestation of European integration has been the European Economic Community (EEC). And while it is true that the middle initial of the EEC gradually fell out of use, partly to indicate that the interests of the Community were not confined to economics, the economic co-operation among the member states of the EC/EU remained much more extensive than either foreign-policy co-ordination or efforts to establish a joint European approach to security. There is thus a ring of plausibility in the claim advanced by one prominent historian of the integration process that: 'The true origins of the European Community are economic and social.'[1]

The divided historiography is also partly explained by the nature of the deliberations within the Community institutions, first in Luxembourg and then in Brussels. For the policy agenda of the early European institutions had remarkably little to do with the Cold War. The central concerns of the High Authority of the ECSC were naturally enough the state of Western Europe's coal and steel industries. Those of the early EEC Commission focused on trade and tariffs, the establishment of a complex agricultural subsidy system, and the relations between the EEC and its West European neighbours. East–West relations and the struggle between the 'free world' and its Communist rival were seldom mentioned directly. Those who worked in Community Brussels operated in ways that could seem almost hermetically sealed from the Cold War, despite sharing a city with the NATO headquarters from 1966 onwards. Even European foreign ministers attending meetings of the EEC Council of Ministers appeared inclined to ignore Cold War considerations in favour of an almost total concentration on the predominantly economic agenda of the early Community.

It would be misguided, however, to believe that this day-to-day separation extended to all aspects of the Cold War and European integration. For the two phenomena were in fact deeply entangled with one another in the late 1940s and early 1950s, and went on interacting, albeit less intensely, throughout the years from 1958 to 1990. Furthermore, as this chapter will show, the whole international system into which European integration was born was profoundly influenced by the overarching East–West conflict. It was therefore inevitable that the Cold War had a substantial effect on the ways in which the countries of Western Europe co-operated with one another. There is also evidence suggesting that Western Europe's efforts to unite played a role in the evolution of the Cold War and especially in the way that the East–West struggle came to an end.

An American priority

The first significant evidence showing that the Cold War influenced European integration relates to the role played by the United States in supporting

1 Alan Milward, *The European Rescue of the Nation-State* (London: Routledge, 1992), xi.

European unity. This support was by no means guaranteed. Why, after all, should Washington have looked favourably upon a political and economic process which was quite explicitly intended by some of its proponents to create a rival to American power? There was also a danger that efforts to establish stronger regional ties within Europe might cut across the US-led drive to encourage global co-operation. Yet American backing not only materialised but proved vitally important in getting the process of integration off the ground. This reflected the belief by policy-makers in Washington that neither the economic prosperity nor the political stability that Western Europe required in order to withstand the challenge of Communism could be realised were the continent allowed to fall once more into the type of internecine rivalries which had characterised the interwar years. Franco-German acrimony in particular could not be allowed to fester. The United States thus threw itself with much energy into the promotion of European unity from 1947 onwards.[2]

It is admittedly the case that the first major American initiative designed to bring the countries of Western Europe closer together – the Marshall Plan – fell far short of its ambitious objectives as far as European unity was concerned.[3] Western European governments proved very enthusiastic recipients of US financial largesse. The American aim of transferring to Europe some of the secrets of its economic growth was also partially successful. But US attempts to use Marshall aid as a mechanism to oblige the states of Western Europe to co-operate more closely with one another accomplished little. Washington was not, therefore, presented with one single, jointly designed list of Europe's financial requirements as it had hoped; instead, Europe's desiderata took the form of a patchwork of separate national wish-lists.[4] Nor were the institutions of the Marshall Plan to become the embryo of a united European government. The British and French were able to obstruct such plans and ensure that bodies such as the Organisation for European Economic Co-operation (OEEC) remained weak and purely intergovernmental, unable to impose joint European policies upon unwilling national governments.[5] Western Europe hence proved impossible to push into any form of unity not of its own making.

This initial frustration did not deter the United States, however. For as Washington would quickly discover, it was able to accomplish much more by

---

2 See William Hitchcock's chapter in volume I.
3 See Michael J. Hogan, 'Paths to Plenty: Marshall Planners and the Debate over European Integration, 1947–1948', *Pacific Historical Review*, 53, 3 (1984), 337–66.
4 Alan Milward, *The Reconstruction of Western Europe, 1945–51* (London: Methuen, 1984), 80.
5 Milward, *The Reconstruction of Western Europe*, 169–211.

acting as external sponsor of Western Europe's own, French-led, efforts to move towards greater political and economic unity. No explanation of why the Schuman Plan succeeded, and indeed of why the EDC progressed as far as it did, would be complete without recognition of the substantial backing provided by the United States.

American policy-makers were closely involved with the Schuman Plan from the very outset. Dean G. Acheson, the secretary of state, was the second foreign statesmen to be informed about the scheme, preceded only by the German chancellor, Konrad Adenauer, without whose approval the plan would have been stillborn. Acheson indeed heard of the French initiative before it had even been approved by the full French cabinet. The enthusiasm of the US response was, moreover, of great importance as Robert Schuman, the French foreign minister, and Jean Monnet, the man responsible for devising the plan, sought to rebut both domestic misgivings and criticism from the British in particular. US representatives were also deeply involved in the negotiations which led to the signature of the Treaty of Paris in 1951. Monnet extracted maximum advantage from his extensive network of US supporters. John McCloy, for instance, the US high commissioner in Germany, played a crucial role in pressurising Bonn to give ground over the vexed question of industrial concentration in the coal and steel industries, which threatened to disrupt the whole negotiation. And US lobbying in favour of European integration was even more obvious, if rather less successful, in the lengthy struggle to secure agreement to the planned EDC. John Foster Dulles's celebrated threat to conduct 'an agonising reappraisal' of the American commitment to European security were the EDC not established was just the most famous incident in an energetic and wide-ranging campaign.[6]

Such unsubtle intervention in an ostensibly European decision actually proved counterproductive, as the Americans were to realise once the EDC had been rejected. The United States continued, however, to be involved, albeit rather less obviously, in the diplomacy which was to lead to the 1957 Treaties of Rome and the establishment of the EEC. The United States was, it is true, initially more interested in the proposed European Atomic Energy Community (Euratom) than in the EEC. This US enthusiasm, it has been recently argued, reflected a strong belief that Euratom might constitute an effective mechanism for preventing dangerous nuclear proliferation.[7] The

---

6 Cited in Michael Charlton, *The Price of Victory* (London: BBC, 1983), 186.

7 Gunnar Skogmar, *The United States and the Nuclear Dimension of European Integration* (New York: Palgrave, 2004).

Americans hence took somewhat longer than might have been expected to realise that of the two projects under consideration, the economic community had the greater potential. By 1958, however, Washington was sufficiently aware of the EEC's importance to play an active role in ensuring that the proposed European customs union did not receive too rough a passage when discussed in the General Agreement on Tariffs and Trade (GATT). A pattern of American support for the EEC was thus established which would remain unchanged until the very late 1960s, at least. Both the European institutions, and all of those in favour of greater European unity, would derive substantial benefits from having so powerful an external sponsor.

Rehabilitating Germany

A second vital link between European integration and the Cold War becomes apparent once the motives behind West Germany's participation in the integration process are examined. The Federal Republic favoured European unity primarily for political reasons. Economically, West Germany could have prospered under the status quo. The ECSC after all was partially intended to prevent Germany's steel industry from becoming too dominant, while German participation in the EEC was opposed by Ludwig Erhard, the main architect of the German postwar economic miracle. Under the leadership of Adenauer, however, Bonn pressed ahead with both schemes largely as a result of the belief that integration would further the political rehabilitation of the country and stabilise its international position.

At the heart of Adenauer's strategy lay the notion of *Westbindung* – of using institutional links such as the ECSC or EEC to tie the Federal Republic securely to the Western bloc. This would help ensure that neither the chancellor's successors, nor his international allies, would be able to undo Bonn's Western alignment and pursue the goal of a reunified but neutral Germany, floating between East and West. Instead, the Federal Republic would be firmly bound into a process of intensive economic and political co-operation with its Western partners and would be able to accept reunification only when such a process could occur on its terms and without compromising the country's Western ties. Integration would also, from Adenauer's point of view, enable the Federal Republic to rebuild its economic and political strength without alarming his fellow Western European statesmen unduly. Rehabilitating Germany was very much the policy priority for the first postwar chancellor, but he was acutely aware of the need to do this without reawakening the fears of the French in particular. Renewed Franco-German hostility would, after all, be disastrous in a

Cold War context since it would weaken the solidarity of the whole Western bloc. Accepting French ideas for European integration, by contrast, would create a framework within which West Germany's gradual re-emergence would benefit, rather than harm, its still anxious neighbours.

European unity could also offer an insurance policy should US support for Germany's exposed Cold War position falter. This belief almost certainly lay behind Adenauer's attempts during his last years in power to establish a strong link with the French leader, Charles de Gaulle – a process which would culminate in the signature of the Elysée Treaty between France and Germany in January 1963. Close ties to France strongly appealed to the German leader at a time when US Cold War policy seemed to have become much less dependable than it had been in the era of Dwight D. Eisenhower and Dulles. A European political structure, grounded on a strong Franco-German pairing, could act as a vital second guarantor of Germany's security.

Participation in the integration process could be further used by German leaders to demonstrate their ongoing Western alignment even when a degree of engagement with the Eastern bloc became possible. Willy Brandt, German chancellor from 1969 to 1974, would thus repeatedly stress that his efforts to forge a radical new *Ostpolitik* – or Eastern policy – were conceivable solely because of the success of Bonn's earlier *Westpolitik*. Only a Federal Republic safely anchored within the Western bloc could launch a far-reaching overhaul of its relations with the Eastern bloc. Brandt's activism in a European Community context, moreover, should almost certainly be seen partly as an attempt to reassure his Western partners that his government's new strategy towards the East did not imply any weakening of older allegiances. The multiple treaties which the German leader would sign normalising the Federal Republic's relations with the Soviet Union, Poland, and East Germany were thus flanked by energetic – if largely unsuccessful – efforts to push forward Western Europe's quest for monetary integration and greater foreign-policy co-ordination. This tactic foreshadowed Helmut Kohl's attempt to use an energetic commitment to European unity to reassure those alarmed by the haste with which he seized the opportunity to reunify Germany. As Kohl put it, 'German unity can only be achieved if the unification of the old continent proceeds. Policy on Germany and on Europe are but two sides of one coin.'[8] The Federal Republic's ongoing commitment to European

---

8 Cited in Helga Haftendorn, 'German Unification and European Integration are but two sides of one coin: the FRG, Europe, and the Diplomacy of German Unification', in Frédéric Bozo, Marie-Pierre Rey, N. Piers Ludlow, and Leopoldo Nuti (eds.), *Europe and the End of the Cold War: A reassessment* (London: Routledge, 2008), 136.

integration was thus an essential element in minimising the international alarm provoked by Germany's Eastern policies and by its eventual reunification in 1990.

Restoring French power

French policies confirm the interplay between the East–West conflict and integration, especially during the late 1940s and early 1950s. In the French case, the clearest link is to be found in Paris's enforced volte-face towards Germany between 1947 and 1950. The French had not wanted a powerful and sovereign German state to reappear after the Second World War. Their capacity to resist the Anglo-American drive to reconstitute a viable West German state was decisively reduced by the Cold War context, however. The breakdown of East–West relations both made it much more difficult for the French to join forces with Moscow in arguments over Germany and emphasised French dependence on American financial help. The fact that the French military campaign to cling onto its colonies in Indochina was being bankrolled by Washington – for Cold War reasons – only weakened the French position further. By the late 1940s, the French thus had no option but to accept the birth of the Federal Republic. And it was in order to accommodate this defeat that France would resort to European integration and launch the Schuman Plan. At a very basic level, France's turn to Europe – a policy innovation that was to remain fundamental to French foreign policy for decades to come – was thus Cold War-inspired, despite the seemingly economic nature of the first European institutions created. The subsequent EDC project only confirms this argument.

The Cold War context, and the way in which the possession of nuclear weapons became one of the key symbols of status in the East–West confrontation, also helps explain initial French enthusiasm for the Euratom project. This mattered greatly for the overall advance of European integration because without the lure of the proposed European atomic energy community, it is highly unlikely that France would have participated in the discussions which were eventually to culminate in the 1957 Treaties of Rome and the launch of the EEC. Euratom would, of course, have been primarily concerned with the civilian uses of nuclear power. The French were well aware, however, that advances in their understanding of peaceful nuclear power generation would also have positive effects on their parallel effort to develop atomic weaponry. European money and expertise – not to mention the substantial American assistance that Euratom at one stage looked likely to enjoy – could therefore be of benefit in France's quest to become a nuclear power. The French decision to resume discussions about far-reaching co-operation with their European partners so soon after the humiliating parliamentary rejection of the EDC had much to do with their ambition to regain a position of influence within a Cold War world.

The interconnections between the Cold War and French European policy continued after 1958 and the return to power of Charles de Gaulle. The general's dislike of 'integration' spanned both NATO and the EEC. He deeply mistrusted the role of the United States and of American allies, like Monnet, in the genesis of European integration. He also regularly attributed to American interference any incident in which his partners objected to French European priorities. Those German politicians who opposed his desires were for instance dismissed as 'the Americans' men'.[9] And he seems to have regarded the closeness of ties between the European Commission and the US government as further evidence of its unsuitability to hold any real power. The structures of European integration hence needed to be transformed, in de Gaulle's eyes, just as much as those of Atlantic military co-operation. The result was the double crisis of 1965 to 1966 when the French president engaged in a seven-month boycott of the EEC, followed almost at once by his unilateral decision to withdraw his country from NATO's integrated military command.

Paradoxically, though, the results of his systematic campaign against Western orthodoxies highlight important differences between Atlantic co-operation and European integration. In the former, France was able to assume a semi-detached position, protected by the Atlantic alliance but limited in its engagement with NATO activities. Its half-membership neither seriously undermined the strength of NATO nor had any real adverse effect on French security. Within the EEC, by contrast, the much greater centrality of the French meant that the boycott soon led to a situation in which both Gaullist France and its partners were confronted with a choice between accepting serious and possibly fatal damage to the Community system or finding a compromise that would allow their co-operation to resume. Each chose to give ground, thus protecting the multiple national interests which all of the member states had tied up in the integration process. France's need of the EEC *and* the EEC's need of France stood in stark contrast to France's relatively marginal position within the Atlantic alliance.

Intriguingly, this last reality demonstrates how European integration could affect the Cold War rather than vice versa. For some of France's more

9 Alain Peyrefitte, *C'était de Gaulle* (Paris: Fayard, 1997), vol. II, p. 264.

conventionally Atlanticist European partners appear to have concluded that they needed to be relatively accommodating towards French requests within an EEC context so as to avoid a situation in which Gaullist France drifted too far away from its Western moorings.[10] The very real economic rewards France gained from the EEC could, in other words, be used to deter de Gaulle from taking any irrevocable step in his intermittent flirtation with the Soviet Union and the Eastern bloc.[11] The notion of *Westbindung*, originally conceived as the use of European integration to tie West Germany solidly to the West, could hence be seen as applying to Gaullist France in the 1960s as much as to the Federal Republic.

British ambivalence

A fourth interconnection between European integration and the Cold War emerges from British European policy, both during the years up until 1960, when the United Kingdom chose to remain aloof from its neighbours' European policies, and during the subsequent decade when it struggled to gain belated admittance to the EEC. In the earlier period, Cold War considerations seem to have played a significant role in ensuring that Britain's own dislike of supranational integration did not spill over into hostility towards the participation of others in such a process. Thus UK suspicions of the Schuman Plan were partially held in check by the realisation that any move which helped France to accept Germany's rehabilitation and which eased the highly strained relations between Paris and Bonn was of immense value for Western unity at a time of high Cold War tension. Both the British ambassador to Paris and the Chiefs of Staff counselled UK benevolence towards the scheme for precisely these reasons.[12] Similarly, Anthony Eden's 1952 claim that 'on balance I had rather see France and Germany in a confused but close embrace, than at arm's length' is best understood in a Cold War context where Western solidarity mattered greatly and Franco-German hostility could be disastrous for Western defence.[13] The origins of Britain's stance of so-called 'benevolent detachment' towards the efforts of its neighbours to unite – its readiness to

---

10 Memorandum of conversation between US and EEC officials, January 11, 1966, US Department of State, *Foreign Relations of the United States 1964–1968* (Washington, DC: US Government Printing Office, 1998), vol. VIII, 804–09.

11 See Frédéric Bozo's chapter in this volume.

12 Roger Bullen and M. E. Pelly (eds.), *Documents on British Policy Overseas, Series II, Vol. I, The Schuman Plan, the Council of Europe and Western European Integration 1950–1952* (London: Her Majesty's Stationary Office, 1986), 30 and 73–75.

13 *Ibid.*, 846–47.

stand aside but to let its European neighbours proceed in their chosen direction without obstructing their path – are thus closely connected to the Cold War-centred priorities of British foreign policy during the early 1950s.

It would be in their initial reaction to the EEC that the British would most clearly demonstrate the way in which their European policy could be swayed by Cold War considerations. In 1955, unlike five years earlier, London no longer felt strong enough to watch benignly from the margins as six of their continental neighbours went ahead with economic integration. Equally, the British remained certain that they could not participate in the customs union being debated by the Six. They thus briefly but disastrously experimented with a policy of actively opposing the planned EEC and of urging the Six to pursue their ideas of economic co-operation in a wider European forum such as the largely ineffective OEEC. One of the key factors which brought to an end this abortive British attempt to strangle the EEC at birth proved to be American pressure, however. It was thus only when Washington made quite clear that it strongly supported the Six in their endeavour, that the UK realised that to press ahead with its European priority of halting the formation of a European customs union might well be to endanger its Cold War priority of preserving the closeness of its ties to the United States. British pressure on the Six was immediately discontinued and London began a search for a more constructive form of engagement with the emerging EEC. Within six years this quest led to the first UK application to join the EEC.

Cold War considerations played a significant role in both Harold Macmillan's and Harold Wilson's applications to the EEC. Multiple factors lay behind the Conservative government's decision to approach the Community in 1961. These ranged from Britain's growing awareness that the British Commonwealth was unlikely to remain the tightly knit and loyally supportive group of countries that had been initially foreseen to the increased salience of exports to and imports from continental Europe in the UK's trade figures. But central to the calculations of the prime minister in particular was the belief that Britain needed to become involved in the discussions then under way amongst the Six about extending their successful economic co-operation into the field of foreign-policy co-ordination – the so-called Fouchet Plan negotiations. Were Britain to remain excluded from an EC which acquired a more overtly political dimension, the UK would either see itself marginalised in an Atlantic relationship ever more dominated by discussions between the United States and a more united Europe or, still worse, find itself powerless to prevent de Gaulle from pushing the Six away from the Americans and British and into a new and dangerous Third Force

12. De Gaulle and British prime minister Harold Wilson meeting in London in 1965. De Gaulle never gave up his opposition to British membership in the EEC.

position between the two superpowers.[14] For evident Cold War reasons, neither of these eventualities could be easily accepted by London. It was therefore vital for Britain to end its isolation from the Six, if necessary by accepting full Community membership. A clear strand of Cold War logic thus ran through the soul-searching which preceded the UK's 1961 bid.

Labour's decision to submit a new membership request in 1967 also had a Cold War dimension. Again, it would be unnecessarily reductionist to

14 See, e.g., Minutes and papers, Cabinet office records 134/1853; Economic Steering (Europe) Committee, June 1960, UK National Archives (UKNA), Kew, Richmond, Surrey.

suggest that Cold War factors were the sole or even the most important cause of Wilson's rethink on British EEC membership. Disillusionment with the Commonwealth and the near total collapse of Labour's economic policy options following the sterling crisis of July 1966 were probably even more central. But there is strong evidence to suggest at least one factor that pushed the Wilson government to reconsider its European options was the diplomatic fall-out from de Gaulle's March 1966 withdrawal from NATO's integrated military command. For in both Washington and London, it was realised that the UK would only be able to play a central role in countering the Gaullist challenge and ensuring that no other countries were tempted to follow de Gaulle's independent path if London could underline its European credentials by moving closer to the EEC.[15] Britain's Cold War role as the United States' loyal lieutenant, alert to any serious threat to NATO solidarity, required a UK presence within the key European structure, the EEC, rather than a semi-detached position on the margins of European co-operation. Atlantic calculations were thus once more a factor as Britain reapplied to join the Community.

A further linkage between the Cold War and early development of European integration arose from the way in which the East–West conflict limited the number of countries that could participate in the formation of the ECSC and EEC. One of the direct effects of the division of the European continent brought about by the Cold War was to make it impossible for any of the members of the Soviet bloc to consider or be considered for inclusion in the institutions of European co-operation. European unity after 1947 was thus pursued without the participation of Poland, Czechoslovakia or Hungary, despite the manifest European credentials of each of these countries. Also progressively excluded from the integration process were those countries which chose to stand aside from the East–West conflict, like Sweden, as well as those, such as Austria or Finland, which had neutral status thrust upon them. The Cold War thus substantially reduced the number of countries which could participate in the initial stages of European integration. This was almost certainly a necessary precondition of European integration's success. For while it may be possible for the twenty-first century EU to cope with a membership of twenty-seven states, it is inconceivable that so large an entity would have been able to get off the ground five decades earlier. The way in

---

15 James Ellison, 'Stabilising the West and Looking to the East: Anglo-American Relations, Europe and Détente, 1965–67', in N. Piers Ludlow, ed., *European Integration and the Cold War: Ostpolitik and Westpolitik, 1965–73* (London: Routledge, 2007), 105–27.

which the Cold War division of Europe thus narrowed the list of countries involved in the opening acts of the ECSC and EEC drama was a vital element in its initial success.

Of similar utility to the early integration process was the way in which the artificial and Cold War-induced division of Germany ensured a de facto equivalence in population and geographical size between France and Germany. This proved extremely valuable in allowing the structures of European co-operation to be set up on the basis of equality of representation and voting weight amongst all four 'large' member states: France, Germany, Italy and (from 1973 onwards) Britain. The sensitivity of the post-1990 readjustment of voting and representation rules to acknowledge Germany's renewed status as the EU's largest state only confirms how useful in minimising tension within the nascent Community structures the earlier limitation of its size had been.

A protective Atlantic cocoon

The final and most important connection between the development of the Cold War and the evolution of European integration that this chapter will discuss was the way in which the East–West conflict shaped the very international system into which the first European bodies were born.[16] European integration may well, as argued above, have been an important factor in bringing political and economic stability to Western Europe in the decade or so after the end of the Second World War. But it was also the beneficiary of the wider Western economic and political system which developed during the same period. This system was centred on US foreign-policy leadership. Each participating country enjoyed a close bilateral relationship with the United States and tended to treat Washington rather than another European capital as the first port of call whenever foreign-policy concerns arose. The fact that virtually every European country maintained its largest embassy in the US capital rather than elsewhere in Europe and appointed its most seasoned diplomats to Washington underlined the closeness of these transatlantic relationships. This web of bilateral linkages was reinforced by a network of Atlantic institutions, some of which, such as Bretton Woods bodies, predated the Cold War but had developed into purely Western structures, and others,

---

16 The argument that follows is an adaptation of one first advanced by Peter Ludlow. See *Beyond 1992: Europe and its Western Partners* (Brussels: Centre for European Policy Studies, 1989), 5–18.

like NATO, which were clear Cold War creations. These too highlighted US dominance – the United States was very clearly *primus inter pares* in each of these collective bodies – and provided an Atlantic forum within which each European country could express its concerns, grievances or desires. Bodies such as NATO, the International Monetary Fund (IMF) or the GATT also provided a range of obvious public goods for Western Europe, guaranteeing security, monetary stability and a degree of commercial liberalisation.

This environment proved a highly congenial one for the nascent European institutions. The combination of clear US foreign-policy leadership and the very obvious ideological and military threat from the USSR helped maintain a high degree of foreign-policy uniformity among the Western European powers during the early Cold War years. Compared to previous eras, there were few bilateral foreign-policy disputes or disagreements amongst the French, Germans or Italians during the formative years of the integration process, and even when they did occur – as in the case of the ongoing Franco-German argument over the fate of the Saar, for instance – strong American pressure helped prevent the issue from spiralling out of control. The dominant role of the United States also helped minimise the scope for intra-European squabbles about leadership. Within the Atlantic institutions, all were able to accept that the United States should have the lion's share of power, and this clear hierarchy at the very top made the issue of who else held positions of responsibility somewhat less contentious and divisive than it would otherwise have been.

Most fundamentally of all, the institutions of Atlantic co-operation removed the need for the early European structures to handle some of the most problematic aspects of international co-operation. Once the issue of German rearmament had been solved, there was thus no need for the Europeans to discuss defence or security matters amongst themselves, since this could be left to NATO. Nor, after 1958 and the introduction of full monetary convert-ibility across Western Europe, was it necessary for the early EEC to concern itself with the preservation of monetary stability. This was an IMF task, and one which seemed initially to be carried out very effectively: for most of the 1960s, the six countries that made up the EEC experienced almost total exchange-rate stability with each other. The potentially vexed topic of mon-etary co-operation could be left almost exclusively to the Atlantic-level insti-tutions. As a result, the European Community could benefit from a generalised climate of macroeconomic stability and focus most of its initial energies on the eminently attainable tasks of creating a customs union and a common agricultural policy. Both of these targets had been reached by 1968.

Quite how valuable this protective Atlantic cocoon was to the early stages of European integration became apparent once the overarching system began to show signs of strain from the mid-1960s onwards. The first sign of change was the way in which détente, growing Western European confidence, and the United States' ever-greater involvement in Southeast Asia started to erode European willingness to accept US foreign-policy leadership and to encourage individual European countries to experiment with their own, more autonomous, approaches to East–West relations. De Gaulle's wide-ranging rebellion against the US role in Europe was the most obvious and extreme manifestation of this development, but was not entirely unique. Other Western European leaders also harboured misgivings about the direction of US policy, particularly in Vietnam, and aspired to a degree of influence on East–West relations. A great deal of that Western uniformity on the key foreign-policy issues of the day that had existed during the 1950s and early 1960s disappeared as a result. And disagreements among Western Europeans about the best approach to the Eastern bloc or the degree to which Europe should seek autonomy from the United States easily spilled over into disagreements within the EEC.[17] Some of the disharmony in Brussels in the late 1960s reflected declining US hegemony and greater foreign-policy divergence amongst the countries of Western Europe.

The difficulties of European unity outside the protective Atlantic framework became even more apparent at the very end of the decade and into the early 1970s as European confidence in American leadership declined still further and as the Atlantic institutions that had ensured monetary stability fell apart. Together these developments helped encourage the EEC to broaden its policy agenda and to begin to concern itself with both foreign-policy co-ordination and with monetary co-operation. But while from a long-term perspective both of these steps can be seen to have been crucial to the EC/EU's subsequent development, they were not easy ones to take. On the contrary, Western Europe's initial experiences of both EEC monetary co-ordination and foreign-policy co-operation were deeply dispiriting and did much to contribute to that mood of gloom and disillusionment which characterised the Community for much of the 1970s. Co-operation in Brussels had in other words been much easier when difficult issues such as global currency fluctuations or questions about the best stance for Western Europe to adopt towards the crises in the Middle East could be dealt with elsewhere. The

---

17 N. Piers Ludlow, *The European Community and the Crises of the 1960s* (London: Routledge, 2006), esp. 110–14. For more on these matters, see the chapters by Bozo and Jussi M. Hanhimäki in this volume.

uncomfortable realities of operating without the protective Atlantic cocoon – realities which would become even more evident after 1990 – did, however, serve to underline the extent to which the Cold War system was a highly supportive environment for Europe's nascent institutional structures.

Shaping the Cold War

If European integration was significantly affected by the Cold War, it also had an impact upon the evolution of the East–West conflict itself. There are at least three instances where the growth of co-operation amongst the states of Western Europe had a discernable effect on the character of either East–West or West–West relations within the Cold War. The first of these was the impact of the EEC's early success on Western Europe's economic prosperity and political self-confidence; the second was the way in which West Germany used the Community framework to begin the slow process of regaining the will to act autonomously in the foreign-policy field; and the third was the importance of Western Europe's all-too-visible success in eroding the cohesion and, eventually, the stability of the Eastern bloc. Each of these deserves to be examined a little more closely.

Many factors contributed to the changing relationship between Western Europe and the United States in the late 1950s and early 1960s. Changing patterns of trade and investment, the steady advance of decolonisation, and the shifting nuclear balance were all of some importance, as was the tendency of both superpowers to play out their rivalry in theatres ever further removed from Western Europe. But the dramatic success of the EEC, especially during the 1958–64 period, was undoubtedly a major ingredient in the growing confidence of many Western European politicians during the 1960s. No longer did the six member states of the Community feel bound to look, both individually and collectively, to the other side of the Atlantic in order to learn how a modern and advanced economy should be run. Instead, their own, largely home-grown recipe for growth and development seemed to be functioning extremely well. Indeed, there were even signs that the United States might be ready to copy aspects of Western Europe's policy recipe success rather than vice versa: John F. Kennedy, for instance, was quite open about the way in which his vision of a new drive for trade liberalisation at a global level borrowed ingredients from the EEC's success. And this new, slightly smug, gratification of Western European politicians at Western Europe's economic and political progress all too easily inclined them to look askance at US policy more generally and to steer a somewhat more autonomous international course. The debates about NATO reform, nuclear non-proliferation, the multilateral force (MLF), the merits of collective bloc-to-bloc as opposed to bilateral détente, and the best response to Eastern bloc calls for a European security conference were all influenced by this diminished European subservience vis-à-vis the United States.

Germany's steady emergence as a foreign-policy actor ready to speak its own lines internationally, which occurred during much the same period, also owed a great deal to the European integration process. For it was in Brussels and in response to the exigencies of EEC politics that the Federal Republic made its postwar diplomatic debut as a player of note. In the early years of both the Cold War and the integration process, Bonn's international profile had been kept deliberately low. On East–West questions as well as on the key European controversies, the West Germans had seldom sought the limelight and had preferred whenever possible to join their voices with a larger chorus rather than to behave in a fashion which brought to the fore their national interests, aspirations or fears. Germany's role in defusing the EEC crisis of 1963 had, however, been the first significant break in this pattern.[18] With France in temporary disgrace and the Community all but paralysed after the row that had broken out following de Gaulle's veto of Britain's first membership application, the German foreign minister, Gerhard Schröder, took the lead in calming the situation and creating an environment in which the EEC could resume its onward movement. In the process, Bonn acquired a taste for Community leadership. It took a while for this new German confidence to extend to diplomacy beyond the confines of the EEC. But it does seem likely that the foreign-policy activism demonstrated by Brandt, first as foreign minister and then as chancellor, was built in part upon the foundations laid by Schröder and others within an EEC context.

European integration also contributed to that image of Western European success, stability and prosperity that did so much to destabilise Communist rule in Eastern Europe as the Cold War came to an end. Few East German dissidents, Polish trade-unionists or Czech demonstrators are likely to have known much about the European integration process as they began the chain of actions which was to lead to the collapse of the Eastern bloc. They would, however, have been conscious of the way in which the quality of life within the other half of their continent vastly outstripped their own. They were probably also aware of the disparity between Western Europe's renewed international confidence in the latter half of the 1980s, built on the back of

18 Ludlow, *The European Community and the Crises of the 1960s*, 17–24.

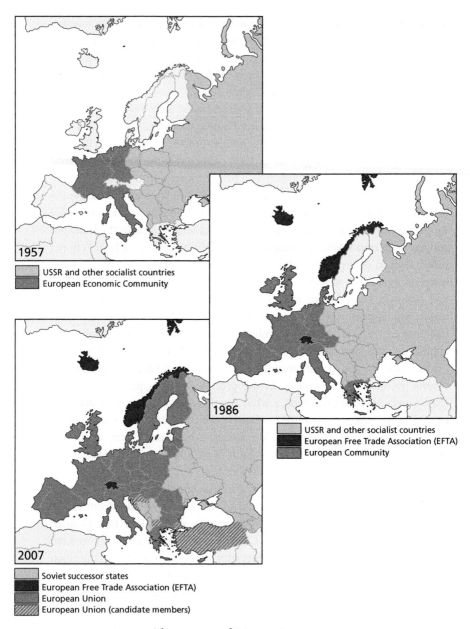

USSR and other socialist countries
European Economic Community

1986

USSR and other socialist countries
European Free Trade Association (EFTA)
European Community

2007

Soviet successor states
European Free Trade Association (EFTA)
European Union
European Union (candidate members)

1. The expansion of European integration

progress in Brussels, and the ever-greater gloom and pessimism that characterised debate about the future of the Soviet bloc. And the fear of Germany, which had been so heavily used by the Soviets in earlier eras to justify their military presence in Eastern Europe, seemed steadily more anachronistic in the face of a Federal Republic which, thanks in part to the success of its own European policies, had become the great advocate of multilateralism and international co-operation rather than national expansion.

All of these factors seem likely to have played some part in both the surge of popular protest and the total loss of nerve on the part of the ruling regimes that was to so dramatically alter the political face of Europe in 1989–90. Certainly, it was notable how quickly the successor regimes that emerged from the revolutions that had brought the Cold War to its end both adopted the rhetoric of a 'return to Europe' and began the practical steps that would lead in the first part of the twenty-first century to their adherence to the EU. The expansion of the EU in May 2004 to include eight former members of the Communist bloc should in many ways be seen as the moment when the Cold War division of Europe was definitively consigned to the history books.

European integration and the Cold War have thus never been entirely immune from interaction. They were certainly both autonomous processes. Neither caused the other, and the end of one has not brought about the collapse of the other. Each was also open to multiple other influences and dynamics, whether internal or external. But it appears clear that their paths intersected at multiple points throughout the four decades of their simultaneous evolution. No detailed analysis of either can therefore afford to disregard both those instances when the East–West struggle had an impact upon the development of European integration and those where the transformation through integration of the western half of the European continent deeply influenced both its rapport with the Western superpower and its standing as a rival and magnet to the countries of the Soviet bloc. European integration was profoundly shaped by the early Cold War and continued to be affected by the East–West struggle over the next forty years; its success, moreover, played a role in bringing the Cold War to a peaceful end and has guided the destinies of both halves of the once divided continent in the years since 1989.

10

Détente in Europe, 1962–1975

JUSSI M. HANHIMÄKI

The main purpose of this chapter is to argue that European détente was, first and foremost, a *European* project. While there is no denying the significance of the United States and the Soviet Union in the shaping of Europe's fortunes in the 1960s and 1970s, détente actually began (and continued far longer) in Europe. In some ways this should be no surprise to any student of the Cold War: after all, the Cold War had commenced to a large extent in the Old World and would, in the late 1980s, wither away there as well. So, why should the "middle cold war" have been any different? In fact, one can push the argument slightly further: while the division of Germany lay at the heart of the Cold War division of Europe and the unification of that country marked the end of that era, then something profound took place in the status of Germany as a result of the *Ostpolitik* practiced, in particular, by West German chancellor Willy Brandt (1969–74). It was ultimately his policy of multiple "openings" – most significantly to the USSR, Poland, and East Germany – that ushered in an era of détente in Europe.

More precisely, the basic argument in this chapter is that the relaxation of East–West tensions in Europe was a result of a European challenge to the excesses of bipolarity. Some of these challenges came in the form of nationalistic needs – be it Charles de Gaulle's effort to lift France's international status or, most significantly, Willy Brandt's pursuit of *Ostpolitik*. There was, as Henry Kissinger observed, no obvious unity among Europeans beyond their general resentment of being treated as pawns by the United States and the Soviet Union in a game of global geopolitics.[1] Yet, as such agreements as the Harmel Report of 1967 and the Davignon Report of 1970 would indicate, most Europeans

---

1 This is a reference to the Year of Europe controversy that followed Kissinger's April 1973 speech in which he declared that the United States had "global responsibilities," while the Europeans were limited to having "regional interests." See Jussi M. Hanhimäki, *The Flawed Architect: Henry Kissinger and American Foreign Policy* (New York: Oxford University Press, 2004), 275–77.

agreed with each other on the general need for improved East–West relations and better interallied cooperation. The most evident culmination of the new era in European politics during the period discussed in this volume was the conclusion of the Conference on Security and Cooperation in Europe (CSCE) in 1975. It was there that Europe's postwar era finally came to an end.

The shadow of superpowerdom

The early 1960s saw some of the worst crises of the Cold War. In 1961, the issue of divided Berlin and the persistent brain drain of young East Germans to the West ultimately resulted in the erection of the Cold War's most grotesque symbol, the Berlin Wall. A year later, another drama unfolded in the Caribbean after American planes photographed evidence of Soviet nuclear installations in Cuba. For a few weeks, the world – or at least those Americans tuned in to the coverage of the crisis – held their breath as a nuclear exchange appeared imminent. Both crises were, fortunately, solved (or at least diffused) through diplomatic channels. Yet, if the term "bipolarity" carried a true meaning, it was there and then, in the crisis-ridden early 1960s, when the Soviets and the Americans confronted each other "eyeball to eyeball," as Secretary of State Dean Rusk put it during the Cuban missile crisis, that bipolarity had the potential of escalating into a true global confrontation.

In Europe, the twin crises of 1961–62 were cruel reminders of the central role that the Soviet Union and the United States continued to play in deter-mining the course of international relations. It may have been the Germans (East and West) that were most immediately touched by the tension over Berlin; it was surely the Europeans (East and West) that would suffer most should war break out. But it was Soviet and American tanks that faced each other at Checkpoint Charlie in the fall of 1961. A year later, no ally – not even Britain despite the ruminations of London's erstwhile ambassador David Ormsby-Gore – was truly consulted in the course of the Cuban missile crisis. Nikita Khrushchev, for his part, had naturally seen little point in asking the members of the Warsaw Pact for their views on the matter. Europeans appeared as powerless bystanders in crises that had the potential of destroying not only their way of life, as nuclear theorists reminded people in the age of mutual assured destruction (MAD), but all kinds of life.[2]

Consequently, the Cold War appeared primarily, if not exclusively, as a game which could be decided only by the two principal protagonists.

2 See James Hershberg's chapter and Marc Trachtenberg's chapter in this volume.

Europeans were held hostage to the irreversible division of their continent, confirmed by the presence of Soviet and American troops in the center of Europe, and by the guardianship of officials in Washington and Moscow over massive and ever-growing nuclear arsenals. Worse, Europe seemed increasingly like a sideshow in the context of international relations in the 1960s. There were many other more urgent, more controversial, and, ultimately, more important issues. The Vietnam War, numerous postcolonial conflicts in Africa, and the never-ending scuffles in the Middle East commanded far more attention from American and Soviet policymakers than the diplomacy of a continent divided yet stable. To the chagrin of Europeans, policymakers in Washington and Moscow were also assigning more and more importance to the emerging triangular relationship between the United States, the Soviet Union, and the People's Republic of China (PRC).

Compounding their plight, Europeans – East and West – were economically dependent on the two superpowers. Although the place of the United States in the international economic structure was undergoing a major transformation in the 1960s and 1970s with the collapse of the Bretton Woods system,[3] the United States retained a sizable positive trading balance vis-à-vis Western Europe. Similarly, the record of foreign direct investment (FDI) shows a continued European dependency on the United States.[4] In the Soviet bloc, economic dependency was based on the continued dominance of the USSR over its Warsaw Pact client states who were compelled to follow the rules of the Soviet-led Comecon. Prevailing practices prevented any meaningful contacts between East European economies and Western Europe.[5] Europe, then, was most definitely in the shadow of the superpowers.

What is then missing from the above description is the simple fact, increasingly documented by historians in recent years, that the Cold War international system was not a simple hierarchical construction. As John Gaddis puts it: "the 'superpowers,' during the Cold War, were not all that 'super.'"[6] There was much more fluidity and bargaining within the blocs than is usually portrayed. Multipolarity existed under the cloak of bipolarity, and the weak influenced the policies of the strong. To a large extent it had been the East

---

3 For more detailed discussions of the international economy, see Wilfried Loth's and Richard Cooper's chapters in this volume.
4 These figures are from Alfred Eckes and Thomas Zeiler, *Globalization and the American Century* (New York: Cambridge University Press, 2003), 261–67.
5 This is another under-researched area of Cold War history. The best place to start is Anthony Kemp-Welch's chapter in this volume.
6 John Gaddis, "A Naïve Approach to Studying the Cold War," in Odd Arne Westad (ed.), *Reviewing the Cold War: Approaches, Interpretations, Theory* (London: Frank Cass, 2000), 30.

Germans who "drove the Soviets up the wall," as one historian has summed up the outcome of the Berlin crisis.[7] Likewise, American restraint during the Cuban missile crisis – the Kennedy administration's decision not to use airstrikes to destroy nuclear installations – was in part a result of sensitivity to the concerns of NATO allies about the consequences that might follow (for example, Soviet retaliation against Western forces in Berlin). And, perhaps most important of all, the Sino-Soviet split of the early 1960s was as clear an indication as any that the idea of a monolithic Communist bloc was but an imaginary construction.[8]

In the end, the crises of the early 1960s offered a great many challenges and opportunities to which Europeans responded in a variety of ways. In both East and West, though, it was evident that the caricature-like division of Europe and the world did not always conform to the interests and aspirations of individual nations and their leaders. Most importantly for the present discussion, East–West détente in Europe was in large part a response to the alternative policies advanced by a number of countries in the aftermath of the "Crisis Years." Indeed, any analysis of European détente needs to employ Tony Smith's concept of "pericentrism," the idea "that junior actors may have interests, passions, and types of leaders wanting to take advantage of what they perceive to be an international contest to give shape to domestic, or regional, or even global organizations of power that they conceive of in their own nationalist or ideological terms." In the 1960s and 1970s, there were several such "junior actors" in Europe, pursuing either their own national interests or the economic and political integration of the continent (or, more often, a mixture of both).[9]

Centrifugal pressures in the West: de Gaulle and early *Ostpolitik*

President Charles de Gaulle, at times described as "a neutralist for nationalistic reasons," hardly requires an introduction.[10] De Gaulle ruled France for over a

---

7 Hope M. Harrison, *Driving the Soviets up the Wall: Soviet–East German Relations, 1953–1961* (Princeton, NJ: Princeton University Press, 2004).
8 On the Sino-Soviet split, see Sergey Radchenko's chapter in this volume.
9 Tony Smith, "A Pericentric Framework for the Study of the Cold War," *Diplomatic History*, 24, 4 (Fall 2000), 591. On European integration, see Piers Ludlow's chapter in this volume.
10 A term used by the former French foreign minister, Christian Pineau. Memorandum of conversation, April 9, 1963, box 3907, Central Foreign Policy File, 1963, RG 59, National Archives, College Park, Maryland (NA). See also Erin Mahan, *Kennedy, De Gaulle and Western Europe* (London: Palgrave Macmillan, 2003).

decade after 1958, during which time he attempted to raise his country into a new position of prominence in Europe. The flip side of this was, of course, that de Gaulle wished to limit the American and (if less obviously so) Soviet roles on the continent. He withdrew France from NATO's integrated military structure, pursued the development of an independent French nuclear capability, strengthened the Franco-German special relationship (for example, the 1963 Franco-German Treaty), and embarked on independent initiatives with regard to Eastern Europe (Romania, in particular) and the Soviet Union.[11] De Gaulle even stirred trouble in America's backyard: while visiting the city of Montreal in 1967, he declared that the Francophone bastion should move towards independence ("Vive le Québec Libre"), thus helping to stir the pot of nationalism. And there were many other tense moments over Vietnam, over foreign investment, over de Gaulle's decision to recognize the PRC without consulting the United States. President Lyndon B. Johnson undoubtedly agreed with his confidant, Senator Richard Russell, when he said that "we've really got no control over their (France's) foreign policy."[12]

De Gaulle was ultimately unsuccessful because his policies were often either contradictory or overtly ambitious. He could neither make Western Europe independent of the United States nor claim for France an unambiguous leadership position among European countries. Even with the *force de frappe*, even when he took France out of NATO's unified military command in 1966, even when he attempted to practice independent détente with the USSR, de Gaulle was unable to claim that he had removed the American 'yoke' from Europe. Nevertheless, of all the centrifugal tendencies in the history of NATO during the Cold War, it was the prominent role embraced by France under de Gaulle to lead a more independent Europe that caused the severest headaches in Washington. His *potential* impact on American–European relations might have been very far-reaching. As Assistant Secretary of State William Tyler put it, de Gaulle: "gave expression to a certain sentiment not only in France but in Free Europe as a whole in varying degree: a confused sense that it is possible, indeed natural and necessary, for Europe to have interests within the framework of an alliance with the United States which do not in all cases spring from a conception of the world identical with that held by the United States."[13]

---

11 For a fuller account of French policies, see Frédéric Bozo's chapter in this volume.

12 Cited in Thomas Schwartz, *In the Shadow of Vietnam: Lyndon Johnson and Europe* (Cambridge, MA: Harvard University Press, 2003), 31.

13 Tyler's commentary in reaction to Charles Bohlen's memo, "Reflections on Current French Foreign Policy," March 11, 1964, box 169, France, vol. I, Country Files, National Security Files (NSF), Lyndon B. Johnson Library, Austin, Texas (LBJL).

American diplomats did not "panic" as a result of France's withdrawal from NATO in March 1966, and they were equally calm when de Gaulle visited Moscow a few months later. They were confident that de Gaulle's talk of a "Europe from the Atlantic to the Urals" was likely to remain just that, talk. As a May 1966 intelligence memorandum confidently maintained: "[It is] unlikely that Moscow overestimates De Gaulle's value. [It] recognizes that America is the real power, and would prefer to deal directly with Washington."[14] Indeed, had de Gaulle been the only one in Western Europe challenging the logic of bipolarity, his impact, direct or indirect, on East–West relations in Europe would likely have been limited.

Alas, he was not alone. In the 1960s, West German policymakers were expressing increased doubts about American leadership. To be sure, the leaders in Bonn had none of the global pretensions that were so evident in de Gaulle's politics and, in particular, the Frenchman's grand rhetoric. West German politicians, whether Christian Democrats or Social Democrats, were ultimately concerned over a nationalist goal, reunification. De Gaulle may have removed France from NATO's integrated military structure and embarked on an independent course with regard to Moscow in order to enhance France's significance as a player in international relations, but Ludwig Erhard, Kurt Kiesinger, Willy Brandt, and other West German leaders gradually established independent ties to the East largely because the policies of Konrad Adenauer had failed to substantially advance the unification of Germany.[15]

The first steps towards *Ostpolitik*, the so-called "policy of movement," was in large part a reaction to the Wall, the apparent lack of Western commitment to German unification, and the failure of the Hallstein Doctrine to advance the cause of unification. From the West German point of view, it must have seemed as though the rest of the world, their American allies included, were in fact quite happy to see Germany divided.[16] Some observers predicted in 1963 – in the aftermath of de Gaulle's first veto of British membership in the European Economic Community (EEC) and his signing of the Franco-German friendship treaty – that a strengthening of the Bonn–Paris axis might

---

14 National Intelligence Estimate (NIE) 11-7-66, "Trends in Soviet General Policies," April 28, 1966, box 3: 11-66, USSR, NIEs, NSF, LBJL; CIA Intelligence Memo No. 1354/66, May 20, 1966, box 172: France memos, vol. IX, Country Files, National Security Council (NSC) Files, LBJL.

15 For a discussion of Adenauer's foreign policies see, among others: Ronald Granieri, *The Ambivalent Alliance: The CDU/CSU and the West, 1949–1966* (London: Berghahn Books, 2004).

16 CIA Memo 14-64 (Office of National Estimates), "Bonn Looks Eastward," November 10, 1964, box 185, Germany memos, vol. IX, Country Files, NSF, LBJL.

result in the rupture of NATO and the unification–neutralization of Germany.[17] From the US perspective, the worst-case scenario was that:

> external events could cause neutralist feeling in West Germany to grow. In time, and especially if the sense of direct Soviet threat to Western Europe continues to diminish, the West Germans' conviction that NATO is essential for their security could weaken. Conceivably even the necessity for the continued presence of American forces might be put in question.[18]

During the following year there were, of course, a number of such "external events": de Gaulle announced France's withdrawal from NATO and made his visit to Moscow, America's involvement in Vietnam deepened, and the Soviets – facing an increasingly threatening situation in Asia (that is, the Sino-Soviet split) – appeared more amenable to developing better relations with the West. There was, then, adequate reason for the growing concern about "losing" West Germany, through unification, neutralization, or the maneuverings of de Gaulle.

While France and West Germany represented the most profound political challenges to American dominance, historians have also illustrated the increasingly limited control that Washington exercised over Western trade policy. For example, by the late 1950s, Britain had taken a leading role in the transatlantic bargaining process over export controls vis-à-vis the Soviet bloc. Thus, the utility of the so-called Coordinating Committee (COCOM) – the Western grouping established at the onset of the Cold War to control the export of "strategic" items to the USSR and its satellites – was being increasingly challenged. By the 1960s, the Americans faced a virtually unanimous – and increasingly more prosperous – West European front calling not only for improved political relations with the Soviet bloc, but also seeking to challenge American leadership on matters of East–West trade.[19] Ironically, there was similar tension within the Soviet bloc.

17 Thomas Schwartz, "Victories and Defeats in the Long Twilight Struggle: The United States and Western Europe in the 1960s," in Diane B. Kunz (ed.), *The Diplomacy of the Crucial Decade: American Foreign Policy in the 1960s* (New York: Columbia University Press, 1994), 131.

18 NIE 23-65, "Prospects for West German Foreign Policy," box 5: "23 West Germany," NIEs, NSF, LBJL.

19 See Ian Jackson, *Economic Cold War: America, Britain and East-West Trade, 1948–1963* (Basingstoke: Palgrave, 2001); Michael Mastanduno, *Economic Containment: CoCom and the Politics of East–West Trade* (Ithaca, NY: Cornell University Press, 1992).

Unity and division in the East

To a lesser degree than in Western Europe, the Soviet bloc experienced its own centrifugal tendencies in the 1960s.[20] This was the case despite the fact that even contemplating a possible exit from the Soviet-led military alliance could have bloody consequences; the Hungarians had experienced this in 1956. But the repression ultimately underlined the fragility of the alliance; it illuminated the fact that the American "empire" in Western Europe was built upon a multi-lateral invitation by the founding members of NATO, whereas the Soviet empire was based upon a unilateral imposition of Moscow's hegemony.[21]

The 1960s saw, though, an effort on the part of East European leaders to find room for independence. As early as 1960, Enver Hoxha, the Stalinist dictator of Albania, openly criticized the USSR. Although Albania remained nominally a member of the Warsaw Pact until 1968, its "defection" was symbolic of the – admittedly minor – cracks in the Soviet hold on Eastern Europe. The average Albanian did not benefit very much. Chinese aid was limited and Hoxha used the increased isolation of his country to strengthen his personal hold on power. In 1966, the Albanian dictator even launched his own cultural revolution, emulating Mao's model. Little changed: Albania remained Europe's poorest country and did little to trouble the Soviets. Nor did Hoxha have any interest in détente; if anything he called for a more confrontational approach to the West.[22]

Potentially more disconcerting than Albania's "defection" to the Chinese camp was Romania's independent course. Romanian leaders George Gheorghieu-Dej and, after 1965, Nicolae Ceauşescu were ruthless authoritarians, who combined repression at home with an independent foreign policy. The latter, at least partly geared toward increasing their domestic popularity, resulted in Romania's consistent resistance to any kind of economic integration in the Soviet bloc. In 1967, Ceauşescu took riskier action by recognizing the Federal Republic of Germany (FRG) and thus breaking Soviet bloc unity on this issue (the USSR

---

20 See Kemp-Welch's chapter in this volume.
21 The 'empire by invitation' thesis is usually associated with Geir Lundestad, but it has many adherents. Lundestad, "'Empire' by Invitation? United States and Western Europe, 1945–1952," *Journal of Peace Research*, 23, 3 (1986), 263–77. On the Warsaw Pact see Vojtech Mastny and Malcolm Byrne (eds.), *A Cardboard Castle? An Inside History of the Warsaw Pact* (Budapest: Central European University Press, 2005).
22 Very little has been written about Albania during the Cold War. For a general account, see, for example, R. J. Crampton, *The Balkans since the Second World War* (London: Longman, 2002).

though, had recognized the FRG earlier). While refusing to participate in the 1968 Warsaw Pact invasion of Czechoslovakia and inviting President Richard M. Nixon for a state visit the following year, Romania nonetheless remained a member of the alliance. It was no wonder that Ceauşescu was often described as the Eastern version of de Gaulle; someone willing to issue a challenge to the dominant superpower in the name of national pride, but unwilling to risk a complete breakdown in relations.[23]

A desire to break away from the political straitjacket of Soviet domination was further strengthened by the need to increase the limited economic links that East European countries enjoyed with the West. By the 1960s, it was clear to most Warsaw Pact leaders that Comecon – the economic organization of socialist states that had been founded in 1949 as a Soviet response to the Marshall Plan – had failed to become an engine of prosperity in the Eastern bloc. Comparisons with the EEC were negative. The EEC quickly became an integrated trading bloc with impressive economic growth; countries like Britain lined up to join it by the early 1960s.[24] In contrast, the Comecon shifted from being a vehicle of Soviet economic exploitation of Eastern Europe in the late 1940s and early 1950s to being an organization through which the USSR essentially subsidized its satellites in the late 1950s and 1960s. While trade and energy subsidies played a role in keeping the Soviet empire together, they also illustrated the vast difference between West and East European economic integration. While the former lacked a central actor and was multilateral in nature, the latter was driven and controlled from Moscow.

The important point, though, is that by the 1960s Soviet policy was clearly failing. Instead of creating uniformity across the Soviet "empire," Moscow had produced a competition among Comecon countries over the size of each nation's subsidy. Moreover, once dependent on Soviet subsidies, East European leaders (who personally relied upon Moscow's support) were reluctant to let them go. As Randall Stone puts it: "the satellites became a growing drain on the Soviet economy [that] undermined the viability of the system."[25] This burden, however, made economic détente – increased East–West trade and Western investment in Eastern Europe – more acceptable, even desirable, to the USSR. Pushing in the same direction was the constant

---

23 On Romania, see Vladimir Tismeanu, *Stalinism for All Seasons: A Political History of Romanian Communism* (Berkeley: University of California Press, 2003).

24 See the chapters by Ludlow, Richard Cooper and Wilfried Loth in this volume.

25 Randall W. Stone, *Satellites and Commissars: Strategy and Conflict in the Politics of Soviet-Bloc Trade* (Princeton: Princeton University Press, 2002), 238.

demand for high-technology goods from the West; the need for sophisticated machine tools and electrical equipment was a significant driving force behind trade liberalization across the Soviet bloc.

In sum, there was dissent in the East, as there was in the West. Throughout the 1960s, yearnings for national independence were increasing throughout the Soviet bloc. The Iron Curtain stood firm, yet minor cracks were already appearing as renegade leaders – de Gaulle and Ceauçescu in the forefront – made forays across the East–West divide. In addition, the Soviet bloc was caught in a set of economic circumstances that demanded the reduction of Eastern Europe's dependency on the high level of Soviet subsidies. With the bloc's economic integration proceeding less than smoothly, an opening to the West – that would yield economic benefits in the form of increased trade and investment – was viewed more positively by the late 1960s, exactly at the time that Brandt was beginning to pursue his *Ostpolitik*.

Bridges, reforms, and crackdown

The apparent loosening of Soviet bloc unity did not go unnoticed in the West. Already in 1961, Zbigniew Brzezinski and William Griffith had called for a policy of "peaceful engagement" with Eastern Europe designed to result "in the creation of a neutral belt of states." In June 1963, John F. Kennedy asked Americans to "reexamine our own attitude toward the possibilities of peace, toward the Soviet Union, toward the course of the cold war."[26] A year later, Secretary of State Dean Rusk pointed out that "[t]he Communist world is no longer a single flock of sheep following blindly one leader," and that, in particular, "[t]he smaller countries of Eastern Europe have increasingly asserted their own policies." President Lyndon Johnson harped on the same theme and called for extending bridges of "trade, travel and humanitarian assistance" to Eastern Europe.[27] In 1966, however, the momentum toward peaceful engagement and bridge building in the United States collapsed. When Congress defeated the East–West Trade Bill, the Johnson

---

26 "Toward a Strategy of Peace," Commencement Address by President Kennedy at American University, Washington, DC, June 10, 1963, quoted in Richard P. Stebbins (ed.), *Documents on American Foreign Relations, 1963* (New York: Harper & Row, 1964), 117; Zbigniew Brzezinski and William E. Griffith, "Peaceful Engagement in Eastern Europe," *Foreign Affairs*, 39 (July 1961). See also Jussi M. Hanhimäki "The First Line of Defense or a Springboard for Disintegration: European Neutrals in American Foreign and Security Policy, 1945–1961," *Diplomacy and Statecraft*, 7, 2 (July 1996), 378–403.

27 Quoted in Joseph F. Harrington, "Romanian–American Relations During the Kennedy Administration," *East European Quarterly*, 18, 2 (June 1984), 225.

administration's most ambitious effort to use US economic power as a tool to build bridges to the Soviet bloc ended.[28]

While the Americans balked, West Europeans rapidly expanded their links to the East. In 1964, Britain signed a fifteen-year credit agreement with the USSR. In 1965, France negotiated a series of trade and technological exchanges; the following year, as de Gaulle visited Moscow, the French dropped many import quotas from Eastern Europe. The Italians, having signed similar agreements, invited Soviet president Nikolai Podgornyi to Rome in early 1967. Indeed, among the large European countries, the Germans were the one exception.

The Harmel Report, adopted by NATO in late 1967, was the logical culmination of the growing Western interest in détente. While maintaining the emphasis on continued military preparedness, the Harmel Report's major "new" offering was to stress the significance of negotiations with the Warsaw Pact as a means of enhancing European security. This codification of a loosely coordinated dual-track policy – maintaining military strength and pursuing détente – can therefore be seen both as a road map to a different kind of East–West relationship in Europe and as a way of meeting the challenges to NATO's unity in the 1960s. In a sense, the Harmel Report illustrated the flexible nature of NATO as well as the US leadership role in the alliance. It also served as an opportunity to link French and West German initiatives to a unified approach that the alliance embraced. As Andreas Wenger puts it, the Harmel exercise represented, quite simply, the "multilateralization of détente." Furthermore, in June 1968, at a NATO foreign ministers' meeting in Reykjavik, the alliance reaffirmed its commitment to détente and declared itself in favor of Mutual Force Reductions talks with the Warsaw Pact.[29]

Significantly, it appeared that the Eastern bloc was readying itself for détente as well. In addition to unilateral Soviet contacts with a number of West European countries, there were other moves toward détente with the West. In the summer of 1966, the Warsaw Pact issued the so-called Bucharest Declaration, reaffirming its interest in an all-European security conference that

28 Joseph Harrington and Bruce Courtney, "Romanian–American Relations during the Johnson Administration," *East European Quarterly*, 22, 2 (June 1988), 225. US exports to Eastern Europe (excluding the USSR and Yugoslavia) grew from about $ 87.5 million in 1961 to $135 million in 1967. Bennett Kovrig, *Of Walls and Bridges: The United States and Eastern Europe* (New York: New York University Press, 1991), 251.

29 See Frédéric Bozo, "Détente versus Alliance: France, the United States and the Politics of the Harmel Report," *Contemporary European History*, 7, 3 (1998), pp. 343–60 and Andreas Wenger, "Crisis and Opportunity: NATO and the Multilateralization of Détente, 1966–68," *Journal of Cold War Studies*, 6, 1 (Winter 2004), 22–74.

had first been broached in 1954. In 1967, a month after Romania's recognition of the FRG, another Warsaw Pact foreign ministers' meeting repeated this call. Although these appeals undoubtedly encouraged NATO to move toward the adoption of the Harmel Report, the intended exclusion of the United States and Canada from these Pan-European security talks dampened the enthusiasm of the West. But such sticking points appeared minor when compared to the tensions of the early 1960s. Détente, it seemed, was about to break out.

Not even the August 1968 Warsaw Pact crackdown on Czechoslovakia – discussed in more detail elsewhere in this volume – could change the momentum toward European détente that had been built over the preceding years. Of course, the ruthless intervention that destroyed the internal Czech efforts to build socialism with a human face – the so-called Prague Spring – was a brutal reminder of the limits of internal reform within the Soviet zone. The public justification – the so-called Brezhnev Doctrine – made it clear that any threat to the socialist system was not to be tolerated. As Anatolii Dobrynin, at the time the Soviet ambassador to Washington, recorded in his memoir, the Prague invasion was "a true reflection of the sentiments of those who ran the Soviet Union" at the time, i.e.: "[a] determination never to permit a socialist country to slip back into the orbit of the West."[30]

Initially it seemed that the crackdown on Czechoslovakia also marked a death blow to détente in its European and Soviet–American varieties. The possibility that a Strategic Arms Limitation Treaty (SALT) – preliminarily outlined at a Soviet–US summit meeting a year earlier – could have been negotiated during the Johnson administration was blocked. West Europeans involved in "bridge building" were naturally taken aback by the invasion as well as Soviet accusations that their détente policy was tantamount to "interference" in the internal affairs of socialist countries. As Chancellor Kurt Kiesinger's envoy to the United States, Kurt Birrenbach (Christian Democratic Party [CDU] member of *Bundestag*) told Secretary of State Rusk in September 1968: "*Ostpolitik* is completely blocked."[31]

Ostpolitik in the spotlight

Birrenbach could hardly have been more wrong. *Ostpolitik* was battered by the events in Prague, but as events during the next few years illustrated, its

---

30 Anatoly Dobrynin, *In Confidence: Moscow's Ambassador to America's Six Cold War Presidents* (New York: Random House, 1995), 183; for more on the Prague Spring and Eastern Europe, see Kemp-Welch's chapter in this volume.
31 Memorandum of conversation, Rusk, Birrenbach *et al.*, September 9, 1968, Germany memos, vol. XVI, Country Files, NSF, LBJL.

progress suffered hardly at all. Following the Bundestag elections in the fall of 1969, the Social Democrats formed a new government with Willy Brandt as the chancellor. Subsequently, there was plenty of *Annäherung* (rapprochement), although to most Germans' taste, perhaps not enough *Wandel* (change).[32] With Washington's knowledge – if not always approval – Brandt and his confidant Egon Bahr initiated contacts with the Soviet Union and its East European satellites. They then proceeded to negotiate groundbreaking agreements. The German–Soviet Treaty of August 1970, the September 1971 Four Power agreement on Berlin, and the December 1972 Basic Treaty between East and West Germanies were dramatic examples of the unfolding of Brandt's *Ostpolitik*.

While Brandt proceeded from breakthrough to breakthrough, his American counterparts had mixed feelings. Although Nixon and Kissinger were bent on pursuing bilateral détente with the Soviet Union, they were not keen on seeing themselves overshadowed by an independent German policy. More substantively, the Nixon administration wanted to make sure that there were no cracks in a unified Western position that the USSR might exploit. Already during his February 1969 trip through Europe, Nixon warned (the then foreign minister) Brandt that the Soviets' interest in *Ostpolitik* was part of "a major Soviet objective to weaken the [NATO] alliance and especially the FRG."[33]

Brandt had much the same concern. He had no intention of breaking away from NATO, but sought to find ways of aligning *Ostpolitik* with NATO policy, most specifically with the 1967 Harmel Report. Brandt well understood the need to coordinate his actions with the United States. In discussions in October 1969, Bahr outlined to Kissinger his vision of *Ostpolitik*, detailing the planned West German overtures toward the USSR, Poland, and East Germany. Writing to Nixon, Kissinger warned that the planned German initiatives "could become troublesome if they engender euphoria, affect Germany's contribution to NATO and give ammunition to our own détente-minded people here at home. The Germans may also become so engaged in their Eastern policy that their commitment to West European unity may decline. The Soviets, and with some apparent prodding by Moscow, [East German leader Walter] Ulbricht, seem willing enough to receive Bonn's overtures."[34]

---

32 An allusion to the crucial idea underlying *Ostpolitik, Wandel durch Annäherung* (change through rapprochement).

33 Memoranda of conversation, Nixon, Rogers, Kissinger, Brandt, Kiesinger, February 26, 1969, box 484 Conference Files, 1966–72, CF 340-CF342, RG 59, NA.

34 Kissinger to Nixon (drafted by Sonnenfeldt), October 14, 1969, box 917, VIP Visits, NSC and Kissinger to Nixon, October 20, 1969, box 682: Germany vol III, Country Files, NSC, Nixon Presidential Materials Project, NA (soon to be moved to Yorba Linda, California). Bahr's memorandum of conversation in *Akten zur Auswartigen Politik der Bundesrepublik*

13. West German chancellor Willy Brandt kneeling at the monument to those killed by German troops in the uprising in Warsaw during World War II. Brandt's December 1970 tribute did much to allay Polish anxieties about an ongoing German threat.

Indeed, the Soviets, East Germans, and other Warsaw Pact countries were eager to see Brandt succeed, thus contributing to the success of *Ostpolitik* in 1970–72. But their motives differed. To Brandt, *Ostpolitik* was a means to a larger end; a step on the way toward the ultimate unification of Germany. To East Germans, *Ostpolitik* represented an opportunity for greater legitimacy, for true "statehood."[35] For the Soviets and a number of East Europeans, the treaties of 1970–72 meant the consolidation of the division of Germany and the recognition of postwar borders, while increasing access to high-technology items that were still available only in the West. In short, the aims of the leaders were almost diametrically opposite: if Brandt wanted to transform the existing situation, most of his counterparts in the East were hoping to freeze it.

Deutschland 1969, vol. II, 1114–18. Kissinger's and Bahr's versions are also in their memoirs. See Henry Kissinger, *White House Years* (Boston: Little, Brown, 1979), 410–12; Egon Bahr, *Zu Meiner Zeit* (Munich: Karl Blessing Verlag, 1996), 271–73.

35 The best account about East German thinking is Mary E. Sarotte, *Dealing with the Devil: East Germany, Détente, and Ostpolitik, 1969–1973* (Chapel Hill, NC: University of North Carolina Press, 2001).

But how much change did *Ostpolitik* bring about? After all, Germany remained deeply divided, something that most of Germany's neighbors probably welcomed. In fact, in 1973 both the FRG and the German Democratic Republic (GDR) joined the United Nations, a conspicuous sign that they were, in fact, two separate and independent countries. From this perspective, one might easily argue that the main outcome of *Ostpolitik* was to give added legitimacy to the GDR at the expense of the reunification hopes of the FRG. Certainly, the policy-makers of 1973 did not think that they had set in motion an irreversible process that would result in the reunification of Germany less than two decades later.

Since officials could not foresee the future, the debates regarding the long-term significance of détente are frustrating: they go around in circles. How does one interpret the changes that took place? Were they radical or conservative, transformative or stabilizing? Did détente accelerate or prolong the collapse of the Cold War order in Europe (whether the collapse was inevitable is quite another matter)? It is impossible to answer any of these questions with certainty. We know that the Cold War ended after détente, so it is, of course, tempting to maintain that the simple sequence of events proves a causal link. But we cannot 'prove' that such a link necessarily exists. In terms of *Ostpolitik* and German reunification, such links are (as they were at the time) intimately tied to domestic politicking, which, in turn, is not the best possible stimulus for objective historical assessment.

Nevertheless, one can surely assert that by opening doors and building bridges, *Ostpolitik* made the eventual *peaceful* unification of Germany easier (even if not inevitable). But its impact – as well as its origins – went far beyond the narrow boundaries of German–German relations. By improving relations with a number of East European governments as well as the Soviet Union, Brandt and his *Ostpolitik* set in motion the process of increased exchanges and contacts across the Iron Curtain that paved the way to the successful conclusion of the Conference on Security and Cooperation in Europe, a key event in the era of détente.

CSCE and the rise of human security

The signing of the Helsinki Accords on August 1, 1975, represented a seminal moment in Europe's Cold War. With thirty-five nations represented, including the United States and Canada, most of them by their respective heads of state, it was the biggest (and first) European multilateral gathering since World War II. While it did not result in the signing of formal treaties, the CSCE was perhaps the most high-profile expression of the fact that the Cold

War had moved to an entirely new stage. While observers disagreed (and historians continue to do so) about whether the Helsinki Accords were a move toward undermining the Cold War order or an effort to stabilize it, the sheer magnitude of the undertaking spelled the birth of a new kind of Europe, one no longer exclusively dominated by East–West rivalries.

The CSCE had a long history. The original proposal for a Pan-European security conference had been made by the Soviet foreign minister, Viacheslav Molotov, in 1954. Because the United States (and Canada) were not invited, the proposal was turned down by NATO countries (as they rejected Warsaw Pact appeals in the 1960s). In the aftermath of the crackdown on Czechoslovakia in 1968 and virtually coinciding with the Sino-Soviet border clashes, the Warsaw Pact issued, on March 17, 1969, the Budapest appeal, which, for the first time, did not include specific preconditions (that is, it did not exclude any countries from the list of participants). Two months later, the Finnish president Urho Kekkonen, at the USSR's urging, acted as a neutral go-between, offering Helsinki as the site for such a conference. Most significantly, the latter invitation was directed to all European countries as well as the United States and Canada.[36] Finally, in November 1972, the initial Multilateral Preparatory Talks began at the Dipoli conference centre, outside of Helsinki. After several years of arduous negotiations in Geneva and Helsinki, involving representatives of thirty-five countries, the CSCE finally concluded with a high-level three-day summit in Helsinki (Stage III) that opened on July 30, 1975.

Both the process and the outcome were remarkable in highlighting the birth of a new kind of East–West relationship in Europe. The four 'Baskets' (or parts) of the Helsinki Accords dealt with virtually every aspect of Pan-European security. While Basket I, for example, dealt with such "traditional" security issues as the inviolability of borders, Baskets II and III dealt with economic issues and, perhaps most controversially, human rights. Basket IV – rarely mentioned – was perhaps the most important of all: it called for follow-up conferences, thereby ensuring that the accords would become a "living" document. In other words, the signing ceremony at Helsinki's Finlandia Hall on August 1, 1975, was as much the beginning of a process as it was an end of the multilateral negotiation that had stretched far beyond the time limits anticipated in 1972.

Nor should one underestimate the significance of the process itself. It was quite a feat to bring together the diplomatic representatives of countries as

---

36 For useful overviews of these developments, see Wilfried Loth, *Overcoming the Cold War: A History of Détente* (London: Palgrave-Macmillan, 2002), and John van Oudenaren, *European Détente* (Durham, NC: Duke University Press, 1992).

different as Britain and Romania, or Belgium and Yugoslavia. Equally importantly, by involving both Germanies in the process, the CSCE negotiations
offered the first significant opportunity for addressing the division of the
country. Of course, the Helsinki Accords did not solve the question of
Germany's division; in fact, many in Western Germany were concerned lest
the process, by adding further legitimacy to the East German regime, actually
served to solidify the division. The CSCE did, though, fit nicely with Brandt's
Ostpolitik by offering yet another means for strengthening the Federal
Republic's ties to the East (both the GDR and other Soviet bloc nations).

Remarkable – and perhaps somewhat overrated – though the CSCE's final
document was, it was also inherently contradictory, producing diametrically
opposite interpretations. The Helsinki Accords were widely criticized in the
United States for allegedly recognizing Soviet control over Eastern Europe. In
the Soviet bloc, the provisions on human rights were basically ignored.
Nevertheless, the CSCE was of major long-term significance: it signaled the
emergence of human security as an important and recognized aspect of
international relations. The agreements would later serve as a manifesto by
numerous dissident and human rights groups inside the Soviet Union and its
satellites. The fact that the CSCE did recognize the possibility that borders
might be changed through "peaceful means" also satisfied the minimum
demands of those Germans who still held up unification as a realistic goal.[37]

Not everyone, however, was excited (or concerned) about the CSCE. Iurii
Andropov, the head of the Soviet KGB and later secretary-general of the Soviet
Communist Party, dismissed the notion that Basket III would ever have an
appreciable impact inside the USSR. "We are the masters in this house," he
reportedly told the Politburo members who doubted the wisdom of signing a
protocol that recognized freedom of speech. Others, like Kissinger, did not
even bother reading the Helsinki Accords. The American secretary of state,
whose lack of enthusiasm for the CSCE was notable throughout the process,
at one time even quipped that the Helsinki Final Act might just as well be
written "in Swahili."[38]

Such missives notwithstanding – and Kissinger himself would later
provide a rather positive assessment of the CSCE – the CSCE did mark a
certain rebirth of Europe. For the first time since the end of World War II,

37 For a thorough analysis, see Daniel C. Thomas, *The Helsinki Effect: International Norms,
Human Rights, and the Demise of Communism* (Princeton: Princeton University Press,
2001).
38 Jussi M. Hanhimäki, "'They Can Write it in Swahili': Kissinger, the Soviets, and the
Helsinki Accords, 1973–1975," *Journal of Transatlantic Studies*, I, I, (Spring 2003), 37–58.

the CSCE provided a forum in which all-European negotiations could take place. In Helsinki and Geneva, under the umbrella of the CSCE, East–West contacts were fostered in a way that could hardly have been foreseen a decade earlier. West Europeans, in particular, found the CSCE to be a vehicle for putting the recommendations of the 1970 Davignon Report into practice, in effect launching what today is called a European Common Foreign and Security Policy. NATO members and neutrals tended to dominate much of the negotiating process because the Americans showed but minimal interest and the Soviets (and selected East European governments) tried to keep the agenda – and the results – as limited as possible.[39]

At the same time, the Iron Curtain was punctured economically. Already, by the late 1960s, the unity of the Atlantic alliance regarding its trade embargo against the Soviet bloc in strategic goods had evaporated. Europeans had gradually drifted away from the rigid American approach to the embargo.[40] Consequently, aggregate East–West trade (exports plus imports) rose nearly sixfold in nominal terms from 1970 through 1979. The increase, however, was imbalanced in at least two ways. First, only a few key countries (such as West Germany and Romania) saw a substantial increment in their trade with countries outside their own bloc. Second, while Western Europe produced a host of goods in demand in the East, there was little that Soviet bloc countries could offer in return. Unlike the USSR, they had no massive energy sources (gas or oil). Thus, Eastern Europe's purchases from the EEC countries were financed heavily with loans provided by banks in Western Europe. In the 1980s, the credits would effectively bankrupt a number of Soviet bloc countries and deepen the crisis of Communism.[41]

Perhaps most importantly, West Europeans were able to include questions of individual freedom and political rights in the CSCE agenda, an important – if initially perhaps mainly cosmetic – victory. As T. A. K. Elliott, the British ambassador to Finland who was deeply involved in the negotiations, put it in

---

39 This is evident both from the documentation now available as well as from the memoirs of most participants. See the sources cited above, especially Thomas, *Helsinki Effect*; for the Davignon Report and European foreign policy cooperation, see Michael E. Smith, *Europe's Foreign and Security Policy: The Institutionalization of Cooperation* (New York: Cambridge University Press, 2004).

40 See Mastanduno, *Economic Containment*.

41 See Harriet Friedmann, "Warsaw Pact Socialism: Détente and the Disintegration of the Soviet Bloc," in Allen Hunter (ed.), *Re-Thinking the Cold War* (Philadelphia: Temple University Press, 1998), 213–31.

1974: "One thing the Conference has already achieved: to get it accepted for the first time by Communist states that relations between peoples – and therefore the attitudes of Governments towards their citizens – should be the subject of multilateral discussion." This principle, he added, was important because it might "eventually be able to get the Soviet Union to lower, even a little, the barriers to human contacts and the flow of information and ideas between East and West."[42]

Herein lay the key to the long-term significance of the CSCE and of European détente. Unlike superpower détente, it did not focus on nuclear weapons or traditional security issues. What the CSCE, one of the key products of European détente, brought clearly to the international arena was a focus on human security, on the rights of people rather than the prerogatives of states.

Complexities of European détente

Détente in Europe was a complex and constantly evolving process. It sprang from the national aspirations of several countries; it represented a rebellion of sorts against the formation of tight blocs that had emerged in previous decades. De Gaulle's efforts to lift France's status and Ceauşescu's attempts to take Romania down a more independent road were two examples of such nationalism. But so was the *Ostpolitik* of Willy Brandt, at least if one regards the chancellor's policies as an effort to advance the cause of German reunification. Still, men like Brandt touched chords and inspired people beyond their national boundaries. Among a large number of Europeans, whether they were members of NATO or the Warsaw Pact or neutrals, there was a strong desire to overcome the rigidities of the blocs and to puncture holes in the Iron Curtain. Because of his unique background, Brandt in many ways was the perfect symbol of the new European era: a social democrat and victim of Nazi persecutors, he had served as the mayor of Berlin in the early 1960s when the Soviets and East Germans had erected the wall. Because he had earned his anti-totalitarian and anti-Communist credentials, Brandt was the right person to talk peace to the Soviets.

---

42 T. A. K. Elliott to J. Callaghan, July 29, 1974, in *Documents on British Policy Overseas*, Series III, vol. II, *The Conference on Security and Cooperation in Europe, 1972–1975*, ed. G. Bennett and K. A. Hamilton (London: Whitehall History Publishing, 1997), 317–26.

Recognizing the aspirations of its allies to reach out to their brethren in East Germany and Eastern Europe, US officials were impelled to pursue a policy of building bridges to the eastern part of the continent. When they put their weight behind the Harmel Report in 1967, American officials were saying that they accepted détente as an appropriate policy to be undertaken multilaterally to relax tensions in Europe while they focused on other parts of the world that they now deemed increasingly important. The détente in Europe that was launched in the late 1960s, however, was very different from its Soviet–American counterpart. It was nurtured and driven by European leaders like Brandt and was embodied in European institutions like the CSCE, setting it apart from its superpower variant.

The practical results of European détente, however, are difficult to measure. Unlike Soviet–American détente, which had its specific mileposts like SALT I and the Anti-Ballistic Missile (ABM) Treaty, the relaxation of East–West relations in Europe was a relatively open-ended process. Because it was not propelled by a single country, it did not have a single coherent goal. Although economic intercourse grew between East and West, it did not transform continent-wide patterns. Although Brandt signed numerous agreements with his counterparts in the East, they were, in the end, less important for what they stated or recognized than for the contacts and processes that were begun. Likewise, the CSCE was not a formal treaty and could be interpreted in numerous contradictory ways; yet the Helsinki Accords for all their ambiguities – perhaps because of their ambiguities – were of great consequence.

Perhaps because it did not have such identifiable and formal "end products," European détente did not suffer a rapid decline and collapse. Unlike Soviet–American détente which was widely proclaimed dead by 1979 (if not earlier), the European process lingered on into the 1980s. The CSCE, for example, was institutionalized in the framework of the follow-up conferences (Belgrade, 1977–78; Madrid, 1980–83; Ottawa, 1985). These had been outlined in Basket IV of the Helsinki Final Act. Indeed, unlike the ABM Treaty of 1972, the CSCE still exists in the form of the Organization for Security and Co-operation in Europe (OSCE). This, in turn, reflected one of the most important developments in the all-European process that had gradually emerged in the 1960s and early 1970s. Getting to the point of signing the Helsinki Final Act on August 1, 1975, had required a collective change in the mindsets of leaders on both sides of the Iron Curtain. Although the division of Europe remained intact for another decade and a half, détente and the Helsinki process had begun to nurture an all-European challenge to the division of the continent.

When Willy Brandt accepted the Nobel Peace Prize in December 1971, he said: "Europe has its future ahead of itself. In the West it will grow beyond the European Economic Community and develop into a union which will be able to assume part of the responsibility for world affairs, independently of the United States but firmly linked with it. At the same time there are opportunities for developing cooperation and safeguarding peace through the whole of Europe, perhaps of establishing a kind of European Partnership for Peace."[43] Later events would show that Brandt's vision was far more prophetic than that of most of his counterparts in the West or the East.

43 Willy Brandt, "Peace Policy in Our Time," Nobel lecture, December 11, 1971, in Irwin Abrams (ed.), *Nobel Lectures: Peace, 1971–1980* (Singapore: World Scientific, 1997), 24–25.

Eastern Europe: Stalinism to solidarity

ANTHONY KEMP-WELCH

Suppression of the Hungarian uprising in 1956[1] gave Eastern Europe a harsh reminder of the ground rules operating within the Soviet bloc.[2] First, no member could leave the Warsaw Pact. Second, the states of Eastern Europe had to maintain a Communist monopoly at all times. These two principles were designed to prevent radical change within Eastern Europe. They secured Moscow's geostrategic interests in the region by setting boundaries that could not be crossed. That did not prevent leaders from taking local initiatives should they so wish, but their willingness to do so differed markedly between countries.

The Polish leader Władysław Gomułka had been brought back to power in October 1956. One of his first external acts was to renegotiate Poland's relations with the Soviet Union. Though the relationship remained subservient, a degree of formal sovereignty was restored. At home, he preserved the main domestic changes made during 'October': the return of agriculture to private hands and improved relations between Church and state. However, realising that the invasion of Hungary was a fate that Poland had missed perhaps by only a few days, he rejected any further reforms. Even modest proposals to reintroduce market elements into central planning were dismissed as attempts to 'undermine socialism'. Poland entered a decade of stagnation.

By contrast, the East German leader Walter Ulbricht became somewhat more flexible. Having gained the reputation of a dogmatist during the 1950s, he began to emerge as more open-minded. Building the Berlin Wall in 1961 helped to stabilise the domestic labour market. The new economic programme unveiled in 1963 introduced new criteria for efficiency. It used financial indicators, profits, sales and costs, rather than the Stalinist quantitative targets. Although under increasing attack from 1965, and quietly

---

1 See Csaba Békés' chapter in volume I.
2 East Germany, Poland, Czechoslovakia, Hungary, Romania and Bulgaria.

terminated at the end of the 1960s, its focus on consumerism and material improvements continued. Economic benefits for the population included modest wage rises and increased leisure, with the introduction of the five-day week, though these achievements were overshadowed by West Germany's 'economic miracle'.

Similarly, the Hungarian leader János Kádár began to relax the regime that brought him to power in 1956. While anxious to avoid workers' councils (a key feature of the Hungarian uprising), he tried to extend industrial democracy through extending trades union rights, including a right to veto management decisions. Greater openings to the West were permitted, particularly for credits and technology, leading 'New Left' activists to criticise the increasing 'commercialisation' of the Hungarian way of life.

The main barrier to change, both in Hungary and across the bloc, was party officials. Fearful of losing their power and privileges, apparatchiks fought fiercely to retain their role in managing the planned economy. Whenever radical reform was proposed, they would appeal to Moscow to support the status quo. The effectiveness of such lobbying depended on the prevailing climate in Soviet politics.

The early 1960s seemed a propitious time for change. Nikita Khrushchev's second round of de-Stalinisation, launched in 1961, addressed systemic questions that his 'secret speech' attacking Iosif Stalin in 1956 had evaded. A much fuller account of Stalinist crimes started to appear. Khrushchev agreed to publish Aleksandr Solzhenitsyn's first stories of Gulag life. As Soviet literature began to include Stalin's collectivisation campaign and consequent mass famine (1932–34), the false optimism of socialist realism went into terminal decline. Stalinist orthodoxies were discarded, and there was a recovery of intellectual vitality unknown in Soviet life since the 1920s.

Khrushchev's new party programme boldly declared that the Soviet Union was on the road to full Communism, which would see material abundance, equality and self-government. Completion dates were even provided: public transport and education were to be free by 1980. But meeting such ambitious targets required radical restructuring, starting with the economy.

Soviet economists began to question the ability of central planning to cope with the complexity and speed of change required by modernity. A seminal article by Professor Y. G. Liberman suggested that Soviet enterprises should be geared to profits earned, not merely to output targets. He suggested that state enterprises be opened to market forces; prices and other performance indicators should no longer be set by the centre. His publication in the party daily[3] led East European reformers to believe that radical changes in economic management were becoming possible.

However, a fundamental question for both the friends and the foes of change was how far economic devolution could go without similar changes in the political sphere. Following Khrushchev's ouster in October 1964, grand reforms were shelved. Instead of his dramatic, if sometimes erratic, shifts of policy, the new leadership sought stability. Their first test in Eastern Europe was Czechoslovakia. The impulse for reform from above, which eventually grew into the Prague Spring, came from economic failure.

Reform from above

In 1963, Czechoslovakia became the first country in postwar Eastern Europe to record negative growth. The Five-Year Plan was abandoned. Faced with the collapse of its economic policies, an outspoken Czech economist, Professor Ota Šik, proposed far-reaching reforms.

Šik stated that the all-powerful Planning Commission should no longer set targets for the whole economy but concentrate on long-term trends and perspectives. This would free up the microeconomy in which individual enterprises could take genuine initiatives. Šik proposed the centre should listen and respond to popular opinion. There should be consumers' rights and 'the right and real possibility of various groups of the working people and different social groups to formulate and defend their economic interests in shaping economic policy'. The workforce should also have real power. Employees should be able to replace factory directors.[4]

Though such reforms gained formal acceptance in 1965, middle-ranking officials started to dilute them. They could not envisage a 'socialist market economy' in which their own commanding voice was muted and might one day disappear. Faced with their delaying tactics, Šik stated publicly in the summer of 1966 that economic reform could not take place without political reform.

Similar conclusions had been drawn by a commission on the political system, whose chief author was Zdeněk Mlynář, a fellow student at Moscow State University in the early 1950s with Mikhail Gorbachev. His report called the political system dictatorial and monopolistic. It was based on the 'false thesis that the Party is the instrument of the dictatorship of the proletariat'.

---

3 'Plan, profit and bonuses', *Pravda*, 9 September 1962.
4 H. G. Skilling, *Czechoslovakia's Interrupted Revolution* (Princeton, NJ: Princeton University Press, 1976), 114.

This was tantamount to admitting that Lenin's concept of the party as a 'proletarian dictatorship' meant in practice the party's dictatorship over the proletariat.

Mlynář urged the party to engage in genuine discussion at all levels. The Central Committee should hold authentic debates rather than simply ratify decisions taken in advance. But it should not decide everything. 'The Party does not want to, and will not, take the place of social organizations.'[5] On the contrary, it should introduce a more democratic system allowing 'different social interests and needs to play a real part in the creation and execution of policy'.

How such a transformation could come about was unclear. Mlynář admitted it was a social and political experiment. He later noted: 'this was a development towards political pluralism under conditions in which the economic, social, political and institutional supports of classic bourgeois political pluralism had been destroyed'.[6] He hoped that the party could gradually build up new supports from below. Meanwhile, the Soviet reaction to the burgeoning Prague Spring was crucial.

Leonid Brezhnev came to accept that Antonín Novotný, Czechoslovak Party leader since 1953, had lost touch with the popular mood. He was replaced by the Slovak Party leader Alexander Dubček. On the twentieth anniversary of the 'Prague coup' that had installed Communism in Czechoslovakia, Dubček called for 'a true invigoration and unification of all constructive and progressive forces in our Republic'. He called on the Communist Party to make 'a new start to socialism'. Nobody should be shielded from scrutiny: all problems should be looked 'boldly in the face'.[7]

The Soviet Politburo soon became doubtful about Dubček's capacity to control events. The Soviet ambassador in Prague reported in mid-January 1968 that while Dubček was 'unquestionably an honourable and faithful man and a staunch friend of the Soviet Union', his leadership was weak. Faced with divisions in the party, Dubček was 'vacillating'.[8] The Kremlin resolved to keep a close watch on developments. Alarm bells rang when Dubček started to replace orthodox party officials in key ministries, including the Interior and in

---

5 *Ibid.*

6 Z. Mlynář, 'Notions of Political Pluralism in the Policy of the Communist Party of Czechoslovakia in 1968', Working Paper No. 3 (Vienna, 1979), 3–4.

7 J. Navrátil (ed.), *The Prague Spring 1968: A National Security Archive Documents Reader* (Budapest: Central University Press, 1998), 53–54.

8 M. Kramer, 'The Czechoslovak Crisis and the Brezhnev Doctrine', in C. Fink, Philipp Gassert and Detlef Junker (eds.), *1968: The World Transformed* (Cambridge: Cambridge University Press, 1998), 122–23.

the armed forces. Their replacements were all reformists and less amenable to Soviet pressure. Worse still for the Soviets, Moscow was not being consulted over their appointments.

As Czechoslovak censorship was lifted and a wide range of opinions began to appear in journals and the press, fears of 'democratic infection' started to be expressed by East European leaders. Ulbricht complained that Czech writers admired the West and frequently became 'a tool for Bonn's global strategy against the socialist countries'. Their uncensored writings were being beamed back to East German audiences by West German television. Like Moscow, Ulbricht lacked confidence in Dubček's ability to restore control. Gomułka warned Dubček, 'If your situation gets worse, our hostile elements will rear their head again. We already have trouble with writers and students'.[9]

The trouble in Poland began with a classical drama staged at Warsaw's National Theatre about the country's struggle for freedom under the Russian partition. Audience reactions to the anti-Russian passages steadily grew and alarmed the authorities who banned the play. After the last performance, three hundred spectators marched to the playwright's statue nearby, festooning it with flowers and banners. This first street manifestation for more than a decade shook the party leadership.

Fliers appeared stating 'Poland awaits her own Dubček'.[10] A mass meeting was held at Warsaw University in defence of democratic freedoms and university autonomy. Speakers pointed out that freedom of speech, press and assembly were guaranteed by the Polish Constitution (Article 71). But as students started to leave, heavily armed police charged them, chasing many across the campus, some down to the river, beating and clubbing indiscriminately all they could reach. There were dozens of arrests.

Academics supporting the student protest were dismissed and the faculties of Economics, Philosophy, Sociology and Psychology were disbanded. Hundreds of students were expelled and the purge was extended to other university cities. A parallel purge took place in the high offices of state when hundreds of senior officials were summarily sacked for alleged 'pro-Zionist' views, Jewish origin, or both. As a result of the pogrom, Poland lost about 13,000 citizens through emigration.

Whilst Gomułka used repression, Dubček pressed on with reform. An 'Action Programme', published on 10 April 1968, outlined a new role for the

---

9 A. Garlicki and A. Paczkowski (eds.), *Zaciskanie pętli: Tajne dokumenty dotyczące Czechosłowacji 1968r.* [The Tightening of the Noose: Secret Documents Concerning Czechoslovakia in 1968] (Warsaw: Wydawnictwo Sejmowe, 1995).
10 Jerzy Eisler, *Marzec 1968* (Warsaw: PWN, 1991), 346.

Communist Party. Rather than holding a monopoly of power, it would compete for influence. The competition was to be strictly circumscribed: the party would not share power and its 'leading role' would be retained. But although alternative parties were still forbidden, the Communist Party began to acknowledge the legitimacy of non-party institutions. Organisations under its formal tutelage, such as the Socialist and People's Parties and trade unions, began to show some signs of autonomy. New associations were set up outside party auspices. Most prominent were the Club of Non-Committed Party Members (KAN) and Club K-231 (an organisation of former political prisoners). In short, the Prague Spring was becoming pluralistic.

Under pressure from Moscow, the Czechoslovak leaders tried to rein in these developments. Even the reformist Mlynář agreed that the police should investigate the new formation K-231, on the grounds that at least some of those arrested in the Stalinist period had deserved their sentences. Dubček made clear that all new organisations should come under the rubric of the National Front, a party-controlled body. He also assured Moscow that the Action Programme based foreign policy on the firm alliance and further co-operation with the Soviet Union and other socialist states.

Prague tried to placate its allies in the Warsaw Pact with repeated assurances that the country's international alignment would not change. In return for loyalty to the Warsaw Pact, Czechoslovak reformers hoped that Moscow would accept domestic initiatives. Above all, they wanted a significant expansion of personal freedoms and civil liberties, including equal status for Czechs and Slovaks within a federal state. Their economic priority was to shift from over-concentration on heavy industry to consumer production. They sought to boost living standards through the liberalisation of foreign trade.

Instead of being reassured, Soviet leaders began to plan military intervention. They announced manoeuvres on Czechoslovakia's borders. In the Kremlin's view, 'reactionaries and counter-revolutionaries abroad' were blocking normalisation in Czechoslovakia. If not stopped at once, they would move on to destabilise the other socialist states. Moscow insisted that Dubček rein in public debate by restoring censorship. He could hardly do so without jettisoning a major vehicle of the Prague Spring. Instead, he simply appealed to the press and journals to rally round the party's Action Programme.

To this appeal, a prominent writer responded bluntly that after twenty years of unchallenged rule, party leaders had lost the public's confidence. The only remedy for political stagnation was grass-roots renewal. Officials who acted brutally, embezzled, or were simply incompetent should be removed by popular pressures. Ordinary citizens should use peaceful means such as non-violent strikes and picketing to achieve political and economic change. However, in a clear reference to threats from the country's allies, the writer's manifesto declared, 'We can show our Government that we will stand by it, with weapons if need be.'[11]

Soviet leaders watched with alarm as the Czechoslovak Party moved away from orthodox Leninism towards social democracy. They feared this process would be completed by an Extraordinary Party Congress, summoned for early September. Other Warsaw Pact leaders had concerns about 'contagion'. They knew the spread of political freedoms in Czechoslovakia would ignite similar aspirations among their own population. At their behest, an emergency summit was held in Warsaw. Unlike earlier summits, Dubček declined to attend.

The Romanian leader Nicolae Ceauşescu was also absent. From the late-1950s, Romania had pioneered a more independent foreign policy. All Soviet troops stationed in the country left by agreement, and Romania skilfully used space opened up by the Sino-Soviet dispute to differentiate itself from Moscow. Ceauşescu took the line that since there was no longer a single 'model' of socialist development, the Warsaw Pact had no right of intervention to end 'deviations'. When Czechoslovakia was invaded, Ceauşescu later condemned the action.

But all those attending the summit had lost patience with Prague. Even the Hungarian leader Kádár was no longer supportive. His New Economic Mechanism had launched a fresh era of liberal economic reform at home. But he saw the Czechoslovak Party as endangered by 'revisionist forces' tending in a social-democratic direction. Though reluctant to call the Prague Spring 'counter-revolutionary', he thought the next stage would be a 'restoration of the (pre-war) bourgeois order'.[12]

The Bulgarian leader, Todor Zhivkov, had fewer inhibitions. 'We cannot agree with the view offered by Comrade Kádár or with his conclusions,' said Zhivkov. He thought 'counter-revolutionary centres controlled by the American and West German imperialists' were seeking to tear Czechoslovakia from the Soviet bloc. Only armed force by the Warsaw Pact could retrieve the situation. In their 'Warsaw Letter', the summit leaders informed Prague that attempts to remove Czechoslovakia from the 'socialist commonwealth' would meet a sharp rebuff.

Preparations for an invasion had been honed by extensive Soviet manoeuvres on Czechoslovak soil since early summer. To differentiate it from 1956, when Soviet forces acted alone, some 80,000 soldiers from Poland, Bulgaria,

---

11 Ludvík Vaculík, 'Two Thousand Words that Belong to Workers, Farmers, Officials, Scientists, Artists, and Everybody', in Navrátil (ed.), *The Prague Spring 1968*.
12 Warsaw Pact Meeting (14–15 July 1968), in Navrátil (ed.), *The Prague Spring*, 217.

14. A Soviet tank in Prague, August 1968. Moscow intervened to curb the independence of the Czechoslovak Communist Party.

Hungary and East Germany were added to the force. However, the great bulk came from the USSR and the whole operation was under Soviet command.

Leonid Brezhnev called the August 1968 invasion 'an extraordinary step, dictated by necessity'. He explained the unprovoked attack through a convoluted ideological timescale. The historical struggle between socialism and imperialism, foreseen by Marx and Lenin, had reached a 'new stage'. Having been held at bay by the threat of nuclear retaliation by the North Atlantic Treaty Organization (NATO), Western imperialism was still playing its old game. Western leaders were using 'anti-socialist' elements in senior positions in Prague to subvert the Communist Party. They intended its gradual conversion to a Western orientation, through economic ties, and its eventual secession from the Warsaw Pact. The Kremlin claimed that the Prague Spring would be followed by a change of regime in Poland, assimilation of East into Western Germany and further departures from the Warsaw Pact. Faced with these audacious aspirations, the socialist commonwealth acted in self-defence. Czechoslovakian state sovereignty had to take second place to the 'sacred duty' of acting on behalf of 'socialist solidarity'.[13]

13 'Sovereignty and the International Responsibility of Socialist Countries', *Pravda*, 26 September 1968.

Brezhnev's argument was circular. The Warsaw Pact would invade (itself) wherever socialism was in danger: but the meaning of danger, and of social-ism, was defined in Moscow. In 1956, the Hungarians had abandoned the monopoly of their Communist Party and left the Warsaw Pact. The Czechs and Slovaks had done neither, yet the outcome was just the same. Brezhnev's Doctrine seemed a *carte blanche* for interventionism.

The invasion did not cause a superpower crisis. NATO members accep-ted Moscow's reassurances that the invasion posed no threat to them. There was not even a general alert. US forces in Europe were pulled back some 200 kilometres. Yet for home consumption, the Soviet Union argued that the invasion was to forestall Western 'revanchism'. The Kremlin also informed incredulous Czechs that West German divisions were massing on their borders.

But the invasion was a major crisis for East–West relations in Europe. For the first time, the Soviet Union, in collusion with other powers, acted as a deliberate aggressor without even the pretence of international legality behind it. Czechoslovakia had remained loyal to the Warsaw Pact. A joint Soviet–Czechoslovak document, signed in Bratislava on 4 August 1968, reaffirmed the country's sovereignty and the inviolability of its borders. Since this had been torn up by the invasion three weeks later, Western leaders wondered whether the Soviet government could be trusted in inter-national relations again.

The invasion also marked a watershed within Eastern Europe. It exposed the hopelessness of attempts since Stalin to revive the Communist Party, planned economy and Marxism from above. It invalidated the assumption of 'revisionist' Communists that divisions between the party apparatus and wider society could be overcome by party-led reforms. Eastern Europe seemed to be at an impasse with the Yalta division of the continent unchal-lengeable. However, a surprising new development began to upset the apparently immutable status quo. In movements variously entitled civil society, a parallel *polis*, and political opposition, citizens started to influence politics from below. Their actions were not easy to suppress.

Unlike Western writers, who had largely discarded the notion of 'totalitarianism', East European activists began to challenge their 'neo-totalitarian regimes'. They started to criticise Communist state mecha-nisms for extinguishing civil society and smothering public life by censor-ship and political monopoly. They argued that politics had been replaced by an empty pantomime of ritualised claims. But the public realm could nonetheless be recovered through independent movements from below.

The first signs of such resistance came in response to the crushing of the Prague Spring.

Change from below

Czechoslovak leaders had instructed their forces and militia to offer no armed response to the Warsaw Pact invasion. But they also refused to give way to the political puppets Moscow wanted to install in their place. Thus, Moscow's military operation went smoothly, but the political objective was not easily attained. A campaign of non-violent civilian resistance to the invasion was sustained until the following spring.

In the autumn of 1968, the Czechoslovak reform movement assumed a mass character. Thousands of people took part in street demonstrations in Prague and other cities. They were dispersed violently by the police, assisted by the Czechoslovak army. Hundreds of students and young workers were arrested. Following such repression, protestors moved indoors. Students held a nation-wide sit-in strike on International Students' Day (17 November) to demand renewal of reforms and respect for civil rights.

Student protesters were supported by local trade union representatives who called a fifteen-minute sympathy strike on their behalf in hundreds of workplaces. The students' national union agreed with the metalworkers' union to call a general strike should the popular chairman of the National Assembly, Josef Smrkovský, be deposed on Soviet orders. At a freely elected Union Congress in the spring of 1969, delegates resolved that the Communist Party's 'leading role' should be respected, but only on the condition that reforms continued. It took relentless pressure from the new party leader, Gustáv Husák, who replaced Dubček in April 1969, to bring the autonomous student and worker unions back under party control.

While Czechoslovakia was being 'normalised', Polish Communism encountered its most severe challenge since 1956. A new political force appeared: the working class. For the first time in history, a Communist leadership was removed by protests from below.

In December 1970, Gomułka's Politburo announced 40 per cent increases on the price of basic foodstuffs. After a decade of stagnation in real wages, most families could not afford to pay. The timing was also critical: the measures were announced a fortnight before the Christmas holiday. Spontaneous workers' protests took place across the country. Those on the Baltic Coast were brutally suppressed when the police and the army fired live rounds into peaceful crowds. In Gdynia, the port of Gdańsk, thousands of commuters answered a televised appeal for a 'return to normal work' but were fired on outside the locked shipyards. The official death toll of forty-four people was an underestimate. Soviet leaders had not approved this use of force and expressed disquiet that protests had not been ended by peaceful means. Their confidence in Gomułka was exhausted and he went into enforced retirement, as did Józef Cyrankiewicz, prime minister since 1956. However, the price increases were not rescinded.

When protests resumed in the early New Year, the political authorities adopted a more reasonable approach. The new leadership under Edward Gierek travelled to the Szczecin and Gdańsk Shipyards for discussions with workers' representatives. Workers poured out their grievances to the visiting dignitaries. In response, Gierek mentioned his own working-class origins and called on workers to help him in overcoming Poland's economic crisis. The strikers responded positively, identifying with Gierek as one of their own, and returned to work. But the country as a whole was not pacified. Major protests by textile workers in Łódź eventually forced the new government to withdraw the December price increases. Workers' protests not only forced a change of leadership but also compelled the new government to reverse a major economic decision.

During two months of protest, Polish workers started to articulate political demands. They condemned the passivity of the state-run trades unions. Unions had lost their original purpose of defending workers against 'both big and little bosses who disregard our vital interests'. They had become bureaucratic, merely implementing production norms, doing paperwork and, at most, organising recreation. Rank-and-file members asked how their union dues were being spent. They questioned whether 'those gentlemen in high posts may have forgotten whose money they live on'.[14]

Strikers believed that unions should become independent of party and state control. Their officials should be elected; they should not be time-servers. Workers should also have the right to strike and to form inter-factory strike committees so that the authorities could not crush enterprises on strike by picking them off one by one. In Gdańsk, the workforce produced a popular tribune: Lech Wałęsa.

In additional to astonishing oratorical talents, entirely untutored, Wałęsa injected into Polish politics a set of attitudes that had not been articulated before. His generation, reaching adulthood in the 1960s, was ready for dialogue and compromise but was 'unreceptive to officially-launched doctrines and

14 Radio Gdańsk, 13 January 1971.

mistrustful of their empty declarations and senseless slogans'.[15] Wałęsa became the emblematic figure of working-class discontent.

Aware of the threat that independent workers posed to its own authority, the party fought back with every means at its disposal. The purpose was to re-surrect the barrier of fear which coastal workers had managed to overcome. In a sustained and brutal process of recriminations, strike leaders of 1970–71 were weeded out, demoted or sacked. In several cases, they were murdered by 'persons unknown'. Others were forced to emigrate.

The fate of Polish workers underlined the atomisation of social groups. In 1968, students had been largely unable to take their protests to the working class. In the winter of 1970–71, workers had received scant support from other groups. But co-operation between classes now began.

The opposition leader, Jacek Kuroń, advocated 'self-organisation' by soci-ety. His notion was that autonomous groups and social movements could arise to constitute an opposition. Expressing themselves freely, citizens with a sense of common purpose might reclaim the public space monopolised by the party and promote democratic values.[16]

Student leader Adam Michnik, a veteran of 1968, thought the future of Eastern Europe would depend upon a convergence of working-class self-organisation with that of other independent groups. It was not possible to predict how and when more permanent workers' representation might be achieved, but it was already clear that Polish workers had grown more politi-cally aware.[17] Michnik realised that there were limits that Eastern European reformers could not cross. But there was also a wider context. Rejecting the 'spheres of influence' established at the end of the Second World War, Michnik and other advocates of civil society wanted Eastern Europe to 'return to Europe' as a whole. This view found resonance with some leaders in the West.

Détente and Eastern Europe

The West German foreign minister, Willy Brandt, argued that détente in Europe should continue despite the 1968 invasion. An increase of

15 A. Drzycimski, 'Growing', in The Book of Lech Wałęsa, intro. Neal Ascherson (trans. from Polish) (Harmondsworth: Penguin, 1982), 69.
16 Jacek Kuroń, 'Polityka i opozycja w Polsce', [Politics and the Opposition in Poland] Kultura (Paris), (11 November 1974).
17 Adam Michnik, 'A New Evolutionism', in Adam Michnik, Letters from Prison and other Essays (Berkeley, CA: University of California Press, 1987), 135–48 (essay written October 1976).

communication between the blocs could lead to gradual change in the East. But he acknowledged that if the West had legitimate strategic interests on the continent, so too did the other side. West German openings to the East began in Moscow.

A Bonn–Moscow treaty (August 1970) declared the inviolability of existing European borders, including those between East and West Germany. According to Western critics of détente, this was a brilliant diplomatic success for the Soviet Union, legitimising its East European empire. But defenders of détente saw the results as more positive. Recognition of the postwar status quo in Europe could be the precondition for overcoming it. The first beneficiary was Poland.

A Bonn–Warsaw treaty (December 1970) recognised Poland's Western frontier and declared existing borders inviolable 'for now and for the future'. The countries had 'no territorial claims on each other and will not raise such claims in the future'. The treaty granted Poland access to the largest and most dynamic economy in Europe. West Germany agreed to promote and help finance Poland's economic growth.

Moscow was also interested in greater East–West collaboration. Brezhnev declared a new openness in economic relations with the capitalist West. In June 1973, he told business leaders in Washington that the Soviet Union sought a new era of international relations based on stability. An initial package of agreements with the United States included a grain deal to compensate for disappointing Soviet harvests and other failures of collective agriculture.

Détente offered rich pickings to the West. Even if it were a trick by the Communists, as hawks insisted, Brezhnev's offer provided opportunities. Some in the West believed that mutual self-interest through bilateral trade, credits, and even shared technology would eventually lead to a convergence of the two systems. It also gave Western governments new leverage in the East. They began to condition their willingness to share technology and extend credits on improved treatment of East European citizens. Officials in Washington, for example, argued that most-favoured-nation status should be extended to those Communist governments which had gone furthest to liberalise their rule.

Perhaps the most lasting legacy of détente was the least expected: the long-anticipated Conference on Security and Co-operation in Europe. Once the Soviet Union dropped its objections to the United States and Canada attending, its implicit agenda of excluding and eventually dissolving NATO disappeared. At Helsinki (August 1975), thirty-five governments adopted a new set of principles on security in Europe. Echoing the United Nations Charter, they declared that states would not intervene in sovereign 'affairs falling within the domestic jurisdiction' of another signatory. A special section of the agreement, popularly known as Basket III, guaranteed 'respect for humans rights and fundamental freedoms, including the freedom of thought, conscience, religion or belief'. A further paragraph committed all participating states to 'promote and encourage the effective exercise of civil, political, economic, social, cultural and other rights and freedoms all of which derive from the inherent dignity of the human person and are essential for his free and full development'.[18]

The Helsinki Accords provided the incipient opposition in Eastern Europe with a new defence for human rights. They enabled dissidents to challenge their governments: 'We are merely asking you to keep your international agreements,' they could now say. Although persecuted by the authorities, Helsinki monitoring groups were founded in Moscow, Kiev, Tbilisi, Erevan and Wilno. Similar groups were formed in Eastern Europe. The most notable was in Czechoslovakia.

In Prague, the proponents of 'Charter 77' gave a comprehensive account of violations of both the Helsinki Accords and the UN Charter. They stated that freedom of expression in Czechoslovakia was violated by the centralised control of media and cultural institutions. Tens of thousands of citizens had been excluded from their professions during the 'normalisation' that followed the 1968 invasion. Similarly, numerous young people had been denied entry to universities because their parents' opinions did not accord with official views. A novel feature of 'Charter 77' was its informality. To avoid official charges of illegality, it remained a 'virtual' organisation, without rules for membership, subscriptions or administration. It was open to all those 'united by the will to strive, individually and collectively, for the respect of civic and human rights in our own country and throughout the world'. In deliberate contrast to the Communist Party, the Chartists sought 'informal, non-bureaucratic, dynamic and open communities'.[19]

'Charter 77' championed inclusion. Seeking to build consensus rather than emphasise difference, contacts were made with Western Europeans, in particular peace activists interested in fostering détente. Czech dissidents also sought linkages with like-minded people elsewhere in Eastern Europe. Emboldened

18 *Conference on Security and Cooperation in Europe: Final Act* (London: Her Majesty's Stationary Office, 1975) 1–5.
19 H. G. Skilling, *Samizdat and an Independent Society in Central and Eastern Europe* (London: Macmillan, 1989).

by Helsinki's statements on the free movement of peoples and ideas, oppositionists started to communicate across frontiers. Border meetings took place between East Europeans. Despite much police harassment and frequent arrests, Poles and Czechs managed to edit a joint publication.

Their volume included Václav Havel's seminal essay, *The Power of the Powerless* (1978). Circulated widely at home, it soon came out in Hungary and Poland, and was translated in the West. Havel distinguished between two types of powerlessness. The first type, to which Havel himself belonged, was best described as 'a category of sub-citizen outside the power system'. These outsiders were known in the West as 'dissidents'. But his second category was much larger: conformists at every level who hid behind comforting phraseology and reiterated the soothing official ideology that claimed all citizens were living in the best possible world.

When a greengrocer placed the sign 'Workers of the World Unite!' amongst the onions and carrots in his window, he ignored its semantic content. The slogan was simply delivered to his shop, along with the vegetables. Not to display it would invite the charge of disloyalty. So he engaged in passive acceptance. He comforted himself with the thought that there would be nothing wrong with workers of the world uniting. Yet one day he might reconsider and remove the sign from the window. He could go further and refuse to vote in single-party elections. He might begin to express his real views at public meetings. By thus refusing to live the public lie, he would recover his personal identity and dignity.

Another Chartist, Václav Benda, advocated the construction of an alternative public sphere. He noted that a parallel – or black market – economy had always existed alongside the state-regulated one. Likewise, alternative social institutions could be set up. Independent forms of higher education were already taking place in underground ('flying') universities in Czechoslovakia and Poland. Actions by independent citizens could create a 'parallel polis' alongside the Communist one. This was beginning to happen in Poland.

Rise of Solidarity

Polish opposition reached a new stage in 1976. After a quiescent five years, in which living standards rose steadily, the authorities felt confident enough to raise basic meat prices by 50 per cent and other staples by 30 per cent. Despite careful preparations, the measures were emphatically rejected by Polish workers. After spontaneous nationwide protests, the prime minister appeared on television to state that the increases had merely been 'consultative'. Their withdrawal was an unprecedented admission by a Communist leader that workers now had the ability to veto a major policy.

As before, strike leaders and their supporters were dismissed or demoted. This time, however, a group of Warsaw intellectuals formed a Committee for the Defence of Workers (KOR). They offered medical, financial and legal help to those being persecuted and to their families. In an 'Appeal to Society', KOR declared that 'solidarity and mutual aid' were the only means for social self-defence against the arbitrary actions of the authorities.

KOR leaders set up an independent information network that escaped censorship. They published a thick factual bi-monthly *Information Bulletin*, modelled on the Russian dissident *Chronicle of Current Events*, to record and publicise all cases of government persecution and violence. These initiatives were extraordinarily successful. By the autumn of 1977, their original demands had been met. All those dismissed for the 1976 protests were released and reinstated, though sometimes to lesser positions. Rather than disband, as the authorities no doubt hoped, KOR then widened its agenda to cover all forms of persecution. It was renamed the Committee for Social Self-Defence (KSS).

The major innovation of KOR and its successor was that they acted openly. Its leaders signed their own names on public statements and listed their professions, addresses and home telephone numbers. While this information opened the authors to police repression, it also gave them greater credibility. In calling for civic courage, they showed the way themselves. They demonstrated to a wider public that Communist claims to subservience and obedience could be resisted. It became possible to say 'no' to demands from the state. This theme was also being stated openly by the Polish Catholic Church.

After the election of a Polish pope, the first non-Italian for 455 years, the Church began to play a more active role in Polish political life. John Paul II devoted his first encyclical *Redemptor Hominis* to the dignity of man and the protection of human rights, 'which can be trampled on so easily and annihilated'. This heralded a Vatican *Ostpolitik*.

The pope's first pilgrimage to his homeland (June 1979) became a massive festival in which the nation experienced itself as a community. Twelve million Poles saw the pope in person and heard his cycle of thirty-two speeches and sermons. He called for an authentic dialogue between Church and state, while recognising their 'diametrically opposed concepts of the world'. Though tactful towards the Soviet Union, the papal message was clear: 'It is necessary to work for peace and understanding amongst peoples and nations of the whole world. It is necessary to seek reconciliation. It is necessary to open the borders.'

15. Strike at Gdańsk shipyard, 1980. Poland exemplified burgeoning East European resistance to Soviet domination. The Church played a key role in nurturing dissent.

Although thousands of Czechoslovak Catholics had been prevented from crossing the frontier to hear him, the pope addressed them: 'Remember, Father, all your Czech children.' Broadening his message, he spoke to all the peoples of Eastern Europe – to Bulgarians, whose Prince Boris was baptised a century before any Poles, to Moravians and Ruthenians and others. He alluded to the 'forgotten and neglected nations'. 'There can be no just Europe,' he said, 'without the independence of Poland marked on its map'. The divided continent needed to be reunited. The 'balance of forces' might be changed without using force itself.

The pope told his congregations that the future of Poland would depend upon how many people were 'mature enough to become non-conformists'. Two million watched his departure from the Kraków meadows. The authorities had left stewarding of these vast gatherings to the Church itself. There had been a temporary suspension of the Communist state.

Emboldened by the visit, Polish oppositionists promulgated a Charter of Workers' Rights. This document, with signatories from twenty-six towns and cities, including the founders of a Free Trade Union on the Baltic Coast, remonstrated against inequality and social injustice. The Charter called for institutions to defend working people. The official trades unions were failing in their mission. Moreover, workers were deprived of a basic instrument they needed for self-defence, the right to strike. Working people had to have the capacity to defend themselves, above all to form independent trades unions.[20] These unions emerged much sooner than anyone expected. The greatest of all Polish strikes in August 1980 led to the birth of Solidarity.[21]

Diversity and nonconformism

By the late 1970s, Eastern Europe presented a differentiated picture. The most repressive country in the region was Romania. A rare miners' strike was sparked in the Jiu Valley by legislation ending disability payments for miners and raising the retirement age to fifty-five. Some 35,000 strikers attended a mass meeting on 1 August 1977. Their demands included a reduction of working hours, improved medical facilities and a return to the retirement age of fifty. They called on the party leader to come to the mines for direct talks.

Faced with this unprecedented stoppage, Ceaușescu arrived to face a hostile crowd. He purported to make concessions, including the promise that there would be no punishment of those who had organised the strike. Once the miners had returned to work, however, the army and secret police moved in. Several hundred activists were transferred to other mines and the longer working day was reinstated. There was no response from other social groups. In contrast to Poland, the lack of social solidarity in Romania was stark.

Although Romania remained neo-Stalinist at home, civil resistance became more common, and better co-ordinated, elsewhere in the bloc. A growing role was played by Protestant churches in East Germany. Though a Church–State Agreement (1978) appeared to give the political authorities greater scope to curtail its independence, the reverse occurred. Under church protection, a public sphere began to develop outside the official realm. Starting with discussion groups on economic and environmental issues, this gradually grew into an unofficial peace movement, including other groups defending human rights. Elsewhere, new forms of counter-culture proliferated, such as unofficial art shows, street theatre and popular musical concerts. Such 'happenings' often arose from connections with the West.

When dissidents sent 'Open Letters' to prominent intellectuals and political leaders in the West, they often received a positive and public response. This helped to remove the sense of international isolation behind which Communist governments sought to confine their citizens. At the intergovernmental level,

20 *Robotnik* [The Worker], 35 (18 July 1979).
21 See Jacques Lévesque's chapter in volume III.

Eastern Europe's 'return to Europe' was legitimised by the biannual monitoring of the Helsinki Accords, starting at Belgrade in the summer of 1977.

Even at the height of the Cold War, East Europeans retained their sense of universal values. They did not respond to their imposed political isolation with passivity. Repression made resistance most difficult in Romania and Bulgaria, but even in those countries there was growing understanding of the need for independence. The founding father of 'Charter 77', Jan Patočka, advised East Europeans in his valedictory statement to behave with civic dignity and courage, to live without fear and to speak the truth. As he put it: 'Let us be frank about this: in the past no conformity has ever led to any improvement in the situation.'[22]

22 Deathbed Statement (Prague, 8 March 1977).

12

The Cold War and the transformation of the Mediterranean, 1960–1975

ENNIO DI NOLFO

If one takes a long-term view of the Mediterranean region between 1960 and 1975, it is characterized by its transition from one defined by the European colonial system and menaced by Soviet encroachment to one that became, fifteen years later, a vital conduit of communication and a channel for shipping Middle Eastern oil into a wider world dominated by the United States. The convergence of Mediterranean history with the global dynamics of the Cold War inspires the consideration of the *longue durée*. From the early decades of the eighteenth century, the Russian Empire had exerted continuous pressure from the Black Sea toward the Mediterranean. The Soviet Union inherited this geostrategic imperative. The messy decolonization of the Ottoman Empire in the Middle East and the Balkans in the early part of the twentieth century, and subsequently that of European empires in Northern Africa after World War II, added further complexity to the region. As a result, newly independent Mediterranean states faced the problem of developing foreign and commercial policies compatible with their own interests while recognizing the influence of often distant naval powers that dominated their coasts. During the period considered here, the global rivalry of the two superpowers – with the United States always being the strongest, with unprecedented capabilities to project its power – gradually imposed itself on complicated regional dynamics with roots going back to the ancient world.

To a certain extent, the Soviet–American confrontation in the Mediterranean began during World War II. Iosif Stalin bitterly resented the exclusion of the Soviets from the Italian armistice negotiations in August 1943, and their de facto exclusion from the Allied Control Commission for Italy (October 1943 to January 1944).[1] In April 1945, pro-Soviet Titoist partisans

---

1 B. Arcidiacono, *Le "précédent italien" et les origines de la guerre froide. Les Alliés et l'occupation de l'Italie 1943–1944* (Bruxelles: Bruylant, 1984).

occupied Trieste, but Stalin was greatly displeased when American pressure forced them to vacate the city, which the 1947 Peace Treaty with Italy placed under international (i.e., Western) control. Moreover, Moscow tried unsuccessfully to obtain from the United Nations (UN) a trusteeship in either Tripolitania or Cyrenaica (both in present-day Libya). During these negotiations, the Soviet foreign minister, Viacheslav Molotov, complained that "You [the Western powers] do not want to give us even a corner of the Mediterranean." This was neither polemical retort nor improvisation, for the Soviet leadership had long coveted the strategic potential of former Italian Mediterranean colonies.[2]

Some of the Cold War's early points of tension were thus located in the Mediterranean basin. Soviet designs were checked by the Truman Doctrine of March 1947, which extended US protection to Greece and Turkey and, in general, warned the Soviets off further attempts at influencing Mediterranean affairs. Subsequently, for several years, the Mediterranean seemed set to return to its imperial past, with France and Britain seeking to reimpose their grip on Africa's northern littoral.[3]

Yet, throughout the 1950s, it was evident that the Mediterranean remained a priority of Soviet diplomacy. In March 1959, the Dwight D. Eisenhower administration countered Soviet plans for the region by deploying medium-range Thor and Jupiter missiles aimed at the USSR in Italy and Turkey.[4] In the Kremlin, meanwhile, Nikita Khrushchev had, since 1955, been conceiving a new political offensive against Western domination of the Mediterranean. He wanted to play a direct role in Mediterranean affairs, prepared to increase the Soviet naval presence in the region, and tried to establish close ties with North African and Middle Eastern countries.

2 V. O. Pechtanov, *"The Allies are Pressing on You to Break Your Will …"*. *Foreign Policy Correspondence between Stalin and Molotov and Other Politburo Members. September 1945–December 1946*, Cold War International History Project (CWIHP), Working Paper No. 26, (Washington, DC: Woodrow Wilson Center, 1999).

3 For a general appraisal of these problems, see E. Calandri, *Il Mediterraneo e la difesa dell'Occidente 1947–1956. Eredità imperiali e logiche di guerra fredda*, 2nd ed. (Florence: Manent, 1997); A. Brogi, *A Question Of Self-Esteem: The United States and the Cold War Choices in France and Italy, 1944–1958* (Westport, CT: Praeger, 2002). M. Leffler, *A Preponderance of Power: National Security, the Truman Administration and the Cold War* (Stanford, CA: Stanford University Press, 1992).

4 D. N. Schwartz, *Nato's Nuclear Dilemma* (Washington DC: Brooking Institution, 1983), 73–74.

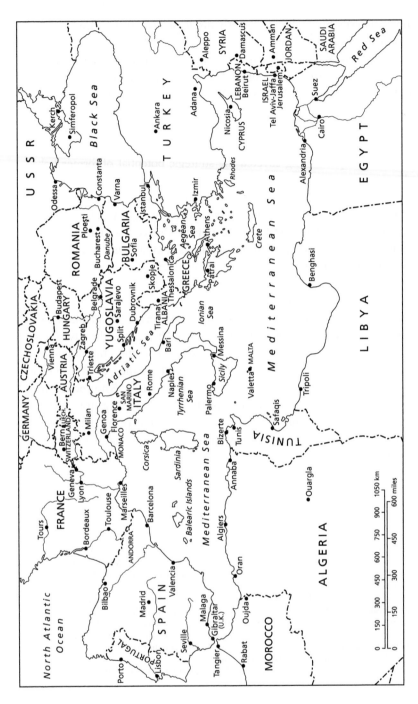

2. The Mediterranean Basin

The 1960s: competition intensifies

In the early 1960s, two developments shaped events in the Mediterranean: the Cuban missile crisis and the erosion of the Europeans' position in North Africa. The Cuban crisis was settled by a secret agreement between Khrushchev and John F. Kennedy that obliged the United States to dismantle its missile bases in Turkey and Italy. Although Washington was planning to replace these missiles with Polaris submarines in the near future, the withdrawal of the missiles was a setback for the Atlantic alliance.[5] At the same time, after meeting the Israeli foreign minister, Golda Meir, Kennedy began preparing to deploy advanced surface-to-air Hawk missiles to Israel, thereby putting an end to a policy of equidistance between the two sides of the Arab–Israeli conflict. The missiles were deployed in 1965, giving Israel a decisive defensive advantage over its Arab neighbors.[6]

Kennedy's decision to link the Jupiter missiles in Turkey to Soviet missiles in Cuba had significant ramifications. Thomas Finletter, the US ambassador to the North Atlantic Treaty Organization (NATO) noted that

> Turkey regards these Jupiters as symbols of the alliance's determination to use atomic weapons against a Russian attack on Turkey ... [The] fact that Jupiters are obsolescent and vulnerable does not affect present Turkish thinking. My impression is that the symbolic importance represents a fixed Government view ... Unless we can avoid such patterns, this could foreshadow a dangerous and divisive situation for NATO alliance because other members may wonder if they too might not be asked give up some military capability at the time of the next Soviet manufactured crisis.[7]

Likewise, Robert W. Komer, a key aide to McGeorge Bundy, Kennedy's national security adviser, observed that, "from a strictly military point of view these missiles are near irrelevant," but the act of removing them "prematurely" might create negative repercussions. "Our Cuba performance to date," he said, "has greatly bucked up our allies, and increased their confidence we will act if vital US interests are threatened. But they are not

5 Memorandum of conversation, January 16, 1963, US Department of State, *Foreign Relations of the United States, 1961–1963*. (Washington, DC: US Government Printing Office, 1994), vol. XIII, *Western Europe and Canada*, 864 (hereafter, *FRUS*, with year and volume number).
6 A. Fursenko and T. Naftali, *"One Hell of a Gamble": The Secret History of the Cuban Missile Crisis* (London: John Murray, 1997).
7 Thomas Finletter to Dean Rusk, October 25, 1962, and Charles Bohlen to Rusk, November 11, 1962; National Security Files (NSF), box 226, John F. Kennedy Library, Boston, Massachusetts (hereafter, JFKL).

fully convinced that we will regard other situations than Cuba as involving the same degree for action." It was the old problem, linked to the formulation of Article 5 of the Atlantic Pact, i.e., the problem of American credibility. "However wrong this sensitivity may be," Komer added, "this point is painfully clear. Doubt as to U.S. intentions is at the core of our NATO problems, and we have not swept it away by our recent actions ... The Soviet target is our [whole network of] overseas bases structure, and the degradation of confidence in our will to act."[8]

After Kennedy's death in November 1963, a confrontation between Greece and Turkey over Cyprus shook the region. Britain had granted the island independence in 1960, and it was divided into two administrative districts, with Archbishop Makarios III elected president of the new state. However, disputes between Greek majority and Turkish minority inhabitants caused a series of international crises. After Britain's withdrawal from its other bases east of Suez, Cyprus had assumed a new importance to the Atlantic alliance. Both Greece and Turkey separately asked for Washington's help in support of their national kin on the island, while the United States sensed hidden danger in Makarios's neutralist approach. In 1964, fighting broke out between the two communities, prompting Ankara to threaten to invade the island in order to defend the Turkish minority. Makarios rejected an Anglo-American proposal to send a NATO peacekeeping force, but accepted one under UN authority instead. The tensions inherent in the situation strained Turkish–American relations. On the Greek side, where the annexation of Cyprus (*enosis*) was eagerly expected, suspicions of American plans for a division of the island increasingly shaped domestic politics.

Other dramatic changes had taken place in the western part of the Mediterranean during the same period. The policies of the French president, Charles de Gaulle, had a great impact on the region. Although he put an end to the war between the Algerian National Liberation Front and France in March 1962, this conflict bequeathed a series of problems. The sudden influx of almost one million white refugees was manageable by dint of France's continued economic expansion. But with the independence of Algeria on July 5, the northwestern coast of the Mediterranean was now fully decolonized, as Spain had left Morocco in March 1956 (except for the harbors of Ceuta and Melilla). There was a vacuum of power in the region.

---

8 R. W. Komer, memorandum to McGeorge Bundy, November 12, 1962, NSF, box 226, JFKL.

Freed from the Algerian nightmare, de Gaulle prepared a global strategy, premised not only upon French resources, but also upon an evolving European Community. His plans had significant consequences for the Western position in the Mediterranean. On April 27, 1964, the French military representative in NATO's Maritime Standing Group, Admiral Max Douguet, announced that French naval officers would "no longer serve in NATO naval headquarters or in units under non-French naval command." According to the US secretary of state, Dean Rusk, the French decision struck "at the heart of NATO defense system." Rusk and other US officials, such as Secretary of Defence Robert McNamara, feared that French action might invite Soviet military incursions into the Mediterranean.[9] These fears mounted when de Gaulle, in March 1966, said that he intended to withdraw French forces from the Atlantic integrated army. Although this did not mean that France was abandoning the Atlantic alliance, the Central Intelligence Agency (CIA) suspected that de Gaulle was seeking to exploit the growing crisis between Israel and the Arab countries to project French influence among Muslim countries bordering the Mediterranean.[10]

The American reaction to de Gaulle's decision reflected Washington's alarm at the political and military changes in the Mediterranean region. The Soviets were exploiting anti-Western and anticolonial feelings and nurturing new political, economic, and military relationships. To Syria and Egypt, Moscow had supplied economic and financial aid with the hope of securing future naval facilities. Algeria quickly became another target of Soviet ambitions. Libya, too, although leaning towards neutralism, was open to Soviet influence, especially after Muammar al-Qaddafi's coup in 1969.

These developments, in combination with the growth of the Soviet fleet in the Mediterranean, engendered pessimism in Washington. While the United States was entangled in Southeast Asia and the West Europeans were preoccupied with the creation of the European Economic Community (EEC) the Soviets were becoming serious political and military players in the Mediterranean region. Washington worried that none of its regional allies could be counted on in the event of military conflict. Turkey was bitterly

---

9 "NATO Ministerial Meeting," December 1964, and "Comments by Secretary McNamara on Issues and Questions Raised by the Progress Report of the Defence Planning Committee," December 16, 1964, NSF, box 34, International Meetings and Travel File, Lyndon B. Johnson Library, Austin, Texas (hereafter, LBJL).

10 W. W. Rostow to L. B. Johnson, Washington, June 16, 1967, and enclosure CIA Intelligence Information Cable, box 17, vol. 31, Files of Walt W. Rostow, Memos to the Presidents, NSF, LBJL. See also M. Vaisse, *La Grandeur: Politique étrangère du général de Gaulle 1958–1969* (Paris: Fayard, 1998), 615–47.

disappointed by the outcome of the Cuban and Cypriot crises; Syria and Egypt were at best neutral or more likely pro-Soviet; and the pro-Western countries, Tunisia and Morocco, were motivated principally by the exigencies of regional rivalries. At the same time, Franco's Spain was entering an uncertain phase of transition, and France seemed to be a diffident ally. Italy was probably the country closest to the United States in this period, but politics in Rome were increasingly shaped by the influence of leftist parties. Josip Broz Tito's Yugoslavia was neutral, Greece was disappointed by America's response to the Cyprus situation, and newly independent Malta was ruled by a pro-Qaddafi government. In the entire Mediterranean basin, Israel alone stood out for its dependence on American assistance and its willingness to cooperate with Washington's policies. By the mid- to late 1960s, therefore, the United States had reason to be worried. Despite the efforts of the Eisenhower and Kennedy administrations, the retreat of French and British power left the door ajar to the advance of Soviet influence in the Mediterranean.

Crises in the Middle East and Southern Europe

When considering the impact of the 1967 Arab–Israeli war on the Mediterranean system, the main problem to address is whether the conflict was instigated by the Israeli government in order to weaken the Arabs, or whether it was a response to a carefully crafted Soviet–Syrian–Egyptian plan to strike at both Israeli and US power in the region. There is some evidence that the Soviets were prepared to accept or even abet the destruction of Israel in order to cement their newly acquired influence with Arab states.[11] At the end of February 1967, about forty Soviet naval vessels had been moved from the Black Sea to the Mediterranean, and, on June 4, they received orders for full battle alert. The US ambassador in Moscow believed that the Kremlin's objective was "to transform the Arab/Israeli struggle into a showdown between Communists and anti-Communists for control of the Middle East, and the Soviets [were] succeeding. If Nasser wins this one, monarchies and western oil interests will go."[12]

Nevertheless, the government in Tel Aviv was not wholly innocent. Although not preparing their forces for an offensive before the crisis became acute, the Israelis had been receiving American increased missile assistance

---

11 See I. Ginor, "The Cold War's Longest Cover-up: How and Why the USSR Instigated the 1967 War," *Middle East Review of International Affairs*, 7, 3 (September 2003), 34–59.

12 Lewellyn Thompson, American Embassy, Moscow, to Secretary of State, May 28, 1967, confidential, Department of State incoming telegram 029479. "Middle East Crisis," vol. II, box 105, Country File, NSF, LBJL.

since the first Hawk battery was set up around Dimona in 1965; research for developing a nuclear weapon had been underway since the mid-1950s.[13] The Israeli high command was aware of Egyptian troop movements and decided to act without informing the United States. The Israelis even attacked the US naval intelligence vessel, the *Liberty*, either by mistake or to hinder US intelligence gathering in the conflict.[14]

The devasting Israeli aerial blitz and its swift and comprehensive military victory in the Six Day War was a humiliating defeat for the Egyptians and their Soviets backers. During the war, the United States maintained a very restrained public position in order to avoid recriminations from its oil-rich Muslim allies, Saudi Arabia and Iran. Yet it was increasingly evident that, with Moscow supplying Egypt's military buildup, Israel was abandoning its neutral attitude and becoming a forward base for US interests in the Mediterranean.[15]

In hindsight, therefore, the Six Day War was a decisive occasion for an American reappraisal of the importance of NATO's southern flank. In the midst of the conflict, the State Department urged Washington's permanent representative to NATO, Harlan Cleveland, to remind European allies of their common interest in the long-term stability in the Middle East region. Cleveland was instructed to emphasize how vital the Middle East region was in view of NATO's need for overflight privileges, sea communications, and oil resources. This did not mean that NATO should intervene directly in the Arab–Israeli conflict, but it was necessary to create a consultative mechanism inside NATO to facilitate the discreet coordination of Middle East policies even when member governments desired to avoid public controversy.[16]

The totality of Israel's military victory changed the fundamentals of regional politics. Gamal Abdel Nasser's resounding defeat forced him into greater dependence on the Soviet Union. For its part, Moscow assessed the Arab–Israeli crisis in terms of a wider global strategy, and saw it as "a confrontation between progressive Arab regimes and the vanguard of world imperialism, Israel."[17] Before 1967, the Soviets viewed regional dynamics from

13 A. Cohen, *Israel and the Bomb* (New York: Columbia University Press, 1998), 268, 470.
14 The question of the attack against the *Liberty* has not yet been fully clarified. See J. Ennes, Jr. *Assault on the Liberty: The Story of the Attack on an Intelligence Ship* (New York: Random House, 1979); A. Jay Cristol, *The Liberty Incident: The 1967 Israeli Attack on the U.S. Navy Spy Ship* (Washington, DC: Brassey's, 2002), 126–35.
15 S. L. Spiegel, *The Other Arab–Israeli Conflict: Making American Middle East Foreign Policy from Truman to Reagan* (Chicago: University of Chicago Press, 1985), 94–314.
16 Dean Rusk to Harlan Cleveland, June 8, 1967, *FRUS, 1974–1968*, vol. XIII, 612–15.
17 I. Ginor, "Under the Yellow Arab Helmet Gleamed Blue Russian Eyes," *Cold War History*, 3 (2002), 127–56.

a geopolitical calculus, but after the war, they injected an ideological fervor into their Mediterranean policy. They strengthened their naval fleet and provided more aid to African and Arab countries, thereby suggesting that Leonid Brezhnev and his comrades wanted the Soviet Union to become an even more powerful force in the Mediterranean. From 1967 on, the Soviets embraced anticolonialism with renewed fervor claiming they were fighting for the liberation of all peoples oppressed by imperialism and neo-imperialism. Since Nasser was a leader of the anticolonial movement in the Third World, the Kremlin overlooked the fact that he outlawed the Egyptian Communist Party. The Soviets willingly collaborated with dubious allies of world Communism such as Syria, Egypt, Iraq, Libya, and Algeria in opposing Israel.

There was, however, a flaw in this plan, the importance of which was soon to appear. During the 1967 war, the Soviet government severed its diplomatic relations with Tel Aviv and failed to grasp the significance of Israel now occupying Sinai and the Golan Heights. These facts could be changed only by another war or by diplomacy. The first option was not likely to prove successful, and the second could not occur so long as the Kremlin eschewed direct negotiations with the Israelis. Although severing relations with Israel proved to be a serious miscalculation and although Egypt's defeat reflected poorly on the merits of Soviet military assistance, it seemed for a while that Moscow had profited from the Six Day War by solidifying its position in the Arab world.

Profound changes took place in Israel and Egypt, the two most important states of the Middle East. The extension of the territory that Israel controlled encouraged the idea of creating a greater Israeli state. This vision did not take into account a newly aroused Palestinian nationalism, embodied in the growing importance of the Palestinian Liberation Organization (PLO), headed by Yasser Arafat. Meanwhile, the defeat had a deep psychological and political impact on Nasser, who suddenly resigned from power, only to be compelled by public demonstrations to reverse his decision. Yet his physical health deteriorated, and in September 1970 he died of a heart attack. Anwar Sadat, his friend and successor, inherited a difficult domestic situation and a rapidly changing international environment. He quickly realized the benefits and the liabilities of Soviet protection.[18]

Elsewhere in North Africa, Tunisia and Morocco were kept in the Western orbit by two pro-Western leaders, Habib Bourguiba and King Hassan II, but

18 D. Hopwood, *Egypt: Politics and Society. 1945–1981* (London: Allen and Unwin, 1982), 180 ff.

Libya and Algeria became more radical in the late 1960s and possessed significant energy resources. In 1967, Algeria's Houari Boumedienne became the main sponsor of Palestinian nationalism, as well as a supporter of other revolutionary movements around the world. On September 1, 1969, Captain Qaddafi deposed King Idris of Libya and established a rigid "Islamic socialist" dictatorship. Both Algeria and Libya pursued socialist economic policies and nationalized their oil and gas reserves at the expense of Western companies. Qaddafi also seized control of the US Wheeler Air Force base and he and Boumedienne ostentatiously engaged in a non-aligned policy that inclined toward the Soviets, while continuing – much to American irritation – to work with France.[19]

In the Balkans, schisms within the Communist world persisted, but the West was unable to capitalize on them. Although Tito and Khrushchev improved Soviet–Yugoslav relations, they increasingly alienated Enver Hoxa's regime in Albania. After a bitter attack by Khrushchev, Hoxa decided to denounce Soviet "revisionism." In December 1961, Moscow broke diplomatic relations, and Albania became an isolated Chinese ally in Europe.[20]

Bickering inside the Communist world was little consolation to the United States as each of Washington's southern European allies was plagued by internal unrest. Turkey, Greece, Italy, France, Spain, and Portugal gave the United States cause for concern. All of these countries, moreover, were exposed politically and economically to the turmoil in the Middle East. The emergence of the Soviet Union as a Mediterranean power, the polarization of the Middle East by the 1967 war, and the radicalisation of economic policy in much of the Arab world combined to magnify the vulnerability of US strategic and economic interests in the Mediterranean region.

In Turkey, militarily the most powerful US ally in the eastern Mediterranean, politics remained unstable after a military coup in 1960. The civilian governments that followed were a series of unstable government coalitions alternating between the Justice Party of Süleyman Demirel on the right and the Republican People's Party of İsmet İnönü and Bülent Ecevit on the left. The economy was left to founder. After another coup in 1971, the military continued to have a distinct say in the country's politics. The lack of political stability and the poor economy created increasing tension between the extremes in Turkish politics, with open clashes between leftists and nationalists,

19 M. Cricco, *Il Petrolio dei Senussi: Stati Uniti e Gran Bretagna in Libia dall'indipendenza a Gheddafi (1949–1973)* (Florence: Polistampa, 2002), 164–223.
20 B. Jelavich, *History of the Balkans*, 2 vols. (Cambridge and New York: Cambridge University Press, 1983), vol. II, *The Twentieth Century*, 392–93.

while in the east the Kurdish population began campaigning for greater national rights.

Greece continued to be a weak link in the NATO alliance throughout this period. Anti-Communism had been a salient feature of Greek foreign policy since the Civil War of the 1940s,[21] but the fragility of the Greek state became clear after the electoral success of the leftist Progressive Centre Union Party (EK), led by Andreas Papandreou, in 1964. Escalating tension between the left and right wings of Greek politics culminated in the military coup of April 1967. The new strong man, Colonel Georgios Papadopoulos, was as anti-Communist as can be and had longstanding contacts with the CIA, but his regime's regressive approach to civil liberties soon became an embarrassment both for the Americans and for their main European partners. Worse, Papadopoulos did nothing to ease tensions with Turkey, which had been exacerbated by his civilian predecessor, thereby presenting the Soviets with golden opportunities for propaganda victories and for playing on the ongoing feud on the southern flank of NATO.

The Iberian peninsula's right-wing dictatorships had been an even greater source of embarrassment for the West since the end of World War II. In Spain, the Fascist-inspired dictatorship of General Francisco Franco had – in spite of newfound economic growth from the mid-1960s on – never attained general legitimacy at home or abroad. While having a military agreement with the United States, Franco was never able to elbow his way into the new Europe that was coming into being two decades after the war ended. For Washington, though, a main concern was what would happen after Franco, born in 1892, faded from the scene. Some policymakers feared that Spain would fall apart in ethnic and political strife when the general's chosen successor, the young and untested Bourbon prince Juan Carlos, took over. Although Basque separatists assassinated the prime minister in December 1973, the government did not crumble and the transition continued, although how it would end remained unpredictable in the early 1970s.

Political change in Portugal was even more ominous for American interests. The end was approaching for the long-running dictatorship of Antonio Salazar, a staunch conservative inspired by Fascist ideologies and a rigid defender of the Portuguese Empire, who spent up to 40 percent of the limited national revenue on the preservation of colonial possessions in Africa. In 1968, Salazar suffered a stroke and was succeeded by the conservative Marcelo Caetano, who seemed even more clueless than his predecessor about how to

---

21 See Svetozar Rajak's chapter in volume 1.

end the colonial wars and get the economy in Western Europe's poorest country on its feet. His limited reforms satisfied very few Portuguese, even within the army, where many officers were disgusted with having to fight unwinnable wars in Africa while the country deteriorated at home. By the early 1970s, some of these officers began contacting the illegal left-wing opposition to Caetano's regime.

The major European powers did not buttress US efforts to counter the worsening trends in the Mediterannean. Dependent on oil and gas reserves in the hands of Arab states, Western European governments sought to cooperate with their former colonies in ways that would preserve their interests as much as possible. The Yaoundé Agreement of 1964 between the EEC and eighteen African states was designed to create an area of special economic cooperation and therefore caused some concern in the United States where it was seen as creating a preferential economic zone from which the United States was excluded. Washington feared that members of the EEC might form a closed market, protected by a high tariff wall, that might at least in some ways include their former colonies.

France and Italy took care not to alienate the Arab states on whose oil their economies depended and who constituted an important export market. It was also a natural instinct for the Mediterranean nations, Spain included, to preserve their relationship with the southern shore, which was increasingly the source of substantial immigration. Under de Gaulle, Paris reversed France's pro-Israel tilt of the 1950s and assumed a diplomatic posture more friendly to the Arabs. Likewise, Italy began to assume a more ambiguous position. This shift was due in part to the influence of the Socialist Party, whose role in the Italian government had grown since it broke with the Communists in 1956. In October 1970, the British ambassador in Rome sent London the following synopsis of Italian foreign policy in the Mediterranean:

> Peace in the Middle East is a major Italian interest, though those responsible for Italian foreign policy recognise that there is little which they can do by themselves to bring this nearer. But they do not think that peace is round the corner. They will be careful meanwhile not to become too identified with the Americans in order to avoid damaging their position with the Arabs. For this reason, and because of domestic political pressure from the Left, the Italians will continue to fight shy of any increase in Nato's Mediterranean role … Despite this restrictive definition, there is no question at present of the Italian Government wishing Nato to abandon its principal bases at Naples. The Nato embrace may sometimes be an embarrassment … but no Italian

Government, foreseeable up to the 1973 elections, at least, is likely to wish to escape from it.[22]

In sum, from Washington's perspective, prospects for the Mediterranean had taken a real turn for the worse during the late 1960s. The Arab–Israeli crisis, culminating in the 1967 war, had given the Soviets an entrée as super-power patron to counter US support for Israel. At the same time, Moscow's moralistic and ideological approach to the region appealed to regimes in Cairo, Tripoli, Algiers, and even Belgrade. This rhetorical campaign capital-ized on the differing economic agendas of the Western powers and high-lighted their awkward reliance on the dictatorships of southern Europe.

Oil, power politics, and democratization (1973–1975)

Notwithstanding the difficulties the United States faced in Vietnam, Washington embarked on a strategic counteroffensive. "Neither Europe nor we can afford these days to be provincial in our thinking," wrote John McCloy to Walt Rostow, President Lyndon Johnson's national security adviser, on August 11, 1967.[23] Provincial they were not, because in these months they set forth a policy to roll back Soviet influence in the Mediterranean and to transform the sea into an "American Lake." Faced with European unwill-ingness to adopt military measures, the State Department recommended "modest, non-provocative political-military responses." It also decided to resume military aid to Greece despite the internal political situation of the country.[24]

The Warsaw Pact invasion of Czechoslovakia, in August 1968, and the election of Richard M. Nixon as US president in November created additional opportunities for the American counteroffensive. The invasion of Czechoslovakia shocked European public opinion. Although NATO govern-ments had embraced a common policy of détente at their ministerial meeting in 1968, Nixon primarily viewed détente as a strategy "for enabling America to regain the diplomatic initiative while the war in Vietnam was still in pro-gress."[25] Moreover, the American president was prepared to move ahead

22 The British ambassador in Italy, Sir Patrick Hancock, to the Foreign Office, October 19, 1970, PRO, FCO, 33/1094.
23 J. J. McCloy to W. W. Rostow, August 11, 1967, LBJL, NS, AF, NATO, General, box 36, vol. 5, No. 8.
24 Paper prepared in the Department of State, "The Reykjavik Ministerial Meeting of Nato" [no date], FRUS, 1964–1968, vol. XIII, 712–16; Memorandum for the Record, "Summary of NSC Meeting on Nato," June 19, 1968, ibid., 716–18.
25 H. Kissinger, Diplomacy (New York: Simon & Schuster, 1994), 713.

unilaterally.[26] For him, the Atlantic alliance was more a formal structure than a real cooperative body in the search for solutions to the problems of the Mediterranean region. When he embarked on his offensive in the Mediterranean, three concerns shaped his policy: the need to have access to reasonably priced oil, the threat of Communism in the moderate Arab countries, and the state of relations with Israel.

Meanwhile, the leaders of Egypt and Saudi Arabia became convinced that they could not defeat Israel militarily and were inclined toward compromise.[27] Yet this compromise could only occur in a wholly different psychological environment than the one that prevailed after the 1967 war. A deal with Israel could be reached only if the Arabs could negotiate from a more advantageous position. Sadat was convinced that oil could be a powerful tool for gaining Western support; he also believed that dependency on Soviet economic and military aid constrained his options. In the early 1970s, he reduced his military ties with the Soviet Union while discussing with the Saudis the use of the oil weapon to force the West into a more flexible attitude.

When the Yom Kippur War erupted in October 1973, Egyptian successes in the first phase of the conflict caused Washington to fret over the extent of Soviet support, precipitating a partial mobilization of US forces in order to send a message to the Kremlin. Yet the Egyptian president's aim was not actually to win the war, which he knew to be unrealistic given the danger of sparking a wider international conflict. Rather, his objective was to achieve enough on the battlefield to erase the Egyptian (and Arab) inferiority complex vis-à-vis Israel, thus setting up a new psychological balance in the negotiations that were likely to follow.[28] The Soviets, in fact, were prepared to resupply his army immediately, but Sadat did not want it. Although Israeli forces managed to reverse their fortunes and gain the upper hand militarily in the war's second phase, the situation was transformed. The Egyptians shattered the aura of Israeli invincibility, thereby making it possible to put the diplomatic option on the table.

The Paris conference of December 1973 was the first occasion when Americans, Soviets, Egyptians, Jordanians, and Israeli representatives met to settle the problems of the region peacefully. At that time, Europe faced severe oil shortages, with price hikes instituted by the Organization of the Petroleum Exporting Countries (OPEC) threatening economic growth. EEC members

---

26 For more on Nixon's policies, see Robert D. Schulzinger's chapter in this volume.
27 See Douglas Little's chapter in this volume.
28 W. Bundy, *A Tangled Web: The Making of Foreign Policy in the Nixon Presidency* (New York: Hill and Wang, 1998), 428–34.

were unable to agree on a common approach to the oil-producing countries, and Franco-American tensions were exacerbated by the harsh clash between Henry Kissinger and the French foreign minister, Michel Jobert. In this situation – with their role in Middle East affairs seemingly acknowledged – Soviet leaders believed they were on the verge of a substantial international victory. In reality, however, the fragility of their diplomatic position was revealed: the absence of diplomatic relations between Moscow and Tel Aviv meant that only the Americans could deal with the Egyptians and the Israelis at the same time. Kissinger's diplomacy, which brokered the Egyptian–Israeli negotiations, demonstrated the restoration of American primacy – and Soviet haplessness – in Mediterranean affairs.

On January 18, 1974, Egyptians and Israelis signed a ceasefire agreement that provided for the withdrawal of the Israelis to 30 kilometres east of the Suez Canal. Kissinger's strategy was well defined, as he explained to a panel of US experts before the negotiations began:

> We can reduce Soviet influence in the area and can get the oil embargo raised if we can deliver a moderate program and we are going to do it. If not, the Arabs will be driven back to the Soviets, the oil will be lost, we will have the whole world against us. We must prove to the Arabs that they are better off dealing with us on a moderate program than dealing with the Russians.[29]

His strategy succeeded: in 1974, Sadat reestablished official relations with the United States, and two years later he renounced the treaty of alliance with the Soviet Union. It was a stunning changing of sides by Moscow's most important ally in the region.

Sadat's realignment coincided with a wider deterioration of the Soviet position in the Mediterranean. Cairo's dumping of the Kremlin did much to discredit the Soviets in the eyes of other Arab states. The USSR continued to supply Syria, Algeria, and Libya with substantial quantities of military *matériel*, but the illusion was shattered that, in times of crisis, Moscow could match the Americans diplomatically and stategically. Henceforth, Moscow would pay more for less credibility in the Arab capitals.

On the northern shore of the Mediterranean, the Western long-term strategic position proved to be more successful than that of the Soviets. Political developments in Europe's dictatorships – Greece, Spain, and Portugal – validated the liberal project of the Atlantic alliance and the attraction of European integration, while the implementation of the Brezhnev Doctrine and the invasion of

---

29 H. Kissinger, *Years of Upheaval* (Boston, MA,: Little, Brown, 1982), 205–27, 532ff.

16. The 1974 coup in Cyprus and the Turkish intervention that followed split the island in two. Here a Greek-Cypriot woman is looking for a relative lost in the fighting.

Czechoslovakia in 1968 ended the Soviet allure in Europe. Greece's right-wing government had been an element of weakness in the Western system and became even more of a burden after Colonel Dimitrios Ioannides took power in another coup in 1973. The strongly nationalist Ioannides helped organize a coup against the government of Cyprus in 1974, aiming at the unification of that island with Greece.

But the Cyprus coup backfired after Turkey sent in its military in July 1974 to force a division of the island between Greek and Turkish Cypriots. Despairing of the incompetence of the Greek junta and fearful of the return of the Cypriot government under Archbishop Makarios III, whom they considered lukewarm toward the West, the US government acquiesced in the Turkish occupation of the northern part of the area in spite of the massive displacement of Cypriots from both parts of the island that followed. The Greek junta was ousted from power soon after the Cyprus debacle. The old liberal leader, Constantine Karamanlis, then formed a new government which slowly restored democracy to Greece, reestablishing confidence with the Western allies and joining the EEC in 1981.[30]

The runaway inflation and the economic downturn caused by the 1973 oil crisis proved the end of the Portuguese dictatorship. On the morning of April

30 C. M. Woodhouse, *The Rise and Fall of the Greek Colonels* (London: Granada, 1985).

17. Mário Soares, the leader of the Portuguese Socialist Party, campaigning in Lisbon in 1975. Soares's party was supported by most of the West European Left.

25, 1974, a group of officers calling themselves the Movement of the Armed Forces (Movimento das Forças Armadas – MFA) took power in Lisbon in a bloodless coup. The Carnation Revolution, which they initiated, aimed at a full-scale withdrawal from Africa and a gradual move toward full democracy guided by the MFA. In reality, the officers soon lost control of the situation in the colonies, with a civil war breaking out in the most important of them, Angola.[31] The collapse of the empire also meant a large influx of refugees into an already impoverished home country.

By late 1974, it seemed as if Portugal was heading toward political chaos, with the Portuguese Communist Party (PCP) as the best-organized political force. In early 1975, right-wing officers launched a failed coup, which seemed to put the MFA radicals and the the hardline Communists in the political driver's seat. But through hard campaigning and substantial help from a motley group of international helpers – including the US government and various West European socialists and social-democrats – the Socialist Party under Mário Soares became the biggest party after the April 1975 elections. In November 1975, moderate army officers disbanded the MFA organization.

31 See Piero Gleijeses's chapter in this volume.

The leader of the centre-right within the military, Colonel António Ramalho Eanes, was elected president in June 1976. Eanes invited Soares to become premier in the first democratically elected Portuguese government for more than fifty years.

This progression of events had a significant impact upon the Cold War in the Mediterranean. From a strategic point of view, Portuguese air bases and ports were vital for NATO's forces on the continent. Even more important was control of Madeira because it protected the North Atlantic routes to Gibraltar, while the Azores provided refuelling facilities for rapid deployment of US troops to the Mediterranean and the Middle East. As a result, when the MFA had begun cooperating with the Moscow-oriented Portuguese Communists, there had been deep-seated alarm in NATO circles. Soares's government did much to calm these fears. He kept Portugal within NATO, while moving quickly toward membership in the EEC, which the country achieved in 1986.

In Spain, when Franco died on November 20, 1975, the country had already entered a period of economic growth, and this eased the political transition and strengthened the Western position in the Mediterranean. At first, it was very unclear which direction the young king, Juan Carlos, would move in. He appointed an old Franco supporter, Carlos Arias Navarro, as his prime minister, and himself swore allegiance to Franco's principles and the political movement the general had founded, the Movimiento Nacional (National Movement). The political opposition – including the well-organized and Euro-Communist oriented Spanish Communist Party – prepared for a long struggle ahead.

Soon, however, it became clear that Juan Carlos was ready to move beyond the confines of his mentor's policies. In the summer of 1976, during a visit to Washington, the king made clear his commitment to rapid democratization and appealed for American support. On his return home, he replaced Navarro with the younger Adolfo Suárez as prime minister. Together, the king and Suárez began to dismantle Franco's system methodically and move toward free elections, releasing political prisoners and legalizing the political opposition as they went along. The enormous outpouring of popular support for the young king made the transformation possible; it was Juan Carlos who became the guarantor of a democratic Spain in alliance with the United States and Western Europe.

Following the invasion of Czechoslovakia, the Italian Communist Party had been beset with internal debates. A long period of disillusionment ended only when Enrico Berlinguer became general secretary in 1972 and began to construct the Euro-Communist initiative,[32] In 1973, for the first time, Berlinguer spoke in favor of the Atlantic alliance. Although terrorists from both the left wing and right wing had the country under siege and the liberal center seemed to be collapsing, something new was happening in Italian politics. In 1978, the kidnapping and assassination of Aldo Moro, the head of the Christian Democrats, marked the moment of greatest peril. But the government succeeded in crushing terrorism without impairing democracy, and a new consensus emerged regarding Italy's appropriate place in the Western bloc.[33]

France also became more amenable to Washington's wishes than it had been during the presidency of de Gaulle. After the general resigned in 1969 and died the following year, his successor, Georges Pompidou, did not share the anti-American spirit of his predecessor. Although a fervent Gaullist, Pompidou realized that his predecessor's ambitious foreign policy, including the pursuit of leadership in Europe and Africa, aroused substantial public opposition and had been costly. Pompidou sought to cooperate with les Anglo-Saxons in Europe. He reconsidered Britain's application for membership in the EEC and collaborated with Washington and London in the Mediterranean.[34] After Algeria nationalized its oil and gas reserves in 1971, France was as vulnerable to OPEC's diplomacy and as dependent as the rest of Western Europe on America's arbitration of Middle Eastern affairs.

The Americanization of the Mediterranean

During the period dealt with in this chapter, roughly 1960–1975, there was no direct confrontation in Europe between the United States and the Soviet Union. On the contrary, Moscow and Washington began to cooperate on broader disarmament issues and they negotiated a Strategic Arms Limitation Treaty (SALT) and an Anti-Ballistic Missile (ABM) Treaty as well as a series of other agreements.[35] Yet, it was also a period of rivalry in the Mediterranean, and the Soviet Union ultimately suffered substantial political setbacks after making serious advances up to the late 1960s. In the aftermath of the 1967

---

32 See Silvio Pons's chapter in volume III.
33 C. Sterling, *The Terror Network: Secret War of International Terrorism* (New York: Holt, Rinehart and Winston, 1981).
34 See N. Piers Ludlow's chapter in this volume. G.-H. Soutou, *La Guerre de Cinquante Ans: Le conflit Est-Ouest,1943–1990,* (Paris: Fayard, 2001), 470–77.
35 See Robert D. Schulzinger's chapter and Marc Trachtenberg's chapter in this volume.

Arab–Israeli war, the Kremlin had a chance to solidify its relations with the oil-producing Arab states. At the same time, Moscow could capitalize diplomatically on America's association with Israel and the US collaboration with European fascist, authoritarian, and neocolonial regimes. Soviet leaders hoped to align themselves with the exploited "South" against a rapacious "North." But the Soviets miscalculated and their ambitions collapsed. They mistakenly severed diplomatic relations with Tel Aviv and weakened their diplomatic leverage. They overestimated the ideological affinity between themselves and Arab nationalists and did not have the economic power and geopolitical leverage to exert significant influence. In effect, the United States was able to combine its "hard" and its "soft" power to regain its position of supremacy in the Middle East. The Western European states, meanwhile, were unable to adopt a unified Mediterranean policy due to their conflicting agendas and imperial legacies. Their response to the Arab–Israeli crisis was confused and reflected their vulnerability to the Arab oil weapon. The United States alone was strong enough to exert its will in the region diplomatically, economically, and politically.

Henry Kissinger's declaring 1973 to be the "year of Europe" has often been met with criticism. But although transatlantic relations were at a low ebb and although US actions often antagonized its NATO partners, the accession of Britain, Ireland, and Denmark to the EEC opened the way for the subsequent inclusion of southern Europe's former dictatorships. No longer did the West have a vulnerable southern flank. Seeing the region as one integrated whole helps us understand the significance of the transformations that took place: the Soviet Union lost its position in the Middle East, and Spain, Portugal, and Greece transformed themselves politically, strengthened democratic institutions, and became a bulwark against Soviet designs. The Cold War entered a new phase. With the Mediterranean solidly in the US orbit, Africa became the new battlefield.

13

The Cold War in the Third World, 1963–1975

MICHAEL E. LATHAM

In 1958, only one year after his country gained independence from Britain, the Ghanaian prime minister, Kwame Nkrumah, delivered a speech before the Council on Foreign Relations in New York. In addition to a resolute anti-imperialism, he emphasized that two related imperatives would play a crucial role in shaping the orientation of Africa toward the wider world. First, the tremendous "industrial and military power concentrated behind the two great powers in the Cold War" demanded that the new states of Africa pursue a policy of non-alignment. In Africa, Nkrumah insisted, "the opportunities of health and education and a wider vision which other nations take for granted are barely within reach of our people." To preserve their impoverished continent from devastating violence, African nations would have to remain apart from the Cold War's military alliances, rivalries, and strife. Second, Africa would have to seek dramatically accelerated development. Colonial overlords had failed to deliver promised advances, but "now comes our response. We cannot tell our peoples that material benefits and growth and modern progress are not for them. If we do, they will throw us out and seek other leaders who promise more. And they will abandon us, too, if we do not in reasonable measure respond to their hopes. We have modernize."[1]

In the late 1950s and early 1960s, the goals of non-alignment and rapid development shaped the ambitions of a wide range of postcolonial leaders. From the Asian–African Conference at Bandung (1955) through the Non-Aligned Conferences at Belgrade (1961) and Cairo (1964), figures like Indonesia's Ahmed Sukarno, India's Jawaharlal Nehru, Algeria's Ahmed Ben Bella, and Egypt's Gamal Abdel Nasser articulated a shared vision of anti-imperialism, disarmament, accelerated development, expanded trade, and economic cooperation among those emerging from colonial domination. Above all, they

---

1 Jussi Hanhimäki and Odd Arne Westad (eds.), *The Cold War: A History in Documents and Eyewitness Accounts* (Oxford: Oxford University Press, 2003), 355–56.

rejected the ideological rigidity of the Cold War and insisted on the right to define freely their own paths to progress in a world of different social systems. As the official declaration from the Belgrade conference put it, "aware that ideological differences are necessarily a part of the growth of the human society, the participating countries consider that peoples and governments shall refrain from any use of ideologies for the purpose of waging cold war, exercising pressure, or imposing their will."[2]

That hope, however, would go unrealized. For the United States, the Soviet Union, and the People's Republic of China (PRC), the Cold War was a *fundamentally* ideological conflict, a struggle over the direction of global history and the definition of modernity itself. At the very same moment that the first generation of postcolonial leaders articulated their ambitions for non-aligned, self-determined development, each of the Cold War's main adversaries approached the phenomenon of decolonization through hegemonic, universalistic models of social change. In that context, Third World elites made a variety of difficult choices. Some, attracted to the Soviet Union's impressive record of industrialization and eager to centralize their authority in strong state and party structures, sought ties to Moscow. Others gravitated toward the vastly superior economic resources and development funds offered by the United States and international financial bodies. A final group of states, wary of the military alliances that were often linked to development aid, drew selectively from the different camps, played the superpowers off against each other, and tried to maintain an independent course. In the ideologies through which American, Soviet, and Chinese policymakers interpreted the world, decolonization expanded the scope of the Cold War and created new fields in which the struggle over the acceleration and destination of global change would be fought. In the upheavals of Third World revolution, each of the major powers came to perceive crucial test cases in which liberal capitalism and diverse forms of state socialism would engage in a contest of universal and lasting significance. As a result, places like Cuba, Vietnam, Indonesia, Congo, and Angola all became points of intense Cold War conflict.

Cold War interventions in the Third World would also become more lethal over time. In the early 1960s, the major Cold War adversaries approached the postcolonial world with striking ambitions. Despite the obvious differences in their objectives, US, Soviet, and Chinese policymakers all believed that

---

2 "Declaration of the Heads of State or Government of Non-Aligned Countries," in Henry M. Christman (ed.), *Neither East Nor West: The Basic Documents of Non-Alignment* (New York: Sheed and Ward, 1973), 57.

decolonization provided them with a moment of profound opportunity, a window in which they might draw on their own historical experience to identify the crucial levers of social change and transform the future of Asia, Africa, Latin America, and the Middle East. By the mid-1960s, however, their expectations became increasingly frustrated. The Third World, they learned, was not nearly as malleable as they had anticipated. American policymakers found themselves unable to promote a modernizing turn to liberal, democratic capitalism in Latin America and Southeast Asia. Soviet leaders faced growing tensions with Cuba and watched in dismay as governments they supported in Southeast Asia and Africa were overthrown. Chinese policymakers, finally, witnessed diplomatic reversals in Africa and the erosion of their relationship with North Vietnam.

The result, by the late 1960s, was a reorientation in Soviet, American, and Chinese policies that only amplified the ideological polarization of the Third World. As the first postcolonial governments were replaced by repressive military dictatorships or radical Marxist regimes, the space for nationalist elites to pursue viable, non-aligned development diminished. By the middle of the decade, US policymakers increasingly shifted from approaches stressing modernization and accelerated development to a greater reliance on direct coercion and military force. The Soviet Union also turned from a pluralistic embrace of anticolonial movements toward a more rigid insistence on Marxist–Leninist party-building. China, meanwhile, emerged from the chaos of the Cultural Revolution willing to support nearly any cause in the campaign against its Soviet rival. By the late 1960s, superpower-supported violence escalated dramatically. The struggle to determine the course of the Third World helped destroy the foundations for détente, but the greatest damage was done by its contribution to a tragic pattern of expanded militarization, civil war, and human suffering across some of the poorest regions of the globe.

Ideology and the acceleration of history

As many historians have argued, the policies that the major powers directed toward the Third World were shaped by a complex range of factors. Evaluations of strategic demands, material and economic objectives, domestic political forces, bureaucratic politics, and the variables of personality all played significant roles. Yet the fact that countries such as Vietnam and Angola, on the distant periphery, far from national borders and vital markets, became points of intense superpower conflict also suggests the value of taking ideology seriously. The Cold War, as one scholar explains, was driven by "fundamentally incompatible conceptions of the organization of political, economic, and social life … Indeed, power came in large measure to be defined in ideological terms, gains or losses during the Cold War being measured by the global advance or retreat of regime types to an extent that would confound an orthodox realist."[3] Ideology alone certainly did not wholly determine superpower policies. But as David Engerman argues, recognizing its significance can provide us with a better understanding of the way policymakers defined and pursued a broad range of national interests.[4]

The American, Soviet, and Chinese conceptions of security at home were also intimately tied to the expansion and preservation of their social systems abroad. As European empires collapsed, US policymakers feared that Communists would prey on conditions of poverty and instability to subvert fragile new states. They also worried that a failure to counter such designs with a compelling response of their own would do immense damage to American credibility, emboldening radical aggressors, disheartening allies, and jeopardizing the domestic political consensus needed to support what John F. Kennedy famously called a "long twilight struggle." By the early 1960s, Soviet and Chinese strategists had also concluded that the Third World was an arena of crucial significance. While Soviet capabilities did not enable the same reach, Nikita Khrushchev determined that the rapid decolonization of the world had created a moment in which the "transition to socialism" might be promoted abroad in ways that would help secure the historical foundations of the Soviet state. Mao Zedong, profoundly impressed by the global anti-imperial struggle, also concluded that "only when China's superior moral position in the world had been recognized by other peoples would the consolidation of his continuous revolution's momentum at home be assured."[5] These ideologies certainly did not preclude Cold War powers from pursuing more pragmatic policies, nor did they remain fixed in stone. At different points in time each government supported regimes or movements that had little interest in their own social ideals. As this chapter will explain, these ideologies also changed over time. At the high tide of decolonization, however, they played crucial roles as conceptual frameworks through which policymakers made sense of a rapidly changing world and sought to act upon it.

3 Nigel Gould-Davies, "The Logic of Soviet Cultural Diplomacy," *Diplomatic History* 27 (2003): 195.
4 See David C. Engerman's chapter in volume I.
5 Chen Jian, *Mao's China and the Cold War* (Chapel Hill, NC: University of North Carolina Press, 2001), 15.

Central to the thinking of policymakers in Washington, Moscow, and Beijing as well was a common tendency to interpret decolonization as evidence of history's global direction. While each power defined that direction in sharply different terms, they all concluded that history was ultimately on their side, and that its course might be profoundly accelerated. In the United States, the ideology of modernization was especially significant in this regard. From the late 1940s through the mid-1960s, American social scientists drew on older, Enlightenment assumptions to frame theories defining a fundamental transition from "traditional" worlds shaped by the contours of family, ascribed status, religion, and fatalism to "modern" orders characterized by individualism, achieved status, rationalism, and scientific confidence in the promise of progress. Sociologists such as Talcott Parsons and Daniel Lerner, political scientists like Gabriel Almond and Lucian Pye, and economists like Max Millikan and Walt Rostow all concluded that the world was moving along a single, universal trajectory in which the impact of Western ideals and technology was creating a "revolution of rising expectations." By positioning the liberal, democratic, capitalist United States at the endpoint of their historical scale, they also gave this framework a decidedly encouraging cast. The United States, theorists maintained, had experienced the world's first "modern" revolution, and others might now follow in its wake.

That conclusion went down well in an American culture that had long defined its own history in prophetic, regenerative terms. It also fit well in the Cold War context. Social scientists, working on projects often funded by the state itself, were quick to point out the strategic significance of their work. While necessary and beneficial, they explained, the transition toward modernity could also be disruptive and chaotic. Societies caught in the anxiety and uncertainty generated by the erosion of traditional worldviews often sought new forms of belonging, substitutions for their fallen faiths, and shortcuts to modernity, and that fact kept the field open for the dangers of Communist subversion. The Communists, as Rostow argued, were "scavengers of the transitional process," a malevolent force that preyed on societies at their most vulnerable moment. But the United States did not have to stand idly on history's sidelines. Using the tools of foreign aid, development planning, and technical assistance, the United States could dramatically accelerate the passage of traditional societies through a crucial "take-off" toward the modern endpoint. By accelerating the great transition, it could slam shut the narrow window of opportunity that Communist aggressors sought to exploit and produce a safer, liberal, more democratic world of thriving capitalist societies.

The Kennedy administration took those ideas to heart and prominent social scientists took on significant roles in US policymaking. But their theories were probably most compelling because they crystallized a set of core assumptions about the transformative power of American ideals that was already widely shared among Cold War liberals. As Kennedy himself argued before the US Congress, "We live at a very special moment in history. The whole southern half of the world – Latin America, Africa, the Middle East, and Asia – are caught up in the adventures of asserting their independence and modernizing their old ways of life." The world's "new nations," moreover, needed American help because they were "under Communist pressure ... But the fundamental task of our foreign aid program in the 1960s is not negatively to fight Communism: Its fundamental task is to help make a historical demonstration that in the twentieth century, as in the nineteenth – in the southern half of the globe as in the north – economic growth and political democracy can develop hand in hand."[6]

The acceleration of modernity also became a fundamental policy goal. As part of an American-sponsored "Decade of Development," the Kennedy administration launched an Alliance for Progress with Latin America, a ten-year program designed to raise economic growth rates, promote education, improve health care, provide housing, and engineer comprehensive development planning through democratic institutions. The Peace Corps sent thousands of young Americans to promote modernization through "community development" programs in Asia, Africa, Latin America, and the Middle East. The administration also promoted modernization as a counterinsurgency strategy in South Vietnam, linking military objectives to an ambitious vision of social engineering. In Iran, finally, US policymakers hoped that the Shah's "White Revolution" would promote economic growth and diversification as well as form a liberalizing alliance between the monarch and a newly educated, progressive-minded peasantry. American policymakers deeply feared Communist movements in the Third World. But by accelerating the course of modernization they hoped to contain Communism and possibly drive the world into a historical stage in which it would no longer have any appeal.

To an even greater extent than their American counterparts, Soviet strategic thinkers envisaged a world of opportunity in the early 1960s. Following Iosif Stalin's death, the Soviet leadership embarked on a prolonged ideological reassessment. Several related factors shaped that process. First, Soviet strategists came to believe that the advent of tremendously destructive nuclear

6 Hanhimäki and Westad (eds.), *The Cold War*, 361.

weapons made the inevitability of total war between Communist and capital-ist states less certain. That conclusion, in turn, placed a new premium on the development of activist policies designed to accelerate the longer-term spread of socialism in conditions of "peaceful coexistence." Where Stalinists had defined a world rigidly divided between a "socialist" camp constituted by the Soviet Union and the Marxist–Leninist states loyal to it and a "capitalist" camp made up of all others, Khrushchev believed that Third World leaders, even determinedly nationalist ones, were not mere "stooges of imperialism" or pawns of their former colonial masters. As Mark Bradley argues, for Khrushchev, decolonization marked a decisive, global turning point.[7] The new, postcolonial states of the world, he concluded, could potentially become elements of a "vast zone of peace," a broad coalition of progressive forces standing in opposition to the powers of imperialism. As Khrushchev declared in 1956, "the new period in world history, predicted by Lenin, when the peoples of the East would play an active part in deciding the destinies of the entire world and become a new and mighty factor in international relations has arrived."[8]

From the late 1950s through the mid-1960s, Soviet leaders worked to put these new concepts in practice. As they debated the possibility that the historical path to socialism might take on a variety of different forms, strate-gists such as Boris Ponomarev, head of the International Department of the CPSU Central Committee, joined Khrushchev in considering the implica-tions of the new thinking for Soviet Third World policy. Soviet analysts often disagreed with each other, but like their American counterparts, they came to define the decolonizing world as fundamentally "transitional" and concluded that time was ultimately on their side. Postcolonial and especially non-aligned states, one scholar explains, "were not conceived to be static in equilibrium between capitalism and socialism. Instead, struggling 'progressive forces' within these historically transitional states were expected to encourage them over time to cooperate ever more closely with the socialist camp."[9] Soviet leaders believed that their country's record of steadfast opposition to coloni-alism and impressive economic growth would appeal to Third World elites seeking an alternative to global capitalism and collaboration with imperial powers. They also expected that as working-class and proletarian forces

---

7 See Mark Philip Bradley's chapter in volume I.
8 Bruce D. Porter, The USSR in Third World Conflicts: Soviet Arms and Diplomacy in Local Wars, 1945–1980 (Cambridge: Cambridge University Press, 1984), 17–18.
9 Roy Allison, The Soviet Union and the Strategy of Non-Alignment in the Third World (Cambridge: Cambridge University Press, 1988), 9–10.

gained strength, bourgeois nationalists might form alliances with them and help convert anti-imperialist revolutions into anticapitalist ones. The result would be a trend toward socialism that did not necessarily require armed struggle, a firm allegiance to Marxist principles, or the instrumental, vanguard role of Communist parties.

Following that optimistic vision, the Soviet Union moved quickly to develop close ties with a wide range of postcolonial states. Nehru's India, Sukarno's Indonesia, Nasser's Egypt, Ben Bella's Algeria, and Nkrumah's Ghana all received significant amounts of Soviet military and economic aid. While many Third World recipients of Soviet assistance embraced radical economic policies, the vast majority of them were not Marxist states. Many of them also declared their firm commitment to policies of non-alignment and even suppressed local Communist parties. The Soviets hoped, however, that anti-imperial, nationalist movements would ultimately turn in socialist directions. As Piero Gleijeses explains, Fidel Castro's Cuba became the greatest and most famous source of Soviet enthusiasm in the early 1960s.[10] Although Castro had taken power without Moscow's support, Khrushchev and his colleagues quickly came to perceive the Cuban revolution as both a reflection of the Soviet past and a vision of the future.

The Soviet commitment to "national liberation movements" also led to an intervention in the former Belgian colony of Congo. In the summer of 1960, only weeks after Congo gained independence, the mineral-rich province of Katanga seceded with help from Brussels. Newly elected prime minister and former labor leader Patrice Lumumba then requested that the United Nations (UN) intervene to end the rebellion and expel Belgian military forces from the country. Worried that Lumumba might follow in Castro's footsteps and fearful that he would export his country's uranium to the Soviets, Washington helped ensure that the UN peacekeeping mission would not support his goals. In frustration, Lumumba then accepted a Soviet aid offer, and Khrushchev moved quickly to intervene. The Soviets delivered hundreds of trucks, some two dozen aircraft, and several helicopters to enable Congolese troops to mount an offensive against Katanga. In September, as Lumumba began to make progress, the United States made plans to assassinate him and supported a coup by Colonel Joseph Mobutu of the Congolese army. Lumumba's subsequent capture and murder by his Congolese and Katangese adversaries was a severe blow for Moscow's policy. By delivering arms to Congo and criticizing the UN for supporting the colonizers, however,

10 See Piero Gleijeses's chapter in this volume.

Khrushchev challenged the West and appealed to the Third World with a
clear, anti-imperial stance.

Chinese policymakers also perceived decolonization as a force for tremendous revolutionary change. Yet in contrast to Washington and Moscow,
Beijing did not suddenly come to that conclusion in the mid-1950s and early
1960s. For Mao Zedong, China's own long historical experience in the revolutionary struggle against Western imperialism made his nation a "natural ally"
of the world's "oppressed peoples." From the time the People's Republic was
founded, Mao defined the promotion of national liberation as a core element
of China's revolutionary mission. In the late 1940s, Mao placed China within
the vast "intermediate zone" of oppressed, non-Western countries standing
between the threat of US imperialism and the Soviet socialism he admired.
Promoting national liberation in the decolonizing world, Mao believed, would
help ensure the survival of China's own revolution and defend socialism as a
whole. In this regard, Mao and his prime minister, Zhou Enlai, sought close
relations with decolonizing countries even before that objective became a
major Soviet priority. At the 1955 Bandung Conference, for example, Zhou
eagerly pursued a common "united front" against imperialism among postcolonial states that often had little interest in the formal ideology of the
Chinese Communist Party.

Starting in the late 1950s, as Sergey Radchenko notes, the growing Sino-
Soviet schism also affected Chinese Third World policy.[11] When the Soviets
declined to back China in a Sino-Indian border conflict in 1959, and
Khrushchev appeared to value his relationship with the non-aligned Nehru
over solidarity with Mao, underlying ideological tensions burst into the open.
Mao attacked Khrushchev's "revisionism" and insisted that war with the forces
of imperialism remained inevitable. "Peaceful coexistence," he argued, was
merely a temporary condition, and the "transition to socialism" could only
proceed through armed struggle and class conflict. More fundamentally, Mao
also viewed the question of Third World revolution through a domestic lens.
Worried about the potential for bureaucratic stagnation and a loss of momentum, he sought to accelerate China's own drive from socialism to genuine
Communism and feared that Soviet backsliding might infect and corrupt his
own government's revolutionary commitments. Just as he promoted the
disastrous Great Leap Forward at home, he sought to mobilize his country
behind a more radical policy abroad.

11 See Sergey Radchenko's chapter in this volume.

Chinese Third World activism in the early and mid-1960s, therefore, reflected a desire to counter American imperialism and demonstrate Beijing's claim to global revolutionary leadership, a project pursued most aggressively in Vietnam and Africa. While Mao had supported Vietnam's revolution since 1950, as the Sino-Soviet split deepened China dramatically increased its commitment. China's experience, Mao believed, was an essential model for the Vietnamese, and support for that revolution became a "litmus test for 'true communism.'"[12] Worried that higher levels of Soviet aid would draw the North Vietnamese closer to the Kremlin, Mao increased China's own weapons deliveries and deployed a total of over 320,000 engineering, anti-aircraft, transportation, and logistic troops starting in 1965. In the event of an American invasion of North Vietnam, Mao also promised that China would send its own combat units to defend the revolution. In the early 1960s, Zhou Enlai also made three separate trips to Africa, visiting Algeria, Ethiopia, Egypt, Ghana, Guinea, Mali, Morocco, Somalia, Sudan, and Tunisia in one journey that lasted from December of 1963 through February of 1964. Anticolonial guerrilla commanders were invited to train in China, the PRC sent doctors to Africa despite their shortage at home, and huge shipments of Chinese rice and maize arrived in Guinea and the Sudan even as famine afflicted China itself. In Southeast Asia and Africa, China aimed to promote revolutions that would embody its own experience. As Politburo member Lin Biao confidently declared in 1965, the revolutionary encirclement of the cities by triumphant rural forces during China's civil war was about to be replicated on a global scale. As the "people's revolutionary movement in Asia, Africa, and Latin America" continued "growing vigorously," it would steadily surround and overwhelm North America and Europe, putting both the Americans and the Soviets on the defensive.[13]

By the mid-1960s, American, Soviet, and Chinese policymakers perceived decolonization and national liberation as forces of immense significance. Where Americans envisioned modernization as a means to confront the Communist inroads they so feared, Soviet strategists optimistically defined the Third World as a rich field for socialist transformation. Chinese policymakers, finally, insisted on the wider validity of their own anticolonial revolution in opposition to the United States as well as their Soviet rivals.

12 Chen, *Mao's China*, 211.
13 George T. Yu, "China and the Third World," *Asian Survey*, 17 (1977), 1038.

Failures and reassessments

Ambitions to direct and channel postcolonial aspirations, however, were soon disappointed. As they learned, often painfully, that the Third World was not nearly as malleable as they had assumed, both American and Soviet policy-makers struggled to reorient their approaches. Chinese policy, consumed by domestic turmoil, also underwent a major shift. The result, by the end of the 1960s, was a sharp escalation in armed conflict and violence.

Much of the frustration experienced by the great powers stemmed from the fact that Third World elites were never simply passive recipients of modernizing or revolutionary models. While they certainly were attracted to the promises of accelerated development and state-building, postcolonial leaders often played the superpowers off against each other and adapted their ideologies for their own purposes. Where Soviet, American, and Chinese policymakers tended to see their models as complete, indivisible packages, Third World leaders displayed a remarkable proclivity for selecting and blending diverse elements while combining them with their own historically and culturally defined priorities.

American policymakers found that phenomenon particularly troublesome. Modernization, in their view, was a single, integrated process in which step-by-step advances in capitalist structures, psychological transformations, and political democracy would each reinforce the other. But leaders like Nehru, willing to "skip stages" and experiment in the pursuit of rapid change, eagerly combined ideas drawn from both Soviet and American experience. In an attempt to contain China and demonstrate its commitment to postcolonial Asia, the Kennedy administration provided substantial support for India's economic development. The problem, however, was that Americans and Indians had fundamentally different understandings of what "development" itself meant. Nehru was deeply impressed by the Soviet record of rapid industrialization, embraced Soviet-style centralized planning, and strongly emphasized the production of steel, machinery, and capital goods. Indian planners also rejected the advice of American economists that instead of a crash drive toward industrialization, long-term development required greater attention to agriculture and balanced growth. Along with Nehru's sharp criticism of US intervention in Vietnam, his leftward economic turn alienated many American supporters. US aid helped alleviate an Indian economic crisis, but the relationship between the two countries remained tense. Through Nehru's death in 1964, the ideology of modernization prevented much of the US government from recognizing that Nehru's interest in Soviet economics did not extend to Soviet politics.[14]

The internal contradictions and failures of modernization, experienced across different regions, also contributed to a reassessment of US Third World policy during the Johnson administration. Modernization, in the Kennedy period, was frequently considered as an alternative to the direct deployment of American military force, a way to promote structural solutions and win the Cold War in the Third World by speeding up the course of history itself. Lyndon Johnson and his advisers did not completely abandon that perspective, but they did determine that the risk of Communist gains and the potential damage to American credibility required far more immediate and coercive action. As scholars such as Nils Gilman have argued, the ideology of modernization was always ambivalent at best regarding the question of democracy, and by the mid-1960s it increasingly became "the intellectual equivalent of hitting the gas pedal on a skidding car: an attempt to accelerate out of a problem. As moderate solutions to development failed again and again, hard-core solutions found more and more advocates."[15]

In Latin America, Johnson responded to the failures of the Alliance for Progress by reorienting the program away from its original reformist ambitions. By the mid-1960s, few Latin American nations had reached targeted economic growth rates or made expected increases in popular living standards. A handful, such as Rómulo Betancourt's Venezuela, did reduce unemployment, promote modest agrarian reform, and increase the share of the national budget devoted to education and health care. But many Latin American liberals found that their ability to fund further reforms was seriously constrained by the declining terms of trade between exports of primary goods and the imports of manufactured products. The program's economic contradictions were compounded by political ones. Kennedy had warned that "those who make peaceful revolution impossible will make violent revolution inevitable," but the idea of promoting "revolution" of any kind threatened conservative, anti-Communist oligarchs. In Guatemala, for example, Alliance-sponsored community leadership training, literacy programs, and financial cooperatives empowered Indians and poor peasants to challenge the dominance of merchants and landowners. At the same time, however, elites red-baited their adversaries and used the steady flow of US

14 David C. Engerman, "The Romance of Economic Development and New Histories of the Cold War," *Diplomatic History*, 28 (2004), 23–35.
15 Nils Gilman, *Mandarins of the Future: Modernization Theory in Cold War America* (Baltimore, MD: Johns Hopkins University Press, 2003), 12, 50–51.

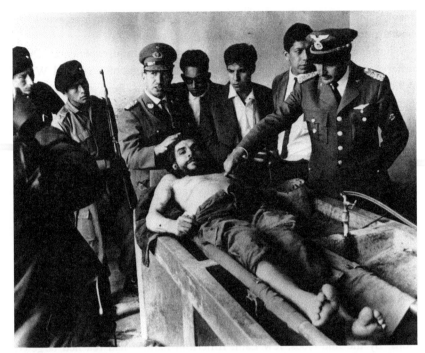

18. The body of Che Guevara. He was executed after being captured in Bolivia in 1967. Guevara was regarded as the most dangerous opponent of US influence in Latin America.

counterinsurgency aid to make war against them. Johnson did little to correct these failings, and as US-sponsored repression gutted the developmental gains that modernizers had sought, anti-Communist anxieties killed the "peaceful revolution" in its infancy.[16]

The promotion of authoritarian regimes may not have been Johnson's first choice, but as modernization ran aground in Latin America he concluded that such a policy would certainly be preferable to the uncertainties of long-term, democratic development. Thomas Mann, Johnson's new assistant secretary of state for Latin American affairs, outlined the administration's approach in 1964 by declaring that the United States would no longer make democratic reforms a condition for the delivery of US military and economic aid under the Alliance. In the struggle to prevent a "second Cuba," order and anti-Communist stability would have to precede

16 Stephen M. Streeter, "Nation Building in the Land of Eternal Counterinsurgency: Guatemala and the Contradictions of the Alliance for Progress," *Third World Quarterly* 27, (2006), 57–68.

progress. Accordingly, the administration moved quickly to recognize military coups against left-leaning governments in Brazil, Bolivia, and several other states. More dramatically, in April 1965 the Johnson administration invaded the Dominican Republic with 33,000 troops to prevent the possible return to power of Juan Bosch, a progressive who had been democratically elected in late 1962 and overthrown by a conservative junta ten months later. Although evidence of Communist activity among the pro-Bosch forces was very thin, Johnson concluded that the risk of subversion was simply intolerable.

In Vietnam, Johnson also determined that America could not wait for modernization to produce its expected miracles. While deeply concerned about Communist gains, in 1961 Kennedy planners still believed that it might be possible to derail the Vietnamese revolution through a blend of development and counterinsurgency programs. As the United States increased the flow of arms and advisers, it also stepped up civil service training programs and urged Ngo Dinh Diem toward liberal reforms. The heart of the effort, however, unfolded in the countryside where the United States directed a massive plan to relocate the Vietnamese peasantry in "strategic hamlets" that would separate them from the insurgents and allow for government-sponsored development programs to win their loyalty and support. That ambitious mix of military tactics and social engineering failed miserably. South Vietnamese government and military leaders frequently abused the peasantry they were supposed to protect and assist, but the more fundamental causes were grounded in an ideology that ignored the realities of Vietnamese history and culture. Although US officials continued to define Diem as the root of the problem and hoped for greater success after his removal in late 1963, the National Liberation Front continued to gain ground and American pessimism steadily grew.

Johnson's response was a forceful one. As Fredrik Logevall explains, Johnson feared that a withdrawal from Vietnam would do irreparable damage to America's global credibility as well as his own domestic political power and personal authority.[17] Development-centered counterinsurgency programs continued in South Vietnam, and in April of 1965 Johnson dramatically offered to build a Tennessee Valley Authority on the Mekong Delta. Yet, the president concluded that long-term, structural efforts at "nation building" were simply not enough. In early 1965, he ordered the sustained bombing of North Vietnam, and by 1967 more than a half million US combat troops were in the field. Modernizing ambitions did not vanish, but visions for structural

---

17 See Fredrik Logevall's chapter in this volume.

change were largely eclipsed by a massive war of attrition designed simply to kill revolutionaries faster than they could be replaced.

In Indonesia, the United States also turned toward a more aggressive policy. By 1964, Sukarno's political confrontation with British-supported Malaysia, his mismanagement of the Indonesian economy, and his declared promise to shift Indonesian politics to the left all alarmed Washington officials. Where US policymakers had previously tolerated Sukarno's neutralism and seen his government as a viable alternative to the Indonesian Communist Party, they now began to work covertly for his removal. In 1965, when General Suharto and other Indonesian army leaders put down a revolt by junior officers and crippled Sukarno's power, the Johnson administration was elated. The United States also threw its firm support behind the army's relentless, sweeping campaign to expose and execute Indonesia's Communists and suspected sympathizers. A resolute American stance in Vietnam, US officials concluded, had emboldened Indonesia's military and might help promote a crucial turn throughout the rest of Southeast Asia as well.

In Vietnam, Latin America, Iran, and Indonesia, US policymakers also discarded even the tentative steps they had previously made to promote liberal reforms. By strongly supporting a string of dictators in Saigon, backing the Shah of Iran's political repression, supporting an anti-Communist, military-driven bloodbath in Indonesia, and embracing right-wing coups across Latin America, the United States steadily turned toward "bureaucratic author-itarian" solutions. Modernization promised stability through long-term pro-gress, but by the mid-1960s US policymakers concluded that the immediate preservation of anti-Communist order required a much more direct approach.

The Soviets also engaged in a revision of their Third World policy during the mid-1960s. Like their American counterparts, Soviet strategists were dismayed by the willingness of postcolonial elites to chart independent courses. Mao Zedong's growing hostility, in particular, raised wider questions about the wisdom of committing precious Soviet resources to build alliances with regimes that might refuse to follow the Soviet political line, or, worse, become potential adversaries. Soviet aid to self-proclaimed, non-aligned socialists like Sukarno and Nkrumah also raised doubts. Neither Indonesia nor Ghana had embarked on a disciplined "transition" to "scientific" Marxist socialism, and both governments had proven unstable enough to fall victim to military coups in the mid-1960s, a result that destroyed years of Soviet political and capital investment.

Frustrated relations with Cuba also played a significant role in triggering a Soviet reevaluation. Castro's fury, when Khrushchev removed Soviet missiles from Cuban soil without consulting him, and his decision to block the international inspections intended to resolve the missile crisis alarmed Kremlin leaders. Protests by Che Guevara over the terms of Soviet aid, Cuba's refusal to follow the USSR in signing the Nuclear Test-Ban Treaty, Cuban criticism of Soviet trade with its Latin American enemies, and state trials of members of the old, pre-revolutionary Cuban Communist Party all strained relations between Havana and Moscow. Where Soviet policymakers had once envisioned the Cuban revolution as a wondrous sign of socialist advance and solidarity, by 1966 they found themselves listening to a doggedly independent Castro attack the USSR for its failure to recognize the need for armed struggle in the cause of global revolution.

The Soviet investment in Egypt did not live up to Khrushchev's expectations either. Starting in the 1950s, the USSR took significant steps to cultivate an alliance by providing funding for the Aswan High Dam and supporting Egypt during the Suez crisis. Nasser, however, held firmly to his policy of non-alignment and cracked down aggressively on Egyptian Communists, imprisoning many of them. After Cairo and Damascus created the United Arab Republic in 1958, Nasser spread his anti-Communist campaign into Syria and condemned Soviet support for Communist elements in Iraq as well. While Khrushchev hoped that Egypt would take a more radical turn to the left, Nasser angrily accused the Soviets of hindering the cause of Arab unity and interfering in internal Arab affairs. Although relations improved in the mid-1960s, serious tensions persisted over the terms of Soviet support for the Arab conflict with Israel. Egypt, moreover, never embarked on the kind of thoroughgoing revolutionary transformation that Khrushchev hoped for.

As Svetlana Savranskaya and William Taubman explain, the growing doubt with which Soviet leaders viewed Khrushchev's revolutionary adventurism contributed to his downfall.[18] Doubt also produced a political reconsideration. The "transition to socialism," many strategists concluded, was far more complex than Khrushchev had assumed. Feudalistic forces were more tenacious, peasants less politically mobilized, and the goals of rapid industrialization and land reform far more difficult to achieve than anticipated. Yet the USSR did not retreat from engagement with the Third World under Leonid Brezhnev, nor did Soviet policymakers cease to believe that history was on their side. Indeed, analysts, like Karen Brutents, argued that the USSR should pursue an activist approach. The key, however, would be for the USSR to direct its longer-term, comprehensive support more carefully to movements grounded in explicitly Marxist–Leninist ideology and to place a stronger

18 See Svetlana Savranskaya and William Taubman's chapter in this volume.

emphasis on the role of "vanguard parties" in providing the political structure essential to drive revolutions forward and defend them against imperialist resistance.

As its aspirations for global revolutionary change were chastened, the Soviet Union also shifted its emphasis toward military aid and arms sales, a tool that it often used for shorter-term, instrumental purposes. During the Khrushchev era, the amount of funding for economic development that was offered to a broad range of anticolonial movements and postcolonial states had slightly exceeded levels of military assistance. By the late 1960s, however, the value of military aid surpassed that of development funding, a trend that strongly increased over the next decade. Under Khrushchev limited military capabilities prevented the USSR from playing a larger role in far-flung regions, but under Brezhnev the Soviets used new assets in air transport, shipping, communications, and naval vessels to intervene at much greater levels. Following the American escalation in Vietnam in 1965, the Soviet Union dramatically amplified its military assistance to its Communist ally there, providing the North Vietnamese with surface-to-air missiles, jet fighters, field artillery, and radar as well as technicians and pilots. Thousands of North Vietnamese soldiers and officers also trained in Soviet military schools. But Soviet arms sales, military aid, and advisers also poured into non-Marxist states and fueled wars fought by Egypt, Syria, India, and Iraq. In these cases, the USSR shelved its longer-term, historical vision in favor of the more practical goals of gaining leverage in diplomatic negotiations, obtaining access to naval and air bases, raising hard currency, and frustrating US efforts to build regional alliances. As ideological ambitions cooled, the Soviet Union, like the United States, placed an increasing premium on the utility of force.

From the mid-1960s through the early 1970s, Chinese policymakers endured a series of setbacks of their own in the Third World. The 1965 overthrow of Algeria's Ben Bella eliminated a regime that China had helped come to power and had seen as a model for further armed struggle in Africa. The coup against Sukarno and the decimation of the Indonesian Communist Party in 1965 and 1966 also destroyed a government China hoped would become part of a strong anti-Western alliance in Asia. Several moderate African governments broke relations with the PRC in protest over China's support for insurgencies on that continent, and China's confrontation with India alienated other members of the Non-Aligned Movement. Chinese officials also watched in frustration as their relationship with North Vietnam deteriorated. After Mao dismissed a Soviet proposal for a collaborative approach to assisting the Democratic Republic of Vietnam (DRV) and Soviet arms shipments steadily increased,

Hanoi stopped criticizing Soviet "revisionism." When Le Duan traveled to Moscow in 1966 and referred to the Soviet Union as a "second motherland," Chinese officials were deeply angered. The DRV's 1968 decision to enter into peace negotiations with the United States, over strenuous Chinese objections, also amplified fears of Soviet influence.

As China plunged into the Cultural Revolution from 1966 to 1969, Beijing's Third World policy fell into disarray. While aid to North Vietnam continued, all Chinese ambassadors, with the single exception of the one in Cairo, were recalled to engage in studies of Maoist doctrine, effectively paralyzing the country's diplomatic organization. When China finally emerged from the chaos, Mao and Zhou replaced their earlier, more flexible promotion of a broad anti-American, anti-imperial united front with an overriding and rigid insistence on the dangers of Soviet aggression. Alarmed by the 1968 Soviet invasion of Czechoslovakia and worried that violent border clashes with the Soviets in 1969 might lead to general war, Chinese officials also began to emphasize the need for the PRC and the entire Third World to struggle against the "dual hegemony" of the world's two superpowers. By 1973, after the famous meeting between Mao and Richard Nixon in Beijing, Chinese officials also downplayed armed struggle, deemphasized the cause of national liberation in favor of interstate relations, and subordinated their previous revolutionary goals to the overriding campaign against Soviet "social imperialism."

From Vietnam to Angola, and the demise of détente

The combined American and Soviet turn away from ambitious, open-ended visions of decolonization to a more immediate emphasis on coercion, force, and control in the mid-to-late 1960s intersected with the passing away of the first generation of postcolonial leaders. As non-aligned nationalists were replaced in coups by military juntas or revolutionary regimes, the Third World became increasingly polarized. Resolute, dictatorial anti-Communists like Suharto in Indonesia, Mobutu in Zaire, and the Shah of Iran received substantial US support and, under the Nixon administration, came to be seen as regional bulwarks against the dangers of Marxist insurgency. At the same time, however, revolutionary ideologies, often introduced through the writings of dissident intellectuals in the West, made new headway among activists and students across Southeast Asia and Africa and helped turn liberation movements in more clearly Marxist directions.

Vietnam in particular became a source of inspiration for revolutionaries and guerrilla movements. While few Third World radicals devoted close, serious study to Vietnam's experience, Hanoi's determined stand in the face of American technological might became an appealing symbol of determined resistance and the power of popular revolutionary war. Despite Johnson's massive deployment of US combat troops and Nixon's sharp intensification of the bombing campaign and invasion of Cambodia, the revolutionaries had struggled on. As Che Guevara proclaimed, the Vietnamese offered a lesson to the world: "Since the imperialists are using the threat of war to blackmail humanity, the correct response is not to fear war. Attack hard and without let-up at every point of confrontation – that must be the general tactic of the people."[19] Where radicals came to see Soviet policies as too conservative and fainthearted, the 1968 Tet Offensive stirred revolutionary imaginations across Southeast Asia and Africa.

Impressed by Hanoi's resilience and the effect of the war on American politics, Soviet leaders also drew important conclusions of their own in Vietnam. With Soviet help, a disciplined Marxist–Leninist party like that in the DRV was capable of raising the political costs of war to the point that the United States would ultimately decide to pull back its forces. If the United States proved unwilling or unable to stop a revolution in Vietnam, where it had made an immense commitment, then the chances of successful revolutions in other areas looked to be on the rise.

As several scholars have argued, the beginnings of superpower détente also made increased Cold War conflict in the Third World more, not less, likely. America's growing frustration in Vietnam contributed to the rise of détente, and Nixon and Henry Kissinger hoped that a diplomatic engagement with the Soviets might persuade them to hold their North Vietnamese allies in check. They hoped, through a strategy of "linkage," to offer the Soviets "recognition of their strategic parity" and "a promise of access to Western capital and technology." In return, "they asked Moscow to recognize the mutuality of superpower interest in stability, especially in maintaining order in the Third World."[20] Yet as Raymond Garthoff explains, détente was "not a clearly defined concept held in common." While Soviet policymakers did expect that détente might help prevent war between the superpowers, they also "insisted loudly that peaceful coexistence among states did not mean an end to 'the class struggle' or the 'national liberation movement' in colonial or neo-colonial situations." Where Nixon and Kissinger anticipated that détente

19 Odd Arne Westad, *The Global Cold War: Third World Interventions and the Making of Our Times* (Cambridge: Cambridge University Press, 2005), 190.
20 Warren I. Cohen, *America in the Age of Soviet Power, 1945–1991* (Cambridge: Cambridge University Press, 1993), 183.

would result in a Soviet acceptance of the status quo in the Third World, Brezhnev believed that the Soviet Union retained a free hand to challenge the United States' global engagement there. Convinced that the Communist victory in Vietnam demonstrated that the "correlation of forces" in the world was shifting to the benefit of the USSR, Brezhnev thought it would be a mistake not to press the advantage.[21]

The conflicting expectations came to a head most dramatically in Angola. When the Portuguese dictatorship collapsed in April 1974 and that country erupted into civil war among three competing independence movements, the United States and South Africa both intervened in an attempt to prevent the Marxist-oriented Popular Movement for the Liberation of Angola (MPLA) from coming to power. An MPLA victory, South Africa feared, might promote radical attacks on apartheid in Namibia and South Africa itself. Worried about the damage to American credibility done by defeat in Vietnam, Kissinger hoped that an easy win in Angola might repair the domestic Cold War consensus and restore US prestige abroad. By the following summer, US weapons deliveries, CIA advisers, and South African military trainers were deployed there. When it appeared that the MPLA was still edging toward victory, South African troops invaded the country in October 1975 with US approval.

Although they were concerned by the factional splits within the MPLA, the USSR provided the movement with essential military equipment. The decisive contribution, however, came from Cuba. Since the early 1960s, Castro's commitment to anti-imperialism, vision of Third World solidarity, and opposition to white supremacy had led Cuba to support revolutionary movements in Algeria, Zaire, and Guinea-Bissau. Acting on its own initiative, Cuba responded to the South African invasion in November 1975 by deploying 36,000 troops, repelling the assault, and winning the war for the MPLA. As Piero Gleijeses points out, the Soviet Union did not direct Cuban policy.[22] Yet once it became clear that victory was in sight, Moscow was quick to proclaim the triumph in Angola as evidence of Soviet leadership in the cause of Third World liberation.

The wider international ramifications of the Angolan war were significant. Among the immediate losers was the People's Republic of China. By the early 1970s, the PRC had become so committed to opposing Soviet influence that

---

21 Raymond L. Garthoff, *Détente and Confrontation: American–Soviet Relations from Nixon to Reagan* (Washington, DC: Brookings Institution, 1994), 27, 45.

22 See Gleijeses's chapter in this volume.

it sacrificed previous commitments to anticapitalist liberation as well as regional diplomatic objectives. As the Soviets and their Cuban allies backed the MPLA, China threw its weight toward the rival National Union for the Total Independence of Angola (UNITA), a nativist, populist movement, and the National Front for the Liberation of Angola (FNLA), a nationalist organization without a clearly defined ideological stance. When South Africa invaded Angola, the PRC then found itself in the untenable position of fighting on the same side as the United States and, more crucially, Pretoria's white supremacist regime. Although China stopped training FNLA soldiers within days of the South African attack, the result was a diplomatic disaster: "Its erstwhile clients, the FNLA and UNITA, had been defeated, its relations with the victorious MPLA had been destroyed, and its image as a disinterested and principled friend of African causes had been badly damaged."[23] Gerald Ford's administration also watched in frustration as the US Congress voted in January 1976 to cut off all funding for further US covert action in Angola. The failed attempt to bolster American credibility had only succeeded in further solidifying the anti-interventionist political climate at home. The American cooperation with apartheid South Africa also did grave damage to US relations with other African states, most of which moved quickly to recognize the MPLA government.

The MPLA victory in Angola, however, also had ironic results. Although the USSR gained little in a strategic sense, the Angolan war helped harden a growing perception among US policymakers that the Soviets were exploiting the process of détente and violating its terms. When the USSR went on to promote the Ethiopian revolution, especially after its declaration of Marxist–Leninist principles in 1976, the concept of détente came under fierce political attack in the United States, a process that helped push Jimmy Carter's administration toward a harder line and contributed to the rise of a powerful, right-wing, moralistic, anti-Soviet consensus under Ronald Reagan. Gains in Angola and Ethiopia, therefore, helped jeopardize the arms-limitation agreements that, ultimately, were of far greater value to Moscow. Perhaps even more seriously, those victories encouraged the Soviet conviction that by supporting Marxist parties and moving quickly with new military capabilities they could continue to reshape the course of the Third World, an expectation that would lead to disaster in Afghanistan. The Soviets, in that sense, were about to learn the hard lessons that intervention in Vietnam had taught the United States. Overwhelming military and technological superiority would prove a poor

23 Steven F. Jackson, "China's Third World Foreign Policy: The Case of Angola and Mozambique, 1961–93," *China Quarterly* (1995), 411.

vehicle with which to support a regime lacking real political legitimacy. The forces of culture, religion, and history at work in the Third World, moreover, were not subject to easy manipulation or rapid transformation. The result, moreover, would contribute to the overextension and final crisis of the Soviet state.

The greatest damage done by the Cold War in the Third World, however, was surely suffered by those who lived there. American and Soviet policymakers,

19. The image of Che Guevara, already dead for four years, decorating a Chilean slum in 1971. Guevara and the Cuban revolution continued to provide inspiration for many Third World radicals in the 1970s.

viewing the postcolonial world as inherently malleable, promoted competing ideologies of accelerated development. Believing that their national security depended on the spread of their visions of modernization or socialist transformation, they also deployed tremendous force to propagate them. Many Third World elites, eager for rapid economic and social progress, also embraced those approaches and employed repression in the name of transformation. The sources of violence in Africa, Asia, and Latin America were often grounded in anticolonial movements and domestic conflicts along lines of class and ethnicity that pre-dated the Cold War itself. But the intervention of the United States, the Soviet Union, and China made them far more devastating. In this respect, the worry that Nkrumah expressed before his New York audience in 1958 appears prophetic. As the Cold War arrived in Africa and the rest of the Third World, the goals of peaceful, independently charted material advance receded into the distance.

14

The Indochina wars and the Cold War, 1945–1975

FREDRIK LOGEVALL

The struggle for Indochina after 1945 occupies a central place in the international history of the twentieth century. Fought over a period of three decades, at the cost of millions of lives and vast physical destruction in Vietnam, Laos, and Cambodia, the conflict captured in microcosm all of the grand political forces that drove the century's global history: colonialism, nationalism, communism, and democratic-capitalism. It was both an East–West and a North–South struggle, that is to say, intimately bound up with the two most important developments in international relations after World War II, the Cold War and the breakup of the colonial empires.

It took time, however, for Indochina to become a major cockpit of tensions in the international system. In the early years, the conflict was largely a Franco-Vietnamese affair, resulting from Paris leaders' attempt to rebuild the colonial state and international order from before World War II, and Vietnamese nationalists' determination to redefine that state in a new post-colonial order. France had lost colonial control when, after the fall of France in 1940, Japan swept southward and gradually gained effective control of the whole of Southeast Asia. The Tokyo authorities initially found it convenient to leave the day-to-day control of Indochinese affairs in French hands, but in March 1945 the Japanese brushed aside the French in favor of ruling Indochina themselves. By then the tide of the Pacific War had turned against them, however, and in the weeks and months that followed, the French government and various Vietnamese nationalist groups – the most powerful of which was the Communist-led Vietminh under Ho Chi Minh – jockeyed for power. They continued to do so after Japan's surrender until, in late 1946, large-scale war broke out.

East–West tensions were by then becoming serious in Europe and the Near East, and one might have expected the same to be true in Vietnam, because Ho Chi Minh and his chief lieutenants were dedicated Marxists. In fact, though, Paris leaders cared little that the Vietminh was Communist-led;

what mattered was that Ho refused to accede to French colonial control. The British government backed the French less out of concern for Ho Chi Minh's political philosophy than out of fears for what a Vietnamese nationalist victory could to do to their own colonial holdings. As for Soviet leader Iosif Stalin, he showed scant interest in Southeast Asia; it was for him always a backwater. He did not extend diplomatic recognition to the Democratic Republic of Vietnam (DRV) that Ho proclaimed in September 1945, and instead continued to regard France as the legitimate ruler of Indochina. His attention on European issues, and distrustful of Ho Chi Minh (for being too independent and nationalist-oriented), Stalin early on offered the Vietminh neither material nor diplomatic support and, indeed, endorsed the French Communist Party's backing of the first war budget and emergency measures related to the prosecution of the struggle.

Stalin's pawns?

If Ho Chi Minh's Communist orientation mattered significantly in any major world capital in this early period, it was in Washington. Soviet–American relations had deteriorated sharply in 1946 and early 1947, as Moscow and Washington clashed over a range of issues: over European reconstruction, over the division of Germany, over Iran, and over the civil war in Greece. By spring 1947, Soviet hostility was a staple of both American policy documents and much journalistic reporting. Equally important in historical terms was the fact that, by then, there was no mistaking the growing salience of apocalyptic anti-Communism in American political discourse. French leaders, always keen to find favor in Washington, shifted their public diplomacy on Indochina in response to this emerging US–Soviet confrontation and this changing American mood. In Vietnam, Admiral Thierry d'Argenlieu, the French high commissioner, early in the year moved what was then still a localized and strictly Franco-Vietnamese conflict to the highest international level, that of East versus West. He insisted before all comers that Ho and the Vietminh were mere pawns in Stalin's struggle for world supremacy, and that Indochina was where the West must make a stand.[1]

That basic message, articulated also by other French officials – including some who didn't believe in it, who thought anti-Communism would be a useless weapon against a nationalist uprising – found a receptive audience in

1 Philippe Devillers, *Le Viet-Nam contemporain* (Paris: Comité d'etudes des problems du Pacifique, 1950), 2; Thierry d'Argenlieu, *Chroniques d'Indochine* (Paris: Albin Michel, 1985).

Washington. Despite the fact that the State Department found no evidence of mass popular support for Communism within Vietnam, and further that it was not ideology but a desire for independence and a hatred of the French that drove the unrest, the principals in US decisionmaking proceeded on the basis of worst-case assumptions. Losing Indochina to Communism, senior planners worried, could upset the strategic balance in Southeast Asia, particularly if, as these officials anticipated, other countries in the area were to succumb as well. It would also harm the economic recovery of Japan and other key allies, who were dependent on maintaining commercial ties with the primary producing areas of Southeast Asia.

American strategists also feared the effects in France itself of a French defeat in Indochina. Might a loss cause Western-oriented moderates to lose their grip on power in Paris and enhance the prestige of the Soviet-supported French Communist Party (FCP), maybe even bring that party to power? The thought made US officials shudder, and made them reluctant to quibble with Paris over its pursuit of a military solution. True, these men acknowledged, Stalin showed only modest interest in fomenting revolution in France and, indeed, kept the FCP at arm's length, but this was only because he sought to avoid an international crisis while the future of Germany remained an open question; once that issue was resolved, he would surely turn his focus to France.

Yet senior officials were loath to simply throw US support behind the French war effort. It was too much a colonial affair. Harry Truman's team ruled out direct assistance to the military campaign and told Paris planners that any attempt to retake Vietnam by force of arms would be wrongheaded. At the same time, the administration knew full well that a sizable chunk of the unrestricted US economic assistance to France ($1.9 billion between July 1945 and July 1948) was being used to pay war costs. In this way, though American leaders declared themselves to be neutral in the conflict, theirs was a neutrality that tilted toward the European ally. French messages were always answered, while those from Ho Chi Minh – who had modeled his declaration of independence on the American version of 1776, and several times in 1945–46 pleaded for US help – were ignored.

And so, the Vietminh fought alone, largely isolated in non-Asian world opinion. The French had a massive superiority in weapons and could take and hold any area they really wanted. But they were fighting far from home and could never deploy sufficient numbers of troops to secure effective control. The war quickly reached a stalemate. The French dominated the cities and towns but were unable to extend their control to the villages and countryside, where most Vietnamese lived and where the Vietminh had broad popular support. It soon became clear that the French would have difficulty achieving victory by conventional military means. Far-reaching political concessions to a Vietnamese government – involving the transfer of genuine executive and legislative authority – would be essential to achieving early pacification, yet successive French governments were unwilling to grant such concessions.

In June 1948, the French did go partway, facilitating the creation of the first central government for Vietnam in opposition to Ho Chi Minh's DRV. Rightly seen by most Vietnamese as largely a French creation, it marshaled little national support. In March 1949, the French struck another deal, this time with Bao Dai, the former Vietnam emperor who had abdicated in 1945. Under this deal, Vietnam was brought into the French Union without reference to the wishes of Ho Chi Minh. Real power, however, remained in French hands. The same was true in Laos and Cambodia, whose monarchs agreed in 1948 to bring their respective countries into the French Union. Together, the three formed the Associated States of Indochina (les États Associés de l'Indochine).

An internationalized war

If French leaders hoped these various agreements with Indochinese monarchs would have a galvanizing effect on the anti-Vietminh effort, they were soon disappointed. In Vietnam, Bao Dai's government won little public backing, while in Cambodia and Laos the DRV countered France's Associated States by facilitating the creation of two of its own: the "governments of resistance" led by the Khmer Issarak (Son Ngoc Minh) and the Lao Issara (Prince Soupha-nouvong). More ominously still, in 1949, Mao Zedong's Communists won control of China, which meant that the DRV would now have a friendly government across Vietnam's northern frontier. In early 1950, both Beijing and Moscow extended diplomatic recognition to Ho's government; soon thereafter, Mao moved to support the Vietminh with arms, advisers, and training. No longer would the Vietminh be dependent on weapons it could manufacture in the jungle or capture on the battlefield; no longer would they have to rely solely on their own limited resources and facilities for the training of their men. On the flip side they would now have to put up with increased Chinese influence over military planning and strategy. Beijing sought through its support for the Vietminh to promote the People's Republic of China (PRC) as an international power in Asia and to enhance the security of its southern border.

The internationalization of the conflict also served French strategy in Indochina, for in early 1950 Paris, too, landed a major outside patron – the

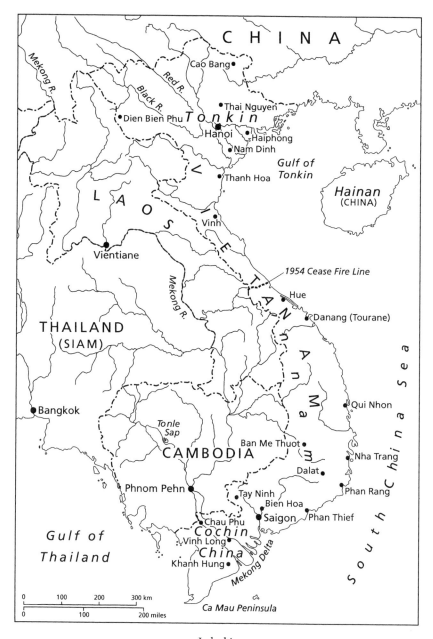

3. Indochina

United States. Washington officials chose this time to move beyond their French-leaning neutrality in favor of open support of the anti-Vietminh effort. Since 1948, US analysts had watched with concern as insurgencies erupted in Burma and Malaya and as Mao's armies gained ground in China. In early 1950, the Truman administration made the first step toward direct American involvement in Indochina – it opted to prop up an embattled colonial regime in order to prevent a Communist victory and also to retain French support in the European theatre of the Cold War. In February, the administration granted diplomatic recognition to the French-sponsored Bao Dai government. In early March, it pledged to furnish France with military and economic assistance for the war effort. The outbreak of the Korean War in late June, together with concern about the intentions of the Chinese Communists, solidified Washington's commitment.

A watershed moment it was. Henceforth, the First Indochina War was simultaneously a colonial conflict and a Cold War confrontation. The arrival of Chinese Communist aid and advisers across the frontier was one reason for this transformation; the other was the decision by Washington, spurred by fears of further Communist expansion in Asia and beyond, to throw its support behind the French war effort. A National Security Council (NSC) report penned in mid-1949 speculated on the meaning of Mao's victory: "If Southeast Asia is also swept by communism, we shall have suffered a major political rout the repercussions of which will be felt throughout the rest of the world, especially in the Middle East and in a then critically exposed Australia … the colonial-nationalist conflict provides a fertile field for subversive Communist movements, and it is now clear that Southeast Asia is the target for a coordinated offensive directed by the Kremlin."[2]

There was in fact no such coordinated offensive. Stalin's interest in Southeast Asia remained minimal, and his feelings about the Chinese developments were decidedly mixed. Still, it was not altogether fanciful for Washington analysts – and many non-Communist leaders in Southeast Asia – to think that Communism was on the march in the region. In addition to Mao in China and Ho in Vietnam, there were Communist-led rebellions in Indonesia, in newly independent Burma, in Malaya, and in the Philippines. All four rebellions would fail in due course, but in late 1949 their mere existence fueled Western fears. Did the historical momentum now lie with the

---

2 A portion of this report is in *The Pentagon Papers: The Defense Department History of Decisionmaking on Vietnam*, Senator Gravel ed. (Boston, MA: Beacon Press, 1971), vol. I, 82.

Communists? Even if it didn't in objective terms, might the perception gain hold that it did, sending messages that could have a pernicious impact on American national security interests? It seemed all too possible.

Domestic political pressures also inclined the Truman White House to link Indochina developments to broader developments. What historians would call the Second Red Scare was now underway, and Truman experienced ferocious partisan assaults for supposedly "abandoning" Chiang Kai-shek and "losing" China. He and his aides felt pressure to show their firmness elsewhere in the region, and providing aid to the French was one way to do so. It is of considerable significance in this regard, as historian Robert McMahon has noted, that the initial American dollar commitment to the French effort in Vietnam came from funds designated by the president's congressional critics for containment of Communism "within the general area of China."[3]

American strategists were not the only ones to see the Indochina conflict through a Cold War lens. DRV officials did too. Senior Vietminh theoretician Truong Chinh, for example, welcomed the coming of the Cold War to Vietnam and declared that the war against France was now not just a national liberation conflict but an integral part of the international Communist struggle against the United States in Asia. Vietnamese Communist sources make clear that leaders were keen to push the revolution not merely in Vietnam but beyond, and that their views on this score jibed with those of leaders in Beijing.

Important though the Chinese and American assistance was to the fighting capabilities of the two sides, it did not change the overall strategic situation: the Vietminh continued to hold the advantage, notwithstanding the fact that US aid to the French war effort was massively larger than that of Beijing to the DRV. The French in 1951 achieved some tactical successes under General Jean de Lattre de Tassigny, beating back daring offensives by General Vo Nguyen Giap, but these results did not seriously impair Vietminh capabilities. By early 1953, with the fighting now entering its seventh year, and with no end in sight, French popular disenchantment with the war grew markedly. From across the political spectrum came proposals for early withdrawal from Indochina. The proposals were rejected. The French government, feeling pressure from Washington to remain steadfast in the struggle, insisted that its policy of holding on in Indochina was working and that the war-weary Vietnamese were bound sooner or later to accept any arrangement that promised a stable regime and

3 Robert J. McMahon, *The Limits of Empire: The United States and Southeast Asia since World War II* (New York: Columbia University Press, 1999), 40.

security. The Vietnamese would rally to Bao Dai, Paris officials vowed, if the Communists could only be held back by military action a little longer.

Privately, these same Paris leaders were much more circumspect about the prospects. Many wanted to end the war by negotiation, a notion that found no favor in Washington (this despite the fact that the Americans were themselves pursuing the diplomatic option in Korea). And so the fighting raged on, while the United States kept raising the level of its material aid until American taxpayers were carrying, by the spring of 1954, about three-quarters of the financial cost of the French effort. Bombers, cargo planes, trucks, tanks, naval craft, automatic weapons, small arms and ammunition, radios, hospital and engineering equipment plus financial aid flowed heavily. Between 1950 and 1954, US investment in the war in Indochina reached a total of approximately $3 billion.

Dominoes, anyone?

By 1953, if not before, American planners were in fact far more committed to the French war effort than the French were. The apocalyptic scenario depicted in the 1949 NSC report quoted above remained operative, even though its dire warning of a "coordinated offensive" in Southeast Asia directed by the Kremlin had not come true. The NSC report had been an early version of the so-called domino theory, and it was followed by other, similar articulations in the years thereafter, all arguing the same point: If Vietnam was allowed to "fall," other countries would inevitably and perhaps swiftly follow suit.

It was, of course, Dwight Eisenhower who famously used the metaphor of falling dominoes at a press conference on April 7, 1954, as French forces faced the prospect of a major military defeat at Dien Bien Phu in northwest Tonkin. Even before that date, his administration had pushed the theory harder than did its predecessor. In August 1953, for example, Eisenhower declared: "If Indochina goes, several things happen right away. The Malayan peninsula, the last little bit of the end hanging on down there, would be scarcely defensible ... all India would be outflanked. Burma would certainly, in its weakened condition, be no defense."[4] Vice President Richard Nixon and Secretary of State John Foster Dulles spoke in similar terms, with the latter telling Congress that defeat in Indochina could trigger a "chain reaction throughout the Far East and Southeast Asia."[5]

---

4 Quoted in *Pentagon Papers*, vol. I, 591–92.
5 Allan B. Cole (ed.), *Conflict in Indo-China and International Repercussions: A Documentary History, 1945–55* (Ithaca, NY: Cornell University Press, 1956), 171.

It is curious that the passage of time since 1949 had only made US officials more attached to this kind of theorizing. Never mind that in no previous case had the fall of a country to Communism triggered the rapid fall of a whole string of other countries. Even in a weaker form, envisioning only a short row of dominoes, in this case only those countries nearby in Southeast Asia, the theory seemingly bore little relation to reality. China, the world's most populous country, had gone Communist in 1949, but that event had not caused dominoes to fall.

Just how much Eisenhower believed in a mechanistic domino theory is a matter of debate. But it's clear he endorsed the general proposition that Communism was expanding, and that this was dangerous and should be prevented. Hence, the close consideration he and his secretary of state, John Foster Dulles, gave to intervening militarily in Vietnam in the spring of 1954 – in April they asked Congress for authority to use, if necessary, US troops to save France's position. The lawmakers refused to go along unless the British also joined, and Winston Churchill's government declined, on the ground that the intervention might precipitate a disastrous war with China if not with the Soviet Union too. British officials were dubious in any case that limited military intervention had any real hope of salvaging the French position and, accordingly, pinned their hopes on a negotiated settlement. Eisenhower refused to go in alone, and no US military intervention occurred that spring.

Important though Cold War strategic concerns were in shaping Eisenhower's policy on Indochina in 1953–54, he – like all six US presidents between 1946 and 1975 – also acted partly out of domestic political concerns. Savvy politician that he was, Eisenhower understood that he could face criticism at home from two different directions if he downplayed Indochina's importance. On the one side, the American public and their representatives in Congress would be reluctant to allocate funds on a matter not deemed critically important to US national security concerns. On the other, McCarthyism remained a force to be reckoned with in American politics, and the president had no desire to see the "Who lost China?" question posed again, this time with respect to Vietnam. Eisenhower knew he was already suspect among some in the Republican old guard for agreeing to an armistice in Korea the previous summer – an action, they grumbled, that constituted snatching defeat from the jaws of victory.

Interregnum

On May 7, 1954, Giap's forces overran the French garrison at Dien Bien Phu. The following day, an international conference already in session in Geneva began to discuss a basis for a ceasefire in the war. Although the conflict was approaching its climax and Vietminh leaders vowed to continue fighting until they won a definitive victory, there was reason to hope that a negotiated settlement might be possible. France was plainly losing the will to continue a war that many of its leaders doubted could be won. Many NATO powers wanted Paris to cut its losses in Southeast Asia to concentrate its attention instead on pressing matters close to home, such as the proposed European Defense Community. Neutralist Asian states likewise wanted an end to the fighting, which they saw as retarding the development of newly independent countries in South and Southeast Asia. Most important, both China and the Soviet Union saw, for different reasons, much to gain from a political settlement. Moscow leaders worried that a prolongation of the fighting would only increase Chinese and American influence in the region, while officials in Beijing saw in the Geneva Conference a chance to demonstrate simultaneously their great power credentials and avoid indefinitely matching in Indochina the stepped-up pace of US military aid, with the attendant risk of a general war.

The Vietminh and the Americans were less enthusiastic participants. Hanoi leaders were reluctant to agree to a compromise settlement when military victory seemed within reach but were persuaded by Moscow and Beijing to accept a settlement that left them in control of only a part of the country. Take one half of the loaf now, the Communist powers in effect told them, and count on getting the other in the not-too-distant future. The senior American representative at Geneva, Secretary of State Dulles, meanwhile had grave misgivings about the negotiations, and he encouraged the French to continue the struggle in Indochina in the interest of the "free world." The French refused, and after ten weeks a peace settlement was signed. Vietnam was partitioned at the seventeenth parallel pending nationwide elections in 1956. The Vietminh took control north of the parallel, while the southern portion came under the control of the Catholic nationalist Ngo Dinh Diem, who had the backing of the United States.

And with that, the struggle for Indochina entered a kind of interregnum; a war had ended but what replaced it was not quite peace. In the North, the DRV leadership set about consolidating its control, while Diem sought to do the same in the South. The Eisenhower administration, meanwhile, tried to salvage what it could from what senior officials considered a major Cold War setback for the United States. Accordingly, in September, it took the lead role in the formation of the Southeast Asia Treaty Organization (SEATO), a largely toothless anti-Communist alliance intended to signal resolve to Beijing and Moscow. The other members were France, Britain, Australia, New Zealand,

20. French prisoners of war and their Vietnamese captors, July 1954. Losing the battle of Dien Bien Phu made France withdraw from Indochina.

Pakistan, and, as the only Southeast Asian representatives, Thailand and the Philippines. In South Vietnam, the administration moved swiftly to supplant French influence with American dollars, advisers, and *matériel*. All too aware that Ho Chi Minh would likely win a nationwide election, the administration supported Diem's refusal in 1955 to hold even the consultations with the DRV that had been envisioned in the Geneva Accords.

Diem's truculence caused consternation in the other major world capitals, but none of these governments were willing to push the matter. The new Soviet leader Nikita Khrushchev did not want a fracas over elections in Vietnam to interfere with his policy of "peaceful coexistence" with the West. Chinese officials also stayed largely silent, content to issue tepid protests. Britain, with the Soviet Union the sponsor of the Geneva Conference, initially worked to ensure the implementation of the accords, but backed off when Washington made its position clear. Prime Minister Anthony Eden griped that his government was being "treated like Australia" by the Americans, but he was not willing to risk a serious falling out with his powerful ally on account of Indochina.[6] The July 1956 deadline for national elections in Vietnam came and went with no balloting taking place.

6 Anthony Eden, quoted in Arthur Combs, "The Path Not Taken: The British Alternative to US Policy in Vietnam, 1954–1956," *Diplomatic History*, 19 (Winter 1995), 51.

The Saigon leader and his American patrons had what they wanted, and for a time it looked like the young Republic of (South) Vietnam would become a stable and prosperous entity. The other world powers seemed content to keep the country divided indefinitely, with the Soviets in 1957 even floating the idea of admitting both Vietnams into the United Nations. (The Western powers, fearful of the implications for Germany, said no thanks.) As American aid dollars, technical know-how, and products poured into the South in the second half of the 1950s, some US officials spoke hopefully about a "Diem miracle," about South Vietnam being a "showcase" for America's foreign aid program.

Appearances deceived. US aid, necessary though it was, inevitably fostered a dependent relationship, which undercut the Saigon government's legitimacy with the southern populace. Though a man of principle and personal courage, Diem had a limited concept of political leadership and was inflexible and despotic. His policies – which favored the Catholic minority and showed little sensitivity to the needs of the Vietnamese people – alienated many. He demonstrated limited interest in enacting meaningful political reform. From time to time, American officials pushed him in that direction, but usually they got nowhere. Contrary to many historical accounts, it was Diem, not the United States, who was the dominant voice in South Vietnamese politics. Washington never had as much influence over Vietnamese affairs after 1955 as the French had before.

Slowly, beginning in 1957, a guerrilla insurgency arose in the South to challenge Diem's rule. The fighters included former Vietminh who had remained in the South after partition, but also included new recruits, non-Communists alienated by Diem's repressive actions. The insurgency was not imposed by Hanoi; on the contrary, the DRV leadership went through a wrenching series of deliberations about whether to support it, with some Politburo members arguing for the need to focus exclusively on building a socialist state in the North. Precisely when Hanoi leaders gave their approval for armed struggle in the South remains a matter of debate (many accounts point to the 15th Plenum of the Party Central Committee in early 1959), but give it they did, although through the end of 1960 Hanoi still emphasized the political over the military struggle. Only in January 1961 did the Politburo assert that "the revolution in the South is moving along the path toward a general insurrection with new characteristics, and the possibility of a peaceful development of the revolution is now almost nonexistent."[7] Henceforth, military struggle should thus be placed on equal footing with political struggle.

---

7 *Cuoc Khang Chien Chong My Cuu Nuoc 1954–1975* [The Anti-American National Salvation Resistance 1954–1975] (Hanoi: Army Printing House, 1988), 81.

The Second Indochina War

By the start of 1961, then, the Second Indochina War was underway. A new American president, John F. Kennedy (JFK) took office at just this time, and Indochina was from the start an important foreign-policy issue for his administration. Initially, however, it was not Vietnam but Laos that loomed largest. Laos had been declared neutral by the Geneva conferees in 1954, and Washington had thereafter sent aid and advisory personnel to try to secure stable, pro-Western rule in the small, landlocked country. The Vietnamese countered by building up the Pathet Lao in the east. By the time of Kennedy's inauguration, the US-sponsored government of Phoumi Nosavan faced imminent defeat at the hands of Pathet Lao guerrillas, heavily backed by the DRV. Outgoing president Eisenhower and several senior US officials urged JFK to intervene militarily, but he demurred, in part due to opposition from the British and French governments. Instead, Kennedy opted to back a Soviet-sponsored initiative to convene a new Geneva conference on Laos for the purpose of negotiating a settlement among the competing factions. In July 1962, a deal was signed. It did not bring lasting peace, but it did remove Laos from the list of Cold War hot spots.

For Kennedy, diplomacy seemed the only viable option on Laos. But he feared that by choosing this course he had opened himself up to charges of being "soft on communism" from his domestic opponents, many of whom were also attacking him for the failed effort to overthrow Fidel Castro in 1961. He determined to stand firm in Vietnam. The administration consequently stepped up aid dollars to the Diem regime, increased the air-dropping of raiding teams into North Vietnam, and launched crop destruction by herbicides to starve the Vietcong (as the insurgents in the South became known) and expose their hiding places. Kennedy also strengthened the US military presence in South Vietnam, to the point that by 1963 more than 16,000 military advisers were in the country, some authorized to take part in combat alongside the US-equipped Army of the Republic of Vietnam (ARVN).

Meanwhile, opposition to Diem's repressive regime increased. Peasants objected to programs that removed them from their villages for their own safety, and Buddhist monks, protesting the Roman Catholic Diem's religious persecution, poured gasoline over their robes and ignited themselves in the streets of Saigon. Intellectuals complained that Diem countenanced corruption in his government and concentrated power in the hands of family and friends, and blasted his policy of jailing critics to silence them. Eventually US officials, with Kennedy's approval, encouraged dissident ARVN generals to remove Diem and his influential brother Ngo Dinh Nhu. On November 1, 1963, the generals struck, ousting Diem and then murdering him and Nhu. Less than three weeks later Kennedy himself was assassinated in Dallas.

The timing and suddenness of Kennedy's death ensured that Vietnam would be a particularly controversial aspect of his legacy. Just what would have happened in Southeast Asia had Kennedy returned from Texas alive can never be known, of course, but that has not stopped historians (including this one) from speculating. Consensus is usually elusive in such counterfactual exercises, and even more so in this case given the contradictory nature of Kennedy's Vietnam policy. He expanded US involvement and approved a coup against Diem, but despite the periodic urgings of top advisers he refused to commit US ground forces to the struggle. Over time he became increasingly skeptical about South Vietnam's prospects and hinted that he would end the American commitment after winning reelection in 1964. Some authors have gone further and argued that he had commenced an American withdrawal from Vietnam even at the time of his death, but the evidence for this claim is thin. More likely, JFK arrived in Dallas still uncertain about how to solve his Vietnam problem, postponing – as veteran politicians often do – the truly difficult choices until later.

Lyndon Johnson (LBJ), too, sought to put off the tough decisions for as long as possible. In the early months, he viewed all Vietnam options through the lens of the 1964 election. "Stay the course" seemed to be the wisest strategy in that regard, far less risky than either precipitous withdrawal or major escalation. Yet Johnson also wanted victory, or at least to avoid defeat, which in practice amounted to the same thing. As a result, throughout 1964, the administration secretly planned for an expansion of the war to North Vietnam and never seriously considered negotiating a settlement. In early August, the president launched the first direct US military attacks on North Vietnam, after two American destroyers reported coming under attack in the Gulf of Tonkin. He did so despite conflicting evidence as to what had occurred in the Gulf and why. Johnson also pushed through Congress the Gulf of Tonkin Resolution, which gave him the authority to "take all necessary measures to repel any armed attack against the forces of the United States and to prevent further aggression." In so doing, Congress essentially surrendered its war-making powers to the executive branch. The resolution, Secretary of Defense Robert McNamara later noted, served "to open the floodgates."[8]

---

8 Robert McNamara, *In Retrospect: The Tragedy and Lessons of Vietnam* (New York: Crown, 1995), 141.

Johnson, delighted with the broad authority the resolution gave him, also appreciated what the Gulf of Tonkin affair did for his political standing – his public approval ratings went up dramatically, and his show of force effectively removed Vietnam as a campaign issue for the Republican Party's presidential nominee Barry Goldwater. On the ground in South Vietnam, however, the outlook remained grim in the final weeks of 1964, as the Vietcong continued to make gains. US officials responded by fine-tuning the secret plans for an escalation of American involvement.

In Hanoi, as well, plans were laid in 1964 for stepped-up military action. Already in December 1963, in the aftermath of the Diem coup, DRV leaders had decided to escalate the fighting in the South, in the hopes that further deterioration would either cause the Americans to give up the ghost and go home or leave them insufficient time to embark on a major escalation of their own.

Having made this decision, Hanoi officials were slow to carry it out, in part because their allies in Beijing and Moscow urged caution. Neither Communist giant was keen to see an Americanized war in Vietnam, one that could confront them with difficult choices and potentially bring them into direct contact with the US Seventh Fleet. Their own bilateral relationship deeply fractious, they also each sought to keep the other from gaining too much influence in Hanoi. Both advised the DRV to go slowly, and to avoid provoking Washington. The North Vietnamese professed to agree, even as they used the final weeks of 1964 to step up the infiltration of men and *matériel* into the South. Premier Pham Van Dong said during a meeting with Mao Zedong in October 1964: "If the United States dares to start a [larger] war, we will fight it, and we will win it. But it would be better if it did not come to that."[9]

Americanization

But come to that it did. In early December, after Johnson's massive election victory, he and his aides agreed on a two-phase escalation of the fighting. The first involved "armed reconnaissance strikes" against infiltration routes in Laos – part of the so-called Ho Chi Minh Trail that carried men and *matériel* into the South – as well as retaliatory airstrikes against North Vietnam in the event of a major Vietcong attack. The second phase anticipated "graduated military pressure" against the North, in the form of aerial bombing and,

9 O. A. Westad, Chen Jian, Stein Tønnesson, Nguyen Vu Tung, and James G. Hershberg (eds.), *77 Conversations between Chinese and Foreign Leaders on the Wars in Vietnam*, Cold War International History Project Working Paper No. 22 (Washington, DC: Woodrow Wilson Center, 1998), 83–84.

almost certainly, the dispatch of US ground troops to the South. Phase one would begin as soon as possible; phase two would come later, after thirty days or more.

In February 1965, following Vietcong attacks on American installations in South Vietnam that killed thirty-two Americans, Johnson ordered Operation Rolling Thunder, a bombing program planned the previous fall that continued, more or less uninterrupted, until October 1968. Then, on March 8, the first US combat battalions came ashore near Danang. The North Vietnamese met the challenge. They hid in shelters and rebuilt roads and bridges with a tenaciousness that frustrated and awed American officials. They also increased infiltration into the South.

That July, Johnson convened a series of high-level discussions about US war policy. Though these deliberations had about them the character of a charade – Johnson wanted history to record that he agonized over a choice he had in fact already made (and many historians have obliged him) – they did confirm that the American commitment would be more or less open-ended. On July 28, the president publicly announced a significant troop increase, disclosing that others would follow. By the end of 1965, more than 180,000 US ground troops were in South Vietnam. In 1966, the figure climbed to 385,000. In 1967 alone, US war planes flew 108,000 sorties and dropped 226,000 tons of bombs on North Vietnam. In 1968, US troop strength reached 536,100. The Soviet Union and China responded by increasing their material assistance to the DRV, though their combined amount never came close to matching American totals.

The 1965 Americanization came despite deep misgivings on the part of influential and informed voices at home and abroad. In the key months of decision (November 1964 through February 1965), Democratic leaders in the Senate, major newspapers such as the *New York Times* and the *Wall Street Journal*, and prominent columnists like Walter Lippmann warned against deepening involvement (though, in the case of the lawmakers, they did so quietly, behind closed doors). Inside the administration, the opponents included Under Secretary of State George W. Ball and Vice President Hubert H. Humphrey. The latter assured Johnson that the Republican right's dismal showing in the November elections gave the administration ample maneuverability on Vietnam. Abroad, all of America's main allies cautioned against escalation and urged a political settlement, on the grounds that no military solution favorable to the United States was possible. Remarkably, even many of the proponents of the escalation shared this pessimism. They knew that the odds of success were not great, that the Saigon government was weak and getting weaker, lacking even the semblance of popular support.

Why, then, did Johnson and his advisers choose war? Think domino theory again, only in a new form. The worry now was less tangible, more amorphous than in the early 1950s, as US officials began to expound what Jonathan Schell has called the "psychological domino theory."[10] To be sure, from the start, the domino theory had contained an important psychological component; now, however, that component became supreme. *Credibility* was the new watchword, as policymakers declared it essential to stand firm in Vietnam in order to demonstrate America's determination to defend its vital interests not only in the region but around the world. Should the United States waver in Vietnam, friends both in Southeast Asia and elsewhere would doubt Washington's commitment to their defense, and might succumb to enemy pressure even without a massive invasion by foreign Communist forces – what political scientists call a "bandwagon" effect. Adversaries, meanwhile, would be emboldened to challenge US interests worldwide.

Vietnam, in this way of thinking, was a "test case" of Washington's willingness and ability to exert its power on the international stage. Even the incontrovertible evidence of a deep Sino-Soviet split, which affected the strategic balance in the Cold War in the mid-1960s in serious ways, evidently did not lessen the importance of the credibility imperative. Beijing appeared to be the more hostile and aggressive of the two Communist powers, the more deeply committed to global revolution, but the Soviets, too, supported Hanoi; any slackening in the American commitment to South Vietnam's defense could cause an increase in Soviet adventurism. Conversely, if Washington stood firm and worked to ensure the survival of a non-Communist Saigon government, it could send a powerful message to Moscow and Beijing that indirect aggression could not succeed.

Many of the aforementioned opponents of the 1965 escalation rejected this line of argument. They rebuffed the notion that US credibility was on the line in Vietnam and that a setback there would inevitably cause similar losses elsewhere. Some said US credibility would *suffer* if Johnson made Vietnam a large-scale war, as audiences around the world questioned Washington's judgment and its sense of priorities. On occasion, top officials allowed that the critics might be right, but they pressed the credibility argument anyway. One reason was that for many of them, it was not merely *America's* credibility that was perceived to be at stake; it was also the administration's *domestic political* credibility and officials' own *personal* credibility. Johnson

10 Jonathan Schell, *The Time of Illusion* (New York: Knopf, 1976), 9.

worried that failure in Vietnam would harm his domestic agenda; even more, he feared the personal humiliation he imagined would inevitably accompany a defeat – and for him, a negotiated withdrawal constituted defeat. Senior advisers, meanwhile, many of whom had for years publicly trumpeted Vietnam's importance, knew that to start singing a different tune now would expose themselves to potential ridicule and endanger their careers.

What, then, of the stated objective of helping a South Vietnamese ally repulse external aggression? That too figured into the equation, but not as much as it would have had the Saigon government – racked with infighting among senior and mid-level officials and possessing little broad-based support – done more to assist in its own defense. Talented and courageous anti-Communists dedicated to the war effort certainly existed in the South, including in the halls of power, but never in sufficient numbers, even after the ascension to power in 1965 of a more stable regime under Air Marshal Nguyen Cao Ky and General Nguyen Van Thieu. The Ky–Thieu government, a rueful Robert McNamara would remark two years later, in June 1967, "is still largely corrupt, incompetent, and unresponsive to the needs and wishes of the people."[11]

To the Paris Accords

The American forces fought well, and their entry into the conflict in 1965, together with the aerial bombardment of enemy areas, helped stave off a South Vietnamese defeat. In that sense, Americanization achieved its most immediate and basic objective. But if the stepped-up fighting in 1965–66 demonstrated to Hanoi leaders that the war would not swiftly be won, it also showed the same thing to their counterparts in Washington. Chinese and Soviet military and economic aid now flowed into North Vietnam in increased amounts, and Beijing also sent – beginning in June 1965 – support units to assist the war effort. Until March 1968 they would come, ultimately totaling some 320,000 troops – including anti-aircraft artillery units, defense engineering units, railway units, and road-building units.

As the North Vietnamese matched each American escalation with one of their own, the war became a stalemate. The US commander, General William Westmoreland, proved mistaken in his belief that a strategy of attrition

11 Robert McNamara, quoted in Larry Berman, *Lyndon Johnson's War: The Road to Stalemate in Vietnam* (New York: Norton, 1989), 51.

represented the key to victory – the enemy had a seemingly endless supply of recruits to throw into battle. Worse, the American reliance on massive military and other technology – including carpet bombing, napalm, and crop defoliants that destroyed entire forests – alienated many South Vietnamese and brought new recruits to the Vietcong. A major Communist offensive coinciding with the Tet lunar New Year in early 1968, though inconclusive in its military effects, inflamed American domestic opinion and indirectly caused an embattled LBJ to rule out (publicly at least) a run for reelection.

This was the situation that confronted Richard Nixon when he assumed the presidency in January 1969. "I'm not going to end up like LBJ," Nixon vowed before the inauguration, recalling that the war had destroyed Johnson's political career. "I'm going to stop that war. Fast." He didn't, and the main reason is he wanted to win it first. Nixon and his national security adviser, Henry Kissinger, understood that the conflict was generating deep divisions at home and hurting the nation's image abroad, and that they had to begin withdrawing American troops. The difficulties of the war signified to them that American power was limited and, in relative terms, in decline. Yet the two men feared, just like the Johnson team before them, that a precipitous disengagement would harm American credibility on the world stage. Nor were they any less committed than their predecessors to preserving an independent, non-Communist South Vietnam, if not indefinitely then at least long enough to get Nixon reelected. To accomplish these aims, Nixon set upon a policy that at once contracted and expanded the war.

A centerpiece of Nixon's policy was "Vietnamization" – the building up of South Vietnamese forces to replace US forces. Nixon hoped such a policy would quiet domestic opposition and also advance the peace talks underway in Paris since May 1968. Accordingly, the president began to withdraw American troops from Vietnam, decreasing their number from 543,000 in the spring of 1969 to 156,800 by the end of 1971, and to 60,000 by the fall of 1972. Vietnamization did help limit domestic dissent – as did replacing the existing draft with a lottery system, by which only those nineteen-year-olds with low lottery numbers would be drafted – but it did nothing to end the stalemate in the Paris negotiations. Even as he embarked on this troop withdrawal, therefore, Nixon intensified the bombing of North Vietnam and enemy supply depots in neighboring Cambodia, hoping to pound Hanoi into concessions. When the North Vietnamese refused to buckle, Nixon turned up the heat: in April 1970, South Vietnamese and US forces invaded Cambodia in search of arms depots and North Vietnamese army sanctuaries.

The president announced publicly that he would not allow "the world's most powerful nation" to act "like a pitiful, helpless giant." Maybe not, but the invasion triggered nationwide protests in cities and on college campuses, and caused an angry US Senate to repeal the Gulf of Tonkin Resolution of 1964. After two months, US troops withdrew from Cambodia, having accomplished little. Another invasion the following year, this one into Laos and involving no regular US ground troops, likewise yielded no appreciable results.

The fighting continued through 1972, but there was also a diplomatic break-through. When Hanoi launched a major offensive across the border into South Vietnam in March, Nixon responded with a massive aerial onslaught against the DRV. In December 1972, after an apparent peace agreement collapsed when the South Vietnamese refused to moderate their position, the United States again launched a furious air assault on the North – the so-called "Christmas bombing." Months earlier, Kissinger and his North Vietnamese counterpart in the negotiations, Le Duc Tho, had resolved many of the outstanding issues. Most notably, Kissinger agreed that North Vietnamese troops could remain in the South after the settlement, and Tho abandoned Hanoi's insistence that the Saigon government of Nguyen Van Thieu be removed. Nixon had instructed Kissinger to make concessions because the president was eager to improve relations with the Soviet Union and China, to win back the allegiance of the United States' allies, and to restore stability at home. On January 27, 1973, Kissinger and Le Duc Tho signed a ceasefire agreement in Paris. Nixon then compelled a reluctant Thieu to accept it by threatening to cut off US aid while promising to defend the South if the North violated the agreement. In the accord, the United States promised to withdraw all of its troops within sixty days. North Vietnamese troops would be allowed to stay in South Vietnam, and a coalition government that included the Vietcong eventually would be formed in the South.

The United States pulled its troops out of Vietnam, leaving behind some military advisers. Soon, both North and South violated the ceasefire, and large-scale fighting resumed. The feeble Saigon government, whose military by the start of 1975 possessed a huge numerical advantage in tanks, artillery pieces, and combat-ready troops, could not hold out. Just before its surrender, hundreds of Americans and Vietnamese who had worked for them were hastily evacuated from Saigon. On April 29, 1975, the South Vietnamese government collapsed, and Vietnam was reunified under a Communist government in Hanoi.

The end came even sooner in Cambodia. The Nixon-ordered invasion of 1970 had set in motion a bloody five-year civil war between a US-sponsored

21. Vietnamese try to get on-board a US helicopter sent to evacuate CIA personnel from a building in Saigon, April 29, 1975. The manner of the US exit from Vietnam was humiliating to many Americans and disastrous to the Vietnamese who had collaborated with the United States.

government under Lon Nol and the Communist-led Khmer Rouge. Massive American bombing of Khmer Rouge and North Vietnamese positions in Cambodia propped up the Lon Nol government for a time but devastated Cambodian society in the process. The physical destruction was enormous, and many hundreds of thousands of refugees flooded Phnom Penh and a few other urban centers. Upon returning from a visit to the war-torn country in early 1975, Republican congressman Paul N. McCloskey said: In Cambodia, the United States had done "greater evil than we have done to any country in the world, and wholly without reason, except for our benefit to fight against the Vietnamese."[12] On April 1, 1975 Lon Nol relinquished power and fled the country for Hawaii; on the tenth, US president Gerald Ford ordered the evacuation of all remaining American personnel; and on the seventeenth, the Khmer Rouge triumphantly entered the capital.

Indochina's third domino fell with much less violence and destruction. In early 1973, soon after the signing of the Paris Accords, Laotian prime

12 Quoted in Arnold R. Isaacs, *Without Honor: Defeat in Vietnam and Cambodia* (Baltimore: Johns Hopkins University Press, 1983), 273.

minister Souvanna Phouma reached a ceasefire deal with the Pathet Lao that gave the Communists a dominant position in Vientiane's coalition government. The departure of the United States further strengthened the position of the Pathet Lao, and following the Communist takeovers in Vietnam and Cambodia in April 1975, the non-Communist leaders fled for Thailand. That December the Pathet Lao announced the creation of the Lao People's Democratic Republic. Truong Chinh's dream of a revolutionary Indochina seemed to have come true.

Indochina and the Cold War

Outside Indochina, however, the dominoes did not fall, and it remains to assess the conception of Indochina as a Cold War battleground – a conception that took shape first in Washington, as we have seen, early in the Franco-Vietminh struggle, and was crucially important to all that occurred in Indochina for the next quarter-century. Ho Chi Minh was a pawn of the Kremlin, so went the argument, and his struggle was one part of a global, Soviet-directed offensive; as such, he had to be stopped. This view of the stakes always had its critics, inside and outside the American government, and it was never a widely held view in official Paris. In retrospect, moreover, it looks decidedly dubious. Stalin had minimal interest in Indochina and, indeed, saw the conflict there as a nuisance. Neither he nor his Kremlin successors had major ambitions in that part of the world, and they sought at all times to avoid a major East–West military showdown over Vietnam. DRV leadership, meanwhile, though dependent on Soviet and Chinese aid after US assistance began flowing to the French, always had considerable (though never complete) success keeping its powerful patrons at arm's length.

There's a deeper problem here. It is not at all clear that had Paris and Washington opted against war, other powers would have concluded that the credibility of US and French commitments elsewhere in the world would be grievously damaged. Harry Truman, it is well to recall, had not vowed to keep China from going Communist in 1949, and that defeat caused no meaningful pro-Moscow realignment in the international system. Nor had the "loss" of Cuba a decade later caused dominoes to fall in Latin America. By the same token, Nikita Khrushchev's humiliation in Cuba in 1962 did not mean that the United States was free to run rampant in Eastern Europe. Nor had French prestige suffered when Charles de Gaulle withdrew from an untenable position in Algeria; if anything, it rose. The list goes on. As George Ball put it in June 1965 in arguing (too late, as it turned out) against Americanization: "[N]o great captain has ever been blamed for a successful tactical withdrawal."[13]

By their repeated public vows of determination regarding Indochina, French and American leaders backed themselves into a corner and reduced their maneuverability. And not merely in geopolitical terms: for successive American administrations, as for many of the governments of the French Fourth Republic, Indochina's importance derived in large measure from the effects failure there could have at home, on elections, on political alignments and agendas, on individual careers. What James C. Thomson, Jr., said of the Vietnam-era US presidents could be said also of French leaders in 1946–54: they feared they were the last domino in line. From 1947 onwards, officials in Paris and Washington always publicly defined the struggle in Cold War terms, in terms of stopping the spread of Moscow-directed Communist expansion. It was a foreign-policy rationale, and it was indeed one reason for the long and bloody and ultimately unsuccessful effort aimed at defeating the forces of Ho Chi Minh. But only one. Other factors also shaped policy, notably careerist and domestic political calculations.

For Ho Chi Minh, too, the Cold War was an early and constant preoccupation, presenting a range of problems, challenges, and opportunities. Like Sukarno in Indonesia, Ho moved quickly after Japan's capitulation to seek American assistance, framing his request in terms of Washington's historic anticolonialism and support for self-determination. Like Sukarno, Ho was disappointed when US leaders chose instead to back their European Cold War allies. But whereas Sukarno subsequently proved his anti-Communist bona fides by suppressing internal Communist bids for primacy in the larger Indonesian independence movement, thereby ultimately earning the Truman administration's backing for independence from the Dutch (granted in 1949), Ho, the veteran Comintern agent and Indochina Communist Party founder, turned instead to Moscow and Beijing. Their assistance was vital but came at a price: the DRV, as a member of the Communist bloc after 1950, would be unable to use the international system to full effect against France and, indeed, had now to contend with a hostile United States. To a degree not fully evident at the time, the superpower actions in Indochina in 1950 had the effect of intensifying the struggle and prolonging it, and of reducing (but not eliminating) the freedom of action of both France and the DRV.

---

13 George Ball, "Cutting Our Losses in Vietnam," June 28, 1965, US Department of State, *Foreign Relations of the United States, 1964–1968* (Washington, DC: US Government Printing Office, 1995), vol. III, 222.

Through it all, year after bloody year, DRV leaders persevered, mobilizing every available resource for the struggle, first against France, then the United States and its Saigon ally. Victory would come in the end, on a spring day in 1975, almost three decades after Ho Chi Minh declared Vietnamese independence. Ho himself would not live to see it. It would be left to colleagues to preside over the celebrations, and to tally up the enormous costs of thirty years of war.

15

The Cold War in the Middle East: Suez crisis to Camp David Accords

DOUGLAS LITTLE

The Cold War saw deepening Soviet–American rivalry in the Middle East from the mid-1950s to the late 1970s on three levels – a geopolitical struggle to recruit allies and secure access to strategic resources (especially oil); diplomatic maneuvers to prevent the Arab–Israeli conflict from escalating into a super-power confrontation; and ideological competition for the future of the Muslim world, where secular nationalists and Islamic radicals shook the foundations of colonial empires and absolute monarchies throughout the region. On three occasions – the 1956 Suez crisis, the 1967 Six Day War, and the October 1973 War – hostilities between Israel and its Arab enemies disrupted world oil supplies, forced Washington and Moscow to contemplate military inter-vention, and briefly sparked fears of nuclear Armageddon. Once the shooting stopped in late 1973, American policymakers undertook "shuttle diplomacy" between Middle Eastern capitals, prompting the Arab members of the Organization of Petroleum Exporting Countries (OPEC) to lift their oil embargo on the United States, reducing the Kremlin's influence among Arab nationalists, and inducing Israel to be more flexible on territorial issues, all of which paved the way for the Camp David summit in September 1978. Diplomatic progress on the Arab–Israeli front, however, was undermined by the Islamic upheavals that rocked Iran and its Muslim neighbors during the late 1970s.

The early Cold War in the Middle East

Because the United States was preoccupied during the early years of the Cold War with crises in Europe and Asia, the Harry S. Truman administration expected Britain to promote and protect Western interests in the Middle East. US expectations notwithstanding, the financial and political consequences of World War II forced UK policymakers to reassess their imperial policies, not only in Asia and Africa but also in the Middle East. In Palestine, where Britain had held a League of Nations mandate for a quarter-century, civil war loomed between Jews and Arabs, each of whom was determined to establish an independent state. Unwilling to bear the costs of empire in the Holy Land, Whitehall turned the problem over to the United Nations (UN), whose plan to partition Palestine paved the way for the creation of Israel in May 1948. Despite Arab objections, the United States recognized the new Jewish state immediately, at least in part, as Truman's counsel Clark Clifford put it, "to steal a march on [the] U.S.S.R.," which had been supporting Zionism as a way to undermine British influence in the region.[1] Meanwhile, Britain's economic interests came under fire a thousand miles to the east in Iran, where in 1951 nationalists led by Mohammad Mossadeq seized control of the Anglo-Iranian Oil Company (AIOC), which provided more than half of the petroleum consumed in the British Isles. Mistakenly interpreting the nationalization of AIOC as a sign that Iran was about to align itself with the Soviet Union, British and American intelligence secretly organized a coup d'état and deposed Mossadeq in August 1953. Having helped Mohammad Reza Pahlavi, the pro-Western shah of Iran, regain undisputed power in Tehran, the Dwight D. Eisenhower administration persuaded Whitehall reluctantly to relinquish AIOC's monopoly over Iranian oil in favor of a new international consortium dominated by US petroleum giants.

Nowhere in the Middle East did the British Empire have more at stake, however, than in Egypt, where the Suez Canal had served as an imperial lifeline facilitating the flow of oil, trade, and troops for seventy-five years. Because Britain exercised what amounted to a protectorate over the nominally independent Egyptian monarchy, the canal was operated by an Anglo-French company and was protected by 30,000 British Tommies stationed at the Suez base, which during the early years of the Cold War also served as home to a Royal Air Force squadron whose atomic bombs were targeted at the Soviet Union. In July 1952, a group of young officers led by Gamal Abdel Nasser seized power in Cairo and vowed to reduce British influence. A secular revolutionary and self-proclaimed pan-Arab nationalist, Nasser pressed Britain in 1954 to withdraw from its Suez base and sought military assistance from the United States a year later following an Israeli attack on Egyptian troops in Gaza. After Washington declined to provide arms, Nasser swapped Egyptian cotton for Eastern bloc weapons provided by Czechoslovakia in September

---

1 Clark Clifford, quoted in George Elsey's memorandum of conversation, May 12, 1948, US Department of State, *Foreign Relations of the United States, 1948* (Washington, DC: US Government Printing Office, 1975), vol. V, 976 (hereafter, *FRUS*, with year and volume number).

1955. His larger goal was not to become a Soviet satellite but rather to place Egypt at the center of three circles – Africa, the Arab world, and the emerging Non-Aligned Movement. With Kremlin support for Israel now ancient history, the Soviet premier, Nikita Khrushchev, was happy to oblige by providing guns and rubles to Nasser, whom he intended to groom as a poster boy among Third World nationalists during the mid-1950s. Indeed, Nasser's support for non-aligned radicals like Indonesia's Sukarno and his opposition to Western regional defense organizations like the recently established British-backed Baghdad Pact fit well with Soviet plans to pit the newly independent nations of Africa and Asia against the European colonial powers and their American allies.

Determined to prevent Russian encroachments in the Middle East, President Eisenhower, Secretary of State John Foster Dulles, and their British counterparts employed economic aid to draw Egypt back toward the West. The United States, Britain, and the World Bank offered Nasser $200 million to build a high dam on the Upper Nile at Aswan, a monumental public works project that would rival the pyramids in its scope and, by controlling seasonal flooding, increase cotton production and generate vast amounts of hydroelectric power. There were implicit strings attached, however. Nasser must tone down his anti-Israeli rhetoric, he must take part in secret peace negotiations with Israel's prime minister, David Ben-Gurion, and he must distance himself from the Kremlin. Nasser's actions during the spring of 1956 gave neither the White House nor Whitehall much cause for optimism. In quick succession, the Egyptian leader refused face-to-face talks with Ben-Gurion, encouraged Jordan's King Hussein to expel British military advisers from Amman, and recognized the People's Republic of China. US and UK officials soon concluded that what Nasser liked to call "neutralism" was really a smoke screen for Soviet subversion in the Middle East.

By the summer of 1956, the Aswan Dam project was dead on arrival both in Washington and London. On Capitol Hill, pressure was building to pull the plug, not only among Republican anti-Communists linked to the China Lobby, but also among southern Democrats, who worried that Egypt's expanded cotton crop would flood the American market, and friends of Israel in both parties, who regarded Nasser as "Hitler on the Nile." On the other side of the Atlantic, Prime Minister Anthony Eden and Foreign Secretary Selwyn Lloyd questioned Nasser's bona fides and promoted pro-Western moderates like Iraqi prime minister Nuri Said to curtail the spread of Pan-Arabism throughout the region. On July 19, Eisenhower decided that "we should withdraw the U.S. offer." After alerting Whitehall, John Foster Dulles informed the

Egyptian ambassador that "no single project was as unpopular today as the Aswan Dam." Even if American officials regarded Egypt as creditworthy (and Dulles emphasized that they did not), the United States was no longer willing to provide financial support.[2]

Nasser was not surprised by America's decision, but he did resent the abrupt and condescending manner in which it was communicated. To prepare for just such an eventuality, he had quietly secured a $400 million commitment from the Kremlin in early June. Bolstered by Soviet military and economic aid, on July 26 Nasser announced that Egypt was expropriating the Anglo-French company that operated the Suez Canal and would use the tolls to finance the Aswan Dam. British officials were apoplectic. During a late-night cabinet meeting, Anthony Eden and his colleagues vowed never to accept Egyptian control of the waterway and "agreed that our essential interests in this area must, if necessary, be safeguarded by military action."[3] Eisenhower also regarded Nasser's actions as outrageous, but he worried that armed intervention would backfire and instructed Dulles to seek a diplomatic solution. While the diplomats talked, the Egyptians made certain not to disrupt the oil tankers passing through the canal, reinforcing the American view that any resort to military force would be misguided and premature. Should Britain and France send in troops, Eisenhower cautioned Eden on September 2, "the peoples of the Near East and of North Africa and, to some extent, of all of Asia and all of Africa, would be consolidated against the West to a degree which, I fear, could not be overcome in a generation and, perhaps, not even in a century particularly having in mind the capacity of the Russians to make mischief."[4] Counseling patience, US policymakers believed that the crisis could be resolved by diplomacy and covert action. "The Americans' main contention," Eden remarked privately on September 23, "is that we can bring Nasser down by degrees rather on the Mossadeg lines."[5]

Unbeknown to Eisenhower and Dulles, however, Britain and France were conspiring to regain control of the Suez Canal by force with help from Israel. Anthony Eden was desperate to show the world that Britain was still a great

2 Memorandum of conversation between John Foster, Dulles and Dwight D. Eisenhower, July 19, 1956, and Dulles memorandum of conversation, July 19, 1956, *FRUS, 1955–1957*, vol. XV, 862, 867–73.
3 Anthony Eden, quoted in Cabinet Minutes, July 27, 1956, CM(56)54, CAB 128/30, Public Record Office (PRO), National Archives, Kew, Richmond, Surrey.
4 Dwight D. Eisenhower to Anthony Eden, September 2, 1956, *FRUS, 1955–1957*, vol. XVI, 355–58.
5 Anthony Eden to Harold MacMillan, September 23, 1956, vol. 740, Selwyn Lloyd Papers, FO800, PRO.

power, Prime Minister Guy Mollet was eager to curtail Egyptian support for nationalist guerrillas seeking to drive France out of Algeria, and David Ben-Gurion was determined to force Nasser to open the Straits of Tiran at the mouth of the Gulf of Aqaba to Israeli shipping. On October 23, British, French, and Israeli officials met secretly at Sèvres just outside Paris to approve an elaborate tripartite scheme. Israel would invade Egypt and march to the Suez Canal, Britain and France would demand that both sides pull back ten miles from the waterway, and when Nasser balked at withdrawing Egyptian forces from their own territory, British troops with logistical support from the French would intervene. Six days later, the Israelis staged a lightning attack, Eden and Mollet issued their ultimatums, and Nasser scuttled several Egyptian freighters to block the Suez Canal. When Nasser's Syrian allies blew up a British-owned pipeline that carried Iraqi petroleum to the Mediterranean, the oil crisis that Britain and France had hoped to avoid suddenly materialized.

The American response was clear and consistent from the very outset. Washington sought an immediate ceasefire under UN auspices, warned London and Paris not to send in troops, and worked to prevent Moscow from intervening. Outraged by the timing of the crisis, which came just one week before the US presidential election, Eisenhower insisted that whatever happened on November 6, he would condemn the Israelis as aggressors if they did not cease and desist. He was also "extremely angry with both the British and French," who "should be left to work out their own oil problems – to boil in their own oil, so to speak," should they seek emergency access to American petroleum reserves.[6] Meanwhile, Soviet leaders were eager to divert attention from their own impending military intervention to depose a reformist regime in Hungary. To this end, Khrushchev embraced Nasser, issued thinly veiled nuclear threats against Britain and France, and offered to send in Russian "peacekeepers" to guarantee regional stability. "It is nothing less than tragic that at this very time, when we are on the point of winning an immense and long-hoped-for victory over Soviet colonialism in Eastern Europe," Dulles told the National Security Council as the Suez crisis came to a climax, "we should be forced to choose between following in the footsteps of Anglo-French colonialism in Asia and Africa, or splitting our course away from their course."[7]

---

6 Dwight D. Eisenhower, quoted in Andrew Goodpaster's memorandum of conversation, October 30, 1956, *FRUS, 1955–1957*, vol. XVI, 873–74.
7 John Foster Dulles, quoted in minutes of the 302nd NSC meeting, November 1, 1956, *ibid.*, 902–16.

As painful as the choice was, when Whitehall pressed on and tried to retake the canal with gunboats, bombers, and paratroops, the White House employed financial leverage to force the British to stop shooting and start withdrawing from Egypt. Having halted Britain's armed intervention and removed the specter of Soviet troops in the Middle East, the Eisenhower administration managed to reclaim the moral high ground against the Soviets, who were ruthlessly shooting their way back into Budapest at a cost of 4,000 Hungarian dead. The biggest challenge the United States faced, however, was Israel, which refused to pull its troops out of the Sinai and Gaza until Eisenhower threatened to impose economic sanctions in February 1957. Even then, Ben-Gurion would not budge until the UN agreed to station blue-helmeted observers along the Egyptian frontier and the United States guaranteed Israel's right of free passage through the Straits of Tiran.

Seriously at odds with its friends in London and Tel Aviv and deeply mistrustful of the nationalist regime in Cairo, Washington worried that Moscow might move into the vacuum in early 1957. "The leaders of the Soviet Union, like the Czars before them," Eisenhower recalled in his memoirs, "had their eyes on the Middle East," where in the wake of the Suez crisis they intended "to seize the oil, to cut the Canal and pipelines …, and thus seriously to weaken Western civilization."[8] One option for containing the Soviets was formal US membership in the Baghdad Pact, but American policymakers worried that this step would merely drive Nasser more rapidly into the Kremlin's orbit. The preferred option at the White House was what would come to be known as the Eisenhower Doctrine, based on a joint resolution approved by Congress in March 1957, providing up to $200 million in US economic aid and authorizing the use of American troops to assist any Middle Eastern nation threatened by "armed aggression from any country controlled by international communism."[9]

Ironically, Moscow's policies in the Arab world were somewhat less aggressive than Washington imagined. To be sure, Khrushchev proved quite willing to replenish Egypt's depleted arsenal, but he rejected a Syrian request for Soviet MIGs, and pilots to fly them, in March 1957 because this "might involve negative consequences for both the Arab states and the Soviet Union."[10] The

---

8 Dwight D. Eisenhower, *Waging Peace 1956–61* (Garden City, NY: Doubleday, 1965), 177–78.

9 Douglas Little, *American Orientalism: The United States and the Middle East since 1945* (Chapel Hill, NC: University of North Carolina Press, 2004), 132–33.

10 Moscow Foreign Ministry to embassy, Damascus, March 27, 1957, quoted in Aleksandr Fursenko and Timothy Naftali, *Khrushchev's Cold War: The Inside Story of an American Adversary* (New York: Norton, 2006), 143.

Kremlin's more cautious approach stemmed not only from a growing aware-ness that Eisenhower was deadly serious about using military force to protect American interests in the Middle East, but also from a growing suspicion that Nasser's Pan-Arabism might ultimately prove incompatible with Communism.

Nevertheless, many in Washington suspected that the radical regimes in Damascus and Cairo were likely to become Soviet satellites and worked behind the scenes to build up pro-Western moderates like Saudi Arabia's King Saud and Jordan's King Hussein as Muslim counterweights to Nasser. Once Syria agreed in February 1958 to join Egypt as part of the newly created United Arab Republic (UAR), however, pro-Nasser Muslims next door in Lebanon challenged the authority of President Camille Chamoun, a Christian strong-man with close ties to the Eisenhower administration. When left-wing Iraqi officers overthrew Nuri Said and the Hashemite monarchy in Baghdad on July 14, 1958, Chamoun panicked and warned Washington that his own regime was now threatened by international Communism. The next day, Eisenhower sent 14,000 US Marines to Beirut, where they remained for five months without suffering a single casualty.

Although Soviet leaders had not orchestrated events in Baghdad, they welcomed the revolution and worried that American intervention in Lebanon might be merely the prelude to an assault on Iraq. "The destruction of Iraq," Khrushchev told his colleagues on July 18, "would be a reversal for the national self-determination movement in the Arab world" and a blow to the Kremlin's prestige.[11] The Eisenhower administration never seriously considered invading Iraq, but Dulles did confirm that sending US troops to Lebanon was linked to American credibility, not only in the Middle East but throughout the Third World. "Turkey, Iran and Pakistan would feel – if we do not act – that our inaction is because we are afraid of the Soviet Union," Dulles explained to congressional leaders. "Elsewhere, the impact of not going in – from Morocco to Indo-China – would be very harmful to us."[12] Privately, however, senior US policymakers confirmed that the real sources of Lebanese political instability were Chamoun's own autocratic policies, the smoldering antagonism between Christians and Muslims, and the magnetic appeal of Nasserism. "Nasser has won the enthusiastic and even idolatrous support of the largely illiterate populations in the region," Eisenhower acknowledged on July 18, by relying on "the slogan of nationalism, which is one force stronger than communism."[13] And as Under

11 N. Khrushchev, quoted in *ibid.*, 182.
12 Andrew Goodpaster, memorandum of conversation, July 14, 1958, *FRUS, 1958–1960*, vol. XI, 219.
13 Eisenhower to Macmillan, telegram, July 18, 1958, *ibid.*, 330.

Secretary of State Christian Herter pointed out, this meant that "we have to find some way to accommodate ourselves to Pan-Arabism."[14]

For the next two years, the Eisenhower administration sought an accommodation with Nasser, the most vocal advocate of Pan-Arabism. To this end, the United States kept its distance from Israel while making surplus American wheat available to Egypt on favorable terms under the auspices of Public Law 480 (PL 480), the "Food for Peace Program." In September 1960, Eisenhower and Nasser met for the first and only time following a tumultuous session of the UN General Assembly, memorable chiefly for Khrushchev's shoe-thumping opposition to Western intervention in the former Belgian Congo. Although there was no meeting of the minds about the Arab–Israeli conflict or the Congolese civil war, Eisenhower promised to "respect the UAR position as a neutral" so long as it did not "com[e] under Soviet domination" and Nasser headed home hoping for better relations with Washington.[15]

To the Six Day War

How best to reverse recent Soviet gains in the Congo and other Third World trouble spots like Cuba was a hot-button issue in John F. Kennedy's victorious presidential campaign in 1960. Although the Massachusetts Democrat was preoccupied with crises in the Caribbean, Africa, and Southeast Asia, he was determined to expand Eisenhower's rapprochement with Nasser, who proved quite willing to put the question of Israel "in the ice box" after the Kennedy administration offered Egypt a three-year $500 million aid package. As grateful as he was for US economic assistance, however, Nasser was not about to abandon Pan-Arabism, especially after Syria seceded from the UAR and Crown Prince Faisal of Saudi Arabia, the heir apparent to King Saud, challenged Egypt's leadership of the Arab world. During the summer of 1962, Nasser hired West German scientists to develop short-range missiles, asked the Soviet Union for medium-range bombers, and stepped up his long-distance exhortations for revolutionary change in Riyadh.

In late September, pro-Nasser officers seized power in Yemen, a remote land in the southwest corner of the Arabian Peninsula whose ruling family had close ties to the House of Saud. Fearful that Saudi Arabia might be next,

---

14 Christian Herter testimony, July 16, 1958, US Congress, Senate, *Executive Sessions of the Foreign Relations Committee (Historical Series)*, 10, 535.

15 Andrew Goodpaster, memorandum of conversation, September 28, 1960, "United Arab Republic File," International Series, AWF, Dwight D. Eisenhower Presidential Library, Abilene, Kansas (DDEL).

Crown Prince Faisal began running guns to royalist guerrillas inside Yemen and ignited a proxy war with Nasser, who sent 60,000 troops and several squadrons of Soviet-made aircraft to support the new Yemen Arab Republic (YAR). Preoccupied with resolving a nuclear crisis halfway around the world in Cuba, the White House publicly recognized the YAR while privately urging Faisal to stop the flow of Saudi arms and Nasser to start withdrawing his troops. After Egyptian bombers struck royalist base camps inside Saudi Arabia in early 1963, however, Kennedy agreed to provide Faisal with a squadron of US air force jets as a deterrent. Before the year was out, American and Egyptian pilots were playing a high-altitude game of cat and mouse along the Saudi–Yemeni border and Congress was on the verge of banning PL-480 wheat shipments to Egypt.

Relations between Cairo and Washington deteriorated rapidly once Lyndon B. Johnson moved into the White House. Irritated by what he regarded as American economic blackmail, Nasser tilted toward the Soviet Union in 1964, welcoming Khrushchev to Cairo in May to celebrate the completion of the Aswan Dam, endorsing the Kremlin's call for "wars of national liberation" from Southeast Asia to the Middle East, and heralding the creation of the Palestine Liberation Organization (PLO) in Jerusalem. After an Egyptian mob sacked the offices of the US Information Agency in Cairo in December, Johnson froze American grain deliveries. Nasser responded by inviting the Vietcong to open an embassy in Egypt in the spring of 1965 and requesting more military hardware from Moscow. To make matters worse, Hafez al-Assad and the Ba'ath party, a pro-Nasser organization that preached state socialism and Arab unity, seized power in Damascus in February 1966 and quickly concluded an arms deal with the Kremlin that would bring Syria hundreds of tanks and a squadron of MIG-21 jet fighters.

While the Soviets were moving closer to Nasser and the Arab radicals, the Americans were moving closer to the Israelis. Because 1966 would see off-year elections whose outcome might erode congressional support for the war in Vietnam, Johnson was especially sensitive to the security concerns of Israel, whose friends on Capitol Hill could be very helpful on broader diplomatic and defense issues. Geopolitics, however, was at least as important as domestic politics in the emerging "special relationship" between America and Israel. With nearly half a million GI's fighting in Southeast Asia and with the Soviet Union calling for wars of national liberation in Africa, Latin America, and the Middle East, a well-armed Israel could be a real strategic asset for the United States. Moreover, the White House hoped that by providing the Israelis with conventional military hardware, they would be less likely to develop nuclear weapons. With all this in mind, Johnson approved the sale of 210 tanks to Israel in April 1965 and 48 A-4 Skyhawk jet fighters a year later. When PLO guerrillas attacked Israeli villages from base camps in Jordan, Israel struck back, destroying the town of Samua in the Jordanian-controlled West Bank in November 1966. And when Syrian artillery began to shell northern Israel in solidarity with the PLO early in the new year, Tel Aviv prepared to strike back again, this time with Washington's blessing. "The Syrians are sons of bitches," a top Pentagon official told Foreign Minister Golda Meir in March 1967. "Why the hell didn't you beat them over the head when it would have been the most natural thing to do?"[16]

Two months later, Prime Minister Levi Eshkol hinted that Israel's ultimate objective might indeed be regime change in Syria. The Kremlin vowed to defend its new friends in Damascus and warned Nasser that the Israelis had actually mobilized fifteen brigades for an attack on the Golan Heights. Israel strongly denied that it was preparing to invade Syria, and most observers and historians have confirmed that Moscow exaggerated the threat, perhaps purposely, in an effort to stir up trouble for Washington in the Middle East.[17] Based on what was at best misinformation and at worst disinformation, Nasser mobilized the Egyptian army in mid-May, demanded that the United Nations withdraw the observers it had stationed in Gaza and the Sinai ever since the Suez crisis, and closed the Straits of Tiran to all Israeli shipping, something that Levi Eshkol and his colleagues regarded as an act of war. For three weeks, the Johnson administration pressed Israel not to attack and urged the Kremlin to help persuade Egypt to reopen the straits.

Time ran out at dawn on June 5, when dozens of jets marked with the Star of David knocked out Nasser's air force on the tarmac while hundreds of Israeli tanks smashed through Egyptian front lines in the Sinai, seized Gaza, and raced west through sand dunes and scrub brush toward the Suez Canal. Convinced by back-channel signals from the United States that Israel would not strike first, Nasser angrily appealed to the Soviet Union and to other Arab states for help. While the Kremlin condemned Israel as an aggressor and called for a ceasefire, Jordan's King Hussein sent his army into action against the Jewish state, an ill-advised act of inter-Arab solidarity that would backfire when Israeli forces counterattacked, seizing East Jerusalem and occupying the rest of the West Bank. Meanwhile, pro-Nasser demonstrations in Libya and

---

16 Townsend Hoopes quoted in Michael B. Oren, *Six Days of War: June 1967 and the Making of the Modern Middle East* (New York: Oxford, 2002), 45.
17 Galia Golan, "The Soviet Union and the Outbreak of the June 1967 Six-Day War," *Journal of Cold War Studies*, 8, 1 (Winter 2006), 6–8.

Kuwait forced these two staunchly pro-Western regimes briefly to halt oil exports to the United States and sparked calls in other Arab capitals for a much broader embargo. When Minister of Defense Moshe Dayan sent Israeli troops into the Golan Heights on June 9 in a bid for regime change in Syria, which had heeded the Kremlin's advice and remained on the sidelines during the previous four days, the war threatened to escalate into a superpower confrontation. "The Soviets [had] hinted," Secretary of State Dean Rusk recalled grimly in his memoirs, "that if the Israelis attacked Syria, they would intervene with their own forces."[18]

Eager to avert a more serious crisis, the Johnson administration pressed Israel to accept a UN-sanctioned ceasefire on June 10. With Israeli forces just forty miles from Damascus, Aleksei Kosygin, Khrushchev's successor as Soviet premier, used the "hot line" to warn the White House that Soviet intervention was imminent. Lyndon Johnson decided to call the Kremlin's bluff and sent the US Sixth Fleet into the war zone in the Eastern Mediterranean. At the eleventh hour, Israel accepted the ceasefire, Kosygin backtracked, and as one White House aide put it, "everyone relaxed a bit as it became clear that the fighting was petering out."[19] When the shooting finally stopped the next day, the Israelis controlled Gaza, the Sinai, East Jerusalem, the West Bank, and the Golan Heights while Nasser was thoroughly humiliated. Johnson was quite pleased that the Egyptian leader had been "cut down to size," but he was also frustrated by Israel's impetuosity and reminded Prime Minister Eshkol that "it wasn't Dayan that kept Kosygin out."[20]

Two weeks later, Kosygin and Johnson met in Glassboro, New Jersey, to discuss how best to avoid another crisis in the Middle East. On June 19, Johnson had unveiled a five-point peace plan whose chief ingredients were Israeli withdrawal from the occupied territories and an Arab commitment to a formal peace treaty. Kosygin, however, saw things a bit differently. The Soviets were preparing to rearm Egypt and Syria, he told Johnson on June 23, and unless Israel withdrew from all the occupied territories, the Arabs "would be sure to resume the fight sooner or later. If they had weapons, they would use them. If they did not have them, they would fight with their bare hands." Johnson bristled at this threat. "Let us understand one another," he retorted.

18 Dean Rusk, *As I Saw It* (New York: W. W. Norton, 1991), 386.
19 Harold Saunders, memorandum for the record, October 22, 1968, "Hot Line Meeting June 10, 1967," vol. 7, box 19, Middle East Crisis, National Security Files (NSF), National Security Council (NSC) History Files, Lyndon B. Johnson Library, Austin, Texas.
20 Lyndon B. Johnson, quoted in the minutes of the NSC Special Committee Meeting, June 12, 1967, *ibid.*

4. Territories occupied by Israel after 1967

"I hope there will be no war. If there is a war, I hope it will not be a big war. If they fight, I hope they fight with fists and not with guns. I hope you and we will keep out of this matter because, if we do get into it, it will be a 'most serious' matter."[21]

21 Lyndon B. Johnson, quoted in Editorial Note 320, FRUS 1964–1968, vol. XIX, 556–57.

Avoiding another fistfight in the Middle East would not be easy. By July 1967, nearly half a million Palestinians had fled the Israeli-controlled West Bank for crowded refugee camps inside Jordan. Meanwhile, Israeli troops dug in for a long stay from the Golan Heights to the Suez Canal, prompting Nasser to issue his infamous "Three Nos" in late August at an Arab summit held in Khartoum, Sudan – "no recognition of, no negotiations with, and no peace for Israel." Nevertheless, US officials worked behind the scenes to secure support for UN Security Council Resolution 242, which called for the Israelis to withdraw from the occupied territories, for the Arabs to respect the sovereignty of all states in the Middle East, and for both sides to sit down together at the negotiating table. Despite containing some ambiguous language that both the Arabs and the Israelis would later twist to suit their own purposes, Resolution 242 was adopted unanimously by the Security Council on November 22, 1967, and UN Secretary-general U Thant sent Gunnar Jarring, a Swedish diplomat, to the Middle East in December to discuss its implementation. Weeks of haggling ensued, however, and conditions on the ground worsened throughout 1968, with PLO guerrillas led by Yasser Arafat attacking Israeli outposts in the West Bank. By the time Johnson left the Oval Office, Israel and the PLO were engaged in a nasty low-intensity war that under the wrong circumstances might force Washington and Moscow to become involved.

Although the Arab–Israeli conflict was not as high as the Vietnam War on Richard M. Nixon's foreign-policy agenda in early 1969, he and his national security adviser, Henry Kissinger, embraced a policy of détente toward the Soviet Union that they hoped would pay dividends in the Middle East. When the June 1967 war erupted, candidate Nixon had remarked that "the key to peace in the Middle East is now in Moscow."[22] One week after moving into the White House, President Nixon called on the Soviets to support "new initiatives and new leadership ... to cool off the situation in the Mideast," which he likened to "a powder keg, very explosive."[23] The US president initiated back-channel conversations with Russian leaders during 1969, but the much-heralded new approach to the Middle East never materialized, and, as the year drew to a close, American policy retained

22 Richard Nixon to Dean Rusk, June 5, 1967, quoted in William Quandt, *Peace Process: American Diplomacy and the Arab–Israeli Conflict since 1967* (Washington, DC: Brookings Institution, 1993) 65–66.
23 Richard Nixon press conference, January 27, 1969, *Department of State Bulletin*, 60 (17 February 1969), 142–43.

the same old characteristics – more arms for Israel and much huffing and puffing about Arab intransigence.

From the October 1973 War to the Camp David Accords

In early 1970, long-simmering skirmishes between Egypt and Israel erupted into a nasty "war of attrition." Egyptian artillery pounded Israeli positions along the Suez Canal while Israeli warplanes, including supersonic F-4 Phantom jets recently acquired from the United States, carried out "deep penetration" retaliatory raids against Egyptian targets in the Nile Valley. As in 1967, Nasser appealed for Soviet military assistance, and once again, he got it – more MIGs, and pilots to fly them, batteries of surface-to-air missiles (SAMs) for use against Israel's F-4's, and 10,000 Red Army troops to defend the airfields and SAM sites. Soviet motives were complex. On the one hand, Leonid Brezhnev, who had emerged as first among equals at the Kremlin, was frustrated by Egypt's poor performance during the Six Day War, which he attributed to "total carelessness, [and] a lack of understanding of what an army is under modern conditions." Yet Soviet leaders also believed that, with enough help from Moscow, Nasser could rebound from the debacle, regain the upper hand over Israel, and destabilize pro-Western regimes in Saudi Arabia and Jordan.[24]

Worried that the war of attrition would escalate into another Soviet–American confrontation, Kissinger brokered a ceasefire in August 1970, but a few weeks later civil war erupted in Jordan, where the PLO attempted to overthrow King Hussein. When royal troops gained the upper hand against the Palestinian guerrillas, the Soviet-backed regime in Damascus sent its tanks toward the Jordanian border. Deeply disturbed by what they regarded as Russian aggression by proxy, on September 21, Nixon and Kissinger secretly agreed that the Israelis should launch airstrikes against the Syrian armored columns if necessary to save Hussein's throne. At the last minute, however, Brezhnev persuaded the Syrians to reverse course, King Hussein managed to expel the PLO from his realm without any help from Israel's air force, and the "Black September Crisis" ended with a whimper rather than a bang.

Black September grew blacker still for many Arabs when Gamal Abdel Nasser died suddenly of a massive heart attack and was succeeded by Anwar

24 Odd Arne Westad, *The Global Cold War: Third World Interventions and the Making of Our Times* (New York: Cambridge University Press, 2006), 198–99.

Sadat, who proved far less flamboyant and far less committed to Pan-Arabism than his predecessor. Well aware that he would need America's help to secure Israel's withdrawal from the Sinai, in January 1971 Sadat began secretly to communicate with Henry Kissinger through a back-channel link. Convinced that the Kremlin had been the driving force behind both the war of attrition and Syria's recent meddling in Jordan, the Nixon administration now regarded the Soviets as the major obstacle to peace and stability in the Middle East and worked systematically to reduce their influence. The first step came in May 1972 at the Moscow summit meeting, where Nixon warned that another flare-up in the Arab–Israeli conflict could seriously disrupt détente. He won Brezhnev's agreement for a joint communiqué supporting the military status quo. The second step came two months later in Cairo, where Sadat accused the Kremlin of sacrificing its Arab friends at the altar of détente and demanded that Brezhnev withdraw the 10,000 Soviet "advisers" stationed in Egypt.[25] By the end of Nixon's first term, Washington appeared to have disrupted Moscow's longstanding alliance with Cairo. "Our policy [was] to reduce and where possible eliminate Soviet influence in the Middle East ... under the cover of détente," Henry Kissinger told an interviewer two decades later, "and we did it."[26]

If Sadat expected the United States to respond to the expulsion of Soviet forces from Egypt by ratcheting up diplomatic pressure on Israel to withdraw from the Sinai, however, he was sorely disappointed. Preoccupied with the end game in Vietnam, Nixon and Kissinger paid little attention to the Middle East during the first half of 1973, ignoring Sadat's military threats and accepting at face value Israeli assurances that their fortifications along the Suez Canal were impervious to any Egyptian assault. With America either unwilling or unable to deliver on the diplomatic front and with Russia relegated to the sidelines, Egypt and Syria launched a two-front war on October 6. While the Israelis were honoring Yom Kippur, the Egyptian army crossed the Suez Canal shielded by Soviet-supplied MIGs and SAMs. Two hundred miles to the northeast, Hafez al-Assad's tanks overran Israeli positions in the Golan Heights, prompting fresh calls from PLO leaders in Damascus for the liberation of all of "occupied Palestine."

Stunned by the setbacks on both fronts, Golda Meir, who had succeeded Levi Eshkol as prime minister, urgently pressed Washington to replace the

---

25 Christopher Andrew and Vasili Mitrokhin, *The World Was Going Our Way: The KGB and the Battle for the Third World* (New York: Basic Books, 2005), 155–56.
26 Henry Kissinger interview, June 19, 1991, quoted in Richard Ned Lebow and Janice Gross Stein, *We All Lost the Cold War* (Princeton, NJ: Princeton University Press, 1994), 174.

Israeli tanks and planes destroyed on the battlefield. Confident that Israel possessed the wherewithal to handle the Arabs without additional US help, the Nixon administration's initial response was to wait and see. "The best result," Henry Kissinger remarked privately, "would be if Israel comes out a little ahead but got bloodied in the process, and if the U.S. stayed clean."[27] On October 9, however, the Kremlin began to airlift war *matériel* to the Egyptians, hoping thereby to tilt the military balance further in Sadat's favor. During the next twenty-four hours, rumors circulated in Washington that the Israelis might resort to nuclear weapons if their conventional arsenal was depleted. "From where we sat," Secretary of Defense James Schlesinger recalled long afterward, "there was an assumption that Israel had a few nukes and that if there was a collapse, there was a possibility that Israel would use them."[28] With pressure mounting on Capitol Hill to assist the Israelis, on October 13, Nixon ordered the Pentagon airlift ammunition, artillery, and tanks directly to Tel Aviv. Reassured and emboldened by the American airlift, the Israelis quickly regained the upper hand on the Sinai front, where a brilliant but brutal commander named Ariel Sharon drove the Egyptian Third Army back toward the Suez Canal and prepared to encircle it.

Sharon's bid for a knockout punch might well have succeeded had not the Arabs chosen this moment "to play the oil card." Thirteen years earlier, Saudi Arabia had taken the lead in establishing OPEC, a cartel whose principal objective was a more equitable distribution of revenue between the multinational oil companies and the producing states. Just before the October 1973 war erupted, Saudi officials informed oil executives in Vienna that OPEC would insist on greater control over prices and production. A few days later, in a surprising act of solidarity with Sadat and Assad, Saudi Arabia and the other Arab members of OPEC imposed an embargo on all oil exports to the United States until Israel agreed to a ceasefire and withdrew from Egyptian and Syrian territory. Sharply rising gasoline prices and dwindling supplies quickly produced an "energy crisis" that gave the Nixon administration an added incentive to halt the fighting in the Middle East as soon as possible.

The Kremlin, of course, also had a strong interest in an early ceasefire, since the longer the war lasted, the more likely it became that Sadat would request Soviet military intervention to prevent a resounding Egyptian defeat. Although Moscow's credibility as a guarantor in the Arab world was at stake, sending

---

27 Kissinger, quoted in *ibid.*, 189.
28 James Schlesinger quoted in Seymour M. Hersh, *The Samson Option: Israel's Nuclear Arsenal and American Foreign Policy* (New York: Random House, 1991), 230.

in the Red Army was simply out of the question. "It should be clear to everybody," Brezhnev told the Politburo in mid-October, "that this would mean a world war."[29] Determined to avoid a confrontation with the United States, the Soviet leader invited Nixon to send Kissinger to Moscow to work out a ceasefire that the two superpowers would impose on their respective clients. After two days of talks, Kissinger and Brezhnev agreed on the text of what would become UN Security Council Resolution 338, which called for an immediate ceasefire followed by Arab–Israeli peace talks. The UN Security Council passed Resolution 338 unanimously on October 23, and Sadat agreed to implement the ceasefire at once; Israel, however, fought on, hoping to destroy the Egyptian Third Army. Convinced that they had been double-crossed by Kissinger, the Kremlin sent an ominous message to the White House insisting that Moscow and Washington must work together "to compel the observance of the ceasefire without delay." Brezhnev delivered a blunt warning: "I will say it straight," he wrote Nixon on the evening of October 24, "that if you find it impossible to act jointly with us in this matter, we should be faced with the necessity urgently to consider the question of taking appropriate steps unilaterally."[30]

Brezhnev's message had an electric effect in Washington, where US policy-makers were reeling from the "Saturday Night Massacre" that had seen several high-ranking Justice Department officials resign to protest Nixon's defiance of a controversial Supreme Court ruling in the Watergate scandal. Without bothering to awaken the president, Kissinger and White House chief of staff Alexander Haig convened an emergency meeting of the National Security Council in the wee hours of October 25, during which they agreed to place America's nuclear arsenal on a DEFCON III alert, the highest stage of readiness short of all-out war, and drafted a letter from Nixon informing Brezhnev that the United States was deadly serious. Meanwhile, Kissinger warned the Israelis that unless they stopped shooting and implemented the ceasefire at once, the White House might be forced to halt the American resupply effort. Later that morning, the guns finally fell silent.

Soviet officials were shocked by this saber rattling, but despite calls from some Politburo members to up the ante, cooler heads prevailed. "What about not responding at all to the American nuclear alert?" Brezhnev suggested. "Nixon is too nervous – let's cool him down." To this end, the Kremlin

---

29 Leonid Brezhnev quoted in Lebow and Stein, *We All Lost the Cold War*, 182.
30 Leonid Brezhnev to Richard Nixon, October 24, 1973, quoted in Henry A. Kissinger, *Years of Upheaval* (Boston, MA: Little, Brown, 1982), 583.

instructed Soviet ambassador Anatolii Dobrynin to assure Nixon and Kissinger that Moscow had never contemplated military intervention, but also to point out that nuclear threats were antithetical to the spirit of détente.[31] Nevertheless, many US officials blamed the Soviets for triggering the most dangerous superpower confrontation since the Cuban missile crisis. "All you had to do was read [Brezhnev's] ultimatum," Alexander Haig insisted many years later, "to know that we had World War III in the making."[32] Kissinger, however, viewed things somewhat differently in the immediate aftermath. Just two days after the DEFCON III alert, he took a telephone call from Ambassador Dobrynin, who confirmed that "anger in Moscow is still very high" and complained that "you are trying to make this look like it was a Cuban or Hanoi crisis," when it was not. "Too much is at stake for us to be angry with each other," Kissinger replied. Emphasizing that the American reaction "can only be explained in terms of emotional stress over a domestic situation," he reckoned that "if you had no intention of acting unilaterally our letter was a mistake."[33]

Despite the diplomatic fallout from the nuclear alert, however, Kissinger was more convinced than ever that the overarching American goal of eliminating Soviet influence in the Middle East was *not* a mistake. Throughout the fall of 1973 and into the new year, he solidified his back-channel contacts with Anwar Sadat, who quickly concluded that the road to resolution of the Egyptian–Israeli conflict ran through Washington, not Moscow. Relying on what came to be known as "shuttle diplomacy," Kissinger pressed both Tel Aviv and Cairo, step by grudging step, toward a disengagement agreement in the Sinai and then raised the possibility of preliminary conversations about a broader peace settlement. Kissinger's breakthrough on the Egyptian–Israeli front was a crucial factor in OPEC's decision to lift its oil embargo in the spring of 1974, but Nixon's resignation the following August and his replacement by the inexperienced Gerald Ford dissipated America's diplomatic momentum at both the regional and global levels. Although Ford's defeat at the polls in November 1976 stemmed in large measure from the dismal state of an American economy beset by stagflation, the stalemated peace process in the

31 Victor Israelyan, *Inside the Kremlin during the Yom Kippur War* (University Park, PA: Pennsylvania State University Press, 1995), 179–83; Vladislav M. Zubok, *A Failed Empire: The Soviet Union in the Cold War from Stalin to Gorbachev* (Chapel Hill, NC: University of North Carolina Press, 2007), 238–41.
32 Alexander Haig, quoted in Gerald S. Strober and Deborah H. Strober, *Nixon: An Oral History* (New York: HarperCollins, 1994), 154–55.
33 Telephone conversation between Henry Kissinger and Anatolii Dobrynin, October 27, 1973, US Department of State Electronic Reading Room, "Kissinger Transcripts," http://foia.state.gov/documents/kissinger/0000C147.

Middle East and the widely shared perception that détente had become a one-way street favoring the Kremlin helped Jimmy Carter emerge victorious on election day.

Eager to break the deadlock in the Middle East and sustain détente with the Soviet Union, the Carter administration proposed to convene a peace conference at Geneva, where Washington and Moscow could sit down with their regional clients to hammer out a comprehensive settlement. Menachem Begin, Israel's newly elected prime minister, was dead set against the Geneva Conference, not least because representatives of the PLO were likely to be present. For his part, Sadat worried that Carter, in his eagerness to preserve détente, would strike a deal with Brezhnev that might jeopardize Egypt's rapprochement with the United States. In a move even more unexpected than Nixon's opening to China six years earlier, Sadat flew to Jerusalem in November 1977, where he embraced Begin and announced that Egypt was willing to negotiate a peace treaty with Israel.

Carter was delighted by this turn of events, and after bilateral Israeli–Egyptian conversations reached an impasse in the spring of 1978, he invited Sadat and Begin to a summit meeting at Camp David in September. The

22. Egyptian president Anwar Sadat (left) and Israeli prime minister Menachem Begin (right) with US president Jimmy Carter at the White House, March 26, 1979, after signing a peace treaty. Sadat's political courage made the Camp David Accords possible.

terms of a "peace for land" agreement took shape very quickly – Israel would withdraw from the Sinai in exchange for Egypt signing a formal peace treaty. The major sticking point was the fate of the occupied West Bank, where the Palestinians hoped to establish a homeland but where the Israelis were already establishing permanent settlements. Reluctant to make a separate peace, Sadat insisted that the proposed treaty must be contingent on Israel freezing the settlements and opening talks with the Palestinians. After thirteen days of brutal back and forth, Carter proudly unveiled the Camp David Accords on September 17. Sadat and Begin accepted in principle a bilateral peace agreement linked informally to a temporary halt on new Israeli settlements as the first step toward addressing the question of "Palestinian autonomy." Denounced by the PLO and the Kremlin as a traitor to the Arab cause, Sadat signed the formal peace treaty with Israel on March 26, 1979, confirming that, a quarter-century after Nasser seized power in Cairo, Egypt had in effect changed sides in the Cold War and abandoned pan-Arab nationalism.

The Cold War in the Middle East

By the spring of 1979, however, America's triumph over Soviet-backed revolutionary nationalism in Egypt looked more and more like a pyrrhic victory. While Nixon, Ford, and Carter were building an unprecedented partnership with Sadat, the Soviets were strengthening their ties with Arab radicals. Indeed, during the 1970s, the Kremlin established a military alliance with Saddam Hussein's Iraq, restocked the Syrian arsenal that Hafez al-Assad had squandered in his ill-advised war against Israel, and endorsed the PLO as the sole legitimate representative of the Palestinian people. Moreover, while the Americans and Soviets jockeyed for position among Arab moderates and radicals, both Washington and Moscow faced new challenges from an unexpected quarter – radical Islam. For many devout Muslims, Nasser's defeat in the June 1967 war was proof of the bankruptcy of his secular model of reform through Westernization, and by the mid-1970s an Islamic revival was underway throughout the region. In Egypt, the resurgent Muslim Brotherhood, a Sunni group whose top leaders had been executed by Nasser, challenged the legitimacy of Sadat's one-party state, while in Lebanon the downtrodden Shi'a Muslims took up arms against the American-backed Christian-led regime in Beirut. Meanwhile, the Muslim populations of Soviet Central Asia were growing restless after six decades of Communist rule and Islamic guerrillas were mobilizing against the Kremlin-backed regime next door in Afghanistan.

The hotbed of the Islamic revival, however, was Iran, where Shi'a clerics loyal to the exiled Ayatollah Ruhollah Khomeini preached increasingly vitriolic sermons against the Shah, whose pro-Western "White Revolution" they regarded as antithetical to the principles of Islam.

The impending crisis undermined one of the key operating assumptions of American policymakers, who expected Iran to fill the strategic vacuum in the Persian Gulf after Britain relinquished its empire east of Suez in 1971. To this end, the Nixon and Ford administrations sold the Shah nearly $11 billion in US weapons, paid for with rising oil revenues generated by the OPEC price hikes following the October 1973 war. In September 1978, the American-equipped Iranian army fired into a crowd of pro-Khomeini demonstrators in Tehran, leaving 400 dead and 4,000 wounded. Five months later, a full-blown Islamic revolution forced the Shah to seek asylum in Egypt while Khomeini returned home in triumph, vowing to settle old scores with America, which he labeled "the Great Satan." Islam, which US officials had touted as the antidote to Soviet subversion in the Middle East just two decades earlier, had suddenly become more dangerous to American interests in the region than Communism.[34]

From the Suez crisis through the Camp David Accords, the US strategy in the Middle East remained quite consistent. Determined to protect Western access to Persian Gulf oil and promote the security of Israel, Washington sought to reduce Moscow's influence in the region and combat pan-Arab radicalism from Cairo to Damascus. American tactics varied from administration to administration. Eisenhower sent the Marines into Lebanon, Kennedy wooed Egypt with economic aid, and Johnson recruited Israel as a partner in the battle against national liberation movements in the Third World. Nixon, Ford, and Carter each hoped that some variant of Soviet–American détente would prevent the increasingly volatile region from becoming the central arena of the Cold War during the 1970s.

Soviet policies toward the Middle East, by contrast, shifted in noticeable ways during the quarter-century after the Suez Crisis. Long before he was removed in an October 1964 palace coup, Khrushchev realized that Nasserism, Ba'athism, and other forms of Arab nationalism could be anti-Western without necessarily being pro-Soviet. Brezhnev and Kosygin were appalled by Nasser's catastrophic defeat in June 1967, stunned by Sadat's expulsion of Soviet advisers from Egypt five years later, and frustrated by

---

34 For further analysis of the situations in Iran and Afghanistan, see Amin Saikal's chapter in volume III.

their virtual exclusion from the American-backed Arab–Israeli peace process after the October 1973 war. By the late 1970s, Moscow's bold embrace of wars of national liberation throughout the Arab world had been reduced to a series of spoiling operations mounted by unreliable clients like Iraq, Syria, and the PLO. More importantly, both Soviet and American officials had become so preoccupied with their superpower rivalry that they paid far too little attention to regional dynamics and underestimated the significance of the emerging threat represented by radical Islam.

16

Cuba and the Cold War, 1959–1980

PIERO GLEIJESES

Cuba's role in the world since 1959 is without precedent. No other Third World country has projected its military power beyond its immediate neighborhood. Brazil sent a small troop to the Dominican Republic in 1965 as the United States' junior partner; Argentina's generals briefly helped Anastasio Somoza's defeated cohorts in 1980–81 as they sought to regain a foothold in Nicaragua; Vietnam's soldiers never ventured beyond Indochina; China's military activities outside Asia have been limited to the supply of weapons and the dispatch of a few hundred instructors to Africa. During the Cold War, extra-continental military interventions were the preserve of the two superpowers, a few West European countries, and Cuba. Moreover, West European military interventions in the thirty years between the rise of Fidel Castro and the end of the Cold War pale in size and daring compared to those of Cuba. The dispatch of 36,000 Cuban soldiers to Angola between November 1975 and April 1976 stunned the world; in early 1978, 12,000 Cuban soldiers went to Ethiopia; by 1988, there were 55,000 Cuban soldiers in Angola. Even the Soviet Union sent far fewer troops beyond its immediate neighborhood than did Cuba. In this regard, Cuba is second only to the United States.

This chapter focuses on those regions of the world where Cuba's actions had an important, tangible impact – Latin America and Africa. It analyzes Havana's motivations and the extent to which its policy was a function of Soviet demands. It assesses Cuba's relations with the United States and discusses how Cuba affected the course of the Cold War.[1]

---

1 This chapter is drawn from my research in the archives of Cuba, the United States, Britain, Belgium, Germany (including the former German Democratic Republic), and South Africa.

Origins

President Dwight Eisenhower did not hesitate to recognize the government
established by Fidel Castro. On January 7, 1959, six days after Fulgencio
Batista had fled Cuba, the White House extended the hand of friendship to
the victorious guerrillas. Within a year, however, Eisenhower had decided
that Castro must go. It was not Castro's record on political democracy that
bothered the Americans. US presidents, including Eisenhower, had maintained good relations with the worst dictators of the hemisphere – as long
as they accepted US hegemony. Castro, however, would not bow to the
United States. "He is clearly a strong personality and a born leader of great
personal courage and conviction," a US official noted in April 1959.[2] "He is
inspired by a messianic sense of mission to aid his people," a National
Intelligence Estimate reported two months later.[3] Even though he did not
have a clear blueprint of the Cuba he wanted to create, Castro dreamed of a
sweeping revolution that would uproot his country's oppressive socioeco-
nomic structure. He dreamed of a Cuba that would be free of the United
States, which had dominated the island since 1898 when it had intervened in
the Cuban–Spanish war, robbing the Cubans of the independence they were
achieving on the battlefield. (Washington forced the Cubans to accept the
Platt amendment, which granted the United States the right to intervene
militarily and maintain naval bases on Cuban soil; today the Platt amendment lives on, at Guantanamo.)

In 1959, Castro had no assurances whatsoever that the Soviet Union would
befriend Cuba, a fragile outpost in the American backyard. He might have
accepted a modus vivendi with Washington that promised Cuba complete
independence in domestic policy, while setting some limits on its foreign
policy. The Eisenhower administration, however, insisted that Cuba remain
firmly within the US sphere of influence. By early 1960, the Central
Intelligence Agency (CIA) was working on what would become the Bay of
Pigs invasion. In April 1961, three months after John Kennedy's inauguration,
some 1,300 CIA-trained Cuban exiles stormed a Cuban beach, only to surrender en masse three days later.

2 "Unofficial Visit of Prime Minister Castro of Cuba to Washington – A Tentative
  Evaluation," enclosed in Herter to Eisenhower, April 23, 1959, US Department of State;
  Foreign Relations of the United States, 1958–1960 (Washington, DC: US Government Printing
  Office, 1991), vol. VI, 483 (hereafter, *FRUS*, with year and volume number).
3 Special National Intelligence Estimate (NIE), "The Situation in the Caribbean through
  1959," June 30, 1959, 3, National Security Archive, Washington, DC (hereafter, NSA).

Flush from victory at the Bay of Pigs, Castro tendered an olive branch to the United States. On August 17, 1961, Che Guevara told a close aide of Kennedy that Cuba wanted to explore a modus vivendi with the United States. Kennedy was not interested. A few months later, on the president's orders, the CIA launched Operation Mongoose, a program of paramilitary operations, economic warfare, and sabotage designed to visit what Kennedy's adviser, Arthur Schlesinger, has called the "terrors of the earth"[4] on Fidel Castro.

Castro enjoyed widespread support among the Cuban population, as the CIA acknowledged, but he understood that only strong Soviet backing could protect his fledgling revolution from the United States. The fate of the Guatemalan president, Jacobo Arbenz, overthrown by the CIA in 1954, was a bitter reminder of what befell errant presidents in the US sphere. In January 1959, the Soviet leaders knew very little about Castro except that he was not a Communist and his country was in the heart of the American empire. For several months, their only contact was through leaders of the Cuban Communist Party visiting Moscow to vouch for the revolutionary credentials of the new government. In October 1959, a KGB official arrived in Havana, establishing the first direct link between the Kremlin and the new Cuban leadership. Soon, the tempo accelerated: in March 1960 Moscow approved a Cuban request for weapons. That same month, a handful of Soviet officers arrived in Havana to help organize the Cuban armed forces. Diplomatic relations were established on May 8. Over the next year, the relationship grew close and ebullient as Soviet bloc arms and economic aid arrived. Castro was charismatic, he seemed steadfast, he worked well with the Cuban Communists, and he had humiliated the United States at the Bay of Pigs. The Soviet Union would transform the island into a socialist showcase in Latin America. The Soviets' enthusiasm was all the greater because they underestimated the economic cost of the friendship.

It was the missile crisis that brought the honeymoon to an abrupt end. Thirty years later, in 1992, Kennedy's defense secretary, Robert McNamara, finally understood why the Soviets and the Cubans had decided to place missiles in Cuba: "I want to state quite frankly with hindsight, if I had been a Cuban leader [in the summer of 1962], I think I might have expected a US invasion. ... And I should say, as well, if I had been a Soviet leader at the time, I might have come to the same conclusion."[5] As McNamara admitted, Castro

---

4 Arthur Schlesinger, *Robert Kennedy and His Times* (New York: Ballantine, 1979), 516.
5 Robert McNamara, in Laurence Chang and Peter Kornbluh (eds.), *The Cuban Missile Crisis, 1962: A National Security Archive Documents Reader* (New York: New Press, 1992), xi–xii.

had legitimate concerns for his country's security. Added to this was the Kremlin's desire to close the "missile gap," America's well-publicized overwhelming superiority in strategic weapons.

Kennedy learned that there were Soviet missiles in Cuba on October 16, 1962. On October 24, the US Navy quarantined the island. Four days later, when Nikita Khrushchev agreed to remove the missiles, he did not consult Castro. The honeymoon was over. The Cubans confronted their vulnerability: if the United States attacked them (there had been, as McNamara pointed out, "no non-invasion guarantee"[6]), the Soviet Union would not protect them. As Castro told a high-level delegation from the German Democratic Republic in 1968, "The Soviet Union has given us weapons. We are and will be forever thankful ... but if the imperialists attack Cuba, we can count only on ourselves."[7] The missile crisis was followed by a brief détente between the superpowers, but this did not extend to Cuba, where the paramilitary raids, the sabotage operations, and the efforts to cripple the economy continued. So, too, did the attempts to assassinate Castro. US officials were no longer confident that they could eliminate him, but they were determined to teach the Latin Americans that the price of following Cuba's example would be high. "Cuba was the key to all of Latin America," the director of the Central Intelligence Agency told Kennedy in 1962. "If Cuba succeeds, we can expect most of Latin America to fall."[8]

While Kennedy promoted subversion in Cuba, Castro promoted revolution in Latin America. Castro argued that "the virus of revolution is not carried in submarines or ships. It is wafted instead on the ethereal waves of ideas. ... The power of Cuba is the power of its revolutionary ideas, the power of its example."[9] The CIA agreed. "The extensive influence of 'Castroism' is not a function of Cuba's power," it noted in mid-1961. "Castro's shadow looms large because social and economic conditions throughout Latin America invite opposition to ruling authority and encourage agitation for radical change."[10] Cuba, however, did not rely just on the power of its example. "By 1961–1962,

6 Robert McNamara, in James Blight, Bruce Allyn, and David Welch, *Cuba on the Brink: Castro, the Missile Crisis and the Soviet Collapse* (New York: Pantheon Books, 1993), 384.
7 "Aus der Aussprache mit Genossem Fidel Castro am 14. November 1968 während des Mittagessens im Gürtel von Havanna," DY30 IVA 2/20/205, Stiftung Archiv der Parteien und Massenorganisationen der DDR im Bundesarchiv, Berlin (hereafter, SAPMO).
8 McCone, memorandum of meeting with president, August 23, 1962, FRUS, 1961–1963, vol. X, 955.
9 Fidel Castro, *Revolución* (Havana), February 23, 1963, 4.
10 NIE, "Latin American Reactions to Developments in and with Respect to Cuba," July 18, 1961, 5, box 8/9, National Security Files (NSF), NIE, Lyndon B. Johnson Library, Austin, Texas (hereafter, LBJL).

Cuban support began taking many forms," a CIA study noted, "ranging from inspiration and training to such tangibles as financing and communications support as well as some military assistance." Most significant was military training. US intelligence estimated that between 1961 and 1964 "at least" 1,500 to 2,000 Latin Americans received "either guerrilla warfare training or political indoctrination in Cuba."[11]

By 1964, the guerrillas in Latin America had suffered a string of setbacks, and Cuban support for them had become a source of discord with the Soviet Union. The Cubans resented Moscow's growing antipathy for armed struggle in Latin America, and they complained about the shoddy equipment the Soviets sent them. The Soviets were alarmed that Cuba was a far greater economic burden than anticipated, and they were unhappy that Castro's support for guerrilla warfare in Latin America complicated their relations with the United States and Latin American governments. Most Latin American Communist parties, moreover, had come to resent Havana's encouragement of armed struggle.

Castro did not bend. At a meeting of Communist parties in Moscow in March 1965, Raúl Castro, Fidel's brother and the minister of defense, stressed that it was imperative "to organize a global movement of solidarity with the guerrillas in Venezuela, Colombia, and Guatemala who … are fighting heroically for the independence of their countries."[12]

Africa: the beginnings

Castro not only helped the insurgents in Latin America prepare a new revolutionary offensive. He also turned to Africa. Even before coming to power, the Cuban revolutionaries had seen similarities between the Algerian revolution against French rule and their own struggle against Batista and the United States. In December 1961, a Cuban ship unloaded weapons at Casablanca for the Algerian rebels. It returned to Havana with seventy-six wounded Algerian fighters and twenty orphans from refugee camps. In May 1963, after Algeria had gained its independence, a 55-person Cuban medical mission arrived in Algiers to establish a program of free health care for the Algerian people. "It was like a beggar offering his help, but we knew that the Algerian people needed it even more than we did, and that they deserved it," explained the

11 CIA, Directorate of Intelligence, "Cuban Subversive Activities in Latin America, 1959–1968," February 16, 1968, box 19, National Security File Country File (NSFCF), LBJL.
12 "Discurso pronunciado en la reunión consultiva de los Partidos Comunistas y Obreros que se celebra en Moscú," March 3, 1965, 3, Oficina Secreta 2do Sec CC PCC, Havana (hereafter, OS).

minister of public health.[13] In October 1963, when Algeria was threatened by Morocco, the Cubans rushed a force of 686 men with heavy weapons to the Algerians, jeopardizing a contract Morocco had just signed with Havana to buy 1 million tons of Cuban sugar for $184 million, a considerable amount of hard currency at a time when the United States was trying to cripple Cuba's economy.

Cuba's interest in sub-Saharan Africa quickened in late 1964. This was the moment of the great illusion when the Cubans, and many others, believed that revolution beckoned in Africa. Guerrillas were fighting the Portuguese in Angola, Guinea-Bissau, and Mozambique. In Congo Brazzaville, a new government proclaimed its revolutionary sympathies. Above all, there was Zaire, where armed revolt threatened the corrupt pro-American regime that Eisenhower and Kennedy had laboriously put in place.[14] To save the Zairean regime, the administration of Lyndon B. Johnson raised an army of approximately 1,000 white mercenaries in a major covert operation that provoked a wave of revulsion even among African leaders friendly to the United States. In December 1964, Che Guevara went on a three-month trip to Africa. The following February, in Tanzania, he offered the Zairean rebels "about thirty instructors and all the weapons we could spare." They accepted "with delight." Che left with "the joy of having found people ready to fight to the finish. Our next task was to select a group of black Cubans – all volunteers – to join the struggle in Zaire."[15] From April to July 1965, approximately 120 Cubans, led by Che, entered Zaire. In August, 250 Cubans, under Jorge Risquet, arrived in neighboring Congo Brazzaville at the request of that country's government, which feared an attack by the CIA's mercenaries; the column would also, if possible, assist Che in Zaire.

But Central Africa was not ready for revolution. By the time the Cubans arrived in Zaire, the mercenaries had broken the resolve of the rebels, leaving Che no choice by November 1965 but to withdraw. In Congo Brazzaville, Risquet's column saved the host government from a military coup in June 1966 and trained the rebels of Agostinho Neto's Popular Movement for the Liberation of Angola (MPLA) before withdrawing in December 1966.

The late 1960s were a period of deepening maturity in Cuba's relationship with Africa. No longer deluded that revolution was around the corner, the

13 José Ramón Machado Ventura, note to author, Havana, July 12, 1995.
14 I refer to the former French colony as Congo Brazzaville and the former Belgian colony as Zaire.
15 Che Guevara, "Pasajes de la guerra revolucionaria (Congo)," [Dar-es-Salaam, c. December 1965], 13–14, private collection, Havana.

23. Fidel Castro (left), Raúl Castro, and Che Guevara (right) in October 1963, finalizing the plan to send Cuban troops to Algeria to protect it from Moroccan aggression.

Cubans were learning about the continent. In those years, the focus of Havana's attention in Africa was Guinea-Bissau, where rebels were fighting for independence from Portugal. At their request, in 1966 Cuban military instructors and doctors arrived in Guinea-Bissau, where they remained until the end of the war in 1974. This was the longest and most successful Cuban intervention in Africa before the dispatch of troops to Angola in 1975.

Relations with Moscow

Whereas Cuba's support for armed struggle in Latin America in the 1960s provoked the wrath of the United States and angered Moscow, Cuba's activities in Africa drew much less heat. There, Cuban and Soviet policies ran along parallel paths: they supported the same movements and govern-ments. US officials knew that the Cubans were in Africa, but they were confident that a handful of Cubans could not be effective in distant, alien countries. Washington was focused, instead, on Cuban activities in Latin America where, in 1966–67, Cuba continued to fan the flame of armed struggle. By 1968, however, the guerrillas had been crushed in Bolivia, virtually wiped out in Guatemala, and brutally punished in Colombia and Venezuela. These defeats, and Che's death, taught Havana that a few brave men could not ignite armed struggle in Latin America. "By 1970 Cuban assistance to guerrilla groups ... had been cut back to very low levels," US officials concluded.[16]

This removed a major irritant in Cuba's relationship with the Soviet Union, which had become increasingly strained. In the mid- and late 1960s, while US policymakers publicly lambasted Castro as a Soviet puppet, US intelligence analysts quietly pointed to Castro's resistance to Soviet advice and his open criticism of the Soviet Union. "He has no intention of subordinating himself to Soviet discipline and direction, and he has increasingly disagreed with Soviet concepts, strategies and theories," a 1968 study concluded, reflecting the consensus of the intelligence community.[17] Castro had no compunction about purging those who were most loyal to Moscow or about pursuing economic policies that ran counter to Soviet advice. Soviet officials "muttered about pouring funds down the Cuban rathole" and footed the bill, the State Department noted.[18] Castro criticized the Soviet Union as dogmatic and opportunistic, niggardly in its aid to Third World governments and liberation movements, and overeager to seek accommodation with the United States. He made no secret of his displeasure with the inadequacy of Moscow's support of North Vietnam, and in Latin America he actively pursued policies contrary to Moscow's wishes. "If they gave us any advice, we'd say that they were interfering in our internal affairs," Raúl Castro later remarked, "but we didn't hesitate to express our opinions about their internal affairs."[19]

To explain why the Soviets put up with "their recalcitrant Cuban ally," US intelligence reports noted that they were "inhibited by Castro's intractability."[20] The Soviets still saw advantages in their relations with Cuba, a 1967 study observed – as a symbol of Soviet ability to support even "remote allies" and for its "nuisance value vis-a-vis the US." Above all, they drew back from the political and psychological cost of a break: "How could the Soviets pull out of Cuba and look at the world or themselves in the morning? It would be a confession of monumental failure – the first and only Socialist enterprise in the

---

16 US Department of State (DOS), "Cuban Presence in Africa," December 28, 1977, Freedom of Information Act (FOIA), 4.
17 "National Policy Paper – Cuba: United States Policy," draft, July 15, 1968, 16, FOIA.
18 DOS, "Soviet Intentions toward Cuba," March 1965, box 33/37, NSFCF, LBJL.
19 Memorandum of conversation, Raúl Castro, Mengistu et al., Addis Ababa, January 7, 1978, 61, OS.
20 Thomas Hughes to the Secretary of State, "Soviet Intentions toward Cuba," March 12, 1965, box 33/37, NSFCF, LBJL.

New World abandoned – and it would seriously damage Soviet prestige and be widely interpreted as a victory of sorts for the United States."[21]

By the early 1970s, however, Castro became less intractable. Reeling from the twin failures of his revolutionary offensive in Latin America and his economic policies at home, he softened toward the Kremlin. Cuban criticism of Soviet policies ceased, and Havana acknowledged Moscow's primacy within the socialist bloc. At the same time, Havana's abandonment of its revolutionary offensive in Latin America eased relations with the United States. By 1974, Secretary of State Henry Kissinger concluded that US policy toward Cuba had become counterproductive. West European and Latin American governments increasingly resented Washington's heavy-handed pressure to enlist them in its crusade against Cuba, and US public opinion, spearheaded by businesses interested in the growing Cuban market, now favored peaceful coexistence with the island. Kissinger proposed secret negotiations aimed at normalizing relations. In a secret meeting on July 9, 1975, Cuban and US representatives discussed steps that would lead to an improvement of relations and, eventually, full bilateral ties. Four months later, Cuban troops landed in Angola.

Angola

When the Portuguese dictatorship collapsed in April 1974, there were three rival independence movements in Angola: Neto's MPLA, Holden Roberto's National Front for the Liberation of Angola (FNLA), and Jonas Savimbi's National Union for the Total Independence of Angola (UNITA). Although Portugal and the three movements agreed that a transitional government would rule until independence on November 11, 1975, civil war erupted in the spring of 1975. In July, Pretoria and Washington began parallel covert operations in Angola, first by supplying weapons to both FNLA and UNITA, and then, in late August, by sending military instructors. South Africa and the United States were not pursuing identical ends in Angola, but both agreed that the MPLA had to be defeated. Pretoria wanted to shore up apartheid at home and eliminate any threat to its illegal rule over Namibia, sandwiched between South Africa and Angola. South African officials were well aware of the MPLA's implacable hostility to apartheid and of its commitment to assist

---

21 CIA, Board of National Estimates, "Bolsheviks and Heroes: The USSR and Cuba," November 21, 1967, FOIA.

the liberation movements of southern Africa. (By contrast, UNITA and FNLA had offered Pretoria their friendship.) Although US officials knew that an MPLA victory would not threaten US strategic or economic interests, Kissinger cast the struggle in stark Cold War terms: the freedom-loving FNLA and UNITA would crush the Soviet-backed MPLA. He believed that success in Angola would provide a cheap boost to the prestige of the United States and to his own prestige, pummeled by the fall of South Vietnam a few months earlier.

The first Cuban instructors for the MPLA arrived in Luanda at the end of August, but Soviet aid to the MPLA was very limited because Moscow distrusted Neto and did not want to jeopardize the Strategic Arms Limitation Treaty (SALT II) negotiations with the United States. By September, Washington and Pretoria realized that the MPLA was winning the civil war, not because of Cuban aid (no Cubans were yet fighting in Angola) or superior weapons (the rival coalition had a slight edge, thanks to US and South African largesse), but because, as the CIA station chief in Luanda noted, the MPLA was "more effective, better educated, better trained, and better motivated."[22]

Washington urged Pretoria, which might have hesitated, to intervene. On October 14, South African troops invaded Angola, transforming the civil war into an international conflict.

As the South Africans raced toward Luanda, MPLA resistance crumbled. They would have seized the capital had not Castro decided on November 4, to respond to the MPLA's desperate appeals for troops. The Cuban forces, despite their initial inferiority in numbers and weapons, halted the South African onslaught. The official South African historian of the war writes, "The Cubans rarely surrendered and, quite simply, fought cheerfully until death."[23] As the South African operation unraveled and credible evidence surfaced in the Western press that Washington and Pretoria had been working together in Angola, the White House drew back. US officials claimed that they had nothing to do with the South Africans and condemned Pretoria's intervention in Angola. Betrayed by the United States, pilloried as aggressors throughout the world, and threatened by growing numbers of Cuban soldiers, the South Africans gave up. In March 1976, they withdrew from Angola. The US–South African gambit had failed.

22 Robert Hultslander (CIA station chief, Luanda, 1975), fax to author, December 22, 1998.
23 F.J. du Toit Spies, *Operasie Savannah. Angola 1975–1976* (Pretoria: S.A. Weermag, 1989), 108.

24. Four heads of state – Agostinho Neto of Angola, Fidel Castro of Cuba, Luís Cabral of Guinea-Bissau, and Ahmed Sékou Touré of Guinea – at the grave of Amílcar Cabral, who led the independence movement of Guinea-Bissau. Guinea-Bissau and Guinea were the only two countries that sent troops to fight alongside the Cubans in Angola. Conakry, March 1976.

The administration of Gerald Ford responded to the debacle in Angola by unleashing a torrent of abuse against Havana, but Jimmy Carter, upon assuming the presidency in January 1977, changed course and announced that he would seek to normalize relations with Cuba. Relations improved, but Washington insisted that Havana withdraw its troops from Angola, and Havana would not budge. In December 1977, two US congressmen who favored rapprochement with Cuba had a lengthy meeting with Castro. They told him that "though President Carter was 'eager' to normalize relations, some willingness to deescalate Cuban involvement in Angola was needed." Castro gave no ground. Angola was threatened by South Africa and Zaire, he said. "The Cuban mission in Angola was the defense of the country." The congressman insisted: "President Carter simply wanted a statement of Cuba's intention to deescalate." Castro replied that "this could not be done unilaterally ... The Angolan government had to decide this, since the Cubans were not there on their own account. ... If the restoration of relations [with the United States] was presented in the Angolan context, things would not advance."[24] This was the constant refrain: Cuba would not let the United States determine its policy in Africa. What this meant would soon be clear.

The Horn of Africa

In Ethiopia, less than two weeks after Carter's inauguration, the military junta that had overthrown Emperor Haile Selassie in 1974 turned further to the left, quashing any lingering US hope of retaining influence there. In July 1977, the junta was rocked by Somalia's invasion of the Ogaden, a region in eastern Ethiopia inhabited by ethnic Somalis. The invasion had been encouraged by ambivalent signals from Washington. As the National Security Council (NSC) specialist on the Horn wrote in 1980, "The crucial decision [to invade] seems to have been taken only ... when the Somalis concluded they had a good chance of securing American military aid."[25] The Somalis made swift progress, and in late August 1977 Secretary of State Cyrus Vance told the Chinese foreign minister, "I think they [the Somalis] will succeed ... they ... will be in control of the Ogaden."[26] Ethiopia's leader, Mengistu Haile Mariam, turned to Cuba, which had begun sending military instructors and doctors in April. He asked for troops.

Castro's reply was negative. A secret Cuban military history notes, "it did not seem possible that a small country like Cuba could maintain two important military missions in Africa."[27] In an August 16 cable, Castro told the head of the Cuban military mission in Addis Ababa, "We absolutely cannot agree to send Cuban military forces to fight in Ethiopia. You must convince Mengistu of this reality. ... Despite our sympathy for the Ethiopian revolution and our profound indignation at the cowardly and criminal aggression to which it has fallen victim, it is frankly impossible for Cuba to do more in the present

24 "Representatives Fred Richmond and Richard Nolan, Discussions with Cuban President Fidel Castro," enclosed in Richmond to Carter, December 16, 1977, box CO-20, White House Central File, Jimmy Carter Library, Atlanta (hereafter, JCL).
25 Paul Henze to Zbigniew Brzezinski, June 3, 1980, box 5, Horn, Staff Material, NSA, Brzezinski Collection, JCL.
26 Memorandum of conversation, Cyrus Vance, Huang Hua et al., August 23, 1977, 14, FOIA.
27 Ministerio de las Fuerzas Armadas Revolucionarias, "Las misiones internacionalistas desarrolladas por las FAR en defensa de la independencia y la soberanía de los pueblos," nd, 65, Centro de Información de las Fuerzas Armadas Revolucionarias, Havana (hereafter, CIFAR).

circumstances. You cannot imagine how hard it is for us to constantly rebuff these requests."[28]

However, as the Ethiopians' military situation deteriorated, the Cubans reconsidered. On November 25, 1977, Castro decided to send troops to Ethiopia to help repel the attackers. Two days later, the general secretary of the Soviet Communist Party, Leonid Brezhnev, wrote Castro a warm message expressing "our complete agreement with your policy. We are pleased that our assessment of events in Ethiopia coincides with yours, and we sincerely thank you for your timely decision to extend internationalist assistance to Socialist Ethiopia."[29] Over the next three months, 12,000 Cuban soldiers arrived in Ethiopia and helped defeat the Somalis.

The crisis in the Horn marked the end of the tentative rapprochement between Washington and Havana; Cuba's continuing presence in Angola and support for the liberation movements of Namibia and Zimbabwe haunted the Carter administration. Castro was blunt: Cuba would not modify its policy in Africa in response to US threats or blandishments. "We feel it is deeply immoral to use the blockade [the US embargo] as a means of pressuring Cuba," he told two Carter emissaries in December 1978. "There should be no mistake – we cannot be pressured, impressed, bribed, or bought ... Perhaps because the U.S. is a great power, it feels it can do what it wants and what is good for it. It seems to be saying that there are two laws, two sets of rules and two kinds of logic, one for the U.S. and one for other countries. Perhaps it is idealistic of me, but I never accepted the universal prerogatives of the U.S. – I never accepted and never will accept the existence of a different law and different rules." And he concluded, "I hope history will bear witness to the shame of the United States which for twenty years has not allowed sales of medicines needed to save lives. ... History will bear witness to your shame."[30]

US–Cuban relations deteriorated further in the remaining two years of the Carter administration. Through late 1978, US officials considered Cuba's policy in Africa "the most intractable obstacle to significant improvement in bilateral relations,"[31] but following the Sandinista victory in Nicaragua in the summer of 1979, Central America moved to the eye of the storm. By the time Carter stepped down, relations with Cuba were no better than they had been

---

28 Fidel Castro to Arnaldo Ochoa, August 16, 1977, CIFAR.
29 Leonid Brezhnev to Fidel Castro, November 27, 1977, CIFAR.
30 Memorandum of conversation, Peter Tarnoff, Robert Pastor, and Fidel Castro, December 3–4, 1978, 5, 9–10, 25, Vertical File: Cuba, JCL. On May 15, 1964, the United States banned the export of medicines to Cuba.
31 DOS, "Cuban Presence in Africa," December 28, 1978, 19, FOIA.

in Ford's last year. They would worsen through the 1980s, as Havana and Washington clashed in southern Africa and Central America.

Castro's motivations

US intelligence analysts in the 1960s were determined to figure out what was motivating Cuban foreign policy. What is striking about their conclusions is how similar they are to the explanation that emerges from the Cuban documents themselves. Not once did US intelligence reports suggest that Cuba was acting in Latin America or Africa at the behest of the Soviet Union. Occasionally, they referred to Castro's ego – "his thirst for self-aggrandizement"[32] – as a motivating factor for his foreign-policy activism, but they consistently stressed that self-defense and revolutionary fervor were his main motivations. They acknowledged that Castro had repeatedly offered to explore a modus vivendi with the United States – in 1961, 1963, and 1964. With one fleeting and "very tenuous"[33] exception in October–November 1963, he had been rebuffed. The American response was instead to attempt to assassinate Fidel Castro, to launch paramilitary operations against Cuba, and to cripple the island's economy.

The Cuban leaders concluded that the best defense was offense – not by attacking the United States directly, which would be suicidal, but by assisting revolutionary forces in the Third World, thereby gaining friends and weakening US influence. When Che Guevara went to Africa in December 1964, Thomas Hughes, the director of the State Department's bureau of intelligence and research (INR), noted that this "three-month trip was part of an important new Cuban strategy." The strategy, he argued, was based on Cuba's belief that Africa was ready for revolution and that it was in Cuba's interest to spread revolution there: it would win Havana new friends and it would challenge US influence on the continent.[34] "It was almost a reflex," Che's second-in-command in Zaire remarked. "Cuba defends itself by attacking its aggressor. This was our philosophy. The Yankees were attacking us from every side, so we had to challenge them everywhere. We had to divide their forces, so that

32 George Denney to the Secretary of State, "Cuban Foreign Policy," September 15, 1967, 4, Pol 1 Cuba, Subject – Numeric Files: 1963–73, RG 59, National Archives II, College Park, Maryland (hereafter, NA).
33 McGeorge Bundy, quoted in Chase, "Meeting with the President, December 19, 1963," FRUS, 1961–1963, vol. XI, 907.
34 Thomas Hughes to the Secretary of State, "Che Guevara's African Venture," April 19, 1965, box 20, NSFCF, LBJL.

they wouldn't be able to descend on us, or any other country, with all their might."[35]

But to explain Cuban activism in the 1960s merely in terms of self-defense would be to distort reality – a mistake US intelligence analysts did not make. There was a second motive force, as the CIA and INR freely acknowledged: Castro's "sense of revolutionary mission."[36] Report after report stressed the same point: Castro was "a compulsive revolutionary,"[37] a man with a "fanatical devotion to his cause,"[38] who was "inspired by a messianic sense of mission."[39] He believed that he was "engaged in a great crusade."[40]

History, geography, culture, and language made Latin America the Cubans' natural habitat, the place closest to Castro's and his followers' hearts, the first place where they tried to spread revolution. But Latin America was also where their freedom of movement was most circumscribed. Castro was, as the CIA observed, "canny enough to keep his risks low" in the backyard of the United States.[41] This is why fewer than forty Cubans fought in Latin America in the 1960s and why Cuba was extremely cautious about sending weapons to Latin American rebels.

In Africa, Cuba incurred fewer risks. Whereas in Latin America Havana challenged legal governments, flouted international law, and faced the condemnation of the governments of the hemisphere, in Africa it confronted colonial powers or defended established states. Above all, in Africa there was much less risk of a head-on collision with the United States. US officials barely noted the Cubans in Africa, until Cuban troops landed in Angola in November 1975.

Moreover, the Cuban leaders were convinced that their country had a special empathy for the Third World beyond the confines of Latin America and a special role to play there. The Soviets and their East European allies were white and, by Third World standards, rich; the Chinese exhibited the hubris of a rising great power, and they were unable to adapt to African and Latin American culture. By contrast, Cuba was nonwhite, poor, threatened by a powerful enemy, and culturally Latin American and African. It was,

---

35 Interview with Víctor Dreke, Havana, July 11, 1994.
36 Denney to the Secretary of State, "Cuban Foreign Policy," 5.
37 Special NIE, "Cuba: Castro's Problems and Prospects over the Next Year or Two," June 27, 1968, 3, box 8/9, NSF, NIE, LBJL.
38 CIA, Directorate of Intelligence, "Cuban Subversive Policy and the Bolivian Guerrilla Episode," May 1968, 3, box 19, NSFCF, LBJL.
39 Special NIE, "The Situation in the Caribbean through 1959," June 30, 1959, 3, NSA.
40 NIE, "The Situation in Cuba," June 14, 1960, 9, NSA.
41 Special NIE, "Cuba: Castro's Problems and Prospects over the Next Year or Two," June 27, 1968, 3, NSF, NIE, box 8/9, LBJL.

therefore, a unique hybrid: a socialist country with a Third World sensibility. This mattered in a world that was dominated, as Castro rightly understood, by the "conflict between privileged and underprivileged, humanity against 'imperialism'"[42] and where the major fault line was not between socialist and capitalist states but between developed and underdeveloped countries.

These, then, were the dual motivations of Cuban activism in the 1960s: self-preservation and revolutionary idealism. When Realpolitik clashed with revolutionary duty, sometimes the former prevailed: the Mexican government did not join the US crusade against Cuba, and in return Cuba did not criticize Mexico's corrupt and repressive regime or support armed struggle against it. At other times revolutionary duty prevailed: in 1961, Cuba risked the wrath of the French president, Charles de Gaulle, by helping the Algerian rebels, and, in 1963, it went to the defense of the Algerian Republic, even though this jeopardized an important sugar contract with Morocco.

It is impossible to know what would have happened to Cuba's foreign-policy activism in the 1960s had the costs suddenly escalated, that is, had Kennedy or Johnson been willing to consider a modus vivendi with Castro if he abandoned his support for revolution abroad. INR director Hughes wrestled with this question in the spring of 1964:

> On the one hand they [Cuba's leaders] are still dedicated revolutionaries. ... Many would rather be remembered as revolutionary martyrs than economic planners. Yet on the other hand these same men are aware that the current pressing problems demand amelioration that can only be brought by muting the call to revolution, by attempting to reach live and let live arrangements with the US, and by widening trade and diplomatic contacts with the free world. Tensions between the two paths, between peaceful coexistence and the call for violent revolution will continue to exist within the Cuban hierarchy, both within and between individuals, for the foreseeable future.[43]

In the 1960s, Cuba did not have to choose between Realpolitik and idealism because the United States consistently rebuffed its attempts to discuss a rapprochement. Realpolitik and idealism ran along parallel tracks as the main motivations of Cuba's foreign policy.

But does this hold true for the 1970s? More precisely, does it help explain the dispatch of Cuban troops to Angola in November 1975? Two difficulties are apparent. First, the argument of self-defense loses much of its power because,

---

42 "National Policy Paper – Cuba: United States Policy," draft, July 15, 1968, 15 (quoting Castro), FOIA.

43 Hughes to the Secretary of State, "Cuba in 1964," April 17, 1964, 10–11, FOIA.

by 1975, the United States had decided to seek accommodation with Cuba. Furthermore, whereas Castro's fierce independence from the Soviet Union in the 1960s was evident for all to see, by the early 1970s Cuban criticism of Soviet policies had ended. This may suggest that the Cubans intervened in Angola in response to Soviet demands.

This might seem plausible – until you study the documents. Havana's intervention in Angola was in fact a sterling example both of Cuban independence from the Soviet Union and of Cuban idealism. It is now beyond question that, as a Soviet official states in his memoirs, the Cubans sent their troops "on their own initiative and without consulting us."[44] The evidence is so compelling that even Kissinger, who habitually dismissed the Cubans as Soviet proxies, has reconsidered. "At the time we thought he [Castro] was operating as a Soviet surrogate," he writes in his memoirs. "We could not imagine that he would act so provocatively so far from home unless he was pressured by Moscow to repay the Soviet Union for its military and economic support. Evidence now available suggests that the opposite was the case."[45]

What motivated Castro's bold move in Angola? Not Cuba's narrow interests; not realpolitik. By deciding to send troops Castro challenged Brezhnev, who opposed the dispatch of Cuban soldiers to Angola. He faced a serious military risk: Pretoria, urged on by Washington, might have escalated, and the Cuban soldiers might have faced the full South African army without any guarantee of Soviet assistance; indeed, it took two months for Moscow to begin providing very needed logistical support to airlift Cuban troops to Angola. Furthermore, the dispatch of Cuban troops jeopardized relations with the West at a moment when they were markedly improving: the United States was probing a modus vivendi; the Organization of American States had just lifted the sanctions it had imposed in 1964; and West European governments were offering Havana low-interest loans and development aid. Realpolitik required Cuba to rebuff Luanda's appeals. Had he been a client of the Soviet Union, Castro would have held back.

Castro sent troops because he understood that the victory of the Pretoria–Washington axis would have meant the victory of apartheid, tightening the grip of white domination over the people of southern Africa. It was a defining moment. As Kissinger now says: Castro "was probably the most genuine revolutionary leader then in power."[46]

---

44 Anatoly Dobrynin, *In Confidence: Moscow's Ambassador to America's Six Cold War Presidents* (Seattle, WA: University of Washington Press, 1995), 362.
45 Henry Kissinger, *Years of Renewal* (New York: Simon & Schuster, 1999), 816.
46 Kissinger, *Years*, 785.

The contrast between the Soviet reaction to the dispatch of Cuban troops to Angola in November 1975 and to Ethiopia in November 1977 is stark: in Angola, Cuba acted without even informing the Soviet Union, whereas in Ethiopia there was close consultation; in Angola, for two harrowing months the Cubans operated without any logistical support from the Soviet Union, whereas in Ethiopia Moscow supported the airlift of Cuban troops from day one; in Angola, the Cubans planned military operations without any Soviet input, whereas in Ethiopia, Soviets and Cubans worked together to help the Ethiopians plan military operations. As Castro told Neto, "In Angola we took the initiative, we acted on our own ... It was a decision full of risks. In Ethiopia, our actions were coordinated from the very beginning with the Soviets."[47]

That Havana and Moscow agreed about what policy to pursue in Ethiopia does not mean that the Cubans were subservient to the Soviets. Arguably, the key to explaining Cuban motivations is provided by National Security Adviser Zbigniew Brzezinski, who told Carter in March 1977, "Castro ended up more favorably impressed by the Ethiopians. He found the Somalis, who pressed their longstanding territorial demands on Ethiopia, more irredentist than socialist."[48] Indeed, Castro had been very impressed by the Ethiopian revolution, and by Mengistu, whom he had met in March 1977. He told East German leader Erich Honecker, "a real revolution is taking place in Ethiopia. In this former feudal empire the land has been given to the peasants ... Mengistu strikes me as a quiet, honest and convinced revolutionary leader."[49] Hundreds of Cuban documents covering the critical period from late 1976 through the spring of 1978 make clear that Castro's feelings were shared by the three top Cuban officials in Addis Ababa: the ambassador, the head of the military mission, and the head of intelligence. With hindsight, we know that the Cubans' impression of what was happening in Ethiopia was wrong. But this was not clear in 1977: though the process was undeniably bloody, the Ethiopian junta had decreed a radical agrarian reform and had taken unprecedented steps to foster the cultural rights of the non-Amhara population.

While the evidence is not conclusive – this would require the minutes of conversations among Cuban leaders or between Cuban and Soviet leaders in the days preceding the decision – it strongly suggests that the Cubans

47 Memorandum of conversation, Fidel Castro, Agostinho Neto, Havana, January 24, 1979, 23, Archivo del Consejo de Estado, Havana, Cuba.
48 Zbigniew Brzezinski to Jimmy Carter, [March 1977], FOIA.
49 "Niederschrift über das Gespräch zwischen Genossen Erich Honecker und Genossen Fidel Castro am Sonntag, dem 3. April 1977, von 11.00 bis 13.30 Uhr und von 15.45 bis 18.00 Uhr, im Hause des ZK," April 3, 1977, 20–21, 23, DY30 JIV 2/201/1292, SAPMO.

intervened because they believed, as Cuban intelligence stated in March 1977, that "the social and economic measures adopted by the country's [Ethiopia's] leadership are the most progressive we have seen in any underdeveloped country since the triumph of the Cuban revolution."[50] The Cubans considered the Somali invasion "unjustified and criminal,"[51] and they correctly understood that it had been encouraged by Washington. They knew that Mogadishu had violated the most sacred principle of the Organization of African Unity – the respect for the borders inherited at the time of independence. Without this principle, there could be no peace in Africa. As the NSC specialist on the Horn told Brzezinski, "The Soviets and Cubans have legality and African sentiment on their side in Ethiopia – they are helping an African country defend its territorial integrity and countering aggression."[52]

In my years of research on Cuban foreign policy I have not discovered one instance in which Cuba intervened in another country at Moscow's behest. As an NSC interagency study concluded in August 1978, "Cuba is not involved in Africa solely or even primarily because of its relationship with the Soviet Union. Rather, Havana's African policy reflects its activist revolutionary ethos and its determination to expand its own political influence in the Third World at the expense of the West (read U.S.)."[53] Castro did not send troops to Ethiopia to do the Soviets' bidding, but Soviet military and logistical support allowed him to pursue the course he wanted to take. Cuban actions in Latin America and Africa in the 1960s – small-scale operations involving a limited number of people – were conducted without direct Soviet assistance, as was the dispatch of the first Cuban troops to Angola, but they would not have been possible without the military and economic aid that Moscow gave to the island. Cuba's ability to act independently was made possible by the existence of a friendly superpower on which it depended for its economic and military lifeline, a situation reminiscent of the fact that Israel's freedom of maneuver has been made possible by the support of the United States. Although Cuba and Israel have very different foreign policies, they have one thing in common: this economic and military dependence did not translate into being a client.

---

50 "Síntesis analítica sobre la revolución etiopica. Proposiciones" [early March 1977], CIFAR.
51 Fidel Castro to Neto, March 7, 1978, CIFAR.
52 Henze to Brzezinski, March 1, 1978, box 1, Horn, Staff Material, NSA, Brzezinski Collection, JCL.
53 "Response, Presidential Review Memorandum 36: Soviet–Cuban Presence in Africa," August 18, 1978, 15, NSA.

Cuba and the Cold War

This brings us to the interesting question: How did the existence of a Soviet ally in the very heart of the US empire affect the Cold War? Surprisingly, the impact was minor in the 1960s, with one major exception: in 1962, Kennedy's reckless policy of aggression against Cuba precipitated the decision to install missiles in the island and brought the world to the brink of nuclear war. But the tentative détente between Moscow and Washington that followed the missile crisis was not influenced by Cuban actions. Cuba's support for armed struggle in Latin America was only an irritant in relations between the two superpowers. It did, however, change US policy in the hemisphere. The fear of a second Cuba haunted US policymakers, particularly in the early 1960s; it was midwife to the Alliance for Progress and triggered Kennedy's decision to strengthen Latin America's two most repressive institutions – the military and the police.

It was in the 1970s that Cuban foreign policy did significantly influence – twice – relations between the superpowers. The Ford administration responded to the Cuban victory in Angola by placing the SALT II negotiations and détente in the deep freeze. Cuba, it claimed, was a Soviet proxy, and the Cuban intervention a gross violation of the rules of détente. Two years later, the Carter administration responded in a similar way to Cuba's intervention in Ethiopia. In Brzezinski's famous expression, "SALT lies buried in the sands of the Ogaden."[54]

Clearly, Cuba's actions in Angola and Ethiopia damaged détente. But what lay behind America's anger? If indeed the "rules" of détente were violated in Angola, the principal culprit was the United States, which had encouraged South Africa to invade. It was this invasion that persuaded Castro to send troops. In the Horn, US ambivalence encouraged the Somalis to invade Ethiopia, threatening the principle of the inviolability of the territorial integrity of African states. The Cuban troops upheld that principle. What died in the sands of the Ogaden was the delusion of a one-sided détente, in which the enemies of the United States did not have the right to send troops anywhere, whatever the provocation, whatever the violation of international law, whereas the friends of the United States did, as, for example, when the French and Belgians sent troops to Zaire in 1978 (aboard US planes) and the South Africans invaded Angola in 1975.

54 Zbigniew Brzezinski, *Power and Principle: Memoirs of the National Security Adviser 1977–1981* (New York: Farrar, Straus & Giroux, 1983), 189.

What did the Soviets gain from their alliance with Cuba? Not much. Khrushchev's attempt to use Cuba to close the missile gap ended in abject failure. Soviet hopes that Cuba would be a springboard for further advances in Latin America backfired – Havana's support for armed struggle hindered Moscow's diplomatic efforts in Latin America in the 1960s. Angola and Ethiopia became a drain on scarce Soviet resources; true, they bought billions of dollars of Soviet weapons, but mostly on credit, and the debts were never paid. The major benefit that the Soviet Union derived from its alliance with Cuba – an obstreperous, proud, and difficult ally that did not shy from confrontation – was enhanced prestige in the Third World.

If we view the Cold War as a global struggle rather than merely a bipolar one, Cuban foreign policy had a profound impact. In this struggle, Castro's battalions included tens of thousands of Cuban doctors and other aid workers who labored in some of the poorest regions of the world, at no cost or at very little cost to the host country. And they included the tens of thousands of underprivileged youths from Latin America, Africa, and Asia who studied in Cuba, all expenses paid. This aid began in the 1960s, became massive in the late 1970s, and continues despite the collapse of the Soviet Union.

Cuba's support for armed struggle failed in Latin America, but not in Africa: Cuban troops helped restrain Morocco in 1963; they provided valuable aid to the MPLA in Congo Brazzaville in 1965–66; and they lent decisive assistance to the rebels of Guinea-Bissau in their quest for independence. Havana's most impressive success was to change the course of southern African history in defiance of Washington's best efforts to stop it. In 1975, Cuba prevented the establishment of a government in Luanda beholden to the apartheid regime. Cuba's victory unleashed a tidal wave that washed over southern Africa. "Black Africa is riding the crest of a wave generated by the Cuban success in Angola," noted the *World*, South Africa's major black newspaper. "Black Africa is tasting the heady wine of the possibility of realizing the dream of total liberation."[55]

The impact was more than psychological. Cuba's victory forced Kissinger to turn against the white minority regime in Rhodesia and spurred Carter to tirelessly work for majority rule there. It also marked the real beginning of Namibia's war of independence. For the next twelve years, Cuba assisted the Namibian rebels, and Cuban troops helped the Angolan army hold the line against bruising South African incursions into Angola. Finally, in 1988, Cuban diplomatic skill combined with its prowess on the battlefield were

55 *World* (Johannesburg), February 24, 1976, 4.

instrumental in forcing Pretoria to withdraw from Angola and to agree to the independence of Namibia.

This was Cuba's contribution to what Castro has called "the most beautiful cause,"[56] the struggle against apartheid. There is no other instance in modern history in which a small, underdeveloped country has changed the course of events in a distant region – humiliating one superpower and repeatedly defying the other. There is no other instance in which an underdeveloped country has embarked on a program of technical assistance of such scope and generosity. The Cold War framed three decades of Castro's revolutionary zeal, but Castro's vision was always larger than it. For Castro, the battle against imperialism – his life's *raison d'être* – is more than the struggle against the United States: it is the war against despair and oppression in the Third World.

56 Fidel Castro, in "Indicaciones concretas del Comandante en Jefe que guiarán la actuación de la delegación cubana a las conversaciones en Luanda y las negociaciones en Londres (23–4–88)," 5, CIFAR.

17

The Sino-Soviet split

SERGEY RADCHENKO

By 1962, the once robust Sino-Soviet alliance had cracked up, revealing serious conflicts beneath the façade of Communist solidarity. This split was a remarkable development in a Cold War context. It was not the first time that the Soviets had fallen out with their allies: the Yugoslavs were thrown out of the "camp" in 1948; Hungary had tried but failed to leave in 1956; Albania quarreled with Moscow in 1961. But, in spite of their intrinsic importance, these issues were small compared to the red banner of Sino-Soviet unity, the symbol of the power and appeal of socialism worldwide. The demise of the alliance represented the broken promise of Marxism. Ideological unity and conformity were so essential to the Soviet-led socialist world that a quarrel between its two principal protagonists – the Soviet Union and the People's Republic of China – undermined the legitimacy of the socialist camp as a whole, and of the intellectual notions that underpinned its existence.

So inexplicable did the split appear from a Marxist perspective that both Chinese and Soviet historians in retrospect would blame the debacle on the other side's betrayal of Marxism.[1] But from a realist perspective, Marxism had nothing to do with the rift: the Soviet Union and China were great powers with divergent national interests. No amount of Communist propaganda could have reconciled these competing interests, so it was not surprising, indeed it had been predictable, that the Soviets and the Chinese would fall out and the alliance would crumble.[2] The realist perspective is simple and convenient; yet it does not fully explain the extremely intricate process of the Sino-Soviet split: how it was influenced by key personalities, how it related to the domestic environments of the Soviet Union and China, and how it was affected by cultural contexts of policymaking. These complex matters

---

1 For example, Oleg Borisov and Boris Koloskov, *Soviet-Chinese Relations, 1945–1970* (Bloomington, IN: Indiana University Press, 1975).
2 For example, David Floyd, *Mao against Khrushchev: A Short History of the Sino-Soviet Conflict* (New York and London: Frederick Praeger, 1963).

SERGEY RADCHENKO

are addressed in this chapter – not to refute but rather to refine the realist paradigm, and to do justice to the twists and turns of the road, which, from 1962 to 1969, took the Soviet Union and China from a troubled alliance to a violent military confrontation.

The end of the alliance

On October 13, 1962, Nikita Khrushchev had told the departing Chinese ambassador, Liu Xiao, that "our most cherished dream is to get rid of the cold current which is separating us, and to return to the close and intimate relations we had before 1958."[3] But if Khrushchev had anyone to blame for the "cold current," he could well blame himself, although he was too narrow-minded ever to admit that he had played a significant role in the decline of the Sino-Soviet alliance. Since the historian Shu Guang Zhang has addressed Khrushchev's misguided policies in volume I, we shall not spend too much time on the Soviet leader's blunders here, except in the way of a short summary.

Between 1958 and 1962, Khrushchev's disastrous handling of the Soviet relationship with China had seriously exacerbated the tensions in the alliance. He had angered Mao Zedong with his inconsiderate proposition to build a joint submarine flotilla and a military radio station on China's soil. He had tacitly supported India in the 1959 Sino-Indian border war. In 1960, he had hastily withdrawn Soviet experts from China in a fit of rage. He had rallied his allies in Europe to criticize China in international forums. He had pulled out of a deal to deliver a prototype atomic bomb to the Chinese, and had desperately tried to stall the Chinese nuclear weapons program. From the Chinese perspective, these policies consistently spoke of Khrushchev's high-handed arrogance and his chauvinistic disdain for China.

In late 1962, Khrushchev was portrayed in internal Chinese assessments as "a traitor, not a proletarian."[4] His loyalty to China was no longer taken for granted. "Who knows toward whom he will fire rockets one day? You never can tell," said Deputy Foreign Minister Zhang Hanfu to one audience in November 1962 – and such sentiments prevailed throughout the Chinese

3 Conversation between Nikita Khrushchev and Liu Xiao, October 13, 1962, Arkhiv vneshnei politiki Rossiiskoi Federatsii [Archive of Foreign Policy of the Russian Federation], Moscow (hereafter, AVPRF): fond 0100, opis 55, papka 480, delo 4, list 34.
4 Cited in Wang Dong, *The Quarrelling Brothers: New Chinese Archives and a Reappraisal of the Sino-Soviet Split, 1959–1962*, Cold War International History Project (CWIHP) Working Paper No. 49 (Washington, DC: Woodrow Wilson Center, 2006), 65.

foreign-policy establishment.[5] But this did not mean that the Sino-Soviet alliance was a dead letter in Beijing. Rather, Chinese policymakers believed that the realities of a bipolar world order and the intensity of the Soviet–US confrontation made continued Sino-Soviet cooperation indispensable to both their country and to Moscow. For all of Khrushchev's blunders, he was still considered to be on the same side of the barricades as the Chinese.

On October 16, 1962, President John F. Kennedy learned that the Soviet Union had secretly stationed nuclear missiles in Cuba. Whatever Khrushchev's intentions, sending missiles to Cuba had been his personal decision; he had barely consulted with his colleagues in the Party Presidium, as James G. Hershberg explains.[6] Khrushchev did not ask the Chinese for their opinion on the issue, nor did he inform them that a secret operation was underway. When Kennedy declared the naval quarantine of Cuba and demanded withdrawal of the missiles, the Soviet leader first wavered and then agreed to pull them out. Castro was not consulted, while the Chinese were once again completely out of the loop. Khrushchev bent over backwards to show how his handling of the Cuban missile crisis was a great triumph of Soviet foreign policy. But the Chinese accused him of capitulating and betraying the cause of the Cuban revolution.

Khrushchev resented the accusation. After all, he had pulled back from the brink to save the world from a nuclear catastrophe. He had avoided a world war. Would Mao not have done the same? In fact, Khrushchev believed that Mao was "afraid of war like the devil is of holy water."[7] If so, the barrage of propaganda about Khrushchev's "capitulationism" was only a smoke screen for a sinister Chinese plot, which he could not quite decipher. Khrushchev explained his uncertainties in a meeting with the new Chinese ambassador, Pan Zili, shortly after New Year's Day of 1963: "We find the policy of the Chinese Communist Party somewhat hard to understand."[8] Later he voiced his frustration at a party gathering: "On what question do we have disagreements with China? Ask me! I don't know, don't know!"[9] Unable to fully make

5 *Ibid.*   6 On this matter, see James G. Hershberg's chapter in this volume.
7 Conversation between John Gollan and Nikita Khrushchev, January 2, 1963, CP/CENT/INT/02/04, Archives of the Communist Party of Great Britain, Labour History Archive and Study Centre, Manchester, UK.
8 Conversation between Nikita Khrushchev and Pan Zili, January 3, 1963, AVPRF: fond 0100, opis 55, papka 480, delo 4, list 13.
9 Nikita Khrushchev's speech to a Party Plenum, December 13, 1963, Rossiiskii gosudarst-vennyi arkhiv noveishei istorii [Russian State Archive for Contemporary History], Moscow (hereafter, RGANI): fond 2, opis 1, delo 679, list 118.

sense of the hostile propaganda coming from Beijing, Khrushchev concluded that "the Chinese are dimwits."[10]

Khrushchev's difficulties had their root in a curious intellectual handicap. Soviet policymakers, Khrushchev among them, believed Marxism to be a scientific truth based on immutable and self-evident principles. As a Marxist, Khrushchev struggled against imperialism, aided national liberation movements, and strengthened the unity of the socialist camp. By definition, his policies could not be opportunistic, adventurist, or chauvinistic. By claiming a monopoly on absolute truth in politics, he overlooked the possibility that someone else might challenge his views using the same all-embracing and yet ambiguous Marxist banner.

In the fall of 1962, Mao's perceptions exerted a decisive impact on China's foreign-policy rhetoric. Nationwide statistics for 1962 indicated that China was well on its way to economic recovery after three years of chaos and famine caused by the "Great Leap Forward." Mao had observed this reversal from the sidelines. He had distanced himself from economic policymaking after the traumatic debacle of his radical vision for China's "Great Leap" into Communism. Having eyed the waves created by the headwinds of his ideological tirades, Mao had graciously permitted his comrades-in-leadership to steer the boat to the nearest shore. To increase productivity, Mao's second-in-command, Liu Shaoqi, and Chinese Communist Party (CCP) general secretary, Deng Xiaoping, had pragmatically endorsed new practices in the countryside under the banner of "farming as household responsibility." Premier Zhou Enlai and Foreign Minister Chen Yi had reached out to China's wary intellectuals, silenced by the anti-rightist campaign, and had once again called for a united front with the national bourgeoisie. Sober voices in the foreign-policy establishment called for a less confrontational foreign policy and a rapprochement with the Soviet Union.[11] Mao was upset by these "revisionist" tendencies of his party comrades. He resented that his colleagues failed to consult with him on important issues, content with his semi-retirement.

In August 1962, Mao came back with force. At a party conference at Beidaihe, he drew attention to the importance of class struggle. Khrushchev had earlier put forward the notion that class struggle did not apply to an

---

10 Aleksandr Fursenko (ed.), *Prezidium TsK KPSS: 1954–1964* [Presidium of the CC CPSU: 1954–1964] (Moscow: Rosspen, 2003), 696.

11 Roderick MacFarquhar, *The Origins of the Cultural Revolution: The Coming of the Cataclysm, 1961–1966* (Oxford: Oxford University Press, 1997), chs. 11–12.

25. Mao Zedong and the man he purged twice, but who lived to succeed him, Deng Xiaoping.

advanced socialist society, where the party and people lived in harmony. Finding this view thoroughly fallacious, Mao announced that the Soviet retreat from class struggle amounted to revisionism and to the restoration of capitalism in the USSR. He feared that the same fate might befall China one day if the rightist policies peddled under the banner of "adjustment" after the Great Leap were allowed to continue. The following month, at the 10th Party Plenum, Mao made his views clear: "We must acknowledge that classes will continue to exist for a long time. We must also acknowledge the existence of a struggle of class against class, and admit the possibility of the restoration of reactionary classes."[12] Mao's radical pronouncements stemmed the tide of policy pragmatism. He wanted to assure the continuation of the Chinese

12 Cited in *Ibid.*, 283.

revolution at home and of a revolutionary outlook on relations with foreign countries – first and foremost the "revisionist" USSR.

Chinese criticism of Khrushchev's performance in Cuba in November– December 1962 touched a sensitive chord. Khrushchev, no less than Mao, aspired to greatness and loathed public criticism. He used the occasions offered by party congresses in Eastern Europe to counter Chinese allegations in ways reminiscent of Stalin's handling of the dispute with Yugoslavia. The Soviets clearly commanded the support of the Eastern Europeans; each congress was choreographed to isolate the Chinese delegate and praise the wisdom of Khrushchev's foreign policy. Officials in Beijing resented the hard-handed Soviet tactics, which so clearly undermined Khrushchev's claims of goodwill toward China.

In the fall of 1962, China and India went to war over their disputed mountain frontier. The borderline was less of an issue in the conflict, perhaps, than Beijing's determination to show India who was the greater power in Asia. The war came at a bad time for Khrushchev who had just negotiated a deal to sell India MiG-21 jet fighters. He had also supplied India with helicopters and transport planes, and the Chinese sighted those Soviet planes on the border. The Soviet premier initially claimed that he wanted to keep India away from the US embrace but hurriedly cancelled the MiG deal when he learned of Chinese anger.[13] Departing from previous neutrality in the conflict, the Soviet press then condemned India. Khrushchev wanted to convey the impression that he would go out on a limb for China: "In relations between us," he stressed, "there is no place for neutrality ... We shall always be in one camp and share joys and sorrows."[14] These statements failed to impress Chinese policymakers who concluded that Khrushchev had "betrayed [an] ally."[15]

Betrayal of Chinese interests, as Mao viewed it, was only a short distance from betrayal of Marxism. Was Soviet great power arrogance a cause or a symptom of Soviet revisionism? On the one hand, Khrushchev's high-handed and reckless foreign-policy moves provided solid evidence for Mao's theoretical denunciation of Soviet revisionism. If Khrushchev was a Russian chauvinist, he could not be a real Marxist, Mao thought, because Marxism and chauvinism were not compatible. On the other hand, ideology constrained the scope of permissible Chinese interpretations of Soviet behavior, so that Khrushchev's

---

13 Conversation between Stepan Chervonenko and Zhou Enlai, October 8, 1962, AVPRF: fond 0100, opis 55, papka 480, delo 7, list 69.
14 Conversation between Nikita Khrushchev and Liu Xiao, October 13, 1962, AVPRF: fond 0100, opis 55, papka 480, delo 4, list 37.
15 Wang Dong, The Quarrelling Brothers, 64.

genuine gestures of goodwill toward China invariably encountered suspicions. If Khrushchev was not a real Marxist, the Chinese leaders thought, his claims of acting on the basis of Marxist solidarity with China could only be a fake pretension, a cover for Khrushchev's real, un-Marxist nature. The mutually reinforcing relationship between ideology and power in Sino-Soviet relations paralleled Chinese domestic developments in late summer of 1962 when the increasingly insecure Mao unleashed his struggle against the "revisionist" policies of his unduly self-confident colleagues. In both cases, Mao resorted to radical ideology to shape power relationships; yet, unquestionably, his radical ideas had their own dynamic and were not just a smoke screen for a brutal power struggle.

Fidel Castro's visit to the Soviet Union in April–May 1963 gave Khrushchev the opportunity to polish his revolutionary credentials, badly stained since the Cuban missile crisis. Castro agreed to mend fences and received assurances of further Soviet economic aid. In repeated discussions of China, Khrushchev went out of his way to convince Castro that the Soviets were better than the Chinese in struggling against imperialism, and he sensed that Castro agreed with his point of view. Khrushchev told Castro that he knew what the Sino-Soviet quarrel was really about: it was "a question of nationalism, a question of egoism. This is the main thing. They want to play the first fiddle."[16] And then, he made a remarkable admission:

> Even, say, among friends, 5–10 people are friends and one of them is the chief; they do not elect him, they simply recognize him for some sort of qualities … [T]here will be different colours and different characters, and different mental capabilities among people, there will be inequality as in all species of nature.[17]

The Soviet Union was the birthplace of the socialist revolution; it had defeated Nazism; it had launched satellites into space. The Chinese could never match Soviet greatness, and Mao could never hope to wrestle the mantle of leadership from Khrushchev personally. Khrushchev was the chief. He played the "first fiddle."

In July 1963, a high-level Chinese party delegation arrived in Moscow for talks with Soviet leaders. None of the outstanding issues in Sino-Soviet relations were resolved, or even profitably discussed. The delegations talked past each other. The Chinese – Deng Xiaoping, Beijing mayor Peng Zhen, and Politburo member Kang Sheng – defended Mao's ideological position: Khrushchev wronged Iosif Stalin who had been a great "sword" for socialism;

---

16 Fursenko (ed.), *Prezidium TsK KPSS*, 720.   17 *Ibid.*

he substituted peaceful coexistence with the West for resolute struggle against imperialism; he abandoned national liberation movements and gave up on class struggle inside the Soviet Union. Peng Zhen voiced grievances about Soviet "great power chauvinism" and "bourgeois nationalism," and blamed Moscow for ordering other parties about with the "arrogance of the father party" and even for trying to be the "god of the international communist movement."[18] The talks were suspended on July 20, 1963, and the Chinese delegation returned to Beijing. It was a turning point in Sino-Soviet relations. Mao used the failure of the talks to show that he had been correct all along about Khrushchev's irreparable revisionism. Khrushchev, for his part, had to show that his efforts to find a compromise with the United States could be successful in spite of the Chinese criticism. After the failed talks with the Chinese, he hurried to sign the Limited Test-Ban Treaty with US and British representatives, inaugurating détente in Soviet–American relations.

From conflict to confrontation

As Khrushchev pursued détente with the West with some success, Sino-Soviet relations went from bad to worse. In September 1963, the Chinese began publishing a series of polemical articles detailing Soviet violations of Marxism. The Soviets responded in kind. The battle lines were drawn and the two sides exchanged long-range ideological salvos. Many Western observers imagined that Sino-Soviet relations could not get any worse. But over the next few months they did.

On July 10, 1964, Mao told a visiting Japanese delegation that he appreciated Japan's territorial claims against the Soviet Union. China, too, had suffered at the hands of Russian expansionism: "About a hundred years ago the area east of Baikal became Russian territory, and since then Vladivostok, Khabarovsk, Kamchatka and other points have become territories of the Soviet Union. We have not yet presented the bill for this list."[19] Mao Zedong probably had no intention of "reclaiming" Siberia and the Soviet Far East. As he explained to one foreign visitor, "this is called firing empty cannons to make him [Khrushchev] nervous."[20]

18 Peng Zhen's speech at the July 1963 Sino-Soviet talks in Moscow, July 15, 1963, National Security Archive, Washington DC, REEADD, October 26, 1962–64.
19 Pravda, September 2, 1964, 2–3.
20 Cited in Sergei Goncharov and Li Danhui, "EZhong Guanxi Zhong de 'Lingtu Yaoqiu' he '"Bu Pingdeng Tiaoyue,"' [The "Territorial Demands" and "Unequal Treaties" in Sino-Russian Relations] Ershiyi Shiji, No. 10 (2004), 110; the author's conversations with Chen Jian.

Mao's comments were, of course, leaked to the press and in August reached Khrushchev, who was not inclined to interpret these claims philosophically. On August 19, the Soviet leader addressed his colleagues in the Presidium: "have you read [this] hideous document about borders? ... I read [it] yesterday and became indignant." In a passionate speech he condemned Mao's irredentism:

> Let us look at these things. The Russian Tsar grabbed some territories. [Today] there is no tsar, and there are no Chinese feudal lords, there is no Chinese emperor. They [the Chinese] also grabbed territories, just like the Russian Tsar. It is not the Chinese who live there, but the Kyrgyz, the Uighurs, the Kazakhs. How did it happen that they ended up in China? It is a clear thing. Mao Zedong knows that the Chinese emperor conquered these territories.[21]

Mao's "unsettled bill" touched a sensitive chord. The Soviet Union inherited the vast territorial expanse of the Russian Empire. Stalin resorted to brutal piecemeal annexation of neighboring countries in a restless pursuit of territorial security. But in place of security the Soviet leadership grappled with a profound sense of insecurity, aggravated by collective Soviet memories of the Western intervention in the Civil War and the traumatic experience of the German invasion. Any hint of change to postwar borders aroused Moscow's ire and bitter resentment. This was the case for European borders, especially in the postwar context of the division of Germany. In Asia, the Soviets had felt reasonably secure since Japan's defeat in World War II – until Mao's unprecedented demarche. The specter of Chinese territorial claims to the under-populated and yet strategically essential Siberia and Far East shocked Soviet leaders. Khrushchev likened Mao to Adolf Hitler for his expansionist views.[22]

In October 1964, Khrushchev was overthrown by his Kremlin comrades, who were fed up with his erratic leadership and unnerving bureaucratic shake-ups. The split with China was low on the list of the ousted premier's sins, though he was not spared criticism on that account. The new thinking among the party heavyweights was that if Khrushchev had ordered about his own colleagues, and failed to consult with them on issues of importance, then one could not blame the Chinese for hating his arrogance. The key figures in the new leadership arrangement – First Secretary Leonid Brezhnev and Prime Minister Aleksei Kosygin – both had very little experience in foreign affairs. Facing a complex international situation, Khrushchev's successors looked for guidance in ideological prescriptions and tried to rebuild Soviet relations with

21 Fursenko (ed.), *Prezidium TsK KPSS*, 849–50. 22 *Pravda*, September 20, 1964, 1.

foreign countries on a solid Marxist basis, which, they claimed, Khrushchev had opportunistically abandoned.

Brezhnev summarized the Soviet challenge in a speech in November 1964:

> As far as the socialist system is concerned, our main task remains the strengthening of its unity, and of the cooperation and mutual help among fraternal countries, accepting the necessary conditions of respecting equal rights, independence and sovereignty. It is well known that in the past precisely these conditions were frequently not fulfilled. Let us honestly admit that up to now we have not fully freed ourselves from these kinds of problems. Not only pressure and unceremoniousness, but any posture of superiority, "fatherly" teaching, untactful questions or forgetting to consult in time on questions of common interest – all this must be resolutely eliminated from relations with fraternal countries and parties. Only on such a basis can a real friendship be strengthened, [and the] voluntary cooperation of the socialist countries be developed.[23]

Brezhnev's and Kosygin's rediscovered enthusiasm for China was not shared by the wider foreign-policy community, certainly not by the experienced diplomats and China specialists in the Foreign Ministry who tended to be far more reserved about the prospect of a rapprochement with their eastern neighbour. But the skeptical voices from below were not heard at the top when in October–November 1964 the new Soviet leadership set out once again to heal the Sino-Soviet rift. It was thus with high hopes that Brezhnev and Kosygin welcomed a Chinese delegation, headed by Zhou Enlai, for talks in Moscow in early November 1964.

Mao made no secret of his disdain for the toppled Khrushchev, but the fall of the Soviet leader did not change the equation of power between the two states. The alliance was intrinsically unequal, a partnership of a superpower, endowed with military, economic, and technological advantages, and a junior partner haplessly limping along. In China, the news of Khrushchev's downfall was published alongside the announcement of the successful test of China's first atomic bomb. But one bomb did not compensate for the development gap. As before, the relationship between Moscow and Beijing was, to borrow Mao's own words, that of a father and son. Beijing and Moscow operated in the same system of coordinates, defined by both sides' proclaimed adherence to Marxism. Their economic performance served to bolster their respective ideological postures.

---

23 Leonid Brezhnev's speech to a Party Plenum, November 14, 1964, RGANI: fond 2, opis 1, delo 758, list 19.

In this system of coordinates, Mao aspired but never matched Soviet achievements. To build the relationship with Moscow on the basis of equality, China needed either to outperform the USSR or to abandon the ideological system of coordinates. Mao hopelessly failed the first option but could not bring himself to consider the second. His ideological commitment to combating Soviet revisionism immensely constrained China's foreign-policy options and prevented an early Sino-Soviet rapprochement. Yet Mao agreed to send a delegation to Moscow to probe the intentions of the new Soviet leaders, and perhaps at the same time probe the intentions of his own comrades, some of whom, he may have suspected, shared neither his delusions of grandeur nor his leftist beliefs and would have not shrunk from pragmatically mending fences with the USSR, for all their shared resentment of Soviet arrogance.

By sending Zhou Enlai to Moscow in November 1964, Mao tested his loyalty. When Mao required it, Zhou was always able to put aside his pragmatism and embrace the chairman's radical ideas. He came to the talks prepared to struggle against revisionism. But before the premier had a chance to fire his guns at the negotiating table, an embarrassing incident ruined any prospects for an agreement. At a Kremlin reception on November 7, 1964, the Soviet defense minister, Rodion Malinovskii, evidently intoxicated, proposed to a member of the Chinese delegation, Marshal He Long, that they get rid of Mao Zedong just as the Soviets had thrown out Khrushchev. Then, he said, Sino-Soviet relations would necessarily improve.[24] He Long complained to Zhou Enlai who, in turn, protested to the Soviets. The Soviets tried to persuade the Chinese that Malinovskii did not represent the views of the Soviet leadership, while Zhou Enlai insisted that the defense minister's drunken remarks showed what the Soviets really thought about China and Mao Zedong.

The Malinovskii incident revealed the Soviets at their undiplomatic worst. No foreign delegation could tolerate such insults, especially a Chinese delegation keenly sensitive to any hint of Soviet disrespect. The Soviet leaders, judging from Brezhnev's subsequent explanations, never grasped how outrageous Malinovskii's behavior appeared to the Chinese. Brezhnev expressed "c[omrade] Malinovskii's apologies for the incorrectly formulated thought," but Malinovskii was not punished in any obvious way.[25] Insulting as Malinovskii's remarks were, their real importance can only be understood in the context of Chinese domestic politics. He Long and, in particular, Zhou

---

24 Andrei Aleksandrov-Agentov, *Ot Kollontai do Gorbacheva* [From Kollontai to Gorbachev] (Moscow: Mezhdunarodnye otnosheniia, 1994), 169.
25 Leonid Brezhnev's speech to a Party Plenum, November 14, 1964, RGANI: fond 2, opis 1, delo 758, list 16.

Enlai could not do anything less than vigorously defend Mao Zedong against the Soviet accusations. The chairman did not tolerate disloyalty.

Mao's demand for class struggle at the 10th CCP Plenum in September 1962 spurred a political campaign to save China from revisionism. The campaign entailed a series of initiatives, initially in the countryside, and, from early 1963 on, also in the cities, to eradicate grassroots corruption and suppress capitalist tendencies, which, Mao perceived, were on the rise throughout China and threatened her revolution. Yet the so-called Socialist Education Movement did not give the chairman any peace of mind. In early 1964, Mao became increasingly concerned that revisionism had already found its way into the party, and that the Socialist Education Movement, by focusing on low-level problems, overlooked the more fundamental danger of revisionism very close to the levers of power. In February 1964, he claimed that "there are some people who do not make a sound, but wait for the opportunity; therefore, one must heighten one's vigilance." If people like the ousted defense minister, Peng Dehuai, were allowed "like Khrushchev, to control the party, the army and the political power – well, today ... we could be done away with."[26]

Mao thought that Marshall Peng, whom he had purged in 1959 for Peng's outspoken criticism of the Great Leap policies, was Khrushchev's ally inside the Chinese leadership. But Peng Dehuai's downfall had not made Mao feel more secure. In April 1964, he lamented that "Khrushchev has comrades inside the Chinese [Communist] Party," who aimed at removing Mao from the CCP leadership.[27] Mao's apprehension of this scenario probably became more pronounced after Khrushchev's fall from power. After having taken China through the disaster of the Great Leap Forward, he may have suspected that he could not count on unswerving loyalty from his comrades in power; what if they had been secretly plotting to overthrow him? Malinovskii's drunken remarks touched on a sensitive subject. Mao, after years at the apex of political power in China, after repeated rectification campaigns, and after removing his real and imagined opponents, was still not sure that he exercised absolute authority in his own party. He worried that one day he would find himself sidelined by a Soviet-style collective leadership with un-Maoist pluralism and intraparty democracy, and that his revolutionary legacy would be abandoned for the Soviet model of socialist development.

26 Li Danhui, "1964 nian: ZhongSu guanxi yu Mao Zedong waihuan neiyou silu de zhuan-bian" [1964: Sino-Soviet Relations and Mao Zedong's Turn towards the "Trouble Within, Problems Without" Mentality], in Luan Jinghe (ed.), *ZhongSu guanxi de lishi yu xianshi* [History and Reality of Sino-Soviet Relations] (Kaifeng: Henan Daxue, 2004), 557–74.
27 *Ibid.*

In December 1964, Deng Xiaoping, concerned that Mao had been ill, suggested to the chairman that he not attend a routine conference to discuss the progress of the Socialist Education Movement. Mao took this as further evidence that his Politburo colleagues had decided to push him aside. He made a point of attending the conference, which began in mid-December and lasted until January 1965. During the sessions, Mao criticized Liu Shaoqi for limiting the purges to the corrupt cadres in the countryside. Mao believed the campaigns should target the higher ranks of the party bureaucracy – the "people in positions of authority within the party who take the capitalist road." Though Liu usually deferred to Mao in such matters, this time the chairman's chief deputy was more forceful in support of his own propositions. It appeared to the participants of the conference that Mao and Liu were at odds.[28] But what was at stake in this debate – Mao's ideological convictions or simple power calculations? Mao identified himself with the revolution. He had made it possible. He sustained its momentum throughout the years. He saw any challenge to his personal power as a challenge to the revolution itself. Mao regarded the dispute with Liu Shaoqi as one aspect of a revolutionary struggle that he had to intensify. The Sino-Soviet split was another aspect that needed to be looked after.

The new Soviet leaders had no idea about these dramatic developments in China. After the November 1964 meeting failed miserably, they spent months debating the merits of a new approach to China. Premier Aleksei Kosygin still wanted to mend fences. Dismissing Brezhnev's growing skepticism, Kosygin argued that the Soviet Union and China had no fundamental disagreements because both countries adhered to Marxist policies. Whatever disagreements they did have, these had to be put aside now, at a time when Washington was dramatically escalating its involvement in the Vietnam War: the two countries had to act together to oppose "US imperialism." Cold War imperatives must prevent Sino-Soviet rupture at this time of danger, or so Kosygin thought. Perhaps, the prime minister was also keeping an eye on considerations of his own prestige. If he were to repair the Sino-Soviet alliance, Kosygin's political standing in the Soviet leadership would certainly improve, and this was important in the context of a subtle competition for influence between himself and Brezhnev. For these reasons, Kosygin went to China in February 1965 to meet with Mao Zedong to work out their differences.

On February 11, Kosygin had his chance. In a long meeting with Mao he argued that "the most important thing to us is the union of forces. As a result

28 MacFarquhar, *Origins of the Cultural Revolution*, 428.

of this, they [our forces] will be ten times bigger. ... [I]deology is stronger than any weapon."[29] Kosygin reportedly told Mao: "we are both Marxist–Leninists. Why can't we have a good talk?"[30] But the good talk went nowhere. Soviet participants in the conversation recalled that Mao was "emphatically sarcastic," at times even "insulting."[31] In response to Kosygin's pleas for unity, Mao promised that his struggle against revisionism would continue for ten thousand years. Downplaying Cold War constraints, Mao confidently placed the Soviet Union on the other side of the barricades, next to the United States:

> The US and the USSR are now deciding the world's destiny. Well, go ahead and decide. But within the next 10–15 years you will not be able to decide the world's destiny. It is in the hands of the nations of the world, and not in the hands of the imperialists, exploiters or revisionists.

World destiny, Mao thought, was in the hands of China, in his own hands. His struggle against revisionism was at the same time a struggle for recognition, a struggle for greatness, against Soviet efforts to keep China down and out.

Disappointed, Kosygin returned to Moscow to face growing skepticism about China. But remarkably, even after the failed meeting with Mao, Soviet leaders continued to initiate proposals for practical Sino-Soviet cooperation, such as provision aid to North Vietnam. On February 16, 1965, the Soviets probed China on the desirability of arranging another peace conference on Vietnam.[32] On April 3, Brezhnev and Kosygin signed a letter to the Chinese and the Vietnamese with a proposal to meet at the highest level to discuss joint actions to oppose the escalatory actions of the United States. In the meantime, Soviet leaders peddled ideas for military cooperation with the Chinese despite the sorry state of Sino-Soviet relations. On February 27, 1965, Moscow requested Chinese permission to send forty-five transport planes via China to Vietnam with weapons and advisers.[33] Another Soviet proposal (on February 25) entailed the establishment of a Soviet air force base in Kunming in southern China with twelve MiG-21 aircraft to protect the Sino-Vietnamese

---

29 Conversation between Aleksei Kosygin and Mao Zedong, February 11, 1965, Archiwum Akt Novych (Modern Records Archive), Warsaw, Poland, KC PZPR, XI A/10; obtained by Douglas Selvage; translation by Malgorzata Gnoinska.

30 Wu Lengxi, *Shinian lunzhan, 1956–1966: ZhongSu guanxi huiyilu* [Ten Years of Polemics, 1956–1966: Memoir of Sino-Soviet Relations] (Beijing: Zhongyang wenxian, 1999), 915.

31 Oleg Troianovskii, *Cherez gody i rasstoianiia: istoriia odnoi sem'i* [Through Years and Distances: One Family's History] (Moscow: Vagrius, 1997), 352.

32 Conversation between Stepan Chervonenko and Liu Xiao, February 16, 1965, AVPRF: fond 0100, opis 58, papka 516, delo 5, list 29.

33 Conversation between Stepan Chervonenko and Zhou Enlai, April 13, 1965, AVPRF: opis 0100, fond 58, papka 516, delo 5, list 114.

border.[34] The idea behind these approaches, besides the obvious Soviet concern with the military situation in Vietnam, was to show the Chinese that they were not selling out to US imperialism.

Nearly all Soviet approaches regarding Vietnam encountered determined Chinese resistance. A new conference on Indochina did not get off the ground because, in Chinese opinion, the time was not ripe for Hanoi to negotiate – the US had to be defeated on the battlefield first. The Sino-Soviet-Vietnamese summit did not take place, Zhou Enlai explained, because the Chinese had their own channel of communication with Hanoi to discuss whatever concerns they had.[35] A Soviet request to permit passage of military transport planes through their airspace, moreover, angered the Chinese. Zhou Enlai said that the plan amounted to a military operation, and the Chinese had not been consulted in advance.[36] Soviet shipments of arms by rail was grudgingly allowed, but bureaucratic obstacles kept Soviet weapons at the border crossings for weeks. The Chinese feared that the massive flow of Soviet weapons into Vietnam would weaken Hanoi's dependence on China.

The Soviet proposal for an air force base in Kunming triggered a storm of indignation. Chinese leaders claimed that the real purpose of the twelve planes was not to cover the Sino-Vietnamese border against US incursions but to put China under Soviet military control. As absurd as this idea sounded to puzzled Kremlin policymakers, it indicated Chinese apprehension of a foreign military presence on Chinese soil, an apprehension rooted in the turbulent history of the late Qing and Republican China, when the country was overrun time and again by foreign troops. It also stemmed from more recent memories of Soviet meddling in Xinjiang and Manchuria since the 1920s. In fact, if Brezhnev and Kosygin had recalled the problems Khrushchev had in 1958, when the Soviet Union had put forward proposals for a joint submarine fleet and a Soviet-manned military radio station in China, they would have thought twice before proposing ambitious plans for military cooperation. But considerations of class solidarity at the time of the Vietnam War prevented the Kremlin from drawing proper conclusions from past Soviet experiences. Deng Xiaoping later smirked that "the Soviets forgot that we had a certain experience in this respect." Kang Sheng drove the point home: "the Soviets do not respect the sovereignty of our country; ... they look upon our country as a province of the Soviet Union."[37]

---

34 *Ibid.*, list 141.   35 *Ibid.*, list 110.   36 *Ibid.*, list 114.

37 Conversation between Nicolae Ceauşescu and a Chinese delegation, July 26, 1965, Materials of Conference on European Evidence on the Cold War in Asia, Budapest, Hungary, October 30–November 1, 2003.

Mao's resistance to a united front with the Soviets in spite of the Vietnam War reveals his strategic calculations. US involvement in Vietnam posed a potential security threat to China. In 1965, Chinese leaders repeatedly signalled to Washington through various channels their interest in containing the war in Southeast Asia, promising to stay out of the conflict as long as the Americans did not violate China's borders. Of course, no one in Beijing could be confident that the United States would heed these signals, but Mao felt reasonably sure that China itself would not come under American attack.[38] But Soviet military plans were another matter.

Since 1963, Mao had become increasingly concerned with a potential Soviet threat to Chinese security. He may have received intelligence of a military buildup along the Sino-Soviet border, or perhaps learned of Khrushchev's awkward attempts to bring Mongolia into the Warsaw Pact in the summer of 1963. Moscow's improving relations with the West at the time of its worsening quarrel with Beijing would not have appeared particularly reassuring to Chinese policymakers – it looked to Mao as if the Soviets and the Americans were ganging up on his revolution. In February 1964, he told Kim Il Sung sarcastically that all of the measures the Soviet Union took to pressure China into submission had failed, "but there is still one – going to war." By July, his sarcasm disappeared. He felt that "we cannot only pay attention to the East, and not to the North, only pay attention to imperialism and not revisionism, we must prepare for war on both sides." In October 1964, Mao was clearly worried: "Can Khrushchev invade us or not," "can [he] send troops to occupy Xinjiang, Manchuria, and even Inner Mongolia"?[39] To prepare for war, Mao called for the construction of a "third line" of defense – a massive effort to relocate crucial Chinese industries in the interior, faraway from all borders, including the border with the USSR. Indeed, by 1965, Mao was probably as much concerned with the Soviet threat in the north as with the American threat in the south. If so, it should not be surprising that he opted out of joint actions with the Soviet Union in Vietnam; if he did not, he might have been going to bed with an enemy.

38 James G. Hershberg and Chen Jian, "Informing the Enemy: Sino-American 'Signaling' and the Vietnam War, 1965," in Priscilla Roberts (ed.), *Behind the Bamboo Curtain: China, Vietnam, and the World beyond Asia* (Washington, DC, and Stanford, CA: Woodrow Wilson Center Press and Stanford University Press, 2006).
39 Li Danhui, "1964 nian: ZhongSu guanxi yu Mao Zedong waihuan neiyou silu de zhuanbian," 557–74.

The Cultural Revolution and Sino-Soviet military clashes

After his confrontation with Liu Shaoqi over the direction of the Socialist Education Movement, Mao began to prepare the ground for a showdown with his perceived enemies in China. These enemies were to be found in all positions of authority – among senior party officials, and among Mao's long-time revolutionary comrades. Mao chose a circuitous way of achieving his objectives. He encouraged a radical attack on the party bureaucracy under the pretext of a struggle with revisionism in the ruling circles. The campaign had been in planning since at least February 1965, though the opening shots were fired in November when Shanghai-based radicals, incited by Mao's wife, Jiang Qing (who was acting on Mao's instructions), criticized Wu Han, a prominent historian and deputy mayor of Beijing, for revisionism. In the struggle that followed, the mayor of Beijing, Peng Zhen, tried to protect Wu Han but lost the battle to Mao whose real target was the party leadership. Peng Zhen was the first to find that nobody was safe when Mao orchestrated a full-scale purge of the Beijing Party Committee (including Peng) in May 1966. But as the movement, now called the Great Proletarian Cultural Revolution, gained momentum, Liu Shaoqi and Deng Xiaoping also felt the heat. Liu was branded "China's Khrushchev" and deposed; he was to die from medical neglect in a prison in Kaifeng in 1969. Deng lost his position, but not his life. Countless officials were publicly humiliated, tortured, imprisoned, and sometimes killed. The party center disintegrated by late 1966. The radical "Cultural Revolution Group" assumed unprecedented powers with Mao's blessing, and the country descended into chaos as millions of youths took to the streets to worship Chairman Mao and carry through their struggle against revisionism. Was the Cultural Revolution a struggle of ideas or a struggle for power? It was probably both: a complex interplay of Mao's concern for the fate of the Chinese revolution and for his own political power. The Cultural Revolution was born of the same ingredients that fueled Mao's previous anti-revisionist exploits in 1962 and 1964. Now the stakes were higher, and heads rolled on a far grander scale.

From the beginning, there was a clear anti-Soviet angle to the Cultural Revolution, since Mao made an explicit connection between Soviet "capitalist restoration" and Chinese revisionism. Radicals singled out Soviet-style revisionists in China as Moscow's allies who tried to help the USSR "climb on China's back" so as to again make China a "colony or semi-colony."[40] But Moscow

---

40 *Renmin Ribao*, July 1, 1966, 3.

did not play any practical role in the power struggle; Soviet leaders, in fact, did not know what to make of events in China nor with whom to sympathize. By late 1965, the Chinese problem had lost its urgency for Moscow: rapprochement was nowhere in sight, but a turn for the worse was also not expected. The Soviet leaders eyed China with a new sense of confidence, in part because of their advances elsewhere in Asia. Soviet relations with Hanoi had improved substantially compared with those of the Khrushchev era (thanks, no doubt, to the persuasive power of Soviet aid). North Korea was not to be left behind: Kim Il Sung's visit to Vladivostok for talks with Brezhnev in the spring of 1966 laid the groundwork for better relations between Moscow and Pyongyang. In January 1966, the Soviet Union and Mongolia signed a treaty, permitting the stationing of Soviet military forces in that country. The same month Kosygin mediated the Indo-Pakistani conflict in a bid to gain influence with both countries. These foreign-policy achievements compensated for the Soviet failure to mend fences with China.

The Cultural Revolution dealt a major blow to Soviet complacency. The most visible aspect of the chaos – massive rallies of the Red Guards – projected an image of aggressive xenophobia. The revolutionary mobs besieged the Soviet embassy for days at a time. Plans were in the making to burn it down, but in August 1967, Zhou Enlai personally persuaded the leader of the Red Guards besieging the embassy, a pig-tailed girl of sixteen, to call off the attack.[41] To the Soviets, it was not clear whether they faced unsanctioned mob violence or state policy. Moreover, reports were trickling in to Moscow about the buildup of Chinese forces along the Sino-Soviet frontier, the construction of roads leading to the border, and militant propaganda among the troops.

Faced with these threatening developments, the Soviet Politburo decided to upgrade defense capabilities in the East. A resolution was passed on February 4, 1967, to station troops in Mongolia, strengthen the Soviet forces in the Far East, Zabaikal'e, and Eastern Kazakhstan, and build protected command centers.[42] The timing of these decisions is telling: they came in the immediate aftermath of Red Guard violence around the Soviet Embassy. Xenophobic demonstrations agitated Soviet leaders, though otherwise Moscow exercised patience. For example, the request to station troops in Mongolia had first been made in 1965 by the Mongolian government, which was even more

41 Ma Jisen, *The Cultural Revolution in the Foreign Ministry of China* (Hong Kong: Chinese University Press, 2005), 189.
42 On the stationing of the Soviet forces on the territory of the MPR, February 4, 1967, RGANI: fond 2, opis 3, delo 67, list 149.

apprehensive of Chinese intentions than the Soviets.[43] This request had been shelved for more than a year until the chaos of the Cultural Revolution made Soviet policymakers rethink their strategy toward China in the direction of more active military containment. Brezhnev summarized this strategy in one sentence: "we assume that the stronger the defense of our borders, the less danger there is of a really serious military confrontation on our eastern frontiers."[44]

This assumption worked against Moscow. The more forces the Soviet Union stationed along the frontier with China, the more Chinese leaders became convinced of aggressive Soviet intentions. The Soviet invasion of Czechoslovakia in August 1968 deepened Beijing's concerns. In response to the perceived Soviet threat, the Chinese military adopted the strategy of "active defense" that entailed a show of force to dissuade the opponent from hostile action. Active defense also helped Mao mobilize the Chinese population for his domestic agenda – revamping the power structure in the aftermath of the chaos of the Cultural Revolution. In the winter of 1968–69, the Central Military Commission approved a plan to create a border incident; in this context, on March 2, 1969, Chinese troops ambushed a Soviet border patrol near Zhenbao Island. The Soviets retaliated with force some days later; scores were killed on both sides. On August 13, 1969, another armed incident occurred on the Sino-Soviet border in Xinjiang, and a few days later Moscow made veiled threats of a preemptive nuclear strike against China.

In a tense atmosphere, Kosygin and Zhou Enlai met in Beijing airport on September 11 and assured each other that neither side wanted to go to war. They also agreed to reopen border talks in Beijing. But Mao was not convinced by the Soviet assurances and suspected that Moscow might launch a first strike on China, perhaps under the cover of the forthcoming border talks. In September–October, amid war fever, the People's Liberation Army prepared for a Soviet invasion.[45] The attack did not come, and it is unlikely that plans for it were ever seriously entertained by the Soviet leadership. But the experience of 1969 left Mao intensely insecure. In an effort to counterbalance the Soviet threat, Mao turned to China's former enemy, the United

---

43 Resolution of the Mongolian People's Revolutionary Party Politburo, December 1, 1965, Mongol Ardyn Khuvsgalt Namyn Arkhiv [Archive of the Mongolian People's Revolutionary Party]. Ulaanbaatar, Mongolia: fond 4, dans 28, kh/n 173b, khuu. 35–37.

44 Leonid Brezhnev's speech to a Party Plenum, June 26, 1969, RGANI, fond 2, opis 3, delo 159, list 37.

45 John Wilson Lewis and Xue Litai, *Imagined Enemies: China Prepares for Uncertain War* (Stanford, CA: Stanford University Press, 2006), 59–65.

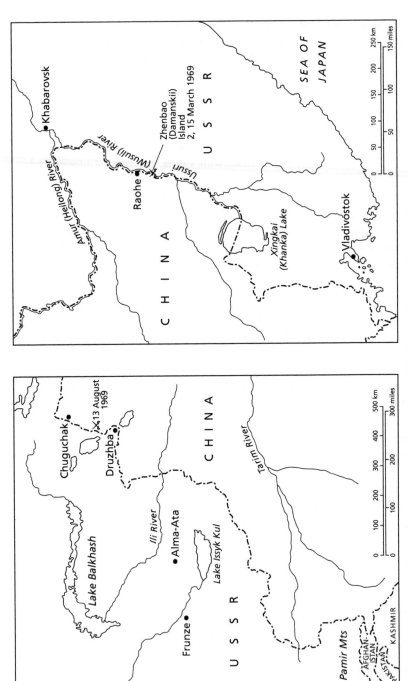

5. Sino-Soviet border clashes on the eastern and western sectors of the frontier, March and August 1969

States. The two countries mended fences in the early 1970s.[46] In the meantime, border talks failed to bring about any substantial improvement in Sino-Soviet relations, which by 1970 had attained a degree of icy stability.

The Sino-Soviet split and new international scenarios

By the end of the 1960s, the Sino-Soviet split transformed international politics. Fear of facing conflict on both the Western and Eastern fronts prompted Soviet leaders to choose the lesser of two evils, and by the turn of the decade the United States was seen as a more limited threat. Many factors shaped Soviet thinking. Moscow interpreted American setbacks in Vietnam and the US economic recession as sure signs of Washington's decline. Meanwhile, China's military buildup and displays of nuclear power served as constant reminders to Moscow of the Soviet Union's vulnerabilities in Siberia and the Far East. Despite their differences, Moscow and Washington could reach agreement on many issues of importance; for example, substantial progress was achieved in strategic arms-limitation talks. Negotiations with China proved more difficult; China was unpredictable and unstable. The lack of progress in the Sino-Soviet border talks suggested to Soviet leaders that China was not genuinely interested in a compromise. A Soviet reassessment of external threats underpinned Brezhnev's efforts – first subtle, and then increasingly blatant – to recruit the United States as an ally, or at least a fellow traveller, in the struggle against China. Similar developments occurred on the Chinese side. After the 1969 war scare, internal assessments in Beijing concluded that the USSR was China's greatest external threat. Mao moved swiftly toward a rapprochement with Washington, seeking improved relations with the United States as a measure of security against perceived Soviet expansionism.

These policy changes involved more than a simple change of threat perception. Since the early years of the Cold War, the United States had not only been the USSR's primary strategic opponent but its ideological adversary. The Cold War had been a struggle of ideas, not merely a confrontation of great powers. Previously, the Soviet Union had allied itself with ideological adversaries to counter a more immediate danger – during World War II, for example, the Kremlin embraced its capitalist foes to withstand the assault from Nazi Germany. In times of crisis Soviet policymakers were capable of

---

46 Yang Kuisong, "The Sino-Soviet Border Clash of 1969: From Zhenbao Island to Sino-American Rapprochement," *Cold War History*, 1, 1 (August 2000), 21–52.

26. Soviet border guards at the Chinese border on the Ussuri river, May 1969. Skirmishes with China encouraged Soviet leaders to opt for détente with the United States.

shelving ideological prescriptions and acting on the basis of strictly realist calculations. The Sino-Soviet conflict created that kind of crisis. Ironically, Moscow played power politics against a former comrade in arms still bound to the Soviet Union by a treaty of alliance. The Chinese now also placed considerations of national interest above the revolutionary dimensions of their foreign policy. Devaluation of a common ideology as a meaningful point of reference in Beijing and Moscow marked a turning point for the Cold War and, as Chen Jian argues, possibly the beginning of its end.[47]

47 See Chen Jian's chapter in volume III.

The forces that brought about this remarkable transformation had deep roots. The Sino-Soviet alliance contained the seeds of its own destruction. Shared Marxist ideology – the strength of the alliance – proved insufficient to hold it together. The principles of equality and fraternity that the alliance stood for were in practice difficult to achieve. Pretense of equality did not compensate for staggering inequalities: China was of course the underdog in the alliance. But whereas the Soviet leadership considered this state of affairs entirely natural, the Chinese resented bitterly such a state of perpetual subordination. Moreover, in place of fraternity, Chinese leaders too often encountered Soviet arrogance and great power pressure. It did not take a leap of imagination to connect Soviet blunders with Russia's historical record of expansion and imperialism in Asia. Meanwhile, Soviet leaders blamed the Chinese for monstrous ingratitude.

The importance of these fundamentals was not immediately apparent when Sino-Soviet relations turned sharply for the worse in the early 1960s. The larger problems were buried beneath a barrage of ideologically charged polemics. In retrospect, Deng Xiaoping, who had passionately defended Mao's revolutionary ideals in the polemical clashes with Moscow, characterized the rhetoric of the 1960s as "konghua" (empty words). As he told Mikhail Gorbachev on May 16, 1989, when the Soviet leader visited him in Beijing to mend fences: "From the mid-1960s, our relations deteriorated; they were practically broken off. It was not because of the ideological disputes; we do not think now that everything we said at that time was right. The basic problem was that the Chinese were not treated as equals and felt humiliated."[48] Deng thus pointed to what was the most important reason for the collapse of the Sino-Soviet alliance – its inequality.

The problems created by the inequality in the relationship were exacerbated by the cultural sensibilities of policymakers in both Beijing and Moscow. Soviet leaders occasionally made blatantly racist remarks about China. Khrushchev and Brezhnev cited the writings of early Russian explorers of China to illustrate how the Chinese had always been "sly" and "perfidious."[49] The impact of these stereotypes on policymakers in Moscow cannot be

---

48 Deng Xiaoping's Remarks to Mikhail Gorbachev, May 16, 1989, Leng Rong *et al.* (eds.), *Deng Xiaoping nianpu, 1975–1997* [Deng Xiaoping Chronology], vol. II (xia) (Beijing: Zhongyang wenxian, 2004), 1275.
49 For instance, conversation between Richard Nixon and Leonid Brezhnev, June 23, 1973, Brezhnev visit, June 18–25, 1973, Memoranda of conversations, Nixon Presidential Materials Project, National Security Council Files, Henry A. Kissinger Office Files, Country Files: Europe–USSR, box 75, National Archives, College Park, Maryland. (Materials will be moving to Nixon Presidential Library, Yorba Linda, California.)

quantified with precision, but their recurrence in Politburo discussions and memoranda of conversations between the Soviet leaders and foreign dignitaries suggests that subtle racism was a factor in policy formulation. Chinese stereotypes of Russia as aggressive and arrogant, though probably confirmed by Soviet actions in some instances, on other occasions precluded clear understanding of Soviet motives and policies.

Finally, the Sino-Soviet split was intrinsically related to the domestic context of policymaking in Beijing and Moscow. China was a factor in the Soviet power struggle, just as the Soviet Union was a factor in the Chinese power struggle. Mao's campaign against Soviet leaders and against Liu Shaoqi were closely connected. Soviet policymakers did not have the same dilemmas, but they, too, played the China card in internal political maneuvers; after Khrushchev's fall, a rapprochement with China briefly promised untold political dividends to anyone who could bring it about. The Sino-Soviet split also made it necessary for the Soviets to distinguish with greater precision genuine (or Soviet) socialism from a Chinese "perversion." Mao, for his part, employed his struggle against "Soviet revisionism" to effect a revolutionary transformation at home. In turn, upheavals in China made Sino-Soviet reconciliation very unlikely so long as Mao remained in control.

But this is not the same as to say that domestic politics drove foreign-policy decisions. Mao's revolution was only a means to an end, not an end in itself. The end was to bring to a close the Chinese "century of humiliation," to make China a great power in its own right. The Sino-Soviet alliance initially helped, but eventually hindered progress toward this goal. Over time, both Chinese and Soviet leaders came to realize that a true great power cannot have allies of equal rank.

18

Détente in the Nixon–Ford years, 1969–1976

ROBERT D. SCHULZINGER

President Richard M. Nixon declared in his inaugural address on January 20, 1969, that "after a period of confrontation, we are entering an era of negotiations" with the Soviet Union.[1] Privately, he told the Soviet foreign minister, Andrei Gromyko, that in the United States "whenever elections approached, political leaders were tempted to take a belligerent anti-Communist line," but that Nixon himself "did not consider such an approach to be in the interests of world peace or of Soviet–American relations."[2]

These conciliatory words toward America's Cold War rival seemed surprising at the time, since Nixon had played important parts in Congress from 1947 to 1952 and as vice president from 1953 to 1961 in shaping confrontational American policies toward the Soviet Union and Communism. As president, Nixon put aside his earlier criticism of the Communist system, choosing to focus instead on expanding areas of common interest between the Cold War rivals in order to promote what he characterized as a "structure of peace." He developed personal relationships with Soviet leaders, and the United States and the Soviet Union reached a series of agreements on arms control, commercial relations, and political cooperation that fostered a fragile détente between them.

Nixon and Henry Kissinger, a former Harvard University professor of government who became his national security adviser, later secretary of state, and his principal foreign-policy lieutenant, believed that the international situation had changed dramatically in the previous decade. The United States and the Soviet Union were no longer the only powers that

---

1 Richard Nixon, "Inaugural Address," January 20, 1969, *Public Papers of the President of the United States, Richard Nixon, 1969* (Washington, DC: US Government Printing Office, 1970), 3.

2 Memorandum of conversation, Nixon, Gromyko, *et al.*, October 22, 1970. US Department of State, *Foreign Relations of the United States, 1969–1976 (FRUS)* (Washington, DC: US Government Printing Office, 2003), vol. I, 270 (hereafter, *FRUS*, with year and volume number).

mattered, as Europe and Japan recovered their strength, and the People's Republic of China (PRC) emerged as a growing challenge in the world Communist movement.

Nixon and Kissinger started détente as a recognition of the relative, not absolute, decline of US power and the growth of multipolarity. They responded to European desires for improved economic relations and reduced political tensions with the Soviet Union and the Eastern bloc. They valued state sovereignty, and they believed that international stability required that great powers like the United States and the Soviet Union avoid interfering in the internal affairs of each other. This advocacy of the rights and responsibilities of great powers collided with a growing popular movement for human rights.

Détente succeeded at first, because it reduced popular anxieties about the dangers of war between the United States and the Soviet Union. Yet even as it enjoyed widespread popularity in the years 1971–73, its foundations were weakened by Nixon's and Kissinger's personalities. The two men manipulated others and worked in secrecy. Détente encountered opposition from both those who wanted a more forthright stand against abuses of human rights and those who continued to fear Soviet military power. When Gerald R. Ford became president in 1974, détente was already losing popularity domestically. In the aftermath of the Communist victory in Vietnam, détente suffered even more. In fact, Nixon's, Kissinger's, and Ford's realistic assessment of growing multipolarity did not rest on a belief in US decline. The Helsinki Final Act, so reviled when it was signed in 1975, actually helped set in motion forces that led to the demise of Soviet-style Communism.

Intellectual foundations of détente

In 1967, Nixon observed the "winds of détente have blown so strongly from the East to the West that ... most Europeans no longer fear" a Soviet threat. As a result, the North Atlantic Treaty Organization (NATO), a long-time cornerstone of American Cold War policy, had weakened.[3] Kissinger also believed that the United States no longer had the dominant world position it had enjoyed in the early days of the Cold War. The growing nuclear arsenals of the United States and the Soviet Union had altered traditional ideas about the relationship between the use of or the threat of military force to achieve political ends. In the past, the greater a nation's military power, the greater its ability to influence others. Now, with both the United States and the Soviet

3 "Address by Richard Nixon to the Bohemian Club," July 29, 1967, *FRUS, 1969–1976*, vol. I, 2.

Union capable of destroying each other, the threat to use nuclear weapons to achieve ordinary political aims had become less credible.

For Nixon and Kissinger, the Soviet invasion and occupation of Czechoslovakia in August 1968 presented a dilemma. On the one hand, the suppression of "socialism with a human face" indicated that the Soviet Union still posed a threat to Europe and that the Cold War competition between East and West continued. On the other hand, both sides possessed enough nuclear weapons to destroy each other, making nuclear war a grave danger. The two nuclear superpowers were mortal rivals, to be sure, but they also had common interests in managing their relationship to prevent war.

The promotion of "peace" became a central theme of the Nixon administration. Nixon campaigned for president on a platform of achieving "peace with honor" in Vietnam. He recognized a popular yearning for an end to the war in Vietnam and to avoid nuclear war with the Soviet Union. While president, he regularly asserted that he sought to create a "structure of peace," which would apply to the whole world and which would reduce the terror of the Cold War. Peace with the Soviet Union principally meant the reduction of the danger of nuclear war.

Nixon was also responding to changes in European attitudes toward the Soviet Union. When he spoke of the winds of détente blowing across Europe, he referred to recent efforts by traditional NATO partners – France, West Germany, Italy, and Britain – to improve relations with the Soviet Union. These overtures combined political, military, and economic openings. The West German government led by the Social Democratic chancellor, Willy Brandt, launched its policy of *Ostpolitik* (policy toward the East) in 1970. The West German government stopped insisting that the East German government was illegitimate and should be isolated. It recognized the frontiers between East Germany and Poland. Kissinger alerted Nixon to the "worrisome ... long range" dangers of an *Ostpolitik* that might detach West Germany from its NATO allies.[4] Across Europe, governments and citizens responded to French president Charles de Gaulle's call for an end to threats or the use of force to resolve political differences in Europe. West German, Italian, French, and British firms invested in and exported goods to Communist countries in Eastern Europe and the Soviet Union. American businesses feared being left behind by competitors in the increasingly prosperous Western European countries, and they demanded that the United States government do more to improve the climate between East and West.

4 Henry Kissinger, *White House Years* (Boston, MA: Little, Brown, 1979), 530.

In this new atmosphere, Nixon and Kissinger resolved to treat the Soviet Union as an ordinary state with reasonable national goals and interests. This meant that the United States would no longer highlight its objections to Communism as a social or political system inside the Soviet Union. It would avoid condemnations of the Soviet government's abuse of its citizens' human rights. It would expect the Soviet Union to show similar restraint in avoiding bombastic criticism of the American political and social system. All the while, the United States would continue to try to contain Communism and oppose the spread of Soviet global influence.

The Nixon–Kissinger relationship

Nixon and Kissinger developed a close personal relationship that profoundly affected the way in which they conducted their foreign policy. On many days they met together alone or with only a handful of aides present for hours, and they spoke at length to one another on the phone. They criticized officials, members of Congress, journalists, and the public. Each man came to office deeply suspicious of elected officeholders, foreign affairs officials, or members of the public who commented on foreign affairs. Nixon was uncomfortable with most people, hating direct disagreement or confrontation with subordinates. He believed that most permanent officials in the government opposed him and his policies. He told his cabinet in 1971, "we've checked and found that 96 percent of the bureaucracy are against us; they're bastards who are here to screw us."[5]

Kissinger was a surprising member of Nixon's inner circle because he had supported Nelson Rockefeller, Nixon's rival for the presidency. In addition, he had taught at Harvard and written extensively for the Council on Foreign Relations, two of the principal institutions of the Eastern establishment that Nixon distrusted. Unlike Nixon, Kissinger could be highly personable, and during his tenure as national security adviser and secretary of state, he often had excellent relations with news reporters. He had, however, other reasons to want to work behind the scenes. He quickly realized that the more he and Nixon spoke to one another, the more indispensable he seemed to become, especially when Kissinger joined the president in complaining about the inadequacies of others.

Kissinger's academic writings belonged to the Realist school of foreign-policy analysis. His research added to his sense that most Americans could not

5 "President's Talk to Cabinet, " June 29, 1971. H. R. Haldeman, *The Haldeman Diaries: Inside the Nixon White House* (New York: Putnam, 1994), 309.

be trusted to understand foreign affairs or to support what he believed to be a foreign policy that promoted American interests. Among the major tenets of Realism are the ideas that power matters most in international relations; ideology has little importance. Regrettably, from Kissinger's point of view, Americans paid too little attention to power relations in international affairs, and they stressed too often unworkable moral maxims or legalistic formulations. In 1968, he disparaged the idealism of American youth who "considered the management of power irrelevant, perhaps even immoral." A generation gap had opened between students opposed to American participation in the war in Vietnam and their elders whose remembered lesson of World War II was the danger of unchecked aggression. "Partly as a result of the generation gap," Kissinger wrote, "the American mood oscillates dangerously between being ashamed of power and expecting too much of it."[6]

During the 1960s, public discussion of Soviet–American relations often focused on efforts to cap the nuclear-arms race. Kissinger, however, expressed skepticism that arms-control agreements by themselves would reduce tension between the two nuclear superpowers. Concentration on arms control, he believed, got the story backward. Improved political relations, he argued, would lead to arms control. But since there was such widespread public support for arms control, Kissinger pursued it.

Nixon and Kissinger sought to embed US–Soviet agreements on arms control in a larger web of mutual interest. At his first press conference on February 6, 1969, Nixon explained that the United States wanted to go forward with the Soviets on political agreements and arms control. This policy became known as "linkage," in which the US government would connect progress in different areas. Kissinger explained that Nixon meant linkage to convey the idea that "there be enough movement in the political field to indicate that arms control negotiations do not unwittingly, instead of reducing the danger of war, offer a means by which conflict can be intensified."[7]

At its most ambitious, the Nixon administration expected that progress toward better bilateral relations with the Soviet Union would encourage the leaders of the Kremlin to apply pressure on the government of the Democratic Republic of (North) Vietnam to agree to end the Vietnam War on terms the Americans would accept. These hopes proved to be illusory. The Soviet Union did not push North Vietnam very hard, and the North Vietnamese could resist Soviet pressure since they also enjoyed the backing of the PRC, Moscow's rival for leadership in the Communist world. Nixon and Kissinger

---

6 "Essay by Henry Kissinger," *FRUS, 1969–1976*, vol. I, 47.   7 Editorial note, *ibid.*, 58–59.

hoped to exploit this intra-Communist rivalry through "triangular diplomacy" among Washington, Moscow, and Beijing.

Triangular diplomacy failed in its original goal of gaining Soviet and Chinese pressure on Hanoi to settle the war in Vietnam on terms agreeable to the United States. Triangular diplomacy did, however, expand US–Soviet détente. American steps toward détente with the Soviet Union proceeded side by side with secret efforts to open relations with China. This behind-the-scenes diplomacy culminated in Kissinger's trip to Beijing in July 1971, which paved the way for a celebrated visit by Nixon to China in February 1972. Soviet officials observed the burgeoning US–PRC rapprochement with alarm. They often warned Nixon and Kissinger against making friends with the Chinese at the Soviets' expense. Nixon and Kissinger offered only tepid reassurances to the Soviet leadership that closer ties between Washington and Beijing would not harm Soviet interests. As the United States and China ended their decades'-long estrangement in 1971 and 1972, Soviet leaders became more inclined than they had been before to reach agreements with the United States.

Nixon and Kissinger built upon their views of politics and international affairs to develop détente. They responded to public anxieties about the costs and the dangers of the continuing confrontation between the United States and the Soviet Union. Their methods became as important as their goals. They built their structure of peace in a way that shut out professional diplomats and cabinet secretaries ostensibly in charge of foreign affairs. Their tight control of foreign policy led to dramatic and unexpected breakthroughs. But their antagonism toward professional advisers also left them without vital support when opponents criticized détente.

Arms control and US–Soviet summit meetings, 1969–1972

In early 1969, at the beginning of the Nixon administration, National Security Adviser Kissinger informed the Soviet ambassador, Anatolii Dobrynin, that the president wanted to conduct business with the Soviet Union personally and directly through a "back channel" line of communication. Kissinger explained that he had the authority to speak for the US government regardless of what other officials said. The back channel became the principal means through which the United States and the Soviet Union communicated over the next five and one-half years. The back channel's advantages were that it gave Kissinger and Nixon control over the setting of foreign policy, and its secrecy enabled them to make dramatic announcements which captured public attention. The disadvantage of conducting foreign affairs through the back channel was that it was far too personal. By ignoring and undermining the professionals within the State Department, Nixon and Kissinger lost out on important technical advice. Their penchant for secrecy and their distrust of professional advice also made it harder than necessary for them to build support for their policies. When domestic opposition to elements of détente intensified, Nixon became vulnerable to complaints that the agreements he had signed were deeply flawed.

In the mid- and late 1960s, the race between the United States and the Soviet Union to deploy more intercontinental ballistic missiles (ICBMs) and submarine-launched ballistic missiles (SLBMs) and to develop anti-ballistic missiles (ABMs) provoked worldwide public anxiety. As soon as he became president, Nixon tried to dampen these fears when he announced within days of taking office that US policy was to have "sufficiency" not "superiority" in nuclear weapons. He downsized the Johnson administration's plan for a large ABM system directed against the Soviet Union, called Sentinel, to a smaller Safeguard system intended to be deployed against a possible threat from China.

In 1970 and 1971, Kissinger negotiated with Ambassador Dobyrnin and Foreign Minister Gromyko through the back channel. In a series of discussions with Dobrynin, Kissinger argued that the Soviet Union and the United States should try to reach an agreement, first, on limiting the potential deployment of ABMs and call a freeze on further deployment of ICBMs. In May 1971, Kissinger and Dobrynin reached what Kissinger called a "conceptual break-through" by separating ABM and Strategic Arms Limitation Treaty (SALT) negotiations. They promised to reach an agreement on an ABM treaty within the next year and make "progress" on SALT.[8]

Nixon announced in May 1971 that he would attend a Moscow summit meeting in May 1972. He and the Soviet Communist Party general secretary, Leonid Brezhnev, would sign arms-control agreements worked out between the two sides over the previous year. During the fall and winter of 1971 and 1972, Kissinger used the back channel without the knowledge of the official US arms-negotiating team meeting with their Soviet counterparts in Helsinki. Kissinger told Dobrynin, "the main problem is to get concrete about something."[9] He believed that the fact of an agreement would do more than

8 Raymond L. Garthoff, *Détente and Confrontation: American–Soviet Relations from Nixon to Reagan*, rev. ed. (Washington: Brookings Institution, 1992), 146–47.
9 Kissinger, *White House Years*, 525.

anything to persuade the public that the United States had not been paralyzed by Vietnam; the actual details of an agreement were less important.

As Nixon and Kissinger prepared for the late-May summit in Moscow, they agreed to steer clear of discussions of human rights. Kissinger told Nixon, "I don't think it is proper for you to start lecturing them about freedom of speech." Nixon concurred: "oh no, no, no, no, no, no, no."[10] Nixon's insistence that he personally negotiate the final terms of agreements to provide dramatic impact lent a frenzied and improvised tone to the Moscow summit meetings from May 23 to 29, 1972. Kissinger, Nixon, Gromyko, and Brezhnev hammered out the final details of several treaties, agreements, and statements in late-night bargaining sessions in the Kremlin and Brezhnev's country house. Nixon told Kissinger that Congress "will watch every line of the agreement to see if we were placed at a disadvantage," but like the national security adviser, he believed the fact of having reached an agreement was more important than the details of it.[11]

Nixon and Brezhnev signed the Interim Agreement on the Limitation of Strategic Arms (SALT I) at an elaborate late-night ceremony on May 26. This agreement was a framework document in which each side froze the number of missiles it had as of the date of its signing. The United States would be allowed 1,054 ICBMs and 656 SLBMs, and the Soviets would be permitted 1,618 ICBMs and 950 SLBMs. Despite what appeared to be a Soviet advantage in SALT, the United States had no plans to increase the number of missiles in its current arsenal. While the Soviets were permitted to increase the number of their ICBMs to about 50 percent more than Americans had in 1972, the United States had an advantage in multiple independently targetable re-entry vehicles (MIRVs). This emerging MIRV technology allowed missiles to carry multiple warheads that would be easier to evade an enemy's defenses. SALT I had a term of five years, during which time the two sides agreed to work to develop a full-fledged treaty limiting, and possibly reducing, offensive nuclear arms.

Nixon and Brezhnev also signed an Anti-Ballistic Missile Treaty. They agreed that each party would construct no more than two ABM sites. One of them would protect the capital and the other would protect a missile base. These provisions allowed for each side to maintain a credible deterrent against a first strike that would permit national governments to continue to function in the event of war.

10 Transcript of telephone conversation between President Nixon and Kissinger, May 17, 1972, *FRUS, 1969–1976*, vol. XIV, 922.
11 Memorandum of conversation, May 23, 1972, Kissinger Transcripts (KT) 100494, Digital National Security Archive (hereafter, DNSA), For additional discussion of the arms race and arms control, see William Burr and David Alan Rosenberg's chapter in this volume.

27. US president Richard Nixon (left) and Soviet leader Leonid Brezhnev at Nixon's home in San Clemente, California, in June 1973. Nixon saw détente as a key breakthrough in relations with the Soviet Union.

The United States and the Soviet Union reached several other understand-ings that expanded détente. They signed agreements on reducing pollution and enhancing environmental quality, on cooperation in medicine, science, and technology, and on space exploration. They set up a joint commercial commission that would negotiate a comprehensive trade agreement. They agreed to convene a Conference on Security and Cooperation in Europe (CSCE), a meeting the Soviets had long advocated as a way of finally acknowl-edging the international borders established in Europe after World War II. CSCE gained little attention when it was announced, but as it developed it became a major element in eroding public support for US–Soviet détente.

The two leaders issued a twelve-point statement of Basic Principles of Relations between the United States and the Soviet Union, a document which broadly defined the ways in which they would treat each other in an era of détente. The Basic Principles committed each power to conduct "normal relations" on the basis of "peaceful coexistence" and the principles of "sover-eignty, equality, non-interference in internal affairs, and mutual advantage."[12]

12 Basic Principles of Relations between the United States of America and the Union of Soviet Socialist Republics, May 29, 1972, *FRUS, 1969–1976*, vol. I, 389.

Kissinger and Nixon thought the Basic Principles had at most a symbolic value. In a press briefing immediately after Nixon and Brezhnev signed the Basic Principles, Kissinger said the document represented "an aspiration and an attitude, and if either the aspiration or the attitude changes, then ... either side can change its course."[13] Unfortunately for the future of détente, Kissinger's attitude toward the Basic Principles proved to be far too nonchalant. Domestic opponents of détente soon used the principle of equality to undermine support for several of the agreements Nixon had signed.

Public reaction to détente, 1972–1973

The meetings in Moscow solidified Nixon's public position as a masterful statesman who had grown far beyond his early anti-Communism to usher in a new era of stability and peace and to dampen the tensions of the Cold War. Kissinger told senators that the SALT agreement was "not merely a technical accomplishment ... but it must be seen as a political event of some magnitude." He encouraged lawmakers to drop what he considered to be sterile old habits of measuring who was ahead and who was behind in the arms race. "Catastrophe has resulted," he warned "far less often from conscious decisions than from the fear of breaking loose from established patterns." He feared that the "paralysis of policy which destroyed Europe in 1914 would surely destroy the world if we let it happen in the nuclear age."[14]

Despite Kissinger's warnings that the world stood on the brink of annihilation if Congress did not support the Nixon administration's approach to arms control, détente faced serious challenges from domestic critics in the months and years following the summit. Opponents considered sufficiency in nuclear weapons to be a dangerous delusion. Representative John M. Ashbrook (R–Ohio), a conservative who was running against Nixon for the Republican presidential nomination, complained that SALT would "lock the Soviet Union into unchallengeable superiority, and plunge the United States and its allies into a decade of danger."[15]

---

13 *Ibid.*
14 "Congressional Briefing by Dr. Henry A. Kissinger," June 15, 1972, Frank Church Papers, box 166, folder 14, Boise State University Library, Boise, Idaho.
15 Quoted in Jussi M. Hanhimäki, *The Flawed Architect: Henry Kissinger and American Foreign Policy* (New York: Oxford University Press, 2004), 220.

Senator Henry M. Jackson (D–Washington) led the opposition to arms-control agreements and détente in general for the remainder of Nixon's presidency. He insisted that the United States had accepted an unfavorable deal with SALT, one in which the United States had made commitments to limit its missiles but the Soviets had not made reciprocal ironclad guarantees. He told Secretary of Defense Melvin Laird that "the total number of ICBM missiles [listed in SALT] represents a unilateral position on our part and does not represent a bilateral agreement with the Russians ... This kind of ambiguity can breed suspicion and lead to an unstable situation rather than to a more stable one."[16]

Jackson used the equality provisions of the Basic Principles of US–Soviet relations to develop an amendment to the congressional joint resolution endorsing SALT. The amendment stipulated that the United States would sign a future treaty only if it guaranteed that the missile forces of each side be equal. It required that US SALT negotiators maintain "the principle of United States–Soviet equality reflected in the anti-ballistic missile treaty." The amendment stated that the United States would consider any new deployment by the Soviet Union of weapons that could destroy American missiles to be contrary to American interests. In September, the Senate passed the amendment by a vote of fifty-six to thirty-five.[17]

Economic relations, emigration, and the Middle East, 1971–1974

While Jackson's amendment to the congressional resolution in support of SALT indicated that not everyone favored Nixon's approach to the Soviet Union, détente was popular in the United States in 1972. Improved relations between the two superpowers promised a more peaceful and more prosperous world. From 1971 to 1974, the two countries completed more than ten pacts dealing with World War II debts, shipping, taxes, and grain purchases. The most significant of these was the October 1972 bilateral trade agreement under which they opened commercial and trade offices in the other nation's capital and the Soviet Union promised to pay its $772 million World War II Lend Lease debt over the next thirty years. The United States promised to extend most-favored-nation (MFN) status to the Soviet Union. (MFN status, a

16 US Senate, Committee on Armed Services, *Hearings on Military Implications of the Treaty on the Limitation of Anti-Ballistic Missiles and the Interim Agreement on the Limitation of Strategic Offensive Arms*, June 20–July 8, 1972, 92nd Congress, 2nd session.
17 Public Law 92–448 as amended by Senator Jackson.

position enjoyed by most US trading partners, meant that the United States would grant a most-favored nation the lowest tariffs it extended to any other country.) But the Soviet Union would become a most-favored nation only with congressional approval.

Congress grew increasingly unhappy with Nixon's conduct of commercial relations with the Soviet Union in 1972 and 1973. Word spread that the Soviet Union had purchased one quarter of the American wheat supply, in part by using commercial credits supplied by the United States under its trade agreement. Wheat prices shot up in the United States and critics charged that the Soviets had engineered a "Great Grain Robbery" with the Nixon administration's connivance or negligence.

Unhappiness with the grain deal contributed to anti-détente sentiment. This hostility grew when the issue of Soviet mistreatment of its own citizens roused attention. In October 1972, Senator Jackson gained the support of seventy-two of his colleagues to pass an amendment to the Trade Reform Act that would deny the Soviet Union MFN status unless it permitted free emigration of its citizens. The issue of emigration from the Soviet Union had become embroiled in the Arab–Israeli conflict. The Soviet Union and its Eastern European allies gave political and military support to the Arab nations after Israel's victory in the 1967 Six Day War against Egypt, Syria, and Jordan. Coinciding with this Communist support of the Arab side had been a rise in anti-Semitism throughout the Eastern bloc, which had prompted many Jews within the Soviet Union to seek to emigrate to the United States or Israel. Between 1968 and 1972, the number of Jewish emigrants from the Soviet Union had exploded from 400 to 35,000 per year. Then, in August 1972, the Kremlin imposed a steep tax amounting to thousands of dollars on anyone wishing to leave.

In April 1973, Congressman Charles Vanik (D–Ohio) introduced in the Houses of Representatives an amendment to the trade bill similar to the one Jackson had sponsored in the Senate. It passed in December by a wide margin. This Jackson–Vanik amendment went through several revisions until both houses of Congress finally adopted it as part of an omnibus Trade Reform Act in 1974. The Soviet Union reacted angrily. It cut the number of Jewish emigrants from 35,000 in 1973 to 20,000 in 1974. It also canceled the 1972 trade agreement with the United States. The Jackson–Vanik amendment directly challenged the Nixon administration's policy of disregarding the Soviet Union's internal affairs or its restrictions on human rights. The amendment and the large issue of the Middle East played major roles in undermining détente throughout the rest of Nixon's term.

Watergate, the Middle East War, and the end of the Nixon administration, 1973–1974

In May 1973, the Senate began televised hearings on the June 1972 break-in at the Democratic National Committee headquarters at the Watergate office complex. As public interest in Watergate intensified, General Secretary Brezhnev came to the United States for another summit meeting with Nixon from June 16 to June 24, 1973. They met at the White House, Camp David, and at the president's summer house in San Clemente, California. Nixon extended lavish hospitality for his Soviet guest, but the two men's conversations lacked the drama of the Moscow summit of May 1972, and they were overshadowed by the growing Watergate scandal.

At their meetings the leaders discussed nuclear arms, the status of the SALT negotiations, and the Middle East. They made little progress on nuclear arms or SALT. Much to Nixon's and Kissinger's discomfort, Brezhnev raised the issue of the Middle East. The Soviet leader said that his allies in Egypt and Syria found the continued Israeli occupation of the Sinai Peninsula (Egyptian territory) and the Golan Heights (Syrian territory) increasingly galling. He urged the United States to apply pressure on Israel to withdraw. "If we agree on Israeli withdrawals, everything will fall in place," Brezhnev said. He added that he was "categorically opposed to a resumption of the war. But without agreed principles" of what a settlement should look like, Brezhnev said, he could not guarantee that a new war would not erupt.[18]

The two leaders signed an agreement on the Prevention of Nuclear War (PNW). The PNW agreement was of indefinite duration and it committed the two countries to conduct themselves in ways "to prevent the development of situations capable of causing a dangerous exacerbation of their relations." They promised to avoid threats against each other and each other's allies. They also agreed that if it appeared as if relations between them or other countries risked a nuclear conflict, they would "immediately enter into urgent consultations with each other and make every effort to avert this risk."[19]

Like the Basic Principles of US–Soviet relations signed at the Moscow summit of 1972, the PNW agreement set forward the aspirations of both sides to work together in an era of détente. Each document held hidden dangers, not fully appreciated by their authors at the time of the signing. As

---

18 Memorandum of conversation, Nixon, Brezhnev, *et al.*, June 23, 1973, KT00765, DNSA.
19 Garthoff, *Détente and Confrontation*, 334.

Raymond L. Garthoff, one of the American arms-control negotiators, noted in *Détente and Confrontation*, "the Basic Principles in 1972 and the PNW agreement of 1973 contributed to the launching and development of détente, but before long they also contributed to its failure."[20]

The United States and the Soviet Union collaborated, but they also approached a confrontation as they backed opposing belligerents during the war between Israel and Egypt and Syria that began on October 6, 1973. The two nuclear superpowers worked together at the United Nations to call for a ceasefire, but it was slow in coming. The Egyptian and Syrian forces made great gains in the first five days of the war, capturing Israeli soldiers and driving scores of kilometers into Israeli-occupied positions. The Soviet Union sent arms to Egypt and Syria as a way of assuring its Arab allies of its support, and also to gain leverage with them to accept a ceasefire.

Israel's government, shocked by the success of the Arab armies, ran low on war *matériel*, and desperately applied to the United States to resupply its losses in planes, tanks, and ammunition. The United States airlifted military equipment on October 12. Once Israel was assured of American arms, it launched a counterattack.

Brezhnev then proposed to Nixon that the two sides jointly sponsor a ceasefire. Nixon sent Kissinger, who in September had become secretary of state in addition to continuing as national security adviser, to Moscow to work out the details. By the time Kissinger began meetings in the Kremlin on October 20, Israel's armed forces were threatening to advance on the Egyptian and Syrian capital cities. Kissinger's visit coincided with a climactic moment in the Watergate scandal. Nixon refused to turn over tapes of conversations he had had with aides discussing the break-in and the cover-up. He fired Special Prosecutor Archibald Cox. This "Saturday Night massacre" provoked an outraged public to demand Nixon's impeachment.

Kissinger, Gromyko, and Brezhnev developed a UN resolution calling for a ceasefire and negotiations for a peaceful solution to the Arab–Israeli conflict. Israel delayed implementing the ceasefire until its forces had pressed their advantage against the Egyptian army. Egypt's president, Anwar Sadat, asked the Soviet Union and the United States jointly to send troops to enforce the ceasefire. The Soviets stepped up their airlift of supplies, and the United States responded by putting its Mediterranean forces on the highest level of alert. Kissinger eventually persuaded Israel to agree to a ceasefire on October 27.

---

20 *Ibid.*, 338.

Over the next several months, Kissinger traveled between the capitals of Israel and Egypt and Israel and Syria to arrange an Israeli withdrawal from the territory it had captured at the end of the war. He convinced Israel to withdraw from the east bank of the Suez Canal, enabling Egypt to reopen that waterway, and from some Syrian territory on the Golan Heights.

Soviet–American cooperation during the October War demonstrated the ways détente operated. Both sides recognized that their need to avoid a confrontation that could lead to a catastrophic nuclear war took precedence over their commitments to their allies. Insofar as the two nuclear super-powers had followed through on their commitments to consult in the Basic Principles and PNW agreements, détente had worked. On the other hand, each side had threatened the other and had armed its allies. Supporters of Israel were especially distressed by the way in which the United States had cooperated with the Soviet Union to deny Israel the opportunity to rout the Egyptian and Syrian armed forces. As Garthoff observes, "many politically significant supporters of Israeli interests thus became disenchanted with the policy of détente."[21]

Congressional opponents of détente stepped up their campaign against Nixon's and Kissinger's efforts to cooperate with the Soviet Union in the winter and spring of 1973 and 1974. Kissinger told his staff on March 18, 1974, that "the Soviets are getting nothing out of détente and what can I deliver in Moscow?" The Jackson–Vanik amendment to the trade bill had proven to be a far greater irritant to the development of détente than Kissinger had expected. Kissinger lamented that "Jackson has obviously been convinced that I am a hostile country." Kissinger derided Jackson as one of "these bastards on [Capitol] Hill who ignore the fact that 400 Jews were leaving the Soviet Union in 1969 and now say that 30,000 a year is inconsequential." Since the trade relationship with the Soviet Union now "is no good, SALT can't go down the drain," because if that happened détente would end.[22]

Kissinger traveled to Moscow in March 1974 to try to make progress on SALT before Nixon's June visit to the Soviet Union. The Soviets rejected his proposal that they allow equality in warheads by granting the Americans superiority in MIRVs. He also did not get Soviet agreement to a proposal for "offsetting symmetries," in which the Soviet Union would have the advantage in ICBMs and the United States would have more MIRVs.

---

21 *Ibid.*, 406. For further discussion of US and Soviet policies in the Middle East, see Douglas Littles's chapter in this volume.
22 Secretary Kissinger's staff meeting, March 18, 1974, KT01072. DNSA.

When Nixon visited the Soviet Union in late June, the days of his presidency were numbered as the Watergate scandal reached a crescendo. Nixon told Brezhnev not to worry about the Jackson–Vanik amendment. "On MFN," Nixon said, "we will get it." Brezhnev called his statement "a good sign."[23] But SALT II was garnering serious criticism in the United States. Before Nixon left for Moscow, Secretary of Defense James Schlesinger endorsed Senator Jackson's position on equality of weapons systems in SALT, thereby publicly undercutting Nixon's and Kissinger's policy of sufficiency. Paul Nitze, a veteran foreign-policy adviser who deeply distrusted the Soviet Union's military intentions, resigned from the US SALT negotiating team. He said that "the traumatic events now unfolding" in the Watergate scandal might encourage Nixon to agree to a disadvantageous SALT treaty with the Soviets just to obtain favorable publicity.[24]

Nixon and Brezhnev made no progress on the details of offensive weapons systems. They amended the ABM Treaty, reducing the number of sites each side could have from two to one. They also signed agreements on commercial, technological, energy, housing, and medical research cooperation, but these accords generated little of the earlier excitement over improving US–Soviet relations. The public was not impressed with their work. Commentators considered the trip to be part of a clumsy effort by Nixon to revive his fading fortunes as a foreign-policy leader. On August 9, 1974, five weeks after Nixon returned from the Soviet Union, he was forced to resign the presidency rather than be convicted in the Senate on three articles of impeachment likely to be approved by the House of Representatives.

The Ford administration and the decline of détente, 1974–1976

Détente did not die with the end of Nixon's presidency, but it was encountering stiffer opposition. Vice President Gerald Ford succeeded Nixon and vowed to continue the foreign policies lain down by Nixon and Kissinger. Kissinger remained secretary of state and national security adviser.

In the first few months of Ford's presidency, he pressed forward with US–Soviet negotiations on strategic arms. The new president met Brezhnev at the Siberian city of Vladivostok in late November and early December 1974, and the two men promised to sign a SALT II agreement within a year. This treaty

23 Memorandum of conversation, Nixon, Brezhnev, Kissinger, Gromyko, et al., June 28, 1974, KT01232, DNSA.
24 Garthoff, Détente and Confrontation, 411.

would limit each side's nuclear delivery vehicles (ICBM's, SLBMs, and long-range bombers) to 2,200. Ford told Brezhnev that a signed SALT II agreement before the 1976 election would strengthen détente and prevent "people such as Senator Jackson" from undercutting favorable trends in US–Soviet relations.[25]

But support for détente, diminishing in 1974, declined even more over the remainder of Ford's term. A series of events at home and abroad undermined Ford's public standing and seriously shook the confidence of administration officials. Opposition Democrats, already in the majority in both houses of Congress, made large gains in the congressional elections of November 1974. In 1975, the Ford administration was preoccupied with the deteriorating situation in Vietnam. In March, the armed forces of North Vietnam intensified an offensive against the South, and the Army of the Republic of Vietnam retreated in disarray from positions it held in the northern part of the country. In late April, North Vietnamese and National Liberation Front troops surrounded Saigon, forcing the last Americans to leave. On April 30, the Communist forces captured the presidential palace in Saigon and declared victory in the war. The mood in Washington was grim in the wake of the revolutionaries' triumph in Vietnam. Philip Habib, one of Kissinger's top deputies, said in May 1975 that long-time allies who had prospered under US military alliances and support "are all concerned that the U.S. shield does not provide them the protection they think is necessary for their own development."[26]

For the remainder of 1975, the Ford administration became more confrontational toward the Soviet Union and its allies. In July, Kissinger insisted that the Central Intelligence Agency (CIA) provide additional financial and military aid to the National Front for the Liberation of Angola (FNLA), one of three armed factions trying to supplant the Portuguese authorities in that West African country. Kissinger advocated intervention in the Angolan civil war as a counter to the Soviet Union which supported the Popular Movement for the Liberation of Angola (MPLA), a rival faction. Kissinger believed that the Soviets supported the MPLA because they felt emboldened by the American defeat in Vietnam. US intervention in Angola generated public fear of involvement in another distant war, similar to Vietnam, and in December, Congress blocked additional CIA funding for the FNLA.

In the summer of 1975, Ford was criticized when he continued Nixon's policy and did not ridicule the Soviets' record on human rights. Ford declined to meet with expelled Soviet dissident writer Aleksandr Solzhenitsyn. The

25 Quoted in Hanhimäki, *Flawed Architect*, 371.
26 Secretary Kissinger's staff meeting, May 7, 1975, KT101611, DNSA.

novelist was widely admired in the United States for his vigorous condemnations of the Kremlin's history of repression. Domestic foes of détente accused Ford of hurting the cause of human rights in the Soviet Union. Solzhenitsyn then further eroded American support for détente when he denounced the upcoming CSCE meeting in Helsinki as a "betrayal of Eastern Europe."[27]

The Helsinki ceremony of August 2, 1975, at which representatives from thirty-five states in Europe and North America signed the Final Act of the CSCE, reflected the culmination of years of negotiations. The Soviets had originally proposed a meeting to resolve all disputes in Europe in the mid-1950s, and they agreed to US participation in the talks in the early 1970s. At the insistence of several Western European and neutral countries, the scope of the discussions expanded from traditional security concerns over borders and the use of force (what came to be known as Basket I of the Helsinki Final Act) to include trade and scientific cooperation (Basket II), and humanitarian and other fields (Basket III).

American foes of the Helsinki agreements did not like the Final Act's recognition of prevailing territorial borders in Europe. Many Americans of Eastern European ancestry were fiercely anti-Communist and opposed to Soviet influence in Eastern Europe. They complained that the acknowledgment of current borders validated the 1940 Soviet occupation and annexation of the Baltic states of Lithuania, Latvia, and Estonia. These criticisms of the Helsinki Final Act made Ford's trip to the conference unpopular, and he sought to recover by adopting a more confrontational stance toward the Soviet Union. When he spoke to the delegates there, he reversed Nixon's practice of refraining from criticizing Soviet domestic policies. He looked directly at Brezhnev during his speech and insisted that the Soviets "realize the deep devotion of the American people and their government to human rights and fundamental freedoms."[28]

Still, Ford's statements at Helsinki did not calm critics of CSCE. To Helsinki's opponents, it seemed that the Final Act condemned the Eastern European and Baltic states to permanent domination by the Soviet Union. Senator Jackson predicted that the human rights provisions of Helsinki were "so imprecise and so hedged" that they would never be implemented. Former California governor Ronald Reagan, who was preparing to challenge Ford

27 Quoted in Anne Hessing Cahn, *Killing Détente: The Right Attacks the CIA* (University Park, PA: Pennsylvania State University Press, 1998), 32.
28 Quoted in Robert Greene, *The Presidency of Gerald R. Ford* (Lawrence, KS: University Press of Kansas, 1995), 153.

for the Republican presidential nomination in 1976, asserted that "all Americans should be against" the Helsinki Final Act.[29]

The attacks on détente and on Kissinger as the architect of US foreign policy continued after Helsinki. Some of them came from within the administration. Secretary of Defense James Schlesinger sided with members of the Joint Chiefs of Staff who argued that the arms-control agreements of recent years had left the United States in a militarily inferior position to that of the Soviet Union. In early November, Ford replaced Schlesinger as secretary of defense with White House chief of staff, Donald Rumsfeld. To assuage the concerns of Kissinger's opponents, Ford replaced him as national security adviser. Kissinger remained secretary of state, but his authority was clearly diminished. Reagan continued to assail détente as a "one way street" and complained that "Henry Kissinger's recent stewardship has coincided with the loss of U.S. military supremacy."[30] In February 1976, Ford explained that officials in his administration would no longer use the word "détente" to characterize US–Soviet relations.

Brezhnev did not visit the United States after the Vladivostok meeting of November 1974. Nor did the United States and the Soviet Union sign the SALT II Treaty by 1976, as they had promised at Vladivostok. Presidential politics interfered with further progress toward détente. The way in which Nixon, Ford, and Kissinger conducted détente became a contentious issue during the presidential election campaign of 1976. Jimmy Carter, the Democratic Party's candidate, assailed the three leaders for acquiescing to the Soviet Union's mistreatment of its own citizens. Carter condemned Ford for declining to meet with Solzhenitsyn in the summer of 1975. Carter said that the Soviets had known what they wanted to achieve from détente, but "we have not known what we've wanted and we've been out-traded in almost every instance."[31] Ford blundered in a televised debate with Carter when the president, attempting to defend the Helsinki Final Act, denied that the Soviet Union dominated Eastern Europe. The Democratic challenger retorted that he would like to see the president convince Hungarian-, Czech-, or Polish-Americans that their former homelands did not live under Soviet control. Carter defeated Ford in November 1976, and he owed his election in part to the public's sense that détente gave unfair military advantages to

---

29 Quoted in Hanhimäki, *Flawed Architect*, 436, 437.
30 Statement by Ronald Reagan at Orlando, Florida, March 4, 1976. box 26, Ronald Reagan folder, Robert Hartman Files, Gerald R. Ford Presidential Library, Ann Arbor, Michigan.
31 Second Carter–Ford Presidential Debate, October 6, 1976, The American Presidency Project, www.presidency.uscb.edu.

the Soviet Union while betraying traditional American commitments to expand human rights abroad.

Assessments of détente

When Richard Nixon left office in August 1974, newspaper commentators were scathing in their denunciations of his domestic abuses of power. They also, however, gave him high marks for reducing the danger of nuclear war and making the world safer. An August 12, 1974, editorial in the *Christian Science Monitor*, a paper highly critical of Nixon's abuse of power, noted that "Nixon risked alienating many of his long-time Cold War supporters by opening America's door to the Communist world."[32] But détente had lost much of its domestic popularity by the time Gerald Ford traveled to Helsinki to sign the Final Act of the CSCE. By then, the public mood in the United States had turned sour and a significant number of Americans believed that the Soviet Union was in the stronger position in the Cold War.

Paradoxically, the Helsinki process undermined Soviet power. Helsinki transformed the discussion of behavior throughout Western and Eastern Europe and the Soviet Union over the next decade. After Helsinki, the protection and advancement of human rights within countries became generally accepted international standards. The political scientist Daniel C. Thomas expressed a widely accepted point of view when he observed in 2001 that this emphasis on human rights "contributed significantly to the demise of Communist rule in 1989–1990."[33]

Yet the end of Soviet-style Communism was not visible on the horizon in the decade after Nixon left office. Nixon's and Kissinger's foreign policy gradually lost popularity in the late 1970s and 1980s. Some of the criticism involved complaints about their deceptive and manipulative style. Garthoff's *Détente and Confrontation* praised Nixon and Kissinger for initiating détente, but Garthoff argued that they undermined support for it by their secretive style and by their belittling the advice of foreign affairs experts.

Later observers, who benefited from the abundance of original documentation on the Nixon and Ford presidencies that became available in the 1990s and the early twenty-first century, noted that these men conducted foreign affairs in order to maintain what the historian Jeremi Suri

---

32 *Christian Science Monitor*, August 12, 1974, editorial page.
33 Daniel C. Thomas, *The Helsinki Effect: International Norms, Human Rights, and the Demise of Communism* (Princeton, NJ: Princeton University Press, 2001), 272.

characterized as "a conservative world order." This arrangement "addressed the fears and served the interests of the largest states."[34] While Nixon and Kissinger spoke often about the changing circumstances of the Cold War in which the United States no longer had unrivaled military superiority over the Soviet Union, they expected to manage a prolonged, even indefinite rivalry with the Kremlin. Jussi Hanhimäki, one of Kissinger's biographers, concluded that the policy of détente with the Soviet Union was essentially backward looking and lacked "understanding of the underlying forces that were shaping the direction of international relations in the 1970s."[35] Popular movements for political freedom and economic prosperity were surfacing in the Communist world and they would culminate in the unexpected collapse of Soviet rule and the end of the Cold War a decade later. Other subsequent observers have been even more critical. The historian Jeffrey Kimball concluded that "the Nixinger grand design was not well conceived in the beginning, was not fully realized in the end, and was as much, if not more, a product of reaction, improvisation, bureaucratic infighting, and political and economic realities, as it was proactive, farsighted planning and wise coolheaded statesmanship."[36]

Negative assessments such as these raise serious questions about the quality of Nixon's and Kissinger's statesmanship. They also are retrospective judgments made in the post-Cold War era through the prism of the end of Soviet-style Communism. The end of the Cold War has led other historians to more favorable judgments of détente. John Lewis Gaddis argued in 2005 that "détente did not free the world from crises, but the new spirit of cooperation, did seem to limit their frequency and severity."[37] The leaders of both the United States and the Soviet Union committed themselves to manage their nations' relations responsibly. They recognized that each was a legitimate state. Henceforth, they would compete for influence throughout the world, but they would limit their rivalry and reduce the danger of nuclear war between them. They would expand trade, cultural, and scientific relations in order to modulate the acrimony in their day-to-day relations. Robert Dallek in his 2007 joint biography of Kissinger and Nixon harshly criticized the two for their secretiveness and

---

34 Jeremi Suri, *Power and Protest: Global Revolution and the Rise of Détente* (Cambridge, MA: Harvard University Press, 2003), 258.

35 Hanhimäki, *Flawed Architect*, 490.

36 Jeffrey Kimball, *Nixon's Vietnam War* (Lawrence, KS: University Press of Kansas, 1998), 370.

37 John Lewis Gaddis, *The Cold War: A New History* (New York: Penguin, 2005), 198.

manipulations of others. He also characterized détente as one of the central elements of US policy toward the Soviet Union. Dallek observed that "détente did not end the Cold War, but in conjunction with containment and deterrence ... it set a process in motion that came to fruition under Mikhail Gorbachev at the end of the 1980s."[38]

---

38 Robert Dallek, *Nixon and Kissinger: Partners in Power* (New York: HarperCollins, 2007), 618.

19

Nuclear proliferation and non-proliferation during the Cold War

FRANCIS J. GAVIN

At first glance, understanding the dynamics of how nuclear weapons spread during the Cold War, and what was done to slow this proliferation, should not be difficult. Weren't nuclear weapons a threat to international stability, inducing widespread support for efforts to hem in this menace to world peace? The real story was not so simple. As scholars have long recognized, nuclear weapons influenced international politics in complex and often contradictory ways during the Cold War. On the one hand, atomic weapons have an enormous destructive power – the capacity to kill millions of people and destroy the fabric of civilized life. On the other, this weapon of terror, may have induced caution among the states that possessed them. Many analysts believe the prospect of mutual destruction prevented World War III, serving as a foundation for what John Lewis Gaddis famously labeled "the Long Peace."[1]

This dilemma was just one of many that policymakers, strategists, and outside observers wrestled with as they tried to understand the military and political purposes of such fearful weapons. These issues were never resolved during the Cold War, as analysts joined government officials in devising the most intricate, sophisticated military strategies for weapons they hoped would never be employed and believed had no meaningful battlefield purpose. These fears also inspired millions around the world to join grassroots, nongovernmental efforts to prevent the bomb from ever being used.

This essay explores the history of efforts to come to terms with the puzzles and tradeoffs involved in confronting nuclear proliferation and non-proliferation during the Cold War. Many of these dilemmas have still not been resolved. For example, scholars vigorously debate whether

---

[1] John Lewis Gaddis, "The Long Peace: Elements of Stability in the Postwar International System," *International Security*, 10 (Spring 1986), 99–142.

proliferation threatens global security or stabilizes international politics and prevents war. Questions persist as to the reasons why states attempt to acquire nuclear weapons, the leading explanations being security, prestige, or bureaucratic/organizational impulse. Disagreement continues over whether the bipolar structure of the international system during the Cold War encouraged or hindered nuclear proliferation. Perhaps most maddening, no one has been able to accurately predict the "who and when" aspect of proliferation. Forecasters have almost always been caught off guard by who did, and did not, enter the nuclear club. Fears of tipping points, nuclear dominoes, and proliferation epidemics have existed from the start of the nuclear age, with worry accelerating in recent years, despite the fact that there are far fewer nuclear powers today than anyone could have reasonably hoped for thirty or forty years ago. Similarly, fears of rogue states with atomic weapons and nuclear terrorism have worried policymakers since the earliest days of the atomic age.

As this chapter reveals, nowhere are these nuclear puzzles more challenging than in the area of non-proliferation policy. If nuclear proliferation should and can be stopped – not universally held beliefs, particularly in the earlier part of the Cold War – what were the best policies to achieve this goal, appeasement or force? Did it make sense to apply the same non-proliferation policy toward democratic, neutral Sweden as toward the People's Republic of China (PRC)? These dilemmas were especially sharp when viewed through the contours of the Cold War alliance system. Arms-control advocates argued that global non-proliferation could only be achieved when states that already had nuclear weapons reduced and eventually eliminated their stocks of atomic weapons, avoided anti-ballistic missile (ABM) defenses, and promised never to use nuclear weapons first. Countries that were asked to forgo these weapons, however, demanded robust and credible protection from the superpowers' nuclear umbrella in return for their abstinence. In the US case, providing extended deterrence to states like West Germany, Japan, and South Korea demanded strategic superiority and a willingness to craft military strategies based on the early and massive use of nuclear weapons in a conflict with the Soviet Union.

The most intriguing feature of non-proliferation, however, was that it became a shared goal of two bitter Cold War enemies, the United States and the Soviet Union. Moreover, they pursued it at the expense of, among others, their closest friends and allies. A West German official complained that US efforts to enlist the Soviet Union in non-proliferation lent to "concessions from the wrong side and to the wrong address."[2] This shared interest, however, proved so powerful that at times it trumped traditional Cold War rivalries, attitudes, and policies; it also provided much of the impetus to détente.

Nuclear non-proliferation and the early Cold War

In the early days of the Cold War, neither US nor Soviet officials pursued non-proliferation efforts with any vigor. In hindsight, their policies appear unsophisticated and unrealistic. Some American officials believed the United States could maintain its nuclear monopoly indefinitely, while others proposed preventative war against the Soviets before they acquired their own weapons. For their part, the Soviets saw disarmament proposals as a propaganda tool while engaging in espionage and a full-scale crash program to develop their own atomic bomb. Despite the terrible destruction brought by the atomic bombing of Hiroshima and Nagasaki, the epoch-changing nature of these new weapons went largely unrecognized or misunderstood in official military circles during the first years of the Cold War.

There were attempts to regulate this fearsome new weapon, although it is difficult to gauge how serious these efforts were. In January 1946, the United Nations Atomic Energy Commission (UNAEC) was created during the first meeting of the UN General Assembly. During this session, the United States submitted the Baruch Plan, based on the Acheson–Lilienthal Report, which proposed UN control of all uranium-235 and plutonium facilities, extensive monitoring in all member states, and eventually global disarmament. The Soviets responded on June 19, 1946, with what came to be known as the Gromyko Plan, which required the United States to disarm. The United States modified the Baruch Plan and President Harry S. Truman signed the Atomic Energy Act of 1946, which created the Atomic Energy Commission (AEC) and banned all sharing of nuclear technology and information, even with Britain.

Cold War tensions between the superpowers increased and even half-hearted disarmament and arms-control efforts were largely dropped. Members of the Western alliance were stunned when the Soviets tested an atomic device on August 29, 1949, and, less than four years later, developed a hydrogen, or thermonuclear, bomb. Britain tested its own nuclear device

2 Matthias Peter and Harald Rosenbach (eds.), *Akten zur Auswärtigen Politik der Bundesrepublik Deutschland, 1966* (Munich: Oldenbourg Verlag, 1997), vol. II. "Notes of Ambassador Schnippenkoetter: Non-Proliferation of Nuclear Weapons (NP)," September 7, 1966, Document 277.

in October 1952. The United States also continued to build its nuclear stockpile, a long moribund UNAEC was formally dissolved, and by the end of the Truman administration little hope existed for any bilateral or international effort to control the spread of nuclear weapons. The war on the Korean Peninsula generated new fears that atomic weapons could be used again.

US president Dwight D. Eisenhower's non-proliferation legacy was mixed at best. On December 8, 1953, Eisenhower announced his Atoms for Peace program, which envisioned the sharing of nuclear technology for peaceful purposes through international channels. Eisenhower's plan was criticized for its naïve belief that knowledge and technology provided to countries for their civilian nuclear efforts would not advance their weapons programs. While the United States provided civilian technology to dozens of countries, it did require most of them to adhere to safeguards and inspections. Most importantly, the Atoms for Peace program led to the creation of the International Atomic Energy Agency (IAEA), which monitors global proliferation to this day.

On the other hand, Eisenhower's defense strategy did not rule out the use of nuclear weapons in future military conflicts; in fact, the president believed general war was inevitable if the Soviets and the North Atlantic Treaty Organization (NATO) clashed in Europe.[3] As late as 1960, Eisenhower told Robert Bowie "we must be ready to throw the book at the Russians should they jump us." We would be fooling our allies and ourselves, Eisenhower continued, if "we said we could fight such a war without recourse to nuclear weapons."[4] This view had implications for the spread of atomic weapons. As the historian Marc Trachtenberg has pointed out, Eisenhower not only did not discourage nuclear proliferation; he actively sought to share nuclear weapons with close NATO allies. The military strategy of massive retaliation called for immense and preemptive use of nuclear weapons if there was clear evidence the Soviet Union was planning to attack. This meant authorization for the use of US nuclear weapons was pre-delegated to non-American forces, including the Federal Republic of Germany (FRG). Eisenhower also strongly supported the European Atomic Energy Agency (Eurotam) and the so-called France–Italy–Germany (FIG) agreements to

---

3 See David Holloway's chapter in volume I.
4 "Minutes of Meeting between D. Eisenhower and R. Bowie," August 16, 1960, US Department of State, *Foreign Relations of the United States*, 1958–1960 (Washington, DC: US Government Printing Office, 1993), vol. VII, 614 (hereafter, *FRUS*, with year and volume number).

advance nuclear cooperation in Europe. According to Trachtenberg, the administration's attitude toward nuclear sharing went beyond Britain and France to include the FRG.[5]

Fears that the FRG would gain access to nuclear weapons prompted both the Soviet Union and its Eastern European allies to propose non-proliferation agreements for Europe. On November 17, 1956, the Soviet prime minister, Nikolai Bulganin, announced a comprehensive disarmament plan that required the destruction of all nuclear forces. After the United States rejected the proposal as propaganda, Bulganin proposed a less ambitious plan that prohibited nuclear weapons tests and created a collective security arrangement that included a nonaggression pact between NATO and the Warsaw Pact. On October 9, 1957, Poland's minister of foreign affairs, Adam Rapacki, proposed a nuclear-weapons-free zone for central Europe. Rapacki modified the proposal twice more in response to criticism from NATO, proposing a nuclear freeze and gradual reductions. The United States and its NATO allies rejected these proposals on the grounds they did nothing to counter the Warsaw Pact's superiority in conventional military forces, nor did they make any substantial progress toward German reunification. Soviet unhappiness about the FRG's increased access to nuclear weapons was one of the reasons that the Soviet premier, Nikita S. Khrushchev, initiated pressure on Berlin.[6]

Despite these proposals and tensions, it is surprising to see how little attention was paid to the issue of nuclear proliferation among journalists, academics, and strategists at that time. Most of the so-called "wizards of Armageddon" studied the effects of the strategic nuclear balance between the Soviet Union and the United States and spent very little time thinking about what was then called the "Nth country" problem. The so-called bomber and missile gap, the tradeoffs between nuclear and conventional forces, the fear of an arms race, the nature of strategic vulnerability, the requirements of deterrence, and the merits of different nuclear strategies occupied the time of policymakers and strategists.

While the strategic community was slow to understand the importance of nuclear proliferation, by the late 1950s and early 1960s profound changes in world politics were forcing policymakers to confront new nuclear challenges. US and Soviet officials began to recognize that their early, lackadaisical

---

5 Marc Trachtenberg, *A Constructed Peace: The Making of the European Settlement, 1945–1963* (Princeton, NJ: Princeton University Press, 1999), esp. 146–211.
6 *Ibid.*, 246–47.

attitudes toward non-proliferation were no longer prudent. The question of who would and would not get access to nuclear weapons became an issue of fundamental importance, not only between the superpowers, but also within each alliance and the non-aligned world as well.

The road to the Nuclear Non-Proliferation Treaty

Prospects for effective global nuclear non-proliferation policies improved in the early 1960s. There were four reasons for this change. First, as Lawrence Wittner has shown in his path-breaking work, *Resisting the Bomb*, grassroots antinuclear groups gained popularity throughout the world. The development of thermonuclear weapons, and the dangers associated with nuclear testing, brought emerging environmental groups together with peace advocates to demand governments ban the bomb. Nongovernmental organizations in the West, as well as political leaders from the Non-Aligned Movement, were especially important in advocating a nuclear test-ban treaty.[7] This grassroots, global antinuclear movement was to expand and increase its influence in the decades to come.

Second, the tense confrontations between the Soviets and Americans between 1958 and 1962, initially over the status of Berlin and culminating in the Cuban missile crisis, brought the world close to the first use of nuclear weapons since 1945. Approaching the nuclear precipice – the US secretary of state, Dean Rusk, called it "the most dangerous crisis the world has ever seen," the only time when the nuclear superpowers came "eyeball to eyeball" – both the Soviets and the Americans recognized the need to reduce tensions, halt arms racing, and limit the chances of an accidental nuclear war.[8] A world with fewer nuclear weapons and fewer atomic powers, it was thought, would be much safer. Both governments increasingly made bilateral and global nuclear-arms control a priority after the October 1962 missile crisis. This led to the third factor – the idea that if proliferation was not stopped, there could be a domino, snowball, or tipping point phenomenon resulting in dozens of new atomic powers. President John F. Kennedy told the world in 1963 that he "was haunted by the feeling that by 1970, unless we are successful, there may be ten nuclear powers instead of four, and by 1975, fifteen or twenty."[9]

---

7 Lawrence Wittner, *Resisting the Bomb: A History of the World Nuclear Disarmament Movement, 1954–1970.* (Stanford, CA: Stanford University Press, 1997).
8 See William Burr and David Alan Rosenberg's chapter in this volume.
9 "President's News Conference, 21 March 1963," *Public Papers of the Presidents of the United States: Kennedy* (Washington, DC: US Government Printing Office, 1964), 280.

The fourth and most important reason for the shift toward stronger non-proliferation polices was geopolitical. Until the early 1960s, it could be argued that the countries that had developed nuclear weapons – the United States, the Soviet Union, Britain, and France – were status quo powers, unlikely to change postwar borders through force. Other potential proliferators – Sweden, India, Australia, even Israel – had understandable (if controversial) security motivations to acquire weapons for defensive and deterrent purposes. However, two other potential nuclear powers, the FRG and PRC, fell into a much different category. The possibility that either or both of these states would gain access to nuclear weapons threatened the stability of Europe and East Asia and challenged both American and Soviet interests.

The FRG was a divided land, only a generation removed from the Nazi legacy of terror and war, feared by its Eastern bloc neighbors, and mistrusted even by its closest European allies. The FRG demonstrated an interest throughout the 1950s in having access to the most modern weapons available.[10] Policymakers in the United States worried about the political consequences of openly discriminating against West Germany, especially when Britain and France were atomic powers. The efforts to make the FRG feel it could participate in nuclear decisionmaking, without actually giving them the bomb, created much anxiety in both the East and the West. Even more alarming to the Soviets, as we have seen, was the attitude of President Eisenhower, who believed that a nuclear-armed FRG was inevitable.

The German question was at the heart of almost all discussions over what to do about nuclear proliferation. As the 1960s progressed, most everyone came to believe that the FRG could not be allowed to possess its own nuclear weapons. The Berlin crisis made it quite clear that the Soviets would simply not stand for a nuclearized Bundeswehr. In the words of a US official, "German national nuclear capability is virtually a Soviet obsession, based upon a deep-seated emotional fear of resurgent German militarism."[11] Could the United States, however, tell the FRG it could never have the most modern weapons, while neighbors France, Britain, and the Soviet Union continued to build their stockpiles? How would the Germans react when smaller or less economically advanced countries like Israel and India attained nuclear status and the security and respect that came with it? US officials, like

---

10 Trachtenberg, *A Constructed Peace*, 232–38.

11 "The Value and Feasibility of a Nuclear Non-Proliferation Treaty," December 12, 1964, p.14, box 2, Committee on Non-Proliferation, National Security Files (NSF), National Security Council (NSC), 2, Lyndon B. Johnson Library, University of Texas, Austin, Texas (hereafter, LBJL).

Under Secretary of State George Ball, realized it was not "safe to isolate Germany or leave it with a permanent sense of grievance," which could result from "her forced exclusion from the nuclear club." Such policies, Ball noted, "would provide a fertile ground for demagogues."[12] Ball and others proposed nuclear-sharing schemes such as the multilateral force (MLF) that they believed would satisfy West German needs.[13] Others believed the MLF would only encourage the FRG's nuclear ambitions. Resolving this dilemma – preventing a German national nuclear force without awakening dangerous resentments – created a great political struggle, both within the NATO alliance and between the United States and the Soviet Union.

At least the FRG was a liberal democracy. China was in many ways the original rogue state. Veering between the ironclad rule of Mao Zedong and the anarchy of the Great Leap Forward in the 1950s and the Great Proletarian Cultural Revolution of the 1960s, China's successful program to develop its own atomic weapons worried its neighbors and both Cold War superpowers. China, with a population of more than 700 million by the early 1960s, had already fought the United States in Korea, attacked India, and threatened Taiwan, Indochina, and Indonesia. The PRC's emerging nuclear status threatened the US position in East Asia and could affect the escalating conflict in Vietnam. President Kennedy had considered a nuclear-armed China a grave threat that would "so upset the world political scene [that] it would be intolerable."[14] In November 1962, US national security adviser McGeorge Bundy said that Chinese nuclear weapons would be "the greatest single threat to the status quo over the next few years."[15] Mao's internal policies had led to the death of millions of his own citizens, and he had already declared that he did not fear nuclear war with the United States: "If the worse came to the worst and half of mankind died, the other half would remain while imperialism would be razed to the ground and the whole world would become

12 Couve de Murville, Charles Lucet, George Ball, and Charles Bohlen, "Memorandum of conversation," December 2, 1964. box 7, lot 67D2, RG 59, US National Archives, College Park, Maryland (hereafter, USNA).
13 The multilateral force, or MLF, was a US proposal, originally floated by the Eisenhower administration, and taken up with varying degrees of enthusiasm by the Kennedy and Johnson administrations, to produce a fleet of surface ships and submarines manned by international NATO crews and armed with ballistic nuclear missiles.
14 William Burr and Jeffrey T. Richelson. "Whether to Strangle the Baby in the Cradle: The United States and the Chinese Nuclear Program, 1960–64," *International Security*, 25 3 (Winter 2000), 54–99.
15 "Memorandum from M. Bundy to J. Kennedy," November 8, 1962, *FRUS, 1961–1963*, vol. VII, 598.

socialist."[16] From the US perspective, a nuclear-armed PRC could become even more aggressive and harder to deter. According to one analyst, the Chinese appeared "determined to eject the United States from Asia" and were sure to "exploit their nuclear weapons for this end." By 1970, China would have "thermonuclear weapons," and by 1980, "it [would] be necessary to think in terms of a possible 100 million U.S. deaths whenever a serious conflict with China threatens."[17] China's attitude toward the Soviet Union was hardly better, as the bitter rhetoric between these ideological and geopolitical competitors threatened to spill over into conflict throughout the 1960s. Tensions grew so heated between these former allies that by 1969, the Soviet Union contemplated a "pre-emptive strike" against China's nuclear forces.[18]

Concerns about West Germany and China motivated the Soviet Union and the United States to seek a common stance in limiting the spread of nuclear weapons. The Kennedy administration began distancing itself from Eisenhower's willingness to share nuclear weapons within NATO. Secretary of State Rusk told Khrushchev, "the Germans should not have a national nuclear capability."[19] Kremlin leaders, of course, concurred. An FRG with nuclear weapons was a grave threat to their interests in Europe. Moreover, they shared a long and often disputed border with China. As relations with the PRC deteriorated, they faced the possibility of nuclear-armed adversaries on two fronts. Furthermore, most prospective proliferators were in the Soviet Union's near abroad, in East and South Asia, the Middle East, and Europe. The superpowers had compelling reasons to cooperate on nuclear non-proliferation.

They also increasingly recognized that uncontrolled nuclear proliferation offered challenges that went beyond traditional geopolitical concerns such as China and Germany. By the mid-1960s, nuclear experts sensed that major powers, such as the United States and the Soviet Union, understood the responsibilities of nuclear ownership and recognized the deadly logic of mutual vulnerability and deterrence, but they wondered whether the same

---

16 Mao Zedong, "We Must Not Fear Nuclear War," as cited in Richard Wyn Jones, *Security, Strategy, and Critical Theory* (Boulder, CO: Lynne Rienner Publishers, Inc., 1999), 137.
17 "China as a Nuclear Power (Some Thoughts prior to the Chinese Test)," October 7, 1964, box 5, Committee on Non-Proliferation, NSF, NSC, LBJL.
18 See William Burr (ed.), National Security Archive Briefing Book, *The Sino-Soviet Border Conflict, 1969: U.S. Reactions and Diplomatic Maneuvers*, June 12, 2001, www.gwu.edu/~nsarchiv/NSAEBB/NSAEBB49/.
19 "Record of D. Rusk and N. Khrushchev Meeting," August 8, 1963, *FRUS, 1961–1963*, vol. XV, 567.

would hold for smaller, less developed countries, or even non-state actors. In 1965, analyst Fred Iklé warned that if proliferation went beyond the "middle powers," it could lead to "owners of nuclear weapons who cannot be deterred because they feel they have nothing to lose." These might include a group "fanatically dedicated to some revolutionary cause which may have no concern for the survival of their country ... To carry out such 'nuclear anarchism' or acts of personal revenge, modern delivery systems would not be needed; it would suffice if the weapons could be sneaked close enough to a target clandestinely."[20] A study led by Thomas Schelling in 1963 argued that the future would hold complex or unforeseen nuclear threats. "(N)uclear weapons will become increasingly economical for smaller countries to produce" and may become available by "theft, commercial purchase, or diplomatic trading." These new nuclear powers would not need sophisticated strategic forces or ballistic missiles. "A fishing boat or a cheap airplane might have been an adequate means of delivery for, say, the Algerian Nationalists against Marseilles, or Castro's Cuba against Baltimore or Miami."[21]

The Soviet Union and the United States had to overcome significant barriers before they could negotiate a nuclear non-proliferation policy, and they moved slowly at first, building upon earlier international efforts. In 1961, Ireland proposed a UN resolution, the Prevention of the Wider Dissemination of Nuclear Weapons, which banned the spread of nuclear technology to additional states and prohibited all countries from acquiring nuclear weapons. In 1962, the Eighteen Nation Disarmament Committee (ENDC) was formed to encourage the Soviet Union and the United States to adopt arms-control measures. A year before, President Kennedy created a new agency, the Arms Control and Disarmament Agency (ACDA) headed by William Foster, and the same year named John McCloy as his special adviser on disarmament. McCloy negotiated a set of arms-control principles with his Soviet counterpart, Valerian Zorin, in September 1961. The McCloy–Zorin principles, as they were called, built upon the efforts of others such as British prime minister, Harold Macmillan, to pave the way for serious negotiations to ban nuclear testing.

The Soviet Union, United States, and Britain negotiated a Limited Test-Ban Treaty that was opened for signature on August 5, 1963. The treaty was not

---

20 Fred C. Iklé, "Possible Consequences of a Further Spread of Nuclear Weapons," January 2, 1965, box 7, Committee on Nuclear Proliferation, NSF, NSC, LBJL.

21 "A Report on Strategic Developments over the Next Decade for the Interagency Panel", October 1963, 51–53, box 376, NSF, John F. Kennedy Library, Boston, Massachusetts (hereafter, JFKL).

perfect. The Soviets and Americans disagreed about the number and types of inspections that would be allowed, and underground tests were not banned. Nothing was done about China's emerging nuclear program. More ambitious arms-control measures, such as a comprehensive test ban or limitations on the growth of strategic weapons, were beyond the reach of the superpowers for the time being.

The Limited Test-Ban Treaty, however, was a good start toward the goal of a global non-proliferation regime, and its timing was propitious. By the mid-1960s, several developed and developing states were considering or actually constructing active nuclear weapons programs. In Europe, Sweden, Switzerland, Italy, Yugoslavia, and even Romania were seen as candidates for the bomb. It was speculated that Brazil, Argentina, and perhaps Mexico were motivated to develop atomic weapons as well. Regional arms races in the Middle East and South Asia were feared if Israel and India successfully tested a weapon. China's capabilities and the conflict in Vietnam made East Asia fertile soil for new nuclear powers, such as Japan, Taiwan, South Korea, Indonesia, and even Australia.[22] There was great concern that China's test – which took place in October 1964 – could initiate a nuclear domino effect if vigorous action were not taken.[23] Not only might this destabilize key regions of the globe by initiating local arms races; the increased number of smaller states acquiring nuclear weapons could put pressure on West Germany to follow suit.

President Lyndon B. Johnson signaled a renewed US commitment to non-proliferation on January 21, 1964, in a message to the ENDC calling for a worldwide treaty based on the Irish resolution. Real movement on the policy front, however, did not come until exactly one year later, when the blue ribbon Committee on Nuclear Proliferation, or Gilpatric committee, delivered its findings to the White House. This committee of influential officials had been put together to construct a new US non-proliferation policy in the wake of the PRC's atomic test in October 1964. The group explored a broad menu of alternatives. On the one hand, it considered the consequences of accepting or even aiding nuclear proliferation. At the other end of the spectrum, the group weighed the implications of a far tougher non-proliferation policy. The committee examined a wide range of policies,

---

22 R. Murray, "Problems of Nuclear Proliferation Outside Europe," December 7, 1964, Document #CK3100281620, 1, Declassified Documents Reference System (hereafter, DDRS), www.columbia.edu.
23 Henry Rowen, "Memorandum – India's Nuclear Problem," December 24, 1964, Document #CK3100154493, *DDRS*.

including appeasement, sanctions against emerging nuclear powers, preemption against the PRC, and even sabotaging French nuclear-testing sites.[24]

There were divergent views within the US government, including skepticism in some quarters about whether nuclear non-proliferation was even desirable. State Department official George McGhee suggested in 1961 that it would be advantageous "if a friendly Asian power beat Communist China to the punch" by testing a nuclear device first, and there was "no likelier candidate than India."[25] Dean Rusk argued that it "was easy for the U.S. to speak out against proliferation, but the Prime Minister of India or Japan must look on the question quite differently." For the secretary of state, "nonproliferation [was] not the overriding element in U.S. relations with the rest of the world."[26] A briefing paper for the Gilpatric committee wondered if it was in "the U.S. interest in all cases" to prevent other countries from obtaining nuclear weapons, "or might it be in the U.S. interest for particular nations to acquire such capability?"[27]

The committee, however, concluded, "preventing the further spread of nuclear weapons is clearly in the national interest, despite the difficult decisions that will be required." The report "as a matter of great urgency" recommended the administration "substantially increase the scope and intensity" of its non-proliferation efforts. "The world is fast approaching a point of no return in the prospects of controlling the spread of nuclear weapons." A program that included formalizing multilateral agreements, applying pressure on individual states considering nuclear acquisition, and making changes to the United States' own policies was recommended.[28]

In order to implement the committee's recommendations, controversial policies would have to be adopted. The Soviet Union would have to be accepted as the key partner in a global effort to stem the spread of atomic weapons. A comprehensive test-ban treaty and regional nuclear-free zones would have to be supported. Nonnuclear powers would have to be given something in return for their pledge to abstain from acquiring nuclear

---

24 Roger Fisher, "Memo on Possible Action: Action Directed against Further French Atmospheric Tests," December 19, 1964, box 10, Personal Papers of Roswell Gilpatric (hereafter, PPRG), JFKL.

25 "Memorandum from G. McGhee to D. Rusk," September 13, 1961, Freedom of Information Act (FOIA) Files, India, National Security Archive, Washington, DC.

26 "Secretary's Meeting with the Gilpatric Committee on Non-Proliferation," 7 January 1965, box 24, lot 67D2, RG 59, USNA.

27 Untitled memo, box 5, Committee on Non-Proliferation, Selected Issues, NSF, LBJL.

28 "Report to the President by the Committee on Nuclear Proliferation," January 21, 1965, Box 8, NSF, LBJL.

weapons. Neutrals like India would have to be offered some form of guarantee against nuclear attack. Japan would have to be reassured. Israel's and Egypt's nuclear ambitions would need to be confronted. Carrots and sticks would have to be employed both to appease and deter potential proliferators. On the most controversial question of all, the status of the MLF and its relationship to West Germany's nuclear ambitions, the committee was divided. Most of its members understood, however, that the MLF would have to be sacrificed to obtain the Non-Proliferation Treaty (NPT) with the Soviet Union.

The Gilpatric committee's conclusions were controversial, especially among those in the US State Department who supported the MLF. Secretary of State Rusk argued the report was as "explosive as a nuclear weapon" and worked to keep it secret. President Johnson, however, strongly supported the group's recommendations, and the thrust of the committee's findings became official US non-proliferation policy when Johnson approved National Security Action Memorandum (NSAM) 335, "Preparation of Arms Control Program." The policy built upon the president's speech celebrating the twentieth anniversary of the United Nations, where he had called upon other governments to join the United States to negotiate "an effective attack upon these deadly dangers to mankind." With NSAM 335, Johnson ordered a program to halt the further spread of nuclear weapons. He assigned the task to the Arms Control and Disarmament Agency, and gave it direct access to the White House, an arrangement that signaled Johnson's keen interest and that prevented the State Department from sabotaging the effort.[29]

The United States submitted a draft non-proliferation treaty to the ENDC on August 17, 1965. The Soviet Union made its own proposal to the UN General Assembly on September 24, 1965. The proposals were similar except for one key provision – how they viewed collective nuclear forces such as the MLF or the Atlantic Nuclear Force (ANF). While the US proposal allowed for the MLF, the Soviet plan prohibited nonnuclear-weapon states from participating in "the ownership, control, or use of nuclear weapons." The Soviet draft even challenged the right of nonnuclear states in an alliance to participate in nuclear planning and targeting. Soviet and American negotiators wrestled over the precise language governing US–NATO nuclear arrangements for almost two years. The difficulty of these negotiations surpassed only the problem both superpowers had in convincing their alliance partners and neutrals to embrace the treaty.

---

29 "National Security Action Memo 335: Preparation of Arms Control Program," June 28, 1965, www.lbjlib.utexas.edu/Johnson/archives.hom/NSAMs/nsam335.asp.

A non-proliferation treaty faced great challenges, particularly within the Western Alliance. Japan expressed grave concerns about the PRC's nuclear status and indicated it was interested in its own atomic weapons. Britain was adamant that there must be a treaty at any cost, even if it jeopardized the FRG's interests. France's position was most vexing. De Gaulle did not believe that states could be prevented from acquiring nuclear weapons if they really wanted them, and he did not support the treaty. On the other hand, France was adamantly opposed to the possession of nuclear weapons by the FRG. Furthermore, de Gaulle supported the Soviet position on the MLF and did whatever he could to undermine the scheme.

The West Germans were not pleased with the renewed focus on their intentions in the nuclear field. Hadn't the FRG already promised, West German officials complained, not to produce atomic, biological, and chemical weapons in the Paris Accords of 1954? Why should the FRG, its leaders asked, sign an agreement without something tangible from the Soviets in return? The FRG was bitterly disappointed that none of her "allies" were making an effort to link non-proliferation to a European settlement beneficial to Germany. Furthermore, West Germany had an emerging civilian nuclear sector, and it did not want to see an NPT harm its economic interests in this area.

The pressure to terminate talks regarding the MLF and to accept the NPT, combined with clashes over military and international monetary policy, brought US–West German relations to a low point in the late 1960s. The new chancellor of the FRG, Kurt-Georg Kiesinger, accused the United States of "complicity" for its overtures to the Soviets on the NPT.[30] The former chancellor, Konrad Adenauer, publicly called the NPT proposals "the Morganthau Plan squared." The FRG's attitude toward the NPT threatened a crisis between the blocs and within NATO.

Though less well known, the Soviet Union had its own difficulties with socialist countries over the issue of nuclear proliferation, resulting in similar alliance tensions. On January 17, 1955, the Council of Ministers of the USSR authorized the sharing of peaceful nuclear technology with its allies. The Soviets offered nuclear technology and information, including research reactors, to Hungary, East Germany, Czechoslovakia, and even Egypt. The most important beneficiary of this policy, however, was China. In exchange for Chinese exports of uranium, the Soviets provided more than 10,000 experts, technical drawings,

---

30 "Conversation between the Federal Chancellor Kiesinger and the American Special Envoy McCloy," March 4, 1967, Document 87, *Akten zur Auswärtigen Politik der Bundesrepublik Deutschland, 1967*.

and refined fuel. This aid is estimated to have expedited China's weapons program by ten to fifteen years.

This program was abruptly ended in the late 1950s, as relations between Russia and China deteriorated.[31] In addition, promises to improve Hungary's and Czechoslovakia's atomic energy programs were not fulfilled. Khrushchev's concerns about China's military prowess and aggressive intentions created another source of tension with his allies. As the historian Douglas Selvage has shown, in 1963 and 1964 the Soviet leader was willing to accommodate American desires for the MLF plan in order to achieve an NPT aimed at China. Eastern European countries, particularly Poland, were furious. They insisted that the NPT must guarantee the FRG's nonnuclear status. The Soviets heeded these concerns and once again made eliminating the MLF a key goal of an NPT.[32]

The MLF issue and the looming appearance of new nuclear powers gave the non-proliferation question a sense of urgency throughout 1966. The evidence indicated both India and Israel would expand their efforts to build nuclear weapons in the absence of a global regime. While it was clear that the Soviets wanted a nuclear NPT, it was just as clear they would not accept an arrangement that allowed for a meaningful MLF. In the fall, negotiations intensified, with Gromyko and Rusk struggling to find compromise language that prevented the transfer of nuclear weapons to individual states but allowed for individual European national programs to be folded into a single larger European scheme. The United States wanted to protect existing US–NATO nuclear arrangements and allow for the creation of the Nuclear Planning Group (NPG).

A rough understanding between the Soviets and the Americans on treaty language and interpretation emerged during the winter of 1966/67. That did not mean, however, that a working treaty agreeable to all major powers was in sight. The West Germans continued to object to an NPT on a number of grounds, and demanded revision of key articles. The so-called Gaullist wing of the new government, led by Finance Minister Franz-Josef Strauss, dismissed the treaty as a "Versailles of cosmic proportions."[33] Disagreements over the

---

31 See Sergey Radchenko's chapter in this volume.
32 Douglas Selvage, *"The Warsaw Pact and Nuclear Nonproliferation, 1963–1965,"* Cold War International History Project Working Paper No. 32 (Washington, DC: Woodrow Wilson Center, 2001).
33 Shane Maddock, "The Nth Country Conundrum: The American and Soviet Quest for Nuclear Nonproliferation, 1945–1970," Ph.D. dissertation, University of Connecticut (1997), 501.

inspection and safeguard regime, peaceful uses of nuclear energy, and the length of the treaty were sticking points for a number of countries. The non-aligned nations highlighted other problems with the treaty and demanded that the United States and the Soviets offer security guarantees, reduce their nuclear stockpiles, and direct the savings into economic aid for the under-developed world. These disagreements proved time-consuming and conten-tious. Negotiations dragged on throughout 1967 and the first half of 1968.

The superpowers were joined by sixty-two other states, giving pre-liminary approval to the NPT, when it was signed on July 1, 1968. The Johnson administration hoped for rapid ratification, both domestically and internation-ally, but the Soviet invasion of Czechoslovakia in August 1968 undermined those hopes. The US Senate voted in October 1968 to delay ratification, and key countries such as Italy, Israel, and the FRG refused to sign the treaty. As Richard M. Nixon succeeded Johnson as US president, the fate of the NPT was uncertain.

The Nixon administration was ambivalent toward both the NPT and the issue of nuclear proliferation in general. A briefing paper for Nixon argued that there were cases where "independent nuclear weapons capability might be desirable."[34] A National Security Council (NSC) memo pointed out that, regarding the NPT, the "problems with the FRG are under-stated."[35] A Kissinger aide claimed that "Henry believed that it was good to spread nuclear weapons around the world" and argued Japan and Israel would be better off with atomic weapons.[36] The president himself argued "treaties don't necessarily get us very much" and if countries wanted to "make their own weapons," they could "abrogate the treaty without sanction."[37] In the end, while the United States would continue to support the treaty, Nixon made it clear that he would "not pressure other nations to follow suit, especially the FRG."[38]

Despite this ambivalence, the Nixon administration formally presented the NPT to the US Senate for advice and consent on February 5, 1969. After a vigorous internal debate and the victory of Willy Brandt's Social Democratic

34 "Summary of NPT Issues Paper," January 28, 1969, 1–2, box H-019, NSC Meetings File, Nixon Presidential Materials Project (NPMP), USNA (materials moving to Yorba Linda, California).
35 "Memorandum: H. Sonnenfeldt to H. Kissinger," January 27, 1969, box 366, NSF, NPMP, USNA.
36 Maddock, *The Nth Country Conundrum*, 523.
37 "Minutes of the National Security Council," January 29, 1969, 6, box H-12, NSC Draft minutes, NPMP, USNA.
38 "List of Actions Resulting from Meeting of the National Security Council," January 29, 1969, box H-019, NSC Meetings File, NPMP, USNA.

Party in national elections, West Germany signaled its intention to sign the treaty in November 1969. The last major hurdle was cleared for both the United States and the Soviet Union to sign, and both superpowers deposited the treaty on March 5, 1970.

The simple act of negotiating and signing a treaty did not, in itself, end the threat of nuclear proliferation. There were immediate setbacks. The Nixon administration did not make non-proliferation a priority. Israel's burgeoning weapons program was ignored, as were South Africa's nascent efforts. US–French nuclear cooperation was resumed. Western European companies offered advanced nuclear technology to potential proliferators, including Argentina, Brazil, and Pakistan. India detonated a peaceful nuclear explosion in 1974, triggering considerable protest but few sanctions.

In spite of these problems, nuclear proliferation began to slow. Many potential proliferators suspended their weapons programs, and Japan, Australia, Sweden, and Egypt, among others, did not go nuclear as had been feared. Significantly, the complex and difficult NPT discussions helped spur other important arms-control negotiations. The Johnson administration pursued the so-called Outer Space Treaty, banning the militarization of space.

28. In May 1974, India became the second Third World country, after China, to successfully test a nuclear weapon. Here Indian prime minister Indira Gandhi visits the testing sites in Rajasthan. She is flanked by the defense minister, Krishna Chandra Pant (left), and Homi Sethna, chairman of the Indian Atomic Energy Commission (right).

The first regional nuclear-free zone was established in Latin America through the Treaty of Tlatelolco in February 1967. Strategic arms-control talks were initiated between the Soviet Union and the United States during the summer of 1968, culminating in Nixon and Brezhnev signing treaties in Moscow on May 26, 1972, limiting both strategic offensive and defensive nuclear weapons. While challenges remained, there was no denying the extraordinary shift in policies and attitudes against the horizontal and vertical spread of nuclear weapons that had taken place in little over a decade.

Proliferation puzzles

How did the new emphasis on non-proliferation influence Cold War global politics? And how effective was the NPT in slowing the spread of nuclear weapons? In the years since the treaty was signed, many critics have emerged and have pointed out the treaty's weaknesses. According to them, the original treaty did not create a rigorous enough inspections regime. Given the hopes for peaceful uses of atomic energy, not enough was done to recognize how easily civilian projects could be turned into weapons programs. Further, the treaty was inherently discriminatory, particularly against countries outside of the Cold War alliance system. The superpowers were not held to their promise to reduce their nuclear arsenals and to plan for their eventual elimination. Little was done to sanction new nuclear countries, such as Israel and India.

US non-proliferation policy was often a target of sharp criticism. Close allies, like West Germany, Taiwan, and South Korea, chafed at the pressure applied on them to forgo weapons, while other geopolitical interests seemed to cause the United States to overlook Israel's and Pakistan's efforts. Although few experts fully accepted the logic of Kenneth Waltz's argument that "more may be better," many observers in the United States argued that the robust nature of nuclear deterrence made undue attention to nuclear proliferation misguided. Even after the Cold War, the United States has been unwilling to deemphasize the role of nuclear weapons in its national security strategy. While countries including India, Russia, Israel, and even China have moved toward full or modified promises to eschew the first use of nuclear weapons, the United States still maintains its right to do so if it sees fit. These and other positions have caused critics to argue that US nuclear strategy undermined the goal of nuclear non-proliferation.

What they ignore is how difficult it is to construct an effective global nuclear non-proliferation regime that is not riddled with puzzles and paradoxes. As a 1964 Hudson Institute report explained, "retarding the spread of nuclear weapons" is a process where "the best may be the enemy of the good." The study continued, an "attempt to get 'everything' may risk achieving substantially less than it would be possible with more modest ambitions."[39] Most everyone believed that nuclear non-proliferation was an admirable principle. But constructing policies that generated worldwide support for it was difficult. How could states be convinced to forgo the perceived prestige and national security advantages that came with becoming a nuclear power?

What the critics have failed to fully understand is that any successful nuclear non-proliferation policy would be burdened with paradoxes and contradictions. Consider the US position toward nuclear strategy, non-first use, and anti-ballistic missile defenses as it related to its efforts to prevent nuclear proliferation among its allies. On the one hand, the United States needed to emphasize "the political unattractiveness of nuclear weapons, to convince populations that they are ugly, dirty, immoral, illegal, dangerous, sickening and not very useful." On the other hand, US policies undermined this message. "As one US expert noted at the time, having a nuclear sub visit Tokyo is like bringing a shiny new motorcycle home to show it off to your teenage son, while trying to convince him that he doesn't want one."[40]

From Japan's perspective, however, the issue was not quite so simple. Japan was near two enemies who had nuclear weapons, the Soviet Union and China. If it was going to give up its own weapons, Japan needed a serious and credible commitment that the United States would protect it if attacked, even if it meant using nuclear weapons. This commitment could hardly be credible in the face of much larger Soviet and Chinese conventional forces without a robust nuclear capability. According to this logic, if the United States reduced its nuclear forces, it might actually encourage proliferation. A smaller US strategic force increased the incentives for small countries to become a "first rank nuclear power."[41] To keep Japan nonnuclear, a "clearly superior US nuclear capability in Asia" had to be maintained.[42] The United States also needed to be willing to use its nuclear weapons first to protect allies surrounded by nuclear adversaries that also had conventional military superiority.

39 Hudson Institute, "Measures for Retarding the Spread of Nuclear Weapons: Proposal to the Arms Control and Disarmament Agency," March 13, 1964, 5, box 5, NSF, LBJL.
40 R. Fisher to S. Keeney, November 5, 1964, Box 5, NSF, LBJL.
41 "Problems Concerning Alternative Courses of Action," undated, 3, box 1, Committee on Nuclear Proliferation, NSF, LBJL.
42 "Japan's Prospects in the Nuclear Weapons Field: Proposed US Courses of Action," June 24, 1965, box 24, lot 67D2, RG 59, USNA.

Deploying strategic missile defenses would also have uncertain effects on nuclear proliferation. Building an ABM system might accelerate an arms race between the United States and the Soviet Union. On the other hand, a US ABM deployment could "decrease U.S. vulnerabilities to possible Chinese threats of attack and thereby enhance the credibility of our [US] commitments to Japan and other friendly nations."[43] A limited ABM could be justified so that "those countries which fear the growth of Chinese nuclear capabilities should not feel that their only alternative is to create a costly nuclear arsenal themselves."[44]

In order to prevent proliferation, the superpowers had to guarantee allies and potential friends that they would come to their defense if attacked. Since few potential proliferators outside of the Eastern bloc were interested in any sort of guarantee from the Soviet Union, the burden fell upon the United States to craft military policies that would reassure countries such as Japan, West Germany, Australia, Indonesia, South Korea, and Taiwan that they could live safely within the new non-proliferation regime. This led to expensive deployments of forces abroad, and justified the buildup of US nuclear capabilities. Security guarantees, however, threatened to pull the United States into regional conflicts it might have otherwise avoided.

What about states that did not want or trust superpower security commitments? And what factors motivated states whose primary concern was *not* the Cold War – diverse countries ranging from Argentina to Sweden? Much more historical research remains to be done to fully understand why some states forgo nuclear weapons while others embrace them.

The Cold War nuclear proliferation legacy

Despite great progress, we still know less than we would like about why states develop nuclear weapons and what policies are most effective at preventing nuclear proliferation. As we have seen, efforts during the Cold War to halt the spread of atomic weapons pulled policy in different, often contradictory, directions. Despite some failings and continuing puzzles and paradoxes, however, a strong case can be made that the NPT was a watershed event in international affairs with two major consequences. Negotiated between two ideological enemies, the NPT was a key part, for better or worse, of the

43 "Contingency Paper on the Arms Control Considerations of a U.S. ABM Deployment Decision," August 25, 1967, box 231, Country File: USSR, NSF, LBJL.
44 "Telegram from the Secretary of State to U.S. Embassy in Paris," September 14, 1967, box 1, NSF, Committee File, LBJL.

stabilization of power politics that began with the Limited Test-Ban Treaty in 1963 and was fully manifested in the Helsinki Accords of 1975. This comes through clearly in the Gilpatric committee deliberations. Neither the Soviets nor the Americans alone could halt proliferation, but "both ha[d] much to lose" if "lesser powers" acquired nuclear capabilities. The Soviet Union and the United States had "multiple, overlapping interests" that suggested the "timeliness of early steps to achieve an essentially bi-polar entente, resembling the Concert of Europe, the informal coalition based on limited mutuality of interests that kept the peace in Europe for more than half of the nineteenth century."[45] The need to stem nuclear proliferation brought these bitter enemies together and helped give rise to détente.[46]

Equally important, the treaty made nuclear non-proliferation a shared value of the international community in the same way human rights, anti-terrorism, and maintaining a stable international economic order have come to be seen as globally shared interests. While hard to quantify, it is clear that this global norm has helped slow (and in some cases, reverse) nuclear proliferation over the past few decades. In 1961, the famous strategist Hermann Kahn claimed that with "the kind of technology that is likely to be available in 1969, it may literally turn out that a Hottentot, an educated and technical Hottentot it is true, would be able to make bombs."[47] What is striking, however, is how wrong the predictions made by Kahn, President Kennedy, and others turned out. Writing in 1985, the National Intelligence Council noted that for "almost thirty years the Intelligence Community has been writing about which nations might next get the bomb." While "some proliferation of nuclear explosive capabilities and other major proliferation-related developments have taken place in the past two decades," they did not have "the damaging, systemwide impacts that the Intelligence Community generally anticipated they would."[48] Over time, non-proliferation, and not nuclear possession, has developed into a well-respected global norm. We have witnessed an extraordinary shift in attitudes about nuclear weapons from the earliest days of the nuclear age.

This points to another important but largely unrecognized fact: the history of the nuclear age is not the same thing as the history of the Cold War. While

---

45 "A Comparable Rationale for Course III (and Beyond)", box 10, PPRG, JFKL.
46 See Jussi M. Hanhimäki's chapter and Marc Trachtenberg's chapter in this volume.
47 "Into the Open," *Time Magazine*, January 2, 1961, www.time.com/time/magazine/article/0,9171,895206,00.html.
48 National Intelligence Council, "The Dynamics of Nuclear Proliferation: Balance of Incentives and Constraints," September 1985, www.foia.cia.gov/docs/DOC_0000453458/0000453458_0001.gif.

they obviously overlapped and interacted, different dynamics were at play in each arena. By the mid-1960s, the goal of non-proliferation at times made the Soviets and Americans less ideological rivals than realistic partners in what often appeared to be a concert or condominium to manage the most important military question in world politics. And when states like Britain, France, China, Israel, India, South Africa, and Pakistan developed nuclear weapons, and others ranging from Brazil to Taiwan toyed with weapons programs, Cold War considerations were only one factor, and often not the most important motivation. Even though the nuclear programs that have caused the most worry in the past decade, those of Iran, Iraq, Libya, and North Korea, began during the Cold War, the persistence of these programs after the disappearance of the Soviet Union reveals other motives were at play.

It is difficult to untangle the relationship between the two parallel drivers of postwar world politics, the Cold War and the nuclear revolution. Most historians would accept that no account of the Cold War is complete without understanding the influence of the bomb on world politics. But the history of the nuclear age reveals a narrative that is both part of yet outside the story of the US–Soviet rivalry. The Cold War is long finished, but the drama of the nuclear age continues, with untold, uncertain endings.

20

Intelligence in the Cold War

CHRISTOPHER ANDREW

Intelligence is probably the least understood aspect of the Cold War, sometimes sensationalised, often ignored. It is also the only profession in which a fictional character is far better known than any real practitioner, alive or dead. Cold War intelligence was, of course, not usually as exciting as the career of James Bond. Like all forms of information, the impact of intelligence is more often gradual than dramatic – though it does from time to time suddenly produce such spectacular revelations as the Soviet acquisition of the plans of the first US atomic bomb or the Soviet construction of missile sites in Cuba in 1962. Sometimes intelligence adds information of real importance to what is available from more conventional sources. Sometimes it adds little or nothing. But, whether intelligence is used, abused or simply ignored, historians of the Cold War can never afford to disregard it. The many studies of policy-making in East and West which fail to take intelligence into account are at best incomplete, at worst distorted.

Signals intelligence (SIGINT)

The starting point for any attempt to assess the role of intelligence during the Cold War is to recognise how much we still do not know. Signals intelligence is perhaps the prime example. Though SIGINT was far more voluminous than intelligence from human sources (HUMINT), it is still entirely absent from most histories of the Cold War. At the end of the Second World War, GCHQ (the British SIGINT agency) wanted to keep secret indefinitely the wartime ULTRA intelligence derived from breaking the German Enigma and other high-grade enemy ciphers but expected the secret to be uncovered within a few years.[1] It was already well known that the British cryptanalysts had broken

---

1 Richard J. Aldrich, *The Hidden Hand: Britain, America and Cold War Secret Intelligence* (London: John Murray, 2001), 1–3.

German ciphers during the First World War, and GCHQ believed that the clues to the even greater British code-breaking successes of the Second World War were too obvious for historians to miss. But, until the revelation of the ULTRA secret in 1973, historians remained so baffled by SIGINT that the clues were overlooked.

The study of the Cold War nowadays suffers from much the same neglect of SIGINT that diminished and sometimes distorted our understanding of Second World War intelligence a generation ago. Though most historians acknowledge the wartime significance of SIGINT, their interest in it usually ceases at V-J Day. None of Harry S. Truman's biographers, for example, mentions that he was so impressed by his brief experience of the wartime British–American SIGINT alliance that on 12 September 1945 he approved its peacetime continuation – and in so doing profoundly influenced the development of the Special Relationship. Throughout the Cold War (and beyond) the United States and Britain shared more secrets than any two independent powers had ever shared before. Their SIGINT accords of March 1946 and June 1948 (the latter known as the UKUSA agreement), which also involved Australia, Canada and New Zealand, still lack their rightful place in the historiography of the Cold War.[2] Though studies of Cold War US foreign policy invariably mention the Central Intelligence Agency (CIA), there is rarely any reference to the National Security Agency (NSA). At the end of the Cold War, President George Bush (the elder) publicly acknowledged that the SIGINT produced by NSA was a 'prime factor' in his foreign policy.[3] The small circle of those in the know in Washington used to joke that NSA stood for 'No Such Agency'. Most histories of the Cold War reflect a similar amnesia.

The amnesiac approach to the role of SIGINT has distorted understanding of the Cold War in significant ways. That point is illustrated by the very first Cold War SIGINT to be declassified: the approximately 3,000 intercepted Soviet intelligence and other telegrams (code-named VENONA) for the period 1939 to 1948, partially decrypted by American and British code-breakers in the late 1940s and early 1950s. The decrypts have large implications for American political history as well as for Soviet–American relations. Through his outrageous exaggerations and inventions, Senator Joseph McCarthy became, albeit unintentionally, the KGB's most successful Cold War agent of influence, making most American liberals sceptical of the significance of the Soviet intelligence offensive against the United States – despite its success in stealing the plans of the first atomic bomb. The evidence of Elizabeth Bentley and Whittaker Chambers, who had worked as couriers for Soviet intelligence, was widely but mistakenly ridiculed. VENONA provides compelling corroboration for both.[4]

Remarkably, the successes of US code-breakers at the beginning of the Cold War were far better known by their British allies than by the Truman administration. The VENONA secret was shared with Clement Attlee, the British prime minister, and all three British intelligence agencies but, due chiefly to the obstinacy of J. Edgar Hoover, not with President Truman or, until November 1952, the Central Intelligence Agency. When Kim Philby was posted to Washington as the representative of the British Secret Intelligence Service (SIS) in 1949, he was thus told that he could discuss VENONA with the Federal Bureau of Investigation (FBI), but not with the CIA. Philby obeyed instructions not to mention the decrypts to the Agency but revealed them to his KGB case officer. Thanks to Philby and a Soviet agent in US SIGINT, William Weisband, Iosif Stalin was thus better informed than Truman about early Cold War American cryptanalysis.[5]

Though the highest-grade cipher systems of the Cold War were less vulnerable than those of the Second World War, the volume of SIGINT generated by both Soviet intelligence and the UKUSA alliance greatly increased. Much of the diplomatic traffic of Third World states was vulnerable to cryptanalysts in both East and West. On the eve of the 1956 Suez crisis, the British foreign secretary, Selwyn Lloyd, formally congratulated GCHQ on both the 'volume' and 'excellence' of its decrypts 'relating to all the countries of the Middle East. I am writing to let you know how valuable we have found this material ...'[6] Soviet cryptanalysts seem to have been equally successful. There was probably never a year during the Cold War, at least from the 1950s onwards, when the KGB sent less than 100,000 diplomatic decrypts to the Central Committee

---

4 Though declassification of the VENONA decrypts began only in 1995, their existence and some of their contents had been known a decade earlier but ignored by most US historians. On the controversies aroused by VENONA since declassification, far greater in the US than in the UK, see John Earl Haynes and Harvey Klehr, *In Denial: Historians, Communism and Espionage* (San Francisco: Encounter, 2003).

5 Christopher Andrew, 'The VENONA Secret', in K. G. Robertson (ed.), *War, Resistance and Intelligence: Essays in Honour of M. R. D. Foot* (Barnsley: Pen and Sword, 1999).

6 Selwyn Lloyd to E. M. Jones (Director, GCHQ), 30 September 1956, AIR 20/10621, UK National Archives, Kew, Richmond.

(chiefly, no doubt, to its International Department). By 1967, it was able to decrypt 152 cipher systems employed by a total of seventy-two states.[7]

The KGB owed much of its SIGINT success to its recruitment of cipher clerks and other personnel in foreign embassies in Moscow. Few, if any, embassies escaped some degree of KGB penetration. The US embassy was penetrated virtually continuously from the beginning of Soviet–American diplomatic relations in 1933 until at least the mid-1960s. Remarkably, most studies of US–Soviet relations continue to take no account of the haemorrhage of diplomatic secrets from the Moscow embassy for more than thirty years. Though security at the US embassy improved after the mid-1960s, that at many other Moscow embassies did not. Soviet SIGINT throughout the Cold War was also assisted by the penetration of foreign ministries in the West as well as the Third World. In 1945, the KGB's Paris residency recruited a 23-year-old cipher officer, codenamed JOUR, in the Quai d'Orsay who was still active in the early 1980s. DARIO in the Italian Foreign Ministry had an almost equally long career as both KGB agent and talent-spotter. The incomplete evidence currently available suggests that, at a number of periods during the Cold War, France and Italy were conducting towards the Soviet Union something akin to open diplomacy. In 1983, for example, the French embassy in Moscow discovered that bugs in its teleprinters had been relaying all incoming and outgoing telegrams to the KGB for the past six years.[8]

Imagery intelligence (IMINT)

Intelligence operations served, in different ways, both to stabilise and to desta-bilise the Cold War. Perhaps the most important stabilising factor was the development of IMINT. Studies of the Cold War frequently forget the truth of Dwight D. Eisenhower's dictum that intelligence on 'what the Soviets *did not* have' was often as important as information on what they did. Ignorance of a feared opponent invariably leads to an overestimation of the opponent's strength. Shortage of reliable intelligence in the early 1950s generated the dangerous American myth of the 'bomber gap', soon followed by that of the 'missile gap' – the delusion that the Soviet Union was increasingly

7 Raymond L Garthoff, 'The KGB Reports to Gorbachev', *Intelligence and National Security*, 11, 2 (1996), 228.
8 Christopher Andrew and Vasili Mitrokhin, *The Mitrokhin Archive: The KGB in Europe and the West* (London: Allen Lane / Penguin, 1999; published in the United States as *The Sword and the Shield* by Basic Books, New York). On DARIO, see the additional information in the Italian edition, *L'Archivio Mitrokhin* (Milan: Rizzoli, 1999), 693–94.

29. U2 spy plane in flight. The U2 overflights of Soviet territory started in 1956 and delivered critical intelligence about the military buildup of the USSR.

out-producing the United States in both long-range bombers and interconti-nental ballistic missiles (ICBMs). In 1955, US Air Force intelligence estimates calculated that by the end of the decade the Soviet Long-Range Air Force would be more powerful than the US Strategic Air Command, whose head, General Curtis LeMay, speculated irresponsibly about the possibility of a pre-emptive strike to prevent the Soviet Union achieving nuclear superiority.

The ability of both superpowers by the middle years of the Cold War to monitor each other's nuclear strike force was crucially dependent on a revolution in imagery intelligence, which began with the construction of the U-2, the world's first high-altitude spy-plane, fitted with the world's highest resolution cameras. U-2 missions over the Soviet Union, which began in 1956, followed four years later by the launch of the first spy satellites, convinced the Eisenhower administration that the Soviet nuclear strike force was not in fact overtaking that of the United States.[9] Without the IMINT revolution, US policy to the Soviet Union would doubtless have continued to be confused by destabilising myths about the extent of Soviet nuclear capability. The course of the 1962 Cuban missile crisis would also have been different. But for IMINT

9 Andrew, *For The President's Eyes Only*, chs. 6, 7.

from U-2s (whose interpretation owed much to top-secret documents supplied by the British–American agent in Moscow, Oleg Penkovskii),[10] Nikita S. Khrushchev would almost certainly have achieved his ambition of concealing the construction of the missile bases until they were fully operational. The world would have come even closer to thermonuclear warfare.

After the missile crisis, the intelligence available to both East and West on the extent and deployment of their opponents' nuclear strike force became an essential element in stabilising the Cold War arms race. Without what were euphemistically termed 'national technical means' (NTMs), based on a combination of IMINT and SIGINT, verification of the arms-control and arms-limitation agreements of the later Cold War would have been impossible. The crucial importance of NTMs was explicitly recognised by the START treaty of 1989, which cut strategic nuclear arsenals by about 30 per cent and required both the United States and the Soviet Union 'not to interfere with the national technical means of verification of the other Party' and 'not to use concealment measures that impede verification by national technical means'. A protocol laid down detailed conditions designed to ensure that each side was able to monitor unhindered the other's missile telemetry.[11]

Covert action

The intelligence operations that did most to embitter, rather than to stabilise, the Cold War involved the use of 'covert action': secret attempts to manipulate the course of events by methods ranging from bribing opinion-formers to paramilitary operations. Covert action played a central role in the establishment of the Soviet bloc in Eastern and Central Europe. The East German Communist leader, Walter Ulbricht, announced to his inner circle after returning to Berlin from exile in Moscow on 30 April 1945, 'It's got to look democratic, but we must have everything under our control.' Because a democratic façade had to be preserved in all the states of the new Soviet bloc, the open use of force to exclude non-Communist parties from power had, so far as possible, to be avoided. Instead, Communist-controlled security

---

10 All the evaluations of the 'Soviet Missile Threat in Cuba' circulated to Excomm during the Cuban missile crisis carry the codeword IRONBARK – a reference to the documents on missile site construction supplied by Penkovskii which had been used in interpreting the U-2 imagery. Mary S. McAuliffe (ed.), *CIA Documents on the Cuban Missile Crisis 1962* (Washington, DC: CIA, 1992). On the missile crisis, see James G. Hershberg's chapter in this volume.

11 START Treaty, 31 July 1989, Articles IX,X; Protocol on telemetric information (text published by US Arms Control and Disarmament Agency).

services, newly created in the image of the KGB (then known as the MGB) and overseen by Soviet 'advisers', helped to implement the postwar transition to so-called 'people's democracies' by intimidation behind the scenes. Finally, the one-party Stalinist regimes, purged of all visible dissent, were legitimised as 'people's democracies' by huge and fraudulent Communist majorities in elections rigged by the new security services.[12]

The United States began covert action on a very much smaller scale with the attempt, by bribery and other 'influence operations', to ensure the defeat of the Communists in the 1948 Italian general election. (Though the Italian Communists, who themselves received secret subsidies from Moscow via the KGB, did indeed lose the election, there is no evidence that US covert action had a significant influence on the outcome.) Within five years, the Korean War and the arrival of Eisenhower in the Oval Office had turned covert action into a major arm of US foreign policy. Between 1951 and 1975, there were, according to the 1976 Church Committee report, about 900 major covert actions, as well as many minor ones.

The apparent success of covert action in overthrowing supposedly pro-Soviet regimes in Iran and Guatemala during the first eighteen months of the Eisenhower administration led it to ignore the warning signs later left by other, less successful, operations. After a failed attempt to overthrow President Sukarno of Indonesia in 1958, the future CIA deputy director for intelligence (DDI), Ray Cline, wrote prophetically:

> The weak point in covert paramilitary action is that a single misfortune that reveals CIA's connection makes it necessary for the United States either to abandon the cause completely or convert to a policy of overt military intervention.[13]

Failure to learn that lesson led to humiliation at the Bay of Pigs in April 1961. After the failed invasion by a CIA-backed 'Cuban brigade' of anti-Castro exiles, President John F. Kennedy despairingly asked his special counsel, Theodore Sorensen, 'How could I have been so stupid, to let them go ahead?' The American people, however, rallied round the flag and the president. It did not occur to Congress to investigate the debacle.

Fourteen years later, in the wake of the Vietnam War and Watergate, the mood had changed dramatically. The sensational disclosures during 1975, the

---

12 Christopher Andrew and Oleg Gordievsky, *KGB: The Inside Story of its Foreign Operations from Lenin to Gorbachev*, paperback ed. (London: Sceptre, 1991), ch. 9.
13 Ray Cline, *Secrets, Spies, and Scholars: Blueprint of the Essential CIA* (Washington, DC: Acropolis Books, 1976), 182.

'Year of Intelligence', of CIA 'dirty tricks' – among them assassination plots against foreign statesmen (notably Fidel Castro) and illegal spying on US citizens during Operation CHAOS – caused widespread public revulsion. Senator Frank Church, chairman of the Senate Select Committee set up to investigate the abuses, declared: 'The Agency may have been behaving like a rogue elephant on the rampage.' A later congressional report concluded more accurately that the CIA, 'far from being out of control', had been 'utterly responsive to the instructions of the President and the Assistant to the President for National Security Affairs'.[14]

Alongside revelations of the real abuses of US covert action, there emerged other ill-founded allegations of CIA dirty tricks which, by dint of frequent repetition, became conventional wisdom and still appear in otherwise reliable Cold War histories. President Richard M. Nixon infamously told the CIA in 1970 to try to prevent the election of Chile's Marxist president, Salvador Allende, and to make the Chilean economy 'scream'. But, as recent research by Kristian Gustafson has demonstrated, the regularly repeated claims that the CIA orchestrated Allende's overthrow (and even his death) in 1973 and the rise of his successor, General Augusto Pinochet, are mistaken. The Chilean military's *amour propre* would have been offended by the notion that they either needed the United States to run the coup for them or were taking instructions from the CIA. As Pinochet acknowledged after the coup, 'he and his colleagues, as a matter of policy, had not given any hints to the U.S. as to their developing resolve to act'.[15]

The 'Year of Intelligence' also gave rise to bestselling but woefully inaccurate conspiracy theories – chief among them the claim, which a majority of Americans believed and the KGB did its best to encourage, that the CIA was responsible for the assassination of John F. Kennedy. If the CIA had been involved in killing its own president, it was reasonable to conclude that there were no limits to which the agency would not go to subvert foreign regimes and assassinate other statesmen who had incurred its displeasure. KGB 'active measures' (covert action) successfully promoted the belief that the methods that the CIA had used to attempt to kill Castro and destabilise his regime were being employed against 'progressive' governments around the world. Indira

14 The extensive literature on US covert action includes *Final Report of the Select Committee to Study Governmental Operations with Respect to Intelligence Activities* [Church Committee], 94th Cong., 2nd Sess., Report no.755 (26, April 1976); Gregory F. Treverton, *Covert Action* (New York: Basic Books, 1987); Andrew, *For The President's Eyes Only*.
15 Kristian Gustafson, *Hostile Intent: US Covert Operations in Chile 1964–1974* (Washington, DC: Potomac Books, 2007).

Gandhi was one of a number of Third World leaders who became obsessed by supposed CIA plots against them. In November 1973, she told Fidel Castro, 'What they [the CIA] have done to Allende they want to do to me also.' Tragically, Mrs Gandhi paid more attention to the imaginary menace of a CIA-supported assassination attempt than to the real threat from her own body-guards, who murdered her in 1984.[16]

Just as the history of intelligence collection in the Cold War has been distorted by the neglect of SIGINT, so the history of covert action has been distorted by over-concentration on the US experience. No account of American Cold War policy in the Third World omits the role of the CIA. By contrast, covert action by the KGB passes almost unmentioned in most histories both of Soviet foreign relations and of developing countries. The result has been a curiously lopsided history of the secret Cold War in the Third World – the intelligence equivalent of the sound of one hand clapping. The admirable history of the Cold War by John Gaddis, for example, refers to CIA covert action in Chile, Cuba and Iran, but makes no reference to the extensive KGB operations in the same countries.

In reality, from at least the early 1960s onwards, the KGB played an even more active global role than the CIA. The belief that the Cold War could be won in the Third World transformed the agenda of Soviet intelligence. In 1961, the youthful and dynamic chairman of the KGB, Aleksandr Shelepin, won Khrushchev's support for the use of national liberation movements and other anti-imperialist forces in an aggressive new grand strategy against the 'Main Adversary' (the United States) in the Third World. Though Khrushchev was soon to replace Shelepin with the more compliant and less ambitious Vladimir Semichastnyi, the KGB's grand strategy survived. It was enthusiastically embraced by Iurii Andropov from the moment he succeeded Semichastnyi as KGB chairman in 1967.[17]

By contrast, the long-serving Soviet foreign minister, Andrei Gromyko, as his almost equally long-serving ambassador in Washington, Anatolii Dobrynin,

16 Andrew and Mitrokhin, *The Mitrokhin Archive*, ch. 14; Max Holland, 'The Lie that Linked CIA to the Kennedy Assassination', *Studies in Intelligence*, 11 (Fall/Winter 2001–2), www.cia. gov/library/center-for-thestudy-of-intelligence/csi-publications/; Christopher Andrew and Vasili Mitrokhin, *The Mitrokhin Archive II: The KGB and the World* (London: Allen Lane and Penguin, 2005; published in the United States as *The World Was Going Our Way* by Basic Books, New York), 18, 326.

17 Andrew and Mitrokhin, *The Mitrokhin Archive*, 236–37; Andrew and Mitrokhin, *The Mitrokhin Archive II*, 10, 40; Nikolai Leonov, Eugenia Fediakova and Joaquín Fermandois, 'El general Nikolai Leonov en el CEP', *Estudios Públicos*, No. 73 (1999).

recalls, had limited interest in the Third World.[18] At most of the main moments of Soviet penetration of the Third World, from the alliance with the first Communist 'bridgehead' in the western hemisphere (to quote the KGB's codename for Castro's Cuba) in the early 1960s to the final, disastrous defence of the Communist regime in Afghanistan in the 1980s, the KGB, usually supported by the International Department of the CPSU Central Committee, had greater influence than the Foreign Ministry. Castro preferred the company of Soviet intelligence officers to that of Soviet diplomats, telling the first KGB resident in Havana, Aleksandr Alekseev, that their meetings were a way of 'bypassing the Ministry of Foreign Affairs and every rule of protocol'. In 1962, largely at Castro's insistence, Alekseev replaced the unpopular Soviet ambassador. Other Latin American leaders who, like Castro, preferred KGB officers to Soviet diplomats included Allende in Chile, Juan Josè Torres in Bolivia, Omar Torrijos (not to be confused with his son) in Panama and Josè Figueres in Costa Rica. The first Soviet contact with Juan and Isabel Peron before their return to Argentina in 1973 was also made by the KGB rather than by a diplomat. KGB support for the Sandinistas began almost two decades before their conquest of power in Nicaragua in 1979.

In Asia, Africa and the Middle East, the main initiatives in Soviet policy during the 1960s and 1970s were also more frequently taken by the KGB than by the Foreign Ministry. India, the world's largest democracy, was described by General Oleg Kalugin, who in the mid-1970s was the youngest general in Soviet foreign intelligence, as 'a model of KGB infiltration of a Third World government'. As in India, most of the KGB's Third World operations led to transitory successes rather than enduring influence. That, however, was not how it seemed in the 1970s. Vladimir Kriuchkov, head of the KGB First Chief (Foreign Intelligence) Directorate (FCD) from 1974 to 1988, described the Non-Aligned Movement (NAM) as 'our natural allies'. In 1979, the NAM elected the unmistakably aligned Fidel Castro as its chairman – prompting a complaint from the KGB Havana residency that, 'F. Castro's vanity is becoming more and more noticeable.' Only a decade before the Soviet Union fell apart, the KGB leadership remained rashly optimistic about the success of its Third World operations. Andropov boasted in 1980 that the 'liberation' of Angola, Mozambique, Ethiopia and Afghanistan demonstrated that 'the

18 Anatoly Dobrynin, *In Confidence* (New York: Times Books, 1995), 404–05; cf. N. S. Leonov, *Likholete: sekretnye missii* (Moscow: Mezhdunarodnye otnosheniia, 1995), 141.

30. Iurii Vladimirovich Andropov, a water engineer born in the Caucasus, was chairman of the KGB from 1967 to 1982.

Soviet Union is not merely talking about world revolution but is actually assisting it.'[19]

Just as the KGB's enthusiasm for Castro a generation earlier had helped to launch the Soviet forward policy in the Third World, so the disastrous military intervention in Afghanistan, for which the KGB leadership bore much of the responsibility, was to bring it to an end. CIA covert action, in particular its supply of shoulder-launched Stinger missiles to the mujahedin beginning in the summer of 1986, probably hastened the Soviet withdrawal from Afghanistan. During 1986, the CIA station in Islamabad co-ordinated the provision of over 60,000 tons of arms and other supplies to the mujahedin along more than 300 infiltration routes by trucks and mules. The station chief,

19 Andrew and Mitrokhin, *The Mitrokhin Archive II*, passim.

31. William Casey, a corporate lawyer from New York, was director of US Central Intelligence from 1981 to 1987.

Milton Bearden, complained that the agency 'needed more mules than the world seemed prepared to breed'.[20]

American covert action against the Sandinista regime in Nicaragua, first authorised by President Ronald Reagan in December 1981, was far less successful than against the Russians in Afghanistan. Secret CIA support for the inept Contra guerrilla campaign against the Sandinistas was revealed by the US media and banned by Congress. Robert Gates, then the CIA DDI

20 Milton Bearden and James Risen, *The Main Enemy: The Inside Story of the CIA's Final Showdown with the KGB* (New York: Random House, 2004); quotation from p. 312; Odd Arne Westad, *The Global Cold War: Third World Interventions and the Making of Our Times*, paperback ed. (Cambridge: Cambridge University Press, 2007), 353–57, 375–77; Andrew and Mitrokhin, *The Mitrokhin Archive II*, chs. 21, 22.

(head of analysis), reported to the director of Central Intelligence, William Casey, in December 1984 that covert support for the Contras was counter-productive and would 'result in further strengthening of the regime and a Communist Nicaragua'. The only way to overthrow the Sandinistas would be overt military support for the Contras combined with US airstrikes. Neither Casey nor Reagan was willing to face up to this uncomfortable truth. The attempt to circumvent the congressional ban led the White House into the black comedy of 'Iran-Contra' – an illegal attempt to divert to the Contras the proceeds of secret arms sales to Iran. The revelation of the Iran-Contra scandal in November 1986 provoked the most serious crisis of the Reagan presidency. Vice President George Bush dictated for his diary a sequence of staccato phrases which summed up the despondency in the White House: 'The administration is in disarray – foreign policy in disarray – cover-up – Who knew what when?'[21]

Scientific and technological intelligence (S&T)

The greatest success of Soviet bloc intelligence operations in the West during the Cold War was probably in the field of scientific and technological intelligence. Though the West had little to learn from Soviet technology, the Soviet Union had an enormous amount to learn from the West and from the US defence industry in particular. The plans of the first US atomic bomb, obtained for Moscow by British and American agents at the end of the Second World War and used to construct the first Soviet atomic bomb in 1949, were perhaps the most important scientific secret ever obtained by any intelligence service. The early development of Soviet radar, rocketry and jet propulsion was also heavily dependent on the covert acquisition of technology from the West.

For most of the Cold War, the American defence industry proved much easier to penetrate than the US federal government. By 1975, FCD Directorate T of the First Chief Directorate (FCD), which ran KGB S&T operations, had seventy-seven agents and forty-two confidential contacts working against American targets. SIGINT was also a major source. The SIGINT stations within the Washington, New York and San Francisco KGB residencies succeeded in intercepting the telephone and fax communications of a series of major US companies and laboratories. The United States was a more important – and more productive – S&T target than the rest of the world

---

21 Andrew, *For The President's Eyes Only*, 478–93, 497; Westad, *The Global Cold War*, 339–48, 374.

combined. In 1980, 61.5 per cent of the S&T received by the Soviet Military-Industrial Commission (VPK), which was mainly responsible for tasking in the military field, came from American sources (some outside the United States), 10.5 per cent from West Germany, 8 per cent from France, 7.5 per cent from Britain and 3 per cent from Japan. Documents provided by a French penetration agent in Directorate T, Vladimir Vetrov, provided proof of the huge scale of Soviet S&T operations. In 1980, the VPK gave instructions for 3,617 S&T 'acquisition tasks', of which 1,085 were completed within a year, benefiting 3,396 Soviet research and development projects.[22]

During the 1980s, there were increasing attempts to use S&T in the Soviet civilian economy. Kriuchkov told a meeting of senior FCD staff in 1984 that, 'In the last two years the quantity of material and samples handed over to civilian branches of industry has increased by half as much again.' This, he claimed, had been used 'to real economic effect', particularly in energy and food production. In reality, the sclerotic nature of Soviet management made it far harder to exploit S&T in the civilian economy than in military production.[23] The Soviet armed forces, by contrast, became dependent on S&T. According to one KGB report in 1979, over half the development projects of the Soviet defence industry were based on S&T from the West. The Pentagon estimated in the early 1980s that probably 70 per cent of all current Warsaw Pact weapons systems were based in varying degrees on Western – mainly US – technology.[24] *Both* sides in the Cold War – the Warsaw Pact as well as the North Atlantic Treaty Organization (NATO) – thus depended on American know-how. Intelligence is central to understanding the military as well as the political history of the Cold War.

Political intelligence analysis

The Soviet bloc had an inbuilt advantage over the West in intelligence collection. The authoritarian and secretive political systems of one-party

22 Andrew and Mitrokhin, *The Mitrokhin Archive*, 167–70, 280–87; Philip Hanson, *Soviet Industrial Espionage: Some New Information* (London: RIIA, 1987). On Vetrov, see also Christopher Andrew and Oleg Gordievsky, *Le KGB dans le monde* (Paris: Fayard, 1990), 619–23.

23 Christopher Andrew and Oleg Gordievsky (eds.), *Instructions From the Centre: Top Secret Files on KGB Foreign Operations, 1975–1985* (London: Hodder and Stoughton, 1990); slightly revised US edition published as *Comrade Kryuchkov's Instructions: Top Secret Files on KGB Foreign Operations, 1975–1985* (Stanford, CA: Stanford University Press, 1993), 37, 49–50. East Germany found similar difficulty in exploiting Western S&T. See K. Macrakis, 'Does Effective Espionage Lead to Success in Science and Technology? Lessons from the East German Ministry of State Security', *Intelligence and National Security*, 19, 1 (2004), 52–77.

24 Andrew and Mitrokhin, *The Mitrokhin Archive*, 280–87, 723–25.

states are, by their very nature, harder to penetrate than those of democracies. Equally, however, the Soviet bloc had an inbuilt disadvantage in intelligence assessment. In all one-party states, political intelligence analysis (unlike most S&T) is necessarily distorted by the insistent demands of political correctness. It thus acts as a mechanism for reinforcing, rather than correcting, the regimes' misconceptions of the outside world. Autocrats, by and large, are told what they want to hear. One British SIS chief defined his main role as, on the contrary, to 'tell the Prime Minister what the Prime Minister does not want to know'. Western intelligence agencies, of course, have sometimes fallen far short of this exalted calling. Though the politicisation of intelligence sometimes degrades assessment even within democratic systems, it is built into the structure of all authoritarian regimes.

The lowly status of Soviet intelligence analysis is reflected in the sparse references to it in the lengthy KGB Lexicon.[25] Soviet intelligence reports throughout, and for some years after, the Stalin era usually consisted of selective compilations of raw intelligence that conformed to the views of the political leadership. Though intelligence analysis improved under Andropov, it remained seriously undeveloped by Western standards. Nikolai Leonov, who was dismayed to be appointed in 1971 as deputy head of the FCD assessment department, Service 1, estimates that it had only 10 per cent of the importance of the CIA's Directorate of Intelligence [Analysis]. Its prestige was correspondingly low. To be transferred there from an operational section, as happened to Leonov, was 'equivalent to moving from a guards regiment in the capital to the garrison in a provincial backwater'.[26] Vadim Kirpichenko, who later rose to become first deputy head of the FCD, recalls that pessimistic intelligence reports were kept from Brezhnev for fear that they 'would upset Leonid Ilyich'.[27] When Soviet policy suffered setbacks that could not be concealed, analysts knew they were on safe ground if they blamed them on imperialist machinations, particularly those of the United States, rather than failures of the Soviet system. As one FCD officer admitted at the end of the Cold War, 'In order to please our superiors, we sent in falsified and biased information, acting on the principle, "Blame everything on the Americans, and everything will be OK".'[28]

25 *KGB Lexicon: The Soviet Intelligence Officer's Handbook*, ed. and intro. by Vasiliy Mitrokhin (London: Frank Cass, 2002).
26 Leonov, *Likholete*, 120–22.
27 Interview with Vadim Kirpichenko, *Vremia Novostei*, 20 Dec. 2004; Cf. Leonov, *Likholet'e*, 129–31.
28 Andrew and Mitrokhin, *The Mitrokhin Archive*, 722; *Izvestiia*, 24 Sept. 1991.

The damaging effects of political correctness were made worse by the KGB's recurrent tendency to conspiracy theory, which in times of crisis escalated into a paranoid tendency. Looking back on the Cold War, Sir Percy Cradock, former chairman of the British Joint Intelligence Committee and Margaret Thatcher's foreign policy adviser, rightly identifed 'the main source of weakness' in the Soviet intelligence system as 'the attempt to force an excellent supply of information from the multifaceted West into an oversimplified framework of hostility and conspiracy theory'.[29]

For most of the Cold War, one of the main weaknesses of Western intelligence analysis was its failure to grasp the degree to which political correctness and conspiracy theory degraded Soviet intelligence assessment. On 29 June 1960, Shelepin, the KGB chairman, personally delivered to Khrushchev a horrifyingly alarmist assessment of American policy that may have owed something to wild speculation by General Curtis LeMay:

> In the CIA it is known that the leadership of the Pentagon is convinced of the need to initiate a war with the Soviet Union "as soon as possible" ... Right now the USA has the capability to wipe out Soviet missile bases and other military targets with its bomber forces. But over the next little while the defence forces of the Soviet Union will grow ... and the opportunity will disappear.

Khrushchev took the warning seriously. Less than a fortnight later he issued a public warning to the Pentagon 'not to forget that, as shown at the latest tests, we have rockets which can land in a preset square target 13,000 kilometres away'. In March 1962, the GRU claimed that the United States had actually taken the decision to launch a surprise nuclear attack on the Soviet Union in September 1961 but had been deterred at the last moment by Soviet nuclear tests which showed that the USSR's nuclear arsenal was more powerful than the Pentagon had realised.[30]

Had Western analysts in the early 1980s been aware of the KGB and GRU assessments of twenty years earlier, they would doubtless have been quicker to recognise the extent of Soviet fears of the Reagan administration. In a secret speech to a major KGB conference in May 1981, a visibly ailing Brezhnev denounced Reagan's policies as a serious threat to world peace. He was followed by Andropov, who was to succeed him as general secretary eighteen

---

29 Sir Percy Cradock, *Know Your Enemy: How the Joint Intelligence Committee Saw the World* (London: John Murray, 2002), ch. 17.
30 Aleksandr Fursenko and Timothy Naftali, *'One Hell of a Gamble': Khrushchev, Kennedy, Castro and the Cuban Missile Crisis, 1958–1964* (London: John Murray, 1997), 51–52, 155, 168.

months later. To the astonishment of most of the audience, the KGB chairman announced that, by decision of the Politburo, the KGB and GRU were for the first time to collaborate in a global intelligence operation, code-named RYAN – a newly devised acronym for *Raketno-iadernoe napadenie* ('Nuclear Missile Attack'). RYAN's purpose was to collect intelligence on the presumed, but non-existent, plans of the Reagan administration and its NATO allies to launch a nuclear first strike against the Soviet Union.[31] 'Not since the end of the Second World War', Andropov informed foreign residencies, 'has the international situation been as explosive as it is now.'[32] As Brezhnev's successor in November 1982, Andropov retained control over the KGB; his most frequent visitors were senior intelligence officers. Throughout his term as general secretary, RYAN remained the first priority of Soviet foreign intelligence. For several years Moscow succumbed to what its ambassador in Washington, Anatolii Dobrynin, described as a 'paranoid interpretation' of Reagan's policy.[33]

Intelligence operations in the rest of the Soviet bloc were distorted by the requirement to assist Operation RYAN. Markus Wolf, the able, long-serving head of the East German Hauptverwaltung Aufklärung (HVA: GDR foreign intelligence service), found KGB liaison officers 'obsessed' by RYAN and the threat of a NATO first strike:

> The HVA was ordered to uncover any Western plans for such a surprise attack, and we formed a special staff and situation centre, as well as emergency command centres, to do this ... Like most intelligence people, I found these war games a burdensome waste of time, but these orders were no more open to discussion than other orders from above.[34]

Like Wolf, most KGB residencies in Western capitals were less alarmist than Andropov and KGB headquarters. When Oleg Gordievskii, who had been recruited as a British agent in the KGB in 1974, joined the London residency in June 1982, he found all his colleagues in Line PR (political intelligence) sceptical about Operation RYAN. None, however, was willing to risk his career by challenging the Centre's assessment. RYAN thus created a vicious circle of intelligence collection and assessment. Residencies were, in effect, ordered to search out alarming information. The Centre was duly

---

31 Andrew and Gordievsky (eds.), *Instructions from the Centre*, ch. 4.
32 Oleg Kalugin, *My 32 Years in Intelligence and Espionage against the West* (London: Smith Gryphon, 1994), 302–03. Kalugin considered Andropov's cable 'paranoid'.
33 Dobrynin, *In Confidence*, 523.
34 Markus Wolf (with Anne McElvoy), *Man without a Face: The Autobiography of Communism's Greatest Spymaster* (London: Jonathan Cape, 1997), 222.

alarmed by what they supplied and demanded more. The Washington resident, Stanislav Androsov, among others, was at pains to provide it. Alarm within the Centre reached a climax during the NATO exercise 'Able Archer 83', held in November 1983 to practise nuclear release procedures. For a time the KGB leadership was haunted by the fear that the exercise might be intended as cover for a real nuclear first strike. Some FCD officers stationed in the West were by now more concerned by the alarmism in the Centre than by the threat of a Western surprise attack.[35]

The first reliable intelligence on RYAN to reach the West came from Oleg Gordievskii. Following his posting to London, Gordievskii was able to supply not merely oral information but also RYAN directives from the Centre which he regularly smuggled out of the residency.[36] Though his case officer, who later rose to become chief of SIS, was initially 'astonished and scarcely able to believe' the intelligence he provided,[37] it was quickly accepted as of vital importance by the prime minister, Margaret Thatcher, and her foreign secretary, Sir Geoffrey Howe, as well as by the British intelligence community. When the intelligence was shared with Washington, however, a major difference of view quickly emerged. On the British side, as Howe wrote later, during Able Archer 'Gordievsk[y] left us in no doubt of the extraordinary but genuine Russian fear of real-life nuclear strike'.[38] Most CIA analysts disagreed – probably because of the difficulty they found in crediting the role of conspiracy theory in Soviet intelligence analysis.[39] Later reassessment of the intelligence from Gordievskii and other sources led to a drastic revision of that conclusion. Robert Gates writes in his memoirs:

> Information about the peculiar and remarkably skewed frame of mind of Soviet leaders during those times that has emerged since the collapse of the Soviet Union makes me think there is a good chance – with all of the other events in 1983 – that they really felt a NATO attack was at least possible ...

US intelligence had failed to grasp the true extent of their anxieties. A re-examination of the whole episode by the president's Foreign Intelligence

---

35 Andrew and Gordievsky, *KGB*, 582–605; Andrew and Gordievsky (eds.), *Instructions from the Centre*, ch. 4; Yuri Shvets, *Washington Station: My Life as a KGB Spy in America* (New York: Simon & Schuster, 1994), 29, 74–75.

36 Some of the KGB RYAN directives are published in Andrew and Gordievsky (eds.), *Instructions from the Centre*, ch. 4.

37 Oleg Gordievsky, *Next Stop Execution: The autobiography of Oleg Gordievsky* (London: Macmillan, 1995), 262.

38 Geoffrey Howe, *Conflict of Loyalty* (London: Macmillan, 1994), 349–50.

39 'Implications of Recent Soviet Military-Political Activities', Special National Intelligence Estimate (SNIE) 11-10-84/JX.

Advisory Board in 1990 concluded that the intelligence community's confidence
that this had all been Soviet posturing for political effect was misplaced.[40]

There is no better evidence of the extent of Mikhail Gorbachev's 'new
thinking' in foreign policy after he became general secretary in March 1985
than his dissatisfaction with the bias of the KGB's political reporting. In
December 1985, Viktor Chebrikov, KGB chairman since 1982, summoned a
meeting of the KGB leadership to discuss a stern memorandum from
Gorbachev 'on the impermissibility of distortions of the factual state of affairs
in messages and informational reports sent to the Central Committee of the
CPSU and other ruling bodies' – a damning indictment of its previous political
correctness. The conferees sycophantically agreed on the need to avoid
sycophantic reporting and declared the duty of the KGB both at home and
abroad to fulfil 'the Leninist requirement that we need only the whole truth'.[41]
According to Leonid Shebarshin, who succeeded Kriuchkov as head of foreign
intelligence in 1988, the FCD 'no longer had to present its views in a falsely
positive light'[42] – though it is difficult to believe that all its officers instantly
threw off the habits of a lifetime.

Intelligence asymmetry in East and West

In KGB jargon, the United States was the 'Main Adversary' (*glavnyi protivnik*) –
just as the CIA regarded its main adversary as the Soviet Union. Unlike
Western intelligence agencies, however, the KGB had not one but two 'Main
Adversaries'. The second was what the KGB called 'ideological sabotage' –
anything which threatened to undermine the authority of the Communist one-
party states in and beyond the Soviet bloc.

The asymmetry between the priorities of the intelligence communities in
East and West reflected their radically different roles within the states they
served. The Cheka, founded six weeks after the Bolshevik Revolution, and
its successor agencies were central to the functioning of the Soviet system in
ways that intelligence communities never were to the government of Western
states. Their fundamental role within the one-party state was to monitor and
repress dissent in all its forms, whether by violence or more sophisticated
systems of social control involving huge surveillance networks. Informers in

40 Robert Gates, *From the Shadows: The Ultimate Insider's Story of Five Presidents and How
  they Won the Cold War* (New York: Simon & Schuster, 1997), 273.
41 Garthoff, 'The KGB Reports to Gorbachev', 226–27.
42 Interview with Leonid Shebarshin, *Daily Telegraph*, 1 December 1992.

the German Democratic Republic were seven times more numerous even than in Nazi Germany. The KGB and its intelligence allies played a central role in the suppression of the Hungarian uprising of 1956, the crushing of the Prague Spring in 1968, the invasion of Afghanistan in 1979 and the pressure on the Polish Communist regime to strangle the democratic Solidarity movement in 1981. More of the KGB's elite corps of illegals (deep-cover intelligence personnel posing as foreign nationals) were used to penetrate dissident movements within the Soviet bloc than were ever deployed against the United States or other Western targets during the Cold War.

The war against the dissidents was a major part of KGB foreign as well as domestic operations. Indeed, some of the most important of the foreign operations were jointly devised by senior officers of the First Chief and Fifth Directorates, responsible respectively for foreign intelligence and countering ideological subversion. Early in 1977, for example, no less than thirty-two 'active measures' designed to discredit and demoralise the leading dissident, Andrei Sakharov ('Public Enemy Number One', as Andropov described him), and his wife, Elena Bonner, were either in progress or about to commence both within the Soviet Union and abroad. Seeking to discredit every well-known dissident who managed to get to the West was a major KGB priority – irrespective of whether the dissident's profession had, in Western terms, anything to do with politics at all. At the world chess championship in the Philippines in 1978, when the dissident Viktor Korchnoi committed the unforgivable sin of challenging the orthodox Anatolii Karpov, the KGB sent eighteen operations officers to try to ensure his defeat.[43]

Only when the vast apparatus of Soviet social control began to be dismantled under Gorbachev did the full extent of the KGB's importance to the survival of the USSR become clear. The manifesto of the hard-line leaders of the August 1991 coup, of which the KGB chairman, Vladimir Kriuchkov, was the chief organiser, implicitly acknowledged that the relaxation of the campaign against ideological subversion had shaken the foundations of the one-party state: 'Authority at all levels has lost the confidence of the population ... The country has in effect become ungovernable.' Crucial to the change of mood was declining respect for the intimidatory power of the KGB, which had hitherto been able to strangle any Moscow demonstration at birth. The most striking symbol of the collapse of the August coup was the toppling of the giant statue of the founder of the Cheka, Feliks Dzerzhinskii, from its plinth in the middle of the square outside KGB headquarters. A large crowd, which

43 Andrew and Mitrokhin, *The Mitrokhin Archive*, chs. 15, 16, 19, 20, 31.

a few years earlier would never have dared to assemble, encircled the Lubyanka and cheered enthusiastically as 'Iron Feliks' was borne away, dangling in a noose suspended from a huge crane supplied by the Moscow city government.

Intelligence and the Cold War

The Cold War was a global conflict between intelligence agencies as well as governments. From the construction of the Soviet bloc in the aftermath of the Second World War to the war in Afghanistan and US operations against the Sandinistas in the 1980s, the course of that global conflict cannot be adequately interpreted without an understanding of its intelligence dimension. Attempting to resolve the most difficult problem posed by the Cold War – why it did not end in hot war – also requires an understanding of the stabilising role of secret 'national technical means' based on a combination of IMINT and SIGINT. There were major differences, however, between intelligence assessment, as well as the priority given to scientific and technological intelligence, in East and West. Intelligence communities also had a far more central role in the one-party states of the Soviet bloc than in Western democracies, even at their most irresponsible. At the end of the Cold War, the speed of the collapse of the Soviet system took almost all observers (including Western intelligence agencies) by surprise. What now seems most remarkable, however, is less the sudden disintegration of the Soviet Union at the end of 1991 than its survival for almost seventy-five years. Without the KGB's immense system of surveillance and social control, the Soviet era would have been significantly shorter. The KGB's most enduring achievement was thus to sustain the longest-lasting one-party state of the twentieth century. By postponing the collapse of the Soviet Union, the KGB also prolonged the Cold War.

21

Reading, viewing, and tuning in to the Cold War

NICHOLAS J. CULL

For many years the historiography of Cold War culture was dominated by two rather parochial clichés. The first held that studying the Cold War and culture meant discussing the impact of the McCarthy-era purges on cultural production in the United States; the second, that it meant the study of films or literature with explicit Cold War content. Recent scholarship has taken a much broader approach. Within the United States, the Cold War has provided the dominant framework for thinking about culture in the 1950s. President Harry S. Truman's notion of containment is now as readily applied to the lives of American women of the era as to their government's relations with the Soviet Union.[1] Beyond this, the cultural Cold War has emerged as a major concern of international history. The literature, film, and broadcasting of the Cold War period is at last being understood by historians, as it was by protagonists, not only as a product of the politics of the era but also as a front in the Cold War as real as that which divided Berlin, bisected Korea, or ran through the straits of Miami. With this in mind, this chapter will consider, first, how the governments of East and West shaped culture during the Cold War and, then, how writers, filmmakers, and broadcasters responded to the conflict. The analysis will focus on the middle years of the conflict, but the conclusion will examine the ways in which these influences played out in the 1980s.

The Soviet propaganda machine

By 1962, the world had become used to the cultural manifestations of the clash between East and West.[2] International exchanges of exhibitions, intellectuals,

I am grateful to Tony Shaw and James Chapman for their feedback on and engagement with this chapter.

1 For example, see Elaine Tyler May, *Homeward Bound: American Families in the Cold War Era* (New York: Basic Books, 1988).
2 See Jessica C. E. Gienow-Hecht's chapter in volume I.

and artists, and the intense competition to boost one's own prestige and diminish that of the enemy had transformed culture into war by other means. The old professionals in the culture game were the Soviets. The Soviet Union had been exporting its political culture since founding the state-run International Book Company (known by its Russian abbreviation as *Mezhkniga*) in 1923 and had followed it up by creating the All-Union Association for Cultural Relations with Foreign Countries (*Vsesoiuznoe obshchestvo kulturnykh sviazei s zagranitsei*, known by the acronym VOKS) in 1925. The Communist International (also known as the Third International) had sought to coordinate the leadership of Communist parties around the world, though purges crippled this organization long before Iosif Stalin formally closed it down as a gesture of goodwill to his wartime allies.

In the postwar period, Moscow's international political propaganda was the province of the Department of Propaganda and Agitation within the Communist Party of the Soviet Union and of COMINFORM (the Communist Information Bureau set up in 1947 to coordinate the efforts of local Communist parties around the world). The system had its problems. The competing bureaucracies struggled to settle the issue of the role of the Ministry of Foreign Affairs. In 1953, the ministry assumed direction of VOKS through a new Department for Ties with Foreign Communist Parties. In 1956, Nikita Khrushchev launched a major cultural offensive around the world, which taken alongside his simultaneous denunciation of Stalin, looks rather like a re-branding campaign by a twenty-first century multinational corporation. He dissolved COMINFORM and, in 1957, replaced VOKS with the Union of Soviet Societies of Friendship and Cultural Relations with Foreign Countries (SSOD) outside the foreign ministry. He also created a new State Committee for Cultural Ties (GKKS) to administer cultural relations with all states, rather than just other Communist countries. This structure was further complicated by the presence of a host of front organizations reaching out in the name of youth or peace or both. The final player in Moscow's propaganda line-up throughout the period was the KGB, which covertly subsidized sympathetic newspapers across the developing world and planted disinformation stories.[3]

In the 1960s, the Soviet state added another layer of international propaganda organizations. In 1961, Moscow created an international press agency, Novosti (News), in order to extend the reach of its version of Soviet and foreign news. Three years later, the SSOD, the Soviet Writers', Journalists',

---

3 Frederick C. Barghoorn, *Soviet Foreign Propaganda* (Princeton, NJ: Princeton University Press, 1964), 238.

and Composers' Unions, and Novosti launched a new international radio station called Radio Peace and Progress that purported to be independent of the government. Few overseas listeners seem to have been persuaded. The structures of Soviet propaganda were not stable for long. In 1967, Leonid Brezhnev replaced GKKS with a Department of Cultural Relations within the Foreign Ministry, but the pace of Soviet cultural outreach did not slacken.[4]

Soviet initiatives in the middle years of the Cold War included displays of technology, the export of certain prestige motion pictures, the mass production of cheap editions of classic Russian literature, and spectacular examples of Soviet ballet. Ironically, movies shown in the West such as *The Cranes Are Flying* (Mikhail Kalatozov, dir., 1957) or *Ballad of a Soldier* (Grigori Chukhrai, dir., 1959) reflected a freedom of form that was frowned on in party circles at home.[5] Literature and ballet which tapped into the Russia past revealed a culture of depth, vigor, and sophistication that belied the tired, grey image of the period immediately following World War II. The Soviet regional minorities were always prominently represented in the international version of life in the USSR as, in public at least, the Soviet Union always celebrated diversity. In such images the maidens were always smiling, the economy was always thriving, and the technology always worked. Moscow found its trump card in its triumph in space from the launch of Sputnik, through the first manned flight in 1961 to the spacewalks of the mid-1960s. The whole effort both challenged stereotypes and concealed truths about the USSR.[6] When audiences failed to respond to Soviet overtures with the requisite admiration, the KGB simply paid for the necessary demonstrations. It helped the Kremlin if their population believed that the USSR was the envy of the world.[7]

The achievements of the Soviet cultural and propaganda offensive during the middle years of the Cold War exceeded the simple objective of selling the Soviet system or reassuring audiences at home. Although the USSR sprang from an internationalist ideology, Moscow leaders painted the United States government as the one-size-fits-all universalists, while presenting themselves as the friends to local nationalism. The USSR enabled the leaders of African liberation movements to speak to their own peoples over the channels of

4 Nigel Gould-Davies, "The Logic of Soviet Cultural Diplomacy," *Diplomatic History*, 27 (2003), 193–214, esp. 203, 205–06.
5 Barghoorn, *Soviet Foreign Propaganda*, 241.
6 Frederick C. Barghoorn, *The Soviet Cultural Offensive* (Princeton, NJ: Princeton University Press, 1960), 336.
7 Christopher Andrew and Vasili Mitrokhin, *The World Was Going Our Way: The KGB and the Battle for The Third World* (New York: Basic Books, 2005).

32. The Soviets were eager to show their progress in education. Here foreign students at the newly opened Patrice Lumumba Peoples' Friendship University in Moscow, 1961.

Radio Moscow. By sponsoring Third World nationalism, Moscow hitched its star to one of the big stories of the era and also exacerbated the tendency in Washington to see every nationalist as a Communist and thereby bungle its relations with much of the developing world as a result. If America's own polls are to be believed, the Soviet effort convinced many that the USSR was the wave of the future. Soviet prestige waxed full with its sporting triumphs, international development projects, and recruitment of foreign students to institutions like Patrice Lumumba University in Moscow.

Yet Soviet outreach had its unintended consequences. It opened the Soviet Union to international influences. Khrushchev probably misjudged the relative benefits and costs of international exchange. His cultural agreements with the Western powers in the late 1950s allowed the Soviets to mount exhibitions in New York, London, and elsewhere, but few people came, whereas the reciprocal events, like the American National exhibition held in Moscow in the summer of 1959, electrified the masses and suggested something of the abundance that flowed from the capitalist system. The evidence of Western prosperity became a ticking time bomb for Moscow. At some point Soviet citizens would demand more than the party could provide.[8]

The US propaganda machine

It could be said that Stalin founded two global propaganda machines, as the US government's Cold War propaganda structure was created in direct response to the scale of Soviet activity. US international propaganda flourished during World War II with institutions like Voice of America radio and the Office of War Information, but the entire effort very nearly folded at the war's end. The ubiquity of Soviet propaganda motivated postwar initiatives like the Fulbright exchanges, the information component to the Marshall Plan, and the wholesale authorization of peacetime propaganda overseas in the Smith–Mundt Act of 1948. The Central Intelligence Agency (CIA) mounted its own covert campaign and established Radio Free Europe and Radio Liberty to use exiles to broadcast propaganda into the Eastern bloc. Yet these efforts were uncoordinated. The threat of Soviet propaganda remained undiminished. In 1953, President Dwight D. Eisenhower responded by establishing the United States Information Agency (USIA) to conduct all overt US information work around the world. As in the USSR, the US information machine had its turf wars. Senator William Fulbright contrived to keep the administration of culture and exchange at the State Department where it remained until 1978. Staff at both USIA and the State Department had wasted much energy on infighting in the interim.[9]

USIA's achievements in the mid-Cold War period included massive programs to translate and publish "helpful" books and promote the teaching of English. USIA worked hard to present the African-American civil rights movement to the world, spinning the story as one of the heroic federal government coming to rescue brave black citizens from localized prejudice. USIA also managed to turn the death of President John F. Kennedy into an opportunity to accentuate the best in America. Voice of America carried American popular music and achieved success broadcasting jazz into the Eastern bloc. USIA and the State Department sponsored tours by jazz musicians, reaching out especially to Africa. In the field of film and television, USIA created documentaries and disseminated them to new and content-hungry TV stations in developing

---

8 Gould-Davies, "The Logic of Soviet Cultural Diplomacy," 213. See also Walter Hixson, *Parting the Curtain* (New York: Macmillan, 1995), 210, 213.
9 For a full account, see Nicholas J. Cull, *The Cold War and the United States Information Agency: American Propaganda and Public Diplomacy, 1945–1989* (Cambridge: Cambridge University Press, 2008).

countries or placed them in cinemas around the world as supporting fare for the biggest Hollywood hits of the era. USIA also secretly subsidized several international newsreels and even created feature material for key audiences, as in 1965 when the agency launched a propaganda soap opera for Mexico called *Nuestro Barrio* (Our Neighborhood) about the struggle between a young doctor and an evil oligarch. The show reportedly soon topped the ratings in Mexico and across Central America.[10] In support of such work, USIA re-branded its activities to allow a clear contrast with Soviet propaganda. From 1965 onwards, USIA commonly called its work Public Diplomacy. There is, however, little evidence that contemporary audiences drew great distinctions between Soviet propaganda and US public diplomacy. Both seem to have been taken with a pinch of salt.

Unlike the Soviet Union's ideological warriors, America's "public diplomats" had to coexist with a lively commercial media emanating from their country. USIA and the State Department worked to enable US culture to reach places where the commercial US media would not or could not go and to balance portrayals of America in countries where the commercial US media could be freely accessed. This meant that in the East and global South, the United States had to overcome stereotypes of heartless capitalism propagated by the Soviets, while in the West the United States had to overcome the impressions of ubiquitous violence and lax morals created by its own popular culture.

USIA had both friends and enemies in the commercial media. News organizations like the Associated Press and Scripps Howard disliked any government role in the news business and lobbied against Voice of America. Hollywood was initially more sympathetic, with the major studios agreeing in the 1950s to shape their output with foreign sensibilities in mind. USIA happily guided script decisions in many export-oriented films. But USIA's informal arrangements with Hollywood did not endure in the 1960s. From the Kennedy years onwards, the gap between the ways in which the US government wished the country to be seen and the images favored by Hollywood remained a major concern for USIA.[11]

European international propaganda: East and West

The European nations had been in the national projection business even longer than the USSR. In the 1880s private groups in France, Germany, and

---

10 Cull, *The Cold War and the United States Information Agency*, 240.
11 Ibid., 84, 184–85, 207, 301–02.

Italy established cultural diplomacy organizations. Britain came late with its quasi nongovernmental British Council in 1934 and foreign-language broadcasts by the BBC which began in 1938. This work continued into the postwar period and acquired a Cold War imperative along with an increased emphasis on cultivating the developing world. West Germany established a new organization: the Goethe Institute, to make a clean break with Nazi cultural propaganda. Student exchanges and overseas student recruitment emerged as a favorite technique of the European cultural propagandists. Europeans also paid particular attention to the idea of establishing twinning agreements between towns across international lines. Such arrangements were an important mechanism of overcoming historical antipathies and building a sense of Europeanness in the shadow of the USSR, but were also used to reach out across Cold War fault lines.

West European cultural diplomacy organizations presented their respective political culture inside the Eastern bloc; Britain and France mounted exhibitions in Moscow in the years following the American exhibition. But these efforts were not simply a product of the Cold War. The British and French were still competing with one another to expand influence and reap material profits. France spent far and away the most money, but the bulk of its budget was allocated to promote French language and culture in its former colonial zone in West Africa.

Eastern European governments set up their own cultural offices, sent cultural attaches abroad, and opened their own exhibition pavilions. They exported their film and television programs, with Czechoslovakia making its mark in the world of animation. They especially focused on sports. Romania's gymnasts, Czechoslovakia's ice hockey team, and East Germany's weight lifters were all presented as symbols of the health and vitality of their system. Sporting events like the contest between the East and West German soccer teams in the first round of the 1974 soccer World Cup gained immense propaganda significance (this particular match was won by East Germany 1–0, but West Germany went on to win the championship). Sometimes sports were a proxy for resistance within the Warsaw Pact. During the 1956 Melbourne Olympic Games, held in the wake of the Soviet invasion of Hungary, the Hungarian and Soviet water polo teams fought so fiercely during their match that it became known as the "blood in the water" match. Hungary went on to clinch the gold medal.

The Cold War cast a shadow over global artistic production. There were moments when art became especially politicized. America's radio stations RFE and RL disseminated the works of dissidents like Boris Pasternak or Aleksandr Solzhenitsyn, and in the same way the Soviet Union used art and literature to publicize America's negative stories from the plight of Vietnamese peasants to the fate of the popularly elected leftist Salvador Allende regime in Chile. US and British propaganda bureaucracies both worked to ensure that the work of the most influential English-language voice of the Cold War – George Orwell – was as widely translated and disseminated as possible. *Animal Farm* and *1984* were invaluable to the Western cause.[12] But Cold War culture was more than this. Artists and audiences across the world gravitated toward certain shared themes which, while already present in the culture, achieved a special prominence in the period and provided a mechanism through which the Cold War experience could be explored. Three broad subjects stand out as characteristic of the era: destruction (and especially nuclear destruction), espionage, and epic renderings of history and fantasy. Stories woven around all three subjects evolved during the period and serve as a window on the development of Cold War attitudes among artists and audiences alike.

Themes of destruction

As soon as the news broke of the atomic bombing of Hiroshima and Nagasaki, Western writers began to ruminate about the horrible potential of nuclear annihilation. The idea had surfaced in Anglo-American fiction as early as 1895, but now nuclear destruction and its consequences became a major theme in Western culture. Almost always the nuclear theme served as a critique of Cold War logic and a plea for peace. Important early manifestations included John Hersey's *Hiroshima*, (1946), and Leonard Engel and Emanuel S. Piller's imagined account of full-scale nuclear war called *World Aflame: The Russian American War of 1950* (1947).

The American imagination ran riot around nuclear fears. Nuclear tests created armies of giant ants in the horror movie *Them!* (Gordon Douglas, dir., 1954), stolen nuclear materials immolate the femme fatale in *Kiss Me Deadly* (Robert Aldrich, dir., 1955), and nuclear war inaugurated a new dark age in Walter M. Miller's remarkable novel *A Canticle for Liebowitz* (1955–59). On the lighter side, in 1959, the satirical songwriter Tom Lehrer released his pastiche hymn "We'll All Go Together When We Go," with such memorable lyrics as: "When the air becomes uranious, we will all go simultaneous ..." It was much the same story elsewhere in the West. Britain produced the thriller *Seven Days to Noon* (John Boulting and Roy Boulting, dirs., 1950) in which a mad scientist tries

12 Daniel J. Leab, *Orwell Subverted: The CIA and the Filming of Animal Farm* (University Park, PA: Pennsylvania State University Press, 2007).

to use a bomb to blackmail the world into disarmament, while Roald Dahl's first novel, *Sometime Never* (1948), contained vivid descriptions of nuclear devastations during World Wars III and IV. Nevil Shute's *On the Beach* (1957) (filmed by Stanley Kramer in 1959) imagined Australia's wait for inevitable death following a nuclear war elsewhere in the world. France produced both Alain Resnais's film *Hiroshima Mon Amour* [Hiroshima My Love] (1959) and the black humor of designer Louis Réard, who dubbed his two-piece swimsuit the "Bikini" (1946) to compare the garment's impact to the US nuclear test at the Pacific atoll of the same name. Japan – whose population knew nuclear devastation at first hand – fixated on the issue. Japanese comics and movies were full of nuclear blasts creating monsters, the most famous being *Gojira* [Anglicized as *Godzilla*] (Ishirô Honda, dir., 1954). In 1972/73, Japan was gripped by the publication of *Hadashi no Gen* [Barefoot Gen], a powerful memoir of the impact of the atomic bomb in *Manga* form by a Hiroshima survivor.

The Cuban missile crisis spurred a series of major films in the West about the danger of a rogue individual or a systems failure triggering a nuclear apocalypse. The most innovative was *Doctor Strangelove or How I Learned to Stop Worrying and Love the Bomb* (Stanley Kubrick, dir., 1964). Similar scenarios were played straight in *Fail-Safe* (Sidney Lumet, dir., 1964). Two major American superheroes created in the 1960s – Spiderman and The Incredible Hulk – gained their powers from nuclear-related accidents. American nuclear fears were also directed toward China, the most extreme example being *Battle Beneath the Earth* (Montgomery Tully, dir., 1967) in which a rogue "Red Chinese" general attempts to attack the US mainland by tunneling under the Pacific Ocean and placing atomic bombs under American military bases.

In Britain, the documentary filmmaker Peter Watkins made *The War Game* (1965) in which he dramatized the effects of a nuclear bomb on London. The BBC thought it too intense to screen on television for another twenty years, but the film was shown theatrically and won the best documentary Oscar. Humorist Spike Milligan created *The Bedsitting Room* (Richard Lester, dir., 1969), a black comedy set in a British nuclear wasteland.

In stark contrast to the West, in the Eastern bloc the subject of nuclear devastation was officially taboo, appearing only in veiled form in science fiction.[13] The regimes hated to allow their populations to dwell on questions which the party could not readily answer. The nuclear theme was explicit only

---

13 See Arkady Strugatsky and Boris Strugatsky, *Obitaemyi ostrov* [Inhabited Island], (1971), published in the West as *Prisoners of Power* (1977). The theme has also been detected in *Stalker* (Andre Tarkovsky, dir., 1979).

in anti-American treatments of the legacy of World War II such as the 1974 film co-produced with Japan, *Moskva, liubov moia* [Moscow my Love] (Aleksandr Mitta and Kenzi Yesida, dirs.), in which a Japanese dancer finds happiness with a Soviet sculptor only to expire from cancer, traced to her mother's presence at Hiroshima before her birth.

Themes of espionage

While nuclear culture argued for peace and restraint, stories of espionage and paranoia shaped the logic of the Cold War conflict and mobilized populations to support (or at least tolerate) their secret states. These stories had deep roots. In West and East alike, spy stories had been an important part of culture during World War II. They were a resource as ready for Cold War deployment as the unfired shells and stockpiled weapons on the inventories of Moscow and Washington.

With the coming of the Cold War, the "enemy" as portrayed in World War II / Great Patriotic War culture simply transmuted from a Nazi into an American or Russian. The first American Cold War film – *Iron Curtain* (William A. Wellman, dir., 1948) – not only played like a remake of *Confessions of a Nazi Spy* (Anatole Litvak, dir., 1939), it had the same writer, Milton Krims. In the United States, this change was driven both by the personal politics of studio bosses like Darryl F. Zanuck and by the eternal quest for box office novelty value. In the Soviet Union, writers of thrillers were more or less obliged to seek out American villains when the minister of cinema, Ivan Bolshakov, let it be known that the time had come to move beyond "Great Patriotic War" stories.[14] Moscow won the dubious distinction of creating the first Cold War hate film with *Russkii vopros* [The Russian Question] (Mikhail Romm, dir., 1947) from a play of the same year by Konstantin Simonov, which dealt with the corruption of the US press rather than spies. Soviet spy stories followed and Hollywood was not far behind. The lead time on film production meant that the respective spy cycles spawned by the state-controlled Soviet industry and patriotic American industry appeared without reference to each other. Each needed the other as an enemy at the same moment. The confluence of mutual prejudice and paranoia would be repeated in the early 1980s.

Notable Russian offerings included *Vstrecha na Elbe* [Meeting on the Elbe] (Grigori Alexandrov and Aleksei Utkin, dirs., 1949), *Sud chesti* [Court of

14 Jay Leyda, *Kino: A History of Russian and Soviet Film* (Princeton, NJ: Princeton University Press, 1983), 398.

Honor] (Abram Room, dir., 1949), and *Sekretnaia missiia* [Secret Mission] (Mikhail Romm, dir., 1950). America's spy cycle included *I Married a Communist* (Robert Stevens, dir., 1949), *My Son John* (Leo McCarey, dir., 1952), and the Red-busting TV show *I Led Three Lives* (1953–56). Themes of paranoia associated with the Cold War were widely disseminated, in science fiction thrillers as *Invasion of the Body Snatchers* (Don Seigel, dir., 1956), and were manipulated in *The Manchurian Candidate* (John Frankenheimer, dir., 1962).

The epicenter of Cold War spy fiction was the United Kingdom. Spy stories became a veritable industry led by intelligence veterans Graham Greene, John LeCarré, and Ian Fleming. This reflected both historical roots – Britain had been thinking about Russian spies since the days of Rudyard Kipling – and contemporary needs. It is easy to read the potency of James Bond as an antidote to the loss of power experienced by the country as a whole. Moreover, espionage stories provided a way to preserve the trope of British opposition to totalitarianism and maintain the political certainties of World War II. Then there was the real world of espionage in which Britain played a special role assisting the United States and fell victim to high-placed enemies within. The spy became an archetypal figure, like America's cowboy, through whom the dramas of national life could be played out.

British spy fiction evolved with the Cold War. In the 1960s, key figures in the genre turned away from Cold War rabble-rousing and began to offer a more complex commentary and reflect the same yearning for peace as that seen in the nuclear destruction narratives. The Communist villains in Ian Fleming's early Bond novels gave way to movies in which Bond battled international crime syndicates, and East and West had to learn to cooperate. Interestingly, the shift in fiction anticipated the genuine political movement to détente. The more serious novels and films such as John Le Carré's *The Spy Who Came in from the Cold* (novel 1963, film 1965), Len Deighton's *The Ipcress File* (novel 1962, film 1965), and Graham Greene's *The Human Factor* (novel 1978, film 1979) presented real moral ambiguity and asked whether the conflict had reduced its players to brute equivalence. Secret agents abounded in increasingly spoofed or tongue-in-cheek form in the adventure television serials of the 1960s, including *The Avengers* (1962–69) and *Danger Man* (1964–68), and even children's programs, as with the glamorous agent Lady Penelope in *Thunderbirds* (1964–65). The genre turned in on itself in the remarkable cult show *The Prisoner* (1967–68) in which an agent (played by *Danger Man*'s Patrick McGoohan) was imprisoned in a mysterious village. It is never clear whether the island is in the East or West, and it did not matter.

This was an exploration of the relationship between individual autonomy and state power.

The United States absorbed most of its spy culture from Britain but also produced homegrown fare, which seemed rather less reflexive and certainly less revealing of any national state of mind toward the Cold War. There were high-budget adventure movies, like Alfred Hitchcock's *North By Northwest* (1959) or *Torn Curtain* (1966), in which Cold War espionage merely provided the logic for placing the hero in jeopardy. There was a steady stream of novels, including full-blown series like Donald Hamilton's long-running Matt Helm stories (1960–93), and by the end of the decade American spy novels had a special taste for Chinese villains and often depicted Americans and Russians teaming up to defeat them.[15] From the mid-1960s on, American culture displayed a penchant for spy spoofs such as the movie *Our Man Flint* (Daniel Mann, dir., 1966) or the risible movie adaptations of Matt Helm. TV series in this vein included *The Man from UNCLE* (1964–68), which gave its American hero a Russian partner, *I Spy* (1965–68), and *Get Smart* (1965–70) with its famous range of wacky gadgets. American children's television delivered the animated *Bullwinkle Show* (1961–73) in which a squirrel and a dimwitted moose foil the plans of stereotyped Soviet spies. These spoofs could be loosely read as reactions against the Cold War stories of the 1950s, albeit while retaining certain stereotypes of evil Russians and Chinese and their cloak-and-dagger intrigue. There was still plenty of mileage in the formal Cold War thriller. In the 1970s, Robert Ludlum began to publish highly successful spy stories, many with a Cold War setting.

Secret agents also loomed large in the Eastern European popular culture. Spy stories had deep roots here, too: Poland had Konrad Wallenrod, the hero of Adam Mickiewicz's great narrative poem of 1828, who lived undetected amid and eventually destroyed the Teutonic Knights. But heritage alone cannot explain the proliferation of the Eastern spy story. Given the pervasive censorship restrictions around the Warsaw Pact, spy fiction must also have been thought useful by the authorities. Bulgaria produced the first great Eastern agent in the form of counter-spy Avakum Zakhov, the creation of Bulgarian writer Andrei Gulyashiki, and a favorite in books and on television across the Soviet bloc from his debut in 1959 in the novel *Sluchayat v Momchilovo* [The Momchilovo Affair].[16] Although his cerebral character was

---

15 George H. Lewis, "Spy Fiction American Style," *Journal of Communication*, 25, 4 (1975), 132–37.
16 Published in English in 1968 as the *Zakhov Mission* (London: Cassell, 1968).

closer to Sherlock Holmes, Zakhov was touted as the Communist James Bond, and Gulyashiki obligingly introduced "agent 07" as a character in Zakhov's world in his 1966 novel *Sreshu 07* (published in English as *Avakoum Zakhov versus 07*). Agent 07 survived the encounter, chastened by his brush with a better man.[17]

Unlike the Western spy stories, Eastern espionage fiction did not shift with the evolution of the Cold War and did not become either subversive fantasy or critical of the state. The Eastern spy story remained a cultural form in which the state was showing its value by secretly protecting the people. Several of the most influential stories did not take place in the Cold War at all, but in the moral certainty of World War II. The contemporary concerns that propelled post-Cuban missile crisis Western narratives into relativism or satire were dodged and the secret state was no less glorified for the historical setting. Poland provided the much-loved character *Kapitan Kloss*, a Polish secret agent operating within the Nazi Abwehr. Kloss appeared in live television plays and twenty comic books but is best remembered from the much-repeated eighteen-episode adventure series *Stawka więększa niż życie* [More than Life Is at Stake] (1967–68).

Soviet spy fiction displayed similar trends. The USSR produced its equivalent to Poland's Kaptan Kloss in Standartenführer Otto von Stirlitz, alias of gallant Russian spy Maksim Isaev, operating in the inner circles of Nazi power. Stirlitz/Iseav was the creation of Iulian Semenov, who produced a string of novels about the character, beginning in 1965 with *Parol ne nuzhen* [No Password Necessary]. Many were adapted to the screen, most notably in 1973 when the television mini-series *Semnadtsat mgnovenii vesny* [Seventeen Moments of Spring] (Tatiana Lioznova, dir.) held Russian audiences spellbound. The plot included a fiendish plan by the United States to make a separate peace with the Nazis. Stirlitz survived his wartime adventures to take part in the Cold War and gained Soviet immortality by becoming a stock figure in jokes.

East Germany produced an adaptation of the adventures of a "real life" spy in *Streng geheim!* [Top Secret!] (János Veiczi, dir., 1963) but scored its biggest hit with the television series *Das Unsichtbare Visier* [The Invisible Visor] (1973–76), starring Armin Müller-Stahl as the agent Achim Detjen. The Stasi reported a wave of new recruits to its ranks citing Detjen as their inspiration. The East German TV bosses hoped that the show would live on for years in sequels and re-runs, but their hopes were dashed when its star defected to

17 Andrei Gulyashiki, *Avakoum Zakhov versus 07* (Sydney, Australia: Scripts, 1967).

the West. Ironically, Müller-Stahl found his niche in Hollywood playing villains in the Cold War films of the 1980s.[18]

Epics of history and fantasy

The third major category of Cold War stories was epic renderings of history and fantasy: stories depicting the past or future in real or imagined worlds told on an immense canvas, frequently with a strong dose of morality and self-righteousness. At the outset of the conflict, such epics helped to sustain wartime cohesion and cement loyalties and identities. As the Cold War progressed, history and fantasy allowed vicarious participation in events and mobilized people behind their leaders' projects through grand narratives of good versus evil and tales of national destiny. In time, as the conflict weighed heavily on its participants, both history and fantasy also provided a language for dissent.

In American television, literature, and film, the Cold War underpinned the production of science fantasy and historically inspired fiction. Biblical / classical epics, war, and western genres all carried obvious ideological freight. The epic had its roots in nineteenth-century pageants and a distinguished career in the silent era, but the Cold War cinema took it to new heights as it became a stage on which the cultural power of America could be displayed. The government did not need to ask Hollywood to do this, but the spirit of national certainty and righteousness which animated Washington was just as much a part of Hollywood life. Major directors, producers, and executives, including Cecil B. DeMille, Daryl F. Zanuck, and the president of the Motion Picture Association of America, Eric Johnston, were true believers in the need for movies to play a role in rallying the nation and disseminating American values around the world.

Cold War Hollywood produced a new generation of biblical and classically themed films. While the stories suggested an American ambivalence toward empire, the films themselves were part of an imperial system displaying the cultural power of the society capable of mounting such a spectacle and showcasing America's religiosity in contrast to Soviet hostility to faith. Cecil B. DeMille presented his remake of *The Ten Commandments* in 1956 as an attempt to assert the common tradition of Christians, Muslims, and Jews in the face of God-less Communism. More than this, American diplomats encouraged the making of biblical epics because the necessary locations happened to

---

18 I owe this story to Patrick Major of the University of Warwick.

be in places where US investment could make a real political difference, most especially in Italy, the one European country where the Communists had a chance to come to power constitutionally. Use of the classical genre to challenge the Cold War status quo was rare, though Stanley Kubrick's *Spartacus* (1960) was open to radical interpretations and suffered during the production process as a result.[19]

The epic war film allowed Hollywood to stage stories of glory on a grand scale and to inject contemporary comment, too. Films of the late 1940s and early 1950s typically included a recruiting scene in which an authority figure spoke of the necessity for each generation to defend democracy, and directors enjoyed the help of the Pentagon to stage mass battle scenes. War films raised some diplomatic difficulties, especially as the villains – Germany and Japan – were now Cold War allies. Hollywood provided a succession of "good Germans" and films like *The Enemy Below* (Dick Powell, dir., 1957) ended with hope for future friendship. Noble Japanese appeared somewhat later. But the American war film was transformed by the Vietnam War. As audiences stayed away from flag-waving pictures like John Wayne's *The Green Berets* in 1968, Hollywood injected counter-cultural satire into its war movies or told stories that could be read as either indictments or celebrations of militarism, the best example being *Patton* (Franklin J. Schaffner, dir., 1970).

The genre of western movies followed much the same trajectory as the war story with films in the immediate postwar period highlighting the "need" for military preparedness. The western that had previously dwelt on the heroic individual now celebrated team work and romanticized army life in a succession of cavalry westerns. As the Cold War shifted to the Third World in the late 1950s, so westerns depicted American heroes saving Mexican farmers from bandits who appeared as thinly disguised Communists. The special status of the western within the American imagination meant that it provided an ideal space to explore responses to the experience of American power, and hence the western was transformed by the US experience in Vietnam into a major site for the reexamination of the sins of America's past and present. Hollywood restaged My Lai by proxy in the West in films like *Soldier Blue* (Ralph Nelson, dir., 1970) in which the 7th Cavalry was seen massacring Native American women and children, long before it tackled such issues head-on in an explicit representation of Vietnam.

19 The 1960s produced one oddity, a contemporary religious film called *Shoes of the Fisherman* (Michael Anderson, dir., 1968), in which a Ukrainian dissident (played by Anthony Quinn) becomes pope. It all seemed terribly far-fetched until the election of John Paul II just ten years later.

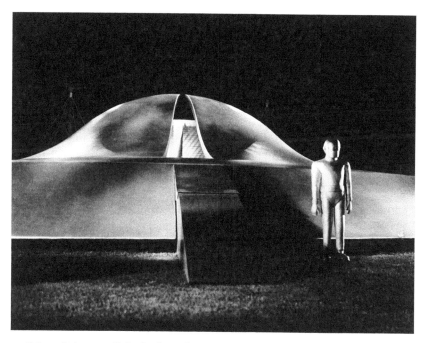

33. Science fiction provided a fertile medium in which to discuss the fears raised by the Cold War, as with Robert Wise's 1951 film, *The Day the Earth Stood Still*, in which aliens help to prevent a nuclear war.

American science fiction also displayed both patriotism and dissent. The epic fantasy films of the 1950s like *This Island Earth* (Joseph M. Newman, dir., 1955) openly displayed the familiar Cold War themes. The world is pulled from the brink of a nuclear war by an alien in *The Day the Earth Stood Still* (1951). American television in the 1960s provided *Star Trek* (1966–69), which mixed both the imperial spirit to "boldly go where no man has gone before" and a pseudo-Soviet enemy in the Klingons, with challenges to Cold War thinking as a Russian crew member and episodes which critiqued the arms race and the balance of terror.[20] When, in the 1970s, Hollywood could no longer display the religiosity of the epic, the patriotic certainty of the war film and the grand narrative of the western, these genres reappeared in hybrid

20 See Nicholas Evan Sarantakes, "Cold War Pop Culture and the Image of U.S. Foreign Policy: The perspective of the Original *Star Trek* Series," *Journal of Cold War Studies*, 7 (2005), 74–103. See also Rick Worland, "Captain Kirk: Cold Warrior," *Journal of Popular Film and Television*, 16, 3 (1988), 109–17.

science fiction form utterly extracted from any political context. The best example of this was *Star Wars* (George Lucas, dir., 1977).

Western Europe also produced Cold War epic histories and fantasies rallying the population for confrontation with the Soviet Union. Innumerable war stories sustained an anti-totalitarian ideology. British science fiction was populated by invading totalitarian races from the Treens of *The Eagle*'s Dan Dare comic strip (1957–69) to the Daleks of BBC TV's *Doctor Who* (1963–89, 2005–). As World War II receded and the Cold War came into question, such stories were increasingly told with a knowing irony that sometimes bordered on camp. The most expansive epic of the period was J. R. R. Tolkien's *Lord of the Rings* trilogy. While Tolkien resisted all attempts to impose allegory on his work and denied that his "Ring of Power" was a cipher for the atomic bomb, his story of virtuous individuals struggling against powers of darkness played into the Cold War self-consciousness of Europeans and Americans. Much of the plot concerned forging and maintaining alliances in ways that would have been instantly recognizable to the politicians of the era.

The Soviet bloc's own epic storytelling trod surprisingly similar terrain to Western culture. Science fiction played a prominent role and innumerable epic dramas recalled the glories of the past. In Brezhnev's Russia, the cult of the "Great Patriotic War" reached unprecedented heights – quite literally – with the erection of vast war memorials and the creation of movies to match. The war continued to be offered to the people as the source of certainty and unity well into the 1970s. It was much the same story in East German film and television with numerous tales of heroic German Communist resistance to Nazi tyranny. The state control of the media in the East meant that any criticism had to be far more veiled than in the West, but nonetheless, some filmmakers used historical stories to air dissent. In Poland, myths of the war (and the ideological foundations of that state) were laid bare in films like *Popiół i diament* [Ashes and Diamonds] (Andrzej Wajda, dir., 1958) and the bleak POW segment of *Eroica* (Andrzej Munk, dir., 1957). In Hungary, director Miklós Jancsó's chose stories that on the surface explored the revolutionary past but underneath allowed Austrian or White Russian villains to stand in for the USSR of 1956. Such films questioned the certainties of the revolution, the Communist state, and the Cold War division of the world, but they were but a shadow of the dissent that would erupt in the later 1970s.[21]

---

21 On Jancsó, see *Kinoeye* 3 (February 2003), esp. Andrew James Horton, "*The Aura of History:* Jancsó's depictions of the year 1919."

The years of détente saw a strange phenomenon in Cold War filmmaking – the East–West co-production. Some of the movies created in this way self-consciously tackled themes of interdependence. In the Italian–Soviet co-production *The Red Tent* (Mikhail Kalatozov, dir., 1969), a Soviet icebreaker strives to rescue the survivors of the *Italia* airship expedition to the North Pole.[22] *Waterloo* (Sergei Bondarchuk, dir., 1970), also a Soviet–Italian co-production, recalled the international coalition against Napoleon. The only big US–Soviet co-production was Twentieth Century Fox's remake of *The Blue Bird* (George Cukor, dir., 1976), made in the USSR and starring Elizabeth Taylor, character actors from both sides of the Iron Curtain, and a line up of Soviet ballet talent. It took millions to make and flopped miserably.

Helsinki: the watershed

An examination of the state of play in the cultural Cold War as of the early 1970s reveals striking successes for the Soviets everywhere except Europe and North America. American prosperity and complacency were eroded by the oil shocks, civil unrest, and visible humiliations of Vietnam and Watergate. In contrast, Soviet woes were largely private. For the developing world, Moscow rode high. The USSR continued to sponsor revolutionary nationalist projects and to paint the United States as the universalist power with the imperial agenda. This was especially manifest in the politics around the United National Educational Scientific and Cultural Organization (UNESCO), that under the leadership of its director-general, Amadou-Mahtar M'Bow, launched a campaign for a New World International Communication Order (NWICO). NWICO promised worldwide protection for international journalistic standards, but also pledged to defend the right to national regulation. The United States detected a Soviet ploy to establish a right to censorship in the name of resistance to the growing power of the Anglo-American communications industries and quit UNESCO in the early 1980s.[23]

The Soviets also seemed to dominate the diplomatic negotiating tables. On August 1, 1975, President Gerald Ford, Leonid Brezhnev, and leaders of thirty-three other states from East and West met in Helsinki, Finland, and signed the

---

22 For a case study of this film, see Paula A. Michaels, "Mikhail Kalatozov's *The Red Tent*: A Study in International Co-production across the Iron Curtain," *Historical Journal of Film Radio and Television*, 26, 3 (2006), 311–26.

23 On UNESCO, see William Preston, Jr., Edward S. Herman, and Herbert I. Schiller, *Hope & Folly: The United States and UNESCO 1945–1985*. (Minneapolis, MN: University of Minnesota Press, 1989).

Final Act of the Conference on Security and Cooperation (CSCE) in Europe. The Helsinki Final Act was the pinnacle of détente and the fruit of two and a half years of negotiation. The accords recognized European boundaries and established principles for East–West trade and scientific cooperation. Brezhnev could proudly show his own people America's acquiescence to the Soviet domination of Eastern Europe and their acceptance of the principle of non-intervention. President Ford paid the price for this in the election of 1976.

But Helsinki was the watershed. In the long term, the Helsinki Accords transformed the Soviet state and its satellites. The Final Act included a so-called "Third Basket" of principles that dealt with promoting East–West contact in the personal (including tourism and freedom of travel), informational, educational, and cultural fields. The document stressed the need for more exchanges. It opened the way for the greater flow of Soviet ideas westward and the spread of Western culture and ideas into the Soviet orbit. The Helsinki principles meant that authors could contact foreign publishers and printed materials could be freely distributed. They also allowed for direct contact between parties arranging educational exchanges and encouraged extensive reform of the working conditions for Western journalists in the East.

The cultural elements of Helsinki were refined and broadened still further at a series of CSCE meetings in Madrid from 1980 to 1983. While the Soviet government dragged its feet, it was obliged to implement these reforms. The numbers of people involved in student exchanges jumped dramatically, and cultural figures found it much easier to travel. Major appearances of Western artists in the East included a legendary concert by the British singer Elton John who stunned his hosts by performing the officially forbidden Beatles number "Back in the USSR" as his encore. The Soviet leaders who thought they would lose little from acceding to increased information flows had clearly miscalculated. As the Soviet economy stalled, the doors opened by Helsinki revealed to the world the grim reality behind the official image of the worker's paradise. The positive image which the Soviets had nurtured at such expense around the world withered away.

Helsinki brought a yet more significant blow to the Soviet system. Following pressure from the countries of the European Economic Community, the "First Basket" of the Helsinki Accords included a pledge by all signatories to "respect human rights and fundamental freedoms." While in the short term the Soviets could reap credit from having publicly embraced such principles, the undertaking opened the Kremlin to a new level of domestic and international criticism when it and its allies systematically ignored their obligations. After 1975, national "Helsinki Watch" committees sprung up around the world to monitor compliance with the accords, including commit-tees inside the Soviet Union and its satellites. In 1982, the national committees formed an International Helsinki Federation for Human Rights. The Helsinki Watch committee in the United States developed into the NGO Human Rights Watch. Helsinki proved a double-edged sword for Moscow: a short-term success bought at the price of the concession of principles that inspired a generation of dissidents, defined a standard by which the USSR could be judged, and facilitated the exchange of ideas across an increasingly transparent Iron Curtain.[24]

Culture and the second Cold War

The second Cold War of the 1980s brought a renewed propaganda battle in which one of the West's strongest tactics was to point to the post-Helsinki dissident movements in the East. The period also saw a resurgence of themes of the Truman/Stalin period in the fiction of both East and West. American political culture reflected the popular culture of the previous phases of the Cold War. Patriotic genres were rediscovered. Empty, ambiguous, or even dissenting stories were given new meanings. President Ronald Reagan echoed *Star Wars* when he spoke of fighting an evil empire, and Senator Edward Kennedy appropriated the film's title to mock the administration's strategic defense initiative. Ironically, the nickname stuck and seems to have rather enhanced the image of that project.[25]

Western popular culture in the second Cold War delivered some new twists on old themes, as the spy thriller overcame its preoccupation with the dark side of human nature to embrace a fixation with technology in the new genre of techno-thriller. Pulp fiction writers and readers embraced the post-nuclear war survivalist story. These new genres displayed a right-wing bias, but there was no shortage of books or films maintaining the spirit of dissent seen in the 1960s and 1970s. Opposition to nuclear weapons flourished. But Western governments had found a way to wage the Cold War in the presence of public skepticism and dissent.

In the new propaganda war between East and West, sports became espe-cially politicized. The United States boycotted the Moscow Olympics in 1980,

24 For a sustained analysis, see Daniel C. Thomas, *The Helsinki Effect: International Norms, Human Rights and the Demise of Communism* (Princeton, NJ: Princeton University Press, 2001) See also Rosemary Foot's chapter in volume III.

25 See Peter Kramer, "*Star Wars*," in David Ellwood (ed.), *The Movies as History: Visions of the Twentieth Century* (Stroud, UK: Sutton, 2000).

and the Soviet Union stayed away from the Olympic Games when they were held in Los Angeles in 1984. The Soviets also made extensive use of disinformation, circulating damaging rumors of assorted conspiracies and assassination plots, most famously claiming that the AIDS virus had been created in an American bio-war lab. The United States responded with an inter-agency effort to expose Soviet fabrications, and President Reagan told Mikhail Gorbachev that he needed to cease Soviet disinformation practices.

The international exchanges survived the renewal of tension. They became ever more significant avenues for increasing Soviet awareness of the West and allowed the world to see exactly what was happening in the East. As the Soviet economy fell ever further short of Moscow's promise, the dissident impulses which had been coded in the novels and films of the 1960s and 1970s became explicit as Helsinki energized a new generation of protest. Filmmakers like Poland's Andrzej Wajda were feted around the world. Meanwhile, American popular culture in the form of blockbuster movies and hit television shows waxed ever stronger presenting a vision of how life might be different.

Western broadcasters played a special role in the denouement of the Cold War. In April 1986, the BBC, RFE/RL, and Voice of America hit home as never before when they carried news of the accident at the Chernobyl nuclear power plant near Kiev to a country whose government remained silent on the story for many days thereafter. As change gathered pace inside the Soviet Union, Western broadcasters told the people of the East what they were missing materially and politically in the West, encouraged dissent, and enabled the dissidents and their countrymen to watch the progress of their neighbors as they too struggled for a better life. A chain reaction followed. It was fitting that the Cold War, which had for so much of its course rendered the people impotent spectators, ended with the people acting and governments, both East and West, watching in amazement.

Popular culture had played an unprecedented role in the Cold War. It was mobilized and manipulated by the bureaucracies of the era, it was deployed by the artists who wished to engage with the great issues of the conflict, and it became a space in which dissenting views could be developed and disseminated. Some of the cultural works created in the process – the writing of Orwell or Greene, the movies of Wajda or Kubrick – transcend their Cold War context, too, but plenty of other Cold War texts merely show the willingness of artists to toe the official line or pander to the prejudice of the masses. There is a certain parallelism between the propaganda of the two blocs in the Cold War. They faced much the same internal turf wars. They traded in similar stereotypes. Both became adept at speaking without really learning to listen to their target audiences. The United States won the race for the image and reality of material prosperity and the USSR manifestly lost, but there was an irony in the victory. In success, the US government neglected its tools of diplomacy, slashing budgets to gain a swift peace dividend and downgrading USIA by folding it into the State Department. The experience of "victory" in the cultural Cold War became a crude talisman of American rectitude rather than a wake-up call to remain engaged with ordinary people around the world. Other players – specifically the European agencies of public diplomacy – fared much better in the post-Cold War world.

22

Counter-cultures: the rebellions against the Cold War order, 1965–1975

JEREMI SURI

In *The Feminine Mystique* – Betty Friedan's 1963 attack on domesticity – the author describes how she "gradually, without seeing it clearly for quite a while ... came to realize that something is very wrong with the way American women are trying to live their lives today."[1] Despite the outward appearances of wealth and contentment, she argued that the Cold War was killing happiness. Women, in particular, faced strong public pressures to conform with a family image that emphasized a finely manicured suburban home, pampered children, and an ever-present "housewife heroine."[2] This was the asserted core of the good American life. This was the cradle of freedom. This was, in the words of Adlai Stevenson, the "assignment" for "wives and mothers": "Western marriage and motherhood are yet another instance of the emergence of individual freedom in our Western society. Their basis is the recognition in women as well as men of the primacy of personality and individuality."[3]

Friedan disagreed, and she was not alone. Surveys, interviews, and observations revealed that countless women suffered from a problem that had no name within the standard lexicon of society at the time. They had achieved the "good life," and yet they felt unfulfilled. Friedan quoted one particularly articulate young mother:

An expanded draft version of this chapter appeared as "The Rise and Fall of an International Counterculture, 1960–1975," in *The American Historical Review* 114:1 (February 2009), 45–68.

1 Betty Friedan, *The Feminine Mystique* (New York: Dell Publishing, 1983, originally published in 1963), 11.

2 Friedan, *Feminine Mystique*, 33–68. For a very insightful analysis of Friedan's writing and advocacy, and the limits of her vision of social change, see Daniel Horowitz, *Betty Friedan and the Making of "The Feminine Mystique": The American Left, the Cold War, and Modern Feminism* (Amherst, MA: University of Massachusetts Press, 2000).

3 Adlai E. Stevenson, "A Purpose for Modern Woman," *Women's Home Companion* (September 1955), 30–31, excerpted at www.wwnorton.com/college/history/archive/resources/documents/ch32_04.htm.

I've tried everything women are supposed to do – hobbies, gardening, pickling, canning, being very social with my neighbors, joining committees, running PTA teas. I can do it all, and I like it, but it doesn't leave you anything to think about – any feeling of who you are. I never had any career ambitions. I love the kids and Bob and my home. There's no problem you can even put a name to. But I'm desperate. I begin to feel I have no personality.[4]

These were the words of the counter-culture, emerging within the United States, Western Europe, and many Communist societies during the middle 1960s. Existential angst was not unique to the period, but it became pervasive in a context of heightened promises about a better life and strong fears about the political implications of social deviance. Ideological competition in the Cold War encouraged citizens to look beyond material factors alone and seek a deeper meaning in their daily activities. Many women, however, did not feel freer in the modern kitchens that American vice president Richard M. Nixon extolled as symbols of capitalist accomplishment.[5] Many men did not feel freer as they went to their daily jobs in the large-scale industries that underwrote the costs of new global responsibilities. Many students did not feel freer as they attended mass institutions of higher education, particularly universities.[6] An international counter-culture developed in response to dissatisfaction with the dominant culture of the Cold War. On the model of Friedan's writing, it gave voice to criticisms of the basic social assumptions – about work, marriage, and family – connected to the politics of the era.[7]

Leaders confront the counter-culture

One must distinguish the counter-culture from various other resistance movements. Many citizens residing in colonial and postcolonial territories had long opposed the great power politics that, in their eyes, contributed to imperial domination over their societies. Nationalist leaders like Jawaharlal Nehru in India, Kwame Nkrumah in Ghana, and Ho Chi Minh in Vietnam were not part of the counter-culture because they never accepted the initial Cold War

---

4 Quoted in Friedan, *Feminine Mystique*, 21.
5 On the famous Khrushchev–Nixon "kitchen debate" of 1959, see William Taubman, *Khrushchev: The Man and His Era* (New York: W. W. Norton, 2003), 416–18.
6 See Jeremi Suri, *Power and Protest: Global Revolution and the Rise of Détente* (Cambridge, MA: Harvard University Press, 2003), 88–130.
7 Theodore Roszak popularized the term "Counter Culture" in his book, *The Making of a Counter Culture: Reflections on the Technocratic Society and Its Youthful Opposition* (Garden City, NY: Anchor Books, 1969). My use of the term draws on Roszak but places it in a broader historical and geographic framework.

framework surrounding Friedan's disillusion. The same could be said for many domestic actors within Western societies, particularly early civil-rights activists. Although figures like Dr. Martin Luther King, Jr., supported the basic tenets of liberal democracy, others – including Robert F. Williams in the United States and Frantz Fanon in Algeria – did not. They were not part of the counter-culture because they advocated full-scale revolution. Social and political change was not enough for them; they wanted to destroy society and rebuild it from the ground up.[8]

The enormous influence of the counter-culture derived from its powerful presence within mainstream society. By the middle of the 1960s, Friedan's problem with no name had become a focus of discussion among leading journalists, intellectuals, and even policymakers. Unlike the Third World nationalists or domestic radicals whom one could dismiss as extreme figures, the suburban housewives, corporate employees, and college students who questioned basic social assumptions were core political constituencies. They were the future of each society – the people whom leaders claimed to serve. These "children of a generally affluent generation – West or East," according to the director of the Central Intelligence Agency (CIA) Richard Helms, "are deeply engrossed in the search for some newer means of arriving at moral values." "For the moment," he warned President Lyndon B. Johnson, "they seem to have settled on a reaffirmation of the dignity of the individual. Most commentators agree that Society's values are in flux; if this is so, restless youth are symptomatic of a deeper current than their numbers alone suggest." The president's special assistant for national security affairs, Walt Rostow, affirmed this judgment, pointing to the "conflict of 'ardent youth' and big machines, causing increasing numbers of young people to ask: 'Where do I fit?'"[9]

These sentiments were not unique to American leaders. As early as 1960, the West German chancellor, Konrad Adenauer, lamented what he called the "most important problem of our epoch" – the "inner political" weakness and superficiality of daily life in the Cold War. East–West rivalries and the

---

8 See Timothy B. Tyson, *Radio Free Dixie: Robert F. Williams and the Roots of Black Power* (Chapel Hill, NC: University of North Carolina Press, 2000); David Macey, *Frantz Fanon: A Life* (London: Granta Books, 2000).

9 Notes of Cabinet Meeting, September 18, 1968, and Attachment A, Folder: Cabinet Meeting, 9/18/68, box 15, Cabinet Papers, Lyndon Baines Johnson Library, Austin, Texas (hereafter, LBJL). See also CIA report, "Restless Youth," September 1968, folder: Youth and Student Movements, box 13, Files of Walt W. Rostow, National Security File, LBJL. Martin Klimke offers an excellent discussion of these materials and the Johnson administration's views of the counter-culture: *The Other Alliance: Student Protest in West Germany and the United States in the Global 1960s* (Princeton: Princeton University Press, 2009).

nuclear-arms race encouraged what he derided as an empty "materialism." Adenauer longed to reawaken public interest in what he called the "Christian" belief in the simple devout life, free from military tensions, superficial consumerism, and impersonal bureaucratic institutions.[10] One of Adenauer's rivals and successors, Willy Brandt, shared this perspective. In September 1968, when he served as West German foreign minister, Brandt observed that: "Young people in many of our countries do not understand why we, the older ones, cannot cope with the problems of an age dominated by science. Not force, but reason alone, can give them an answer." Brandt argued that peace between Cold War rivals was necessary for restoring domestic tranquility among a young discontented generation of citizens.[11]

Soviet leaders had similar concerns about the evidence of growing public disillusionment, despite the repressive control over information in their country. The official Soviet youth journal, *Komsomolskaia pravda*, called attention to problems with the "psychology of contemporary young people." They had apparently lost the combination of pervasive fear and intensive nationalism that had motivated conformity, and even public enthusiasm, during the years after World War II.[12] A public survey conducted by Soviet authorities in 1964 revealed that more than four out of every five students refused, despite severe threats, to heed the leadership's call for the cultivation of "virgin lands" and other patriotic Communist projects. Government leaders, particularly KGB director Iurii Andropov, became obsessed with the regime's domestic vulnerabilities.[13]

10 Konrad Adenauer an dem Herrn Staatssekretär, 9. Dezember 1960, Ordnung III/50, Adenauer Nachlaß, Stiftung Bundeskanzler-Adenauer-Haus, Rhöndorf, Germany (hereafter, Adenauer papers). See also Ansprache des Bundeskanzlers auf dem Festakt anläßlich der 10. Sommertagung des Politischen Clubs an der Evangelischen Akademie, Tutzing, 19. Juli 1963 (Unkorrigiertes Manuskript), 02.31, 1963/Band 1, Reden, Interviews, Aufsätze, Adenauer papers; Adenauer Rede in der Freien Universität, West Berlin, 5. Dezember 1958, 16.25, 1958/Band 2, Adenauer papers; Maria Mitchell, "Materialism and Secularism: CDU Politicians and National Socialism, 1945–1949," *Journal of Modern History*, 67 (June 1995), 287–307.
11 Speech by Willy Brandt at the Conference of Non-Nuclear States in Genf, September 3, 1968, box 288, Egon Bahrs Nachlaß, Archiv der sozialen Demokratie, Friedrich Ebert Stiftung, Bonn, Germany (hereafter, Bahr papers). See also Bahr Entwurf für *Christ und Welt*, Februar 1965, box 9B, Bahr papers; Bahr an Brandt, 15. November 1966, Box 352, Bahr papers.
12 *Komsomolskaia pravda*, April 27, 1961.
13 "Molodoi ukhoditiz kolkhozov v goroda" [Youth Goes from the Collective Farms to the Cities], December 1, 1964, box 80-1-497, fond 300, Records of Radio Free Europe/Radio Liberty, Open Society Archives, Central European University, Budapest, Hungary (hereafter, RFE/RL papers). See also "Molodei Sovetskovo soiuza" [Youth of the Soviet Union] 5–6 November 1962, Institute for the Study of the USSR, Munich, box 80-1-497, fond 300, RFE/RL Papers; Michael Scammell (ed.), *The Solzhenitsyn Files: Secret Soviet Documents Reveal One Man's Fight against the Monolith*, trans. by Catherine A. Fitzpatrick (Chicago: edition q, 1995), esp. xvii–xxxv; Suri, *Power and Protest*, 105–14.

An uprising by citizens in the Russian city of Novocherkassk confirmed these fears. On June 2, 1962, local workers, joined by their families and area youth, seized Communist Party headquarters and the central police station. They demanded reduced food prices, better work conditions, and, most significant, a change in political leadership. In the eyes of many protesters, local authorities were out of touch with the needs and wants of society. They enforced an ideological order that contributed to growing public discontent. To control unrest in Novocherkassk and its "spillover" into other areas, the Soviet army deployed brute force, killing twenty civilians and injuring many more as soldiers fired into crowds of demonstrators. Soviet leaders put down the protests, but they never recovered from the anger and resentment inflamed by these events.[14]

Despite the violence, the citizens who challenged established authorities in the Soviet Union, West Germany, the United States, and other countries lived better lives than prior generations. These were privileged men and women who had unprecedented access to consumer goods, education, and leisure time. They also lived relatively secure lives, even in Communist societies, generally free from the domestic terror of the Stalinist years in the Soviet Union and the deprivations of economic depression in the United States and Western Europe. This was a revolt, in many cases, of the privileged against the leaders who conferred privileges.[15]

The counter-culture was not about material needs. It focused on unrealized spiritual and ideological demands that citizens believed the Cold War, and its dominant leaders, stymied. Competition between capitalism and Communism limited the perceived space for creative programs that combined or subverted the two systems. Foreign interventions also diverted resources and energies from domestic reforms. Most damning, the inherited logics of military and diplomatic strategy gave legitimacy to a group of Cold War "wise men," while undermining the respectability of innovative political leaders who were not "present at the creation."[16]

---

14 For the best account of the events in Novocherkassk, see Samuel H. Baron, *Bloody Saturday in the Soviet Union: Novocherkassk, 1962* (Stanford, CA: Stanford University Press, 2001), esp. 1–127. On the legitimacy crisis confronting Soviet leaders in the 1960s, see Jeremi Suri, "The Promise and Failure of 'Developed Socialism': The Soviet 'Thaw' and the Crucible of the Prague Spring, 1964–1972," *Contemporary European History*, 15 (May 2006), 133–58.
15 This point is echoed in Jessica C. E. Gienow-Hecht's chapter in volume I. See also Nicholas Cull's chapter in this volume.
16 For more on the Cold War "wise men," see Walter Isaacson and Evan Thomas, *The Wise Men: Six Friends and the World They Made* (New York: Simon & Schuster, 1986).

The experience of World War II and its aftermath provided figures from that generation with a political gravity that younger citizens acknowledged but also resented. Students for a Democratic Society in the United States was one of many groups to proclaim that the world faced new challenges – civil rights, nuclear-arms control, decolonization, and others – that the elder statesmen, for all their experience, were unprepared to address. According to this argument, the "wise men" emphasized toughness, rather than peaceful cooperation. The "wise men" focused on military power, not social change. Most of all, the "wise men" were part of a conservative old culture of suits and big band dances, not a new culture of jeans and rock'n'roll. The "wise men" sought to preserve their way of life against challenges from within; the new men and women sought to transform basic assumptions about politics, foreign policy, and daily life. The new men and women also sought to consume a popular culture of personal freedom more fully, without the traditional restrictions imposed by an inherited culture of self-control and public discipline. Dissent was ideological, and it was fun.[17]

Rising expectations and Cold War contradictions

In his analysis of the Old Regime on the eve of the French Revolution, Alexis de Tocqueville predicted the counter-culture of the 1960s and 1970s. Privileged citizens, benefiting from improved material lives, had rising social and cultural expectations. Relative stability and prosperity encouraged increasing demands. The political moderation that supported stability and prosperity came under attack for its very moderation. This is precisely what Tocqueville meant when he pointed to the perils of reform after decades of war and deprivation. The promise of a better life encouraged growing demands among an educated generation of men and women that gradual social improvement could not sustain. Suburban wives had much more than their mothers, but it was not enough. West German students lived more secure lives than their parents, but it was not enough. Soviet laborers had better working conditions

The penetrating phrase "present at the creation" comes, of course, from Dean Acheson's memoirs: *Present at the Creation: My Years in the State Department* (New York: W. W. Norton, 1969).

17 See Students for a Democratic Society, *The Port Huron Statement* (New York: Students for a Democratic Society, 1962), esp. 1–9; Todd Gitlin, *The Sixties: Years of Hope, Days of Rage* (New York: Bantam, 1987); Paul Berman, *A Tale of Two Utopias: The Political Journey of the Generation of 1968* (New York: W. W. Norton, 1996).

than their predecessors, but it was not enough. Citizens blamed their leaders, not their unrealistic expectations, for the limits in their lives.[18]

These popular frustrations were not only a reaction to the Cold War. They were inspired by Cold War rhetoric and encouraged by Cold War leaders – often the same figures the counter-culture would later attack. The Soviet premier, Nikita Khrushchev, offers the best example of this dynamic. In his famous "secret speech" of February 1956, he exposed the horrors of Stalinist rule in the Soviet Union and legitimized freer public expression. Khrushchev explained that the fear and terror of prior years, accompanied by a vicious Stalinist "cult," were "a serious obstacle in the path of Soviet social development."[19] Excessive repression had undermined Communist ideals and it had weakened the Soviet Union in its competition with the United States. Losing its best minds to the Gulag, Moscow could not hope to match Western creativity. The Soviet Union needed to encourage limited new freedoms for the sake of Cold War competition.

Following this logic, Khrushchev temporarily opened up the Communist system, encouraging more innovation and achievement. He disbanded the Gulags, sending prisoners home with amnesty so they could contribute to society. He created new "science cities" where scholars could conduct research with generous resources and freer access to information than they enjoyed before. Most significant, Khrushchev allowed authors, such as Aleksandr Solzhenitsyn, to publish literature that he believed would discredit the Stalinist past and inspire new hope. "In the last years," Khrushchev explained, "when we managed to free ourselves of the harmful practice of the cult of the individual and took several proper steps in the sphere of internal and external policies, everyone saw how activity grew before their very eyes, how the creative activity of the broad working masses developed, how favorably all this acted upon the development of economy and culture."[20] Khrushchev promised that his program of openness – "the thaw," as many referred to it – would produce the first truly Communist society. It would "erase

18 See Alexis de Tocqueville, *L'Ancien Régime et la Révolution* (Paris: Gallimard, 1952), esp. 226–31. On the role of affluence, not deprivation, in the counter-culture, see Arthur Marwick, *The Sixties: Cultural Revolution in Britain, France, Italy, and the United States, c.1958–c.1974* (Oxford: Oxford University Press, 1998), esp. 80–95.
19 Nikita Khrushchev, Special Report to the XXth Congress of the Communist Party of the Soviet Union, trans. by US State Department, repr. in Strobe Talbott (ed. and trans.), *Khrushchev Remembers* (Boston, MA: Little, Brown, 1970), 612–13.
20 *Ibid.*

the essential distinctions between town and country and later on between mental and physical labor."[21]

Khrushchev's policies allowed more freedom for Soviet citizens, and they catapulted popular expectations. He expected to strengthen Soviet rule through these means. Instead, he nurtured a dissident counter-culture. Free of Stalinist terror, citizens could congregate and share their criticisms of the regime. They could organize low-level resistance, often by refusing to follow orders or dropping out of mandatory activities. Most troublesome for Khrushchev and his colleagues in the Kremlin, citizens felt empowered to question the basic legitimacy of the regime. Solzhenitsyn, the former Gulag prisoner whose writing Khrushchev initially approved for publication, made the Gulag into a metaphor for the Soviet Union as a whole. One of Solzhenitsyn's protagonists, Ivan Denisovich Shukhov, employed the existential language that became a hallmark for the counter-culture, and its attacks on leaders like Khrushchev:

> Shukhov stared at the ceiling and said nothing. He no longer knew whether he wanted to be free or not. To begin with, he'd wanted it very much, and counted up every evening how many days he still had to serve. Then he'd got fed up with it. And still later it had gradually dawned on him that people like himself were not allowed to go home but were packed off into exile. And there was no knowing where the living was easier – here or there. The one thing he might want to ask God for was to let him go home. But *they* wouldn't let him go home.[22]

The public circulation of Solzhenitsyn's *One Day in the Life of Ivan Denisovich*, and the enormous attention that it drew, inspired countless other attacks on Soviet authority from scientists, students, and ordinary citizens. Zhores Medvedev, a Soviet biologist who criticized the regime, called Solzhenitsyn's writing "a literary miracle" that had "everybody" talking.[23] "It has become clear," one reader of *Ivan Denisovich* explained in 1962, "that since the appearance of Solzhenitsyn's book we will never again be able to write as we have done till now."[24]

21 Nikita Khrushchev, Report on the Programme of the Communist Party of the Soviet Union, delivered at the XXIInd Congress of the Communist Party of the Soviet Union, October 18, 1961, trans., by Soviet Novosti Press Agency (London: Farleigh Press, 1961), 23.
22 Aleksandr Solzhenitsyn, *One Day in the Life of Ivan Denisovich*, trans. by H. T. Willetts (New York: Farrar, Straus and Giroux, 1991, originally published in Russian in 1962), 178.
23 Zhores A. Medvedev, *Ten Years after Ivan Denisovich*, trans. by Hilary Steinberg (New York: Alfred A. Knopf, 1973), 4, 6.
24 Gregori Boklanov, quoted in Cornelia Gerstenmaier, *The Voices of the Silent*, trans. by Susan Hecker (New York: Hart, 1972), 67. For more evidence of Solzhenitsyn's enormous influence among Soviet citizens, see Leopold Labedz (ed.), *Solzhenitsyn: A Documentary Record*, enlarged ed. (Bloomington, IN: Indiana University Press, 1973).

The government-authorized publication of Solzhenitsyn's book reflected the Cold War pressures on Khrushchev to encourage creativity and some public openness. The reception of the book, however, undermined Khrushchev's purposes – namely the protection of his authority and the strengthening of the Communist system. Cold War politics, in this sense, created a contradictory Cold War culture. The attempt to assure power through openness undermined power. The pressures on leaders to encourage innovation undermined leaders. International Cold War competition created space for the emergence of widespread dissent, even in Communist societies.

Khrushchev's predicament was emblematic, but hardly unique. In West Berlin – the strategic center for Soviet–American conflict – a similar dynamic took shape. At the end of World War II, the United States and the newly created Federal Republic of (West) Germany collaborated to sponsor a self-consciously democratic school: the Free University. Unlike its German counterparts, this institution encouraged student governance. It also emphasized experimental courses and approaches to teaching. The Free University set a new model for post-Fascist education in Germany, and it also served as a showcase for the freedom and dynamism that the sponsoring governments intended to display in West Berlin. The Free University was part of a cultural "magnet" strategy, designed to encourage citizens living under repressive Communist rule to embrace liberal-capitalism. In the unique context of West Berlin – where citizens from the Eastern and Western halves of the city could interact before the construction of the Berlin Wall in August 1961 – this involved the direct attraction of East German men and women through the Free University. Between 1949 and 1961, more than a third of the students attending the institution were citizens of the Communist state.[25]

Democratic education at the Free University helped to subvert Communist authority. The freedom and wealth on display in this institution convinced disgruntled East Germans – particularly the young and ambitious – to defect to the West. In the late 1950s, more than one hundred Communist citizens fled to the Federal Republic each day. Many of them were enrolled at the Free University.[26]

---

25 See James F. Tent, *The Free University of Berlin: A Political History* (Bloomington, IN: Indiana University Press, 1988), 1–176. On the American "magnet" strategy in Europe, see Melvyn P. Leffler, *A Preponderance of Power: National Security, The Truman Administration, and the Cold War* (Stanford, CA: Stanford University Press, 1992), 235–37; John Lewis Gaddis, *Strategies of Containment: A Critical Appraisal of American National Security Policy during the Cold War*, rev. ed. (New York: Oxford University Press, 2005), 64–69.

26 Alexandra Richie, *Faust's Metropolis: A History of Berlin* (New York: Carroll and Graf, 1998), 715–16.

The most famous of these student refugees was Rudolf "Rudi" Dutschke. He came from the East German province of Brandenburg. The Communist government had barred him from higher education when he refused to participate in mandatory military service during the late 1950s. As a consequence, Dutschke attended the Free University – the only post-secondary institution from which he was not barred. In 1961, he fled to West Berlin, continuing his studies in sociology, philosophy, and political science at the Free University.[27]

Dutschke's defection was a Cold War victory for the West, but it also produced a profound challenge to Cold War policy. By the second half of the 1960s, he became a leader of student protests against the West German government, American influence, and what he called the elements of "Fascism" built into capitalist democracy. He condemned the Federal Republic's conservative political culture, its support for repressive foreign regimes (especially the shah's monarchy in Iran), and Bonn's association with the brutal American war in Vietnam. In his diary, Dutschke expressed his desire to create a "third front," a counter-culture, to challenge dominant capitalist and Communist authorities.[28] Mao Zedong, Che Guevara, and idealized images of brave Vietnamese peasant fighters became inspirational symbols for a revolution against not just political institutions, but the basic organization of society. Dutschke proclaimed an "historic opening" for a global "emancipatory struggle and national self-determination."[29]

Dutschke's words articulated the frustrations of many young educated citizens throughout Western Europe who wanted more idealism and less association with Cold War ventures in Vietnam and other places. In February 1968, ten thousand people from various American-allied countries attended a student-organized "Vietnam Congress" at the Free University, designed to mobilize participants for "solidarity" and "revolutionary struggle."[30] Public

---

27 See Ulrich Chaussy, *Die drei Leben des Rudi Dutschke: eine Biographie* (Berlin: Christoph Links Verlag, 1993); Gretchen Dutschke, *Wir hatten ein barbarisches, schönes Leben: Rudi Dutschke, eine Biographie* (Cologne: Kiepenheuer und Witsch, 1996); Bernd Rabehl, *Rudi Dutschke: Revolutionär im geteilten Deutschland* (Dresden: Edition Antaios, 2002).

28 Rudi Dutschkes Tagebuch, 7. Juni 1967, in Rudi Dutschke, *Mein langer Marsch: Reden, Schriften und Tagebücher aus zwanzig Jahren* (Hamburg: Rowohlt, 1980), 70.

29 Dutschke, "Rebellion der Studenten," (1968), in *Mein langer Marsch*, 68–69. See also Jeremi Suri, "The Cultural Contradictions of Cold War Education: The Case of West Berlin," *Cold War History*, 4 (April 2004), 1–20.

30 Dutschke, *Mein langer Marsch*, 122, 71–72. See also Gerhard Bauß, *Die Studentenbewegung der sechziger Jahre* (Cologne: Pahl-Rugenstein Verlag, 1977), 95; Bernd Rabehl, *Am Ende der Utopie: Die politische Geschichte der Freien Universität Berlin* (Berlin: Argon, 1988), 256–68.

protests spread throughout the continent, employing the "third front" rhetoric of Dutschke and others.[31]

In the United States public demonstrations focused on Vietnam and civil rights, but they also employed the attacks on Cold War "imperialism" and "Fascism" that motivated the counter-culture in Western Europe. Antiwar protesters on university campuses throughout America looked to Third World revolutionaries for examples of "liberation." Advocates of Black Power took inspiration from nationalist movements in Africa that attacked the foreign and domestic "colonialism" of white rule. Dutschke's "third front" became the solution of choice for citizens struggling with the frustrations of unfulfilled expectations during a decade of unprecedented social improvements.

Herbert Marcuse, a German émigré to the United States who became one of the most recognized philosophers of the counter-culture, captured this common revolt against Cold War authority. He described what he perceived as the "genuine solidarity" among "young radicals" that drew its "elemental, instinctual, creative force" from guerrilla fighters in the Third World and the Chinese Cultural Revolution, not the traditional centers of influence. Western claims of progress had, according to Marcuse, lost their popular appeal.[32]

For all the violence in Vietnam and other parts of the Third World, the international system had become more stable and less prone to nuclear crisis in the 1960s. For all the continued racism in America and other societies, laws and attitudes had, in fact, changed in powerful ways to protect traditionally disenfranchised groups. This was significant progress, encouraged by Cold War competition. In their desire to make their societies stronger, more creative, and more attractive, leaders worked to make their societies better. Promises of reform in this ideologically overheated environment, however, mobilized citizens beyond the aims of their leaders. Solzhenitsyn's readers, Dutschke's followers, and Marcuse's radicals were empowered by the Cold War reforms they condemned as insufficient. The Cold War provided space for the counter-culture in universities, in public literature, and in other social settings. It even encouraged a counter-culture that showcased freedom and creativity.[33]

By the end of the 1960s, creativity had turned to revolt in nearly every major state. The countries most deeply penetrated by the Cold War confronted pervasive dissent and disaffection, especially among the young. Attempts

---

31 See Suri, *Power and Protest*, 164–212.

32 Herbert Marcuse, *An Essay on Liberation* (Boston, MA: Beacon Press, 1969), 86, 88.

33 On the encouragement of the "rebel" image as a symbol of American freedom in the Cold War, see Leerom Medovoi, *Rebels: Youth and the Cold War Origins of Identity* (Durham, NC: Duke University Press, 2005), esp. 1–51.

by leaders to mobilize their publics for domestic reform and international competition had produced spiraling domestic contention and aspirations to international solidarity among critics. The Cold War had globalized a set of ideological debates, and now a cohort of ideological dissidents.[34]

Counter-cultural violence and backlash

The late 1960s and early 1970s witnessed escalating violence in many societies. Nearly everywhere, established authorities found themselves under siege. National leaders could not travel within large sections of their own countries, for fear of embarrassing protests and personal attacks. Local figures – mayors, businesspeople, and teachers – confronted unprecedented challenges from citizens, customers, and students. Drug usage and crime rose across communities.[35] The British foreign secretary, Michael Stewart, captured the sense of widespread domestic upheaval when he confided to his diary: "The 10 pm television news presents a depressing picture." "The great difficulty of the world," Stewart lamented, "is the moral deficiencies of what should be the free world ... Germany distracted, France selfish, ourselves aimless, U.S.A. in torment."[36] The CIA confirmed this dark assessment, predicting: "The social and political malaise that underlies much of present-day dissidence will not be speedily cured; there are, in fact, striking parallels between the situation today and the conditions of cynicism, despair, and disposition toward violence which existed after World War I and which later helped produce Fascism and National Socialism on the Continent."[37]

The turn to violence among members of the counter-culture in various societies, and their opponents, created nightmarish premonitions. It also severed many of the connections between moderate leaders and critics that had supported effective political reform in prior years. In place of the collaboration between Dr. Martin Luther King, Jr. and President Johnson, open war among the supporters of men like Black Power advocate Stokely Carmichael and southern segregationist George Wallace dominated the years after 1967.

---

34 This point follows the analysis in Odd Arne Westad, *The Global Cold War: Third World Interventions and the Making of Our Times* (Cambridge: Cambridge University Press, 2005), esp. 110–206.

35 For the data on the cross-national increase in crime during the late 1960s, see Ted Robert Gurr and Erika Gurr, "Crime in Western Societies, 1945–1974," www.icpsr.umich.edu.

36 Michael Stewart, handwritten diary, April 17, 1968, STWT 8/1/5, Churchill Archives Center, Churchill College, Cambridge, England.

37 CIA report, "Restless Youth," 37.

34. A crowd of activists give the Black Power salute at a rally for the US Black Panther Party, 1969. Radical African-American leaders made the US political establishment feel that it was under siege.

Violent altercations, riots, and even acts of terrorism engulfed major cities across the United States, Western Europe, and other parts of the world. Cultural dissent produced domestic bloodletting and death. The violence of foreign wars in Vietnam and other places had now come home.

This descent into violence, though shocking, was the extension of the debates begun earlier in the 1960s. If the dominant Cold War culture was stagnant and repressive, as critics claimed, it had to be destroyed and replaced. Overcoming the stubborn resistance of entrenched figures required force. Public violence appeared as a necessary tool to unseat violent oppressors. This is where the image of peasant revolutionaries in Vietnam looked so appealing. This is where the "Great Proletarian Cultural Revolution" in China, initially triggered by Mao Zedong, offered inspiration. Here was a society violently turning itself upside down to eradicate vestiges of an old culture. Here was a society that made violence a purifying force, cleansing itself of "backward" traditions. The Chinese Cultural Revolution was, in fact, one of the most brutal and self-defeating political enterprises of the twentieth century. Its shrill attacks on established wisdom, however, made it attractive for those seeking to change the basic relations between citizens in society. Herbert Marcuse was only one of many to point to China as a model for "liberation."[38]

Counter-cultural groups formed in the early 1970s that treated violence as a means for proving cultural authenticity in an international environment filled with lies. Putting one's life (and the lives of others) on the line demonstrated a depth of personal courage and truthfulness that these critics claimed Cold War society lacked. Instead of working with the "machine" for personal benefit, intelligent young men and women pledged to place their bodies, literally, on the gears – to stop the normal functioning of society with their blood. The Weather Underground embodied this idealization of violence in the United States. Formed in 1969 to promote an "armed struggle" against capitalist society, members of the group declared the need for "a movement that fights, not just talks about fighting." The Red Army Faction emerged in West Germany as a more deadly counterpart. First organized in 1970, it proclaimed: "We will not talk about armed propaganda, we will do it."[39]

These two groups, and those in other countries, mixed counter-cultural politics with paramilitary behavior. They lived communal lifestyles, but they enforced military discipline. They called for political openness, but they violently attacked their critics. They tried to appeal to the public, but they prepared to kill innocent, even sympathetic, citizens in the pursuit of their cause. This is the point when rebels turned into terrorists. This is also the point when violence grew from a tool for resistance into a defining element of the counter-culture. It took on symbolic value as a total rejection of standard, "civilized" authority. It became a marker of status for a small group of men and

---

38 Marcuse, *An Essay on Liberation*, viii.
39 Quotations from Jeremy Varon, *Bringing the War Home: The Weather Underground, the Red Army Faction, and Revolutionary Violence in the Sixties and Seventies* (Berkeley, CA: University of California Press, 2004), 21.

women who came to think of themselves as guerrilla fighters, battling to save society from itself.[40]

This domestic terrorism elicited firm reactions from state authorities and their supporters. They deployed overwhelming force against what they perceived as an apocalyptic threat – violent revolution from within, and domestic terrorism against innocent civilians. State authorities also discredited violent critics by denying them obvious influence on policy. The United States continued to fight in Vietnam, despite resistance at home, for four additional years. The Soviet Union ordered an invasion of Czechoslovakia to repress the reforming government there, despite strong opposition to such a move within the Eastern bloc. The West German government maintained its close partnership with Washington, despite widespread anti-American sentiment. Counter-cultural violence sparked a backlash that raised resistance to change in both domestic and foreign policy.

The backlash was often much more violent than the initial counter-cultural attacks. The August 1968 Democratic Party convention in Chicago offered the most publicized evidence of this dynamic. As groups like the Youth International Party ("Yippies") converged on the city to condemn mainstream politics, in general, and the Democratic Party's continued support for the Vietnam War, in particular, local police prepared to attack the protesters. Abbie Hoffman and other counter-cultural critics mocked and provoked the police, but the response by law enforcement officials was out of proportion to the instigation. Mayor Richard Daley mobilized his entire police force, as well as members of the National Guard, for demonstrations that never included more than 7,000 protesters. Determined to preempt counter-cultural violence, the Chicago police attacked mobs with nightsticks and other implements. They did not wait for the young men and women in the streets to become disruptive. State authorities violently crushed a perceived threat from politically engaged citizens.[41]

Events in Chicago mirrored the expansion of police powers in West Germany and other democratic societies. Counter-cultural disorder created a perceived "emergency" that justified violent, often undemocratic, reactions. Police forces entered university campuses, business offices, and private homes to search for evidence of brewing conspiracy. Domestic intelligence agencies – most notoriously the Federal Bureau of Investigation (FBI) in the United

---

40 See the excellent analysis of this point in Varon, *Bringing the War Home*, esp. 196–289.
41 See the balanced and evocative book by David Farber, *Chicago '68* (Chicago: University of Chicago Press, 1988).

35. French police using force during the student demonstrations in Paris in May 1968. The violent backlash against the counter-culture militarized daily life in the Cold War.

States – increased their surveillance of suspected individuals. Washington, DC, West Berlin, Paris, and Mexico City came under virtual martial law during periods of heightened unrest, as regular army soldiers walked the streets to assure order. The violent backlash against the counter-culture militarized daily life in the Cold War.[42]

In the Communist countries, where politics were already militarized, the domestic deployment of armed forces also expanded. Chairman Mao Zedong had initiated the Great Proletarian Cultural Revolution in China. As the country careened into chaos during the late 1960s, however, he turned to the People's Liberation Army to restore order and assure his continued power. Mao used the military to repress the Red Guards he had sent into the streets. Despite his earlier calls for breaking traditional institutions, Mao warned in 1968 of emerging "anarchy." To reverse this course, he affirmed that "the army is the fundamental pillar of the Cultural Revolution."[43]

---

42 See Suri, *Power and Protest*, 164–212.
43 *People's Daily* editorial, March 1, 1968, in Jerome Chen (ed.), *Mao Papers: Anthology and Bibliography* (New York: Oxford University Press, 1970), 152; Simon Leys, *The Chairman's New Clothes: Mao and the Cultural Revolution*, trans. by Carol Appleyard and Patrick Goode (New York: St. Martin's Press, 1977, originally published in 1971), 106–07. See also Suri, *Power and Protest*, 206–11.

The Soviet Union never returned to the terror of the Stalinist years, but under General Secretary Leonid Brezhnev's leadership, the KGB stepped up its efforts to identify, discredit, and eliminate dissident voices in the early 1970s. The Kremlin's tolerance for domestic criticism diminished as the regime grew more anxious about internal unrest. Brezhnev, in particular, relied on the image of a strengthening Soviet military to bolster his legitimacy (including countless medals he awarded himself) and assure Communist authority. The counter-culture attacked militarization but, ironically, it inspired more of the same.[44]

"Law and order"

If leaders promising to "pay any price" and build Communism dominated the early 1960s, figures pledged to "law and order" shaped the early 1970s. President Nixon popularized the phrase in the United States, but his counter-parts in West Germany, the Soviet Union, and other countries used similar terms. In the wake of the counter-culture, leaders rebuilt their authority around commitments to restore rationality, reasonableness, and domestic peace. As best as we can tell, this is what a "silent majority" of people wanted in many societies, following years of upheaval and violence. Nixon captured this sentiment in his inaugural address of January 20, 1969. Addressing "America's youth" and "the people of the world," the new president argued: "We cannot learn from one another until we stop shouting at one another – until we speak quietly enough so that our words can be heard as well as our voices." "For all our people," Nixon continued, "we will set as our goal the decent order that makes progress possible and our lives secure."[45] Nixon's words received favorable attention at home and abroad, including China, where Mao Zedong sought to rein in the excesses of the Cultural Revolution and open relations with the United States.[46]

---

44 See Dmitrii Volkogonov, *Sem' vozhdei: galereia liderov SSSR* [Seven Leaders: The Gallery of the Leaders of the USSR], 2 vols. (Moscow: Novosti, 1995), vol. II, esp. 41–42; Suri, "The Promise and Failure of 'Developed Socialism,'" 150–58.

45 Richard Nixon, Inaugural Address, *Public Papers of the Presidents: Richard Nixon, 1969* (Washington, DC: US Government Printing Office, 1971), 1–2 [hereafter, *ppp*]. On the "Silent Majority," see Dan T. Carter, *The Politics of Rage: George Wallace, the Origins of the New Conservatism, and the Transformation of American Politics*, 2nd ed. (Baton Rouge, LA: Louisiana State University Press, 2000), esp., 324–414; Bruce J. Schulman, *The Seventies: The Great Shift in American Culture, Society and Politics* (New York: Free Press, 2001), esp. 23–117.

46 See Mao Zedong's comments on an article in *Renmin ribao* and *Hongqi*, January 1969, trans. in *Cold War International History Project Bulletin*, 11 (Winter 1998), 161; Mao Zedong's speech at the First Plenary Session of the Chinese Communist Party's Ninth Central Committee, April 28, 1969, trans. in *ibid.*, 164–65.

"Law and order" was more than just a reaction to disorder and upheaval. It represented a new kind of counter-culture in the 1970s, one that rejected both the standard ideological rhetoric of the Cold War and the oppositional claims of figures like Betty Friedan, Aleksandr Solzhenitsyn, and Rudi Dutschke. "Law and order" meant a return to something more basic – commitment to civility, faith in moderation, and loyalty to nation. These beliefs did not challenge the Cold War per se, but they reframed the conflict in terms of limits rather than possibilities. Instead of proclaiming a mission to improve the lives of diverse people at home and abroad, "law and order" focused on restraining the excesses of the last decades that in Vietnam, on university campuses, and in countless other locales had brought despair and disillusion. "Law and order" was about a sober political and social reassessment that lowered popular expectations and encouraged citizens to accept an imperfect world.[47]

This rhetoric appealed to some of the racist, chauvinist, and ethnocentric instincts that characterized the backlash against the counter-culture. In doing so, it rejected the faith in the possibilities of liberal capitalist and communist "development" that underpinned earlier Cold War conflict. The United States and the Soviet Union continued to intervene overseas – and Moscow, in fact, increased its activities in the Third World – but these undertakings lacked the optimism of prior ventures.[48] The leaders and citizens of the superpowers acted in response to local and allied pressures, often to protect face more than pursue global change. There were exceptions (particularly massive Soviet support for an Ethiopian revolution that promised to lead the African continent to Communism), but the 1970s was not a decade of grand projects or grand expectations.[49] The counter-culture of these years rejected the ambitions shared by advocates and opponents of Cold War policy in prior decades.

Proponents of "law and order" told activists like Betty Friedan that they were indeed mistaken to expect happiness in Cold War suburbia. They were also wrong to pursue an alternative form of liberation. Instead, they should accept their lives as they were and protect what they had against worse possibilities. A culture of pessimism and limits replaced the Cold War culture of optimism and possibilities.

47 See Michael W. Flamm, Law and Order: Street Crime, Civil Unrest, and the Crisis of Liberalism in the 1960s (New York: Columbia University Press, 2005), esp. 31–50, 162–78; Melvin Small, The Presidency of Richard Nixon (Lawrence, KS: University Press of Kansas, 1999), 153–83.
48 See the chapters by Michael E. Latham, Fredrik Logevall, Douglas Little, and Piero Gleijeses in this volume; see also the chapters by Nancy Mitchell, Vladislav M. Zubok, Chris Saunders and Sue Onslow, John H. Coatsworth, and Amin Saikal in volume III.
49 See Westad, The Global Cold War, esp. 250–87.

Détente

This was the social and cultural context for the foreign policy of détente in the 1970s. Scholars of détente generally point to the importance of near nuclear parity and a general balance of power in bringing the United States and the Soviet Union to embrace more stable relations. They also point to the growing rift between Moscow and Beijing, and the opening this created for Washington to position itself between these two states. American desperation to end the Vietnam War surely contributed to détente as well, encouraging citizens and leaders in the United States to accept a less ideologically strident foreign policy.[50]

President Nixon and his special assistant for national security affairs, Henry Kissinger, embraced these strategic transformations, and they attempted to turn them to American advantage. They sought to use improved great power relations for more effective leverage over local events around the globe, with less direct American force. This was the basis for the "Nixon Doctrine," designed to avoid making countries "so dependent upon us that we are dragged into conflicts such as the one that we have in Vietnam."[51] Amidst powerful domestic and allied dissent against American interventions, détente was an attempt to compensate for internal weakness with diplomatic acumen. It was a reaction to domestic pressures for peace and fears of continued Cold War militarization. "We were," Kissinger explained, "in a delicate balancing act: to be committed to peace without letting the quest for it become a form of moral disarmament, surrendering all other values; to be prepared to defend freedom while making clear that unconstrained rivalry could risk everything, including freedom, in a nuclear holocaust."[52]

In his memoirs, Kissinger immediately turns from this description of détente to a discussion about the need to "outmaneuver" domestic dissent – from "liberals" who wanted to see more commitment to peace and reform in American actions, and "conservatives" who demanded stronger confrontation

50 See Robert Schulzinger's chapter in this volume; Jussi Hanhimäki, *The Flawed Architect: Henry Kissinger and American Foreign Policy* (New York: Oxford University Press, 2004), esp. 55–67; Robert Schulzinger, *Henry Kissinger: Doctor of Diplomacy* (New York: Columbia University Press, 1989), esp. 52–74; Gaddis, *Strategies of Containment*, 272–341; Raymond Garthoff, *Détente and Confrontation: American-Soviet Relations from Nixon to Reagan*, rev. ed. (Washington, DC: Brookings Institution, 1994).
51 Richard Nixon, Informal Remarks in Guam with Newsmen, July 25, 1969, *PPP: Richard Nixon, 1969*, 548. For a fuller statement of the "Nixon Doctrine," see Richard Nixon, Annual Foreign Policy Report, February 18, 1970, in *ibid.*, 1970, 118–19.
52 Henry Kissinger, *White House Years* (Boston, MA: Little, Brown, 1979), 1254.

with Communism.[53] Political leaders in West Germany, Britain, and other states faced the same dichotomous pressures. The counter-culture's attack on Cold War assumptions, and the backlash against this challenge, inflamed these debates. The domestic violence and extremism of the period made it difficult to build bridges between points of view. In contrast to their predecessors, leaders in the 1970s had to formulate international policy at a time when their authority was deeply contested at home. President Nixon and West German chancellor Willy Brandt, two of the most powerful international leaders of the 1970s, both resigned from office due to domestic scandals, inflamed by public distrust of leaders. The making of détente reflected the unmaking of the Cold War consensus.

Kissinger admitted this. When asked in 1971 "where the administration wants to end up after four years?" he invoked both the crisis of values and the new international environment that characterized the period. "This administration came into office when the intellectual capital of US postwar policy had been used up and when the conditions determining postwar US policy had been altered," he explained.

> We had to adjust our foreign policy to the new facts of life. It is beyond the physical and psychological capacity of the US to make itself responsible for every part of the world. We hope in the first term to clear away the under-bush of the old period. In the second term, we could try to construct a new international settlement – which will be more stable, less crisis-conscious, and less dependent on decisions in one capital.[54]

The "underbush of the old period" included the assumptions about omnipotent power that the counter-culture condemned. Constructing a "new international settlement" meant applying "law and order" to foreign policy, providing a framework for rationality, reasonableness, and moderation in the relations between societies – despite the contrary pressures at home. Frequent "back channel" communications between leaders would encourage cooperation, establish basic norms for international conduct, and insulate policy from domestic interference. This was an effort, Kissinger and the Soviet ambassador Anatolii Dobrynin agreed, to make international civility "irreversible."[55]

53 *Ibid.*, 1255.
54 Memorandum of conversation between Henry Kissinger and a group of Fellows from the Harvard Center for International Affairs, December 7, 1971, Digital National Security Archive Document Database, http://nsarchive.chadwyck.com.ezproxy.library.wisc.edu (accessed July 26, 2006).
55 Memorandum of conversation between Leonid Brezhnev, Anatolii Dobrynin, Henry Kissinger, *et al.*, Moscow, October 24, 1974, 11:00 am–2:00 pm, folder: 11/74, Japan,

The two superpowers formalized their commitment to international "law and order," rather than revolutionary change, in the Agreement on Basic Principles – officially "The Basic Principles of Relations between the United States of America and the Union of Soviet Socialist Republics" – signed in Moscow on May 29, 1972. The document spoke explicitly about "rules of conduct" that would assure "peaceful coexistence" and avoid any "dangerous exacerbation" of relations.[56] It encouraged consultation among state leaders, and it diminished the importance of ideology, nationalism, and other moral claims. The Agreement on Basic Principles aimed to silence cold warriors and counter-cultural critics at the same time.

In addition to basic strategic considerations, détente represented an effort to build a new culture for international affairs. It was, in this sense, the foreign mirror of domestic change. Internal discontent and disorder forced leaders to reconceptualize their foreign-policy aims and capabilities. Challenges to assumed Cold War values motivated policies that did not hinge on traditional ideological claims. Men like Kissinger and Dobrynin feared the backlash as much as the counter-culture, and they worked to craft a new middle ground. They emphasized "law and order" in the international system. They attempted to isolate policy from public influence. They defined themselves against both the counter-culture of the late 1960s and its opponents.[57]

Counter-cultures and the Cold War

Betty Friedan's famous attack on domesticity was about more than feminism. Her words captured an emerging revolt against authority around the world. Unlike most prior resistance to the dominant Cold War ideas and policies, this rebellion came from within – from the universities, the literary circles, and even the bedrooms of mainstream society. This was Friedan's central insight. Those who appeared to benefit most from the politics of the time were dissatisfied. They were empowered, because of their social centrality, to

Korea, USSR, box A6, Kissinger–Scowcroft Files, Gerald Ford Presidential Library, Ann Arbor, Michigan. See also memorandum of conversation between Leonid Brezhnev, Anatolii Dobrynin, Henry Kissinger, *et al.*, Moscow, October 26, 1974, 7:10pm–10:20 pm, *ibid.* These two documents are also reprinted in William Burr (ed.), *The Kissinger Transcripts* (New York: New Press, 1998), 327–55.

56 "Basic Principles of Relations between the United States of America and the Union of Soviet Socialist Republics," May 29, 1972, repr. in *The U.S. Department of State of Bulletin* 66 (June 26, 1972), 898–99.

57 See Jeremi Suri, *Henry Kissinger and the American Century* (Cambridge, MA: Belknap Press of Harvard University Press, 2007), esp. 197–248.

demand more. They were motivated, because of their rising expectations, to reject cultural limitations.

In the 1960s and 1970s, an international counter-culture, comprising countless local groups, exposed the problem that had no name. The counter-culture challenged not only existing authority, but also the basic assumptions about the "good life" that underpinned social order. The Cold War policies condemned for stagnating social change actually encouraged and legitimized this counter-culture. State leaders sponsored education and innovation for more effective competition against international adversaries. They also made broad ideological claims that they could not fulfill. Citizens, particularly privileged young citizens, now had the means and the motivation to challenge their leaders for failing to meet their stated goals. In nearly every major society, men and women asked why government policies did not produce the promised outcomes, why their country was falling short. A wide spectrum of citizens – from street protesters to members of the "Silent Majority" – questioned not just the competence of their leaders, but also their values.

This was the central contradiction of the Cold War between 1965 and 1975. The pressures for international competition inspired domestic contention. As states built external strength they diminished their internal cohesiveness. Observers frequently treat the social history of the counter-culture as something separate from the political history of the Cold War, but the two were, in fact, deeply intertwined. Cold War ideas, resources, and institutions made the counter-culture. The counter-culture, in turn, unmade these ideas, resources, and institutions. The backlash against the counter-culture furthered this process by contributing to widespread violence and division. In the 1960s and 1970s, the Cold War became more stable in traditional areas of great power conflict, but it grew more disruptive within societies.

Although the counter-culture did not revolutionize the world, it exerted a powerful influence on Cold War policies. Leaders abandoned grand ideological projects and turned to promises of "law and order." At home and abroad, they emphasized rationality and reasonableness. Détente rejected the old political assumptions as well as the radical calls for something new. The counter-culture was both a product of the Cold War and an agent in its transformation.

23

The structure of great power politics, 1963–1975

MARC TRACHTENBERG

John F. Kennedy's most basic goal as president of the United States was to reach a political understanding with the Soviet Union. That understanding would be based on a simple principle: the United States and the Soviet Union were both very great powers and therefore needed to respect each other's most basic interests. The US government was thus prepared, for its part, to recognize the USSR's special position in Eastern Europe. The United States would, moreover, see to it that West Germany would not become a nuclear power. In exchange, the Soviets would also have to accept the status quo in Central Europe, especially in Berlin. If a settlement of that sort could be worked out, the situation in Central Europe would be stabilized. The great problem that lay at the heart of the Cold War would be resolved.

But to reach a settlement based on those principles, Kennedy had to get both the USSR and his own allies in Europe to accept this sort of arrangement. The Soviets, however, were not particularly receptive when it became clear to them, beginning in mid-1961, what the president had in mind. The Americans, in their view, were making concessions because they were afraid the Berlin crisis would lead to war. Why not see what more they might get by keeping the crisis going?

As for the Europeans, they by no means welcomed the new Kennedy policy with open arms. The West German government was especially distraught. Germany was divided and there was obviously not much anyone could do about it. But for years the German government – the conservative government that Konrad Adenauer had led since the founding of the Federal Republic in 1949 – had insisted that those "realities" could not be officially recognized. To do so would put a kind of seal of approval on the division of the country. Nor was the Adenauer government pleased by what the Americans had in mind with

A more heavily footnoted version of this paper is available online at www.polisci.ucla.edu/faculty/trachtenberg/cv/chcw(long).doc.

regard to Germany's nuclear status. A Germany with no nuclear forces under its own control would be utterly dependent on the United States for its security. Could any great nation rely so totally on a foreign power for its protection and accept the sort of extreme political dependence that such a situation implied? The Germans, of course, knew they had to pay a price for what their country had done during the Hitler period, and that meant that for the time being certain constraints in this area had to be accepted. But the German government also felt it had to try to keep the Federal Republic's nuclear options open. It thus did not take kindly to the idea of formalizing Germany's nonnuclear status, above all as part of a general settlement with the USSR.

The French, for other reasons, did not like the way Kennedy was playing the Western hand. It was not that they objected in principle to the sort of understanding with the Soviets he had in mind, but they felt he was giving away too much too quickly at a time when a lot more in the way of backbone was in order. Even the British were somewhat taken aback, in late 1961, by the Kennedy policy. But the president was prepared to move ahead regardless: the Europeans would have to "come along or stay behind."[1]

He was particularly rough with the Germans. The conflict came to a head in early 1963. If the Germans wanted to pursue an independent policy – a policy based on a strong alignment with the France of Charles de Gaulle, a policy, that is, with a distinct anti-American edge – they could just forget about American military protection. If they wanted the United States to provide for their security, they would have to follow America's political lead. They would have to cooperate, in other words, with the policy Kennedy was now pursuing vis-à-vis the Soviet Union. And the Germans made their choice. Adenauer was forced out as chancellor and the Federal Republic more or less formally declared its loyalty to the North Atlantic Treaty Organization (NATO) and to the United States.

By that point, the conflict with the USSR had come to a head. The Cuban missile crisis of October 1962 was the climax of the great Berlin crisis of 1958–62.[2] The Soviets had not been willing to make peace on Kennedy's terms and they had in effect threatened war. But now, after the missile crisis, that Soviet policy was clearly bankrupt. The Soviets were still unwilling to make a formal deal, but the major powers reached certain more or less tacit understandings: the status quo in Berlin would be respected and Germany

---

1 Memorandum from J. F. Kennedy to D. Rusk, August 21, 1961, US Department of State, *Foreign Relations of the United States, 1961–1963* (Washington, DC: US Government Printing Office, 1971), vol. XIV, 359 (hereafter, *FRUS*, with year and volume number).
2 See James Hershberg's chapter in this volume.

would be kept nonnuclear. Indeed, one of the main goals of the Limited Nuclear Test-Ban Treaty of July 1963 – a treaty which the Germans were essentially made to sign – was to make it harder for West Germany to build nuclear weapons.[3] But this was not a simple gift to the Soviets. It was linked to other understandings, most notably relating to Berlin, that mainly benefited the Western powers.

Taken as a bloc, those understandings provided the basis for a relatively stable international order. But many Germans – the German "Gaullists," as now ex-Chancellor Adenauer and those who basically shared his views were called – were bitter about the course that events had taken. German interests, as they saw it, had been sacrificed so that the United States could pursue its own goals. But in West Germany in 1963 that was a minority view, even in Adenauer's own party. Most Germans were coming to see things in a rather different light.

It was important, Kennedy argued, in a speech he gave during his famous visit to Berlin in June 1963, "to face the facts as they are, not to involve ourselves in self-deception." It was "not enough," he said, "to mark time, to adhere to a status quo, while awaiting a change for the better."[4] His meaning was clear: the rigid German policy of the past had to be abandoned. But the Germans, by and large, were not appalled by those remarks. The Adenauer approach had not brought reunification any closer, so maybe it was time for something new. There was also a certain sense that the Federal Republic could not be too out of step with her Western partners, none of whom were (as de Gaulle often put it) in any rush to see Germany reunified. The Federal Republic could not afford to pursue a totally independent policy. She had to frame her policy with an eye to what her allies, especially the Americans, were willing to support.

Egon Bahr, chief adviser to Willy Brandt, mayor of West Berlin and the leading figure in the German Social Democratic Party (SPD), made the key point in a famous speech he gave in July 1963, just three weeks after Kennedy's visit to Berlin. The Americans were pursuing a peace policy, and if the Germans did not want to just sit on the sidelines as America pursued that policy, they would have to pursue an active détente policy of their own.[5] A policy that sought to relax tensions in Central Europe might eventually lead to major changes in the Cold War status quo. At the very least, in the view of people like Bahr, better relations

---

3 For more on the Limited Test-Ban Treaty, see Francis J. Gavin's chapter in this volume.

4 Address at the Free University of Berlin, June 26, 1963, *Public Papers of the Presidents: John F. Kennedy: 1963* (Washington, DC: US Government Printing Office, 1964), 527.

5 Bahr Tutzing speech, July 15, 1963, *Dokumente zur Deutschlandpolitik*, 4th series (Frankfurt/Main: Alfred Metzner, 1978), vol. IX, part 2, 572–75.

with the Soviet Union might reduce the Federal Republic's extraordinary dependence on America and thus might make it possible for the Germans to pursue a policy based more on their own national interests.

By the end of the decade, Brandt had become chancellor and Bahr was his right-hand man. Their way of thinking had strong support not just in their own party but also in the Free Democratic Party (FDP), the junior partner in the governing coalition. It was also supported to one degree or another by important elements in the conservative parties. Brandt and Bahr were thus able to pursue their policy of improving relations with the east – their *Ostpolitik*. The Soviets were receptive, their Western partners were supportive (for the time being at least), and by 1973 a whole package of agreements

36. US secretary of state Henry Kissinger and West German chancellor Willy Brandt in Bonn, March 1974. Kissinger never fully trusted Brandt's Western orientation.

had been signed and ratified: treaties providing for the "inviolability" of existing borders in Central Europe; a treaty establishing a framework for relations between the two German states; a four-power treaty securing the status quo in Berlin; and the Nuclear Non-Proliferation Treaty (NPT), whose importance for the Soviets lay mainly in the fact that it would help keep Germany nonnuclear.

This was very similar to what Kennedy had wanted, and it is tempting to view the *Ostpolitik* treaties as just the icing on the cake – to assume that the system of great power relations in Europe, the heart of the international political system, was already quite stable, and that the only difference now was that this fact was getting a kind of formal recognition. But the system had a basic structural flaw: the military foundation on which it rested was not rock-solid. How stable it would end up being would depend, in large measure, on how that military problem was dealt with.

The NATO nuclear problem

During the Cold War, Western Europe lived in the shadow of Soviet military power and the NATO countries obviously had to be concerned with the military balance on the continent. If there were no effective counterweight to Soviet power in Europe, the Europeans would be at the mercy of the USSR. Even if the Red Army never actually invaded Western Europe, an imbalance of military power, it was assumed, would almost certainly have far-reaching political consequences.

What sort of counterweight could be put in place? During the heyday of American nuclear superiority, the period from late 1952 through mid-1963, the Soviets could be deterred from invading Western Europe by the threat of US nuclear retaliation. This was a threat the US government might actually execute in extreme circumstances: if the attack was massive enough and was launched quickly enough, the United States would not suffer really heavy damage from whatever counterattack the Soviets were able to mount. But by September 1963, the US government had reached the conclusion that even if the United States were to "attack the USSR first, the loss to the United States would be unacceptable to political leaders." It was understood at once that Washington could no longer, even in theory, respond to an act of aggression in Europe with a full-scale attack on the USSR.[6]

6 Summary record of NSC meeting, September 12, 1963 (Report of Net Evaluation Subcommittee), *FRUS, 1961–1963*, vol. VIII, 499–500.

How then could NATO Europe be protected? In principle, the European countries could build deterrent forces of their own and, in fact, a number of NATO countries wanted to go in that direction. The Germans, in particular, were interested in building a nuclear force they themselves would control. Adenauer, for example, certainly wanted Germany to have nuclear weapons – "we must produce them," he said in 1957 – and Ludwig Erhard, who succeeded him as chancellor, told President Lyndon B. Johnson in 1965 that "it was impossible to assume that Germany will go forever without a nuclear deterrent."[7] The Germans very much wanted to keep their nuclear options open; it was for this reason that many German leaders in the late 1960s did not want their country to sign the Non-Proliferation Treaty.

But the Soviets were dead set against the very idea of a German nuclear force and opposed anything that pointed in that direction. This was one issue, it seemed, that the USSR might actually go to war over. As for the Federal Republic's allies, the British were totally opposed to the notion of a German nuclear capability from the very outset. The French attitude, somewhat ambivalent in the late 1950s and early 1960s, hardened dramatically after Franco-German relations went downhill in 1963. By the mid-1960s, de Gaulle was very much against the idea of the Germans getting their hands on nuclear weapons.

And the Americans, by that time, were absolutely determined to keep the Federal Republic from acquiring a nuclear force. President Johnson had no doubt that the Germans would want to build such a force as soon as they could, but he also thought it would be disastrous if Germany went nuclear. The US government tried to deal with this problem by pushing its plan for a "multilateral force" (MLF); the huge effort it put into that very dubious project, especially in 1964, is a good measure of the seriousness with which it took this problem. It eventually gave up on that idea and thus needed to deal with the problem in a more direct way – namely, by laying down the law to the Germans. They were warned that their country "might well be destroyed" if they tried to develop an independent nuclear capability.[8] They could scarcely resist this sort of pressure, and by the end of the decade it was clear that the Federal Republic was not going to become a nuclear power.

But if a German nuclear deterrent was out of the question, and if the American nuclear deterrent could no longer, in itself, keep the Red Army at

---

7 Konrad Adenauer, quoted in Hans-Peter Schwarz, *Adenauer*, vol. II (Stuttgart: Deutsche Verlags-Anstalt, 1991), 396; Memorandum of conversation between L. B. Johnson and L. Erhard, December 20, 1965, *FRUS, 1964–1968*, vol. XIII, 291.
8 Meeting between W. W. Rostow and R. Barzel, February 23, 1968, *FRUS, 1964–1968*, vol. XV, 637.

bay, how then could Europe be protected? US leaders thought that NATO needed to move away from nuclear deterrence and should instead place much greater emphasis on conventional forces. But there were two problems with the conventional strategy. First of all, the forces needed to sustain such a strategy were simply not available. Throughout the 1960s, the United States, and Britain as well, were under pressure to cut back on their military presence in Central Europe for balance-of-payments and other reasons, some connected with the Vietnam War. Indeed, and despite the emphasis American leaders placed on conventional forces at that time, US force levels in Europe declined substantially during that period, and the NATO defense ministers were told in 1968 to get ready for yet further cuts. France's withdrawal in 1966 from the NATO military system, of course, further aggravated the problem.

The second problem was more basic: no matter what sort of conventional defense was put in place, NATO would still have to worry about the possibility of a Soviet nuclear attack. People wanted to build up NATO's conventional defenses because they assumed the United States would not be willing to use nuclear weapons against the USSR no matter what was happening in a conventional war for fear of provoking a Soviet nuclear attack on the United States. But would the threat of escalation be any less great if nuclear weapons were used in response to a Soviet *nuclear* attack on Europe? Why would the United States be more likely, in such circumstances, to take action that could lead to a Soviet attack on America? Wouldn't the Americans in that case be likely to accept defeat, or at most to use nuclear weapons only against battlefield targets and targets in Eastern Europe, avoiding Soviet territory entirely? But if Soviet territory was treated as a "sanctuary," then what exactly was the USSR being threatened with? What deterrent value would the Western forces then have?

US officials generally dismissed this problem out of hand. But the Europeans were not convinced that a nuclear war in which the two superpowers' homelands were spared was simply out of the question and their concerns had some basis in fact. The Soviets, it seems, had by no means ruled out the possibility of a war in which "the use of nuclear weapons would remain restricted to the theater level, leaving both homelands inviolate."[9]

That meant that the nuclear issue could not be dismissed as unreal. One could not just assume that nuclear weapons were "unusable" for both sides, that the two nuclear arsenals simply "cancelled each other out," and that the

9 William Odom, *The Collapse of the Soviet Military* (New Haven, CT: Yale University Press, 1998), 69.

conventional balance was the only thing that really mattered. One had to think about how nuclear weapons would be used, if a conventional defense proved ineffective or if the enemy used nuclear weapons first in a European war. It made little sense to launch an all-out attack in such circumstances; if nuclear weapons were used at all, they would obviously have to be used in a more limited and more controlled way. And NATO, in fact, adopted a strategy of controlled escalation. But how would that strategy work? What "philosophy" would govern the use of NATO's nuclear forces?

The key issue here had to do with tactical nuclear weapons – that is, with the question of how the thousands of such weapons NATO had in Europe would be used in the event of war. But the NATO countries had a hard time coming up with an answer to this question. The basic problem was clear enough. On the one hand, if the goal was to deter a Soviet attack on Europe, the USSR itself could not be treated as a "sanctuary." Use of the weapons, it was sometimes argued, would therefore have to be part of a process, perhaps a process no one could fully control, that might conceivably lead to nuclear attacks on the USSR itself. Those attacks, to be sure, might in turn lead to a Soviet nuclear strike on the United States. But as long as there was only a *chance* of this happening – as long as the US government did not have to take action that it knew with absolute certainty would lead to a general nuclear war – NATO, the argument ran, should be willing to run the risk.

On the other hand, there was a real aversion, not just on the part of the Americans but in practice on the part of the Europeans as well, to deliberately running any serious risk of general nuclear war. Given what was at stake, a strategy of that sort seemed utterly irresponsible. The risk of escalation was not a phenomenon to be exploited; it was a danger to be minimized. The Americans had no stomach for engaging in what Thomas Schelling called a "competition in risk taking" – for deliberately playing on the possibility that events might spin out of control, and thus for arranging things so that no one could be sure that the conflict would not escalate. Nor were the Europeans really committed to such a strategy: as US leaders sometimes pointed out, whatever the Europeans said in peacetime, if the moment of truth ever came they would draw back from any use of nuclear weapons.

So the Americans wanted to keep the lid on the escalatory process – or, as they put it even in official pronouncements, to keep the fighting at the "lowest level of violence consistent with NATO's objectives."[10] But this seemed to

---

10 Secretary of Defense James Schlesinger, "The Theater Nuclear Force Posture in Europe" (April 1974), www.dod.mil/pubs/foi/reading_room/237.pdf, 1.

imply that if the Soviet attack was limited to Europe, the American response would also be limited to Europe. The USSR and the United States would be treated as "sanctuaries," but both Eastern and Western Europe would be incinerated. The problem here, of course, is that with this sort of strategy – with the Soviet homeland insured against attack – NATO's nuclear forces would have little deterrent value. This strategy, moreover, would give the Soviets the upper hand in a crisis: if the two sides were faced with the prospect of a Europe-only war, it was obvious which side would be more likely to draw back. And there was yet another problem with such a strategy, one that contemplated a war in which Europe would be destroyed but America would get off virtually scot-free: it was bound to poison relations between the United States and the European allies, especially if East–West relations were bad and the threat of war had to be taken seriously.

Thus, the problem of controlled escalation had no easy solution. In fact, the US government in this middle period of the Cold War had no clear sense for how the escalatory process was to be managed, and, in particular, for the role tactical nuclear weapons were to play. In 1965, for example, the US secretary of defense, Robert McNamara, told his German counterpart "that in his judgment there exists no rational plan for the use of nuclear weapons now located in Europe." In 1971, Henry Kissinger, President Richard M. Nixon's national security advisor, complained that "we still don't have a clear doctrine for their use."[11] In Kissinger's view, if such issues were not taken seriously – if the United States gave the impression that it was "not interested in fighting" – then the other side would conclude that the United States was just bluffing. Deterrence, he thought, had "to be based on a war-fighting capability."[12]

So the whole military situation was far from satisfactory. It was clear that the security of the NATO allies, and especially West Germany, did not rest on a solid military foundation. As Johnson was told by his top advisers in 1966, there were "gaping holes in all strategic options": massive retaliation would be "virtually suicidal"; an effective conventional defense "seems less attainable than heretofore"; and "tactical nuclear war" was "full of uncertainties."[13] President Nixon, in 1970, felt the same way. Outside observers often made the

---

11 Harlan Cleveland to State Department, November 29, 1965, *FRUS, 1964–1968*, vol. XIII, 280; NSC meeting, August 13, 1971, 3, Kissinger Transcripts (KT), Digital National Security Archive, http://nsarchive.chadwyck.com/home.do, item number KT00332 (hereafter, DNSA).

12 Minutes of Defense Program Review Committee (DPRC) meeting, February 22, 1971, 5, DNSA/KT00236.

13 R. McNamara and D. Rusk to L. B. Johnson, May 28, 1966, *FRUS, 1964–1968*, vol. XIII, 402–03.

same point. Lawrence Freedman's view was typical: "An inadequate conventional defense backed by an incredible nuclear guarantee," – he said, was what the NATO strategy of "flexible response" really boiled down to.[14]

The assumption, in other words, was that nuclear deterrence was something of a sham. The United States would never launch a fall-scale nuclear attack on the Soviet Union in the event of a European war. Kissinger himself, in a famous speech, later admitted that the United States' "strategic assurances" had been empty.[15] Even the tactical nuclear option was unreal. "We will never use the tactical nuclears," Nixon said. The "nuclear umbrella in NATO," in his view, was "a lot of crap."[16]

What all this meant was that in strategic terms, the Western position was not very strong. In the event of a crisis, the West would be at a disadvantage; the Soviets would have the upper hand. The NATO powers thus had an enormous incentive to make sure that they did not come anywhere near the point where an armed conflict was a real possibility. They had an enormous incentive, that is, to reach a political accommodation with the USSR.

The point applied with particular force to the case of West Germany. Brandt thought in 1968 that "West Germany cannot really depend on the Americans"; he thought that "as things now stand the United States would not be in a position to meet by military means a serious Soviet military offensive in Europe."[17] The implication was that Germany could not afford to risk a confrontation with the USSR – that it instead needed to try to mend fences with its great neighbor to the east. Bahr was even more explicit. With nuclear parity, he told Kissinger, the Americans would certainly not launch a nuclear attack on the Soviet Union "if the Russians took Hamburg." Détente, he said, was "our only option."[18] His country thus had a strong "structural incentive," as one astute German observer put it, to pursue a "policy of partial appeasement."[19]

---

14 Lawrence Freedman, "NATO Myths," *Foreign Policy*, 45 (Winter 1981–82), 55.
15 Henry Kissinger, *For the Record: Selected Statements, 1977–1980* (Boston, MA: Little, Brown, 1981), 240.
16 Summary record of NSC meeting, November 19, 1970, 9, DNSA/KT00211; NSC meeting, February 19, 1969, quoted in William Burr, "The Nixon Administration, the 'Horror Strategy,' and the Search for Limited Nuclear Options, 1969–1972," *Journal of Cold War Studies*, 7 (2005), 48 n. 31.
17 "Foreign Minister Brandt's Musings on West German Foreign Policy before Visiting Paris," September 13, 1968, CIA Electronic Reading Room (www.foia.cia.gov/), document number EO-2002–00148.
18 Bahr's account, as reported in Dana Allin, *Cold War Illusions: America, Europe and Soviet Power, 1969–1989* (New York: St. Martin's Press, 1994), 40.
19 Josef Joffe, *The Limited Partnership: Europe, the United States, and the Burdens of Alliance* (Cambridge, MA: Ballinger, 1987), 23.

But a source of weakness for the West was a source of strength for the Soviets. The structural incentives cut both ways. The Western countries, and especially the Germans, might feel that they needed to ease tensions with the USSR. But the Soviets might feel freer to take a tougher line in their dealings with the Western powers, especially on European questions.

What sort of policy would the USSR pursue in such circumstances? The West was basically content to live with things as they were. A threat to the status quo could therefore only come from the East. But would the Soviets try to take advantage of the position they enjoyed? Would they try to draw Western Europe in some way or other into their sphere of influence? Or would they pursue a more relaxed policy, a policy aimed basically at stabilizing the status quo?

The Soviet choice

Given the basic structural weaknesses in the Western system, which way would the Soviets go? Would the Kremlin try to exploit NATO's vulnerabilities by pursuing a forward policy in Central Europe or would it seek instead to stabilize the existing system? As the Soviets grappled with this question, they were pulled in more than one direction. The USSR, to be sure, clearly had a certain interest in expanding its influence in Western Europe. The Soviets would obviously not be upset if the countries there had to live more in the shadow of Soviet power – if the Europeans, that is, had to be more sensitive to Soviet wishes, more accommodating politically, militarily, and economically. The USSR might therefore want to "Finlandize" Western Europe – that is, draw that part of the world, to one degree or another, into the Soviet orbit.

This kind of thinking did, in fact, play a certain role in shaping Soviet policy, especially on the German question, and above all on the German nuclear question. The Federal Republic, clearly, was to have a special status in this area. Not only, in the Soviet view, would West Germany not be allowed to develop a nuclear force of its own. Not only would it not be allowed to participate in any sort of NATO nuclear force, even a force that was something of a charade – a force, like the MLF, explicitly designed to prevent that country from getting its finger on the nuclear trigger. But the Germans, ideally, would not even be allowed to take part in NATO nuclear planning. And later on, in the post-1979 period, Soviet leaders strongly objected to the stationing of medium-range American missiles in Western Europe, including West Germany, even though Soviet missiles had been targeting that area for years. In their view, they had a certain *droit de regard* over that whole region, especially where defense issues were concerned.

And the Soviets could achieve those general goals, in principle, by building up their military power. During the Brezhnev period (1964–82), the Soviets made an enormous effort in this area, steadily building up their forces at every level – strategic nuclear, theater nuclear, and conventional – and straining every muscle to do it. The defense burden was very high: defense spending accounted for a much higher share of the national income than it did in the West.

Observers in the West were bound to ask why the USSR was making that kind of effort. If détente was "truly the Soviet purpose in Europe," one analyst wondered, "then why the steady and unprecedented military build-up at the same time?"[20] The USSR was Clausewitzian to the core: military forces were of value, in large measure, because of the political shadows they cast. If the Soviets were making a major military effort, then presumably this was because they had some major political purpose in mind. And what could that purpose be if not to deepen Soviet influence in Western Europe?

But while the temptation to push ahead in Europe clearly played a certain role, it was not the only factor that entered into the equation. There was, in fact, a whole series of reasons why the Soviet Union might be expected to pursue a less ambitious policy.

First of all, if one were trying to predict the course of Soviet foreign policy, the basic character of the regime would certainly have to be taken into account. Over the years, the USSR had lost most of its revolutionary élan. By the 1970s, the regime had become heavily bureaucratic and conservative, and this was bound to affect the way the Soviet leaders dealt with other countries.

The Soviets, moreover, had a lot to worry about at home. "The Soviet economy," as one scholar put it, "seemed to be gradually running out of steam, being dragged to stagnation and decline by some inexorable under-lying process."[21] American analysts at the time had the sense that a "crisis" was beginning. From the 1960s on, the Soviet leadership itself was receiving "confidential reports critical of the economy's performance."[22] But those

---

20 Eliot Goodman, "Disparities in East–West Relations," *Survey*, 19 (1973), 89.
21 Gertrude Schroeder, "Reflections on Economic Sovietology," *Post-Soviet Affairs*, 11 (1995), 209, 225.
22 For the view of US experts at the time, see *ibid.*, 223–24. Note, in particular, the round-table discussion on "Soviet Economic Performance and Reform," in the *Slavic Review*, 25, 2 (June 1966), esp. 233, 234 (where the term "crisis" was used). The quotation is from Michael Ellman and Vladimir Kontorovich, "The Collapse of the Soviet Union and the Memoir Literature," *Europe–Asia Studies*, 49, 2 (March 1997), 260.

warnings were ignored: the regime seemed unable to deal with the problem. The impact on Soviet foreign policy was enormous. Not only was the self-confidence of the regime shaken, but the Soviets now had to worry more about the USSR's long-term ability to sustain a costly military rivalry with a coalition of much richer and more technologically advanced powers. Consequently, Soviet leaders were under greater pressure thus to avoid actions that might provoke a massive increase in US defense spending. Because of the economic problem, they had a greater incentive to ease tensions with the West, especially since that might help them get access to Western technology and credits, which were particularly important given the nature of the economic problem they faced.

Geopolitical factors, especially the conflict with China, were bound to loom large in Soviet thinking. If the Chinese were hostile, the Soviets would obviously want to improve their relations with the West. The Soviet leadership had a certain interest in getting the United States to side with the USSR in its conflict with China, or at the very least in preventing the Americans from forming a de facto alliance with the Chinese. But to have any chance at all of achieving those goals, they would have to pursue a relatively moderate course of action in other areas, above all in Europe.

The Soviets, in other words, might be tempted in such circumstances to think in terms of a US–Soviet "condominium," and that kind of thinking might have had a certain bearing on how specific political issues, and especially European issues, were approached. They might, for example, be attracted to the idea of a divided Europe, with the USSR controlling the east and the Americans and their friends controlling the west. An American withdrawal from Europe might lead to some kind of European nuclear force and thus possibly to a German finger on the nuclear trigger. It might be better, therefore, to keep the Americans in, so that West Germany could be contained in a structure dominated by American power. Even a Germany unified under Communist rule might not make much sense from the Soviet point of view, given what had happened with China. "We don't need a united Germany at all," Soviet foreign minister Andrei Gromyko told one of his advisers in 1977, "not even a socialist one. The united socialist China is enough for us."[23]

So the Soviets were pulled in both directions: toward exploiting the position they had acquired and toward reaching an accommodation with the West. Which way would they go? The answer might depend to a certain degree on decisions the Western governments made – above all on the policies pursued

---

23 Valentin Falin, *Politische Erinnerungen* (Munich: Droemer Knaur, 1993), 238–39.

by West Germany and the United States. How did those governments try to deal with the USSR during this period, and what effect, if any, did their policies have on Soviet behavior?

What effect, in particular, did the German *Ostpolitik*, certainly one of the most important developments of the period, have on the way the Soviets struck the balance? The Brandt government began with a policy of accepting the status quo, and few people outside Germany had any problem with that policy. But by 1973, with the ratification of the basic treaty between the two Germanies, the goals that the German government had set for itself in that initial period had been achieved, and the question now was what would come next. And many people, both inside and outside Germany, were convinced, not without reason, that Brandt and his associates wanted to go much further: that they wanted to end the bloc system, dissolve both NATO and the Warsaw Pact, and get both American and Soviet forces out of Central Europe. But with the US troops gone, would Germany really be secure? The Red Army, after all, would not be that far away and paper guarantees were no substitute for military hardware. Brandt and Bahr seemed to reject "Cold War thinking" of that sort. Peace, the argument ran, needed to be based more on trust and less on military power. But that was still a minority view in Germany. The SPD was itself divided on the issue, and its coalition partner, the FDP, would not go along with that policy. And this, it seems, was one of the main factors that led to Brandt's fall from power in 1974.

What effect did all this have on the USSR? A Soviet hardliner could interpret the Brandt phenomenon – not just the move toward détente, but even more Brandt's apparent willingness to move toward a "European peace order" in which NATO would no longer exist – as a direct result of the buildup of Soviet military power, as indeed it was to a certain degree. It could be interpreted, in other words, as a good example of "Finlandization" in action. On the other hand, a Soviet leader interested in reaching an accommodation with the West could view the Brandt phenomenon in a very different light – as proving that Germany posed no threat, that a moderate policy was workable, and that there were governments in the West that would cooperate with such a policy. "Without Ostpolitik no Gorbachev!" – that was how a key mid-level Soviet policymaker later put the point.[24] But since both arguments could be made and neither was intrinsically more compelling than the other, it is hard to see

---

24 Valentin Falin, quoted in Timothy Garton Ash, *In Europe's Name: Germany and the Divided Continent* (New York, Random House, 1993), 119.

how the Brandt policy could have played a major role in determining how the Soviets struck the balance.

The same general point can be made about US policy during the Johnson period (1964–68). Johnson wanted peace and was determined, especially toward the end of his term of office, to move ahead, above all on arms control. Non-proliferation was taken quite seriously as a goal, and Johnson also very much wanted to reach a strategic arms-limitation agreement with the Soviets. In 1968, his last year in office, he tried hard to get the arms negotiations started; even the Soviet invasion of Czechoslovakia in August did little to slow him down. The plan for a Johnson visit to the USSR to begin talks on this subject was dropped only after it was made clear to the Soviets in December that the incoming Nixon administration very much disapproved of the idea.

What impact did that policy have on Soviet behavior? Again, one can argue both sides of the issue. On the one hand, with regard to arms control, Johnson in late 1968 focused on strategic weapons – that is, on an area where the stability of the balance was never really in danger. The truly important military questions – above all, those relating to the defense of Europe, an area where there really was a stability problem – did not receive much attention. The administration, in fact, seemed willing to give away the store in what came to be called the "Eurostrategic" area: it was prepared to enter into an agreement that would allow the Soviets to keep the large number of missiles they had targeted on Western Europe, but which would prevent the United States from deploying any missiles of its own on European soil.[25] This sort of policy would scarcely deter the Soviets from trying to "Finlandize" Western Europe. If anything, it would have the opposite effect.

On the other hand, Soviet leaders interested in reaching an accommodation with the United States might have reacted positively to the Johnson policy. They might, in particular, have been encouraged by Johnson's policy of keeping German power limited. The basic idea that the two superpowers had overlapping interests in this area was by no means new. John Foster Dulles himself, despite his reputation as a hardliner, thought that the United States and the Soviet Union had a common interest in making sure that Germany, whether united or divided, was kept under "some measure of external control."[26] But under Johnson that attitude was blunter, cruder, and less nuanced than it had been under Dwight D. Eisenhower or even under

---

25 "Strategic Missile Talks: Basic Position Paper," August 24, 1968, *FRUS, 1964–68*, vol. XI, 706.

26 Notes of NSC meeting, February 6, 1958, 7–8, box 9, NSC Series, Ann Whitman File, Dwight D. Eisenhower Library, Abilene, Kansas.

Kennedy. And the Soviets could reasonably see that policy as providing the basis for a political understanding between the two superpowers. Again, the policy could cut both ways, and what effect it had in practice would depend on how the Soviets were disposed to approach the general problem of their relations with the West.

Can the same be said of US policy during the Nixon period (1969–74)? In principle, Nixon and Kissinger wanted a world where the major powers, pursuing their interests "rationally and predictably," balanced each other's power and kept each other in check. The US government would balance between the other great states. It needed to be able to maneuver between the Soviet Union and China; it had to make sure that each of the Communist giants understood it had something to gain from better relations with the United States and something to lose if relations with Washington were to deteriorate.

Thus, the US opening to China, Kissinger later insisted, was not directed against the USSR. The aim was "not to collude against the Soviet Union but to give us a balancing position to use for constructive ends – to give each Communist power a stake in better relations with us."[27] That meant that the United States had to pursue a relatively complex and nuanced policy, not too militant, but not too committed to "peace" either. "If the quest for peace," Kissinger wrote, "turns into the *sole* objective of policy, the fear of war becomes a weapon in the hands of the most ruthless."[28] The United States should, therefore, be willing to use its power, but in a relatively measured way, in order to bring about the sort of "global equilibrium" that could serve as the basis of a stable international order.[29]

This, of course, was quite different from the policy Johnson had pursued. Nixon and Kissinger obviously disliked the image of the United States as a "reluctant giant," "seeking peace and reconciliation almost feverishly." The Soviets were taking their measure of the United States, and the ability of the US government to influence the sorts of choices the Soviets would be making would depend on the conclusions they reached about the United States. The goal, therefore, was to structure the incentives within which the Soviets would operate – to dangle carrots and brandish sticks, so that when the Soviets made a calculation about the sort of policy that would be in their interest, they would reach what the Americans viewed as the right conclusion.

27 Henry Kissinger, *White House Years* (Boston, MA: Little, Brown, 1979), 192.
28 *Ibid.*, 70; emphasis his.
29 On US policy in this period, see Robert D. Schulzinger's chapter in this volume.

So that was the theory, and if the policy had actually worked that way, it might have had a major impact on Soviet behavior. The problem was that American policy, as it took shape in practice, was not really cut from that cloth. The US government, during the Nixon–Kissinger period, was not actually interested in balancing *between* the Soviet Union and China. It was interested instead in balancing *against* the USSR, by helping China build up its power and by entering into a tacit alliance with the People's Republic of China (PRC). But that policy, US leaders understood, could not be pursued in a straightforward way. The United States needed to make sure the Soviets did not attack China before it became strong enough to deter the USSR on its own. To do that, the United States not only needed to develop a certain relationship with China; it also needed to try to hold back the Soviets by pursuing a détente policy with the USSR at the same time. The American strategy, as Kissinger told French president Georges Pompidou in May 1973, was "perhaps complex, but it was not stupid." The goal was to "gain time, to

37. US president Richard Nixon meets Chairman Mao Zedong in Beijing, February 21, 1972. Nixon hoped to use China to balance Soviet power.

paralyze the USSR."[30] This, Kissinger admitted (especially in talks with the Chinese), was not a particularly heroic policy, but the US government needed to use such "complicated methods." It needed to "maneuver," not just because of the Soviet threat to China, but also because of its domestic situation, and because of the political situation in Europe as well.[31]

The United States, Kissinger said, had to engage in a lot of "shadow-boxing," but it was important, he insisted, to "distinguish between appearances and reality."[32] The US government had "no illusions about the world today."[33] The West, in his view, had to be on its "guard against détente." Indeed, it had to be prepared to use détente "quite cold-bloodedly to justify as hard a policy line" as it could.[34]

It is scarcely surprising, therefore, as Kissinger himself admitted in 1974, that the Soviets were "getting nothing from détente." The United States was "pushing them everywhere." The Soviets, on the other hand, had "tried to be fairly reasonable all across the board." You could not find a single place, Kissinger said, "where they have really tried to make serious trouble for us. Even in the Middle East where our political strategy put them in an awful bind, they haven't really tried to screw us. Their tactics haven't been exactly brilliant but they haven't been particularly destructive either."[35]

The Nixon–Kissinger policy in theory was supposed to draw the Soviet Union into a closer, more cooperative relationship with the West. But there was a huge gap between rhetoric and reality, and the Soviets could scarcely be expected to respond positively to the policy the US government actually pursued during that period. The rhetoric of détente might serve US political purposes in the short run, but in the long run the chickens would probably come home to roost. There was a good chance the Soviets would feel that they had been played for fools and would react accordingly.

---

30 Quoted in Georges-Henri Soutou, "Georges Pompidou and U.S.–European Relations," in Marc Trachtenberg (ed.), *Between Empire and Alliance: America and Europe during the Cold War* (Lanham, MD: Rowman and Littlefield, 2003), 181.

31 See various documents in William Burr (ed.), *The Kissinger Transcripts: The Top Secret Talks with Beijing and Moscow* (New York: Free Press, 1998), 94, 177–78, 303, 386.

32 Memorandum of conversation, Kissinger–Deng meeting, November 26, 1974, in Burr, *Kissinger Transcripts*, 290.

33 Memorandum of conversation, Kissinger–Debré meeting, July 11, 1972, 2, DNSA/KT00525.

34 Kissinger meeting with high British officials, April 19, 1973, 4, DNSA/KT00707 (second document at that location).

35 Kissinger meeting with State Department and White House officials, March 18, 1974, in Burr, *Kissinger Transcripts*, 224–25.

A stable system?

The détente policy was thus something of a charade. Kissinger and Nixon had not set out to build a "global structure of peace" based on cooperation with the USSR. Their goal instead was to keep the Soviets in line by making sure they had to worry about a strong China on their Asian border. The US government, that is, as Kissinger told Pompidou in May 1973, was interested in "playing China against the Soviet Union." It therefore wanted to prevent the Soviets from "destroying China." To do that, the Americans needed to develop a certain political relationship with the PRC, so that the Soviets could not be sure the United States would remain passive if China were attacked. But that would take time, and while that relationship was developing, the USSR would somehow have to be kept from attacking that country. That was why US policy could not "*seem* to be directed against the Soviet Union"; that was why détente had to be "carried on in parallel with the Soviet Union"; that was why (as he told the Chinese) the US government needed to "do enough with the Soviet Union to maintain a *formal* symmetry." While China was making its way through the danger zone, the United States could not seem to be ganging up with that country against the USSR.[36] The United States had to make it seem that it was also developing a relationship with the Soviet Union. The Soviets had to be made to feel they had something to lose if they moved against China.

The focus was thus on appearances, not substance. Kissinger and Nixon were not really interested in working with the Soviets on fundamental political problems. The Arab–Israeli question, for example, was obviously of central importance for all sorts of reasons, and it seemed that the USSR, especially after the 1973 Yom Kippur War, was willing to cooperate with the United States in working out a solution. But the US government was not interested in collaborating with the Soviets in this area no matter what position they took. Indeed, as Kissinger himself said, the United States was not particularly interested in the "merits of the dispute." "Our whole policy," he said, was to avoid "settling it cooperatively with the Soviet Union."[37]

The most important US–Soviet negotiations thus dealt not with political but with military questions. A number of agreements were reached in that latter area, and the Strategic Arms Limitation Treaty (SALT) agreements,

36 Memoranda of conversation, Kissinger–Pompidou meeting, May 18, 1973, 4, DNSA/ KT00728; and Kissinger–Huang meeting, August 4, 1972, in Burr, *Kissinger Transcripts*, 73; emphasis added.
37 Memoranda of conversation, Kissinger–Mao meeting, November 12, 1973, and Kissinger–Deng meeting, October 20, 1975, in Burr, *Kissinger Transcripts*, 188, 382.

limiting the size of each side's strategic nuclear arsenals, were considered quite important at the time. Looking back, though, it appears that their importance had to do mainly with what those agreements seemed to symbolize. They made it seem that the two sides were determined to move away from the Cold War and put their relations on a more solid basis.

But putting symbolism aside, it is hard to see how the SALT agreements had a major stabilizing effect. With or without an agreement, neither side could hope to disarm the other. With or without an agreement, neither side had any incentive to preempt. In such circumstances, what exactly could an agreement in this area hope to accomplish? How exactly could a strategic arms agreement make for a more stable international order? But those fundamental questions were not addressed. The negotiations on offensive weapons, Schelling later wrote, were evidently not governed by any "guiding philosophy." Arms control, he said, was pursued "for its own sake, not for the sake of peace and confidence."[38] It is difficult to quarrel with those judgments. In fact, it is hard to see how even the agreement limiting the deployment of defensive anti-ballistic missile systems – the famous Anti-Ballistic Missile (ABM) Treaty of 1972 – played a major role in stabilizing the US–Soviet strategic relationship. Given that ABM systems could easily and cheaply be overwhelmed by additional offensive weapons, even a massive defensive effort was bound to be futile and would have had little impact on that relationship.

But the arms-control negotiations and the SALT agreements were considered extremely important. Strategic arms control was viewed as the heart of the détente process. It seemed that the two great powers were dealing seriously with the military side of the Cold War, and that made it easier to ignore the fact that the really important military problems, the problems relating to the defense of Europe, were not being dealt with effectively.

Kissinger, of course, understood those problems – not just the military problems in the narrow sense, but the whole complex of problems, political as well as military, rooted in the waning of the American nuclear guarantee. This set of issues had been his main concern as a scholar since the mid-1950s, and those problems were certainly on his mind when he was in power in Washington. Even in December 1976, on the eve of his departure from office, he had no doubt that the European defense problem – and problems relating to the defense of other regions as well – were still of overwhelming importance.

---

38 Thomas Schelling, "What Went Wrong with Arms Control?" *Foreign Affairs*, 64 (1985–86), 225, 228.

But did the European defense problem really have to be taken so seriously? No one, after all, thought the Soviets were about to invade Western Europe. The real problem was less overt. The West, even in the official view, had to worry instead about "a more subtle mix of military, psychological and political pressures."[39] But if that was all there was to the threat, how much danger were the Western countries really facing? Kissinger himself might have thought that Europe was on the verge of an "abyss," that Brandt, if he continued on his present course, would end up giving the Soviets a "veto over German policy," and that in about five years the point would "be reached where no German Chancellor [could] afford the hostility of the Soviet Union."[40] But while those fears were not absurd, they seem exaggerated, and not just in retrospect. The real risk was probably never that great.

But that is not the same as saying that there was nothing to be worried about. Maybe the Soviets would never use nuclear weapons in Europe. Maybe they would calculate that the risk was just too great – that no one, not even the Americans themselves, could tell what the US government would do if those weapons were actually used, and maybe that core uncertainty would have a very powerful deterrent effect. But it was also possible that the Soviets would come to the conclusion that America would never attack Soviet territory, no matter what the Red Army was doing in Europe; maybe they would somehow try to take advantage of that situation. Who could tell what they would do five or ten years down the road? Who could tell how the Western countries would assess the threat or how they would deal with it? Events could take their course in all kinds of ways, and no one could predict with any confidence how things would develop.

Extreme pessimism may not have been warranted, but there was no deep stability in this system. There were just too many unresolved questions – questions about the future of the USSR and the future course of Soviet policy, about the future of Europe and the future of the US commitment to Europe, even about the future of the Sino-Soviet relationship. And one has the sense, studying this period, that those issues would not be left hanging forever – that sooner or later those questions would be answered, and that change, perhaps even fundamental change, was inevitable. But what sort of world would emerge as that process ran its course? Change there would be, but to what?

39 Richard Nixon, "U.S. Foreign Policy for the 1970's: Building for Peace," February 25, 1971, *Department of State Bulletin*, March 22, 1971, 342.
40 Memoranda of conversation, Kissinger meeting with "Wise Men," November 28, 1973, 31, DNSA/KT00928; Kissinger–Zhou meeting, November 11, 1973, in Burr, *Kissinger Transcripts*, 175; and Kissinger–Jobert meeting, May 22, 1973, 13, DNSA/KT00736.

24

The Cold War and the social and economic history of the twentieth century

WILFRIED LOTH

The Cold War was not only about power politics, security, and hegemony – it was also a conflict between differing theories of how to organize economies and societies at the various stages of industrial development. Ideologies and belief systems helped define the Cold War's front lines, but social conflict also largely determined its course and outcome. Beginning with the Marxist challenge to the capitalist system, multiple social concepts emerged during the course of the Cold War without any clear favorite model emerging. In the long run, however, collectivist and centrally planned economies showed some strengths in modernizing less developed societies albeit at great costs, whereas free-market economies showed greater productivity, at least after having accepted state-run systems of social welfare and a certain degree of planning at the national and international levels. That political freedom favored productivity and innovation ought to be one of the major lessons of the twentieth century.

Capitalist system, Marxist movement, and Soviet power

For Karl Marx and Friedrich Engels, history was a story of class struggle. From their nineteenth-century perspective, they saw only two classes exercising an influence on history: the bourgeoisie that dominated society, and the proletariat that was exploited by it. The future, Marx and Engels believed, belonged to the proletariat. They predicted that the concentration of capital would continually increase, as would the exploitation and impoverishment of the proletariat. Finally, there would come a point when there would be no one left who could afford to buy the products of the few remaining big capitalists, and when the ever-expanding working class could no longer contain its indignation. That would be the hour of the revolution, the hour of the "proletariat's elevation to the dominant class," according to *The Communist Manifesto* of 1848. The "dictatorship of the proletariat" would not, however, be long-lasting, since the working class would proceed to eliminate the old conditions of production and thereby also put an end to "the existential conditions of class conflict, to classes altogether." The rule of the working class would thus lead to the classless society in which "the free development of each is the condition for the free development of all."[1]

Here was a message that industrial workers were happy to hear. It addressed everyday experiences in the industrial world such as the significant difference in income between workers and factory owners; the cultural conflicts between the workers' milieu and bourgeois society; the continual concentration of capital; and the cycle of economic depression. The message of *The Communist Manifesto* offered those who were dissatisfied with existing conditions a plausible explanation of the contemporary situation as well as prospects for its alteration. The workers' future dominance, a prediction seemingly based in science, offered consolation in the face of the present day's misery. At the same time, it promoted self-assurance and a rebellious spirit. The prospect of eliminating class-based society added moral energy to the struggle against business-owners and attracted dissatisfied intellectuals.

Hence, it was no accident that Marxism found much resonance with workers and that, with the expansion of industrial capitalism and mass politics in Europe in the late nineteenth and early twentieth centuries, a Marxist movement sought to eliminate the capitalist system through revolutionary battle. Not every faction within the workers' movement embraced socialist ideas, nor did every socialist follow the teachings of Marx and Engels, but their adherents frequently constituted an agenda-setting majority within the various socialist parties. In 1891, the Social Democratic Party of Germany (SPD), the strongest and most influential contingent of the "Second Socialist Internationale," adopted its Erfurt Program, which echoed the notion of a world polarized by capital concentration and proletarian exploitation, and supported the goal of "abolishing class dominance."[2] Likewise, at their founding congress in 1905, French socialists defined themselves as "a party of class struggle and revolution."[3] It did not seem to matter that Marx and Engels had

---

1 Karl Marx and Friedrich Engels, *Werke*, Vol. IV (Berlin: Institut für Marxismus–Leninismus beim ZK der SED, 1957), 481ff.

2 *Protokoll über die Verhandlungen des Parteitages der Sozialdemokratischen Partei Deutschlands, abgehalten zu Erfurt vom 14. bis 20. Oktober 1891* (Berlin, 1891), 3ff.

3 Georges Lefranc, *Le mouvement socialiste sous la troisième république* (Paris: Payot, 1977), 124.

omitted many considerations in their grand analyses, such as the role of all of the other classes and groups seen in contemporary society, the consequences of productivity increases, or the momentum of ideas. On the contrary, it was the superficial unambiguity of the Marxist schema that powered its widespread resonance.

The revolution that brought the Bolsheviks to power in Russia in November 1917 had little to do with the prognostications of Marx and Engels, for Russia was not an advanced industrial society. The industrial working class constituted only a small minority there, and in fact the workers' and soldiers' committees that formed following the abdication of the tsar did not even contemplate taking power on a national scale. In these circumstances, Vladimir Ilich Lenin relied on the idea of the *avant-garde*, a party elite that was to guide the working class along the path of revolution. An assisted socialist revolution in backward Russia would then spark revolution in the main European industrial countries that had long since been "ripe" for it, above all imperial Germany. In reality, the leaders of the October Revolution only managed to remain in power over the long term by relying on armed force and systematic centralization, submitting to a popular desire for an end to the Great War, inflicting rigid terror against all kinds of perceived enemies, and by deftly managing sequential crises.

Lenin's dream of world revolution went unfulfilled. There was, however, a socialist-inspired revolution in Germany and the proclamation of a soviet republic in Hungary. Although neither of those enjoyed lasting success and subsequent attempts failed, it was the case that national Communist parties established themselves practically everywhere, and submitted themselves to the leadership of the Russian avant-garde. Large segments of the socialist workers' movement joined the Communist International (normally referred to as the 'Comintern') in the hope of one day realizing the revolution. New revolutionary movements appeared in the countries of the former Habsburg Empire; in Cuba, Mexico, and elsewhere in South America; as well as in China and Indonesia. Even in Australia and in the United States, small numbers of radicalized workers founded local Communist parties. Lenin and the other Bolshevik leaders, who had in the meantime become the state party of the Soviet Union, dictated the policies of the foreign parties under their authority and organized them in the image of the successful Bolsheviks. In 1922, there were some sixty-one of these parties, and 440,000 members of the Comintern outside the Soviet Union.

Some authors see the beginnings of the Cold War in this cooperation of Soviet state power with the international revolutionary movement. That view is inaccurate in the sense that Communist revolutionary strategies were aimed primarily at seizing power in individual countries, and only then unleashing the world revolution. Furthermore, neither the occasional formation of anti-Bolshevik fronts, nor the liberal-democratic internationalism of the American president, Woodrow Wilson, after World War I, constituted a foe for the international Commun world movement. There existed ideological antagonism, but not a geopolitical threat. Thus, one cannot speak of an international East–West conflict before the formation of the anti-Nazi coalition during World War II.

It is the case, however, that the link between Soviet power and an international movement that sought to topple the bourgeois-capitalist order meant that East–West tensions had social and domestic ramifications in addition to the ideological one. The dictators of the Soviet Union (and later of the other Communist states) regarded themselves as the avant-garde of a world revolutionary movement that sooner or later would also emerge in the capitalist countries. Their dictatorial regimes were not merely held together by force and terror, since they could depend on those who benefited in terms of material gain and social status from the establishment of Communist regimes. At the same time, there were Communist movements of varied significance in the countries beyond the Soviet Union, and these movements counted on the support of Moscow. Thus, those who felt threatened by the Soviet Union feared not only for their independence, but also for their assets and their entire way of life.

The partnership between a revolutionary movement and Soviet state power was not without its tensions and frictions. As early as Lenin's time, the Soviet leadership forced the other Communist parties to accept modes of organization and strategic concepts that did not necessarily correspond to circumstances in their own countries. When in doubt, revolutionary ambitions in individual countries were subordinated to the interests of the Soviet Union, and after the collapse of hopes for a rapid world revolution, those ambitions were no longer at the center of Moscow's policies. Once Communists had taken power in other countries, especially after 1945, traditional conflicts between states as well as other conflicts of interest continued inside the boundaries of the socialist camp. Preserving the authority of the Soviet leadership over the Communist world movement was an unending task, for "renegades" repeatedly popped up and required neutralization by the Soviets. Under Iosif Stalin, such people often faced physical liquidation. Additionally, there were always convinced Marxists who rejected Soviet leadership from the outset exactly because they took their Marxism seriously;

they regarded Lenin's voluntaristic construction of history as an adventurous departure from orthodoxy. Likewise, there were those who sympathized with the Soviet Union but who did not subordinate themselves to any party discipline, and who did not want to tie themselves down ideologically. Connections between the Communist world movement and national societies were thus fluid.

The Great Depression that followed the Wall Street crash of 1929 brought the Communist movement new adherents and sympathizers. This world economic crisis had been set off by a crisis of overproduction in the United States and led to persistent unemployment at levels previously unimaginable. At the deepest point of the crisis (1932–33), some 22 percent of British workers were idle, 27 percent of those in North America, 32 percent in Denmark, and no less than 44 percent in Germany. After this collapse, employment levels recovered only gradually. In Britain, for example, a hard core of 16 to 17 percent remained jobless, as did some 20 percent in Denmark.[4] In contrast, unemployment was nonexistent in the Soviet Union. Indeed, Stalin could point to new achievements year by year in the industrialization of the country. The Marxist crisis theory thus gained plausibility, and many of the unemployed as well as intellectuals set their hopes on the Soviet model as an alternative to the discredited liberal system.

More than Communism, however, it was the Fascists who really profited from the world economic crisis. One after the other, liberal regimes on the European continent were replaced by authoritarian ones or by totalitarian forms of mass mobilization. When this occurred in Germany, the interests of the Soviet state and of Communist sympathizers once again converged. The general interest in countering Fascist threats and containing the expansion of National Socialist Germany reunited them in a common front. At the Seventh World Congress of the Comintern in the summer of 1935, the Communist parties were obliged to commit themselves to the so-called "Popular Front" strategy. Up to that point, they had been instructed to direct their "main thrust" against social democrats and to win the support of workers who were oriented toward social democracy. Now, however, they were to ally themselves not only with the social democrats but also with all anti-Fascist forces, including those of the Right. In France, the Communists thus proceeded to support a moderately leftist anti-Fascist government that initiated social reforms such as the forty-hour week and annual paid vacation. In Spain,

---

4 Walt W. Rostow, *The World Economy: History and Prospect* (Austin, TX: University of Texas Press, 1978), 270.

Communists participated in the defense of the republic against the uprising of a fascistically oriented military. This brought them new adherents and new sympathy. In France, the number of party members rose from 30,000 in 1932 to 330,000 in 1936, the first year of the Popular Front government, while the number of votes they registered jumped from 700,000 to 1.5 million. Literary figures such as Arthur Koestler and André Malraux became involved in the Spanish Civil War on the side of the Communists.

The alliance between Communists and Western democratic forces was plagued by tensions because the former did not by any means give up their hopes for revolutionary upheaval, and hence sought unceasingly to bring the Popular Front under their control. There came a break in the anti-Fascist alliance in August 1939 when Stalin, in an abrupt modification of his containment policy, made a pact with Hitler. The Communist Party (which had been banned in Germany since 1933 and faced persecution there) was now ostracized in the democratic countries. In France, it was banned. The Italian socialists in exile broke their ties to the Communists. After the victory of Francisco Franco's forces in Spain, a cruel persecution of the Left ensued.

The German attack on the Soviet Union in June 1941 led to a new and expanded version of the Popular Front program. It was now to extend to all countries occupied by the National Socialists and was to encompass all national forces fighting Nazism, and not only the Left. Communists therefore participated in the diverse national resistance movements and subordinated themselves to non-Communist leaders where power dynamics necessitated it. In France, the Communists acknowledged the authority of General Charles de Gaulle. In Italy, they joined the 'Committee of National Liberation' and subordinated themselves to the 'Corps of Volunteers.' In order to reduce mistrust on the part of his new Western allies, Stalin even took the step of officially disbanding the Comintern on May 15, 1943. Covertly, foreign party leaders were still required to follow his directives.

Communists played a major role in resisting the National Socialists, and the contribution of the Red Army to the defeat of Germany and its allies was tremendous. The Soviet Union paid for this victory, clutched from the jaws of defeat, with no fewer than 27 million lives, perhaps half the total killed in World War II. Both the Communists' resistance to the Nazis throughout Europe and the decisive role of the Soviet Union brought the Communist parties new members and newfound sympathy in the liberated countries of Europe. The idea of a broad coalition of anti-Fascist forces gained much acceptance. At the beginning of 1944, Ivan Maiskii, returning to Moscow after serving as Soviet ambassador in London, perceived signs that government in the liberated countries would now move in the direction of "a broad democracy in the spirit of the Popular Front idea." As he said, "There are grounds for assuming that these principles will prevail in countries such as Norway, Denmark, Holland, Belgium, France, and Czechoslovakia without external pressure." Elsewhere, the victorious powers, "primarily the USSR, the USA, and England," would need to provide assistance.[5]

It was indeed the case that the Communists managed to make significant gains in the first elections held after the war. In Finland, the Communist-directed People's Democratic Union won a surprising 24 percent of the vote in March 1945. In France, the Communists became the largest party with more than 26 percent of the vote in October 1945. In Czechoslovakia, they gained 38 percent in May 1946, *after* the withdrawal of Soviet occupation forces. In Italy, they registered 19 percent in June 1946. In Scandinavia and in the smaller West European states, the Communist vote ranged between 10 and 13 percent in the period.

The context for these electoral successes was a general shift to the Left in the European political spectrum. After the British Labour Party achieved an impressive victory at the polls in July 1945, social democratic parties in other states also increased their share of the vote and some of the new Christian democratic parties secured their victories under the banner of a "Christian socialism." As the failure of liberalism had now been followed by a failure of Fascism, many Europeans saw their countries on the path to social democracy, not to be built through revolutionary upheaval, but rather by the nationalization of key industries and by the expansion of the welfare state.

This prospect was all the more attractive given that the consequences of the Great Depression had never really been overcome in any European country. Only in Germany had unemployment been eliminated by the end of the 1930s, and the devastation of war had then reduced the country's productive capacity to ashes. Germany had lost 13 percent of its capital equipment, Italy 8 percent, and France 7 percent. The monstrous loss of human life – more than 17 million dead in the European countries alone – signified further decreases in future production potential. One year after the end of the war, by which time transportation systems had largely been reestablished and many American loans had already begun to flow into reconstruction, total production in Britain and in the Scandinavian countries was only marginally above prewar levels. In France and in the Benelux countries, the figure was 89 percent, in

---

5 Report, I. Maiskii to V. Molotov, January 11, 1944, *Istochnik*, No. 4, (1995), 124–44.

southern and Eastern Europe approximately 60 percent, and in Germany still only 40 percent.[6]

The policy of containment and the triumph of the affluent society

In the United States, the leftward trend of postwar European politics caused many to worry that the Communists might seize power in several countries. A strong socialist workers' movement had never existed in the United States because of the primacy of race issues over class issues, and the Communists remained a small splinter party of utopians. Consequently, Americans did not appreciate that a strong majority in favor of socialist reforms was coalescing in Europe, and the large vote gains by the Communists frightened those on the other side of the Atlantic. The danger posed by the Communists appeared all the greater while the war's lasting depravations impeded reconstruction efforts. It seemed certain that the Communists would exploit the impoverishment of Europe for their own purposes. As the assistant secretary for economic affairs at the State Department, William Clayton, put it in a memorandum of March 5, 1947: "Full of hunger, economic misery, and frustration," the majority of European countries were standing "on the very brink and may be pushed over at any time; others are gravely threatened." It was already possible to see that Communists would seize power in Greece and France in the wake of economic collapse in those countries.[7]

As a consequence of this view, the first tool of America's containment policy was economic. The Marshall Plan was intended to promote the resuscitation of Europe to such an extent that revolutionary programs would lose their appeal. The plan thus constituted an economic crisis response with a geostrategic rationale. Economic support for the European countries was desirable in any case in order to revive them as trading partners and foreign markets, and in order to prevent a lasting crisis of overproduction after the cessation of war-footing economic policy. That such motivations converged as a coherent plan in the spring of 1947 – following a series of individual measures – was the result of fears that the impoverishment of Europe might bring Soviet hegemony as far as the eastern shores of the Atlantic. Structural reform of Europe's economies was intended to guarantee that the Western

---

6 Quoted from the compilation in Walter Lipgens, *A History of European Integration 1945–1947* (Oxford: Clarendon Press, 1982), 8.
7 Published in Ellen Clayton-Garwood, *Will Clayton: A Short Biography* (Austin: University of Texas Press, 1958), 115–18.

model would enjoy higher long-run productivity (and thus also legitimacy) than the Communist alternative.

Yet, fears of Communist takeover due to economic privation were greatly exaggerated. Reconstruction actually progressed rapidly after 1946. As early as 1947, most European countries had retrieved the industrial production levels of 1938; the very hard winter of 1946–47 was followed by an exceptionally good harvest in 1947–48, prior to the first deliveries of the Marshall Plan. The Communists did not aim to exploit economic distress but, on the contrary, urged workers to refrain from demanding wage increases so as not to endanger reconstruction. Nevertheless, the Marshall Plan propagated a vision of the future that countered the Marxist one: the model of a liberal society, founded on a market economy and parliamentary democracy, the needs of an advanced industrial society met by state planning for modernization, state-organized social equalization, and the greatest possible integration of national economies within a multilateral free-trade system. It was the American ideal in its ultimately successful New Deal variant rather than a resumption of prewar liberalism, and during conflict-filled negotiations with the democratic governments of Europe it developed into the Western societal model. In the debates on the Marshall Plan, the West perceived itself as an association of powers and as a societal vision, which stood opposed to the embodiment of the Marxist version in the Soviet Union.

Contrary to Western perceptions, the Soviets' campaign against the Marshall Plan was not connected to a turn away from the expanded Popular Front strategy. Yet, intense pent-up frustration over lack of consumer goods during the reconstruction period produced large strike movements in the autumn and winter of 1947, leading to the Communists' long-term isolation in the West. It was impossible for them to get back into government in France or Italy; even in Finland, they found themselves in the opposition once again after the elections of July 1948. This meant that the movement for social democracy lost its parliamentary majority almost everywhere, and that the expansion of the social welfare state proceeded less rapidly than its adherents had expected. Many spoke of a "restoration" of the old order, but, in fact, participation in the Marshall Plan pushed reforms onto a liberal course and promoted the integration of recipient countries into a wider economic and political association.

Two political circumstances strengthened the productivity promoted by the Marshall Plan. First, the outbreak of the Korean War generated a massive demand for capital goods. The Federal Republic of Germany (FRG) was able to satisfy that demand all the more effectively because its productive capacity was not tied up in the armaments sector. Thus, the FRG was able not only to regain market share lost during the war, but also to achieve a strong long-term position in the world market. Second, the supranational nature of the Schuman Plan offered Western Europeans a guarantee that the liberation of German production from the constraints of the Allies' occupation regime would not lead to the return of German political hegemony over the continent. Only by these means was German reconstruction made palatable to its European neighbors in terms of security policy and domestic public opinion.

The newfound climate of trust among the countries of the Organisation for European Economic Co-operation (OEEC) was further strengthened by the high growth rates that Marshall aid had brought about. In order to avoid jeopardizing reconstruction, workers had to restrain their pay demands, entrepreneurs could not seek quick profits, and consumers had to accept higher prices for foodstuffs and other necessities. Investors were forced to accept that the war had obliterated their wealth, and those who depended upon the welfare state had to be satisfied with more modest aid. All of these strictures were easier to bear when the communal pie was getting larger and larger. Thus, high growth rates helped limit dissatisfaction and created a wide consensus about the desirability of reconstruction. It was indeed the case that this consensus remained vague and varied somewhat from country to country within the OEEC. The impression that the benefits of reconstruction were more or less fairly distributed was sufficient to avoid struggles over distribution that would have threatened its success. Unemployment rates fell, and during the 1960s, full employment was achieved almost everywhere in Western Europe.

On the basis of these indices, Western European reconstruction turned into long-term growth. Industrial production expanded at an annual average of 7.1 percent from 1950 to 1970. During the same period, gross domestic product (GDP) grew at an annual rate of 5.5 percent overall and 4.4 percent per capita. These figures reflect advancing industrialization as well as significant rises in productivity and income. In 1970, output per capita was almost two and a half times greater than in 1950, and per capita income had grown at an average of 4.5 percent per year. This growth was more than twice as fast as the rate seen in the United States and exceeded anything previously known in Europe. In the two decades from 1950 to 1970, annual per capita income rose between 250 and 400 percent.[8]

8 Derek H. Aldcroft, *The European Economy 1914–1990* (London and New York: Routledge, 1994), 124, 130, 133.

The rapid rise in real income produced an expansion of consumption. Living standards grew significantly. Durable consumer goods such as refrigerators, televisions, and automobiles became ubiquitous mass-market products, as did one-time luxuries like high-value foodstuffs, tasteful clothing, vacation trips, and investments in social welfare. There was an expansion of education, the disparity between the urban world and the countryside faded, and local and national governments assumed more and more public responsibilities. The diversification of professions, increasing mobility, and widely accessible free-time activities led to a far-reaching dissolution of traditional social milieus. The traditional distinct circles of peasant, bourgeois, and working-class culture faded into history. Instead, a consumer society arose in which differences within existing class cultures became stronger, while the lines between those class cultures began to blur. Now, fine differences in taste and style characterized the many social groupings more strongly than did material contradictions or distinct class consciousness. Western Europe was developing into an advanced industrial society along the lines of the United States.

At the same time, growing prosperity promoted the stabilization of the democratic order. This was especially the case in West Germany, Austria, and Italy, where democracy had been reintroduced under the supervision of the victorious Allied powers, and where embedding the habits of democracy in local society was a major challenge. In those countries with stronger democratic traditions, economic success also preempted the rise of radicalism. The Communists, who in any event no longer held any realistic revolutionary prospects, lost up to two-thirds of their support. In France and Italy, where they did manage to retain the support of 20 to 30 percent of the electorate for a long time, the Communists languished in the isolation of a counter-culture. After the suppression of the Hungarian revolt by Soviet forces in November 1956, most intellectuals also gave up on Soviet Communism. In the social democratic parties, the Marxist prediction of ever-growing antagonism between capital and the masses lost its plausibility. German social democracy established a pluralistic basis for itself in the Bad Godesberg Program of 1959.

Aside from the dictatorships in southern Europea (Portugal, Spain, and, after 1967, Greece), the calculus behind America's containment strategy worked out on a grand scale. Western Europe became "safe for democracy," and at the same time developed into an exceptionally productive trading partner. The region was less susceptible than ever to revolutionary seizures of power based on class conflict; on the contrary, Western Europe became increasingly attractive to the societies of the Eastern bloc.

The competition between the systems

For many contemporaries, these developments were all the more surprising given that they had experienced the failure of many liberal democracies after World War I, as well as difficulty in overcoming the effects of the Great Depression. Moreover, not a few observers had been nervously asking themselves whether a planned economy might not be superior to a market economy after all. It was true that Stalin had brought about a powerful achievement in terms of industrialization. In the twelve years from 1928 to 1940, industrial production in the USSR had risen sharply, while agriculture had been relegated to second place in its contribution to GDP.[9]

Soviet reconstruction also achieved quick and impressive results after the massive destruction of the war. As early as 1945, industrial production had already reached 92 percent of the prewar level. In 1950, it reached 173 percent, some 25 percent more than had been anticipated in the four-year plan of 1946.[10] From 1951 to 1965, agricultural production grew by an average of 4.1 percent per year, the productivity of industry by 6.4 percent, and real income per capita by 5.5 percent.[11] Likewise, there was a tangible economic recovery in the countries under Soviet control. Although the war's devastation was significantly graver east of the Iron Curtain than in the Western European countries, and participation in the Marshall program was out of the question due to Soviet opposition, prewar levels of industrial production returned three or four years after the war's conclusion. Throughout the region, reconstruction translated into sustained growth, supported by a planned economic model which all of the Eastern bloc countries adopted from the Soviets. Between 1950 and 1970, annual GDP growth rates averaged some 7 percent.[12] Altogether, the modernization of the Eastern Bloc proceeded even more rapidly than that of Western Europe.

The West's own achievement of the affluent society soon made Westerners forget the successes of reconstruction in the East. Nikita Khrushchev, however, took the impressive growth rates in Eastern European industrial production as confirmation that the Soviet system was superior to the Western

---

9 Helmut Altrichter, *Kleine Geschichte der Sowjetunion 1917–1991* (Munich: C. H. Beck, 2001), 84.

10 Alec Nove, *An Economic History of the USSR, 1917–1991* (Harmondsworth: Penguin Books, 1992), 298.

11 Manfred Hildermeier, *Geschichte der Sowjetunion 1917–1991* (Munich: C. H. Beck, 1998), 1174.

12 Aldcroft, *European Economy*, 130, 173ff.

one. He thus had high hopes for the victory of socialism by catching up to the West and then surpassing it, with the East bloc developing a society characterized by prosperity and consumption: "We'll bury you," he told Western representatives at a reception in November 1956.[13] What he meant was that the Communists would still be around when capitalism was sent to its grave, and that sooner or later, the people of the West would come to realize the advantages of the Soviet model. He added a prediction to the 1961 program of the Communist Party of the Soviet Union saying that industrial production in the Soviet Union would surpass that of the United States in ten years and would increase sixfold over the next twenty years. In the 1970s, the USSR would thus enjoy a living standard "higher than that of any capitalist country."[14]

Khrushchev's optimism seemed all the more justified given that the crisis of the European liberal system in the 1930s and 1940s had eventually resulted in the loss of the colonies that had added to the strength of the great powers during the height of imperialism. It was often the case that the colonial struggle for independence went hand in hand with an orientation toward the Leninist variant of Marxism. Because such liberation projects were initially the preserve of small Western-educated elites in colonial society, the successful model of the Bolshevik professional revolutionary was appealing. The 1949 victory of Mao Zedong's Communists in China, after a long conflict, served as an inspiration, as did the persistent struggle of the Vietnamese revolutionaries led by Ho Chi Minh, first against French colonial masters and later against American forces. After 1959, Fidel Castro's regime in Cuba developed into an attractive model for revolutionary movements in the southern hemisphere. Even though the Soviet leadership was never able to bring these various revolutionary movements and regimes under its control, there were still good reasons to assign them to the Soviet column when undertaking a "global assessment of power relations," as the Marxists' dialectical view of the world put it. Power rivalries in the Third World thus produced additional Cold War tensions.

However, the impressive industrialization of the Soviet Union suffered from two structural flaws. First, the agricultural sector had been severely hampered by forced collectivization, and investment was lopsidedly allocated to heavy industry and to the arms industry. The result was that the production

---

13 Charles E. Bohlen, *Witness to History, 1929–1969* (New York and London: Norton, 1973), 437.

14 Altrichter, *Kleine Geschichte*, 145ff.

of consumer goods was meager, and standards of living and consumption levels of the masses in both urban and rural areas deteriorated during the 1930s. This situation could not be redressed very rapidly by means of progress in industrialization. The beginnings of a pronounced emphasis on consumer goods in the initial postwar years were snuffed out by the advent of the Cold War and by a tendency to invest in major prestige projects. Agricultural prices were held artificially low, and collective farms, which had previously used the structures of the traditional village, proliferated and expanded rapidly. These factors continually hindered productivity in the agricultural sector. Hence, by 1950, agricultural production and the incomes of non-agricultural workers had only reached prewar levels. It was not until 1953 or 1954 that non-agricultural workers earned as much as they had in 1928.[15] In 1965, the Soviet Union's gross national product (GNP) was about 45 percent as large as that of the United States.[16]

Developments were similar in the countries which had adopted the Soviet model after 1945. They were, at least initially, spared the collectivization of agriculture, but Moscow also imposed high reparations on East Germany, Hungary, and Romania which reduced returns on output. In order to achieve ambitious planning goals, it was typically the case that more was invested in large industrial projects than could be justified in terms of well-balanced growth in consumption. While there were great differences among the various Eastern bloc states, rates of growth in private consumption were only half as high as in the West. On the other hand, poverty vanished, public transportation systems were expanded, and washing machines, refrigerators, and television sets gradually made their appearance in households. Still, skilled workers usually had to accept a certain decline in living standards, while prices and the selection of goods were determined not by the market but by bureaucracies. Hence, quality often left something to be desired, and there was a chronic shortage of the most popular goods, which fetched correspondingly high prices. Only a minority could afford an automobile in this period. The peoples of the Eastern bloc experienced progress toward a modern consumer society, but there remained a significant gap between them and the consumer societies of the West.[17]

Most obvious was the contrast between developments in West Germany and in East Germany. Before the war, consumption levels in the central region of Germany had not been significantly lower than in the western and southern

15 Hildermeier, *Geschichte der Sowjetunion*, 697, 707.　16 Altrichter, *Kleine Geschichte*, 145.
17 Aldcroft, *European Economy*, 177ff.

regions of the country. Yet, in the mid-1960s, the German Democratic Republic (GDR) had rates only 60 percent of those of the West Germans. Germans on both sides of the Iron Curtain took note of this disparity. From the foundation of the GDR, a steady stream of refugees headed west. It was not just fear of repression that caused them to abandon the German "workers' and peasants' state"; many simply wanted to enjoy better living conditions and greater personal freedom. Year after year, between 200,000 and 300,000 people left the GDR for the Federal Republic, mostly via Berlin where one could simply decamp from the eastern sector to one of the western ones. By the summer of 1961, some 2.7 million people had left the East German state, a figure amounting to 15 percent of its 1950 population.

This steady exodus was all the more problematic for the GDR because it was mostly the young and well educated who were leaving. Not only did this hamper productivity growth in the GDR and give extra impetus to that in the FRG, it also unsparingly highlighted the illusionary character of Communist promises for the future. The GDR's refugee problem was therefore of decisive strategic importance for the whole Communist movement. As Soviet deputy prime minister Anastas Mikoyan explained in a conversation with function-aries of East Germany's Socialist Unity Party (SED) in June 1961: "The GDR, Germany, is the country in which it must be decided whether Marxism–Leninism is right, that communism is the higher, better form of social organization for industrial states as well ... If socialism does not triumph in the GDR, if communism does not prove itself superior and viable here, then we have not triumphed."[18]

The Soviet Union therefore assisted the GDR economically, not only for strategic military reasons, but also because of the significance of a successful socialist Germany to the whole bloc. Above all, however, the Soviets helped the GDR by granting approval for the building the Berlin Wall in August 1961. Overnight, the barrier cut off the flow of refugees and enabled the GDR to survive direct comparison with the Federal Republic. Yet, the Wall also made clear that the Eastern side could not win the competition between the systems, a competition it had itself declared.

Moreover, it was now apparent to most observers that the Communist regimes could only survive over the long term if they shielded themselves from Western influences. Whereas Western societies enjoyed growing afflu-ence and a new self-confidence, the leaders in the East had to concentrate on

18 Quoted in Michael Lemke, *Die Berlinkrise 1958 bis 1963. Interessen und Handlungsspielräume der SED im Ost-West-Konflikt* (Berlin: Akademie-Verlag, 1995), 161ff.

preserving their regimes with a mixture of concession and force. The prospect of revolution in the West had definitively proven to be an ideological fantasy, and the containment of encroaching capitalism, rather than revolutionary expansion, now became the Eastern bloc's strategic priority. That which was still officially called the "class struggle" was, in reality, self-defense by men in power of the Eastern bloc regimes against the forces of freedom. In 1958, Milovan Djilas correctly characterized those leaders as a "new class," one which had constituted itself in the aftermath of the Communist seizure of power.

The different ways by which the countries of the East and West profited from the transition to consumer societies became evident when, in the late 1906s, growing prosperity gave rise to a lifestyle revolution for the West's younger generation or, to be more exact, for the student elite of that generation. True, some young Westerners temporarily revived interest in Marxist ideology, but this did not translate into support for the Soviet Union. Instead, the "children of Karl Marx and Coca-Cola" actually accelerated the trends of individualization, democratization, and consumer orientation in the West. In the East, student protests were instinctively interpreted as attacks on the dictatorship of the Communist Party. In Czechoslovakia, student protests coalesced as a movement for a more open form of socialism which, in August 1968, was snuffed out by the tanks of the Warsaw Pact. In the USSR meanwhile, a broad stratum of university graduates imbued with skepticism toward the ruling ideology began long careers in the institutions of the state.

The Soviet model on the defensive

For a time, closing the borders and suppressing opposition of the Prague Spring allowed the Eastern bloc's "new class" to escape the general tendency toward "westernization." In the long term, however, isolation could not be sustained. In order to keep the gap in living standards from growing still larger and to keep popular dissatisfaction below a critical threshold, the regimes of the Soviet bloc were compelled to seek credit from and expand trade relations with the West. Loans were to be had, however, only if the Eastern bloc were to open itself, at least partially, to exchanges of "people, ideas, and views," as Western diplomats put it at the Conference on Security and Cooperation in Europe. Additionally, Radio Free Europe and Western television, which could be received in countries close to the border between the blocs, provided continual information about conditions in the West and the Western view of things, and efforts to jam the signals were not successful.

The leaders of "real existing socialism" thereby found themselves in a dilemma: if they persisted too strongly in sealing off their societies, there would be the menace of unrest due to the backwardness of social conditions. However, if they chose the path of exchange with the West, they could be faced with the destabilization of their regimes due to Western influences. East German foreign minister Otto Winzer insightfully called the West's policy of détente "aggression in slippers."[19] Expansion of relations with the West was thus controversial within the Communist leadership. Openness was inextricably associated with the transformation of the socialist regimes, and it remained an open question as to whether this transformation could be appropriately managed. As KGB chief Iurii Andropov secretly informed Willy Brandt's adviser, Egon Bahr, in February of 1970, "You have no idea at all what is going on within the leadership [of the USSR]. You must give us time. It's more difficult for us than for you."[20]

In order to evade the choice between openness and impoverishment, many of the Eastern leaders chose to focus more intensively on promoting consumption. Western credits were not invested to modernize the economy but instead were spent directly to eliminate supply bottlenecks, to raise wages, and to expand social welfare. Such a course was set by János Kádár in Hungary as early as 1963. In Poland, the emphasis on consumption began after the large strike movement of December 1970, which was sparked by frustration over the lack of consumer goods and the high price of foodstuffs. Again and again, party head Edward Gierek found himself having to make economic concessions to the workers that hindered the success of his modernization program. After Erich Honecker replaced Walter Ulbricht as leader of the GDR in May 1971, a social welfare and prosperity program was put in effect with the aim of preventing disruptions such as those witnessed in Czechoslovakia and Poland.

The crisis-avoidance strategy developed by Kádár, Gierek, and Honecker was only temporarily successful. Kádár became so popular that he could allow a certain amount of openness in the media and an extensive easing of repression. In the early 1970s, contemporaries spoke of "goulash communism." In Poland, where the supply of goods remained more strained, the authorities managed to hold on for another decade, until a new nationwide strike movement arose in the summer of 1980. Even after the emergence of the *Solidarność* movement east of the River Oder, everything remained quiet in the GDR. It was the case, however, that the Communists who emphasized prosperity had to pay for

---

19 Egon Bahr, *Zu meiner Zeit* (Munich: Karl Blessing, 1996), 157.
20 Bahr, *Zu meiner Zeit*, 305ff.

their consumer orientation with an increasing relative lag in productivity and with growing financial dependence on the West. The Soviet leadership around Leonid Brezhnev watched with growing concern as the GDR grew dependent on the steady importation of West German currency. The Soviet ambassador to the Federal Republic, Iulii Kvitsinskii, described this process with a catchy image: "Deeper and deeper, the GDR was swallowing the golden fishhook from which it could no longer free itself."[21]

The West's new approach to the Eastern bloc could be attributed to its economic prosperity. On the one hand, that prosperity was the foundation for the self-confidence required to pursue a policy of open borders and open competition. On the other, it also put Western governments in a position to provide attractive loans to the East, thereby nurturing economic ties. There was, then, a chronological as well as a causational connection between the West's transition to a consumer society and the intensification of the West's détente policy in the late 1960s and early 1970s. This corresponded with the East's increased interest in economic cooperation.

Although the end of the West's postwar boom period of high growth and full employment came in 1973–74, it changed nothing in this dynamic. The people of the West saw the recession of 1974–75 for what it was – the end of an exceptional situation that had arisen from the coincidence of postwar reconstruction, the creation of transnational institutions to promote growth and technological innovation, and low energy costs. The more modest growth rates to which people now had to become accustomed nonetheless constituted continued economic expansion. While unemployment became a chronic problem, it could be mitigated by the advanced social welfare systems now in place. Due to rigid social welfare regulations and a decline in technological innovation, Western Europe found it more difficult to compete internationally. Yet by 1979, an average GDP growth rate of 3.9 percent was once again achieved. Following another decline at the beginning of the 1980s, the level returned to 3.7 percent in 1988.[22]

Positive economic conditions put Western Europeans in a position to pursue their form of détente even as the Americans again embraced an agenda of isolating the East and intensifying the arms race. In December 1981, the West German chancellor, Helmut Schmidt, was able to negotiate increased travel opportunities for GDR citizens in exchange for the extension of overdraft

21 Quoted in Peter Bender, *Fall und Aufstieg. Deutschland zwischen Kriegsende, Teilung und Vereinigung* (Halle: Mitteldeutscher Verlag, 2002), 64.
22 Aldcroft, *European Economy*, 245. See also John W. Young's chapter in volume III.

provisions in trade between the two German states. Under his successor Helmut Kohl, West German banks offered an attractive loan of some one billion marks to the GDR in June 1983, which saved the Communist regime from looming insolvency. Further liberalization of travel followed: in 1987, some 1.2 million East Germans were allowed to visit the Federal Republic, five times as many as the previous year. The number of trips to the West by GDR citizens of retirement age rose from 1.5 million in 1986 to 3.8 million in 1987 and 6.7 million in 1988. Around 30,000 East Germans received permission to emigrate permanently each year. The foreign currency received by the East German government in exchange for permitting such emigration, and for the release of political prisoners, became an indispensable source of income.

The Eastern bloc did not suffer from the rise in energy prices during 1973–74. In fact, the opposite was true because, as net exporters of energy, the Soviet Union, Romania, and Poland profited from price increases. The Soviets and Romanians exploited their oil reserves more intensively, while Poland benefited from higher demand for coal. However, this source of revenue, and secret subsidies to the other states of Comecon (the East's multinational economic organization) made possible by energy exports, could only temporarily hide the creeping exhaustion of the economies of the socialist countries. The Eastern regimes did not know how to use Western loans effectively. Even in cases where those funds were not used directly to promote consumption, there was a lack of qualified personnel and economic infrastructure to produce manufactured goods that would be competitive on the world market. Heavy industry, especially the arms industry, drained away scarce resources of capital and skilled labor, and the easy availability of oil and gas led to careless investment in energy-intensive sectors. Morevoer, the sluggish state economic bureaucracies did not recognize the growing importance of microcomputers and microelectronics. In 1987, there were only about 200,000 microcomputers in use in the Soviet Union, compared to some 25 million of more advanced design in the United States.[23]

Eventually all of the Eastern bloc countries found themselves in a debt crisis. They could not export enough competitive products to pay for their imports and service their debts. Mounting interest repayments ate away at the funds available for internal investment, thus putting a brake on growth and obliging reductions in consumption. In Poland, the first socialist country to be hit by this dilemma, the Ministry of Internal Trade acknowledged in March 1979 that some 280 products were not available in quantities sufficient to meet

---

23 Aldridge, *European Economy*, 266; see also David Reynolds's chapter in volume III.

demand.[24] Consequently, various essential consumer products were rationed. Long lines in front of shops once again became part of everyday experience, and the waiting periods for desired goods became longer and longer.

Those countries in the Third World where direct or indirect Soviet support had established leftist regimes also wound up with severe debt problems. They not only thoughtlessly accumulated large debts by borrowing petrodollars but also had to pay much higher energy prices. Their growing insolvency undermined their ambitious development goals.

At the same time, the Kremlin experienced more and more difficulty providing assistance to its friends in the southern hemisphere. The Red Army, bogged down in support of an unpopular ally in Afghanistan, engendered growing skepticism in the USSR about the efficacy and wisdom of Moscow's other adventures in the Third World. It was hard to see that the Kremlin was gaining much from its vast expenditures in Africa, the Middle East, and Asia (as well as Cuba and Nicaragua). Instead, these commitments set back the creation of "real existing socialism" inside the Soviet Union.

The dissolution of the Soviet bloc

Collectively, the Eastern bloc countries slid into an economic crisis with no easy exit, especially not for state-dominated, centrally planned economies. Whereas in 1970 net material production in the Soviet Union and Eastern Europe had risen by 8 percent on average, average increases dropped to 2.1 percent in 1979. Growth in all sectors shrank to historic lows.[25] In the last three years of the Brezhnev era (1979 to 1982), the number of those in work grew by only 1.4 percent, while worker productivity grew by only 2.3 percent and gross capital investment by only 2.2 percent. Shortages developed in two decisive production factors – labor and capital.[26] Aging machinery made for high repair costs, while a workforce with little motivation and often insufficient qualifications wasted its time on unproductive endeavors. Even in weapons technology, the Soviet Union was no longer able to compete with the United States. Accidents such as the Chernobyl disaster in April 1986 had immediate and dramatic effects on the supply of goods. The fall in oil prices in the second half of the 1980s also led to a worsening of the foreign trade balance.

In light of the growing communication between East and West, the leaders of the Communist dictatorships were no longer in a position to reassure their

24 Aldridge, *European Economy.*, 262.   25 *Ibid.*, 257.
26 Hildermeier, *Geschichte der Sowjetunion*, 886ff.

populations with promises of a better future. Instead, the frustration over new bottlenecks and numerous sharp reductions in living standards found expression in broad protest movements which immediately called into question the legitimacy of "real existing socialism." In Poland, this had been the case since 1980, and, there, the imposition of martial law had been unable to suppress frustration over the long term. When renewed worker unrest in the spring of 1989 inspired the transition to a multiparty system, a general rejection of the ruling order occurred right across the Eastern bloc; first in Hungary, then in the GDR, and then almost simultaneously in the other satellite states. In the Soviet Union, where halfhearted reforms only served to worsen the supply of goods, dissatisfaction encouraged nationalist movements in all directions. Everywhere in the socialist sphere, frustration with material conditions and embitterment toward the political leadership produced the fundamental delegitimization of the ruling order.[27]

The leaderships of the Communist parties either sought salvation in reforms which amounted to adoption of the Western societal model, or capitulated when they were rejected by a working class that they had so long claimed to represent. No more illusions could be maintained in light of the standards of societal openness established by the West, the technological revolution in communications, and the reforms instituted by Soviet leader Mikhail Gorbachev. The peoples of the Eastern bloc liberated themselves from the shackles of a rigid system, sometimes with the cooperation of their leaders, but for the most part at their expense. The people of the GDR, where the Iron Curtain was literally pulled down, quickly voted for annexation into the Federal Republic and the wondrous prosperity of the West that now lay before them.

In retrospect, the implosion of the Soviet bloc was a belated shattering of the illusions and self-deceptions that the leaders of the October Revolution had imposed on post-tsarist Russia, and which thereafter had been believed by generations of Communists the world over. Communist elites nonetheless sought to preserve their leadership role. They failed when a new stage of technological development made apparent to everyone the limited potential of a centrally directed collectivist economy in a strongly interlinked world. The Cold War thus not only had its roots in the conflicts of modern industrial society; it was also made obsolete by the further development of that society.

---

27 See the chapters by Archie Brown, Alex Pravda, Jacques Lévesque, and Helga Haftendorn in volume III.

Bibliographical essay

The bibliographical essays in the three volumes of the *Cambridge History of the Cold War* aim at being selective and critical overviews of the literature available in each subfield of historical investigation. The entries are written by the authors of the chapters in the main text, with additions, deletions, and cross-references suggested by the editors. Readers may want to look at the bibliographical entries in more than one volume to get an overview of the literature on a particular issue or region.

1. Grand strategies in the Cold War

The best edition of Thucydides is Robert B. Strassler (ed.), *The Landmark Thucydides: A Comprehensive Guide to the Peloponnesian War*, revised edition of the Richard Crawley translation (New York: Simon & Schuster, 1996). For modern accounts, see Donald Kagan, *The Peloponnesian War* (New York: Viking, 2003), and Victor Davis Hanson, *A War Like No Other: How the Athenians and the Spartans Fought the Peloponnesian War* (New York: Random House, 2005). Louis J. Halle, in his *The Cold War as History* (New York: Harper & Row, 1967), was one of the first Cold War historians to draw on ancient analogies, including Thucydides.

Geoffrey Roberts, *Stalin's Wars: From World War to Cold War, 1939–1953* (New Haven, CT: Yale University Press, 2006), stresses Iosif Stalin's grand strategic skills, but is thin on the Cold War years. For these, see Vojtech Mastny, *The Cold War and Soviet Insecurity: The Stalin Years* (New York: Oxford University Press, 1996), and Vladislav Zubok and Constantine Pleshakov, *Inside the Kremlin's Cold War: From Stalin to Khrushchev* (Cambridge, MA: Harvard University Press, 1996). See also, on Nikita Khrushchev, William Taubman, *Khrushchev: The Man and His Era* (New York: Norton, 2003), and Aleksandr Fursenko and Timothy Naftali, *Khrushchev's Cold War: The Inside Story of an American Adversary* (New York: Norton, 2006). The best overall history of Soviet grand strategy during the Cold War is now Vladislav M. Zubok, *A Failed Empire: The Soviet Union from Stalin to Gorbachev* (Chapel Hill, NC: University of North Carolina Press, 2007).

Patrick O. Cohrs, *The Unfinished Peace after World War I: America, Britain and the Stabilisation of Europe, 1919–1932* (Cambridge: Cambridge University Press, 2006), explains the failure to shape an effective peacetime grand strategy after World War I. For Franklin D. Roosevelt, see Robert Dallek, *Franklin D. Roosevelt and American Foreign Policy, 1932–1945*

(New York: Oxford University Press, 1979), and, for Harry S. Truman, Melvyn P. Leffler, *A Preponderance of Power: National Security, the Truman Administration, and the Cold War* (Stanford, CA: Stanford University Press, 1992). John Lewis Gaddis, *We Now Know: Rethinking Cold War History* (New York: Oxford University Press, 1997), covers the origins and evolution of the Cold War through 1962. For containment, see John Lewis Gaddis, *Strategies of Containment: A Critical Appraisal of American National Security Policy during the Cold War*, rev. and exp. ed. (New York: Oxford University Press, 2005).

Marc Trachtenberg, *A Constructed Peace: The Making of the European Settlement, 1945–1963* (Princeton, NJ: Princeton University Press, 1999), shows why the post-World War II settlement in Europe proved more durable than its post-World War I predecessor. For the expansion of the Cold War to Asia, see Thomas J. Christensen, *Useful Adversaries: Grand Strategy, Domestic Mobilization, and Sino-American Conflict, 1947–1958* (Princeton, NJ: Princeton University Press, 1996). David Holloway, *Stalin and the Bomb* (New Haven, CT: Yale University Press, 1994), and McGeorge Bundy, *Danger and Survival: Choices about the Bomb in the First Fifty Years* (New York: Random House, 1988), trace the development of Soviet and American strategy regarding nuclear weapons. For superpower strategies in the Third World, see Odd Arne Westad, *The Global Cold War: Third World Interventions and the Making of Our Times* (New York: Cambridge University Press, 2005).

Jeremi Suri, *Power and Protest: Global Revolution and the Rise of Détente* (Cambridge, MA: Harvard University Press, 2003), shows how protest movements of the 1960s encouraged Soviet, American, and Chinese efforts to formalize the Cold War stalemate. Margaret MacMillan, *Nixon and Mao: The Week That Changed the World* (New York: Random House, 2007), documents the Sino-American rapprochement that was part of this process. Aaron L. Friedberg, *In the Shadow of the Garrison State: America's Anti-Statism and Its Cold War Grand Strategy* (Princeton, NJ: Princeton University Press, 2000), discusses domestic mobilization for the Cold War inside the United States, while Matthew J. Ouimet, *The Rise and Fall of the Brezhnev Doctrine in Soviet Foreign Policy* (Chapel Hill, NC: University of North Carolina Press, 2003), examines economic and geopolitical crises within the Soviet Union during the era of détente. For the emerging issue of human rights, see Daniel C. Thomas, *The Helsinki Effect: International Norms, Human Rights, and the Demise of Communism* (Princeton, NJ: Princeton University Press, 2001).

Little has as yet been written on the role of grand strategy in ending the Cold War, but some preliminary attempts to consider these issues include Raymond Garthoff, *The Great Transition: American-Soviet Relations and the End of the Cold War* (Washington, DC: Brookings Institution, 1994), Philip Zelikow and Condoleezza Rice, *Germany Unified and Europe Transformed: A Study in Statecraft* (Cambridge, MA: Harvard University Press, 1995), Don Oberdorfer, *From the Cold War to a New Era: The United States and the Soviet Union, 1983–1991*, updated ed. (Baltimore, MD: Johns Hopkins University Press, 1998), as well as John Lewis Gaddis, *The Cold War: A New History* (New York: Penguin, 2005), and the final chapters of Gaddis, *Strategies of Containment*.

John Patrick Diggins, *Ronald Reagan: Fate, Freedom, and the Making of History* (New York: Norton, 2007), seeks to place Reagan's strategy within a broad historical context, while Paul Lettow, *Ronald Reagan and His Quest to Abolish Nuclear Weapons* (New York: Random House, 2005), focuses on that particular aspect of it. William Taubman is preparing the definitive biography of Mikhail Gorbachev; until it appears, the best sources for Gorbachev's strategy are his *Memoirs* (New York: Doubleday, 1995), and Anatoly

S. Chernyaev, *My Six Years with Gorbachev*, trans. and ed. by Robert D. English and Elizabeth Tucker (University Park, PA: Pennsylvania State University Press, 2000).

For Clausewitz's classic work, the only reliable edition is Carl von Clausewitz, *On War*, ed. and trans. by Michael Howard and Peter Paret (Princeton, NJ: Princeton University Press, 1976), which also contains informative essays by the editors and Bernard Brodie. Brodie's own analysis of Clausewitz's relevance to the Cold War – and that of Thucydides – is in his *War and Politics* (New York: Macmillan, 1973).

2. Identity and the Cold War

The basic work on identity from social psychology is Henri Tajfel, "Social Identity and Intergroup Behavior," *Social Science Information/sur les sciences socials*, 13 (1974), 65–93. See also John Turner and Henri Tajfel, "Social Comparison and Group Interest in Ingroup Favoritism," *European Journal of Social Psychology*, 9 (1979), 187–204, and Henri Tajfel, *Human Groups and Social Categories: Studies in Social Psychology* (London: Cambridge University Press, 1997). Tajfel's basic point is that groups form under even minimal provocation and that people quickly come to see the in-group as more competent, deserving, and moral than the out-group. People also tend to exaggerate the differences between the in-group and the out-group and to police the boundaries between them. For summaries of the research on identity, cohesion, and in-group bias, see Rose McDermott, "Psychological Approaches to Social Identity: Experimentation and Application," in Rawi Abdelal, Yoshiko Herrera, Alastair Iain Johnston, and Rose McDermott (eds.), *Measuring Identity: A Guide for Social Scientists* (New York: Cambridge University Press, 2009), and Leonie Huddy, "Group Relations and Political Cohesion," in David Sears, Leonie Huddy, and Robert Jervis (eds.), *Oxford Handbook of Political Psychology* (New York: Oxford University Press, 2003), 511–58. The topic is so important that there now is a journal *Self and Identity* devoted to it. The best application to international politics is Jonathan Mercer, "Anarchy and Identity," *International Organization*, 49 (1995), 229–52. The importance of interaction for identity is stressed in Alexander Wendt, *Social Theory of International Politics* (New York: Cambridge University Press, 1999), who argues that identities are central to international politics both in the foreign policies of specific states and in the characteristic nature of international politics prevailing in particular eras. David Campbell, *Writing Security* (Minneapolis, MN: University of Minnesota Press, 1992), examines the role of identities in the Cold War.

Louis Hartz, *The Liberal Tradition in America* (New York: Harcourt, Brace & Co., 1955), makes a crucial argument that American political culture is distinctive because its social structure is unique: the country was formed by what he calls a "social fragment" as the founding population that wielded political and social power was essentially middle-class. Unlike Europe, the United States then never experienced feudalism (except for the South, which had a form of it), and therefore never experienced a bourgeois revolution or, concomitantly, working-class radicalism. This also gave the United States a distorted view of other countries, who experienced revolutions in the normal course of their history. Hartz extended his views by comparing the United States to other settler countries in *The Founding of New Societies* (New York: Harcourt, Brace & World, 1964). Hartz's views have been subject to prolonged debate: for a recent summary and defense, see Philip Abbott

"Still Louis Hartz after All These Years," *Perspectives on Politics*, 3 (2005), 93–109, and the comments by Richard Iton and Sean Wilentz, *ibid.*, 117–20. See also *The First New Nation: The United States in Historical and Comparative Perspective* (New York: Basic Books, 1963) and *American Exceptionalism: A Double-Edged Sword* (New York: Norton, 1996) by Seymour Martin Lipset, and Byron E. Shafer (ed.), *Is America Different?: A New Look at American Exceptionalism* (Oxford: Clarendon Press of Oxford University Press, 1991). For analyses of American identity based on survey data, see Donald Devine, *The Political Culture of the United States* (Boston, MA: Little, Brown, 1972), and Herbert McClosky and John Zaller, *The American Ethos: Public Attitudes toward Capitalism and Democracy* (Cambridge, MA: Harvard University Press, 1984).

The literature on the sources of American identity is large and contested. The role of the period before the American Revolution is stressed by Bernard Bailyn in his *The Ideological Origins of the American Revolution* (Cambridge, MA: Belknap Press of Harvard University Press, 1971) and *The Origins of American Politics* (New York: Knopf, 1968), and by Richard Merritt, *Symbols of American Community, 1735–1775* (New Haven, CT: Yale University Press, 1966). David Hackett Fischer, *Albion's Seed* (New York: Oxford University Press, 1989), shows that although the American colonies were indeed settled dominantly by people from Britain, there were four distinct waves of British immigration that brought with them different cultures and ideas. Jill Lepore, *The Name of War: King Philip's War and the Origins of American Identity* (New York: Knopf, 1998), sees events a century before the revolution as crucial. Samuel Huntington among others, *Who Are We? The Challenges to American National Identity* (New York: Simon & Schuster, 2004), sees national identity forming only after the Civil War.

Ted Hopf, *The Social Construction of International Politics: Identities and Foreign Policies, 1955 and 1999* (Ithaca, NY: Cornell University Press, 2002), provides a theoretically informed and empirically well-grounded study of changing Soviet and Russian identities, highlighting 1955 and 1999. He is particularly acute on the changes wrought by Khrushchev and the interconnections among domestic politics, conceptions of collective self, and foreign policies toward the Third World and the West. Hopf shows how the acceptance of a wider range of regimes abroad and a willingness to relax tensions with the West were linked to domestic reforms and how both were reciprocally linked to a broader sense of the Soviet self, a broadened definition of the social classes that supported the Soviet state, and a more relaxed view of class conflict.

Jussi Hanhimäki, *The Flawed Architect: Henry Kissinger and American Foreign Policy* (New York: Oxford University Press, 2004), is a thorough, comprehensive, and even-handed analysis of the Nixon–Kissinger foreign policy, of which détente was the center-piece. Like everyone else, he draws on Raymond Garthoff, *Détente and Confrontation: American–Soviet Relations From Nixon to Reagan*, rev. ed. (Washington, DC: Brookings Institution, 1994). Deeply scholarly, but informed by his knowledge as a former government official, Garthoff argues that the version of détente presented in the two volumes of Henry Kissinger's memoirs available when he wrote are extremely misleading, disguising as they do the degree to which at every turn the United States sought to thwart the Soviet Union's quest for equality, thereby undermining détente. Ironically, the third volume of Kissinger's memoirs, *Years of Renewal* (New York: Simon & Schuster, 1999), written after the fall of the Soviet Union, endorses Garthoff's analysis, although without mentioning it. Mike Bowker and Phil Williams, *Superpower Détente: A Reappraisal* (London: Royal Institute of International Affairs, 1988), is briefer, critical of the United States, and (correctly) stresses the incompatible aspirations and self-images involved. The role of the Third World in the Cold War is most fully developed in Odd Arne Wested, *The Global Cold War* (New York: Cambridge University Press, 2006), which shows both the extent to which the conflict was waged in these areas and the ideological character of the struggle.

3. Economic aspects of the Cold War, 1962–1975

A pro-administration account of contemporary US economic policy, and the public rationale for it, can be found annually in *Economic Report of the President*, and for trade policy since 1963 in the annual reports of the US Trade Representative. The former is mostly devoted to domestic economic policy but typically includes a chapter on foreign economic policy, which is of course conditioned by domestic economic conditions and pressures. The president's proposed budget for the coming year, reflecting his administration's spending priorities, can be found in the annual *Budget of the United States*, along with recent data on actual spending under the same headings. The monthly *Federal Reserve Bulletin* also contains useful contemporary information and analyses.

Developments in the world economy seen from a non-US perspective can be found in the annual reports of the Bank for International Settlements; global trade developments are covered in *International Trade*, published annually by the secretariat of the General Agreement on Tariffs and Trade (GATT). Comparable data on foreign aid can be found in *Development Assistance Efforts and Policies*, published annually (during the 1960s) by the Development Assistance Committee of the Organisation for Economic Co-operation and Development (OECD). Data on US arms trade and estimates for that of the Soviet Union can be found in *World Military Expenditures and Arms Transfers*, published by the US Arms Control and Disarmament Agency (ACDA).

Glimpses into the worldview and thought processes of key decisionmakers can often be found in their memoirs: See, for example, Dwight Eisenhower, *Waging the Peace*, volume II of his *The White House Years* (Garden City, NY: Doubleday, 1965), Lyndon Johnson, *The Vantage Point: Perspectives of the Presidency 1963–1969* (New York: Holt, Rinehart and Winston, 1971), and Richard Nixon *The Memoirs of Richard Nixon* (New York: Grosset & Dunlap, 1978). John F. Kennedy was unable to produce memoirs, but partial substitutes can be found in Theodore C. Sorensen, *Kennedy* (New York: Harper Row, 1965), and in Arthur Schlesinger, Jr., *A Thousand Days: John F. Kennedy in the White House* (Boston, MA: Houghton Mifflin, 1965); both Sorensen and Schlesinger were close to Kennedy and worked for him in the White House. An entertaining discussion of foreign policy, especially foreign economic policy, can be found in *The Past Has Another Pattern* (New York: Norton, 1982), by George W. Ball, under secretary of state in the Kennedy and Johnson administrations. See also Henry A. Kissinger's *The White House Years* (Boston, MA: Little Brown, 1979) and *Years of Upheaval* (Boston, MA: Little, Brown, 1982); and H. R. Haldeman, *The Haldeman Diaries: Inside the Nixon White House* (New York: G. P. Putnam's, 1994) for the Nixon administration. Francis Bator, deputy national security assistant for economics and for Europe in the Johnson administration, has written a series of recollections and reflections on Johnson's approach to foreign economic policy, in Kermit Gordon (ed.), *Agenda for the Nation: Papers on Domestic and Foreign Policy Issues*

(Washington, DC: Brookings Institution, 1968), *Foreign Affairs* (1968), George L. Perry and James Tobin (eds.), *Economic Events, Ideas, and Policies: The 1960s and After* (Washington, DC: Brookings Institution, 2000), and Aaron Lobel and Robert Richardson Bowie (eds.), *Presidential Judgment: Foreign Policy Decision Making in the White House* (Hollis, NH: Hollis Pub., 2001).

A British perspective is provided by Harold Macmillan in *Pointing the Way, 1956–1961* (London: Macmillan, 1972) and *At the End of the Day, 1961–1963* (New York: Harper & Row, 1973), by Harold Wilson, *A Personal Record: The Labour Government 1964–1970* (Boston, MA: Little, Brown, 1971), and by Alec Cairncross, *The Wilson Years: A Treasury Diary 1964–1969* (London: Historian's Press, 1997). A French perspective is given in Charles de Gaulle, *Memoirs of Hope: Renewal and Endeavor* (New York: Simon & Schuster, 1971). Allowance must be made for the likelihood that all memoirs are written with a historical legacy in mind, especially the last.

An overview of world economic growth during the past half-century (and more) can be found in Angus Maddison, *The World Economy: A Millennial Perspective* (Paris: OECD, 2001). For a Federal Reserve insider's account of international monetary developments, see Robert Solomon, *The International Monetary System, 1945–1981: An Insider's View* (New York: Harper & Row, 1977). For an analysis of the effectiveness of economic sanctions, see Gary Clyde Hufbauer, Kimberly Ann Elliot, and Jeffrey J. Schott, *Economic Sanctions Reconsidered*, rev. ed. (Washington, DC: Institute for International Economics, 1990). On the Kennedy Round of multilateral trade negotiations (concluded in 1967), see Ernest Preeg, *Traders and Diplomats: An Analysis of the Kennedy Round of Negotiations under the General Agreement on Tariffs and Trade* (Washington, DC: Brookings Institution, 1970); and on the interplay between trade policy and US domestic politics, *Water's Edge: Domestic Politics and the Making of American Foreign Economic Policy* (Westport, CT: Greenwood Press, 1979), by Paula Stern. Thomas A. Schwartz has written authoritatively on *Lyndon Johnson and Europe: In the Shadow of Vietnam* (Cambridge, MA: Harvard University Press, 2003).

For the performance of the Soviet economy, see Paul R. Gregory and Robert C. Stuart, *Russian and Soviet Economic Performance and Structure*, 6th ed. (Boston, MA: Addison-Wesley, 2001), and Philip Hanson, *The Rise and Fall of the Soviet Economy: An Economic History of the USSR from 1945* (New York: Longman, 2003). The classic study of the Soviet economy, which was parsimonious in providing data, is Abram Bergson, *The Economics of Soviet Planning* (New Haven, CT: Yale University Press, 1964), and Bergson's *Productivity and the Social System: The USSR and the West* (Cambridge, MA: Harvard University Press, 1978). See also Marshall I. Goldman, *Détente and Dollars: Doing Business with the Soviets* (New York: Basic Books, 1975), and the triennial compendia on the Soviet economy produced by the Joint Economic Committee of the US Congress. Anatolii F. Dobrynin provides an insider's view of US–Soviet relations in *In Confidence: Moscow's Ambassador to America's Six Cold War Presidents, 1962–1986* (Seattle, WA: University of Washington Press, 2001). Krushchev's concerns about Soviet agriculture and excessive Soviet military spending, based on much Soviet archival material, are documented in Aleksandr Fursenko and Timothy Naftali, *Krushchev's Cold War: The Inside Story of an American Adversary* (New York: Norton, 2006).

See also entries under sections 6 and 7 in this bibliography, and relevant parts of the bibliographies in volumes I and III.

4. The Cuban missile crisis

For roughly a decade following the crisis, most accounts – by or based on information from government officials – celebrated JFK's "crisis management" and toughness dealing with his Kremlin adversary, and tended to emphasize the nuclear balance (as opposed to US hostility to Fidel Castro) as both causing the crisis and ordaining its resolution. See, e.g., Elie Abel, *The Missile Crisis* (New York: Bantam, 1966), Theodore C. Sorensen, *Kennedy* (New York: Harper & Row, 1965), Arthur M. Schlesinger, Jr., *A Thousand Days* (Boston: Houghton Mifflin, 1965), Roger Hilsman, *To Move a Nation* (New York: Doubleday, 1967), and, posthumously, Robert F. Kennedy, *Thirteen Days* (New York: Norton, 1969). "To the whole world," Schlesinger declared (pp. 840–41), the crisis "displayed the ripening of an American leadership unsurpassed in the responsible management of power ... throughout the crisis [JFK] coolly and exactly measured the level of force necessary to deal with the level of threat. Defining a clear and limited objective, he moved with mathematical precision to accomplish it ... It was this combination of toughness and restraint, of will, nerve and wisdom, so brilliantly controlled, so matchlessly calibrated, that dazzled the world." Graham T. Allison consolidated Kennedy administration perspectives in *Essence of Decision* (New York: Little, Brown, 1971), the dominant secondary account for the next quarter-century.

The pendulum swung toward a harsher view in the 1970s. Vietnam, Watergate, and CIA scandals nourished skepticism toward hardline Cold War policies, and consequently JFK's handling of the crisis and Cuba. Exemplary texts include the November 1975 report of the US Senate Select Committee to Study Governmental Operations with Respect to Intelligence Activities, *Alleged Assassination Plots Involving Foreign Leaders*, which divulged covert operations and schemes to kill Castro during the Kennedy years; Barton J. Bernstein, e.g., "The Cuban Missile Crisis: Trading the Jupiters in Turkey?" *Political Science Quarterly*, 95 (Spring 1980), 97–125, and Garry Wills, *The Kennedy Imprisonment* (Boston, MA: Little, Brown, 1982). In *Robert Kennedy and His Times* (Boston, MA: Houghton Mifflin, 1978), Arthur M. Schlesinger, Jr., acknowledged (p. 530) that the "record demands the revision of the conventional portraits of Kennedy during the crisis: both the popular view, at the time, of the unflinching leader fearlessly staring down the Russians until they blinked; and the later left-wing view of a man driven by psychic and political compulsions to demand unconditional surrender at whatever risk to mankind."

In the 1980s, the historiography swerved again due both to new evidence and political shifts. The uproar over Ronald Reagan's nuclear policies offered Kennedy loyalists a chance to rebut criticism of their hero. Arguing that Reagan was pushing US–Soviet relations back to the brink, former JFK aides cited his missile crisis posture as a model – *not* the Cold War toughness for which they once hailed him, but because, in fact, he had been the Excomm's leading *dove*, willing to make painful compromises (e.g., publicly trading the Jupiters) to avoid nuclear calamity. Contradicting earlier claims, they now argued that the nuclear balance was *not* decisive in 1962, but that, instead, US *conventional* superiority around Cuba forced Khrushchev to back down. See Dean Rusk, Robert McNamara, George Ball, Roswell Gilpatric, Theodore Sorensen, and McGeorge Bundy, "The Lessons of the Cuban Missile Crisis," *Time*, 27 September 1982, Robert McNamara, "The Military Role of Nuclear Weapons," *Foreign Affairs*, 62, 1 (Fall 1983), 59–80, and McGeorge Bundy, *Danger and Survival* (New York: Random House, 1988).

Gorbachev's *glasnost* and the demise of the Cold War (and the USSR) hastened the *internationalization* of missile crisis historiography beyond US sources to incorporate Soviet, Cuban, and other perspectives. A "critical oral history" project gathering US, Soviet, and Cuban veterans between 1987 and 1992 – and an encore in Havana in 2002 – yielded a series of publications: James G. Blight and David A. Welch, *On the Brink*, 2nd ed. (New York: Noonday Press, 1990), James G. Blight, David A. Welch, and Bruce J. Allyn, *Cuba on the Brink* (New York: Pantheon, 1993), Generals Anatoli I. Gribkov and William Y. Smith, *Operation ANADYR* (Chicago: edition q, 1994), James G. Blight and Philip Brenner, *Sad and Luminous Days* (Lanham, MD: Rowan and Littlefield, 2002).

Since the 1990s, the evidentiary floodgates have opened on various aspects of the crisis, even once taboo topics such as intelligence. Works presenting new findings include Dino A. Brugioni, *Eyeball to Eyeball* (New York: Random House, 1991), James A. Nathan (ed.), *The Cuban Missile Crisis Revisited* (New York: St. Martin's Press, 1992), Scott D. Sagan, *The Limits of Safety* (Princeton, NJ: Princeton University Press, 1994), 53–155, Philip Nash, *The Other Missiles of October* (Chapel Hill, NC: University of North Carolina Press, 1997), and James G. Blight and David A. Welch (eds.), *Intelligence and the Cuban Missile Crisis* (London: Frank Cass, 1998).

Fresh secondary accounts of the crisis have supplanted Allison's *Essence of Decision*, most importantly Aleksandr Fursenko and Timothy Naftali, *"One Hell of a Gamble": Khrushchev, Castro, and Kennedy, 1958–1964* (New York: Norton, 1997). Others include *The Cuban Missile Crisis* (New York: New York University Press, 1995), and *Missiles in Cuba* (Chicago: Ivan R. Dee, 1997), by Mark J. White, Graham T. Allison and Philip D. Zelikow, *Essence of Decision*, rev. ed. (Reading, MA: Longman, 1999), Max Frankel, *High Noon in the Cold War* (New York: Presidio Press, 2004), Sheldon M. Stern, *The Week the World Stood Still* (Stanford, CA: Stanford University Press, 2004), Don Munton and David A. Welch, *The Cuban Missile Crisis* (New York: Oxford University Press, 2007), and Michael Dobbs, *One Minute to Midnight: Kennedy, Khrushchev, and Castro on the Brink of Nuclear War* (New York: Knopf, 2008, published after Chapter 4 was completed.

Important compilations of declassified records include Laurence Chang and Peter Kornbluh (eds.), *The Cuban Missile Crisis* (New York: New Press, 1992; rev. ed., 1998); Mary McAufliffe (ed.), *CIA Documents on the Cuban Missile Crisis* (Washington, DC: CIA History Staff, October 1992); and *Foreign Relations of the United States, 1961–1963*, vols. X-XI and microfiche supplement (Washington, DC: US Government Printing Office, 1996–98). For Excomm transcripts, see Ernest R. May and Philip D. Zelikow (eds.), *The Kennedy Tapes* (Cambridge, MA: Harvard University Press, 1997), *The Presidential Recordings: John F. Kennedy: The Great Crises* (New York: Norton, 2001), Vol. II, *September–October 21, 1962*, ed. Naftali and Zelikow, 391–614, and vol. III, *October 22–October 28, 1962*, ed. Zelikow and May; and Sheldon M. Stern, *Averting 'The Final Failure'* (Stanford, CA: Stanford University Press, 2003).

On the Soviet dimension, see, besides Fursenko and Naftali's *"One Hell of a Gamble,"* William Taubman, *Khrushchev* (New York: Norton., 2003), Aleksandr Fursenko and Timothy Naftali, *Khrushchev's Cold War* (New York: Norton, 2006), Sergo Mikoyan, *Anatomiia Karibskogo krizisa* [The Anatomy of the Caribbean Crisis] (Moscow: Academia, 2006), and translated Russian documents available through the websites of the Cold War International History Project and National Security Archive. For other nations, see, e.g., L. V. Scott, *Macmillan, Kennedy and the Cuban Missile Crisis* (Basingstoke, UK: Palgrave

Macmillan, 1999), and James G. Hershberg, "The United States, Brazil, and the Cuban Missile Crisis, 1962," *Journal of Cold War Studies*, 6, 2–3 (Spring–Summer 2004), 3–20, 5–67.

5. Nuclear competition in an era of stalemate, 1963–1975

For overviews of the nuclear era, see McGeorge Bundy, *Danger and Survival: Choices about the Bomb in the First Fifty Years* (New York: Random House, 1988), David G. Coleman and Joseph M. Siracusa, *Real-World Nuclear Deterrence: The Making of International Strategy* (Westport, CT: Praeger Security International, 2006), and Joseph Cirincione, *Bomb Scare: The History and Future of Nuclear Weapons* (New York: Columbia University Press, 2007). Lawrence S. Wittner's, *Resisting the Bomb: A History of the World Nuclear Disarmament Movement, 1954–1970* (Stanford, CA: Stanford University Press, 1997) and *Toward Nuclear Abolition: A History of the World Disarmament Movement, 1971 to the Present* (Stanford, CA: Stanford University Press, 2003) provide a thorough account of antinuclear movements during the period.

For a detailed topical breakdown of US nuclear spending, see Stephen Schwartz (ed.), *Atomic Audit: The Cost and Consequences of U.S. Nuclear Weapons since 1940* (Washington, DC: Brookings Institution, 1998). For decisions on strategic force levels, see Lawrence S. Kaplan, Ronald D. Landa, and Edward J. Drea, *History of the Office of the Secretary of Defense*, vol. V, *The McNamara Ascendancy 1961–1965* (Washington, DC: Historical Office, Office of the Secretary of Defense, 2006), and Desmond Ball, *Politics and Force Levels: The Strategic Missile Programs of the Kennedy Administration* (Berkeley, CA: University of California Press, 1980). For important studies of major ballistic missile systems, see Graham Spinardi, *From Polaris to Trident: The Development of Fleet Ballistic Missile Technology* (Cambridge: Cambridge University Press, 1994), David Stumpf, *Titan II: A History of a Cold War Missile Program* (Fayetteville, AR: University of Arkansas Press, 2000), and Ted Greenwood, *Making the MIRV: A Study of Defense Decision Making* (Cambridge, MA: Ballinger, 1975). Donald MacKenzie, *Inventing Accuracy: A Historical Sociology of Nuclear Missile Guidance* (Cambridge, MA: MIT Press, 1990), is a wonderful history of inertial guidance.

For US nuclear war planning and target strategy, see essays by David A. Rosenberg, including "Nuclear Planning," in Michael Howard, George J. Andreopoulos, and Mark R. Shulman (eds.), *The Laws of War: Constraints on Warfare in the Western World* (New Haven, CT: Yale University Press, 1994). Fred M. Kaplan's *The Wizards of Armageddon* (Stanford, CA: Stanford University Press, 1991) is a path-breaking work on the RAND Corporation and nuclear war planning. For strategy during the early 1970s, see Terry Terriff, *The Nixon Administration and the Making of U.S. Nuclear Strategy* (Ithaca, NY: Cornell University Press, 1995), and William Burr, "The Nixon Administration, the 'Horror Strategy,' and the Search for Limited Nuclear Options, 1969–1972: Prelude to the Schlesinger Doctrine," *Journal of Cold War Studies*, 7 (2005), 34–78.

For the relationship between control of nuclear weapons and nuclear war planning, see Peter D. Feaver, *Guarding the Guardians: Civilian Control of Nuclear Weapons in the United States* (Ithaca, NY: Cornell University Press, 1992). Nina Tannenwald's *The Nuclear Taboo:*

The United States and the Non-Use of Nuclear Weapons since 1945 (Cambridge: Cambridge University Press, 2007) explores the problem of nuclear use. Lynn Eden, *Whole World on Fire: Organizations, Knowledge, & Nuclear Weapons Devastation* (Ithaca, NY: Cornell University Press, 2003), and Scott Sagan, *The Limits of Safety: Organizations, Accidents, and Nuclear Weapons* (Princeton, NJ: Princeton University Press, 1993), are illuminating studies of nuclear weapons effects and safety issues. Bruce Blair, *The Logic of Accidental Nuclear War* (Washington, DC: Brookings Institution, 1993), reviews US and Soviet launch-on-warning policies since the 1970s.

For strategic intelligence and warning systems, see Jeffrey Richelson, *The Wizards of Langley: Inside the CIA's Directorate of Science and Technology* (Boulder, CO: Westview Press, 2001), and *America's Space Sentinels: DSP Satellites and National Security* (Lawrence, KS: University Press of Kansas, 1999). For the Internet's origins in the efforts to improve nuclear command-and-control systems, see Roy Rosenzweig, "Wizards, Bureaucrats, Warriors & Hackers: Writing the History of the Internet," *American Historical Review*, 103 (December 1998), 1530–52.

Raymond Garthoff's *Détente and Confrontation: American–Soviet Relations from Nixon to Reagan* (Washington, DC: Brookings Institution, 1994) remains the fullest account of détente and the SALT negotiations, but see also Jussi Hanhimäki, *The Flawed Architect: Henry Kissinger and American Foreign Policy* (New York: Oxford University Press, 2004).

English-language work on Kremlin decisionmaking and Soviet nuclear history is scarce, but of high quality. Steven Zaloga, *The Kremlin's Nuclear Sword: The Rise and Fall of Russia's Strategic Nuclear Forces* (Washington, DC: Smithsonian Institution Press, 2002), is one of the most valuable studies. Also essential is Pavel Podvig (ed.), *Russian Strategic Nuclear Forces* (Cambridge, MA: MIT Press, 2001). For Soviet nuclear policy in a broad historical context, see Vladislav M. Zubok, *A Failed Empire: The Soviet Union in the Cold War from Stalin to Gorbachev*, new ed. (Chapel Hill, NC: University of North Carolina Press, 2007), as well as R. Craig Nation, *Black Earth, Red Star: A History of Soviet Security Policy, 1917–1991* (Ithaca, NY: Cornell University Press, 1992). Also important are Christoph Bluth, *Soviet Strategic Arms Policy before SALT* (Cambridge: Cambridge University Press, 1992), and Raymond Garthoff, *Deterrence and the Revolution in Soviet Military Doctrine* (Washington, DC: Brookings Institution, 1990).

For retrospective thinking by former top Soviet commanders, see John Battilega, "Soviet Views of Nuclear Warfare: The Post-Cold War Interviews," in Henry D. Sokolski (ed.), *Getting MAD: Nuclear Assured Destruction, Its Origins and Practice* (Carlisle, PA: Strategic Studies Institute, 2004).

For nuclear issues in US–European alliance relations, including nuclear sharing, NATO nuclear strategy, and the origins and development of flexible response, see Marc Trachtenberg, *A Constructed Peace: The Making of the European Settlement, 1945–1963* (Princeton, NJ: Princeton University Press, 1999), Ivo Daalder, *The Nature and Practice of Flexible Response: NATO Strategy and Theater Nuclear Forces since 1967* (New York: Columbia University Press, 1991), and Holga Haftendorn, *NATO and the Nuclear Revolution: A Crisis of Credibility, 1966–1967* (New York: Oxford University, 1996). Also valuable on US–European nuclear relations is Christoph Bluth, *Britain, Germany, and Western Nuclear Strategy* (Oxford: Clarendon Press, 1995). For the important Anglo-American nuclear relationship, see Stephen Twigge and Len Scott, *Planning Armageddon: Britain, the United States, and the Command of Western Nuclear Forces, 1945–1964* (Amsterdam: Harwood Academic Publishers, 2000).

On nuclear weapons and the Warsaw Pact, see Vojtech Mastny, Sven S. Holtsmark, and Andreas Wenger (eds.), *War Plans and Alliances in the Cold War* (London: Routledge, 2006). Also helpful is Christoph Bluth, "The Warsaw Pact and Military Security in Central Europe during the Cold War," *Journal of Slavic Military Studies*, 17 (2004), 299–311.

6. US foreign policy from Kennedy to Johnson

For published sources, in addition to the variety of documents in the *Foreign Relations of the United States* series, see the transcripts of telephone conversations in Michael R. Beschloss (ed.), *Taking Charge: The Johnson White House Tapes, 1963–1964* (New York: Simon & Schuster, 1997), and Michael R. Beschloss (ed.), *Reaching for Glory: Lyndon Johnson's Secret White House Tapes, 1964–1965* (New York: Simon & Schuster, 2001). For the mood in the Kennedy White House, see Andrew Schlesinger and Stephen Schlesinger (eds.), *Journals, 1952–2000: Arthur M. Schlesinger, Jr.* (New York: Penguin, 2007). See also the online recordings available at the sites for the Miller Center Presidential Recordings Project, the John F. Kennedy Presidential Library, and the Lyndon B. Johnson Presidential Library. For transcripts of JFK's Excomm meetings, see Ernest R. May and Philip D. Zelikow (eds.), *The Kennedy Tapes: Inside the White House during the Cuban Missile Crisis* (Cambridge, MA: Harvard University Press, 1997). Be aware, however, that the editors have deleted many of the "umms," "uhhs," and sentence fragments, making the conversations and particularly the president's contributions seem more focused. For less edited transcripts, see "Documentation: White House Tapes and Minutes of the Cuban Missile Crisis," *International Security*, 10 (1985), 164–203.

Biographies that utilize newly available archival materials include Robert Dallek, *An Unfinished Life: John F. Kennedy, 1917–1961* (Boston, MA: Little, Brown, 2003), and Robert Dallek, *Flawed Giant: Lyndon Johnson and His Times, 1961–1973* (New York: Oxford University Press, 1998). More concise is James N. Giglio, *The Presidency of John F. Kennedy* (Lawrence, KS: University Press of Kansas, 2006). Deeply researched and empathetic is Randall B. Woods, *LBJ: Architect of American Ambition* (New York: Free Press, 2006). For an essential perspective, see William Taubman, *Khrushchev: The Man and His Era* (New York: Norton, 2003). Valuable are parts of Melvyn P. Leffler, *For the Soul of Mankind: The United States, the Soviet Union, and the Cold War* (New York: Hill and Wang, 2007), Walter LaFeber, *America, Russia, and the Cold War, 1945–2006* (Boston, MA: McGraw-Hill, 2008), and Thomas J. McCormick, *America's Half-Century* (Baltimore, MD: Johns Hopkins University Press, 1995). Other studies remain pertinent. More critical are Thomas G. Paterson (ed.), *Kennedy's Quest for Victory: American Foreign Policy, 1961–1963* (New York: Oxford University Press, 1989), and Warren I. Cohen and Nancy Bernkopf Tucker (eds.), *Lyndon Johnson Confronts the World* (New York: Cambridge University Press, 1994). More sympathetic is Diane B. Kunz, *The Diplomacy of the Crucial Decade: American Foreign Relations during the 1960s* (New York: Columbia University Press, 1994). Though hagiographic, early biographies by Kennedy's aides offer rich detail. Arthur M. Schlesinger, Jr., *A Thousand Days: John F. Kennedy in the White House* (Boston: Houghton Mifflin, 1965), and Theodore C. Sorensen, *Kennedy* (New York: Harper & Row, 1965).

For Kennedy, Johnson, and Vietnam, start with George C. Herring, *America's Longest War: The United States and Vietnam, 1950–1975* (Boston, MA: McGraw-Hill, 2002), Marilyn

B. Young, *The Vietnam Wars: 1945–1990* (New York: HarperCollins, 1991), Lloyd C. Gardner, *Pay Any Price: Lyndon Johnson and the Wars for Vietnam* (Chicago: Ivan R. Dee, 1995), David Kaiser, *American Tragedy: Kennedy, Johnson, and the Origins of the Vietnam War* (Cambridge, MA: Harvard University Press, 2000), Robert J. McMahon, *The Limits of Empire: The United States and Southeast Asia since World War II* (New York: Columbia University Press, 1999), and Walter LaFeber, *The Deadly Bet: LBJ, Vietnam, and the 1968 Election* (Lanham, MD: Rowman and Littlefield, 2005). On the politics of escalation, see Robert Buzzanco, *Masters of War* (New York: Cambridge University Press, 1996), and Fredrik Logevall, *Choosing War* (Berkeley, CA: University of California Press, 1999). For the Vietnamese perspective, see Robert K. Brigham, *Guerrilla Diplomacy: The NLF's Foreign Relations and the Vietnam War* (Ithaca, NY: Cornell University Press, 1998). On the Soviet connection, see Ilya V. Gaiduk, *Confronting Vietnam* (Stanford, CA: Stanford University Press, 2003).

For the Cuban missile crisis, see entries under section 4 of this bibliography.

Two key books are Stephen G. Rabe, *The Most Dangerous Area in the World: John F. Kennedy Confronts Communist Revolution in Latin America* (Chapel Hill, NC: University of North Carolina Press, 1999), and Stephen G. Rabe, *U.S. Intervention in British Guiana* (Chapel Hill, NC: University of North Carolina Press, 2005). See also Walter LaFeber, *Inevitable Revolutions: The United States in Central America* (New York: W. W. Norton & Co, 1993).

For other Third World areas, Odd Arne Westad, *The Global Cold War* (New York: Cambridge University Press, 2005), offers the best overview. Also pertinent are portions of Peter L. Hahn and Mary A. Heiss (eds.), *Empire and Revolution: The United States and the Third World since 1945* (Columbus, OH: Ohio State University Press, 2001), Andrew J. Rotter, *Comrades at Odds: The United States and India, 1947–1964* (Ithaca, NY: Cornell University Press, 2000), and Douglas Little, *American Orientalism: The United States and the Middle East since 1945* (Chapel Hill, NC: University of North Carolina Press, 2002).

On relations with France and Germany, see Erin Mahan, *Kennedy, de Gaulle and Western Europe* (New York: Palgrave, 2002), Charles G. Cogan, *Oldest Allies, Guarded Friends* (Westport, CT: Praeger, 1994), Ronald J. Granieri, *The Ambivalent Alliance* (New York: Berghahn Books, 2003), Andreas Daum, *Kennedy in Berlin* (New York: Cambridge University Press, 2007), and Frank Costigliola, *The United States and France: The Cold Alliance since World War II* (New York: Macmillan, 1992). For a sympathetic treatment of LBJ, see Thomas Alan Schwartz, *Lyndon Johnson and Europe* (Cambridge, MA: Harvard University Press, 2003). For key monetary issues, see Francis J. Gavin, *Gold, Dollars, and Power* (Chapel Hill, NC: University of North Carolina Press, 2004). Still insightful is David P. Calleo, *The Imperious Economy* (Cambridge, MA: Harvard University Press, 1982).

For the impact of masculine identity, see Robert G. Dean, *Imperial Brotherhood: Gender and the Making of Cold War Foreign Policy* (Amherst, MA: University of Massachusetts Press, 2001). On the consequences of youthful rebellion, see Jeremi Suri, *Power and Protest: Global Revolution and the Rise of Détente* (Cambridge, MA: Harvard University Press, 2003).

7. Soviet Foreign Policy, 1962–1975

To understand Khrushchev's foreign policy, it is important to understand the man and his career, during both his time in power and the years before that. For a full biography, see William Taubman, *Khrushchev: The Man and His Era* (New York: Norton, 2003). Khrushchev's memoirs have been published in three English-language volumes: Nikita S. Khrushchev, *Khrushchev Remembers*, trans. and ed. by Strobe Talbott (Boston, MA: Little, Brown, 1970), *Khrushchev Remembers: The Last Testament*, trans. and ed. by Jerrold L. Schecter (Boston, MA: Little, Brown, 1974); and *Khrushchev Remembers: The Glasnost Tapes*, trans. and ed. by Jerrold Schecter and Vyacheslav Luchkov (Boston, MA: Little, Brown, 1990). The full Russian version of the memoirs is N. S. Khrushchev, *Vospominaniia: vremia, liudi, vlast* [Memoirs: Time, People, Power], 4 vols. (Moscow: Moskovskie novosti, 1999). A collection of articles including several on foreign and military policy is William Taubman, Sergei Khrushchev, and Abbott Gleason (eds.), *Nikita Khrushchev* (New Haven, CT: Yale, 2000). For an additional list of sources concerning Khrushchev's foreign policy both before and after 1962, see the entries in section 15 of this bibliography.

Khrushchev's son has written two memoirs that devote extensive attention to his last years in power: Sergei N. Khrushchev, *Nikita Khrushchev and the Creation of a Superpower* (University Park, PA: Penn State University Press, 2000), and *Khrushchev on Khrushchev* (Boston, MA: Little, Brown, 1990). Khrushchev's chief foreign-policy assistant's memoir is Oleg Troianovskii, *Cherez gody i rasstoianiia* [Over Years, Over Distances] (Moscow: Vagrius, 1997).

The best history of Khrushchev's foreign policy, based on sources from Russian archives, is Aleksandr Fursenko and Timothy Naftali, *Khrushchev's Cold War: The Inside Story of an American Adversary* (New York: Norton, 2006). See also the entries on the Cuban missile crisis in section 4 of this bibliography.

The vast literature on Soviet foreign policy during the Brezhnev years could be divided into memoir publications, some of which provide a great deal of analysis, and scholarly studies and interpretations of the period. The memoir literature was mainly written by Russian authors and published in Russia, and serious analytical studies done mainly in the United States and Britain. Two significant exceptions to this are the monograph by Vladislav M. Zubok, *The Failed Empire: The Soviet Union in the Cold War from Stalin to Gorbachev* (Chapel Hill, NC: University of North Carolina Press, 2007), and by Rudolf G. Pikhoia, who had full access to Soviet documents as head of the Russian Archival Administration, *Sovetskii soiuz: istoriia vlasti, 1945–1991* [The Soviet Union: A History of Power, 1945–1991] (Novosibirsk: Sibirskii khronograf, 2000).

Among the most valuable memoirs of the period are the books written by former members of the Central Committee who were intimately involved in foreign-policymaking. Two most interesting sources, one looking from the inside and one from outside at the formulation of Soviet foreign policy, are by a member of the International Department of the CPSU Central Committee, Anatolii Cherniaev, *Moia zhizn i moe vremia* [My Life and My Times] (Moscow: Mezhdunarodnye otnosheniia, 1995), and by veteran Ambassador Anatolii Dobrynin, *In Confidence: Moscow's Ambassador to America's Six Cold War Presidents* (New York: Times Books, 1995).

Other memoirs of Soviet decisionmakers include the director of the Institute of USA and Canada, Georgii A. Arbatov's *The System: An Insider's Life in Soviet Politics* (New York: Times Books, 1992), deputy head of the International Department of the CPSU Central Committee Karen N. Brutents's *Tridtsat let na staroi ploshchadi* [Thirty Years at the Old Square] (Moscow: Mezhdunarodnye otnosheniia, 1998), Deputy Foreign Minister Georgii

M. Kornienko's *Kholodnaia voina: svidetelstvo ee uchastnika* [Testimony of a Participant] (Moscow: Mezhdunarodnye otnosheniyia, 1994), and a volume of recollections of members of Brezhnev's inner circle edited by Iurii Aksiutin, *L. I. Brezhnev: materialy k biografii* [L. I. Brezhnev: Materials for a Biography] (Moscow: Politizdat, 1991).

Two outstanding eyewitness accounts combining recollection and analysis are by veteran human rights activist Ludmila Alexeeva, *Soviet Dissent: Contemporary Movements for National, Religious, and Human Rights* (Middletown, CT: Wesleyan University Press, 1985), and by chief Soviet arms-control negotiator Nikolai Detinov, and Alexander Saveliev, *The Big Five: Arms Control Decision Making in the Soviet Union* (Westport, CT: Praeger, 1995), providing a detailed account of Soviet decisionmaking on military-industrial and arms-control issues.

Anyone interested in Soviet foreign policy during the Brezhnev years should consult the magisterial study of US–Soviet relations during détente based on extensive interviews and documents in both countries by Raymond Garthoff, *Détente and Confrontation: American–Soviet Relations from Nixon to Reagan* (Washington, DC: Brookings Institution, 1994). Another classic study that has not lost its relevance is Adam Ulam, *Dangerous Relations: The Soviet Union in World Politics, 1970–1982* (New York: Oxford University Press, 1983).

Among the books that focus on Brezhnev as a leader and foreign policymaker more narrowly are the comparative analysis of Khrushchev and Brezhnev by George Breslauer, *Khrushchev and Brezhnev as Leaders: Building Authority in Soviet Politics* (London: George Allen & Unwin, 1982), Harry Gelman, *The Brezhnev Politburo and the Decline of Détente* (Ithaca, NY: Cornell University Press, 1984), and a collection of essays on Soviet decision-making, *The Domestic Context of Soviet Foreign Policy* (Boulder, CO: Westview Press, 1981), ed. Seweryn Bialer.

Among the recent books published after the end of the Cold War that are based on new sources from both sides of the Iron Curtain are publications by Richard Andersen, *Public Politics in an Authoritarian State: Making Foreign Policy during the Brezhnev Years* (Ithaca, NY: Cornell University Press, 1993), Edwin Bacon and Mark Sandle (eds.), *Brezhnev Reconsidered* (London: Palgrave, Macmillan, 2002), and by Ilya V. Gaiduk, *The Soviet Union and the Vietnam War* (Chicago: Ivan R. Dee, 1996).

8. France, "Gaullism," and the Cold War

No single scholarly work specifically covers France's role throughout the Cold War. A broad account of France's postwar foreign policy can be found in Frédéric Bozo, *La Politique étrangère de la France depuis 1945* (Paris: La Découverte, 1997), and an overview on France's role during the first half of the Cold War is given in Georges-Henri Soutou, "France and the Cold War, 1944–1963," *Diplomacy & Statecraft*, 12, 4 (December 2001), 35–52. For a classic (and sympathetic) analysis of de Gaulle's concept and the Cold War system, see Stanley Hoffmann, *Decline or Renewal? France since the 1930's* (New York: Viking, 1974). For the testimony of a veteran French diplomat whose career covered most of the Cold War (with limited sympathy for "Gaullism"), see Henri Froment-Meurice, *Vu du Quai: Mémoires, 1945–1983* (Paris: Fayard, 1998). For a useful introduction to de Gaulle, see Claire Andrieu, Philippe Braud, and Guillaume Piketty, *Dictionnaire de Gaulle* (Paris: Robert

Laffont, 2006); for a biographical approach, see Jean Lacouture, *De Gaulle: The Ruler, 1945–1970* (New York: W. W. Norton, 1992), and Eric Roussel, *Charles de Gaulle* (Paris: Gallimard, 2002).

On France's policies and the origins of the Cold War under de Gaulle and his immediate successors, see John W. Young, *France, the Cold War, and the Western Alliance, 1944–1949* (Leicester: Leicester University Press, 1990), Pierre Gerbet (ed.), *Le Relèvement, 1944–1949* (Paris: Imprimerie Nationale, 1991), and Georges-Henri Soutou, "France," in David Reynolds (ed.), *The Origins of the Cold War in Europe* (Newhaven, CT: Yale University Press, 1994). On the "turn" of 1947, see Serge Berstein and Pierre Milza (eds.), *L'Année 1947* (Paris: Presses de Sciences-Po, 2000). On France, the German question and East–West relations in the early Cold War period, see Cyril Buffet, *Mourir pour Berlin: La France et l'Allemagne, 1945–1949* (Paris: Armand Colin, 1991), Geneviève Maelstaf, *Que faire de l'Allemagne? Les responsables français, le statut international de l'Allemagne et le problème de l'unité allemande (1945–1955)* (Paris: Ministère des Affaires étrangères, 1999), Michael Creswell, *A Question of Balance: How France and the United States Created Cold War Europe* (Cambridge, MA: Harvard University Press, 2006), and Michael Creswell and Marc Trachtenberg, "France and the German Question, 1945–1955," *Journal of Cold War Studies*, 5, 3 (Summer 2003), 5–28. On France, the Cold War, and the beginning of European integration, see Raymond Poidevin (ed.), *Histoire des débuts de la construction européenne 1948–1950* (Brussels: Bruylant, 1986), and Gérard Bossuat, *La France, l'aide américaine et la construction de l'Europe 1944–1954* (Paris: Comité pour l'histoire économique et financière de la France, 1992). On France, the Cold War, and intra-West relations under the Fourth Republic, see Irwin Wall, *The United States and the Making of Postwar France, 1945–1954* (Cambridge: Cambridge University Press, 1991), and William I. Hitchcock, *France Restored: Cold War Diplomacy and the Quest for Leadership in Europe, 1944–1954* (Chapel Hill, NC: University of North Carolina Press, 1998). On the Fourth Republic, the Cold War, and decolonization, see Denise Artaud, Lawrence Kaplan and Mark Rubin (eds.), *Dien Bien Phu and the Crisis of Franco-American Relations, 1954–1955* (Wilmington, DE: Scholarly Resources, 1990), and Irwin Wall, *France, the United States and the Algerian War* (Berkeley, CA: University of California Press, 2001).

For a detailed account of de Gaulle's foreign policy between 1958 and 1969, see Maurice Vaïsse, *La Grandeur: Politique étrangère du général de Gaulle* (Paris: Fayard, 1998). On de Gaulle's early attempts at engaging the Soviet Union, see Thomas Gomart, *Double détente: Les relations franco-soviétiques de 1958 à 1964* (Paris: Publications de la Sorbonne, 2003). On the rise of Gaullist détente policies and the Franco-Soviet rapprochement, see Marie-Pierre Rey, *La Tentation du rapprochement: France et URSS à l'heure de la détente (1964–1974)* (Paris: Publications de la Sorbonne, 1991); on de Gaulle's détente concept, see also François Puaux, "L'originalité de la politique française de détente," in Institut Charles de Gaulle, *De Gaulle en son siècle*, vol. V, *L'Europe* (Paris: Plon, 1992), and Marie-Pierre Rey, "De Gaulle, l'URSS et la sécurité européenne, 1958–1969," in Maurice Vaïsse (ed.), *De Gaulle et la Russie* (Paris: CNRS Éditions, 2006). On France's relations with the United States during the period, see Frank Costigliola, *France and the United States: The Cold Alliance since World War II* (New York: Twayne Publishers, 1992), and Charles G. Cogan, *Oldest Allies, Guarded Friends: The United States and France since 1940* (Westport, CT: Praeger, 1994). On the interplay between de Gaulle's East–West concept and his intra-West policies, see Frédéric Bozo, *Two Strategies for Europe: De Gaulle, the United States and the Atlantic Alliance* (Lanham, MD: Rowman and Littlefield, 2001), "The NATO Crisis of 1966–1967:

A French Point of View," in Helga Haftendorn, Georges-Henri Soutou, Stephen Szabo, and Sam Wells (eds.), *The Strategic Triangle: France, Germany, and the United States in the Shaping of the New Europe* (Washington, DC: Woodrow Wilson Center Press, Johns Hopkins University Press, 2006), and "Détente vs. Alliance: France, the United States and the Politics of the Harmel Report (1966–1967)," *Contemporary European History*, 7, 3 (1998), 343–60; on the interaction with Franco-German and West European policies, see Georges-Henri Soutou, *L'Alliance incertaine: Les rapports politico-stratégiques franco-allemands, 1954–1996* (Paris: Fayard, 1996), Benedikt Schoenborn, *La Mésentente apprivoisée: De Gaulle et les Allemands, 1963–1969* (Paris: PUF, 2007), and Corinne Defrance and Ulrich Pfeil (eds.), *Le Traité de l'Elysée et les relations franco-allemandes, 1945–1963–2003* (Paris: CNRS Éditions, 2005). On de Gaulle and the German question, see Pierre Maillard, *De Gaulle et l'Allemagne: Le rêve inachevé* (Paris: Plon, 1990).

For an analysis of the influence of "Gaullism" after de Gaulle, see Philip H. Gordon, *A Certain Idea of France: French Security Policy and the Gaullist Legacy* (Princeton, NJ: Princeton University Press, 1993). On France's policies in the 1970s, see Jacques Andréani, *Le Piège: Helsinki et la chute du communisme* (Paris: Odile Jacob, 2005), Association Georges Pompidou, *Georges Pompidou et l'Europe* (Brussels: Complexe, 1995), Serge Berstein and Jean-François Sirinelli (eds.), *Les Années Giscard: Valéry Giscard d'Estaing et l'Europe, 1974–1981* (Paris: Armand Colin, 2006), and Michèle Weinachter, *Valéry Giscard d'Estaing et l'Allemagne: le double rêve inachevé* (Paris: L'Harmattan, 2004). On François Mitterrand's France and the last chapter of the East–West conflict, see the following work by Frédéric Bozo: "Before the Wall: French Diplomacy and the last Decade of the Cold War," in Olav Njølstad (ed.), *The Last Decade of the Cold War: From Conflict Escalation to Conflict Transformation* (London: Frank Cass, 2004), "Mitterrand's France, the End of the Cold War, and German Unification: A Reappraisal," *Cold War History*, 7, 4 (November 2007), 455–78, and *Mitterrand, la fin de la guerre froide et l'unification allemande: De Yalta à Maastricht* (Paris: Odile Jacob, 2005) (English translation, Berghahn Books, 2009).

9. European integration and the Cold War

There is as yet little scholarship that directly addresses the issue of the interconnections between European integration and the Cold War. There are a few exceptions to this rule: Klaus Schwabe, "The Cold War and European Integration, 1947–63," in *Diplomacy and Statecraft*, 12, 4 (2001), a relevant chapter in Desmond Dinan (ed.) *Origins and Evolution of the European Union* (Oxford: Oxford University Press, 2006), N. Piers Ludlow (ed.), *European Integration and the Cold War: Ostpolitik/Westpolitik, 1965–1973* (London: Routledge, 2007), and one substantial monograph in Italian, Massimiliano Guderzo's *Interesse nazionale e responsabilità globale: Gli Stati Uniti, l'Alleanza Atlantica e l'integrazione europea 1963–9* (Florence: AIDA, 2000). The two *Power in Europe* volumes, ed. Josef Becker and Franz Knipping, and Ennio di Nolfo (Berlin: Walter de Gruyter, 1986 & 1992), also cover both fields well. But in most cases, the connections have to be unearthed by reading works primarily focused on either the development of the integration process or Europe's role within the wider Cold War.

The linkages between the two fields are at their most obvious in studies on the late 1940s and early 1950s. This is true of at least some of the scholarship on the Marshall Plan: see for instance Michael Hogan, *The Marshall Plan: America, Britain, and the Reconstruction of Western Europe, 1947–1952* (Cambridge: Cambridge University Press, 1987). It is also the case for much of the literature on the foreign policies of individual Western European states in the early postwar era. For France, Gérard Bossuat's immensely detailed *La France, l'aide américaine et la construction européenne* (Paris: Comité pour l'histoire économique et financière de la France, 1992) has been followed by a good English-language study: William Hitchcock, *France Restored: Cold War Diplomacy and the Quest for Leadership in Europe, 1944–54* (Chapel Hill, NC: University of North Carolina Press, 1998). On Germany too, there is now a strong English-language account: Ronald Granieri, *The Ambivalent Alliance, the CDU/CSU, and the West, 1949–1966* (New York: Berghahn Books, 2003). Georges-Henri Soutou's study of Franco-German relations, *L'Alliance Incertaine* (Paris: Fayard, 1996) is also very valuable. For Britain, John Baylis, *The Diplomacy of Pragmatism* (Basingstoke: Macmillan, 1993), needs to be combined with Anne Deighton, *The Impossible Peace* (Oxford: Clarendon Press, 1993), and John W. Young, *France, the Cold War and the Western Alliance* (Leicester: Leicester University Press, 1990). And for Italy, the best overview is provided by Antonio Varsori (ed.), *La politica estera italiana nel secondo dopoguerra (1943–57)* (Milan: LED, 1993). Two good edited volumes also provide a variety of detailed chapters on most of the individual players: David Reynolds (ed.), *The Origins of the Cold War in Europe* (New Haven, CT: Yale University press, 1994), and Dominik Geppert (ed.), *The Postwar Challenge* (Oxford: Oxford University Press, 2003).

Another fruitful approach is to concentrate on a number of the key biographies, since it was at the highest level of leadership that the interplay between the Cold War and European integration was often most apparent. These include Raymond Poidevin's *Robert Schuman: homme d'état, 1886–1963* (Paris: Imprimerie Nationale, 1986), Hans-Peter Schwarz's two volumes on Adenauer (published in English by Berghahn books in 1995), Alan Bullock's still valuable study, *Ernest Bevin: Foreign Secretary, 1945–1951* (London: Heinemann, 1983), and Piero Craveri, *De Gasperi* (Bologna: Il Mulino, 2006). Also helpful in this regard are Alistair Horne's biography of Harold Macmillan, Eric Roussel's studies of de Gaulle, Pompidou and Monnet, Torsten Oppelland's study of Gerhard Schröder, Michel Dumoulin's work on Paul-Henri Spaak, Vincent Dujardin's biography of Pierre Harmel, and François Duchêne's *Jean Monnet: The First Statesman of Interdependence* (New York: Norton, 1994).

For a flavour of recent scholarship about the European Defence Community episode, Michel Dumoulin (ed.), *The European Defence Community* (Brussels: Peter Lang, 2000), is useful, especially if supplemented with David Large, *Germans to the Front* (Chapel Hill, NC: University of North Carolina Press, 1996), and Spencer Mawby, *Containing Germany* (New York: St. Martin's Press, 1999). And the wider context of US enthusiasm for German rearmament can best be understood from Pascaline Winand, *Eisenhower, Kennedy and the United States of Europe* (London: Macmillan, 1993), Geir Lundestad, *Empire by Integration: the United States and European Integration, 1945–1997* (Oxford: Oxford University Press, 1997), and Marc Trachtenberg, *A Constructed Peace: The Making of the European Settlement 1945–1963* (Princeton, NJ: Princeton University Press, 1999). Also interesting, if much more specialised on the US approach, is Gunnar Skogmar, *The United States and the Nuclear Dimension of European Integration* (Basingstoke: Palgrave, 2004).

A lot of the most recent work has focused on the 1960s. The challenge to both the Cold War status quo and European integration posed by de Gaulle is variously explored by

Frédéric Bozo, *Two Strategies for Europe* (Lanham: Rowman and Littlefield, 2001), Eckard Conze, *Die gaullistische Herausforderung* (Munich: Oldenbourg, 1995), Thomas Schwartz, *Lyndon Johnson & Europe* (Cambridge, MA: Harvard University Press, 2003), Wilfried Loth (ed.), *Crises and Compromises* (Baden-Baden: Nomos, 2001), N. Piers Ludlow, *The European Community and the Crises of the 1960s: Negotiating the Gaullist Challenge* (London: Routledge, 2006), and James Ellison, *The United States, Britain and the Crises in Transatlantic Relations: Rising to the Gaullist Challenge, 1963–68* (Basingstoke: Palgrave, 2007). On Brandt, there is new and detailed biography: Peter Merseburger, *Willy Brandt, 1913–1992: Visionär und Realist* (Stuttgart: DVA, 2002); there are also a number of shorter studies of his eastern policies, e.g. Gottfried Niedhart, "Ostpolitik: Phases, Short-Term Objectives, and Grand Design," *Bulletin of the German Historical Institute*, Supplement 1 (2001). Also useful on the 1970s is Jan van der Harst's volume *Beyond the Customs Union: The European Community's Quest for Completion, Deepening and Enlargement, 1969–1975* (Baden-Baden: Nomos, 2008).

Historians have yet really to tackle the late Cold War in Western Europe. But partial and valuable exceptions include Frédéric Bozo, *Mitterrand, la fin de la guerre froide et l'unification allemande: De Yalta à Maastricht* (Paris: Odile Jacob, 2005), Kristina Spohr Readman, "Between Political Rhetoric and Realpolitik Calculations: Western Diplomacy and Baltic Struggle for Independence in the Cold War Endgame," *Cold War History*, 6, 1 (2006), and Marie-Pierre Rey, Frédéric Bozo, Leopoldo Nuti, and N. Piers Ludlow (eds.), *Europe and the End of the Cold War: A Reappraisal* (London: Routledge, 2008).

10. Détente in Europe, 1962–1975

For a general account that covers European détente in some detail, see Raymond Garthoff, *Détente and Confrontation: Soviet-American Relations from Nixon to Reagan* (Washington, DC: Brookings Institution, 1994). The most comprehensive overview of the development of European détente is the thematically structured John van Oudenaren, *European Détente: The Soviet Union and the West since 1953* (Chapel Hill, NC: University of North Carolina Press, 1991), but for a good and brief narrative, readers should consult Wilfried Loth, *Overcoming the Cold War: A History of Détente, 1950–1991* (London: Palgrave Macmillan, 2002). For a sweeping interpretation stressing the interaction between domestic social movements and top policymakers as the root cause of détente, see Jeremi Suri, *Power and Protest* (Cambridge, MA: Harvard University Press, 2003). See also Dana H. Allin, *Cold War Illusions: America, Europe and Soviet Power, 1969–1989* (New York: St. Martin's Press, 1995), Jussi Hanhimäki, "Ironies and Turning Points: Détente in Perspective," in Odd Arne Westad (ed.), *Reviewing the Cold War: Approaches, Interpretations, Theory* (London: Frank Cass, 2000), and Tony Smith, "A Pericentric Framework for the Study of the Cold War," *Diplomatic History*, 24, 4 (Fall 2000), 567–91.

There is no shortage of works on Charles de Gaulle. The most useful for this chapter were Frédéric Bozo, *Two Strategies for Europe: De Gaulle, the United States, and the Atlantic Alliance* (New York: Rowman and Littlefield, 2000), Hugh Gough and John Horne (eds.), *De Gaulle and Twentieth Century France* (London: Edward Arnold, 1994), Erin Mahan, *Kennedy, de Gaulle and Western Europe* (London: Palgrave Macmillan, 2003), and N. Piers Ludlow, *The European Community and the 1960s Crises: The Gaullist Challenge* (London: Routledge, 2006). Other useful works include: Michael M. Harrison, *Reluctant Ally: France and Atlantic Security*

(Baltimore, MD, and London: Johns Hopkins University Press, 1981), Frank Costigliola, *France and the United States* (New York: Twayne's, 1992), Philip Gordon, *France, Germany, and the Western Alliance* (Boulder, CO: Westview Press, 1995).

On West German policies in the 1960s and 1970s, see Ronald Granieri, *The Ambivalent Alliance: The CDU/CSU and the West, 1949–1966* (London: Berghahn Books, 2004), Wolfram F. Hanrieder, *Germany, America, Europe: Forty Years of German Foreign policy* (New Haven, CT: Yale University Press, 1989), Hans W. Gatzke, *Germany and the United States: A "Special Relationship?"* (Cambridge, MA: Harvard University Press, 1980), Avrill Pittman, *From Ostpolitik to Reunification* (Cambridge: Cambridge University Press, 2002), and Angela Stent, *From Embargo to Ostpolitik: The Political Economy of West German–Soviet Relations* (Cambridge: Cambridge University Press, 2003). There is no satisfactory biography of Willy Brandt, but see Barbara Marshall, *Willy Brandt: A Political Biography* (London: Macmillan, 1997). For an interpretation of early *Ostpolitik*, see Arne Hofmann, *The Emergence of Détente in Europe: Brandt, Kennedy and the Formation of Ostpolitik* (London: Routledge, 2007).

American policy in Europe in the 1960s is covered extensively in Thomas A. Schwartz, *In the Shadow of Vietnam: Lyndon Johnson and Europe* (Cambridge, MA: Harvard University Press, 2003), but see also H. W. Brands, *The Wages of Globalism: Lyndon Johnson and the Limits of American Power* (New York: Oxford University Press, 1995), and Diane B. Kunz, (ed.), *The Diplomacy of the Crucial Decade: American Foreign Policy in the 1960s* (New York: Columbia University Press, 1994). For the early 1970s, see Jussi M. Hanhimäki, *The Flawed Architect: Henry Kissinger and American Foreign Policy* (New York: Oxford University Press, 2004), and William Bundy, *A Tangled Web: The Making of Foreign Policy in the Nixon Administration* (New York: New York: Hill and Wang, 1999). American policies toward Eastern Europe are covered in Bennett Kovrig, *Of Walls and Bridges: The United States and Eastern Europe* (New York: New York University Press, 1991).

On moves towards détente within the Western bloc in the late 1960s, see Frédéric Bozo, "Détente versus Alliance: France, the United States and the Politics of the Harmel Report," *Contemporary European History*, 7, 3 (1998), 343–60, and Andreas Wenger, "Crisis and Opportunity: NATO and the Multilateralization of Détente, 1966–68," *Journal of Cold War Studies*, 6, 1 (Winter 2004), 22–74. For alliance politics in general, see Vojtech Mastny, "The New History of Cold War Alliances," *Journal of Cold War Studies*. 4, 2 (2002), 55–84. For a different account of NATO, see Mark Smith, *NATO Enlargement during the Cold War: Strategy and System in the Western Alliance* (London: Palgrave, 2000).

For a brief general treatment of developments in Eastern Europe, see G. Swain and N. Swain, *Eastern Europe since 1945* (New York: St. Martin's Press, 1993). For other issues covered in this chapter, see Ronald J. Crampton, *The Balkans since the Second World War* (London: Longman, 2002), Stephen Fischer-Galati, *Twentieth Century Rumania* (New York: Columbia University Press, 1991), Katherine Verdery, *National Ideology under Socialism: Identity and Cultural Politics in Ceausescu's Romania* (Los Angeles, CA: University of California Press, 1995), Vladimir Tismeanu, *Stalinism for All Seasons: A Political History of Romanian Communism* (Berkeley, CA: University of California Press, 2003). In addition to Harrison's book cited above, the East German question has been treated effectively by Mary E. Sarotte, *Dealing with the Devil: East Germany, Détente, and Ostpolitik, 1969–1973* (Chapel Hill, NC: University of North Carolina Press, 2001). See also Michael J. Sodaro, *Moscow, Germany and the West: From Khrushchev to Gorbachev* (Ithaca, NY: Cornell University

Press, 1991). For an account that focuses on the Warsaw Pact, the best and most recent is Vojtech Mastny and Malcolm Byrne (eds.), *A Cardboard Castle? An Inside History of the Warsaw Pact* (Budapest: Central European University Press, 2005).

For East–West trade and other economic issues, see Randall W. Stone, *Satellites and Comissars: Strategy and Conflict in the Politics of Soviet Bloc Trade* (Princeton, NJ: Princeton University Press, 2002), Ian Jackson, *The Economic Cold War: America, Britain and East–West Trade 1948–1963* (Basingstoke: Palgrave Macmillan, 2001), Michael Mastanduno, *Economic Containment: CoCom and the Politics of East–West Trade* (Ithaca, NY: Cornell University Press, 1992).

The Conference on Security and Cooperation in Europe (CSCE) has attracted much attention in recent years, although mainly because of its assumed significance in undermining the totalitarian order in the Soviet bloc. For different accounts, see John Maresca, *To Helsinki: The Conference on Security and Co-operation in Europe, 1973–1975* (Durham, NC: Duke University Press, 1987), and Vojtech Mastny, *Helsinki, Human Rights, and European Security: Analysis and Documentation* (Durham, NC: Duke University Press, 1986). For different outlooks on the American perspective on the CSCE, see Charles G. Stefan, "The Drafting of the Helsinki Final Act: A Personal View of the CSCE's Geneva Phase (September 1973 until July 1975)," *SHAFR Newsletter*, 31, 2 (June 2000), and Jussi M. Hanhimäki, "'They Can Write it in Swahili': Kissinger, the Soviets, and the Helsinki Accords, 1973–1975," *Journal of Transatlantic Studies*, I, 1 (Spring 2003), 37–58. On the long-term significance in Europe of the CSCE and détente in general, see Daniel C. Thomas, *The Helsinki Effect: International Norms, Human Rights, and the Demise of Communism* (Princeton, NJ: Princeton University Press, 2001), and Michael E. Smith, *Europe's Foreign and Security Policy: The Institutionalization of Cooperation* (New York: Cambridge University Press. 2004).

11. Eastern Europe: Stalinism to solidarity

A full-length study of many of issues discussed in this chapter is Barbara J Falk, *the Dilemmas of Dissidence in East-Central Europe. Citizen Intellectuals and Philosopher Kings* (Budapest: Central European Press, 2003). For a clear overview of political and social uprisings in the region, see Kevin McDermott and Matthew Stibbe (eds.), *Revolution and Resistance in Eastern Europe: Challenges to Communist Rule* (Oxford: Berg, 2006).

On reemerging civil society, see H. Gordon Skilling, *Charter 77 and Human Rights in Czechoslovakia* (London: Allen and Unwin, 1981), and most notably John Keane (ed.), *The Power of the Powerless: Citizens against the State in Central-Eastern Europe* (London: Hutchinson, 1985), which contains Havel's keynote essay.

The most important recent study of Hungary 1956 is Charles Gati, *Failed Illusions: Moscow, Washington, Budapest, and the 1956 Hungarian Revolt* (Washington, DC: Woodrow Wilson Centre Press and Stanford University Press, 2006). Two valuable retrospective collections are György Litván (ed.), *The Hungarian Revolution of 1956: Reform, Revolt and Repression 1953–1963*, trans. from Hungarian by J. Bak and L. Legters, (London: Longman, 1996), and Tamas Aczel (ed.), *Ten Years After: A Commemoration of the Tenth Anniversary of the Hungarian Revolution* (London: Macgibbon and Kee, 1966). For the general background, see Ferenc Vali, *Rift and Revolt in Hungary: Nationalism versus Communism* (Cambridge,

MA: Harvard University Press, 1961), and Ivan Berend, *The Hungarian Economic Reforms 1953–1988* (Cambridge: Cambridge University Press, 1990). Critical and left-inclined writings include Marc Rakovski, *Towards an East European Marxism* (London: Allison & Busby, 1978), and Miklos Haraszti, *A Worker in a Worker's State: Piece-Rates in Hungary*, trans. from Hungarian by Michael Wright (London: Pelican Books, 1977).

The major collection on Czechoslovakia 1968, including numerous new documents from archives, is Jan Navrátil (ed.), *The Prague Spring 1968: A National Security Archive Documents Reader* (Budapest: Central European Press, 1998). Important further research from archives are Mark Kramer, "The Czechoslovak Crisis and the Brezhnev Doctrine," in Carole Fink, Philipp Gassert, and Detlef Junker (eds.), *1968: The World Transformed* (Cambridge: Cambridge University Press, 1998), and Kieran Williams, *The Prague Spring and Its Aftermath* (Cambridge: Cambridge University Press, 1997). Still very valuable is the monograph by H. Gordon Skilling, *Czechoslovakia's Interrupted Revolution* (Princeton, NJ: Princeton University Press, 1978). Two analyses by Western strategists are Philip Windsor and Adam Roberts, *Czechoslovakia 1968: Reform, Repression and Resistance* (London: Chatto and Windus, 1969), and Karen Dawisha, *The Kremlin and the Prague Spring* (Berkeley, CA: University of California Press, 1984). The memoir of a major participant is Zdeněk Mlynář, *Night Frost in Prague: The End of Humane Socialism*, trans. from Czech by Paul Wilson (London: C. Hurst, 1980).

For Poland, especially useful are Jacek Kurczewski, *The Resurrection of Rights in Poland* (Oxford: Clarendon Press, 1993), by a legal sociologist, and Peter Raina, *Political Opposition in Poland, 1954–1977* (London: Poets and Painters Press, 1978). The writings of a leading oppositionist are Adam Michnik, *Letters from Prison and Other Essays* (Berkeley, CA: 1985), and his *Letters from Freedom: Post-Cold War Realities and Perspectives* (Berkeley, CA: 1988). We have valuable accounts of workers' protests in Roman Laba, *The Roots of Solidarity: A Political Sociology of Poland's Working-Class Democratization* (Princeton NJ: Princeton University Press, 1991), and Jerzy Eisler, *Grudzień 1970: geneza, przebieg, konsekwencje* [December 1970: Origins, Course of Events, Outcomes] (Warsaw: Sensacje XX wieku, 2000).

The unique talks between Polish strikers and party officials are transcribed by Ewa Wacowska (ed.), *Rewolta Szczecińska i jej znaczenie* [The Szczecin Revolt and Its Significance] (Paris: Kultura, 1971). Subsequent worker-intellectual cooperation is described by Jan-Józef Lipski, *KOR: A History of the Workers' Defense Committee in Poland, 1976–1981*, trans. from Polish by O. Amsterdamska and Gene M. Moore (Berkeley, CA: University of California Press, 1985). Two overviews are Andrzej Paczkowski, *The Spring Will Be Ours: Poland and the Poles from Occupation to Freedom*, trans. from Polish by Jane Cave (University Park, PA: Penn State University Press, 2003), and A. Kemp-Welch, *Poland under Communism: A Cold War History* (Cambridge: Cambridge University Press, 2008).

On East Germany, see Z. Madarasz, *Conflict and Compromise in East Germany, 1971–1989: A Precarious Stability* (Basingstoke: Palgrave, 2003), and a meticulous social history by Mary Fulbrook, *The People's State: East German Society from Hitler to Honecker* (New Haven, CT: Yale University Press, 2005). Perennial problems of Balkan nationalism are addressed by Paul Lendvai, *Eagles in Cobwebs: Nationalism and Communism in the Balkans* (London: Macmillan, 1970). Important studies of Romania are Dennis Deletant, *Ceausescu and the Securitate: Coercion and Dissent in Romania, 1965–89* (London: Hurst & Co., 1995), and

Vladimir Tismaneanu, *Stalinism for All Seasons: A Political History of Romanian Communism* (Berkeley, CA: University of California Press, 2003). On Bulgaria, see Richard Crampton, *A Concise History of Bulgaria*, 2nd ed. (Cambridge: Cambridge University Press, 2005).

12. The Cold War and the transformation of the Mediterranean, 1960–1975

A truly comprehensive bibliography of the Cold War in the Mediterranean region would need to include a variety of national and topical histories each with voluminous literatures of their own. For the purpose of brevity, this review focuses on the Mediterranean as a region, on southern Europe, and on Africa's northern littoral. The reader is encouraged also to consult the excellent specialized entries found in the bibliographies for all of the volumes for this *Cambridge History*, especially sections 8, 9, 10 of the bibliography in this volume, section 19 of volume I and sections 2, 5, and 14 in volume III.

For the origins of the Cold War in the region, see E. Calandri, *Il Mediterraneo e la difesa dell'Occidente 1947–1956: Eredità imperiali e logiche di guerra fredda* (Firenze: Manent, 1997). For Italy, see B. Arcidiacono, *Le «précédent italien» et les origines de la guerre froide: Les Alliés et l'occupation de l'Italie 1943–1944* (Bruxelles: Bruylant, 1984), A. Brogi, *A Question of Self-Esteem: The United States and the Cold War Choices in France and Italy, 1944–1958* (Westport, CT: Praeger, 2002), Christopher Duggan and Christopher Wagstaff (eds.), *Italy in the Cold War: Politics, Culture and Society, 1948–58* (Oxford and Washington, DC: Berg, 1995), and the still useful James Edward Miller, *The United States and Italy, 1940–1950: The Politics and Diplomacy of Stabilization* (Chapel Hill, NC: University of North Carolina Press, 1986). For Spain, see Boris N. Liedtke, *Embracing a Dictatorship: US Relations with Spain, 1945–53* (Basingstoke: Macmillan, 1998). For Portugal, Luís Nuno Rodrigues has written several overviews; the formative period is covered in his *Salazar-Kennedy: A Crise de una Aliança* (Capa mole: Editorial Noticias, 2002). For Greece, see Jon V. Kofas, *Under the Eagle's Claw: Exceptionalism in Postwar US–Greek Relations* (Westport, CT: Praeger, 2003), and, for a different view, Howard Jones, *"A New Kind of War": America's Global Strategy and the Truman Doctrine in Greece* (New York: Oxford University Press, 1989). For Turkey, see Ekavi Athanassopoulou, *Turkey: Anglo-American Security interests, 1945–1952: The First Enlargement of NATO* (London: Frank Cass, 1999).

In addition to more general studies of American diplomacy, subsequent developments in Washington's approach to southern Europe are explored in M. Guderzo, *Interesse nazionale e responsabilità globale: Gli Stati Uniti, l'Alleanza atlantica e l'integrazione europea negli anni di Johnson 1963–69* (Firenze: Manent, 2000), and L. Nuti, *Gli Stati Uniti e l'apertura a Sinistra. Importanza e limiti della presenza americana in Italia* (Bari-Roma: Laterza, 1999). On Greece and the problem of Cyprus, see G. S. Kaloudis, *The Role of the United Nations in Cyprus from 1964 to 1979* (New York: Peter Lang, 1991), C. M. Woodhouse, *The Rise and Fall of the Greek Colonels* (London: Granada, 1985).

Consideration of the Mediterranean as a single region was most evident in considerations of military strategy. The Mediterranean's role in NATO is specifically examined in L. S. Kaplan, S. W. Clawson, R. Luraghi, *NATO and the Mediterranean* (Wilmington, DE: Scholarly Resources, 1985), and S. Silvestri, M. Cremasco, *Il Fianco Sud della Nato* (Milano: Feltrinelli, 1980).

On the Middle East and North Africa, see Jon B. Alterman, *Egypt and American Foreign Assistance, 1952–1956: Hopes Dashed* (New York: Palgrave, 2002), Nigel J. Ashton (ed.), *The Cold War in the Middle East: Regional Conflict and the Superpowers, 1967–73* (London and New York: Routledge, 2007) (see also Ashton's excellent *Eisenhower, Macmillan, and the Problem of Nasser: Anglo-American Relations and Arab Nationalism, 1955–59* (New York: St. Martin's Press, 1996). For Egypt, see also Laura James, *Nasser at War: Arab Images of the Enemy* (London: Palgrave Macmillan, 2006). Important specific studies of North Africa include Nicole Grimaud, *La Politique extérieure de l'Algérie* (Paris: Karthala, 1984), Abdelaziz Chneguir, *La politique extérieure de la Tunisie: 1956–1987* (Paris: L'Harmattan, 2004), Ronald Bruce St. John, "Redefining the Libyan Revolution: The Changing Ideology of Muammar al-Qaddafi," *Journal of North African Studies*, 13, 1, (March 2008), 91–106, and Massimiliano Cricco, *Il Petrolio dei Senussi. Stati Uniti e Gran Bretagna in Libia dall'indipendenza a Gheddafi (1949–1973)* (Firenze: Polistampa, 2002). For Soviet policy with regard to the Algerian revolution, see E. Obichkina "Sovetskoe rukovodstvo i voina v Alzhire" [The Soviet Leadership and the War in Algeria], *Novaia i noveishaia istoriia*, No. 1 (2000), 19–30. For Soviet diplomacy in the region, see Roy Allison, *The Soviet Union and the Strategy of Non-Alignment in the Third World* (New York: Cambridge University Press, 1988). The covert aspect of Soviet policy in North Africa is discussed to some degree in Christopher M. Andrew and Vasili Mitrokhin, *The Mitrokhin Archive II: The KGB and the World* (London and New York: Allen Lane, 2005).

Transition in Spain and foreign policy are dealt with by P. Preston, *The Triumph of Democracy in Spain* (London: Methuen, 1986), V. Morales Lezcano V., *España de pequeña potencia a potencia media* (Madrid: Uned, 1991), and A. Marquina Barrio, *España en la Política de Seguridad Occidental: 1936–1986* (Madrid: Ed. Ejército, 1986). On the Portuguese revolution, see H. G. Ferreira, M. V. Marshall, *Portugal's Revolution: Ten Years On* (Cambridge: Cambridge University Press, 1986), T. Gallagher, *Portugal. A Twentieth-Century Interpretation* (Manchester: Mancester University Press, 1983), and Bernardino Gomes and Tiago Moreira de Sá, *Carlucci vs. Kissinger: Os EUA e a Revolução Portuguesa* (Lisbon: Don Quixote, 2008). The diplomatic effects of the Iberian transformation are analyzed in H. de la Torre (ed.), *Portugal, España y Africa en los ultimos cien anos* (Merida: Uned, 1992). The standard work in English on Italy is Paul Ginsborg, *A History of Contemporary Italy: Society and Politics, 1943–1988* (New York: Palgrave Macmillan, 2003), but see also Silvio Lanaro, *Storia dell'Italia repubblicana* (Venice: Marsilio, 1997).

Aleksandr Fursenko and Timothy Naftali, *Khrushchev's Cold War: The Inside Story of an American Adversary* (New York: Norton, 2006) is good on Soviet policy toward the region. A critical account of Soviet influence on Egyptian decisionmaking has recently been elaborated by Isabella Ginor, "'Under the Yellow Arab Helmet Gleamed Blue Russian Eyes': Operation *Kavkaz* and the War of Attrition, 1969–70," *Cold War History*, 3, 1 (2002), 127–56; for a deeper analysis see also Isabella Ginor and Gideon Remez, *Foxbats over Dimona: The Soviets' Nuclear Gamble in the Six-Day War* (New Haven, CT: Yale University Press, 2007).

13. The Cold War in the Third World, 1963–1975

The Cold War in the Third World is the subject of a rich body of literature shaped by diverse interpretations and sources. For an international overview drawing on archives from several different countries, see Odd Arne Westad, *The Global Cold War: Third World Interventions and the Making of Our Times* (Cambridge: Cambridge University Press, 2005). Other useful overviews include Mark T. Berger, *The Battle for Asia: From Decolonization to Globalization* (London: RoutledgeCurzon, 2004), and Forrest D. Colburn, *The Vogue of Revolution in Poor Countries* (Princeton, NJ: Princeton University Press, 1994).

United States policy is broadly treated in Peter L. Hahn and Mary Ann Heiss (eds.), *Empire and Revolution: The United States and the Third World since 1945* (Columbus, OH: Ohio State University Press, 2001), and in Gabriel Kolko's critical *Confronting the Third World: United States Foreign Policy, 1945–1980* (New York: Pantheon, 1988). For an account stressing the agency of Third World actors, see Zachary Karabell, *Architects of Intervention: The United States, the Third World, and the Cold War, 1946–1962* (Baton Rouge, LA: Louisiana State University Press, 1999). On American ideology and modernization, see Nils Gilman, *Mandarins of the Future: Modernization Theory in Cold War America* (Baltimore, MD: Johns Hopkins University Press, 2003), David C. Engerman, Nils Gilman, Mark H. Haefele, and Michael E. Latham (eds.), *Staging Growth: Modernization, Development, and the Global Cold War* (Amherst, MA: University of Massachusetts Press, 2003), and Michael E. Latham, *Modernization as Ideology: American Social Science and "Nation Building" in the Kennedy Era* (Chapel Hill, NC: University of North Carolina Press, 2000). Kennedy and Johnson policies are analyzed in Diane Kunz, (ed.), *The Diplomacy of the Crucial Decade: American Foreign Relations during the 1960s* (New York: Columbia University Press, 1994), Thomas G. Paterson (ed.), *Kennedy's Quest for Victory: American Foreign Policy, 1961–1963* (New York: Oxford University Press, 1989); and Warren I. Cohen and Nancy Bernkopf Tucker, *Lyndon Johnson Confronts the World: American Foreign Policy, 1963–1968* (Cambridge: Cambridge University Press, 1994). For US policy toward specific regions and countries, consult Henry F. Jackson, *From the Congo to Soweto: U.S. Foreign Policy toward Africa since 1960* (New York: William Morrow, 1982), Douglas Little, *American Orientalism: The United States and the Middle East since 1945* (Chapel Hill, NC: University of North Carolina Press, 2002), Fredrik Logevall, *Choosing War: The Lost Chance for Peace and the Escalation of the War in Vietnam* (Berkeley, CA: University of California Press, 1999), Robert McMahon, *The Limits of Empire: The United States and Southeast Asia since World War II* (New York: Columbia University Press, 1999), Dennis Merrill, *Bread and the Ballot: The United States and India's Economic Development, 1947–1963* (Chapel Hill, NC: University of North Carolina Press, 1990), Stephen G. Rabe, *The Most Dangerous Area in the World: John F. Kennedy Confronts Communist Revolution in Latin America* (Chapel Hill, NC: University of North Carolina Press, 1999), and Marilyn Young, *The Vietnam Wars, 1945–1990* (New York: Harper Perennial, 1991). On the United States and the problem of race, see Thomas Borstelmann, *The Cold War and the Color Line: American Race Relations in the Global Arena* (Cambridge, MA: Harvard University Press, 2001).

Soviet relations with the Third World are treated in Roy Allison, *The Soviet Union and the Strategy of Non-Alignment in the Third World* (Cambridge: Cambridge University Press, 1988), Mark N. Katz (ed.), *The USSR and Marxist Revolutions in the Third World* (Cambridge: Cambridge University Press, 1990), Edward Kolodziej and Roger E. Kanet (eds.), *The Limits of Soviet Power in the Developing World* (Baltimore, MD: Johns Hopkins University Press, 1989), Andrzej Korbonski and Francis Fukuyama (eds.), *The Soviet Union and the Third World: The Last Three Decades* (Ithaca, NY: Cornell University Press, 1987), Bruce D. Porter, *The USSR in Third World Conflicts: Soviet Arms and Diplomacy in Local Wars, 1945–1980*

(Cambridge: Cambridge University Press, 1984) and Alvin Z. Rubinstein, *Moscow's Third World Strategy* (Princeton, NJ: Princeton University Press, 1988). More recent works, focused on Khrushchev and Brezhnev, include Edwin Bacon and Mark Sandle (eds.), *Brezhnev Reconsidered* (Houndmills, UK: Palgrave, 2002), Aleksandr Fursenko and Timothy Naftali, *Khrushchev's Cold War: The Inside Story of an American Adversary* (New York: Norton, 2006), William Taubman, *Khrushchev: The Man and His Era* (New York: Norton, 2003), and Vladislav Zubok and Constantine Pleshakov, *Inside the Kremlin's Cold War: From Stalin to Khrushchev* (Cambridge, MA: Harvard University Press, 1996). On the USSR and Vietnam, see Ilya V. Gaiduk, *The Soviet Union and the Vietnam War* (Chicago: Ivan R. Dee, 1996). Nigel Jonathan Gould-Davies, "The Logic of Faith: Ideas, Interests, and the Soviet Experience in World Politics," Ph.D. dissertation, Harvard University (2002), analyzes Soviet ideology.

For the significance of the Third World in the wider contours of Chinese policy, Chen Jian, *Mao's China and the Cold War* (Chapel Hill, NC: University of North Carolina Press, 2001), John W. Garver, *Foreign Relations of the People's Republic of China* (Englewood Cliffs, NJ: Prentice Hall, 1993), Kuo-kang Shao, *Zhou Enlai and the Foundations of Chinese Foreign Policy* (New York: St. Martin's Press, 1996), and Thomas W. Robinson and David Shambaugh (eds.), *Chinese Foreign Policy: Theory and Practice* (Oxford: Oxford University Press, 1994), are very useful. On China and Vietnam, see Priscilla Roberts (ed.), *Behind the Bamboo Curtain: China, Vietnam, and the World beyond Asia* (Washington, DC, and Stanford, CA: Wilson Center Press and Stanford University Press, 2006), and Qiang Zhai, *China and the Vietnam Wars, 1950–1975* (Chapel Hill, NC: University of North Carolina Press, 2000). For Africa, consult Steven F. Jackson, "China's Third World Foreign Policy: The Case of Angola and Mozambique, 1961–93," *China Quarterly* (1995), 388–422, and Philip Snow, *The Star Raft: China's Encounter with Africa* (New York: Weidenfield and Nicolson, 1988).

Other valuable studies, based on specific countries and cases, include Matthew Connelly, *A Diplomatic Revolution: Algeria's Fight for Independence and the Origins of the Post-Cold War Era* (Oxford: Oxford University Press, 2002), Jorge I. Domínguez, *To Make the World Safe for Democracy: Cuba's Foreign Policy* (Cambridge, MA: Harvard University Press, 1989), Piero Gleijeses, *Conflicting Missions: Havana, Washington, and Africa, 1959–1976* (Chapel Hill, NC: University of North Carolina Press, 2002), and John Marcum, *The Angolan Revolution* (Cambridge, MA: MIT Press, 1978).

See also section 22 of the bibliography in volume I; sections 14, 15, 16, and 17 in this volume; and sections 2, 7, and 8 in volume III.

14. The Indochina wars and the Cold War, 1945–1975

Linguistic handicaps as well as the general unavailability of Vietnamese archival documentation give a regrettably skewed quality to any bibliographic essay published in the West. Although there are signs of change (on both counts), the process will be slow.

Still the most comprehensive treatment of the whole 1945–75 era is the vivid and journalistic account by Stanley Karnow, *Vietnam: A History* (New York: Viking Press, 1983), which in key respects holds up well. David W. P. Elliott, *The Vietnamese War: Revolution and Social Change in the Mekong Delta, 1930–1975*, 2 vols. (Armonk, NY: M. E. Sharpe, 2003), is a superb in-depth examination of the struggle in a single province in southern Vietnam. Other general histories include A. J. Langguth, *Our Vietnam: The War, 1954–1975* (New York: Simon & Schuster, 2000), Marilyn Young, *The Vietnam Wars, 1945–1990* (New York: Harper Collins, 1990), and George C. Herring, *America's Longest War: The United States and Vietnam, 1950–1975*, 4th ed. (New York: McGraw-Hill, 2001). Robert J. McMahon, *The Limits of Empire: The United States and Southeast Asia since World War II* (New York: Columbia University Press, 1999), helpfully examines American policy in a broader regional context. Also useful on the entire period is Spencer Tucker (ed.), *Encyclopedia of the Vietnam War: A Political, Social, and Military History*, 3 vols. (New York: Oxford University Press, 1999), and Gareth Porter (ed.), *Vietnam: The Definitive Documentation of Human Decisions*, 2 vols. (Ithaca, NY: Cornell University Press, 1993).

The French war in Indochina has received comparatively less attention (including among French historians) than the American one that followed. See Yves Gras, *Histoire de la guerre d'Indochine* (Paris: Plon, 1992), Alain Ruscio, *La Guerre française d'Indochine* (Paris: Complexe, 1992), Philippe Devillers, *L'Histoire du Viet-Nam de 1940 a 1952* (Paris: Le Seuil, 1952), Hugues Tertrais, *Le piastre et le fusil: Le coût de la guerre d'Indochine 1945–1954* (Paris: Comité pour l'histoire économique et financière de la France, 2002), and Mark A. Lawrence and Fredrik Logevall (eds.), *The First Vietnam War: Colonial Conflict and Cold War Crisis* (Cambridge, MA: Harvard University Press, 2007). On early US involvement, the best recent studies are Mark Philip Bradley, *Imagining Vietnam and America: The Making of Postcolonial Vietnam, 1919–1950* (Chapel Hill, NC: University of North Carolina Press, 2000), and Mark Atwood Lawrence, *Assuming the Burden: Europe and the American Commitment to War in Vietnam* (Berkeley, CA: University of California Press, 2005). For the climactic battle of Dien Bien Phu, two classic accounts are Bernard Fall, *Hell in a Very Small Place: The Siege of Dien Bien Phu* (New York: J. B. Lippincott, 1967), and Pierre Rocolle, *Pourquoi Dien Bien Phu?* (Paris: L'Histoire Flammarion, 1968). For the wider regional context of the Indochinese developments in these years, see Christopher Goscha, *Thailand and the Vietnamese Networks of the Vietnamese Revolution, 1885–1954* (London: Routledge, 1999).

The "interregnum" after 1954 is covered well in several books, but see especially David L. Anderson, *Trapped By Success; The Eisenhower Administration and Vietnam* (New York: Columbia University Press, 1991), Kathryn Statler, *Replacing France: The Origins of American Intervention in Vietnam* (Lexington, KY: University Press of Kentucky, 2007), George McT. Kahin, *Intervention: How America Became Involved in Vietnam* (New York: Knopf, 1986), and Seth Jacobs, *America's Miracle Man in Vietnam: Ngo Dinh Diem, Religion, Race, and U.S. Intervention in Southeast Asia, 1950–1957* (Durham, NC: Duke University Press, 2004).

American involvement in Indochina expanded steadily after 1961 and so, as a result, has the literature on this later period. A hugely influential early account was David Halberstam's mesmerizing, sprawling *The Best and the Brightest* (New York: Random House, 1972). On decisionmaking in the Kennedy and Johnson administrations, see also Fredrik Logevall, *Choosing War: The Lost Chance for Peace and the Escalation of War in Vietnam* (Berkeley, CA: University of California Press, 1999), and David Kaiser, *American Tragedy: Kennedy, Johnson, and Vietnam* (Cambridge, MA: Harvard University Press, 2000). The Gulf of Tonkin crisis is expertly studied in Edwin Moise, *Tonkin Gulf and the Escalation of the Vietnam War* (Chapel Hill, NC: University of North Carolina Press, 1996). An important year is examined in Ronald Spector, *After Tet: The Bloodiest Year in Vietnam* (New York: Free Press, 1992). For a Vietcong perspective centered in large part on these years, see Truong Nhu Tang, *A Vietcong Memoir* (San Diego, CA: Harcourt, 1985). And for a relentlessly combative revisionist examination of the period 1954–65, see Mark Moyar, *Triumph Forsaken? The Vietnam War, 1954–1965* (New York: Cambridge University Press, 2006).

Important studies of latter phase of the conflict, culminating with the fall of Saigon in 1975, include Jeffrey Kimball, *Nixon's Vietnam War* (Lawrence, KS: University Press of Kansas, 1998), Larry Berman, *No Peace, No Honor: Nixon, Kissinger, and Betrayal in Vietnam* (New York: Free Press, 2001), and Robert K. Brigham, *Guerrilla Diplomacy: The NLF's Foreign Relations and the Viet Nam War* (Ithaca, NY: Cornell University Press, 1999). The Paris Accords are handled well in Pierre Asselin, *A Bitter Peace: Washington, Hanoi, and the Making of the Paris Agreement* (Chapel Hill, NC: University of North Carolina Press, 2002). On Cambodia and the rise of Pol Pot, see Ben Kiernan, *How Pol Pot Came to Power: Colonialism, Nationalism, and Communism in Cambodia, 1930–1975*, 2nd ed. (New Haven, CT: Yale University Press, 2004). And on the bitter divisions the war generated in the United States, a useful study is Melvin Small, *Antiwarriors: The Vietnam War and the Battle for America's Hearts and Minds* (Washington, DC: Scholarly Resources, 2002).

Not to be missed, finally, are the important biographies and memoirs that have appeared in recent decades. See, for example, in addition to those listed above, William J. Duiker, *Ho Chi Minh: A Life* (New York: Hyperion, 2000), Pierre Brocheux, *Ho Chi Minh: A Biography* (New York: Cambridge University Press, 2007), Daniel Hémery, *Ho Chi Minh, de l'Indochine au Vietnam* (Paris: Découvertes-Gallimard, 1990), Duong Van Mai Elliott, *The Sacred Willow: Four Generations in the Life of a Vietnamese Family* (New York: Oxford University Press, 1999), Neil Sheehan, *A Bright Shining Lie: John Paul Vann and America in Vietnam* (New York: Random House, 1988), Bui Diem, with David Chanoff, *In the Jaws of History* (Boston: Houghton Mifflin, 1987), and Daniel Ellsberg, *Secrets: A Memoir of Vietnam and the Pentagon Papers* (New York: Viking, 2002). Christian G. Appy ably gathers together various oral history perspectives in *Patriots: The Vietnam War Remembered from All Sides* (New York: Viking Press, 2003).

15. The Cold War in the Middle East: Suez Crisis to Camp David Accords

The best concise account of the geopolitical setting for Soviet–American rivalry in the region remains Peter Mansfield and Nicolas Pelham, *A History of the Middle East* (New York: Penguin, 2004). For an engaging examination of the broad social, cultural, and religious forces at work, see R. Stephen Humphreys, *Between Memory and Desire: The Middle East in a Troubled Age* (Berkeley, CA: University of California Press, 1999). Daniel Yergin, *The Prize: The Epic Quest for Oil, Money, and Power* (New York: Simon & Schuster, 1991), details the rise of the petroleum industry and how it shaped Middle Eastern politics. William Roger Louis, *The British Empire in the Middle East 1945–1951: Arab Nationalism, the United States, and Postwar Imperialism* (New York: Oxford University Press, 1984), is the definitive account of Britain's decline as a regional power, the creation of Israel, and the rise of nationalist movements in the Muslim world during the first years of the Cold War. Douglas Little, *American Orientalism: The United States and the Middle East since 1945* (Chapel Hill, NC: University of North Carolina Press), examines broad US interests and policies, while Galia Golan, *Soviet Policies in the Middle East from World War II to Gorbachev* (New York: Cambridge University Press, 1990), does the same for the USSR. For an overview of the Arab-Israeli conflict, see Avi Shlaim, *The Iron Wall: Israel and the Arab World* (New York: Norton, 2001).

At the center of the Soviet–American rivalry in the Middle East during the first decade of the Cold War stood Gamal Abdel Nasser, whose motives are examined in Said K. Aburish, *Nasser: The Last Arab* (New York: St. Martin's Press, 2004), and Laura M. James, *Nasser at War: Arab Images of the Enemy* (London: Palgrave, 2006). Guy Laron, 'Cutting the Gordian Knot: The Post-WWII Egyptian Quest for Arms and the 1955 Czechoslovak Arms Deal,' Cold War International History Project, (CWIHP) Working Paper No. 55 (Washington, DC: Woodrow Wilson Center, 2007) uses Soviet sources to reconstruct decisionmaking in Cairo and Moscow. Abdel Magid Farid, *Nasser: The Final Years* (Reading: Ithaca Press, 1994), provides key Egyptian documents from the 1960s, while Adeed Dawisha, *Arab Nationalism in the Twentieth Century: From Triumph to Despair* (Princeton, NJ: Princeton University Press, 2003), places Nasserism in the broader context of decolonization and national liberation.

To understand the causes and consequences of the Suez crisis, start with Keith Kyle, *Suez* (New York: St. Martin's Press, 1991), a superb narrative emphasizing the importance of personalities. Other aspects of the 1956 showdown are explored in Diane Kunz, *The Economic Diplomacy of the Suez Crisis* (Chapel Hill, NC: University of North Carolina Press, 1991), and Peter Hahn, *The United States, Great Britain, and Egypt, 1945–1956: Strategy and Diplomacy in the Early Cold War* (Chapel Hill, NC: University of North Carolina Press, 1991). On the rise and fall of the Eisenhower Doctrine, see Salim Yaqub, *Containing Arab Nationalism: The Eisenhower Doctrine and the Middle East* (Chapel Hill, NC: University of North Carolina Press, 2004). On the civil war in Lebanon and the upheaval in Iraq, see Malcolm H. Kerr, *The Arab Cold War: Gamal 'Abd al-Nasir and His Rivals 1958–1970* (New York: Oxford University Press, 1971), and William Roger Louis and Roger Owen (eds.), *A Revolutionary Year: The Middle East in 1958* (London: I. B. Tauris, 2002).

For the early 1960s, see Warren Bass, *Support Any Friend: Kennedy's Middle East and the Making of the U.S.-Israeli Alliance* (New York: Oxford University Press, 2003). The definitive account of the June 1967 War is Michael B. Oren, *Six Days of War: June 1967 and the Making of the Modern Middle East* (New York: Oxford University Press, 2002), which draws on a rich array of Israeli and Egyptian sources. In his new book entitled simply *1967* (New York: Metropolitan Books, 2007), Tom Segev makes extensive use of new materials from the Israeli archives to argue that the Six Day War resulted from a crisis of confidence among Israel's leaders, who overreacted to Nasser's bluster. For more on the 1967 war, see Richard B. Parker (ed.), *The Six Day War: A Retrospective* (Tallahassee, FL: University of Florida Press, 1996), which includes the recollections of Soviet and American officials, and Donald Neff, *Warriors for Jerusalem: The Six Days that Changed the Middle East* (New York: Simon & Schuster, 1984). On the late 1960s, see David Korn, *Stalemate: The War of Attrition and Great Power Diplomacy in the Middle East, 1967–1970* (Boulder, CO: Westview Press, 1992), Richard B. Parker, *The Politics of Miscalculation in the Middle East* (Bloomington, IN: Indiana University Press, 1993), and Isabella Ginor, "'Under the Yellow Arab Helmet Gleamed Blue Russian Eyes': Operation *Kavkaz* and the War of Attrition, 1969–70," *Cold War History*, 3, 1 (October 2002), 127–56.

On the 1970s, begin with the first two volumes of Henry Kissinger's memoirs, *The White House Years* (Boston, MA: Little, Brown, 1979) and *Years of Upheaval* (Boston, MA: Little, Brown, 1982), which are especially good on the 1970 Black September Crisis and the October 1973 War. See also William B. Quandt, *Peace Process: American Diplomacy and the Arab–Israeli Conflict since 1967* (Berkeley, CA: University of California Press, 1993) and Donald Neff, *Warriors against Israel: How Israel Won the Battle to Become America's Ally* (Brattleboro, VT: Amana Books, 1988). On Soviet policy during the 1970s, see Victor Israelyan, *Inside the Kremlin during the Yom Kippur War* (University Park, PA: Pennsylvania State University Press, 1995), and Richard Ned Lebow and Janice Gross Stein, *We All Lost the Cold War* (Princeton, NJ: Princeton University Press, 1994). The regional perspective is covered in an excellent biography of a key player, Nigel Ashton, *King Hussein of Jordan: A Political Life* (New Haven, CT: Yale University Press, 2008). See also Rashid Khalidi, *The Iron Cage: The Story of the Palestinian Struggle for Statehood* (Boston, MA: Beacon Press, 2006).

On the demise of Arab nationalism and rise of radical Islam, start with Fouad Ajami's classic account *The Arab Predicament: Arab Political Thought and Practice since 1967* (New York: Cambridge University Press, 1981). Charles Kurzman, *The Unthinkable Revolution in Iran* (Cambridge, MA: Harvard University Press, 2004), captures the crisis and the chaos surrounding Khomeini's triumph over the Shah in 1978–79. For an inside account of Carter's response to the Iranian revolution, see Gary Sick, *All Fall Down: America's Tragic Encounter with Iran* (New York: Random House, 1985). Zachary Lockman, *Contending Visions of the Middle East: The History and Politics of Orientalism* (New York: Cambridge University Press, 2004), provides a broad overview of the symbiotic relationship that developed between academic experts and national security managers as they struggled to come to terms with radical change in the Muslim world during the Cold War.

16. Cuba and the Cold War, 1959–1980

Historians of Cuban foreign policy after 1959 are crippled by the fact that the Cuban archives are closed. The Cubans have declassified documents only on the missile crisis (see section 4 of this bibliography). Unless otherwise noted, none of the studies listed below uses Cuban documents.

The best biography of Fidel Castro, by far, is Tad Szulc's *Fidel: A Critical Portrait* (New York: Avon Books, 1987). Two more recent works should be noted: Leycester Coltman's *The Real Fidel Castro* (New Haven, CT: Yale University Press, 2003) combines insights with factual errors; Ignacio Ramonet's *Cien Horas con Fidel*, 3rd rev. ed. (Havana: Oficina de Publicaciones del Consejo de Estado, 2006) is a very lengthy interview with Castro. Jon Lee Anderson's *Che Guevara: A Revolutionary Life* (New York: Grove Press, 1997) uses a few Cuban documents but is of very uneven quality.

Three accounts of foreign policy written by Cuban protagonists are particularly valuable: Ernesto Che Guevara's *Pasajes de la guerra revolucionaria: Congo*, ed. Aleyda March (Barcelona: Grijalbo, 1999) is Guevara's history, written for Castro, of the Cuban column he led in eastern Zaire in 1965; Jorge Risquet, *El segundo frente del Che en el Congo. Historia del batallón Patricio Lumumba*, 2nd rev. ed. (Havana: Abril, 2006), is a very well-documented and compelling account of the activities of the Cuban column that Risquet led in the former

French Congo in 1965–66; José Gómez Abad, *Como el Che burló a la CIA* (Sevilla: R. D. Editores, 2006), which is written by a member of the Cuban intelligence services, is the only study of Cuban support for armed struggle in Latin America that is based on a large number of Cuban intelligence documents.

The best history of Castro's Cuba is Richard Gott, *Cuba: A New History* (New Haven, CT: Yale University Press, 2004). Aleksandr Fursenko and Timothy Naftali, *"One Hell of a Gamble": Khrushchev, Castro and Kennedy, 1958–1964* (New York: Norton, 1997), is the only study of Cuban–Soviet relations that relies on an important number of Soviet documents, but unfortunately it is marred by serious factual mistakes about the Cuban revolutionary process. For later years, see Jacques Lévesque, *L'URSS et la révolution cubaine* (Montreal: Presses de la Fondation Nationale des Sciences Politiques, 1976).

The best studies on US–Cuban relations are Wayne Smith, *The Closest of Enemies: A Personal and Diplomatic Account of US–Cuban Relations since 1957* (New York: Norton, 1987), which focuses on the Carter years, and Lars Schoultz, *That Infernal Little Cuban Republic: The United States and the Cuban Revolution* (Chapel Hill, NC: University of North Carolina Press, 2009). Also useful are Morris H. Morley, *Imperial State and Revolution: The United States and Cuba, 1952–1986* (Cambridge: Cambridge University Press, 1987), and Don Bohning, *The Castro Obsession: U.S. Covert Operations against Cuba 1959–1965* (Washington DC: Potomac, 2005). Henry Ryan, *The Fall of Che Guevara: A Story of Soldiers, Spies, and Diplomats* (New York: Oxford University Press, 1998), is the best study of the US response to the guerrilla insurgency in Bolivia led by Che Guevara. The only valuable study on Cuban–West European relations is Alistair Hennessy and George Lambie (eds.), *The Fractured Blockade: West European–Cuban Relations during the Revolution* (London: Macmillan, 1993).

Boris Goldenberg's, *Kommunismus in Lateinamerika* (Stuttgart: Kohlhammer, 1971), is a superb analysis of the impact of the Cuban revolution on the Communist movement in Latin America in the 1960s. Richard Gott's *Rural Guerrillas in Latin America* (Harmondsworth: Penguin, 1973), is the best book on armed struggle in Latin America in the 1960s. Régis Debray's *La critique des armes*, 2 vols. (Paris: Seuil, 1974), covers armed struggle in Latin America in the 1960s and early 1970s and is based on the author's privileged access to several guerrilla leaders and to Cuban officials. Also valuable is Daniel James (ed.), *The Complete Bolivian Diaries of Ché Guevara and Other Captured Documents* (New York: Stein and Day, 1968). Che Guevara's Bolivian diary, however, is far less informative than his account of the operation in Zaire; of the other captured diaries included in the volume, the most interesting is by Pombo.

Since 1994, I have been able to conduct research in the closed Cuban archives and photocopy thousands of pages of documents, mainly on Africa, but also, increasingly, on Cuba's relations with the Soviet Union. See especially "The View from Havana," in Gilbert Joseph and Daniela Spenser (eds.), *In From the Cold: Latin America's New Encounter with the Cold War* (Durham, NC: Duke University Press, 2008), 112–33, "Cuba and the Independence of Namibia," *Cold War History* (May 2007), 285–303, "Moscow's Proxy? Cuba and Africa 1975–88," *Journal of Cold War Studies* (Fall 2006), 98–146, *Conflicting Missions: Havana, Washington, and Africa, 1959–1976* (Chapel Hill, NC: University of North Carolina Press, 2002), "Truth or Credibility: Castro, Carter, and the Invasions of Shaba," *International History Review* (Feb. 1996), 70–103.

Three additional works, though not focusing on Cuba, shed light on Cuba's foreign policy: F. J. du Toit Spies' *Operasie Savannah. Angola 1975–1976* (Pretoria: S. A. Weermag, 1989), Sophia du Preez's *Avontuur in Angola. Die verhaal van Suid-Afrika se soldate in Angola 1975–1976* (Pretoria: J. L. van Schaik, 1989), Nancy Mitchell, "Race and Realpolitik: Jimmy Carter and Africa" (forthcoming). Spies and du Preez offer the only two studies of the South African operation in Angola in 1975–76 that are based on South African documents. Mitchell combines an unprecedented array of sources and a sophisticated analysis to offer what is by far the best study on Carter's policy in Africa. She also has significant access to Cuban documents. (See also Mitchell's "Tropes of the Cold War: Jimmy Carter and Rhodesia," *Cold War History*, May 2007, 263–83.)

17. The Sino-Soviet split

The Sino-Soviet split deservedly attracted the attention of political scientists and historians in the West as it developed, in the 1960s, from a war of words to a real border confrontation. Pioneer accounts include Donald Zagoria, *The Sino-Soviet Conflict, 1956–61* (Princeton, NJ: Princeton University Press, 1962), William E. Griffith, *The Sino-Soviet Rift, 1964–65* (Cambridge, MA, and London: MIT Press, 1964), Klaus Mehnert, *Peking and Moscow* (New York: G. P. Putnam's Sons, 1963), and John Gittings, *Survey of the Sino-Soviet Dispute: A Commentary and Extracts from the Recent Polemics, 1963–67* (London: Oxford University Press, 1968). These books work best with a side-reader, a Chinese propaganda pamphlet, *The Polemic on the General Line of the International Communist Movement* (Beijing: Foreign Languages Press, 1965).

The military clashes between China and the Soviet Union in 1969 deepened interest in Sino-Soviet relations in the West, and the historiography thickened by leaps and bounds, with books like Alfred D. Low, *The Sino-Soviet Dispute: An Analysis of the Polemics* (London: Associated University Presses, 1976), and O. Edmund Clubb, *China and Russia: The Great Game* (New York and London: Columbia University Press, 1971). Herbert J. Ellison (ed.), *The Sino-Soviet Conflict: A Global Perspective* (Seattle, WA, and London: University of Washington Press, 1982), offers an interesting analysis of the global impact of the split. Besides, this volume contains perhaps the best bibliographic essay of works on the Sino-Soviet split written up to 1982. To get a sense of the Chinese and the Soviet historiography of the split, it is enough to read, for example, Hsiao Fan *et al. Ugly Features of Soviet Social-Imperialism* (Beijing: Foreign Languages Press, 1976), and Oleg Borisov and Boris Koloskov, *Sino-Soviet Relations, 1945–1973: A Brief History* (Moscow: Progress Publishers, 1975).

Partial opening of the archives in the former Communist bloc in the early 1990s prompted scholarly reassessments of the Sino-Soviet split, and the emergence of new, nuanced interpretations, as in Odd Arne Westad (ed.), *Brothers in Arms: The Rise and Fall of the Sino-Soviet Alliance, 1945–1963* (Washington, DC: Woodrow Wilson Center Press, 1998), which overall rejects the rigidity of realist scholarship and emphasizes the role of domestic politics, personalities, and perceptions in the making of the confrontation. Domestic politics is also of primary concern in Lorenz Luthi's excellent *The Sino-Soviet Split: Cold War in the Communist World* (Princeton, NJ: Princeton University, 2008), but decidedly less so in Sergey Radchenko, *Two Suns in the Heavens: The Sino-Soviet Struggle for Supremacy,*

1962–1967 (Washington, DC: Woodrow Wilson Center Press, 2009), which blames the Sino-Soviet split on the inequality of the alliance.

In addition, a number of important articles appeared in English on the subject: Yang Kuisong, "The Sino-Soviet Border Clash of 1969: From Zhenbao Island to Sino-American Rapprochement," *Cold War History*, 1, 1 (August 2000), 21–52; Wang Dong, *The Quarrelling Brothers: New Chinese Archives and Reappraisal of the Sino-Soviet Split*, Cold War International History Project (CWIHP) Working Paper No. 49 (Washington, DC: Woodrow Wilson Center, 2006), and Mikhail Prozumenshchikov, "The Sino-Indian Conflict, the Cuban Missile Crisis, and the Sino-Soviet Split, October 1962: New Evidence from the Russian Archives," *Cold War International History Project Bulletin* (hereafter, *CWIHP Bulletin*) Nos. 8–9 (Winter 1996–97). The *CWIHP Bulletin* has other articles pertinent to the subject; see http://cwihp.si.edu. Many Chinese articles on Sino-Soviet relations by, among others, Li Danhui, Niu Jun, Shen Zhihua, and Yang Kuisong, can be viewed (in Chinese) at the website of the International Cold War History Research Center at East China Normal University, www.coldwarchina.com.

Beyond comparatively thin new Cold War scholarship on the Sino-Soviet split, there is growing literature on adjacent subjects. Thus, an important recent book on the Chinese foreign policy – Chen Jian, *Mao's China and the Cold War* (Chapel Hill, NC: University of North Carolina Press, 2001) – takes up the Sino-Soviet split as a function of Mao's domestic agenda, in particular, his preoccupation with the future of the Chinese revolution. Parallel arguments stand out in Roderick MacFarquhar, *The Origins of the Cultural Revolution*, vol. III, *The Coming of the Cataclysm 1961–1966* (New York: Columbia University Press, 1997), a book concerned with a major domestic Chinese upheaval, which had a direct relevance for Sino-Soviet relations. Very much out of tune with these studies, but based on impressive research, is a controversial biography of Mao, Jung Chang and Jon Halliday, *Mao: The Unknown Story* (New York: Anchor Books, 2006), which depicts the Sino-Soviet split as essentially a product of a power struggle between Beijing and Moscow.

Other important sources are volume XV of Roderick MacFarquhar and John K. Fairbank (eds.), *The Cambridge History of China* (Cambridge: Cambridge University Press, 1991), in particular the chapter by Thomas Robinson; and John Lewis and Xue Litai, *Imagined Enemies: China Prepares for Uncertain War* (Stanford, CA: Stanford University Press, 2006). Another useful book on China's foreign policy in the 1960s is Barbara Barnouin and Yu Changgen, *Chinese Foreign Policy during the Cultural Revolution* (London and New York: Kegan Paul International; distributed by Columbia University Press, 1998).

There is also a growing number of memoirs by Chinese participants in the policy-making process, of which the most noteworthy for our purpose is Wu Lengxi, *Shinian lunzhan, 1956–1966: Zhong Su guanxi huiyilu* [Ten Year War of Words: A Memoir of Sino-Soviet Relations], 2 vols. (Beijing: Zhongyang wenxian, 1999). Volumes II and III of Zhonggong zhongyang wenxian yanjiushi, *Zhou Enlai nianpu, 1949–1976* [Zhou Enlai Chronology; 1949–1976] (Beijing: Zhongyang wenxian, 1997), are both indispensable for thorough research on any aspect of Chinese foreign policy in the 1960s, including its Soviet angle. By the same token, former Soviet diplomats published a number of interesting accounts or memoirs of Sino-Soviet relations in the 1960s, including Aleksei A. Brezhnev, *Kitai: Tersnistyi put k dobrososedstvu: vospominaniia i razmyshleniia*

[China: The Thorny Path to Good Neighborliness; Reminiscences and Reflections] (Moscow: Mezhdunarodnye otnosheniia, 1998), Boris N. Vereshchagin, *V starom i novom Kitae: iz vospominanii diplomata* [In Old and New China: From the Reminiscences of a Diplomat] (Moscow: In-t Dalnego Vostoka, 1999), G. V. Kireev, *Rossiia–Kitai: neizvestnye stranitsy pogranichnykh peregovorov* [Russia–China: Unknown Pages from the Border Talks] (Moscow: Rosspen, 2006), and Vladimir Fedotov, *Polveka vmeste s Kitaem: vospominania, zapisi, razmyshleniia* [A Half-Century with China: Reminiscences, Notes, Reflections] (Moscow: Rosspen, 2005).

18. Détente in the Nixon–Ford years, 1969–1976

A rich body of documentary evidence on the Nixon administration's foreign policy has been made available. An excellent survey of that record is contained in Edward C. Keefer, "Key Sources for Nixon's Foreign Policy," *Passport: The Newsletter of the Society for Historians of American Foreign Relations*, 38, 2 (August 2007), 27–30. For textual materials in the National Archives in College Park, Maryland, consult the finding aids available at www.nixon.archives.gov/find/textual/presidential/nsc/kissinger/descriptions.html. Lists of tape recordings of President Richard Nixon's conversations are available at www.nixon. archives.gov/find/tapes.html. The National Security Archive has made copies available of thousands of pages of documents on the foreign policy of the Nixon administration in *The Kissinger Transcripts: A Verbatim Record of U.S. Diplomacy, 1969–1977* (Washington, DC National Security Archive, 2006.). This collection is available electronically from the Digital National Security Archive (DNSA) (http://nsarchive.chadwyck.com.html). Major documents on détente from Soviet and United States archives are published in US Department of State, *Soviet–American Relations: The Détente Years, 1969–1972* (Washington, DC: US Government Printing Office, 2007). For a list of volumes relevant to détente in the series *Foreign Relations of the United States*, compiled by the Department of State, consult www.state.gov/r/pa/ho/.

For a general account of the policies and personalities of the Nixon administration, consult Melvin Small, *The Presidency of Richard Nixon* (Lawrence, KS: University Press of Kansas, 1999). A comprehensive and critical discussion of Nixon's foreign policy is William P. Bundy, *A Tangled Web: The Making of Nixon's Foreign Policy, 1968–1974* (New York: Hill and Wang, 1998).

The global background of détente is treated in Jeremi Suri, *Power and Protest: Global Revolution and the Rise of Détente* (Cambridge, MA: Harvard University Press, 2003). The most detailed discussion of détente is found in Raymond L. Garthoff, *Détente and Confrontation: American–Soviet Relations from Nixon to Reagan*, rev. ed. (Washington, DC: Brookings Institution, 1992). Other useful studies of détente and Soviet–American relations are William P. Hyland, *Mortal Rivals: Superpower Relations from Nixon to Reagan* (New York: Random House, 1987), John J. Moresca, *To Helsinki: The Conference on Security and Cooperation in Europe* (Durham, NO: Duke University Press, 1985), Keith L Nelson, *The Making of Détente: Soviet–American Relations in the Shadow of Vietnam* (Baltimore, MD: Johns Hopkins University Press, 1995), Richard W. Stevenson, *The Rise and Fall of Détente: Relaxations of Tension in U.S.–Soviet Relations, 1953–1984* (Urbana, IL: University of Illinois Press, 1986).

Arms-control negotiations with the Soviet Union are covered in Gerard Smith's highly critical *Doubletalk: The Story of the First Strategic Arms Limitation Talks* (New York: Doubleday, 1980), Terry Terriff's analytical and supportive *The Nixon Administration and the Making of U.S. Nuclear Strategy* (Ithaca, NY: Cornell University Press, 1995), George Bunn, *Arms Control by Committee: Managing Negotiations with the Russians* (Stanford, CA: Stanford University Press, 1992), which criticizes the bureaucratic infighting in the Nixon administration; and John Newhouse, *Cold Dawn: The Story of SALT* (New York: Holt, Rinehart, and Winston, 1973), which is based on interviews with the negotiators.

Economic aspects of détente are covered in Marshall Goldman, *Détente and Dollars: Doing Business with the Soviets* (New York: Basic Book, 1975), and Dan Morgan, *The Great Grain Robbery* (New York: Penguin, 1980).

Biographical studies of Richard Nixon and Henry Kissinger are rich sources of insight into their ideas and conduct of foreign relations. The relationship between the two men is covered extensively in Robert Dallek, *Nixon and Kissinger: Partners in Power* (New York: HarperCollins, 2007). For Nixon, see Stephen E. Ambrose, *Nixon*, Vol. II, *The Triumph of a Politician, 1962–1972*, and *Nixon*, vol. III, *Ruin and Recovery, 1973–1990* (New York: Simon & Schuster, 1989, 1991), Joan Hoff, *Nixon Reconsidered* (New York: Basis Books, 1994), is highly critical of Nixon's and Kissinger's methods. Jonathan Aitken, *Nixon: A Life* (New York: Regnery, 1993), is highly favorable. For Kissinger, consult Jussi Hanhimäki, *The Flawed Architect: Henry Kissinger and American Foreign Policy* (New York: Oxford University Press, 2004), which is based on an abundance of declassified documents; Walter Isaacson, *Kissinger: A Biography* (New York: Simon & Schuster, 1992), based on some documents and numerous interviews; and Jeremi Suri, *Henry Kissinger and the American Century* (Cambridge, MA: Harvard University Press, 2007), based on extensive interviews with Kissinger and recently declassified documents.

The memoirs of the officials of the Nixon administration are essential sources. The most important are Richard Nixon, *RN: The Memoirs of Richard Nixon* (New York: Grossett and Dunlap, 1978) and Henry Kissinger, *White House Years* (Boston, MA: Little, Brown, 1979), *Years of Upheaval* (Boston, MA: Little, Brown, 1982), and *Years of Renewal* (Boston, MA: Little, Brown, 1999). Other useful memoirs are John Ehrlichman, *Witness to Power: The Nixon Years* (New York: Simon & Schuster, 1982), H. R. Haldeman with Joseph DiMona, *The Ends of Power* (New York: Times Books, 1978), H. R. Haldeman, *The Haldeman Diaries: Inside the Nixon White House* (New York: Putman, 1994), H. R. Haldman, *The Complete Multimedia Edition of the Haldeman Diaries* [CD-ROM] (Santa Monica, CA: Sony Electronic Publishing Company, 1994), Raymond Price, *With Nixon* (New York: Viking Press, 1977), William Safire, *Before the Fall: An Inside View of the pre-Watergate White House* (New York: Doubleday, 1975), Gerard C. Smith, *Disarming Diplomacy: The Memoirs of Gerard C. Smith, Arms Control Negotiator* (Lanham, MD: Madison Books, 1996).

Important memoirs from the Soviet side include Anatoly Dobrynin, *In Confidence: Moscow's Ambassador to America's Six Cold War Presidents (1962–1986)* (New York: Times Books and Random House, 1995), Andrei Gromyko, *Memoirs* (New York: Doubleday, 1989), and Georgii Arbatov, *The System: An Insider's Life in Soviet Politics* (New York: Random House, 1992).

19. Nuclear proliferation and non-proliferation during the Cold War

The scholarly work on nuclear proliferation and non-proliferation can be divided into three broad (and occasionally overlapping) categories. The first category and arguably the most influential work has been done by international relations scholars, typically from the political science and strategic studies fields. By far the most important book here is the debate between Scott Sagan and Kenneth Waltz in *The Spread of Nuclear Weapons: A Debate Renewed* (2nd ed.; New York: W. W. Norton, 2002). Sagan's article, "Why Do States Build Nuclear Weapons?: Three Models in Search of a Bomb" *International Security*, 21, 3 (Winter 1996/97), 54–86, is also very important. Also useful are T. V. Paul's *Power versus Prudence: Why Nations Forgo Nuclear Weapons* (Montreal: McGill-Queen's University, 2000), and Nathan E. Busch, *No End in Sight: The Continuing Menace of Nuclear Proliferation* (Lexington, KY: University of Kentucky, 2004). There are many articles and collected essays written by strategists on these questions, but several edited volumes are particularly good: Zachary S. Davis and Benjamin Frankel (eds.), *The Proliferation Puzzle: Why Nuclear Weapons Spread (and What Results)* (London: Frank Cass, 1993), T. V. Paul, Richard J. Harknett, and James J. Wirtz (eds.), *The Absolute Weapon Revisited: Nuclear Arms and the Emerging International Order* (Ann Arbor, MI: University of Michigan Press, 1998), Victor Utgoff, *The Coming Crisis: Nuclear Proliferation, U.S. Interests, and World Order* (Cambridge, MA: MIT Press, 2000), and Peter R. Lavoy, Scott D. Sagan, and James Wirtz, *Planning the Unthinkable: How New Powers Will Use Nuclear, Biological, and Chemical Weapons* (Ithaca, NY: Cornell, 2000). The argument that nuclear non-proliferation has become an important global norm is laid out in Nina Tannenbaum's "Stigmatizing the Bomb: Origins of the Nuclear Taboo," *International Security*, 29, 4 (Spring 2005), 5–49.

The second category includes work written by policy participants, arms-control professionals and non-proliferation advocates (often associated with policy organizations and think tanks). The best works by participants include Raymond Garthoff, *A Journey through the Cold War: A Memoir of Containment and Coexistence* (Washington, DC: Brookings Institution, 2001), Glenn T. Seaborg, *Stemming the Tide: Arms Control in the Johnson Years* (Lexington, MA: DC Heath and Company, 1987), and George Bunn, *Arms Control by Committee: Managing Negotiations with the Russians*, (Stanford, CA: Stanford University Press, 1992). For the most interesting and comprehensive report in the arms-control policy, see George Perkovich, Joseph Cirincione, Rose Gottemoeller, Jon Wolfsthal, and Jessica Tuchman Mathews, *Universal Compliance: A Strategy for Nuclear Security* (Washington, DC: Carnegie Endowment, 2004).

The third category is historical work. There is no comprehensive, global history of nuclear proliferation and non-proliferation, although Shane Maddock has written an excellent dissertation from the US perspective, "The Nth Country Conundrum: The American and Soviet Quest for Nuclear Nonproliferation, 1945–1970," Ph.D. dissertation, University of Connecticut (1997). There are terrific histories of both India's and Israel's nuclear programs: George Perkovich, *India's Nuclear Bomb: The Impact on Global Proliferation* (Berkeley, CA: University of California Press, 1999), and Avner Cohen, *Israel and the Bomb* (New York: Columbia University Press, 1998). The Soviet nuclear weapons program is chronicled in David Holloway's *Stalin and the Bomb* (New Haven, CT: Yale University

Press, 1994), while China's program is explained in John Lewis and Litai Xue's *China Builds the Bomb* (Stanford, CA: Stanford University Press, 1988). The US reaction to China's nuclear detonation is best captured in William Burr and Jeffrey T. Richelson's account, "Whether to 'Strangle the Baby in the Cradle': The United States and the Chinese Nuclear Program, 1960–64," *International Security*, 25, 3 (Winter 2000/01), 54–99. For historical treatment's of President Johnson's nuclear non-proliferation policies, see Thomas Schwartz, *Lyndon Johnson and Europe: In the Shadow of Vietnam* (Cambridge, MA: Harvard University Press, 2003), and Francis J. Gavin, "Blasts from the Past: Nuclear Proliferation and Rogue States before the Bush Doctrine," *International Security* (Winter 2005), 100–35. The change in Soviet nuclear non-proliferation policy is covered in Douglas Selvage, *The Warsaw Pact and Nuclear Nonproliferation, 1963–1965*, Cold War International History Project Working Paper No. 32 (Washington, DC: Woodrow Wilson Center, 2001), 6, www.isn.ethz.ch/php/research/RelationsWithAllies/Wp32_Selvage.pdf; William C. Potter "Nuclear Proliferation: U.S.–Soviet Cooperation" *Washington Quarterly*, 8, 1 (Winter 1985), 141–54; and Joseph Nye's "U.S.–Soviet Cooperation in a Nonproliferation Regime," in Alexander L. George, Philip J. Farley, and Alexander Dallin (eds.) *U.S.–Soviet Security Cooperation: Achievements, Failures, Lessons* (New York: Oxford University Press, 1988).

The best works on the influence of nuclear weapons on international politics during the Cold War include Robert Jervis, *The Meaning of the Nuclear Revolution: Statecraft and the Prospect of Armageddon* (Ithaca, NY: Cornell University, 1989), John Lewis Gaddis, Philip H. Gordon, Ernest R. May, and Jonathan Rosenberg (eds.), *Cold War Statesmen Confront the Bomb* (New York: Oxford, 1999), and Marc Trachtenberg's two volumes *History and Strategy* (Princeton, NJ: Princeton University, 1991) and *A Constructed Peace: The Making of the European Settlement, 1945–1963* (Princeton, NJ: Princeton University, 1999). For works that connect nuclear strategy to the question of proliferation and non-proliferation, see Lawrence Freedman's *The Evolution of Nuclear Strategy*, 2nd ed. (New York: St. Martin's Press, 1997), and Francis J. Gavin, "The Myth of Flexible Response: American Strategy in Europe during the 1960s," *International History Review* (December 2001), 847–75. Lawrence Wittner's *Resisting the Bomb: A History of the World Nuclear Disarmament Movement, 1954–1970* (Stanford, CA: Stanford University, 1997) is essential for understanding the global rise of a grassroots movement against nuclear weapons.

20. Intelligence in the Cold War

In terms of a general approach, Sherman Kent, "The Need for an Intelligence Literature;" in Donald P. Steury (ed.), *Sherman Kent and the Board of National Estimates: Collected Essays* (Washington, DC: History Staff, Center for the Study of Intelligence, Central Intelligence Agency, 1994), is a seminal article (written in 1955 and originally classified) arguing that until intelligence had a serious literature it would be an immature profession. Michael Herman, *Intelligence Power in Peace and War* (Cambridge: Cambridge University Press, 1996), is a persuasive analysis of intelligence as integral to the power of the modern state. Jeffrey T. Richelson, *A Century of Spies: Intelligence in the Twentieth Century* (Oxford: Oxford University Press, 1995): the first attempt at a general history; it does, however, require updating by the more specialized work below but is still a useful survey.

The history of Cold War intelligence is a fast-developing field. The best way to keep track of recent research is through the two leading academic journals: *Intelligence and National Security* (the first in the field) and *International Journal of Intelligence and Counter Intelligence*.

For the Soviet Union, see Christopher Andrew and Vasili Mitrokhin, *The Mitrokhin Archive: The KGB in Europe and the West* (London: Allen Lane, 1999); published in the United States as *The Sword and the Shield: The Mitrokhin Archive and the Secret History of the KGB* (New York: Basic Books, 1999); *The Mitrokhin Archive II: The KGB and the World* (London: Allen Lane, 2005); published in the United States as *The World Was Going Our Way: The KGB and the Battle for the Third World* (New York: Basic Books, 2005); Aleksandr Fursenko and Timothy Naftali, *"One Hell of a Gamble": Khrushchev, Kennedy, Castro and the Cuban Missile Crisis, 1958–1964* (London: John Murray, New York, 1997): the first to use Soviet intelligence records for the missile crisis; Michael Scammell (ed.), *The Solzhenitsyn Files: Secret Soviet Documents Reveal One Man's Fight against the Monolith*, trans. Catherine A. Fitzpatrick (Chicago: Edition Q, 1995), a documentary case study of the KGB's obsession with "ideological subversion"; N. S. Leonov, *Likholete: Sekretnye Missii* (Moscow: Mezhdunarodnye otnosheniia, 1995), a very useful memoir; Christopher Andrew and Oleg Gordievsky (eds.), *Instructions from The Centre: Top Secret Files on KGB Foreign Operations, 1975–1985* (London: Hodder and Stoughton, 1990), slightly revised US edition published as *Comrade Kryuchkov's Instructions: Top Secret Files on KGB Foreign Operations, 1975–1985* (Stanford, CA: Stanford University Press, 1993), and Raymond L Garthoff, "The KGB Reports to Gorbachev", *Intelligence and National Security*, 11 2 (1996), 224–44.

For the United States, see Christopher Andrew, *For The President's Eyes Only: Secret Intelligence and the American Presidency from Washington to Bush* (New York: Harper Collins, 1995); Evan Thomas, *The Very Best Men: Four Who Dared: The Early Years of the CIA* (New York: Simon & Schuster, 1995); Mary S. McAuliffe (ed.), *CIA Documents on the Cuban Missile Crisis 1962* (Washington, DC: History Staff, Central Intelligence Agency, 1992), Kristian Gustafson, *Hostile Intent: US Covert Operations in Chile 1964–1974* (Washington, DC: Potomac Books, 2007); Gregory Treverton, *Covert Action: The Limits of Intervention in the Postwar World* (New York: Basic Books, 1987); Robert M. Gates, *From the Shadows: The Ultimate Insider's Story of Five Presidents and How They Won the Cold War* (New York: Simon & Schuster, 1997), memoirs of a former DCI; Ben Fischer (ed.), *At Cold War's End: US Intelligence on the Soviet Union and Eastern Europe, 1989–1991* (Washington, DC: Ross & Perry Inc., 2001); Loch K. Johnson, *Secret Agencies: US Intelligence in a Hostile World* (New Haven, CT: Yale University Press, 1996); Tim Weiner, *Legacy of Ashes: The History of the CIA* (New York: Doubleday, 2007), well-written, up-to-date sources, but unbalanced; see "Sins of Omission and Commission" by Jeffrey T. Richelson in the *Washington DeCoded* blog. September 11, 2007, www.washington decoded.com/site/2007/09/sins-of-omissio.html. Milton Bearden and James Risen, *The Main Enemy: The Inside Story of the CIA's Final Showdown with the KGB* (New York: Random House, 2004)

For the United Kingdom, see Richard J. Aldrich, *The Hidden Hand: Britain, America and Cold War Secret Intelligence* (London: John Murray, 2001), Michael S. Goodman, *Spying on the Nuclear Bear: Anglo-American Intelligence and the Atomic Bomb* (Stanford, CA: Stanford University Press, 2007), Peter Hennessy, *The Secret State: Whitehall and the Cold War* (London: Allen Lane, 2002), Sir Percy Cradock, *Know Your Enemy: How the Joint Intelligence Committee Saw the World* (London: John Murray, 2002), Sir Lawrence

Freedman, *The Official History of the Falklands Campaign*, 2 vols. (London: Routledge, 2005), Philip H.J. Davies, *MI6 and the Machinery of Spying* (London: Frank Cass, 2004), and Christopher Andrew, *The Centenary History of the Security Service, 1909–2009* (London and New York, 2009). Official histories of SIS (1909–1949) by Keith Jeffery and of the JIC (since 1936) by Michael S Goodman are in preparation.

On forms of intelligence collection, see – for HUMINT – Kim Philby, *My Silent War* (London: MacGibbon & Kee, 1968); Jerrold L. Schecter and Peter S. Deriabin, *The Spy Who Saved The World: How a Soviet Colonel Changed the Course of the Cold War* (New York: Maxwell Macmillan International, 1992), the first to gain access to the debriefs of the most important Western agent of the early Cold War, Oleg Penkovskii; Oleg Kalugin, *Spymaster: My 32 Years in Intelligence and Espionage against the West* (London: Smith Gryphon, 1994); Oleg Gordievsky, *Next Stop Execution: The Autobiography of Oleg Gordievsky* (London: Macmillan, 1995), the autobiography of the most important Western agent of the later Cold War; Victor Cherkashin (with Gregory Feifer), *Spy Handler: Memoir of a KGB Officer: The True Story of the Man who Recruited Robert Hanssen and Aldrich Ames* (New York: Basic Books, 2005); Admiral Fulvio Martini, *Nome in codice, ULISSE: trent' anni di storia italiana nelle memorie di un protaganista dei servizi segreti* (Milan: Rizzoli, 1999); and Pierre Lethier, *Argent Secret: L'espion de L'affaire Elf parle* (Paris: Albin Michel, 2001).

For SIGINT, see Christopher Andrew, "The Making of the Anglo-American SIGINT Alliance, 1940–1948", in James E. Dillard and Walter T. Hitchcock (eds.), *The Intelligence Revolution and Modern Warfare* (Chicago: Imprint Publications, 1996); George A. Brownell, *The Origins and Development of the National Security Agency* (Laguna Hills, CA: Aegean Park Press, 1981), is the report which led to the foundation of NSA and is good on the later development of the SIGINT Alliance; Jeffrey Richelson and Desmond Ball, *The Ties that Bind* (Boston, MA: Unwin Hyman, 1990); and Nicky Hager, *Secret Power* (Nelson, New Zealand: Craig Potten, 1996). By far the most closely studied SIGINT success of the Cold War is VENONA: see Roger Louis Benson and Michael Warner (eds), *VENONA: Soviet Espionage and the American Response, 1939–1957* (Washington, DC: National Security Agency and Central Intelligence Agency, 1996); John Earl Haynes and Harvey Klehr, *VENONA: Decoding Soviet Espionage in America* (Cambridge and New York: Cambridge University Press, 2006) Nigel West, *Venona: The Greatest Secret of the Cold War* (London: Harper Collins, 1999); Wilhelm Agrell, *Venona: Spåren från ett underrättelsekrig* (Lund: Historiska Media, 2003); Desmond Ball and David Horner, *Breaking the Codes: Australia's KGB Network 1944–1950* (St. Leonards, NSW: Allen and Unwin, 1998); and John Earl Haynes and Harvey Klehr, *In Denial: Historians, Communism and Espionage* (San Francisco, CA: Encounter Books, 2003). As yet, the study of SIGINT for most of the Cold War is in its infancy. Pioneering case studies include Matthew M. Aid and Cees Wiebes (eds.), *Secrets of Signals Intelligence during the Cold War and Beyond* (London: Frank Cass, 2001), David Stafford, *Spies beneath Berlin* (Woodstock, NY: Overlook Press, 2003), and Jean-Marie Pontaut and Jérome Dupuis, *Les Oreilles du Président: suive de la liste des 2000 personnes écoutées par François Mitterand* (Paris: Fayard, 1996).

For IMINT, see Dino A Brugioni, *Eyeball to Eyeball: The Inside Story of the Cuban Missile Crisis* (New York: Random House, 1991), an insider's account; Dino A Brugioni, "The Unidentifieds", in H. Bradford Westerfield (ed.), *Inside CIA's Private World* (New Haven, CT: Yale University Press, 1995); Kevin D. Ruffner (ed.), *CORONA: America's First Satellite Program* (Washington, DC: History Staff, Center for the Study of Intelligence, Central

Intelligence Agency, 1995); Dwayne A. Day, John M. Logsdon, and Brian Latell (eds.), *Eye in the Sky: The Story of the Corona Spy Satellites* (Washington, DC: Smithsonian Institute Press, 1998); and Jeffrey Richelson, *America's Space Sentinels: DSP Satellites and National Security* (Lawrence, KS: University Press of Kansas, 1999).

21. Reading, viewing, and tuning in to the Cold War

The middle years of the cultural Cold War have not been well served by the historiography, which has focused on the earlier period. Important exceptions include David Caute, *The Dancer Defects: The Struggle for Cultural Supremacy during the Cold War* (Oxford: Oxford University Press, 2003) and Rana Mitter and Patrick Major (eds.), *Across the Blocs: Cold War Cultural and Social History* (London: Frank Cass, 2004). Cultural dimensions are now regularly considered in the core journals of Cold War history, *Cold War History*, *The Journal of Cold War Studies*, and media history journals like *Historical Journal of Film, Radio and Television*.

The mechanics of Soviet international propaganda in the Cold War are well discussed in Nigel Gould-Davies, "The Logic of Soviet Cultural Diplomacy", *Diplomatic History*, 27 (2003), 193–214, but for sustained treatments the researcher should begin with Frederick C. Barghoorn, *The Soviet Cultural Offensive* (Princeton, NJ: Princeton University Press, 1960) and his follow-up *Soviet Foreign Propaganda* (Princeton, NJ: Princeton University, 1964), and Baruch A. Hazan, *Soviet Propaganda: A Case Study of the Middle East Conflict* (Jerusalem: Keter, 1976), and *Soviet International Propaganda* (Ann Arbor, MI: Ardis, 1982).

On US propaganda, Nicholas J. Cull, *The Cold War and the United States Information Agency: American Propaganda and Public Diplomacy, 1945–1989* (New York: Cambridge University Press, 2008) provides a complete overview using recently declassified material. Much the best volume on the cultural dimension is Richard T. Arndt, *The First Resort of Kings: American Cultural Diplomacy in the Twentieth Century* (Washington DC: Potomac Books, 2005). American and Western broadcasting during the Cold War are both treated in Michael Nelson, *War of the Black Heavens: The Battles of Western Broadcasting and the Cold War* (Syracuse, NY: Syracuse University Press, 1997). An invaluable insight into the working of US cultural diplomacy may be gained from the memoir of Lyndon Johnson's assistant secretary of state for cultural relations, Charles Frankel, *High on Foggy Bottom: An Outsider's Insider View of Government* (New York: Harper & Row, 1969). The story of US and Soviet exchanges has been told in Yale Richmond's two studies: *U.S.–Soviet Cultural Exchanges, 1958–1986: Who Wins?* (Boulder, CO: Westview Press, 1987), and *Cultural Exchange and the Cold War: Raising the Iron Curtain* (University Park, PA: Pennsylvania State University Press, 2003). Leader exchanges are analyzed in Giles Scott-Smith's masterly *Networks of Empire: The U.S. State Department's Foreign Leader Program in the Netherlands, France, and Britain 1950–70* (Oxford: Peter Lang, 2008).

European initiatives in the field of cultural diplomacy may be explored in Francis Donaldson, *The British Council: The First Fifty Years* (London: Jonathan Cape, 1984), and François Roche and Bernard Pigniau, *Histoires de diplomatie culturelle des origins à 1995* (Paris: La Documentation Française, 1995). On German cultural diplomacy and language policy from the Weimar Republic to the early Federal Republic, see Eckard Michels, *Von der Deutschen Akademie zum Goethe-Institut: Sprach- und auswärtige Kulturpolitik 1923–1960* (Munich: Oldenbourg, 2005).

While there is a wide literature on the content of Cold War culture, a magnificent starting point from the Anglo-American perspective that integrates culture and politics across the entire Cold War period is Fred Inglis, *The Cruel Peace: Everyday Life in the Cold War* (New York: Basic Books, 1991). The story of the transformation of American culture during the middle Cold War/Vietnam period is explored in Tom Engelhardt, *The End of the Victory Culture: Cold War America and the Disillusioning of a Generation* (New York: Basic Books, 1995).

An excellent introduction to American Cold War culture may be found in Stephen J. Whitfield, *The Culture of the Cold War* (Baltimore, MD: Johns Hopkins University Press, 1996). America's specific nuclear fears have been addressed by Paul S. Boyer, *By the Bomb's Early Light: American Thought and Culture at the Dawn of the Atomic Age*, 2nd ed. (Chapel Hill, NC: University of North Carolina Press, 1994), and Margot A. Henriksen, *Dr. Strangelove's America: Society and Culture in the Atomic Age* (Berkeley, CA: University of California Press, 1997), and, in a comprehensive work that includes global cultural responses, Paul Brians, *Nuclear Holocausts: Atomic War in Fiction 1895–1984* (Kent, OH: Kent State University Press, 1986), updated at www.wsu.edu/~brians/nuclear/.

For an introduction to Cold War cinema across the entire period in the United States and the United Kingdom, see Tony Shaw, *British Cinema and the Cold War: The State, Propaganda and Consensus* (London: I. B. Tauris, 2001), and his *Hollywood's Cold War* (Edinburgh: Edinburgh University Press, 2007). On Cold War classical epics, see Martin M. Winkler (ed.) *Spartacus: Film and History* (London: Blackwells, 2007), and Sandra R. Joshel, Margaret Malamud, and Donald T. McGuire, Jr. (eds.), *Imperial Projections: Ancient Rome in Modern Popular Culture* (Baltimore, MD: Johns Hopkins University Press, 2001).

Those seeking a scholarly treatment of film and TV spies should begin with James Chapman, *Licence to Thrill: A Cultural History of the James Bond Films* (London: I. B. Tauris, 1999), and his *Saints and Avengers: British Adventure Series of the 1960s* (London: I. B. Tauris, 2002). On spy literature more broadly, see John G. Cawelti and Bruce A. Rosenberg, *The Spy Story* (Chicago: University of Chicago Press, 1987). A good starting point for understanding the evolution of American war films is the revised edition of Thomas Doherty, *Projections of War: Hollywood, American Culture, and World War II* (New York: Columbia University Press, 1999). The best starting point on the Western genre in the Cold War remains Richard Slotkin, *Gunfighter Nation: The Myth of the Frontier in Twentieth-Century America* (Norman, OK: University of Oklahoma Press, 1998).

Points of entry in English into the culture of the USSR and Eastern Europe include Richard Stites, *Russian Popular Culture: Entertainment and Society since 1900* (Cambridge: Cambridge University Press, 1992). On Soviet attitudes towards the United States, see Eric Shiraev and Vladislav Zubok, *Anti-Americanism in Russia from Stalin to Putin* (New York: Palgrave, 2000). For Eastern European film, begin with Dina Iordanova, *Cinema of the Other Europe: The Industry and Artistry of East Central European Film* (London: Wallflower Press, 2003).

22. Counter-cultures: The rebellions against the Cold War order, 1965–1975

The historical literature on the counter cultures is dominated by works of cultural and social analysis. Some of the most insightful books in this genre are Gerd-Rainer Horn, *The Spirit of '68: Rebellion in Western Europe and North America, 1956–1976* (New

York: Oxford University Press, 2007), Arthur Marwick, *The Sixties: Cultural Revolution in Britain, France, Italy, and the United States, c.1958–c.1974* (Oxford: Oxford University Press, 1998), David Farber, *Chicago '68* (Chicago: University of Chicago Press, 1988), and George Katsiaficas, *The Imagination of the New Left: A Global Analysis of 1968* (Boston, MA: South End Press, 1987). Theodore Roszak popularized the term "counter-culture" in the late 1960s, and his writings remain valuable as sources of insight into the self-conception of Americans in the movement at the time. See Roszak's *The Making of a Counter Culture: Reflections on the Technocratic Society and Youthful Opposition* (Garden City, NY: Doubleday, 1969). For a collection of international primary sources on the counter-cultures, accompanied by interpretive comments, see Jeremi Suri, *The Global Revolutions of 1968* (New York: W. W. Norton, 2007).

Historians are beginning to address the influence of the counter-cultures on political leaders across societies. For some of the works in this emerging field, see Samuel H. Baron, *Bloody Saturday in the Soviet Union: Novocherkassk, 1962* (Stanford, CA: Stanford University Press, 2001), Andreas W. Daum, Lloyd C. Gardner, and Wilfried Mausbach (eds.), *America, the Vietnam War, and the World* (New York: Cambridge University Press, 2003), Martin Klimke, *The Other Alliance: Student Protest in West Germany and the United States in the Global 1960s* (Princeton: Princeton University Press, 2009), Jeremi Suri, *Power and Protest: Global Revolution and the Rise of Détente* (Cambridge, MA: Harvard University Press, 2003).

The social movements and politics of the 1960s have inspired a broad range of interpretive surveys, some of the most insightful include Paul Berman, *A Tale of Two Utopias: The Political Journey of the Generation of 1968* (New York: W.W. Norton, 1996), Terry H. Anderson, *The Sixties*, 3rd ed. (New York: Longman, 2006), Doug Rossinow, *The Politics of Authenticity: Liberalism, Christianity, and New Left America* (New York: Columbia University Press, 1998), Van Gosse, *Rethinking the New Left: An Interpretive History* (New York: Palgrave Macmillan, 2005), Maurice Isserman and Michael Kazin, *America Divided: The Civil War of the 1960s* (New York: Oxford University Press, 2000), Zhores A. Medvedev, *Ten Years after Ivan Denisovich*, trans. Hilary Steinberg (New York: Alfred A. Knopf, 1973), Ludmilla Alexeyeva and Paul Goldberg, *The Thaw Generation: Coming of Age in the Post-Stalin Era* (Pittsburgh, PA: University of Pittsburgh, 1990), Wolfgang Kraushaar, *1968 als Mythos, Chiffre und Zäsur* (Hamburg: Hamburger Edition, 2000), Ingrid Gilcher-Holtey (ed.), *1968 – Von Ereignis zum Gegenstand der Geschichtwissenschaft* (Göttingen: Vandenhoeck and Ruprecht, 1998), Rolf Uesseler, *Die 68er: APO, Marx und freie Liebe* (Munich: Wilhelm Heyne Verlag, 1998), Roderick MacFarquhar and Michael Schoenhals, *Mao's Last Revolution* (Cambridge, MA: Harvard University Press, 2006), Anita Chan, *Children of Mao: Personality Development and Political Activism in the Red Guard Generation* (Seattle, WA: University of Washington Press, 1985).

A number of authors have examined the comparative dynamics of protest across societies. For some of the most suggestive works, see Jeremy Varon, *Bringing the War Home: The Weather Underground, the Red Army Faction, and Revolutionary Violence in the Sixties and Seventies* (Berkeley, CA: University of California Press, 2004), Carole Fink, Phillip Gassert and Detlef Junker (eds.) *1968: The World Transformed* (New York: Cambridge University Press, 1998), Gerard J. DeGroot (ed.), *Student Protest: The Sixties and After* (New York: Longman, 1998); Klimke, *The "Other" Alliance*; Marwick, *The Sixties*; Katsiaficas, *The Imagination of the New Left*; Suri, *Power and Protest*.

The literature on "law and order" politics is quite large and varied in focus. For some of the best works, see Bruce J. Schulman and Julian E. Zelizer (eds.), *Rightward Bound: Making America Conservative in the 1970s* (Cambridge, MA: Harvard University Press, 2008), Joseph Crespino, *In Search of Another Country: Mississippi and the Conservative Counterrevolution* (Princeton, NJ: Princeton University Press, 2007), Matthew D. Lassiter, *The Silent Majority: Suburban Politics in the Sunbelt South* (Princeton, NJ: Princeton University Press, 2006), Kevin M. Kruse, *White Flight: Atlanta and the Making of Modern Conservatism* (Princeton, NJ: Princeton University Press, 2005), Michael W. Flamm, *Law and Order: Street Crime, Civil Unrest, and the Crisis of Liberalism in the 1960s* (New York: Columbia University Press, 2005), Dan T. Carter, *The Politics of Rage: George Wallace, The Origins of the New Conservatism, and the Transformation of American Politics*, 2nd ed. (Baton Rouge, LA: Louisiana State University Press, 2000), Patrick Moreau, *Les Héritiers due IIIe Reich: L'extrême Droite Allemands de 1945 à nos Jours* (Paris: Éditions du Seuil, 1994), Jacques Schuster, *Heinrich Albertz – der Mann, der mehrere Leben lebte: eine Biographie* (Berlin: Alexander Fest Verlag, 1997), Klaus Hildebrand, *Von Erhard zur Großen Koalition, 1963–1969* (Stuttgart: Deutsche Verlags-Anstalt, 1984), Dmitri Volkogonov, *Sem Vozhdei: Galereia liderov SSSR* [Seven Bosses: A Gallery of Soviet Leaders], 2 vols. vol. II (Moscow: Novosti, 1995), and Edwin Bacon and Mark Sandle (eds.), *Brezhnev Reconsidered* (Houndmills: Palgrave, 2002).

The historiography on foreign policy in the 1960s and 1970s, and détente in particular, is growing rapidly with the opening of new archival sources in numerous societies. For some of the most insightful books, see Robert D. Schulzinger, *A Time for Peace: The Legacy of the Vietnam War* (New York: Oxford University Press, 2006), John Lewis Gaddis, *The Cold War: A New History* (New York: Penguin Press, 2005), Jussi Hanhimäki, *The Flawed Architect: Henry Kissinger and American Foreign Policy* (New York: Oxford University Press, 2004), Thomas Alan Schwartz, *Lyndon Johnson and Europe: In the Shadow of Vietnam* (Cambridge, MA: Harvard University Press, 2003), M. E. Sarotte, *Dealing with the Devil: East Germany, Détente, and Ostpolitik, 1969–1973* (Chapel Hill, NC: University of North Carolina Press, 2001), Qiang Zhai, *China and the Vietnam Wars, 1950–1975* (Chapel Hill, NC: University of North Carolina Press, 2000), Ilya V. Gaiduk, *The Soviet Union and the Vietnam War* (Chicago: Ivan R. Dee, 1996), Raymond Garthoff, *Détente and Confrontation: American–Soviet Relations from Nixon to Reagan*, rev. ed. (Washington, DC: Brookings Institution, 1994), and Suri, *Power and Protest* and *Henry Kissinger and the American Century* (Cambridge, MA: Belknap Press of Harvard University Press, 2007).

23. The structure of great power politics, 1963–1975

Probably the best and most up-to-date introduction to great power politics in the middle period of the Cold War – the period, say, from 1962 to 1975 – is the section dealing with that period in Georges-Henri Soutou, *La Guerre de Cinquante Ans: Le conflit Est–Ouest 1943–1990* (Paris: Fayard, 2001). André Fontaine's *Un seul lit pour deux rêves: Histoire de la "détente," 1962–1981* (Paris: Fayard, 1981), an account by an astute and very well-informed French journalist, is also very much worth reading. For the latter part of this period, Raymond Garthoff's very detailed study, *Détente and Confrontation: American–Soviet Relations from Nixon to Reagan*, rev. ed. (Washington, DC: Brookings Institution, 1994), is fundamental.

There is a vast literature on US–European relations during this period. The middle chapters in Geir Lundestad's *The United States and Western Europe since 1945: From "Empire" by Invitation to Transatlantic Drift* (Oxford: Oxford University Press, 2003), provide a good introduction; the book also has a very useful bibliography. Josef Joffe's *The Limited Partnership: Europe, the United States, and the Burdens of Alliance* (Cambridge, MA: Ballinger, 1987) is another important work on the subject.

A number of recent studies deal with American foreign policy in the 1960s and early 1970s. On the Kennedy period, see the last two chapters in Marc Trachtenberg, *A Constructed Peace: The Making of the European Settlement, 1945–1963* (Princeton, NJ: Princeton University Press, 1999). On the Johnson period, see especially Thomas Schwartz, *Lyndon Johnson and Europe: In the Shadow of Vietnam* (Cambridge, MA: Harvard University Press, 2003), and Frank Costigliola's important article, "Lyndon B. Johnson, Germany, and the 'End of the Cold War,'" in Warren Cohen and Nancy Bernkopf Tucker (eds.), *Lyndon Johnson Confronts the World: American Foreign Policy, 1963–1968* (Cambridge: Cambridge University Press, 1994). On Johnson's non-proliferation policy, see Francis Gavin, "Blasts from the Past: Proliferation Lessons from the 1960s," *International Security*, 29, 3 (Winter 2004–05), 100–35, and Hal Brands, "Rethinking Nonproliferation: LBJ, the Gilpatric Committee, and U.S. National Security Policy," *Journal of Cold War Studies*, 8, 2 (Spring 2006), 83–113, On balance-of-payments and related issues and their political and military implications, see Francis Gavin, *Gold, Dollars, and Power: The Politics of International Monetary Relations, 1958–1971* (Chapel Hill, NC: University of North Carolina Press, 2004), and Hubert Zimmermann, *Money and Security: Troops, Monetary Policy and West Germany's Relations with the United States and Britain, 1950–1971* (Cambridge: Cambridge University Press, 2002).

On the Nixon–Kissinger period, perhaps the best introduction is Jussi Hanhimäki's historiographical survey, 'Dr. Kissinger' or 'Mr. Henry'? Kissingerology, Thirty Years and Counting," *Diplomatic History*, 27, 5 (November 2003), 637–76 Hanhimäki's *Flawed Architect: Henry Kissinger and American Foreign Policy* (New York: Oxford University Press, 2004) is a good scholarly analysis. See also the account by one of Kissinger's collaborators: William Hyland, *Mortal Rivals: Superpower Relations from Nixon to Reagan* (New York: Random House, 1987). Kissinger's three enormous volumes of memoirs should also be noted; the first of the three – Henry Kissinger, *White House Years* (Boston, MA: Little, Brown, 1979) – is one of the most extraordinary political memoirs ever written.

For German foreign policy through 1963, Hans-Peter Schwarz, *Adenauer*, vol. II (Stuttgart: Deutsche Verlags-Anstalt, 1991), is perhaps the best source. That volume is also available now in English translation. For the post-Adenauer period, see the sections on foreign policy in the following three volumes in the *Geschichte der Bundesrepublik Deutschland* series: Klaus Hildebrand, *Von Erhard zur Grossen Koalition, 1963–1969* (Stuttgart: Deutsche Verlags-Anstalt 1984), Karl Dietrich Bracher, Wolfgang Jager, and Werner Link, *Republik im Wandel, 1969–1974: Die Ära Brandt* (Stuttgart: Deutsche Verlags-Anstalt, 1986), and Wolfgang Jäger and Werner Link, *Republik im Wandel, 1974–1982: Die Ära Schmidt* (Stuttgart: Deutsche Verlags-Anstalt, 1987). In English, the most important work covering the *Ostpolitik* period is *In Europe's Name: Germany and the Divided Continent*, by Timothy Garton Ash (New York, Random House, 1993). Note also Arne Hofmann, *The Emergence of Détente in Europe: Brandt, Kennedy and the Formation of Ostpolitik* (New York: Routledge, 2007). On the internal politics of German foreign policy during that period, see especially

Clay Clemens, *Reluctant Realists: The Christian Democrats and West German Ostpolitik* (Durham, NC: Duke University Press, 1989).

On French policy for the period when de Gaulle was in charge, the most important studies are Maurice Vaïsse, *La grandeur: Politique étrangère du général de Gaulle, 1958–1969* (Paris: Fayard, 1998), and Frédéric Bozo, *Deux stratégies pour l'Europe: De Gaulle, les États-Unis et l'Alliance atlantique* (Paris: Plon, 1996). On the Pompidou period (1969–1974), see especially two important articles by Georges-Henri Soutou: "L'Attitude de Georges Pompidou face à l'Allemagne," in *Georges Pompidou et l'Europe* (Paris: Éditions Complexe, 1995), and "Georges Pompidou and U.S.–European Relations," in Marc Trachtenberg (ed.), *Between Empire and Alliance: America and Europe during the Cold War* (Lanham, MD: Rowman and Littlefield, 2003).

On Soviet policy through 1964, see William Taubman, *Khrushchev: The Man and His Era* (New York: Norton, c2003), and Timothy Naftali and Aleksandr Fursenko, *"One Hell of a Gamble": Khrushchev, Castro, and Kennedy, 1958–1964* (New York: W. W. Norton, 1997), as well as the important new book by those authors, *Khrushchev's Cold War: The Inside Story of an American Adversary* (New York: Norton, 2006). The literature on the post-1964 period is still rather thin. For an overview, see the chapters on the Brezhnev period in Vladislav M. Zubok, *A Failed Empire: The Soviet Union in the Cold War from Stalin to Gorbachev* (Chapel Hill, NC: University of North Carolina Press, 2007). Two older books are still quite useful: Adam Ulam, *Dangerous Relations: The Soviet Union in World Politics, 1970–1982* (New York: Oxford University Press, 1983), and Robin Edmonds, *Soviet Foreign Policy: The Brezhnev Years* (New York: Oxford University Press, 1983). A number of important works have come out in recent years dealing with specific aspects of Soviet policy during that period. See, in particular, Hannes Adomeit, *Imperial Overstretch: Germany in Soviet Policy from Stalin to Gorbachev* (Baden-Baden: Nomos, 1998), and Ilya V. Gaiduk, *The Soviet Union and the Vietnam War* (Chicago: Ivan R. Dee, 1996). Mary Sarotte's *Dealing with the Devil: East Germany, Détente and Ostpolitik, 1969–1973* (Chapel Hill, NC: University of North Carolina Press, 2001) is a major study of the détente / Ostpolitik period based largely on East German sources.

Two topics dominate the study of Chinese foreign policy during this period: the deterioration of Sino-Soviet relations in the 1960s and the Sino-American rapprochement in the early 1970s. Thomas Robinson, "China Confronts the Soviet Union: War and Diplomacy on China's Inner Asian Frontiers," and Jonathan Pollack, "The Opening to America," both in Roderick MacFarquhar and John Fairbank (eds.), *The Cambridge History of China*, vol. XV, *Revolutions within the Chinese Revolution, 1966–1982* (Cambridge: Cambridge University Press, 1991), provide very good introductions to those two topics. On Sino-Americans relations, see also the relevant parts of Chen Jian, *Mao's China and the Cold War* (Chapel Hill, NC: University of North Carolina Press, 2001), Gordon Chang, *Friends and Enemies: The United States, China, and the Soviet Union, 1948–1972* (Stanford, CA: Stanford University Press, 1990), and Rosemary Foot, *The Practice of Power: US Relations with China since 1949* (Oxford: Clarendon Press, 1995).

Military issues loomed large in this period. Anyone interested in getting some real insight into these issues should read Thomas Schelling, *Arms and Influence* (New Haven, CT: Yale University Press, 1966), by far the most important work on the subject. The most important historical work in this area has been done by David Rosenberg. For this period, see especially his article "The History of World War III, 1945–1990: A Conceptual

Framework," in Robert David Johnson (ed.), *On Cultural Ground: Essays in International History*, (Chicago: Imprint Publications, 1994). On nuclear strategy during the Nixon period, William Burr, "The Nixon Administration, the 'Horror Strategy,' and the Search for Limited Nuclear Options, 1969–1972," *Journal of Cold War Studies*, 7, 3 (Summer 2005), 34–78, is a major archive-based study. On the evolution of NATO strategy during this period, see Jane Stromseth, *The Origins of Flexible Response: NATO's Debate over Strategy in the 1960s* (New York: St. Martin's Press, 1988); John Duffield, *Power Rules: The Evolution of NATO's Conventional Force Posture* (Stanford, CA: Stanford University Press, 1995), chapter 5; and Helga Haftendorn, *NATO and the Nuclear Revolution: A Crisis of Credibility* (Oxford: Clarendon, 1996). For European views on NATO strategy, see also Christoph Bluth, *Britain, Germany, and Western Nuclear Strategy* (Oxford: Clarendon, 1995), and Beatrice Heuser, *NATO, Britain, France and the FRG: Nuclear Strategies and Forces for Europe, 1949–2000* (New York: St. Martin's Press, 1997), as well as the book by Frédéric Bozo, *Deux Stratégies pour l'Europe* noted above.

There is a vast literature on Soviet military strategy during this period; some key sources are listed in notes 18 and 20 of the Rosenberg article "World War III," cited above. Some recent historical work has been based on archival sources that have become available since the end of the Cold War. See, for example, the studies published in Vojtech Mastny, Sven Holtsmark, and Andreas Wenger, *War Plans and Alliances in the Cold War* (London: Routledge, 2006); note especially Mastny's article there on "Imagining War in Europe: Soviet Strategic Planning." The Warsaw Pact material in the former East German archives provided some important grist for the scholarly mills in this area. See, for example, Christoph Bluth, "Offensive Defence in the Warsaw Pact: Reinterpreting Military Doctrine," *Journal of Strategic Studies* 18, 4 (December 1995), 55–77, and Beatrice Heuser, "Warsaw Pact Military Doctrines in the 1970s and 1980s: Findings in the East German Archives," *Comparative Strategy* 12, 4 (October 1993), 437–57. One important work, with some interesting new information on this subject, is William Odom's *The Collapse of the Soviet Military* (New Haven, CT: Yale University Press, 1998).

As for arms control, the scholarly literature on the SALT negotiations remains surprisingly thin, despite all the archival material that has become available in the last decade. The best introduction to the subject is probably still John Newhouse's *Cold Dawn: The Story of SALT* (New York: Holt, Rinehart, 1973).

24. The Cold War and the social and economic history of the twentieth century

Any reflection on the relationship between the Cold War and the social and economic history of the twentieth century will profit from Eric Hobsbawn's thoughtful *Age of Extremes: The Short Twentieth Century 1914–1991* (London: Michael Joseph, 1994). More detailed narratives of the second half of the twentieth century, including aspects of social and cultural changes, are David Reynolds, *One World Divisible: A Global History since 1945* (London: Penguin Books 2000), and on crucial developments in Europe, Tony Judt, *Postwar: A History of Europe since 1945* (New York: Penguin, 2005.

The best general accounts of the economic history of the twentieth century can still be found in the volumes of the *Penguin History of the World Economy in the Twentieth Century*:

Gerd Hardach, *The First World War 1914–1918*, Derek H. Aldcroft, *From Versailles to Wall Street, 1919–1929*, Charles P. Kindleberger, *The World in Depression 1929–1939*; Alan S. Milward, *War, Economy and Society, 1939–1945*; and Herman Van der Wee, *Prosperity and Upheaval: The World Economy 1945–1980*.

An updated survey on the economic development in Europe is offered in Derek H. Aldcroft, *The European Economy 1914–1990* (London and New York: Routledge, 1994). Economic relations between states and societies are discussed in James Foreman-Peck, *A History of the World Economy: International Economic Relations since 1850* (New York: Harvester Wheatsheaf, 1995).

Among the general accounts of the developments in the Soviet Union, Alec Nove, *An Economic History of the USSR, 1917–1991* (Harmondsworth: Penguin Books, 1992), is a classic, whereas Manfred Hildermeier, *Geschichte der Sowjetunion 1917–1991* (Munich: C. H. Beck, 1998), offers the most reliable integration of recent research, and Jörg Barberowski, *Der rote Terror. Die Geschichte des Stalinismus* (Munich: Deutsche Verlags-Anstalt, 2003), discusses the dynamism of Stalinist terrorism.

The relations between economic, social, and political history during the emergence of the Cold War are discussed in Wilfried Loth, *Die Teilung der Welt: Geschichte des Kalten Krieges 1941–1955*, rev. ed. (Munich: Deutscher Taschenbuch-Verlag, 2000), and John J. Agnew and Nicholas Entrikin (eds.), *The Marshall Plan Today: Model and Metaphor* (London and New York: Routledge, 2004).

Stalin's postwar strategy is discussed in more detail in Wilfried Loth, *Stalin's Unwanted Child: The Soviet Union, the German Question, and the Founding of the GDR* (London and New York: Macmillan and St. Martin's Press, 1998).

On a special aspect of the change in the international system after World War II, see Roy Fraser Holland, *European Decolonisation 1918–1991* (Basingstoke: Macmillan, 1987). On the far-reaching social changes after the post-World War II reconstruction, Jean Fourastié, *Les trentes glorieuses ou la révolution invisible* (Paris: Fayard, 1979), is a classic. Updated details may be found in general accounts of the history of European countries, such as Paul Ginsborg, *A History of Contemporary Italy: Society and Politics 1943–1988* (London: Penguin Books, 1990), L. P. Morris, *Eastern Europe since 1945* (London and Exeter: Heinemann Educational Books, 1984), René Rémond: *Notre siècle 1918–1988*, vol. VI, *Histoire de France* (Paris: Fayard, 1988), Edgar Wolfrum, *Die geglückte Demokratie: Geschichte der Bundesrepublik Deutschland von ihren Anfängen bis zur Gegenwart* (Stuttgart: Klett-Cotta, 2006).

On the consequences of the transition to consumer societies in the late 1960s, see Henri Mendras, *La Seconde Révolution française, 1965–1984* (Paris: Gallimard, 1994), and Stephan Malinowski and Alexander Sedlmaier, "'1968' als Katalysator der Konsumgesellschaft," *Geschichte und Gesellschaft*, 32 (2006), 238–67.

The final crisis of the Soviet system is discussed in Archie Brown, *The Gorbachev Factor in Soviet Politics* (Oxford: Oxford University Press, 1996), and, with more emphasis on the international relations, in Wilfried Loth, *Overcoming the Cold War: A History of Détente, 1950–1991* (Houndsmills and New York: Palgrave and St. Martin's Press, 2002).

Index

Cumulative index for Volumes I, II, and III.
Bold page numbers refer to maps and photographs.

Afghanistan (cont.)
  Islamist opposition groups, III.124–5, 128
  Islamist uprisings, III.128
  royal rule, III.121–3
  Iranian relations
    border dispute, III.122–3
    Communist coup, III.127
    Daoud regime, III.126
  madrasas, III.131
  Pakistani relations
    border dispute, III.122, 123, 125
    Communist coup, III.127–8
    growing influence, III.133
    intelligence services, III.125, 128
    Islamist groups, III.125, 128
  postwar position, III.113
  refugees from, III.471
  Saudi relations, III.126
  Soviet occupation, II.17, 426
    Carter policy, III.70, 83–5, 87, 129
    Chinese response, III.87, 129, 192, 193–4
    CIA operations, II.427–8, III.130–1
    costs, II.19, III.362, 509
    détente and, II.40, III.63, 85, 150–2
    economic impact, III.39–40, 111
    end of Cold War, III.254–6
    Geneva Peace Accords (1988), III.132–3
    Gorbachev, III.131–3, 286
    international sanctions, III.313
    invasion, III.102–4
    Islamist resistance, III.125, 130–1
    military tactics, III.131
    miscalculation, III.90, 102–3
    mujahedin, III.130, **132**, 133
    nationalist resistance, III.532
    political impact, II.522, III.520
    postinvasion politics, III.112
    return of Cold War, III.150–2, 409
    role of intelligence services, II.436
    South Africa and, III.234
    Soviet perceptions, III.128, 239
    technology and, III.41
    US counterintervention, III.40, 67,
      129–34, 272, 275, 286
    US election (1980) and, III.66
    US monetary system and, III.31
    watershed, III.129, 520
    West European response, III.289,
      290–3, 308
    withdrawal, III.133, 239, 254–6, 286,
      318–19, 362, 418, 520
  Soviet relations, II.426–7
    1950s, III.123

  Daoud regime, III.125, 126–7
  Islamic guerrillas, II.324
  Soviet sphere of influence, III.114, 121–2
  Taliban government, III.133–4
  US relations
    1950s, III.122
    2001 invasion, III.554–5
    Communist government, III.127, 128
    counterintervention strategy, III.40, 67,
      129–34, 272, 275, 286
    covert actions, II.427–8, III.130–1
    economic assistance, III.123
    Pakistani border dispute, III.122, 123
    post-Soviet withdrawal, III.133
    Reagan, III.130, 151–2, 273, 275, 517
    Soviet withdrawal and, III.255
Africa
  see also specific countries
  Cold War politics, I.10
  Cuban policy, II.331–4, 340, III.99
  end of Cold War, I.485
  green revolution and, III.428
  historiography, I.7
  human rights and, III.453
  Johnson presidency, II.131
  Kennedy presidency, II.122–3
  neoliberalism and, III.36
  post-Cold War, III.536–7, 556
  refugees, III.471
  Soviet gambles, III.98–9
  uranium mining, III.438
Agat (Soviet computer), III.397
agriculture
  capitalist, I.52
  environment and, III.423–9
  global transition, I.53
  green revolution, I.65, III.425–9, 431–4, 476
  mechanization, III.466
  Poland, I.59
  Soviet Union, I.46, 447, 448, 450, II.514,
    515–16, III.429
  technology, I.13
  United States, II.256
  USSR Virgin Lands, I.450, III.429–31
air traffic, I.12
Akhromeev, Sergei (Soviet marshal),
  III.80, 414
Al Qaeda, III.133–4
Albania
  China and, I.220, 331, II.205, 247
  Hoxha dictatorship, I.220
  New Course, I.338
  post-Stalin, I.216

Bruce, David (US ambassador to France), I.171
Brussels Exhibition (1958), III.496
Brussels Pact (1948), I.122, 169
Brutents, Karen (Soviet politician), II.273
Brzezinski, Zbigniew (US political scientist and national security adviser), III.69
  Afghan invasion, III.129
  anticommunism, III.100
  on Castro, II.344
  China, III.80–1, 147–8, 148, 190, 192
  Eastern Europe, II.207
  Eurocommunism and, III.56
  Horn of Africa, II.345, 346, III.70, 79, 146, 147
  human rights, III.144
  influence on Carter, II.152
  personality, III.68
  Poland, III.105
  Soviet strategy, II.152
Bucharest Declaration (1966), II.208–9
Budd, Alan (adviser to UK prime minister Thatcher), III.33
Bukovina, I.92
Bukovskii, Vladimir (Soviet dissident), III.73, 100, 144, 145, 458
Bulganin, Nikolai (Soviet prime minister), I.212, II.399
Bulgaria
  1953 unrest, I.336
  1989 revolution, III.323, 330–1
  Communist coup (1944), I.177
  de-Stalinization, I.344
  economy, failure, III.98
  Litvinov document, I.176
  New Course, I.338
  Ottoman domination, III.331
  police state, I.72, II.236
  postwar Soviet occupation, I.183, 199
  refusal to reform, III.315
  show trials, I.193, 344
  Sovietization, I.177, 184, 185, 186, 187, 200, 209
  spy fiction, II.449–50
  Stalin and, I.96, 97, 99, 103, 105, 110, 185, 210, 216
  Stalinization, I.194
  Western cultural contacts, I.405
Bullitt, William (US ambassador), II.125
Bundy, McGeorge (US national security adviser), II.71, 77, 80–1, 241, 402, III.479, 487
Bunker, Ellsworth (US ambassador to South Vietnam), III.168, 478

Burgess, Guy (British diplomat and spy), I.125
Burma
  Communist insurgency, II.286, III.187
  Dobama Asi-ayone, I.469
  independence, I.114, 127
  Japan and, I.251
  nationalism, I.470
  US strategy, II.288
  Vietnam and, I.474
  Young Men's Buddhist Association, I.469
Bush, George H. W. (US president), III.281
  Central America, III.219
  China, III.198
  Eastern Europe, III.282–4, 332
  El Salvador, III.220
  end of Cold War and, III.269, 522–3, 533, 542
  foreign policy and intelligence, II.418
  German unification, III.324, 332, 342, 343–4, 345, 348, 354
  Gulf War (1991), III.550
  Hungary, III.324
  on Iran–Contra affair, II.429
  Japan, III.178–9
  Lithuania, III.283, 367
  NAFTA, III.548
  Nicaragua, III.216
  Panama, III.219
  post-Cold War order, III.548
  Soviet relations
    assessment, III.286–8
    bibliography, III.581
    collapse of Soviet Union, III.284–5, 375–6
    Eastern Europe, III.282–4
    German unification and, III.354
    Gorbachev, III.264, 282–8
    objectives, III.277
    Soviet reforms and, III.281–2
  Ukraine, III.367
Bush, George W. (US president), II.25, III.551, 554–5, 556
Bush, Vannevar (US scientist), III.379
Byrnes, James (US secretary of state), I.56, 70, 72, 97, 99, 141, 142–3

cable television, III.389
Cabral, Amilcar (Guinea-Bissau revolutionary leader), II.337
Cabral, Luis (Guinea-Bissau president), II.337
Caetano, Marcelo (Portuguese leader), II.248–9
Cairo Conference (1943), I.267

Iran (cont.)
Islamic Republic, III.121
modernization, II.263
neoconservatives, III.10
oil politics, I.494–6, 498–500, II.306
Shi'ite opposition, III.117
sphere of influence, III.114, 115
support for dictatorship, II.272, 275, 325
Truman, I.61, 88, 495
Iraq
anticolonial movement, I.470
Baghdad Pact, I.207–8, 300, 500, 502
British policy, I.502, II.307
Egypt and, I.300
Gulf War (1991), III.550
human rights violations, III.453
Iran and, III.118
Khomeini, III.117
Kuwait and, I.503
military coup (1958), I.323–4, 502–3, II.311
military coup (1963), I.503
pan-Arab movement, I.480
Soviet relations, II.246, 326
assistance, III.101
Brezhnev era, II.151, 153
Khrushchev, II.311, III.453
militarization, II.274
Saddam Hussein, II.324
United States and
2003 invasion, III.555, 556
economic assistance, I.481
Eisenhower, I.299
military coup (1958), I.502–3
military coup (1963), I.503
Ireland, I.114, II.257, 404, III.301, 472
Iron Curtain, I.36
irrigation, III.433
Ishibashi, Tanzan (Japanese prime
minister), I.257, 262
Islamism
9/11 attacks, III.134
Afghanistan
opposition groups, III.124–5, 128
resistance to Soviet occupation, III.130–1
Soviet policy, III.102
US counterintervention strategy, III.130
birth control and, III.483
Khomeini and, III.119–21
rise of political Islam, II.324–5, III.112, 533,
536–7, 556
Rushdie fatwa, III.22
Israel
creation of state, II.306

Egypt and, *see* **Egypt**
Golan Heights and, II.314, 315, 317, 319, 385
nuclear weapons, II.401, 405
motivation, II.416
NPT and, II.410, 411
US tolerance, II.412
Yom Kippur War and, II.320
Palestinian issue
oil politics, I.496–7
pan-Arab movement, I.480
Paris Conference (1973), II.251–2
Sinai and, II.319, 324, 385
Six Day War, *see* **Six Day War**
Soviet relations, II.252
Jewish emigration, II.55, 384, III.152
Zionism, II.306
US policy
dependence, II.244, 250
economic assistance, II.62
Eisenhower, II.310, 312
Hawk missiles, II.241, 244–5
military assistance, II.63, 318
Six Day War, II.313–18
Yom Kippur War, II.386–7
Yom Kippur War, *see* **Yom Kippur War**
Italy
affluence and democracy, II.513
Allied Control Commission, I.201
American culture, I.412
Anti-Comintern Pact (1936), I.30
borders, I.102
British–American dominance, I.94
Communism, I.75, 81, 156, 170
Communist Party, I.57, 94, 105, 156, 170
Cominform and, I.191, 209
Czech Soviet invasion and, III.45
Czech Velvet Revolution and, III.325
decline, II.513, III.298
Eurocommunism, II.255–6, III.45–51,
53–7, 59, 60–5, 75
Popular Front, II.508
Portuguese carnation revolution and,
III.51
World War II, II.508
Craxi government, III.300
economy
postwar, I.159
steel industry, I.50
unemployment, III.290
emigration, III.470
European integration, I.172, II.191
European policy, I.126
family tradition, III.1

Index

Japan (cont.)

prewar
imperialism, III.546
Korean relations, I.267
rise of authorianism, II.4
Russo-Japanese war (1904–5), I.69
reemergence, III.541
satellites, III.387
Soviet relations, I.69, 261–2
1960 US security treaty and, III.159–60
end of Cold War, III.175–6, 179
Gorbachev, III.252
oil imports, I.505
San Francisco Treaty and, I.251, 253–4
Stalin, I.93, 96, 97, 98, 109
territorial claims, II.356, III.160
trade, III.157
Taiwan and, I.254, 261, 263, III.43, 176
telecommunications, III.391
territory, I.261–2
Third World policy, II.60
birth control, III.483
trade preferences, II.63
trade unions, I.48
trading
GATT, I.257, 258
power, I.68, 257–8
Southeast Asia, I.258
United States, II.53, III.157, 162–3, 171, 177–9
UN membership, I.257, 261, 264
United States and (1945–60)
American bases, I.251, 252, 253, 254, 263–4
anti-Americanism, I.259
assessment, I.265
bibliography, I.529–31
currency, I.251
democracy, I.247–8, 265
economic restructuring, I.45, 251, 257–8, 280
Korean War, I.285, 286–7
legal reform, I.248
Lucky Dragon, I.258–9
military tribunals, I.247, 252
new security treaty (1960), I.262–5, III.158–63
occupation
1945–47, I.246–9
1947–51, I.249–51
MacArthur control, I.77
objectives, I.249
rearmament, I.255–6, III.157–8
reconstruction, II.7
"red purge," I.250
reverse course, I.249–51

San Francisco Treaty, I.84, 251–4, 257, 265, 279, III.159
specters of neutralism, I.258–62
strategies, I.81–2, 86, 87–8
Strike Report, I.249
United States and (1960–91)
bibliography, III.568–70
Kennedy, II.118
loans, III.179
long end of Cold War, III.175–80
new Pacific frontier, III.163–6
new security treaty (1960), I.262–5, III.158–63
renewal, III.175
Nixon shocks, III.171–5
nuclear guarantee, II.396
Pacific alliance, III.156–8
popular opposition, III.160–1, 162
trade, II.53, III.157, 162–3, 171, 177–9
Vietnam trauma, III.166–71
World War II, oil resources, I.488
Zengakuren, III.161
Jarring, Gunnar (Swedish UN diplomat), II.317
Jaruzelski, Wojciech (Polish general, prime minister and president)
1981 coup, III.63, 106, 293, 314
1986 amnesty, III.316
postrevolution role, III.319
presidency, III.318
resignation, III.324
Solidarity and, III.106
Soviet relations, III.107
jazz, I.461, 462, II.442
Jefferson, Thomas, I.470
Jenkins, Roy (British politician), III.11
Jiang Jieshi (Chinese generalissimo and political leader)
1949 defeat, II.8
Chinese Civil War, I.227–30
Eisenhower and, II.13
flight to Taiwan, I.245
fragile postwar peace, I.222–4
Japanese relations, I.263
Sino-Soviet Treaty (1945), I.108–9
Stalin and, I.223, 473
US missiles, I.363
US support, I.222, 224, 226, 229
abandonment, II.287
Jiang Jingguo (Taiwan leader; son of Jiang Jieshi), I.228, III.197
Jiang Qing (Mao Zedong's wife), II.365, III.186

616

Loyalty Day, I.428–9
Lübbe, Hermann (German philosopher),
III.11
Luca, Vasile (Romanian politician), I.188–9
Lucas, George (US film director), II.454
Lucas García, Fernando Romeo
(Guatemalan president), III.216
Lucky Dragon incident (Japanese fishing
vessel, 1954), I.258–9
Ludlum, Robert (US writer), II.449
Luhmann, Niklas (German sociologist), III.4
Lukanov, Andrei (Bulgarian deputy prime
minister), III.331
Lumet, Sidney (US film director), II.446
Lumumba, Patrice (Congolese prime
minister), I.62, 483, II.46, 123, 265–6
Luxembourg, I.167, 169, 172
Lysenko, Trofim (Soviet biologist), I.454,
455, 457, 458–9, III.429
Lysenkoism, III.427, 430, 431

Maastricht Treaty (1992), II.178, III.355
MacArthur, Douglas (US general), I.246, 275
Japan
occupation commander, I.77, 244
rearmament, I.255
San Francisco Peace Treaty, I.249–50
security, I.251
Tokyo military tribunal, I.247
Korean War, I.274–5, 277
dismissal, I.278–9
nuclear weapons, I.381
operations, I.85–6
phraseology, III.177
MacArthur, Douglas II (US ambassador to
Japan), I.263, 264, III.159, 161
McCarey, Leo (US film director), II.448
McCarthy, Eugene (US senator), II.130–1
McCarthy, Joseph (US senator), I.84, 423–4,
428, **429**, 430, 440, II.418–19
McCarthyism, I.423–31, 433, 434, 435, 440, II.30,
289, III.382, 514
McCloskey, Paul (member, US Congress),
II.301
McCloy, John J. (US diplomat), I.74, II.182,
250, 404, III.479
McCone, John (CIA director), II.71, 72, 81
McDonald's, III.489, 506
McFarlane, Robert (Reagan adviser), III.275,
276, 278, 280
McGhee, George (US State Department
official), II.406
McGoohan, Patrick (British actor), II.448

Machel, Samora (Mozambique leader),
III.232, 233, 237
Maclean, Donald (British diplomat and
spy), I.125
Macmillan, Harold (British prime minister),
I.325, II.73, 166, 188, 404
McNamara, Robert (US secretary of
defense), **I.305, II.127**
on Castro, II.121
Cuban missile crisis, II.71, 72, 73, 77, 78, 81,
86, 329–30
flexible response, II.116–17
nuclear weapons, I.310, II.91, 92
ABMs, II.106–7
Europe, II.490
mutual assured destruction, II.86, 93
NATO, II.99
nuclear taboo, II.105–6
strategy, II.95
West Germany and, II.130
population control, III.467, 480
Vietnam War, II.86
Gulf of Tonkin Resolution, II.294
South Vietnamese government, II.298
World Bank, III.487
McNeil, Hector (British politician), I.125
McNeill, John (US historian), I.65
McNeill, William (US historian), III.38
madrasas, III.131
Maiak, III.439–41
Maier, Charles (US historian) I.164, III.397, 494
Maiskii, Ivan (Soviet diplomat), I.92, 93, 102,
175, 176, II.508–9
Maizière, Lothar de (GDR leader), III.352, 354
Makarios III, Archbishop, II.242, 253
Malaka, Tan (Indonesian nationalist), I.467
malaria, III.476
Malaya
Britain and, I.60, 127–8
anticolonial struggle, I.472
intelligence, I.130
retreat, I.114
Communist rebellion, I.83, 127–8, II.286
Chinese support, III.187, 188
US strategy, II.288
Vietnam and, I.474
Malaysia, II.45, III.427
Malenkov, Georgii (Soviet premier)
Eastern Europe, I.340–1
failure, 463
foreign policy, I.313
Gulag economics, I.448
Khrushchev and, I.450

Rakowski, Mieczyslaw (Polish Communist
leader), III.318, 319
Ramadier, Paul (French socialist leader),
II.160–1
Ramalho Eanes, Antonio (Portuguese
colonel and politician), II.255
Ramphal, Sonny (Commonwealth
secretary-general), III.233
Rand, Ayn, III.16
Rapacki, Adam (Polish foreign minister),
II.399
Rau, Johannes (German Social Democrat),
III.305
Rawls, John (US philosopher, III.15, 16
Reagan, Nancy (wife of Ronald Reagan),
III.274
Reagan, Ronald (US president), III.281
1976 election primaries, III.140
abandonment of New Deal, III.31, 33
Afghan strategy, III.130, 151–2, 272, 275, 517
Gorbachev and, III.132
Argentina, III.210
Berlin, III.304–5, 335
budget deficit, III.21, 33
Central America, III.221, 275
Costa Rica, III.210
El Salvador, III.208, 217–18
Guatemala, III.210, 216–17, 218, 451
Honduras, III.210
human rights abuses, III.451
invasion of Grenada, III.294
Nicaragua, II.428, 429, III.208–16, 295, 517
Panama, III.210
Chinese relations, III.194–5
Cold War rhetoric, III.88
détente and, II.19, 20, 41, 390–1
economy, III.299
end of Cold War and, III.267–9
collapse of Soviet Union, III.361
debate, III.523–4
Helsinki Accords and, III.529
ideology, III.517
Japanese policy, III.176–7, 178–9
military expenditure, III.33, 39, 107–8
"morning in America," III.21
neoconservative appointments, III.10
neoliberalism, III.14, 23, 31
nuclear weapons, II.20, III.265
antinuclearism, II.20, III.277–80, 287
arms reduction, III.273–4, 418
Euromissiles, III.271, 296
INF Treaty, III.262–3, 286, 297, 308–9
protests, I.438

SALT II, III.270
SDI, *see* **Strategic Defense Initiative**
START, III.270–1
strategy, III.154–5
technological advantage, III.39
zero-option, III.418
Pakistan, assistance, III.130
Poland, III.293
political propaganda, III.76
population control, III.483
Reagan Doctrine, III.517
rhetoric, III.267, 269–70
southern Africa, III.236–8, 239
Soviet relations
anti-Soviet consensus, II.278
assessment, III.286–8
bibliography, III.580–1
Brezhnev, II.432
cooperation, III.272–7
crusade, III.107–11
"evil empire" discourse, II.457, III.109,
252, 264, 270, 296, 460–1, 523
Geneva summit (1985), III.305
Gorbachev, II.458, III.257, 261–4, 265,
277–88, 517
hardline years, III.269–72, 277, 293–7, 409
KAL007 incident (1983), III.271, 274–5,
278, 295
nuclear world, III.277–86
regional conflicts, III.273
Reykjavik summit (1986), III.257, 262,
265, 275, 279, 288, 305
sanctions, III.293
shift, III.272–7
Soviet fear of attack, II.432–5
Soviet reforms and, III.281–2
trade, III.294
Western Europe and, III.293–5
strong leadership, III.76
support for dictatorships, III.210
Thatcher and, III.293–5
Third World policy, III.222, 271–2, 517
Western Europe and, III.293–5
Realism, I.5, II.376–7
Réard, Louis (French film director), II.446
Red Army, postwar unrest, I.98
Red Army Faction, II.473
Red Brigades, III.61, 256, 290
Rededication Weeks, I.429–30
Reedy, George (Johnson adviser), II.126
**Reischauer, Edwin (US ambassador to
Japan),** III.163–4, 165, 166, 168
relativism, III.11

China and, III.190
defense, I.274
economic assistance, I.477
Eisenhower, I.281, 294, 297, 299, II.13
Ford, III.189
Johnson, III.167
military assistance, II.63
missiles, I.363
Nixon, III.172, 173
Reagan, III.195
Tajikistan, III.532
Takasaki Tatsunoke (Japanese trade official), I.261
Takeshita Noboru (Japanese prime minister), III.158
Talbott, Strobe (US journalist and deputy secretary of state), III.268
Taliban, III.133–4
Tambo, Oliver (ANC leader), III.240
Tanaka Kakuei (Japanese prime minister), III.174, 176
Tanzania, and Namibia, III.230
Taraki, Noor Mohammad (Afghan Communist leader), III.103, 124, 127, 128
Tashkent Declaration (1966), II.152
Tatarescu, Gheorghe (Romanian National Liberal), I.184
Tati, Jacques (French film director), I.412
Taylor, Elizabeth (British actress), II.455
Taylor, Glen (US senator), III.456
Taylor, Maxwell (US general), I.307, II.71–2, 81, 123
Tchaikovsky, Piotr, I.409
technocracy, III.4
Teheran Conference (1943), I.94, 137, 175
telecommunications, III.388–92
television
cable revolution, III.389
China, III.504
civilian and military technology, I.12
Cold War and, I.16, 44
Eastern Europe, I.417, II.518
espionage, II.448, 449, 450–1
satellite broadcasting, III.389
science fantasy, II.451, 453
second Cold War, II.458
Soviet Union, III.411
transnationalism, III.398
United States, II.442–3, 448, 449
consumerism, III.496
Telstar, III.388

Terman, Frederick (US engineer), III.380
terrorism
9/11 attacks, III.134, 537, 550, 554–5
1970s, III.1
countercultures, II.473–4
Red Brigades, II.256, III.61, 290
Texaco, I.491, 493–4
Texas Instruments, III.384–5
Thailand, I.299, 474, II.45, 63, 291, III.187, 480
Thant, U (Burmese UN secretary-general), II.82, 317
Thatcher, Margaret (British prime minister)
détente and, II.20
East European revolutions and, III.308
EC policy, III.302
economics, III.299–300
election, III.298
end of Cold War and, III.523–4
German unification and, III.343
Gorbachev and, III.246, **III.247**, III.304, 524
intelligence services, II.434
liberalism, II.19
NATO policy, III.306
neoliberalism, III.14, 15, 23, 31–2
nuclear policy, III.305, 307
Reagan and, III.293–5
Rhodesia, III.233
Ukrainian independence and, III.367
visit to Soviet Union (1987), III.310
Theater der Zeit, I.405–6
Third Man, The (film), I.398, 419
Third World
see also **liberation movements**
alternatives to bipolar world, I.198
Bandung Conference, I.260–1, 479–82, II.258, 266
China and, I.483
Angola, II.156, 277–8, III.229
failures, II.274–5
hubris, II.341
ideology, II.261–2, 266–7, 275
militarization, I.484, II.327
shifts, II.268
Soviet competition, I.481–2, II.147, 260, 266, III.224
US relations, III.191–2
Cold War (1945–62), I.4, 10–11, 34, 40–1, 43, 52, 474–9
Vienna meeting (1961), II.34
Cold War (1962–75)
acceleration of modernity, II.263

VOKS (Soviet cultural exchange
organization), II.439
Volcker, Paul (chairman of US Federal
Reserve), III.31, 33, 39
voluntarism, II.23
von Hippel, Frank (US physicist and
official), III.419
Voorhees, James (US political scientist),
III.418
Voronov, Gennadii (Soviet Politburo
member), II.143
Vorster, B. J. (South African prime
minister), III.227, 229, 230–1, 232
voting rights, I.18
Vyshinskii, Andrei (Soviet diplomat and
foreign minister), I.179, 180

Wajda, Andrzej (Polish film director), II.458
Wałęsa, Lech (Polish trade union leader and
president), II.19, 20, 229–30, III.312,
316, 319
Wallace, George (US governor), II.471
Wallace, Henry (US secretary of
commerce), I.37, 70
Wallace-Johnson, I. T. A. (Sierra Leonean
political activist), I.468
Waltz, Kenneth (US political scientist),
II.25, 33, 412, III.518, 541
Ward, Angus (US consul in China), I.235–6
Warner, Christopher (British diplomat),
I.119
Warsaw Pact
1981 exercises, III.313
1989 revolutions and, III.327
announcement, I.317
Brezhnev and, II.226–7
Bucharest Declaration (1966), II.208–9
Budapest appeal (1969), II.213
"Buria" exercise, I.330
Bush attitude to, III.332
conventional arms superiority, III.296
Czech Velvet Revolution and, III.327
defensive defense, III.521–2
disintegration, III.308
German unification and, III.324
Harmel Report (1967), II.208
Hungary and, I.351, II.219
INF and, III.305–6
Khrushchev policy, I.318
nuclear weapons, II.100–2
NATO negotiations, II.399
objectives, I.341
Poland and Solidarity, III.106

Polish revolution and, III.319
renewal (1985), III.304
Romania, III.330
weapons systems, II.430
Washington, George, I.21, III.434
Washington Consensus, III.32, 35, 556
Watanuki, Joji (Japanese sociologist), III.3
Watergate, II.55, 385, 388, III.94, 99, 189
Watkins, Peter (British film director), II.446
Watson, Thomas (head of IBM), III.383
Wayne, John (US actor), II.452
Weather Underground, II.473
Weber, Max, I.49
Weinberg, Alvin (US physicist), III.378
Weinberger, Caspar (US secretary of
defense), III.275, 482, 523
Weisband, William (US double agent),
II.419
Weizäcker, Richard von (West German
president), III.336
welfare capitalism, III.499
welfare states, I.47–8
Wellman, William (US film director), II.447
Wells, H. G., III.447
Werner Report (1970), III.301
West African Students' Union, I.468
Westad, Odd Arne (Norwegian historian),
I.485, III.90
Western Electric, III.390
Western Europe
1949 map, I.190
1979–89
Afghan crisis, III.289, 290–3
attractions, III.290, 308–10
bibliography, III.581–3
democracy, III.309
economy, III.290–1, 299–301
Gorbachev and, III.307, 309, 336
growth rates, III.300
INF negotiations and, III.305–6, 308–9
liberalism, III.310
NATO cruise–Pershing deployment,
III.295–7
Reagan's first term, III.293–5
uncertain détente, III.303–6
unexpected revolution (1989), III.306–8
welfare states, III.301
anti-Americanism, I.407–8
colonialism, I.10
Communism, III.297–8, 309
decline, III.297–8
international movement, II.504–10
US containment policy, II.510–13